The Rowman & Littlefield Handbook of Media Management and Business

The Rowman & Littlefield Handbook Series

This contemporary series of academic handbooks provides authoritative guides to relevant and emerging topics across the humanities and social sciences. To encourage greater dialogue across disciplines, this series engages high-quality, original, and multidisciplinary research on topics, themes, and key debates in academia today.

- Each handbook draws together newly commissioned work to provide a comprehensive benchmark for a field or subdiscipline
- Individual handbooks include an international team of contributors with valuable expertise, knowledge, and perspective in their fields
- Handbooks correspond to the latest topics on courses around the world

Each handbook is available for purchase in both print and digital formats. For more information, see www.rowman.com.

The Rowman & Littlefield Handbook of Christianity in the Middle East
Edited by Mark A. Lamport and Mitri Raheb
The Rowman & Littlefield Handbook of Media Management and Business
Edited by L. Meghan Mahoney and Tang Tang

The Rowman & Littlefield Handbook of Media Management and Business

Edited by
L. MEGHAN MAHONEY
and
TANG TANG

ROWMAN & LITTLEFIELD
Lanham • Boulder • New York • London

Published by Rowman & Littlefield
An imprint of The Rowman & Littlefield Publishing Group, Inc.
4501 Forbes Boulevard, Suite 200, Lanham, Maryland 20706
www.rowman.com

6 Tinworth Street, London SE11 5AL, United Kingdom

British Library Cataloguing in Publication Information Available

Library of Congress Cataloging-in-Publication Data
Names: Mahoney, L. Meghan, editor.
Title: The Rowman & Littlefield handbook of media management and business / edited by L. Meghan Mahoney and Tang Tang.
Description: Lanham : Rowman & Littlefield, 2020. | Series: The Rowman & Littlefield handbook series | Includes bibliographical references and index.
Identifiers: LCCN 2020032417 (print) | LCCN 2020032418 (ebook) | ISBN 9781538115305 (hardcover) | ISBN 9781538115312 (epub)
Subjects: LCSH: Social media—Management. | Industrial management.
Classification: LCC HM851 .R69 2020 (print) | LCC HM851 (ebook) | DDC 302.23/1—dc23
LC record available at https://lccn.loc.gov/2020032417
LC ebook record available at https://lccn.loc.gov/2020032418

Contents

PART IV • MANAGEMENT IN A DYNAMIC LANDSCAPE

PART V • THE FUTURE OF MEDIA MANAGEMENT

Acknowledgments

Each year, the field of media management increasingly favors diversity, specialization, technological convergence, and internationalization. The exclusionary dichotomy between "old" and "new" often seems difficult to navigate. However, the multidimensionality of the field makes it an appealing and exciting area of study and practice. As such, Drs. Mahoney and Tang hope that *The Handbook of Media Management and Business* serves as a guide for future practitioners to understand how to converge existing research and practices with the changes and challenges of a new media environment.

We wish to thank all our mentors and colleagues from our doctorate training at Ohio University, who introduced media management using a holistic and interdisciplinary approach. We are particularly grateful to each of the authors who contributed chapters to the handbook, who bring many unique professional and international experiences to their chapters. This handbook would not have been possible without the support of the faculty at Kent State University and West Chester University as well as endless encouragement from our family and friends. We extend utmost appreciation to the anonymous reviewers of the manuscript as well as the editors at Rowman & Littlefield. Finally, to our children—Maxx, Beatrice, Spencer, and Greta—thanks for enriching our lives every single day.

PART I

MEDIA MANAGEMENT IN CONVERGENCE

CHAPTER 1

Scope, Opportunities, and Challenges in Convergent Media Management

L. Meghan Mahoney, West Chester University
Tang Tang, Kent State University

LEARNING OBJECTIVES

1. Introduce and provide an overview of the field of media management.
2. Explain fundamental rules and key changes in media management in today's convergent media environment.
3. Identify opportunities and challenges that convergence brings to future media practitioners and managers.

The field of media management has historically examined the operations and functions within media enterprises. The multidimensionality of these enterprises makes media management an appealing area of study for many creative and business minds alike. Nonetheless, media landscapes operate very differently today than they did just a decade ago. Each year, the field increasingly favors diversity, specialization, technological convergence, and internationalization.

Convergence resulting from technological, legal, and social changes has dramatically altered the structure of media business. The purpose of this book is to connect research and industry practice. It aims to provide a strategic guide for aspiring and current media professionals to solve media management issues in a convergent environment. It is imperative for media students and professionals—regardless of specific interest—to understand how business is conducted in the ever-changing media industry and to be aware of management issues that drive the production and distribution of media content that entertains, informs, and persuades audiences. Thus, we hope this book is relevant to anyone who works (or aspires to work) in any area of media business.

This chapter aims to introduce media management and business through a convergent media approach rather than focusing on medium-specific strategies. Today's media users no longer operate through mutually exclusive enterprises (e.g., TV, radio, web). Users tend to make choices based on content, with the medium/device serving as a secondary consideration in the media selection process. Media organizations also operate in a convergent manner. Thus, instead of discussing electronic media management versus new media management, this book reflects on the management issues in information, sports, and gaming industries and explores the unique opportunities and challenges brought by media convergence and emerging technologies. It also highlights the fundamental management rules and practices unchanged by such a dynamic environment through a global perspective. By understanding how technologies have impacted the field of media management through an examination of relevant traditional theories, changing management practices, and the opportunities and challenges of each, current and future practitioners will be better prepared to direct media business to align with their goals.

Above all, strategic thinking is key for success in media management. The ability to adapt to the changing media landscape, audience behavior, and financial models is essential to industry survival. Understanding when to rely on management foundations in the field and when to adapt to emerging technological changes can be difficult for media managers. Hopefully, this book will serve as a resource in navigating such a dynamic environment. Chapter 1 explores emerging trends in research, evaluation, and application in the field. Adaptability, creativity, and diversity are important for success in all three. Let us explore a case study of how the media giant Disney strategically adapts to an ever-changing digital on-demand industry.

CASE STUDY

Longtime Disney CEO Bob Iger had to navigate one of the world's most historic and well-recognized brands through many turbulent technological shifts. Perhaps best known for its filmmaking, Disney has been forced to adapt its brand for many platforms, including television, web, music, and merchandising. Through the acquisition of Pixar, Marvel, Lucasfilm, ABC, and ESPN, Disney has reconceptualized and strategized about its brand, especially regarding how each individual content market should best navigate new technologies. Each product has a distinct and unique audience with different motivations and content expectations. Rather than apply a one-size-fits-all strategic plan to each service, Iger led Disney through the adaptation to digital media based on audience demand, brand authenticity, and strategic market research.

Today, streaming services are the trend for television content producers. The United States alone had more than 100 streaming services available for customers to choose from in the 2019 marketplace (Cook, 2019). Though Disney was slow to enter the streaming market, Iger was strategic in establishing digital streaming for Disney by first introducing ESPN+ as a test run to help him better understand how to remain profitable in an on-demand and fragmented environment. Through this platform, Disney was able to examine audience expectations and the technological nuances of offering such a service. Iger was then able to use this knowledge to create a quality digital streaming product better suited to Disney's long-term business plan and objectives.

Iger's careful adaption was not only good for the Disney brand but also led ESPN to emerge as one of the most profitable businesses in the company. Given the growth trajectory and success of ESPN+, Disney launched its complete streaming service, Disney+, in November 2019. Despite more than 250 global online video service competitors at the time, over 10 million people registered for Disney+ in just one week (Wingard, 2019). Iger was able to take lessons learned from ESPN+ and adapt them to the larger market of Disney+. This successful integration was noted as one of his biggest achievements before stepping down as Disney CEO in 2020 (Feiner, 2020). His focus on adaptability and audience-centered content is the key to success in any media management field.

> Disruption led by technological advance has had a profound impact on the entire media and entertainment business—what's being created, how it's being created, how it's being distributed, how it's being consumed, and how it's being monetized. The business model that forms the underpinning of media and entertainment has all changed dramatically. (Iger, 2019)

Future media leaders must embrace technological changes and ever-shifting audience expectations and remain strategic and true to the traditional values of media business. This requires media managers to ensure that decisions are made carefully and strategically within a company, even at the expense of being late to enter a technological market. Consumers have limitless options and are quick to switch brands if expectations are not met. Based on this understanding, each chapter of this book will explore "old" concepts that are still relevant in today's digital environment and "new" practices that have disrupted the industry. Additionally, we will explore key opportunities and challenges that media convergence brings to current and future media practitioners and managers.

Something Old

It is important for media managers to have a comprehensive understanding of traditional theories from a variety of fields and perspectives as well as a nuanced understanding of more applied emerging media software and skills. This combination of age-old traditions with technological advancements is difficult to capture. While there are many positions within an organizational chain that may benefit from impulsive off-the-cuff risk taking, media managers should constantly call for goal-oriented initiatives and research. The following "old" media management adages continue to advance the best media business practices. Specifically, media managers should understand the importance of quality content creation, engaging audiences, creating strategic business models, and building a sustainable and authentic brand, even in today's convergent, continually evolving media environment.

CONTENT IS KING

In 1996, Bill Gates famously wrote an essay titled "Content Is King," in which he predicted that future media leaders who succeed "will propel the Internet forward as a marketplace of ideas, experiences, and products—a marketplace of content" (Evans, 2017). Today, this focus on producing and disseminating quality content is just as critical as it was more than 20 years ago. Consumers have filled virtually every gap in their lives with content, whether it serves a utility function to help them plan a future activity or simply as entertainment to relax and pass time. Content informs, entertains, educates, and offers utility (Olenski, 2017). Without strong content, media businesses will lose their audience. Without an audience, there is no media business.

Almost every brand and sector today must consider ways to create engaging content for audiences. Such content must incorporate interactivity, mobility, and on-demand functionality. The content also needs to serve a purpose and be well made, on brand, and easy for users to access and engage with. Audience research is the key to understanding these changing audience expectations as a means for media managers to establish their unique brand and position within the marketplace. As the number of content options and distribution channels available to audiences continues to increase, the quality of media content must continue to improve to avoid getting lost in a world of information overabundance. In today's and tomorrow's media, content remains king.

AUDIENCE ENGAGEMENT

Research is vital at every stage of the production process. With stiff competition across content platforms in today's convergent environment, media managers are tasked with understanding how audiences engage content. For almost a century, numerical ratings have been critical to media decisions. Almost all strategic and financial decisions stemmed from research regarding the number of eyeballs watching media content. While the focus on audience numbers remains important today, managers are even more invested in improving the quality and type of audience engagement.

Rather than simply exposing audiences to content, media practitioners today understand the difference between an active and a passive audience. In fact, the definition of audience engagement has transformed and now has more than 25 variations (Napoli, 2011). Media research now includes the audience reception process of the media experience. Content retention, identification, purpose, and subsequent decision making are all becoming critical pieces to making decisions. In addition, social listening and big data provide new opportunities to measure audience attention (Nelson & Webster, 2016). These metrics are able to provide insights into trends across the audience experience and help answer questions about who, when, and how often audiences engage content. Big data will be discussed throughout this book and specifically in chapter 22, "Big Data and Entrepreneurship."

The days when a practitioner was able to specialize and focus on a single research methodology are gone. Audience engagement metrics require a balance of both quantitative and qualitative approaches. Media ethnographies and in-depth interviews also help practitioners understand the reception process. These changes to audience research are discussed more in chapter 4, "Academic Research Methods in Media Management." The future of media management research includes holistic and hybrid approaches.

FUNDING SOURCES AND MEDIA BUSINESS MODELS

Media companies must continuously develop and adapt their business models to stay successful in a dynamic technological landscape. There is no shortage of how-to guides or strategies for developing media business models, but each of these holds reiterations of the same traditional key insights. All media today exists in a high-velocity environment and must be frequently adjusted (Wirtz, Schilke, & Ullrich, 2010). Media managers must respond to competitive market structures, governmental / regulatory changes, and technological progress. In a converged environment, this remains even more true.

Wirtz et al. (2010) advised media managers to focus on closing gaps between an organization's existing resources and any technological shifts that may impact the long-term prospects of the firm. This forward-thinking approach is imperative to media management. Failure to assess and adapt to these changes will limit the value chain in a prospective new market. While this is true for almost all components of a business model, perhaps the greatest change exists in adapting to potential new media revenue streams. Yet, it is important for media managers to note that rather than revamp business models entirely, practitioners must be strategic and careful, build on existing market structures, and focus attention on potential collaborators with shared business values. Building and sustaining an authentic brand helps organizations reassess business models to highlight shared resources and potential revenue options.

BRAND AUTHENTICITY

Today, there is a media product for everyone. Successful media organizations understand and embrace the uniqueness of their brand and product value, and more important, they work tirelessly to ensure that they market to audiences who embrace the same values. Every sector is saturated with competition, so it is imperative that media professionals understand their brand's authenticity. Specifically, ask the question, What makes your media product different from your competitors'? (Stratten, 2012). Media managers should welcome these differences and accept the qualities that make them a unique voice in the field. This strategy requires a strong, creative organizational team that is able to convey an authentic brand narrative.

Brand authenticity is something that distinguishes a product, service, or organization from its closest competitors (Mahoney & Tang, 2016). An authentic brand narrative should stem directly from a company's objectives; consumer experiences; identity construction; and the physique, personality, and culture of the products and services offered (Kapferer, 1997; Leigh, Peters, & Shelton, 2006; Mahoney & Tang, 2016). An organization's most important assets are their creative professionals and the knowledge, skills, and creativity of the people who design and produce content (Mierzejewska & Hollifield, 2006). While this has always proven true, strict deadlines and fast turnaround of content can often stifle creativity in today's fast-paced society. It is important for media managers to foster strong leadership and allow room for creative growth (Küng, 2008).

In addition, media practitioners should understand that they cannot please everyone. In fact, the more brands attempt to disseminate generic messages that appeal to a common-denominator audience, the more audiences are going to turn attention toward alternative products with niche values and mission statements. In order to survive in a digital marketplace, brands must know who they are, what they stand for, and how they are different from their competitors, and they must create and market a cohesive brand sensory experience for audiences that provides mutual benefits.

Something New

Understanding the foundations of traditional media management is as important as embracing the dynamic, innovative, and creative changes of tomorrow's industry. What's new about media management for today's practitioners? Almost everything. While the previous section pointed to media management foundations that are still important, it is difficult to provide a comprehensive list of all the ways technology has transformed media industries. Changes have impacted all aspects of media business, including organization restructures, shifting audience tastes and consumption habits, diverse and fragmented revenue streams, changing management styles and philosophy, and new approaches in marketing and distribution (Shaver, 2000). Below, we will highlight several key advancements where media managers should focus their attention, including the intersection of convergence, technology and data, new revenue streams, and the global marketplace.

CONVERGENT TECHNOLOGY AND DATA MANAGEMENT

As media continue to remediate themselves across various forms and formats, convergence remains the most significant technological transformation to increase audience interactivity with business. This focus has led to more synchronous content that accompanies more traditional dissemination (e.g., mass media broadcasting + Twitter hashtag conversation). Increasingly, companies have embraced business models that prove "free of charge" for audiences to access broadcast content in the digital marketplace while still benefiting from social media's network-based potential. Here, users are able to access content for less, and media companies have a more direct communication and interaction with their target audiences. So just how are they making money? Often, profit comes in the form of data.

Real-time digital media serve as a big data repository for media companies. Data streams provide access to user interests and information that can be used by media practitioners and sold to marketers. Data is easily compared, analyzed, contextualized, and monetized in today's digital environment (Zelenkauskaite, 2017). While data management is providing new revenue streams and insights for media business, it also offers new challenges to media practitioners, which we will detail later in this chapter.

NEW REVENUE STREAMS

Aside from data management, numerous other alternative new revenue streams have emerged in the era of convergence. Traditionally, media industries have depended on consumer spending or advertising revenues (Mierzejewska & Shaver, 2014). Here, funding sources are based on audience size rather than actual profit. In today's convergent environment, managers must expand on traditional business models that can just as easily be sold to advertisers and capture audience engagement. In addition, media companies need to increase their return on investment by focusing on cost-reduction efforts. For example, many countries (e.g., China, South Korea, the United States) have built low-cost digital infrastructure, such as on-demand streaming services. Often, this results in streamlined operations to make products more profitable (Hoffert, 2005).

Today's media managers are finding more return by balancing traditional and new revenue streams to build profits. Radcliffe (2019) summarized various revenue streams for media businesses, including traditional ones, such as advertising, subscriptions, paywalls, events, and e-commerce, as well as emerging approaches. For example, media managers have been experimenting with TV partnerships, podcasting (which we will discuss in chapter 17, "Podcasting"), online stores, and idea conferences as potential new revenue streams. Often, funding initiatives are multifaceted with multiple approaches.

Crowdsourcing/funding is another new revenue stream practiced by media and technology companies, such as Wikipedia, to sustain and expand their business (Vukanovic, 2011). Crowdsourcing/funding helps media companies not only diversify revenue sources but also cut fixed costs and offers managers nuanced insights about their audiences/consumers (Trefis, 2012). Moreover, virtual goods have generated more than $1 billion a year in the U.S. market and have become a common revenue stream for new media business (Mahoney & Tang, 2016). WeChat, a popular social media site in China, allows users to send virtual goods/money to each other. During the 2019 Chinese New Year, 820 million WeChat users sent or received Red Packet (i.e., virtual money), which contributes to WeChat's $10.7 billion net profit (Iqbal, 2019). Micropayments have also been widely adopted by media companies, such as the *Wall Street Journal* and *New York Times*, to allow their audiences to pay by the story, a complement to the traditional subscription-based revenue model (Hayes & Graybeal, 2011; Mahoney & Tang, 2016). Sponsorships, branded entertainment, and submarkets with different types of profitability could benefit future media business models (Balis, 2015; Krumsvik, 2012).

Understanding and adopting potential new revenue streams requires traditional media organizations to rebrand based on changing audience expectations. It also requires media managers to be willing to learn about the opportunities and risks brought by any new revenue model, conduct "in-market" experiments, evaluate them, and determine how to improve future efforts (Romaniuk, 2012). Simply put, diversifying revenue streams, matching new supply with demand, and making conscious financial decisions are key to the success of today's and tomorrow's media business (Balis, 2015).

GLOBAL MARKETPLACE

In addition to facing technological convergence, media managers are also adapting to a transnational audience. Today, there is no such thing as a truly local media market. While the United States has traditionally dominated the global online entertainment scene through its ownership of Netflix, Amazon Video, YouTube, Facebook, and Twitter

(Cunningham & Craig, 2016), audiences extend across the globe. Netflix has 80 million subscribers in 190 countries; YouTube has 1 billion users in 88 countries; and Facebook has 1.7 billion users, representing more than half of the global online population. Disney's service has extended to more than 100 countries in 37 languages. CNN, a cable news company based in the United States, can be seen in 200+ countries and territories around the world (Hollifield, 2001). Even local crafting hobbyists who wished to sell their goods through the e-commerce platform Etsy marketed to a global audience of more than 39 million buyers in 2018 (Clement, 2019).

Many media production companies have worked to adapt their programs to as many international markets as possible. This is true for genres such as game shows and talent competitions as well as animation, drama, documentaries, reality programs, and even scripted series, such as *The Office* and *Ugly Betty* (Chalaby, 2012). Global media practices have also moved from purchasing finished programs to buying show concepts, brand elements, and production guidelines. Such a transition deepens the globalization of the media industry by requiring media managers to reconceptualize the value chain of international concepts in a local context as well as enhancing the interconnectedness of media organizations across borders (Chalaby, 2012).

Global markets and international audiences should be positioned at the center of any leading media organization's business models (Chalaby, 2012; Gershon, 2019). Yet, globalization has brought many questions about Internet regulation regarding access, content, and advertising. Often, important regional inconsistencies exist (Cunningham & Craig, 2016). Adapting content to various cultural norms, practices, and regulations can be challenging for media managers, especially for products that were not previously considered to be global products. Media practitioners and managers should also consider how expansion into foreign/global markets impacts their home market operations, particularly in terms of the organization's financial management. Investing overseas may lead to restructuring, cost cutting, and changes in the management style of existing domestic operations (Hollifield, 2001).

Convergence has clearly impacted transnational media management through three key technological shifts: Internet and broadband delivery, digital media, and the emergence of transnational media corporations that blend technology and the Internet (Gershon, 2019). The globalization of markets involves full integration of transnational businesses, nation-states, and technologies operating at a high speed, driven by broad deregulation and privatization trends as well as advancements in new technology (Gershon, 2019). The impact of transnational media will be discussed in greater detail in chapter 10, "Transnational Media and Business Strategy."

Opportunities and Challenges

While future practitioners may feel overwhelmed when considering how much technology has changed and is predicted to further change media management, it is truly a promising time to enter the field. Innovative approaches to marketing and distribution continue to improve the relationships among audiences, industry practitioners, and academic researchers. The intersection of convergence, technology, and data; new revenue streams; and the global marketplace requires each of these sectors to rely more heavily on the others. The abundance of changes in the field of media business should not deter aspirants from pursuing a career in the area but rather encourage future practitioners to embrace the many opportunities of such a new market.

OPPORTUNITIES

The success of any organization lies in its ability to predict the future direction of convergence and adapt business models to enrich the entire value chain, including operational innovation, new products/services, new customer values, and new customer bases (Lee, Olson, & Trimi, 2010). While this remains true, more audience-centered studies are adding to these narratives, allowing for a more complete understanding of various markets. As Webb (2015) notably suggests, opportunities in future media industries will come from understanding the answers to the following questions: "Where/how are people wasting their time? Where/how are people having difficulty with technology? Where/how are people looking for information? Where/how are people stuck? How do people want to be perceived?" (p. 3). These questions point out opportunities for future managers, particularly in the areas of algorithms adopted in the information industry and new audience measurement methods that increase shared-value experiences.

ALGORITHMS AND THE INFORMATION INDUSTRY

The news and information industry is facing substantial obstacles due to convergence and digital disruption. Audiences are less interested in news due to their growing distrust of news organizations. This trend has resulted in a decline in revenues for the industry. Thankfully, big data algorithms provide media practitioners with more trustworthy and transparent information about their audience needs and interests from diverse sources. The impact of such changes will be discussed more in chapter 14, "News and Information Industry."

Big data algorithms are a set of computer-instructed rules or processes based on artificial intelligence and deep learning for problem solving. They can be utilized to explore audience information gathering, seeking and sharing patterns that managers have never noted before, and thus offer many opportunities for new information recommendation systems, news products, and services. Future news and information managers must aim to include big data and better algorithms in their product and audience development to provide audiences with more customized, targeted, trustworthy, and balanced information that fits their individual interests and needs. The information industry will overcome the many obstacles it is currently facing. Often this requires managers to incorporate algorithms, data, and emerging technology in their product development while staying true to traditional news values.

NEW AUDIENCE MEASUREMENT METHODS

With the changing expectations and consumption patterns of audiences, it is important for practitioners to make meaningful interpretations of informatics and engagements (Jiang, Luo, & Kulemeka, 2016). Traditional audience research measurements are being adapted to meet the needs of tomorrow's media. As discussed, professionals are no longer singularly interested in ratings metrics. Media and audience fragmentation undermined traditional panel-based audience measurement on exposure (Napoli, 2012; Webster, 2008). Instead, media managers and practitioners are seeking hybrid methods to measure media use, which typically combine traditional audience survey / focus group and technology-based approaches, such as tracking software installed on computers or census-based measures tracked by a website's own servers (Gunzerath, 2012; Tang & Mahoney, 2019). Hybrid research methods provide a more holistic snapshot of the complete media experience.

While big data metrics are often used to measure how well a media product performed in the market after distribution, practitioners are beginning to see the benefit of integrating these insights earlier in the production process. Big data reveal important insights into how and why individuals choose to use a certain medium as well as how audiences navigate a digital environment with abundant content forms and sources. Social listening also provides opportunities to measure timely and accurate information that resonates in stakeholders' emotions. For example, NPR in the United States now uses CrowdTangle, a technology that spots social media trends, to identify audience needs and trending topics, thus informing future reporting ideas and promotion opportunities (Balis, 2015). Extending beyond providing traditional demographics, psychographics, and geodemographics information, these new measurement methods offer insights into strategies that help media managers build a community.

Media practitioners must also examine the content of media texts, research motivations behind business strategy, and measure audience reception to creative products through cross-media use in a convergent environment. Thoughtful analytics will offer new opportunities to media managers in a multifaceted marketplace. Media managers should seek to be trained in various methodological techniques and embrace the opportunities brought by the new hybrid and holistic research approaches (Bartosova, 2011; Napoli, 2012). Industry trends in media management research will be discussed further in chapter 5, "Industry Research Methods in Media Management."

SHARED VALUE EXPERIENCES

New measurement techniques provide opportunities for new media experiences. "The era of convergence is expected to open new opportunities for better products and services, with leaner value chains, enabling creation of new customer values and leading to expanded customer bases" (Lee et al., 2010, p. 224). If media organizations continue to view value creation narrowly, as short-term financial performance, without understanding customer needs and external influences, they will not succeed (Porter & Kramer, 2019). Instead, tomorrow's media managers must prioritize the concept of shared value.

Shared value focuses on connections between societal and economic progress by reconceiving products and markets, redefining productivity in the value chain, and enabling local cluster development. This approach will generate greater innovation and growth for companies and provide larger benefits for society (Porter & Kramer, 2019). The ever-changing media landscape is seen as a challenge to practitioners while also providing many new opportunities, such as revamping stale financial strategies or business goals. By exploring shared value chain concepts, practitioners are able to examine changes in audience expectations and consumption habits.

Overall, media convergence has forced many media businesses to shift from a supply-led to a demand-led market (Kehoe & Mateer, 2015). The direct communication between product and market allows for more customized opportunities for business. This is a refreshing change for practitioners and audiences alike. The focus of media industries has become the consumer experience and the product in the context of the consumer's life experiences, not the product itself (Calder & Malthouse, 2005). Individualized brand relationships are the key to the success of tomorrow's media business, a reassuring change for both audiences and businesses alike.

CHALLENGES

While new media technologies and globalization have brought a wide range of opportunities to the media industry, there is no doubt that media convergence also led to challenging disruptions to the marketplace. The key challenges faced by media managers largely rest in understanding "what the right balance is between humans and technology across the full media and advertising ecosystem; and how to maximize our creativity as an industry while integrating data-driven approaches" (Balis, 2015, p. 3). Specifically, media management decisions will be strategically made by balancing the tension between being creative and technology/data driven, adapting to the global market while serving local audiences, monetizing media products while staying true to their core values, and being ethical and strategic to solve emerging problems brought by data privacy, security, and confidentiality.

CREATIVENESS VS. TECHNOLOGY

Media managers have the advantage of being surrounded by a diverse and talented mix of professionals. Organizations almost always benefit from the creative ideas offered by their staff. Additionally, automation and technologies offer data and information that help guide strategic thinking and overcome human errors. Balancing this tension between creativity and enlarging technology-driven capabilities has become a new challenge for media managers in today's convergent environment (Balis, 2015). Particularly, it seems as though the creativity and technology trajectories are at odds with each other. Both are currently undergoing transformative processes that rely on each other, as digitization and technologies move from the periphery to the center of value creation (Baetzgen, Michel, & Ciepluch, 2018). How media managers pull together information, strategies, and data from different sources; connect the dots; and make a strategic, creative, and data-informed decision will be essential to their success.

Other challenges faced by future media managers lie in adequately training professionals for a convergent workforce. Until media management practitioners work better with each other, it is unrealistic to expect them to embrace inputs from outside disciplines and industries. With so much overlap and transcendence in a convergent environment, future practitioners must adapt to diversity and changes to the field. Teaching values of collaborative learning and team production proves difficult though beneficial.

Chapter 24, "Looking Forward," will cover many strategies for training hard and soft skills for future media practitioners and managers.

LOCALIZED VS. GLOBAL

Overall, new technologies have provided great competition and field saturation to media industries. Internet regulation regarding access, content, and advertising is subject to inconsistent regional and national state-based mediation despite the often Western-centric distribution of media products. As discussed, this dichotomy between local and global media pressures provides a great challenge for future media managers.

The discipline has long described the influence of U.S. cultural imperialism as a one-way street (Cunningham & Craig, 2016). Yet, many media companies, such as YouTube, have embraced the value of nurturing more local content by encouraging the upload of user-generated amateur videos. The result is greater producer diversity that represents a stronger value proposition to the advertising industry. While these changes are happening at the online level, broadcast products tend to continue with the same established players, norms, principles, and practices that yield power and influence. Future practitioners must work to change this status quo.

Convergent audiences utilize media to fulfill a variety of needs and desires. They wish to learn and connect with others around the globe, but they also wish to share personally unique and culturally specific stories. Future practitioners must resist the urge to succumb to media population biases by ensuring that new media remains a space where users can share localized content. This tension between amateur versus professional, authentic versus careful curation, and localized versus global will present great challenges for media institutions of every size. Future media management training must include intercultural understanding and ethics in addition to technological skills and business management.

MONETIZATION

With audience fragmentation, lower entry barriers, declining advertising revenues, and the free digital culture, monetizing media products and services will be an increasing challenge for media managers. Traditionally, media industries have built business models on the concept of a dual-product market. Here, producers sell media products (e.g., TV shows) to audiences and then sell audiences to advertisers (Krumsvik, 2012). Yet, the lack of consistent audience measurement standards due to the fragmented marketplace has brought many challenges for monetizing media products through advertising. In addition, it is evident that many sectors, including technology companies, compete for the same limited advertising dollars, indicating the need for innovative monetization.

In the previous section, we discussed the need for media managers to focus on their products' core values in strategic planning and branding in order to maximize return on investment. Yet, even the ride-sharing company Uber, which has embraced continuous innovation, user-friendly access, and a global platform, has struggled to monetize the platform. The company reported a $615 million net loss in 2019 and is not expected to turn a profit until the end of 2020 (Rapier, 2020). While a strong brand and a loyal audience should be enough to maintain a successful media business, that just has not proven true in the digital marketplace. The movie ticket subscription service MoviePass declared bankruptcy, even after acquiring more than three million subscribers (Duprey, 2020; Tobin, 2018). Despite disrupting how the movie industry sold tickets, the media platform was unable to find a sustained revenue model.

Developing a sustainable revenue stream that still satisfies users' expectations for quality content is difficult. Media managers need to embrace the complexity, uncertainty, and difficulty of the financial future of the marketplace. Careful forecasting, planning, and pacing are required for media managers to make financial decisions for their organizations. These decisions cannot be made solely based on profitability either. Audience concerns and expectations surrounding digital security must also be addressed.

DATA PRIVACY

There are ongoing concerns about data privacy with the ever-increasing uses of big data, artificial intelligence, and machine learning. According to Pew Research Center, more than 90% of Americans believe that there is a privacy issue in gathering consumer data (Webb, 2015). Personal private data acquisition has left many consumers feeling uncertain about media. Audiences have become increasingly privy to the idea that their personal data are sold for money every day without their permission (Leetaru, 2018). However, this knowledge does not translate into acceptance of such practices. Information surveillance provides little transparency of the buying and selling of user data. This process has created an increasing trust gap between users and brands that future media managers must work to minimize. Otherwise, consumers will turn away and become even more critical of engaging media institutions.

As such, media managers need to be transparent about how they collect and use data and may give audiences/consumers the choice to review, move, and delete their data (Webb, 2015). Challenges will rest in regaining trust from audiences and balancing revenue generation and data use. Ethical decision making and transparency will be essential for media business and management, something discussed more in chapter 9, "Making Ethical Choices in News Media."

It is clear that media management is a field with a strong trajectory of foundational practices that have withstood the test of time. It is important that future practitioners adapt and build on these lessons as technologies continue to adapt and change. Based on the overview of these key opportunities and challenges for future practitioners, the following action plan is offered.

ACTION PLAN

1. Future media managers should be lifelong learners of value, creativity, and diverse research evaluation and welcome input from multiple disciplines, industries, and cultural perspectives.
2. The hybrid nature of the media management discipline should be embraced by bridging creative and data-driven initiatives through new evaluation measures.

3. Media managers must work to understand and predict the multiple ways in which convergence impacts value chain and business model characteristics, especially in specific media sectors.
4. It is important to seek out creative and adaptable training programs that will sustain a career in such a disruptive and dynamic environment.

KEY TAKEAWAYS

1. The field of media management is undergoing a period of vast transformation and disruption. Successful practitioners will be those who embrace creativity and technological shifts and best navigate the marketplace of audience-centered content.
2. Convergence has created a plethora of data, new revenue streams, user engagement opportunities, and an increasingly globalized marketplace.
3. Shared value is a key emerging trend in media management. Future practitioners should focus on product convergence, understanding and reconceptualizing the value chain, and enabling local development in a transnational environment.
4. Media management cannot exist in silos of information and must embrace cross-platform applications and be adaptable in a convergent and global marketplace.

CONCLUSION

Facing convergence, media managers must deal with changes in technology, revenue generation, ownership reconfiguration, globalization, and more (Shaver, 2000). This chapter aims to offer insights into media management and business today and into the future. The media landscape is still evolving. We hope this book serves as a catalyst to the continual strategy formulation necessary to better integrate media organizations and the environment in which they exist (Shaver, 2000). Though it is impossible to predict all the disruptions that technological changes will bring to the field, the foundations outlined in this book should serve as a guide for successful management.

Specifically, this chapter summarizes the scope, opportunities, and challenges for convergent media management. Future media managers must understand the importance of quality content creation and storytelling in a digital era. In today's and tomorrow's media, content remains king. More must be done to capture data to better understand how audiences engage media through their preferences, interests, and motivations. This new information should be used to continuously develop and adapt business models.

In order to adapt successfully, media businesses must have a strong brand authenticity consistent with the company's objectives; consumer experiences; identity construction; and the physique, personality, and culture of their products and services. More emphasis must be placed on collaboration, rather than competition, that aids in increasing profit and combining resources. While these recommendations lay a solid foundation for any growing media enterprise, new technological skills and expectations must also be integrated into business practices.

Overall, a key challenge faced by media managers in a convergent environment is the ability to strike a balance between creative and technology-driven initiatives. Today's global marketplace must serve the needs of both a transnational audience and more localized niche audience segments. This is only possible through careful audience research and strategy development. Thankfully, digital media provide big data repositories to professionals and marketers. This information provides insights for developing new revenue streams and can be used to customize trustworthy and transparent information algorithms to better serve individuals' needs and interests. However, overreliance on big data can have many challenges for practitioners. Research points to increasing audience concern over trust, data security, and reliability. Future practitioners must work to repair this trust gap and seek to be trained in various hybrid and holistic research approaches.

Traditional communication research, such as surveys, focus groups, interviews, and ethnographies, will provide more holistic understandings of the media experience. Hybrid methods must be taught and integrated into media management curriculum. This will help practitioners understand trends in the field as well as the reason *why* these trends may occur. Research should be established in every stage of the media production and dissemination process.

Ensuring that media businesses are profitable and sustainable has always been difficult but is even more so in a saturated convergent environment. Managers must be careful and strategic in developing business models that serve the company's interests and changing audience expectations and that make sense in a global marketplace. Alternative new revenue streams have emerged in the convergence era. Deciding how to balance revenue streams with audience expectations is important. Strategic decisions should integrate profit with content and be consistent with a brand's authenticity. Often, this requires brands to enter a market much later than competitors. Disney+ is an example of the successful adoption of the digital streaming marketplace regardless of its late entry.

Furthermore, convergence has established a growing transnational audience for businesses. This results in various cultural norms, practices, and regulations that practitioners must become familiar with. Media managers must understand the shared value of their product by reconceiving markets and enabling local cluster development. Tomorrow's marketplace is truly characterized by global and local trends. Audiences have more access to more information and global concerns than ever before, but they also desire niche customized content. Additionally, media law is beginning to provide more regulations across borders, something discussed further in chapter 8, "Law and Policy."

Hopefully, this chapter successfully provides an overview of the field of media management by introducing the fundamental rules and key challenges in a convergent media environment. Clearly, there are many important opportunities and challenges for future media practitioners. Due to the size, diversity, and complexity of the field, this book focuses on five areas of the discipline: media management in convergence, fundamental issues in convergent media management, globalization, management in a dynamic landscape, and the future of media management. Each section includes diverse experiences and contributions from experts in the field to provide a broader global context.

Technology innovations and disruptions already prove unavoidable in today's convergent media environment. Media practitioners and managers need to embrace both the opportunities and challenges by wholly considering the implications of convergence on an organization. The shifting media landscape requires many changes to media management, and conscious efforts must be made to evaluate organizational structures, technology platforms, revenue models, marketing and evaluations, management styles, and more.

Above all, future managers must work to better serve audiences. Media convergence forces media business to shift from a supply-led to a demand-led market (Kehoe & Mateer, 2015). Today, audience is key. As such, we must learn how technologies transform audience behavior and the relationship between media producers and consumers in this ever-evolving media world. Chapter 2, "The Changing Audience," will provide an overview of such transformations.

REFERENCES

Baetzgen, A., Michel, B., & Ciepluch, M. (2018). *Human resources management as a crucial success factor in the creative and media industry: The new relationship between artistic and technical professions.* European Media Management Association.

Balis, J. (2015, October 5). 3 strategic questions the media industry's future depends on. *Harvard Business Review.* https://hbr.org/2015/10/3-strategic-questions-the-media-industrys-future-depends-on

Bartosova, D. (2011). The future of the media professions: Current issues in media management practice. *The International Journal on Media Management, 13,* 193–201. doi: 10.1080/14241277.2011.576963

Calder, B., & Malthouse, E. (2005). Managing media and advertising change with integrated marketing. *Journal of Advertising Research, 45,* 356–361.

Chalaby, J. K. (2012). Producing TV content in a globalized intellectual property market: The emergence of the international production model. *Journal of Media Business Studies, 9*(3), 19–39.

Clement, J. (2019). *Number of active Etsy buyers*. Statista. https://www.statista.com/statistics/409375/etsy-active-buyers

Cook, S. (2019). *The complete list of streaming services.* Flixed. https://flixed.io/complete-list-streaming-services

Cunningham, S., & Craig, D. (2016). Online entertainment: A new wave of media globalization. *International Journal of Communication, 10,* 5409–5425.

Duprey, R. (2020). *MoviePass goes bankrupt while AMC still thrives.* The Motley Fool. https://www.fool.com/investing/2020/02/01/moviepass-goes-bankrupt-while-amc-still-thrives.aspx

Evans, H. (2017). *Content is king: Essay by Bill Gates 1996.* Medium. https://medium.com/@HeathEvans/content-is-king-essay-by-bill-gates-1996-df74552f80d9

Feiner, L. (2020). *Bob Iger to step down as Disney CEO, effective immediately*. CNBC. https://www.cnbc.com/2020/02/25/disney-names-bob-chapek-next-ceo.html

Gershon, R. (2019). *Transnational media and the economics of global competition.* Global Communication: A Multicultural Perspective. http://globalcomhilda.blogspot.com/2008/10/chapter-4-transnational-media.html

Gunzerath, D. (2012). Current trends in U.S. media measurement methods. *The International Journal on Media Management, 14,* 99–106. doi: 10.1080/14241277.2012.675754

Hayes, J., & Graybeal, G. (2011). Synergizing traditional media and the social web for monetization: A modified media micropayment model. *Journal of Media Business Studies, 8*(2), 19–44.

Hoffert, E. M. (2005). From cost reduction to revenue growth: Shifting priorities for digital asset management. *Journal of Digital Asset Management, 1,* 110–114.

Hollifield, C. A. (2001). Crossing borders: Media management research in a transnational market environment. *Journal of Media Economics, 14,* 133–146.

Iger, B. (2019). *Managing industry disruption: Disney plus case study*. Masterclass. https://www.masterclass.com/classes/bob-iger-teaches-business-strategy-and-leadership/chapters/managing-industry-disruption-disney-plus-case-study#

Iqbal, M. (2019). *WeChat revenue and usage statistics*. Business of Apps. https://www.businessofapps.com/data/wechat-statistics/#3

Jiang, H., Luo, Y., & Kulemeka, O. (2016). Social media engagement as an evaluation barometer: Insights from communication executives. *Public Relations Review, 42*, 679–691.

Kapferer, J. N. (1997). *Strategic brand management*. Kogan Page.

Kehoe, K., & Mateer, J. (2015). The impact of digital technology on the distribution value chain model of independent feature films in the UK. *International Journal on Media Management, 17*(2), 93–108.

Krumsvik, A. H. (2012). Why old media will be funding journalism in the future. *Journalism Studies, 13*, 729–741. doi: 10.1080/1461670X.2012.664331

Küng, L. (2008). *Strategic management in the media: From theory to practice*. Sage.

Lee, S. M., Olson, D. L., & Trimi, S. (2010). The impact of convergence on organizational innovation. *Organizational Dynamics, 39*, 218.

Leetaru, K. (2018, October 25). Social media companies collect so much data even they can't remember all the ways they surveil us. *Forbes*. https://www.forbes.com/sites/kalevleetaru/2018/10/25/social-media-companies-collect-so-much-data-even-they-cant-remember-all-the-ways-they-surveil-us

Leigh, T. W., Peters, C., & Shelton, J. (2006). The consumer quest for authenticity: The multiplicity of meanings within the MG subculture of consumption. *Journal of the Academy of Marketing Science, 34*, 481–493.

Mahoney, L. M., & Tang, T. (2016). *Strategic social media: From marketing to social change*. Wiley.

Mierzejewska, B. & Hollifield, A. (2006). Theoretical approaches in media management research. In A. Albarran, S. Chan-Olmsted, & M. Wirth (Eds.), *Handbook of media management and economics* (pp. 37–65). Routledge.

Mierzejewska, B., & Shaver, D. (2014). Key changes impacting media management research. *The International Journal on Media Management, 16*(2), 47–54.

Napoli, P. M. (2011). *Audience evolution: New technologies and the transformation of media audiences*. Columbia University Press.

Napoli, P. M. (2012). Audience evolution and the future of audience research. *The International Journal on Media Management, 14*, 79–97. doi: 10.1080/14241277.2012.675753

Nelson, J. L., & Webster, J. G. (2016). Audience currencies in the age of big data. *International Journal on Media Management, 18*, 9–24.

Olenski, S. (2017, May 21). Why content will always be king. *Forbes*. https://www.forbes.com/sites/steveolenski/2017/06/21/why-content-will-always-always-king

Porter, M. E., & Kramer, M. R. (2019). Creating shared value. In L. G. Gilbert & N. C. Smith (Eds.), *Managing sustainable business: An executive education case and textbook* (pp. 327–350). Springer.

Radcliffe, D. (2019). *50 ways to make media pay*. What's New in Publishing. https://whatsnewinpublishing.com/wp-content/uploads/2019/09/50-Ways-to-Make-Media-Pay.pdf

Rapier, G. (2020, February 6). Uber says it will be profitable sooner than expected as it tops Wall Street expectations. *Business Insider*. https://www.businessinsider.com/uber-earnings-q4-profit-loss-revenue-total-rides-eats-2020-2

Romaniuk, J. (2012). Are you ready for the next big thing: New media is dead! Long live new media. *Journal of Advertising Research, 52*(4), 377. doi: 10.2501/JAR.52.4.397.399

Shaver, M. (2000). Special issue on trends in media management for the 21st century. *Journal of Media Economics, 13*, 55–56.

Stratten, S. (2012). *UnMarketing: Stop marketing. Start engaging*. Wiley.

Tang, T., & Mahoney, L. M. (2019). Measurement issues and trends in mass communication research. In E. Graham & J. Mazer (Eds.), *Communication research measures III: A sourcebook* (pp. 160–174). Routledge.

Tobin, B. (2018, August 5). Subscribers left shaken, unsure after MoviePass's latest financial turmoil. *USA Today*. https://www.usatoday.com/story/money/2018/08/05/moviepass-can-movie-subscription-service-saved/876087002

Trefis. (2012). *Crowdsourcing: The best business model in the digital age*. Nasdaq. https://www.nasdaq.com/articles/crowdsourcing-best-business-model-digital-age-2012-10-26
Vukanovic, Z. (2011). New media business models in social and web media. *Journal of Media Business Studies, 8*(3), 51–67.
Webb, A. (2015, January 5). The tech trends you can't ignore in 2015. *Harvard Business Review.* https://hbr.org/2015/01/the-tech-trends-you-cant-ignore-in-2015
Webster, J. G. (2008). Developments in audience measurement and research. In B. Calder (Ed.), *Kellogg on advertising and media* (pp. 123–138). Wiley.
Wingard, J. (2019, November 22). The streaming wars: Disney+ and the winning strategy. *Forbes.* https://www.forbes.com/sites/jasonwingard/2019/11/22/the-streaming-wars-disney-and-the-winning-strategy-for-competitive-advantage
Wirtz, B. W., Schilke, O., & Ullrich, S. (2010). Strategic development of business models: Implications of the Web 2.0 for creating value on the Internet. *Long Range Planning, 43*, 272–290.
Zelenkauskaite, A. (2017). Remediation, convergence, and big data: Conceptual limits of cross-platform social media. *Convergence, 23*, 512–527.

CHAPTER 2

The Changing Audience

Louisa Ha, Bowling Green State University

LEARNING OBJECTIVES

1. Understand how the development of media technologies transforms audience behavior and the relationship between media production and media consumption.
2. Learn the different approaches and methodologies audience researchers use to study audiences over time.
3. Examine the different conceptualizations of audiences over time and their implications for studying media effects and audience dynamics.
4. Discuss how the five factors in media technologies turned audiences into multiplatform audiences, social audiences, big data audiences, binge watchers, personalized audiences, and ubiquitous audiences.

With today's mobile technology, we expect constant updates from friends and colleagues and various news sources feeding directly to our smartphone. Did the advances in media technologies cause audiences to change, or did audiences demand a change and the media and technology industries simply respond to those demands? This dialectical question is important when we discuss the change in audiences. Increasingly, interactive technologies will lead to interactive audiences. If the change in audiences is simply caused by the advancement in media technology, we should employ a technology determinism approach to explain the change: Audiences will change according to how media technologies evolve. The more ubiquitous and portable the media are, the more ubiquitous the audience. But if the change in audiences is caused by external factors, such as theoretical assumptions and perspectives or changes in society, political system, or cultural norms and values, then we should conceptualize media technology changes as a response to meet the changing expectations of audiences.

The concept of "audience" comes from a mass communication research tradition in which the same source of information is disseminated to a large audience simultaneously, such as a public speech by a politician, a sports event, or a television program. Abercrombie and Longhurst (1998) suggest a tiered model of audience in which the audience's relationship with the source (media content) progresses from the audience being uninvolved spectators to highly involved and skilled fans who become producers of content. Napoli (2011) attributes changes in media technologies to the evolution of media audiences and rightfully points out that the conceptualizations of audiences are "often negotiated outcomes between key institutional stakeholders, including media firms, advertisers, audience measurement firms and even policymakers and advocacy groups" (p. 18). Based on the purpose of research, there are many different ways media audiences are conceptualized.

As such, this chapter will first review the different conceptualizations of audiences before the advent of converged media technologies, such as the Internet and smartphones. These conceptualizations represent how audiences are conceived in different social contexts and media contexts based on different theoretical approaches. Next, we will examine the five factors in media technologies that are responsible for the changes in conceptualization of audiences: (1) multiplatform and multimodal synergy, (2) customization, (3) traceability, (4) automation, and (5) accessibility. Finally, opportunities and challenges of the implications of changing audiences for media managers and practitioners in a converged media landscape will be discussed. Below is an illustration of the diverse audience conceptualizations and roles in different media content using this author's own experience as a case study.

CASE STUDY

The variety of conceptualizations of the audience is illustrated by its large number of synonyms: citizen, consumer, public, spectator, fan, sharer, participant, user, reader, listener, viewer, surfer, player, and the even more blurry hybrid identities combining production and consumption, such as produsers (Bruns, 2008) and prosumers (Ha & Yun, 2014; Ritzer & Jurgenson, 2010; Toffler, 1980). As we examine each of these below, the terminologies represent different roles of the audience in the process of media production and consumption and the different expectations of their agency roles in society. We will not call a radio listener a participant unless they call in to the program to request a song, enter a contest run by the show, or talk to the radio show host. We will not call a viewer a fan of a TV program until they demonstrate their involvement, loyalty, and enthusiasm for the TV program.

Taking myself as an example, I have multiple audience identities based on different media content. I am a *fan* of the comedy series *Fresh Off the Boat*. I will not miss any episode, and I will do extra research to learn about the cast, the producers, and upcoming episodes. If this show were canceled, I may write to ABC to complain about it. For many YouTube videos, I watch those that are recommended to me by either YouTube or my friends. Therefore, on YouTube, I am the typical *viewer* (Ha, 2018a). Yet I am also a *curator* of YouTube because I try to find videos that are useful for my classes and compile them so that my students can learn about a topic. On Twitter and Facebook, I am a *prosumer* because I post my own pictures and express my views on different topics to my followers and friends there as a content *producer*. I also read their news feeds as a *consumer*. For most books, I just read them as a *reader*. I do not communicate with the author at all.

Very occasionally, I may write a book review on the books I read and let others know my opinion. For print magazine and print newspaper articles, I may just browse them and, if I find them useful, clip them for future reference. On the contrary, for online news and magazines, if I find an article interesting and useful, I may share and recommend it to my friends or students via email or social media. I become a *sharer* or *spreader* of the content. Reading news about the candidates for an election may reinforce my view on the candidates and affect my voting decision as a U.S. *citizen*. For many news topics, such as the #MeToo movement and high-profile sexual assault cases such as those of Bill Cosby and Harvey Weinstein, my opinion on sexual assault will be affected, and I may follow the issue as an informed *public*. Watching an advertisement for a product, depending on how it is featured and whether it is appealing to me, I may be tempted to buy it or reinforce my loyalty to the brand as a *consumer*. The lesson from this example is that if we try to impose a homogeneous role on the audience, we most likely will be heading in the wrong direction because it will not be applicable to all media in all contexts.

Something Old

Audiences emerge naturally, as it is human nature to communicate with each other. We work to reach more people through ever-larger aggregations of audiences. This results in the evolvement of audiences over time, from live to mediated audiences.

FROM LIVE TO MEDIATED AUDIENCES

The live audience is the oldest form of audience. Live musical performances, sports games, and plays in theaters are some of the earliest forms of entertainment that congregated an audience. The congregation of audiences for these performances allows immediate feedback to the performers and the audiences, and performers can have direct contact with audiences during the performance. Each performance is unique and nonidentical. With the emergence of recording technology, printing technology, and motion pictures, performance and other content can be recorded and distributed to a mass audience in a uniform manner. The mediated audience becomes the most examined form of audience in audience research. Mass media's ability to reach a large audience through broadcast and satellite distribution maximizes the value of the media content by exerting influence as the common information and entertainment source of society.

SINGLE-MEDIUM AUDIENCE—READERS, LISTENERS, VIEWERS, AND PLAYERS

As mediated audiences become mainstream, audiences become more medium specific depending on the modality of the medium. For example, *listeners* refers to people who consume music and radio. *Readers* refers to people who consume print text such as books, newspapers, and magazines as well as static visual images. *Viewers* refers to people who watch audiovisual media with motion, such as television shows, video clips, and movies. *Players* refers to people who play video games. By focusing on the modality of the medium's audience, early research about radio listeners would examine the hearing experience of the audience, such as how music affects the listener's mood or how oral communication including news on the radio affects people's knowledge of the world (e.g., Herzog, 1942).

Such single-medium focus seems to be less relevant nowadays, as the Internet is a convergent and multimodal medium. One can read, write, hear, and watch while accessing the Internet. Despite the growth of this convergence medium, people still use single-modal mediums such as books and radio. Different media become complementary to one another and are used for different settings. People still like to listen to music on their phone or in their car. New media technologies did not render the old ones obsolete. Nonetheless, because of the complexity of conducting a media repertoire study, single-medium research still dominates most empirical media audience studies.

It should be noted that *audience* is the medium-neutral term to refer to all kinds of media consumption, from print to broadcast to Internet. People's consumption of media content is the heart of most audience research. The production of media content typically is not part of media consumption. However, with the rise of the Internet and other editing software, user-generated content becomes easy to create and distribute online. Media audiences are no longer confined to being mere consumers or recipients of the content but can also create and distribute their own content in response to the content they receive. The audience can play the roles of consumer, distributor, and producer simultaneously.

AUDIENCE RESEARCH TRADITIONS

Within scholarship there are two main research traditions in the study of audiences. One is the empirical, social scientific approach of measuring audience size and audience behavior, as in advertising and media management research (e.g., Katz & Lazarsfeld, 1955; Lee & Lee, 1995; Napoli, 2011; Webster, Phalen, & Lichty, 2013). The other is the cultural studies approach as audience reception research. These scholars measure an audience's reception of media texts using a resistance or incorporation paradigm proposed by Stuart Hall (1973). Here, scholars examine how audiences make sense of the media content they encounter (e.g., Livingstone, 2018).

PASSIVE VS. ACTIVE AUDIENCE

One important theoretical debate about the audience is whether audiences are passive or active. The passive audience conception is held by political economists and strong media effects researchers (e.g., Cantril, 1940), who examine audiences as recipients of media messages and measure their response to the content that was given to them. However, minimal media effects theories challenge the passive audience conception. Prominent audience scholars such as Elihu Katz and Paul Lazarsfeld (Katz & Lazarsfeld, 1955) examined personal influences on audiences, giving rise to the uses and gratifications perspective (Blumler & Katz, 1974). Here, audiences have their own will and choose media according to their needs. This is the first wave of active audience research. Lee and Lee's (1995) large-scale research with 18 focus groups and a national probability sample reveals how and why people watch television. They propose four levels of TV viewing activity, from having the TV on just as background noise, as a peripheral activity to another activity in the room, as one of the two primary activities (such as reading while watching television), up to watching the TV program being the sole activity in the room.

THE AGENCY OF AUDIENCES

Another way to conceptualize audiences is by the agency of the audience in the media communication process. Sullivan's (2013) book on media audiences categorizes them into four types based on the agency power of the audience from the least to the most: (1) objects, (2) institutional constructions, (3) active users, and (4) producers. When audience members are treated as the objects of persuasion as in media effects, especially during World War II's media propaganda campaign aimed to control and manipulate the public's attitude and knowledge, media audiences are viewed as very passive entities under the control of the political institution.

Media audiences can also be conceptualized as a collective institution that can be measured and monitored. Public opinion and audience ratings are two aggregate measures of audiences' responses to current affairs and media content, respectively. As a result of the need for quantification to examine the degree of consensus in society, public opinion polls have become an important tool for providing input to government policy in a democracy, which is based on its representation of the public's interest.

For audience ratings, the compilation of data and reports by professional research firms such as Nielsen conceive audiences as a commodity to be sold by media companies. Each audience is reduced to a number constituting the total rating figure. Exposure directly translates into the number of audience members that can be sold to advertisers. Audience ratings are simply a currency for business transactions and to be used for comparing performance between programs.

Another theory that explains the active role of users is Stuart Hall's (1973) encoding and decoding theory of audiences from a cultural studies perspective. Here, audiences decode the media message based on their experiences and values. There are different interpretations of the same media message. Selective perception focuses on the audience's individual preference and choice in understanding the content, which may or may not have any predetermined position (Vidmar & Rokeach, 1974).

Active user theories still focus on the audience's consumption of media content. Only when the audience moves beyond the consumption may it directly affect the media production process.

BEYOND CONSUMPTION: AUDIENCE PARTICIPATION AND ENGAGEMENT

Most media audiences do not produce content, especially before the advent of digital technologies, but they can show their enthusiasm and interest in the media content by participating in the media production process. For traditional media, the participation may be a letter to the editor or call in to radio show hosts, which requires more effort from the audience. In online media, the forms of participation include providing direct feedback through likes, shares, comments, participating in polls, taking quizzes, and providing tips to news organizations.

New media audience participation requires less effort and is more a tool for consumer engagement than a tool for creating original content (Ha & Yun, 2014). Ha et al. (2018) advocate a separation between medium engagement and content engagement by proposing a four-level model of audience content engagement, ranging from the basic level of consumption time, to diversity of platform use to consume the same content, to sharing of the content, to the highest form of participation: influencing the content of the media.

Audiences are conceived as producers or prosumers when they generate content in the media. Two types of audiences are likely to produce content. The first are the fans, who have a strong sense of ownership of their favorite media texts or characters and engage in interpretative play with those texts (Fiske, 1992). These individuals are so skilled and knowledgeable in the content that they become petty producers and turn their fan activity into professional content to market to other fans (Abercrombie & Longhurst, 1988). The fans become activists for the program, write fan fiction, and make demands on the producers when they see the program is not heading in the direction they want (Jenkins, 1992). The second type of audience that is likely to produce content is people with production resources and skills who are also actively involved in the community (Ha & Yun, 2014). Creating content enables activists and community leaders to voice their opinion and exert their influence on the community.

AUDIENCE SIZE AND EXPOSURE TO MEDIA CONTENT

Webster et al. (2013) propose a model of audience behavior in which an audience's media exposure is determined by audience factors and media factors. This perspective examines audience accessibility and availability to use media content. For audiences, structural factors include available audiences and potential audiences. Individual factors include program preference, group versus solitary use, awareness of options, and social networks. For media, the structural factors are the station's or network's coverage, content options, and recommendation systems. The individual factors are technologies owned, subscriptions, and repertoire. Media managers can predict their audience size using these factors.

INCIDENTAL EXPOSURE AND DELIBERATE EXPOSURE

The audience's exposure to media content can be incidental or deliberate. Incidental exposure most commonly occurs in advertising when audiences do not seek advertising, but it simply comes with the program. Sometimes people just turn on the television and flip through channels until something catches their attention. When radio or television serve as background noise, the exposure to the content is mostly incidental. Because incidental exposure is effortless for the audience, the engagement is usually low. This does not mean audiences are not influenced by such exposure. Through repetition and low-involvement learning, audiences gradually remember the message and the advertised brand.

Deliberate exposure can be divided into two types: task-oriented or nontask leisure exposure. Task-oriented exposure usually involves obtaining information to accomplish a task or for daily surveillance of the environment, such as watching news and public affairs programs. After the task is complete, the audience will abandon the media outlet altogether. Anything that interrupts the task, such as advertising, will be considered clutter and skipped or totally ignored (Ha & McCann, 2008). In contrast, for leisure consumption and nontask exposure, such as watching a drama series, the excitement motive is clear, but it is not a task. The audiences may sit through other unrelated content and may be open to other options. They may try the next program following the program they just watched. Hence, commercials' prime time is the fringe hours because the resistance to them is the lowest when people are just having their leisure viewing and have time to kill. Media managers and advertisers need to understand the differences in audience behaviors in incidental versus deliberate exposure.

COMPETITION FOR AUDIENCES

Ang's (1991) cleverly titled book *Desperately Seeking the Audience* is one of the most cited works to describe the media industry's quest to understand audiences. She conceptualizes audiences as either markets or publics. Audience is an important resource for all media organizations for revenue (market) and impact (public). But what do media organizations want from the audience? Their subscription or purchase? Their eyeballs for advertisers? Their minds? The answer is probably all three. Without an audience, media content is nothing. Media's power and influence on society is based on its large audience reach and perceived credibility. Every media outlet is trying to capture the attention of the audience, which is a scarce resource as people's lives are getting busier and busier. For example, busy people with tighter time budgets spend more time on mobile media and new technology to save time than individuals with more leisure time (Zhang & Ha, 2015).

Something New

After reviewing these conventional conceptions of audiences, we can see that technology is not the only factor that differentiates audiences. Rather, it is the task, the setting, the involvement in the content, the resources and different class positions, and theoretical perspectives used to explain how audiences process media content that caused the changes in audience conceptions. As we move from linear media to a convergent media landscape, audience agency changes accordingly. Audiences are no longer confined by location or by a schedule imposed by the media firms. Media technologies are responsible for the changes in the new conceptualization of audiences by their multiplatform and second-screen affordance, accessibility and availability on demand, traceability, automation, and personalization.

MULTIPLATFORM AND TRANSMEDIA AUDIENCE

Multiplatform and transmedia audience is the first new conception of audience in a converged media environment. Unlike the single-medium audience we described above, the multiplatform audience uses more than one platform in information and entertainment consumption. The multiplatform audience typically has a converged media device such as a smartphone. After receiving a recommendation from a friend on Facebook or Twitter, people may click on the link and read the news posted by a news website online. If they like it, they may share it to other friends via email, text messages, or social media on the smartphone, all in a few clicks. If you ask where the news comes from, it would be difficult to answer because the individual has used three platforms—mobile news app, social media, and online news site. As you can see, the audience moves seamlessly from one platform to another via the smartphone.

Not only are the platform and media boundaries blurred in a multiplatform media environment but also the audience can play multiple roles sequentially or seamlessly at almost the same time: the content user, the content participant, the content spreader/endorser/annotator, and the content producer. For example, after an individual watches a funny pet video posted by a friend on Instagram, they can "like" it and write comments on it. They can share the video to their followers. They can take another fun video of their own pet in response to that video. Another example is a video game player who plays the game (consumer); records the experience and posts it on YouTube (producer); and sees another player's video, dislikes it, and writes critical comments about that video (participant). Although most people may only perform one or two roles, they still use multiple platforms on the same screen to access different media content from different sources. Uses and gratifications as a theoretical perspective is still applicable because audiences have different expectations for different social media platforms and use them accordingly. For example, Facebook is for family, community engagement, and instant gratification; YouTube is for curation; text message is for instant communication; and email is for work (Ha, Joa, Gabay, & Kim, 2018). Because of the multiple sources accessible at one's fingertips in converged media devices, it is challenging to create identity and loyalty to a media brand. Online news, for example, has a hard time maintaining a brand identity as people get online news from social media and mobile news apps. Understanding the multiplatform repertoire of the audience is necessary.

The multiplatform availability not only facilitates the multiple roles performed by the audience; its multimodality or intertextuality creates a synergy among the platforms. Presenting the same or similar content in different formats with different technological affordances and features transforms the audience experience. The visual learner can now look at the pictures and videos in addition to listening to the narration. The audience may just originally stumble on a news item or a video on their app, but by paying attention, they may internalize the message and then try to externalize it by sharing with more people, such as family and friends (Choi, 2016).

This process may require additional mental effort in selecting who to distribute to and what to write about the shared content. After sharing the content, they may worry about whether the content will be well received by their audience and check their likes. If the content gets many likes, the behavior is rewarded, and they may share similar content in the future. The audience is not only a passive recipient but also an active processor and endorser of the messages as well as a monitor of the response to the post. The increasing complexity of the audience's role in a multiplatform converged media environment is noteworthy. Media managers should understand how the choice of recommendation is being made and how much audience members choose to annotate their shared posts to make good use of such a platform for word-of-mouth messages.

THE SECOND SCREEN AND SOCIAL AUDIENCE

After discussing the use of the same screen (convergent media device), we now turn our attention to the second screen. Second screening occurs when an individual uses one device while simultaneously consuming content from another device. The concept of the second screen will be discussed further in chapter 21, "Second Screening." The most common type of second screen usage is to simultaneously use a TV and smartphone. This type of multitasking behavior increases the audience's cognitive load (Van Cauwenberge, Schaap, & Van Roy, 2014). When the screens are related, such as tweeting about a live sports game (71% of Facebook TV activity is related to sports, according to Nielsen), second screening socially links viewers of the same program in real time. As much as 43% of weekly U.S. Facebook activity and 33% of weekly Twitter activity takes place on Sundays as people discuss NFL games (Nielsen, 2017). A content analysis of tweets on second screen use in the whole season of a political TV talk show found that many viewers use Twitter to address questions directly to politicians (Giglietto & Selva, 2014). Another two-wave panel survey shows that those who second screen during the news are more likely to participate politically, showing social media engagement's positive effects (Gil de Zúñiga, Garcia-Perdomo, & McGregor, 2015).

Second screens often amplify the social role of the media. Audiences use it to coordinate and connect with like-minded friends and share the joy or frustration of the media consumption experience. The response is immediate as well as recorded. The second screen can also serve as a digital memory for people who cherish those specific moments or as an index of the popularity of the show. However, it is not true that the more commonly discussed the show is on social media, the higher the ratings of the show (Hayes, 2014). Some of the shows that are on top of social media activity have a large and loyal following, such as *The Walking Dead* and *Empire* (Nielsen, 2017). These shows motivate a strong community of fans who use social media to share their experience with fellow fans in real time. Social media managers encourage viewer engagement by adding hashtags to the traditional screen without much research on the impact of second screening. Nonetheless, while social media is widely believed to be beneficial for increasing audience engagement and raising awareness, it can also serve as a double-edged sword. Social media content will also amplify discontent and complaints about the program.

For example, during NBC's telecasts of the 2012 Olympic Games, broadcasters tape-delayed major events to prime time, which caused social media engagement backlash, shedding light on the tension between business needs and audience expectations (Nee, 2015). Viewers demanded to see the Games live on TV, but due to the time difference, NBC tried to maximize the audience by showing the main events only on prime-time television. The audience criticized on social media how the network failed to meet the needs of the viewers as early as the Opening Ceremony using a #NBCfail hashtag on Twitter to voice their complaints about tape delays, editing, and other aspects of NBC's coverage.

In addition, research indicates that using a second screen leads to decreased learning and understanding of content. Van Cauwenberge, Schaap, and Van Roy's (2014) experiment shows that using a second screen increases the cognitive load of the audience and reduces their comprehension of news items, even if the second screen content is related to the news. Hence, multitasking or audience engagement with a second screen should only be encouraged in specific moments rather than as a general habit.

THE PERSONALIZED AUDIENCE

With digitization and traceability, customization of media content is more possible than ever before. There are several ways digital media companies are taking advantage of their databases. Recommendation systems based on the previous usage record of the user are one of the major forms of personalization (Ha, 2018a). YouTube's algorithm creates the recommended list automatically based on the individual's past viewing history and selects the most viewed videos similar to past viewed videos. YouTube also has an autoplay feature that immediately plays a similar video after finishing a video. Some audiences like the convenience and continue to watch. YouTube programmers are able to utilize an advertising algorithm so that the same commercial is not shown to the same individual twice. Thus, each person's YouTube viewing experience is different from other users', as each watches different commercials and receives different recommendations. Such personalization may satisfy the audience more, but it leads to the lack of a common, sharable viewing experience.

Opportunities and Challenges

As we can see through the various new and old conceptions of audiences, the competition for and value of the audience to the media organization are greater than ever before. The nature and complexity of audience roles in media consumption and production have increased tremendously. The affordances offered by media technology advancements create many opportunities and challenges for media managers and audience researchers in today's convergent media environment.

OPPORTUNITIES

The early 21st century can be characterized as a time-shifting media technology boom. The launch of stand-alone digital video recorders (DVRs) such as TiVo and DVRs integrated with cable and satellite TV receivers / set-top boxes not only increased the recording and storage capability of their users but also facilitated loyalty to these multichannel services. Audiences are now able to pause live television, repeat watch the same recorded episode, skip commercials precisely, and build their own personal TV program library. Such time-shifting technology means that audiences do not need to follow the broadcast schedule of the TV network or station, and they can even watch several episodes of the recorded series in a row, known as binge viewing.

Along with the rise of DVR technology came the utilization of the 24-hour accessibility of computer systems and improved broadband infrastructure to make online video streaming possible. All devices with a screen and Internet access become the new television set for audiences. The free video portal YouTube offers billions of videos, and low-cost online subscription services such as Netflix and Hulu offer diverse and high-quality programs online on demand. Such convenience of on-demand availability not only increases overall video viewership (Nielsen, 2018) but also facilitates binge-watching behavior. Binge watching is an intensive consumption of TV series by watching multiple episodes consecutively. Netflix even coined a term, *binge racer*, to describe a viewer who aims to finish a full season of a show within 24 hours of its release. About 8.4 million Netflix subscribers have binge raced a series at least once (D'Douza, 2020). Books on marathon watching by Perks (2014) and Netflix by Jenner (2018) both show binge viewers' increased agency, resulting in deeper engagement with the media content and characters in an insulated flow. Indeed, Netflix benefited greatly from binge watching by differentiating itself from traditional linear TV and keeping subscribers. Nonetheless, similar to other addictive behaviors, there are many negative consequences of binge watching, such as increasing social isolation and health issues and interfering with normal daily life (Alter, 2017).

From the perspective of media executives who offer streaming services, binge watching or binge racing can increase audience loyalty and the value of subscriptions. From the producers' perspective, binge watching and binge racing are not the way the program was originally designed to interact with the audience. The ways that intensive exposure to a TV series and movies affect the perception of quality and parasocial relations with the characters and perhaps associated merchandise is unknown. Currently, viewers enjoy the advertising-free experience of binge watching on Netflix. But if streaming services start to insert commercials in between episodes or within episodes, will these commercials be viewed or simply treated as bathroom breaks? For advertisers, whether product placement in these binge-watching series creates a stronger effect than in weekly programs needs to be confirmed (Schweidel & Moe, 2016).

ON-DEMAND AUDIENCES

Similar to binge watchers, on-demand audiences have no concept of schedule as they expect content to be constantly available to them. They have no idea of license period and expect the permanent presence of the content. The video entertainment business is shifting toward license based. To avoid audience disappointment and the unrealistic expectation of permanent availability, video streaming services should specify the time period that the movie or series is available based on the license contract. Unlike digital video recording or downloading, streaming content is not "owned" or "kept" by the audience. The on-demand availability is subject to contractual terms. This also creates pressure for streaming services to produce their own original shows so that they do not need to worry about the expiration of licenses from third-party suppliers.

CHALLENGES

Apart from retrieving content on demand on mobile devices such as smartphones, iPads, and wearable devices, the audience is also accessible to media companies, specifically marketers and advertisers. The location function of smartphones' GPS makes media ubiquitous, and the audience can be "found" or "located" by advertisers. For example, when you search the keyword *restaurant* on Google, Google automatically shows a list of restaurants near you and gives you a map (which you did not ask for), restaurant reviews in your location, or even news stories about restaurants in your location. The automated content, customized to your need at the time, is considered "smart marketing." It also means that users are accessible to these advertisers, who paid to receive higher ranks in the listing. As such, in order not to be buried in the 100th+ listing, advertisers have to compete for a good spot in Google search to get your attention to be on the radar for consideration.

Another important feature to make audiences accessible to marketers or media companies is the alert feature in mobile apps. Although users can choose to disable the alert notifications of the apps, the convenience of the notifications, such as for the Apple News app or messaging apps, is usually welcomed by users who want to know what the latest news and messages are. Unlike audiences in the past, who chose when to read what news, today's audiences are reminded constantly that something new is there and asked to read it. Hence, audiences have a virtual assistant reminding them to do this and do that and a virtual adviser who recommends what to watch and what to read. Instead of being an active audience choosing what to read and watch in the abundant media environment, people are now nurtured by converged media devices to become passive and "lazy" audiences who listen to recommendations and are reminded to consume media content in the name of convenience.

TRACEABILITY AND THE BIG DATA AUDIENCE

Datafication, or the availability of digital traces and records of audiences, is an important trend affecting how much we know about how audiences use converged media (Livingstone, 2018). Big data in audience research are nonintrusive measures of audience behavior that automatically track their digital footprint and amount of time they spent on each digital media outlet. With a subscriber identification, the amount can be linked to an individual IP address and other demographic data on file for the media outlet. Cell phone service providers are among the best at tracking audiences' online content and mobile media app use. Apple, as a market leader and an integrated cell phone manufacturer, operating system, and app store provider, is the audience big data giant. Online streaming services such as Netflix and Hulu have much detailed information about their subscribers. E-commerce giant Amazon is even able to combine online video audience data with shopping behavior. Cable and satellite companies' set-top box is another huge reservoir of audience viewing data. But these big data are all proprietary to the media companies and not accessible to the public or researchers. There is no third-party verification, so there is no more common currency as in the Nielsen era. We have to believe that the log and audience traffic data each media service provider reports is accurate. Advertisers must exercise their clout to demand third-party verification of the data provided by the convergent media companies to get a good understanding of audience behavior as recorded by these companies. Privacy and data-usage standards must be established so that digital audiences will not be exploited in ways that will be detrimental to their lives (Mollen & Dhaenens, 2018).

As academic researchers scramble for audience data especially in big data form, social media such as Twitter, which allows open access for public accounts, become the dominant source. But various messaging apps, such as WhatsApp, iMessenger, and emails, are out of reach to researchers. The audience data availability problem is exemplified in this era of big data with a few entities owning large amounts of data while many are excluded from access to them. We also must remember the limitations of the digital footprint. It only shows behavior, not motives, reasons, personality, and environment of the audience. The sole reliance on digital big data in learning about audiences will severely undermine the complex decision-making process. As such, we recommend the following action plan for media managers when conceptualizing, measuring, and reaching audiences in today's convergent environment.

ACTION PLAN

1. Media managers must make good use of their platform portfolio and understand better how and why audiences use each platform in order to designate complementary content. Such content allocation management can maximize audience engagement of the media brand and facilitate cross-promotion of another platform to achieve a fulfilling transmedia and synergistic media experience for audiences.
2. Media managers should understand the audience's increased control of their schedule of media consumption. When media content is consumed on demand, advertising and other promotion materials should also be presented in a customized way in order to achieve better effectiveness. Audiences have to be educated on the need to have advertising to continue free service, or they should directly pay for the content through subscription or pay per use.
3. Media managers should disclose what data are collected and how the data will be used to increase the audience's confidence in the media services. Providing an option to turn off certain data collection functions, such as location, is useful for increasing transparency and building trust with audiences.

KEY TAKEAWAYS

1. Changes in conceptions of audiences are due not only to the development of new media technologies but also to changes in expectations of the role of audience in society, including cultural norms in their media consumption and behavior.
2. Conceptions of audiences changed from passive to active audience to prosumers.
3. Audience agency is the core of audience theories.
4. Audiences play different roles in the media consumption and production processes over time, with participation and engagement as bridges between consumption and production.

5. Multiplatform and multimodal synergy, traceability, personalization, on-demand availability, and accessibility are the five factors of media technologies that change the audience's media experience and expectation of media use.
6. The second screen is a double-edged sword in engaging audiences.
7. Instead of being an active audience choosing what to read and watch in an abundant media environment, people are now nurtured by converged media devices to become passive and "lazy" audiences who listen to recommendations and are constantly reminded to consume media content in the name of convenience.
8. Media managers and practitioners must convey the value of the media experience to the audience to combat the low cost and free-ride expectations of media audiences.

CONCLUSION

In this chapter, we explained the evolution of the concept of audience, from passive recipients of messages to producers and active participants, from live audiences to mediated audiences, and from single-platform to multiplatform or transmedia audiences. Past research assumes audiences are a commodity to advertisers, citizens in a democracy with opinions that should determine public policy, or people who are negotiating with the media influences on them. Accordingly, researchers focused on different aspects of the audiences, including audience size, exposure, and reception of media messages. Audiences' engagement levels also range from mere exposure as casual viewers to the highly involved audiences of fans who dedicate substantial effort to learning about every aspect of the TV or movie series and loyally following the characters and content.

Within media exposure, we discussed the differences between incidental and deliberate exposure and identified how such differences will impact the time spent on the media content and opportunities for further exploration of media content. Media managers must understand when incidental exposure will occur and learn about the differences in information processing between incidental exposure versus deliberate exposure.

This chapter also emphasizes that media consumption is not just a simple individual behavior but also an important social phenomenon in which media content sharing now becomes an important part of the socializing process for people. Audiences also use media content to find likeminded people and share their joy and frustration with their friends and family. Audience engagement as word of mouth can be both beneficial and harmful to media management. Social media engagement can make audiences more loyal but also more vocal about their dissatisfaction with their media consumption experience.

Audiences reflect their personal preferences and identity through their media choices. Big data allows media managers to predict audiences' preferences and media consumption behaviors and even link them to their product purchasing behavior. Recommendation systems facilitate media content exploration while making the consumption more personalized based on the past media consumption behavioral data.

On-demand and binge watching as new audience behaviors facilitated by streaming service technology present both great opportunities and challenges to media executives. Executives have lost control of the audience when they consume content with on-demand viewing, the serial format designed for weekly consumption has become irrelevant, and on-demand and binge watching has increased total consumption and repeated viewing behavior. Those who missed a show on air can catch the episode later, and those who do not watch it first run on television or in movie theaters can now catch up online. How to monetize such new audiences or repeated exposure and how such viewing will impact the audience's interaction with the characters and media content is still largely unknown.

Audience agency has always been studied in audience research. While the agency of audiences has been enhanced by the emergence of various user-generated content, media platforms, and time-shifting media technologies in a converged media environment, audience autonomy is also lowered through automation and more tracking by the media companies. Most important, the value of media content in the audience's eyes should be increased with the increasing sophistication of services. Audiences have many more media choices and can participate and produce their own content easily now. Yet, what we can see is a general tendency toward "low-cost" or "free" content rather than premium content. Netflix and Hulu are low-cost alternatives to cable subscription, although in recent years they have increased high-budget original programming to attract audiences.

Newsfeeds from social media, mobile news apps, and online news sites, which are free, have become the most dominant sources of news in the United States and globally, according to Pew Research Center (Shearer, 2018) and eMarketer (2017). YouTube's unsuccessful experiment with premium service shows that most audiences are unwilling to pay for an "ad-free" experience if the content is not compelling enough (Jarvey, 2018). Ji's (2018) comparison of 51 countries and how the Internet affected the revenue of traditional media shows that direct payment is on the rise for traditional media whose advertising revenue was displaced by online media. Online media themselves largely depend on advertising support if not cross-subsidy from their sponsoring organizations.

Among online media, those who are able to charge for content subscription are streaming entertainment services, video games, and a handful of elite news media (Ha, 2018b). Audiences are willing to pay for movies, concerts, and sports events because they are social gathering activities that can build relationships with other people. Despite the increasing number of prosumers, still a large majority are passive audience members who only consume media content quietly and heavily without any other manifest response or engagement. Media managers and practitioners must do more work in educating their audiences on the value of "exclusive" or "live" media experiences if they wish the audience to pay for them. They must provide content for which the audience cannot easily find free substitutes, and they must learn about the needs of the quiet audience to convert them to a paying audience. Otherwise, they have to find their sponsors and advertisers in one way or another to support their services to audiences. Chapter 3 will review the theories of media management in light of the changes in media audiences.

REFERENCES

Abercrombie, N., & Longhurst, B. (1998). *Audiences: A sociological theory of performance and imagination*. Sage.

Alter, A. (2017). *Irresistible: The rise of addictive technology and the business of keeping us hooked.* Penguin.
Ang, I. (1991). *Desperately seeking the audience.* Routledge.
Blumler, J. G., & Katz, E. (1974). *The uses of mass communications: Current perspectives on gratifications research.* Sage.
Bruns, A. (2008). *Blogs, Wikipedia, Second Life, and beyond: From production to produsage.* Peter Lang.
Cantril, A. H. (1940). *The invasion from Mars: A study in the psychology of panic.* Princeton University Press.
Choi, J. (2016). News internalizing and externalizing: The dimensions of news sharing on online social networking sites. *Journalism & Mass Communication Quarterly, 93,* 816–835.
D'Douza, D. (2020). Netflix doesn't want to talk about binge-watching. *Investopedia.* https://www.investopedia.com/tech/netflix-obsessed-binge-watching-and-its-problem
eMarketer. (February 1, 2017). *News app usage rises worldwide.* https://www.emarketer.com/Article/News-App-Usage-Rises-Worldwide/1015151
Fiske, J. (1992). The cultural economy of fandom. In L. A. Lewis (Ed.), *The adoring audience: Fan culture and popular media* (pp. 30–49). Routledge.
Giglietto, F., & Selva, D. (2014). Second screen and participation: A content analysis on a full season dataset of tweets. *Journal of Communication, 64,* 260–277.
Gil de Zúñiga, H., Garcia-Perdomo, V., & McGregor, S. C. (2015). What is second screening? Exploring motivations of second screen use and its effect on online political participation. *Journal of Communication, 65,* 793–815.
Ha, L. (2018a). How digital natives watch online videos. In L. Ha (Ed.), *The audience and business of YouTube and online videos* (pp. 41–58). Lexington Books.
Ha, L. (2018b). Advertising in media management. In B. Mierzejewska, A. Albarran, & J. Jung (Eds.), *Handbook of media management and economics* (pp. 144–158). Routledge.
Ha, L., Joa, C. Y., Gabay, I., & Kim, K. (2018). Does college students' social media use affect school e-mail avoidance and campus involvement? *Internet Research, 28,* 213–231.
Ha, L., & McCann, K. (2008). An integrated model of advertising clutter in offline and online media. *International Journal of Advertising, 27,* 569–592.
Ha, L., Xu, Y., Yang, C., Wang, F., Yang, L., Abuljadail, M., . . . & Gabay, I. (2018). Decline in news content engagement or news medium engagement? A longitudinal analysis of news engagement since the rise of social and mobile media 2009–2012. *Journalism, 19,* 718–739.
Ha, L., & Yun, G. W. (2014). Digital divide in social media prosumption: Proclivity, production intensity, and prosumer typology among college students and general population. *Journal of Communication and Media Research, 6,* 45–62.
Hall, S. (1973). *Encoding and decoding in the television discourse.* Birmingham Centre for Contemporary Cultural Studies, University of Birmingham.
Hayes, D. (2014, November 3). Social cachet still no guarantee of mass tune-in. *Broadcasting & Cable,* 16–17.
Herzog, H. (1942). What do we really know about daytime serial listeners? In P. F. Lazarsfeld & F. N. Stanton (Eds.), *Radio Research 1942–1943* (pp. 3–33). Essential Books.
Jarvey, N. (2018, November 27). YouTube to pull back on scripted amid push to ad-supported in 2020. *The Hollywood Reporter.* https://www.hollywoodreporter.com/live-feed/youtube-pull-back-scripted-programming-ad-supported-push-1164256
Jenkins, H. (1992). *Textual poachers: Studies in culture and communication.* Routledge.
Jenner, M. (2018). *Netflix and the re-invention of television.* Palgrave Macmillan.
Ji, S. W. (2018). The Internet and changes in the media industry: A 5-year cross-national examination of media industries for 51 countries. *Journalism & Mass Communication Quarterly,* 96, 894–918.
Katz, E., & Lazarsfeld, P. F. (1955). *Personal influence: The part played by people in the flow of mass communications.* The Free Press.
Lee, B., & Lee, R. S. (1995). How and why people watch TV: Implications for the future of interactive television. *Journal of Advertising Research, 35*(6), 9–19.
Livingstone, S. (2018). Audiences in an age of datafication: Critical questions for media research. *Television & New Media, 20*(2), 170–183. doi: 1527476418811118

Mollen, A., & Dhaenens, F. (2018). Audiences' coping practices with intrusive interfaces: Researching audiences in algorithmic, datafied, platform societies. In R. Das & B. Yire-Arne (Eds.), *The future of audiences* (pp. 43–60). Palgrave Macmillan.
Napoli, P. M. (2011). *Audience evolution: New technologies and the transformation of media audiences.* Columbia University Press.
Nee, R. C. (2015). Gatekeeping the 2012 Olympic Games: Did #NBCfail the social media audience? *Journalism & Mass Communication Quarterly*, 92, 77–98. doi: 10.1177/1077699014560517
Nielsen. (2017, January 17). *Media: A new megaphone: Social media gives consumers a chance to be heard on what they watch.* https://www.nielsen.com/us/en/insights/news/2017/a-new-megaphone-social-media-gives-consumers-a-chance-to-be-heard.html
Nielsen. (2018). *The Nielsen total audience report Q2.* https://www.nielsen.com/us/en/insights/reports/2018/q2-2018-total-audience-report.html
Perks, L. G. (2014). *Media marathoning: Immersions in morality.* Lexington Books.
Ritzer, G., & Jurgenson, N. (2010). Production, consumption, prosumption: The nature of capitalism in the age of the digital "prosumer." *Journal of Consumer Culture, 10*(1), 13–36.
Schweidel, D. A., & Moe, W. W. (2016). Binge watching and advertising. *Journal of Marketing, 80*(5), 1–19.
Shearer, E. (2018, December 10). *Social media outpaces print newspapers in the U.S. as a news source.* Pew Research Center. http://www.pewresearch.org/fact-tank/2018/12/10/social-media-outpaces-print-newspapers-in-the-u-s-as-a-news-source/
Sullivan, J. L. (2013). *Media audiences: Effects, users, institutions and power.* Sage.
Toffler, A. (1980). *The third wave.* Bantam Books.
Van Cauwenberge, A., Schaap, G., & Van Roy, R. (2014). TV no longer commands our full attention: Effects of second-screen viewing and task relevance on cognitive load and learning from news. *Computers in Human Behavior, 38,* 100–109.
Vidmar, N., & Rokeach, M. (1974). Archie Bunker's bigotry: A study in selective perception and exposure. *Journal of Communication, 24,* 36–47.
Webster, J., Phalen, P., & Lichty, L. (2013). *Ratings analysis: Audience measurement and analytics.* Routledge.
Zhang, X., & Ha, L. (2015). Time budget, news search time cost, and news media choice. *Time & Society, 24,* 201–220.

CHAPTER 3

Theories of Media Management

Maria A. Kopacz, West Chester University of Pennsylvania

LEARNING OBJECTIVES

1. Understand the seminal theories applied in the field of media management.
2. Explore the connections between theories and evolving media management practices.
3. Address the opportunities and challenges for theorists and practitioners in a convergent media environment.

The past 20 years of technological advancements have been nothing short of disruptive to media industries. Incumbent firms like newspapers, television stations, and book publishers have had to transform their entire business models in order to stay afloat and compete against the emerging multitude of digital native companies, such as BuzzFeed, Netflix, and YouTube. During such turbulent times, theories of media management can help describe, explain, and even prescribe what media practitioners can do to adapt.

Media management scholars agree that their field of study is unique and distinct from other management contexts (Küng, 2007; Lowe, 2016; Mierzejewska, 2018). This is due to the type of products created by the industry, the professional cultures of people who create them, and the vast array of micro- and macro-level effects that these media products have on society in areas like culture, technology, politics, and economics.

Despite its uniqueness, media management is very much an emergent field and appears to lack a unifying theoretical framework. Mierzejewska (2018) reviewed the media management literature and suggests that researchers have not developed much field-specific theoretical thought, opting instead to rely on perspectives from business management, psychology, marketing, and communication studies. The sections below explore the most relevant of those perspectives and discuss how media managers can apply some of them in their management practices.

CASE STUDY

Guardian News Media (GNM) is a British news organization best known for publishing *The Guardian*, a daily newspaper founded in 1821, and *The Observer*, a Sunday paper. The owner of GNM is the Scott Trust Limited. In that role, the company ensures that the newspaper maintains editorial independence from corporate or public ownership.

Under the editorship of Alan Rusbridger (1995–2015), *The Guardian* was responsible for breaking some of the biggest stories of the time, such as the Wikileaks release of U.S. diplomatic messages, the publication of U.S. National Security Agency files provided by Edward Snowden, and the U.K. phone-hacking scandal involving British tabloids.

Like all other legacy players in the 1990s, *The Guardian* had to face the changes brought by the Internet and other new media technologies. Rusbridger was one of the first editors in chief to establish an online version of the newspaper (Rusbridger, 2018). Around 1994, he called together a team of young journalists and technology specialists and gave the group a degree of autonomy in editing the paper's new online edition, Guardian Unlimited. The online edition allowed *The Guardian* to probe topics in depth and provide the volume of material that would not have been possible in print. A year later, *The Guardian*'s technology section OnLine went live, followed by sites for news, careers, and sports in 1996–1998. The paper became one of the pioneers of user participation. Its digital team created talkboards, where readers were free to discuss a variety of topics.

In 2008, Guardian Unlimited was brought together under the common URL guardian.co.uk, and in 2013, the domain name was changed to theguardian.com. In 2011, the paper added a U.S. web edition, and in 2013, it launched a site in Australia. Today, the organization also publishes a magazine featuring the best content from *The Guardian, The Observer, Le Monde,* and others.

Other digital products GNM has experimented with include mobile apps; products and services, such as the OpenPlatform site, where all its content is archived and available for developers; and a data journalism site called Datablog. In 2011, GNM announced that it was becoming a digital-first organization, prioritizing digital content over print (History of *The Guardian*, 2017).

In the early 2000s, newspaper revenues were dropping worldwide as advertisers turned to the web to reach target audiences. In addition, advertising revenues from the website never came close to what *The Guardian* had been making from its print sector (Davies, 2018a). Like other news outlets, *The Guardian* considered adding a paywall to its website. The expectation was to boost revenues by charging readers directly for reading content. Paywalls, however, are easier to implement on specialist trade sites with highly targeted professional audiences than on general news portals. So, after extensive consultations with its audience, the paper decided instead to follow the philanthropy model. Similar to National Public Radio and Wikipedia (Davies, 2018a), *The Guardian* makes all its content available to readers for free. In turn, readers visiting the site are asked to donate a small amount of money in order to keep *The Guardian*'s content available to everyone. The strategy seems to be working. Guardian Media Group CEO David Pemsel recently reported that the company has more than 800,000 paying supporters,

300,000 of whom are sustaining members (Davies, 2018a), and 200,000 additional readers subscribe to digital and print editions of the newspaper.

In 2014, the paper launched Guardian Labs, a branded content site that publishes content series sponsored by brand clients (Watkins, 2014). After some refining, the Labs now publish in-depth journalism content in a similar fashion to how its news desks operate. Each campaign is handled by a team of four people with diverse skills (sales, project management, editorial, marketing). The content combines text, images, audio, and video and is integrated with other content published on and off *The Guardian* site (Davies, 2018b).

Theguardian.com now ranks third in the newspaper category, after mail.co.uk and sina.cn (Similarweb, 2018). After two years of cutting costs and downsizing in its U.K. and U.S. offices,* as well as ramping up branded content efforts, the newspaper now receives 150 million unique visits per month, and it is on the verge of breaking even for the first time in years.

The Guardian's example sheds light on some of the challenges faced by media companies in this rapidly changing digital environment. It also illustrates some strategies that media outlets can undertake to adapt to these conditions. Often, these adaptations incorporate traditional media management theories, which can still guide practitioners' decisions today.

Something Old

Early media management research reflected the focus on media companies as industrial organizations (Picard & Lowe, 2016). The field relied on perspectives from economics and manufacturing. Theorists examined the media industry as a whole rather than exploring in-depth management processes within individual companies. One notable research interest has been consolidation, a phenomenon that gained attention in the 1990s. Researchers explored the implications of growing conglomerates for content diversity and distribution, especially how consolidation impacts the coverage of political candidates, public controversies, and current events. Overall, this literature found that consolidated ownership did adversely impact the nature of media coverage (Busterna & Hansen, 1990; Glasser, Allen, & Blanks, 1989). For instance, Picard and Van Weezel (2008) found that publicly owned media companies are pressured to reduce newsroom investments, which, in turn, may affect the quality of news coverage.

A key theoretical context in media management research has been strategic management theories. Among strategic management theories, one of the earliest schools of thought is the rational perspective (Küng, 2016). The rationalist perspective examines the nature of competitive environments in which organizations operate and offers implications in developing long-term strategic plans (Küng, 2017a). This approach views management strategy as a product rather than a dynamic process. The goal of strategy development is to identify environmental factors like economics and business cycles and

*That included shrinking *The Guardian*. *The Guardian*'s print edition changed from the Berliner format to the cost-effective tabloid format, and the printing and distribution work were outsourced to the Trinity Mirror Group (Davies, 2018b).

then choose a strategic position for the company that will help it establish equilibrium and function under various contexts and conditions (Chakravarthy & Doz, 1992).

STRUCTURE-CONDUCT-PERFORMANCE FRAMEWORK

The structure-conduct-performance framework (Fu, 2003) is a theory that emerged within the rational approach. It suggests that the structure of the media industry affects how firms within it behave (conduct), which in turn predicts the industry's performance. Mierzejewska (2018) points out that for media organizations, performance can be understood both in economic terms (profits and losses) and in terms of the firms' ability to serve the public good through dissemination of information and culture. A good recent illustration is Netflix, which started out in 1997 by distributing video content on DVDs via home delivery. With the improvement of Internet access and bandwidth, Netflix later switched to a subscription-based streaming service. In 2013, the company started producing its own video content, often tackling controversial topics. Netflix's original shows like *Orange Is the New Black*, *Tidying Up with Marie Kondo*, and *Dear White People* have not only met with enthusiastic audience reception but have also been influencing the public discourse around issues like race, sexual orientation, gender identity, the prison system, and consumerism. As a business innovator, Netflix has pushed other media distribution companies, including Amazon, Hulu, and YouTube, to start creating their own original content. The Netflix distribution system, which gives each user individual recommendations and allows users to access entire content series, has also shaped media consumption trends by popularizing the phenomenon of binge watching video content (Merikivi, Bragge, Scornavacca, & Verhagen, 2019).

The *Seattle Post-Intelligencer* (*SPI*), a local newspaper that was founded in 1863 in Seattle, can also demonstrate the application and usefulness of the structure-conduct-performance theory (Tate, 2009). For more than a century, the newspaper served the Seattle news market, delivering coverage that was somewhat to the left of the area's biggest newspaper, the *Seattle Times*. *SPI* prided itself on serving the public interest by delivering in-depth, investigative journalism that challenged the status quo. In 1921, the newspaper was purchased by the Hearst Corporation. The changing media landscape of the early 2000s resulted in declining revenues until, in 2009, Hearst announced that it would either sell *SPI* or convert it to an online-only newspaper. A sale did not occur, and on March 17, 2009, *SPI* published its last print issue, reduced its staff from 200 to 20, and moved to an online-only model. Seeking to maximize profits from this asset, Hearst pushed *SPI* toward lighter, less ambitious news coverage and an advertising-heavy interface. In the long run, this strategy did not help. In early 2018, Hearst announced further *SPI* staff reductions and a transition to the editorial control of the *Seattle Times*, which Hearst also owns (Kroman, 2018). Senior editor Levi Pulkinnen was among those who resigned during that time. In a retrospective article a few months later, Pulkinnen (2018) reflected that, during the transition, *SPI* failed to view its readers as committed fans and engaged citizens or to mobilize this group to follow *SPI* online in greater numbers. Further damage was done by relying exclusively on the audience-as-product business model, which, Pulkinnen argues, put many readers off its advertising-laden platform.

The examples above illustrate a global trend where major structural shifts in the media marketplace pushed legacy media toward online-based models, and these transitions affected financial performance as well as the social and cultural impact of the content they produce.

FIVE FORCES MODEL

Porter (1979) proposed the five forces model in order to improve an organization's performance and profit potential and assume an optimal strategic position in its industry. To accomplish this goal, the organization must conduct an in-depth analysis of the state of competition within its industry. The state of competition is shaped collectively by five competitive "forces." Together, they predict the firm's potential to succeed within its industry. These forces include (1) the threat of new entrants (i.e., new companies offering rival products), (2) the threat of alternative products, (3) suppliers' bargaining power, (4) buyers' bargaining power, and (5) the competition from industry rivals.

The five forces model can be useful for assessing the potential for profitability in an industry context that is relatively stable and predictable (Küng, 2018). Let us use the online classifieds niche as an example. Since the late 1990s, the online classifieds niche has been saturated with competitors, such as craigslist.com, classifiedads.com, oodle.com, and sites owned by regional papers like *Philadelphia Inquirer*'s Philly.com Marketplace. With multiple entry barriers, one might believe that since there is considerable existing competition, the threat of new entrants is low. However, established media and technology companies can leverage their user bases (economies of scale), easy access to distribution channels, and large capital resources to add classifieds pages to their portfolios. A recent example is Facebook, which relaunched its Marketplace section in 2016. The Marketplace is free, readily available to all Facebook users, and based on extensive user data and artificial intelligence (Olson, 2018). Placing ads on users' Facebook pages also reduces anonymity that comes with typical classified ads. As such, the Facebook Marketplace is fast becoming an attractive alternative to what any local advertising board can provide. While Philly.com offers a limited free classifieds package, most of its classified subscription packages are offered at a fee. Facebook and Craigslist, in contrast, do not charge individuals for placing classified ads on their sites. This gives users, who are both the buyers and suppliers to classifieds services, significant bargaining power. Following the five forces model, it would appear that the state of the competition gives Facebook the opportunity to assume an advantageous position in the industry.

When applied through an in-depth analysis of an industry, the five forces model lets a media player determine opportunities to gain bargaining power over its competition and block new and existing rivals from taking over its market position. Looking at enterprises as industrial organizations can help media managers understand the "big picture" of the external environment and allow a company to exploit opportunities and minimize threats. However, since the digital disruption began, the five forces model has been criticized for its inability to address the dynamic nature of new media environments (Teece, 2007).

RESOURCE-BASED VIEW

While the five forces model examines the industry forces outside of an organization, the resource-based view (Barney, 1991; Penrose, 1959) looks within. It posits that in order to be successful against its competition, an organization must possess resources and capabilities that are valuable, rare, inimitable, and nonsubstitutable (VRIN). The resources may be tangible, such as facilities, raw materials, trademarks, and technologies. They may also be intangible, including knowledge, culture, relationships, people, or capabilities that enable the organization to implement its management strategy and achieve competitive advantage (Barney, 1991). The role of management is to identify the resources that meet those criteria and develop, cultivate, and protect them. Firms adapt to the changing environments and utilize resources within to create comparative advantage (Mierzejewska, 2018).

A good example of a VRIN resource is Google's search algorithm. It's valuable, as it produces exceptionally high-quality search results, thus attracting advertisers. It is unique to Google and, therefore, rare. It is difficult to imitate, as Google keeps the algorithm secret, and there are no readily available substitutes for it. Indeed, Google's global market share across devices in December 2018 topped 80% (Net Marketshare, 2019). As evident in this example, the resource-based view provides a parsimonious framework for analyzing a company's key internal resources.

VALUE CHAIN ANALYSIS

Just like the resource-based view, the value chain framework (Porter, 1985) assumes that organizations use a variety of resources to develop and supply products and services in their markets. The model's focus, however, is on the value chain, a process of sourcing, producing, and distributing products, which results in greater value to customers/users than the combined value of the resources employed. Those added values then translate into profit.

The value chain analysis breaks down a firm's processes into a series of stages and groups them into primary and secondary activities, which are executed by various systems within or outside a media organization. The primary activities directly relate to the products, including operations, logistics, marketing, sales, and customer service. The support activities are those related to human resources, technology and infrastructure, and procurement. They assist in executing one or more of the primary activities. Each of the value chain activities can be examined separately for the costs and values it offers. The more competitive each activity is, the more added value the entire process contributes.

Prior to the diffusion of the Internet, media organizations had more or less predictable, linear value chains and were able to control all or most of their processes in house. This is no longer the case. The next section discusses the theories in the context of technological transformations.

Something New

The plethora of technological advances that occurred during the past three decades have been termed the biggest revolution in mass communication (Scott, 2015). Media ecology is a useful paradigm to understand this ever-evolving media marketplace. For instance, Postman (1985) compared media technologies to environments, which affect human perception, understanding, feeling, and value. They impose structures that specify what individuals can see, say, and do, often in ways that are not very apparent. McLuhan (1964) went as far as to argue that the content conveyed through the media is less important than these structural implications.

Indeed, we now function in a world where one device allows us to perform multiple tasks like making phone calls, writing letters, reading news, watching movies, and paying bills. Companies invest ample capital and human resources in building an Internet presence. Newspapers publish most of their content online. Individuals can produce and publish independent films with almost no budget. Writers release books without the help of a publishing company. Viewers can binge watch television series on demand. Most individuals spend multiple hours each day interacting with one or more digital devices (Nielsen, 2018). One constant in this ever-changing environment is technological innovation.

Rational theories of management assume that an organization can achieve equilibrium and operate in a more or less stable fashion. Yet, in the current technologically determined environment, equilibrium is a rare phenomenon, and change is a constant (Küng, 2017a; Mierzejewska, 2011). Thus, scholars within the adaptive approach posit that media management strategies should reflect this change and operate in an emergent fashion, functioning more as a dynamic process than a static product of the planning process (Fulmer, 2000; Mintzberg, Lampel, Quinn, & Ghoshal, 2003). Küng argues, "Strategy is not primarily about planning. Rather, it is about trying to see the world as it really is and preparing the organization so that it has a chance of a successful future" (2017a, p. 66). Media organizations now need to be able to implement incremental changes over sustained periods of time and translate them into big transformations (Oliver, 2018).

VALUE CHAINS IN EMERGENT ENVIRONMENTS

New technologies have brought significant disruption to industry value chains. The recent technological changes have introduced a high-speed data transmission infrastructure, where users have constant access to wireless-enabled devices with high-speed data capabilities. It is possible to create multimedia content using those very devices and distribute it via the multitude of social platforms, such as Facebook, Instagram, and Snapchat. This becomes particularly challenging for legacy media organizations like newspapers and book publishers. A new cooking blog can enter the same market as an established cooking magazine and offer the same or greater value than the legacy company while omitting quite a few components of a traditional value chain. This process allows newcomers to create new value-adding activities and thus overtake incumbents (Küng, 2017a).

In legacy organizations, the value chain was more or less owned by each individual organization. As a result of technological changes, value chains are being taken apart and outsourced. New players show up in the media environment and specialize in particular elements of a value chain (Bradley & Nolan, 1998). Some elements of the value chain can be eliminated entirely (e.g., print and distribution of printed products), while others can be added in (e.g., distribution via novel formats and platforms). Content production chains can now be unbundled at each stage and managed differently from others. A single stage can be further split into a number of discrete activities.

New players such as Netflix that have grown up with new content distribution platforms are better positioned to handle the complexity of today's convergent media environment than many legacy players. The changes are always more challenging for legacy media organizations, who must learn and integrate the new processes into their existing structures. Some legacy media (e.g., book publishers or music distributors) must reposition themselves and show content creators and consumers their excellence at managing elements of the value chain like marketing and building public profiles—or they must face being pushed entirely out of the market. Despite these challenges faced by legacy media organizations, there are opportunities to reorganize their value chains, add and remove elements, and outsource the ones at which they may not excel (Evans & Wurster, 2000).

STRUCTURAL CONTINGENCY THEORY

Structural theories were originally applied to study how media ownership and organizational structure affect media content and the professional values of media managers and how those, in turn, shape content creation. Donaldson (1996) proposes that organizations shape their structures in response to contingencies in their market environment in such a way as to maximize efficiency and profitability. The effectiveness of a structure depends on the degree to which it fits the contingencies.

Internal contingency factors come into play inside the organization. Examples include job tasks and organization size. Environmental factors come from outside the organization and shape its ability to adapt to its business environment. Examples of environmental factors include changing competition and consumer preferences or uncertain economy. The interaction between these two groups of factors shapes the organizational structure.

Mierzejewska (2011) notes that structural contingency theory has received little attention from media management scholars. Although grounded in older, rational paradigms, it can be a useful heuristic framework to begin understanding convergent media management as the structures of media organizations grow increasingly complex in response to ongoing changes in technology and media ownership.

DYNAMIC CAPABILITIES THEORY

The dynamic capabilities theory assumes that the emergent business contexts drive media companies to innovate and develop dynamic capabilities (Maijanen & Virta, 2017; Teece & Pisano, 1994). Oliver (2018) defines those as "a firm's ability to renew and reconfigure their resources, capabilities, and competencies in response to fast-changing competitive environments" (p. 2). He also argues that in order to be sustainable, media organizations must engage in ongoing learning and adjust their resources, capabilities, and strategy so they can build competitive advantage. The changes may encompass tangible resources (e.g., processes, routines, product development, collaborations, acquisitions) and intangible ones (e.g., the management skills of scanning the environment for threats and opportunities as well as communicating the evolving strategy).

The process of developing competitive advantage is continuous and involves building a series of smaller competitive advantages over time. These advantages are assumed to be temporary and contingent on the changes within the environment and the firm's resources.

In view of this theory, strategy now has to emphasize at its core organizational adaptation over competitive advantages (Hensmans, Johnson, & Yip, 2013). Indeed, a media company's ability to transform itself in order to tap into the prevailing competitive conditions can be considered a key dynamic capability of today, as it produces improved performance and competitive advantages (Wei & Lau, 2010).

New capabilities can be developed from within, for instance, by gaining knowledge from outside and adapting their learning to develop new capabilities (Dixon, Meyer, & Day, 2014). They can also be accessed through mergers, acquisitions, and corporate liaisons. Adaptation often also means divesting strategic resources that do not fit the long-term strategic plan or that fail to perform. For instance, in 2015, the publishing company Pearson sold the *Financial Times* and *The Economist* and divested its 47 stakes in Penguin Random House (Barnato, 2015). These divestments were performed to help the company focus more on its competitive advantage—educational offerings.

Media managers serve several important roles in the adaptation process. First, executives scan the environment for signs of change and identify opportunities for growth. Second, they develop and communicate the upcoming strategy changes to the firm's stakeholders. Third, they provide motivation and oversee the implementation of the strategies.

Developing new capabilities often requires substantial investments. In the short term, such expenditures can put a company in the red financially but can pay off significantly in the long run. A media company's level of strategic reconfiguration can be observed in its development of new services or product offerings, as exemplified by the Netflix example we reviewed earlier.

Managing changes and adaptations can be draining on a company's resources and people. Indeed, following the path of emergent strategy can produce a sense of chaos and instability. Therefore, scholars suggest that media companies should not abandon long-term strategy but rather deploy it in times of relative stability (Lynch, 2015; Oliver, 2018; Perrott, 2008).

ORGANIZATIONAL CULTURE THEORY

The most recent view of organizational strategy assumes that organizations do not exist within objective reality but instead are socially constructed by their members and the public (Küng, 2007). In this light, what happens in organizations is shaped strongly by the values, belief systems, emotions, and politics of their constituents. Effective strategy must, therefore, examine how such forces facilitate or inhibit organizational change.

A helpful concept within this approach is organizational culture, which has been defined as a collection of shared values, practices, symbols, and knowledge that are socially constructed within the organization and are transmitted to new members by more established organizational actors (Bloor & Dawson, 1994). Organizational cultures are shaped by external forces, such as national and popular cultures, and internally, by influx of new technologies, strategic efforts by leadership, or subcultures and professional cultures within the organization, all of which can often be at odds with each other.

The organizational culture can both enhance and impede organizational performance (Achtenhagen & Mierzejewska, 2016). Specific to media organizations, organizational cultures have been shown to influence the selection and framing of news content (Hirsch, 1977). Culture is also an important predictor of media firms' approach to changes, especially the rapid changes brought by convergence and the technological revolution (Küng, 2018).

NICHE THEORY

Niche theory posits that media organizations occupy niches in the industry environment, much like living organisms hold their respective niches in ecosystems (Dimmick & Rothenbuhler, 1984). Organizations choose niches in their environments and adapt to them in order to stay competitive and survive.

According to Dimmick (2003) to maintain hold of a niche, media organizations and technologies must compete for and make efficient use of finite resources in their ecosystem. Such resources include audience attention and spending, advertiser expenditures, and investor capital. An organization can achieve that by differentiating itself from other media outlets via the gratifications it offers (e.g., surveillance vs. diversion) or via time and space dimensions within which it offers gratifications (e.g., using the Twitter mobile app to disseminate news in real time vs. presenting news during scheduled segments on the radio).

Competitive superiority refers to a media outlet's capacity to use its available resources more effectively than other outlets and is crucial for survival within the industry (Dimmick, Feaster & Hoplamazian, 2011). When a large niche overlap exists between two media organizations, the one that carries competitive superiority will displace its competitor.

Just like in a natural ecosystem, industry resources are subject to fluctuation. A decade ago, Dimmick et al. (2011) found little niche overlap between traditional and mobile news channels, such that mobile technologies were used mostly during workdays by users on the go and traditional channels remained popular during off-peak hours by users at home. Since then, mobile technologies have changed the patterns of news consumption, thus blurring these niche boundaries. Consequently, news outlets that pivot their use of resources to address these changes stand a greater chance of persisting in the industry.

DIFFUSION OF INNOVATIONS

Digital technology is now an inherent part of the media business (Küng, 2017b). All legacy media organizations have developed online outlets, and the vast majority of company revenue is now derived from the consumption of online content. Pure technological companies, such as Amazon, Google, and Facebook, now either produce media content themselves or at least develop platforms where other media companies publish their content. Given the disruptive pace of technological changes, it is helpful to apply theoretical frameworks that will help us integrate technology adoption more effectively into the organizational strategies.

Diffusion theory is a well-established framework (Rogers, 1962). It posits that most innovations (including new technologies) diffuse in society in a predictable pattern, following the so-called diffusion curve. Technology adopters can be divided into five categories depending on when during the diffusion process they adopt the technology. Innovators are the first group to adopt an innovation. They include the creators of the innovation and those with high tolerance for risk, ample resources, and strong orientation toward experimenting. Early adopters are well integrated into the social fabric. They possess higher social status, and they influence the opinions of other groups. The early majority group is the critical mass—it is the largest group of adopters, and once an innovation is adopted by this group, it typically sees ongoing success. The late majority are those more cautious and risk averse, with more limited resources, who need to ensure that innovations are well tested by the system before adopting them. The laggards are the last group to adopt the innovation. They are less socially integrated and resistant to adoption, often due to their cultural and personal values. It is important to note that an adopter of two innovations may fall into two different categories of adopters. For instance, a user may be an early adopter of podcasts because they provide utility value while driving to work. The same user may also be a laggard on the adoption of virtual reality games due to a personal belief about adverse effects of video gaming.

Diffusion theory is useful because it helps us address numerous questions, including how a media technology diffuses in the industry, what pattern the diffusion follows, what is the individual process of adoption, and what circumstances increase the likelihood that an individual will adopt.

Diffusion of innovations is a complex process, as adopters include not only end users but also media organizations themselves. For instance, some newspapers, like *The Guardian,* were quick to implement online forums on their websites, while others delayed adoption in order to observe its opportunities and risks, and yet others did not adopt it at all. Only a few media management scholars, however, have used diffusion of innovations to look at organizational adoption processes within media companies. For example, Ferguson and Greer (2011) examined how local radio stations use Twitter, while Lawson-Borders and Kirk (2005) studied blogs in campaign communication.

TECHNOLOGY ACCEPTANCE MODEL

The technology acceptance model, developed by Davis (1989), sheds further light on the circumstances of technology adoption by individuals. According to Davis, the extent to which an individual is ready to accept a technology depends on its perceived usefulness and ease of use. Perceived usefulness may be applied to professional goals (e.g., work performance) or personal ones. For instance, a social media user might choose Facebook as a way to stay in touch with family members but may use Twitter as the primary channel for receiving news. The ease of use is defined as the extent to which a person expects using a technology to be effort free. An example of a media technology that has been slow to gain widespread adoption is the QR code. It allows one to embed information, such as web links, product details, or contact information into a small square containing a black-and-white geometric pattern. A person with a QR code reader can scan the code to access the data embedded in it. Unfortunately, until recently, most mobile devices required users to download a separate QR reader app, which posed an adoption barrier. This may change in the future since smartphone developers are starting to integrate QR reading capabilities into native camera apps.

Opportunities and Challenges

As Bauman (2000) points out, we are operating in a time of liquid modernity where profound changes are constant and rapid. Picard and Lowe (2016) note that media markets are volatile and difficult to control. They are continuously affected by entrepreneurial and technological innovations initiated by media companies on one hand and by audience behavior on the other. Küng (2017a) argues that this creates a management environment that is emergent in nature, one with blurred distinctions among industry actors, constantly changing business and audience models, and new and unexpected competitors (Eisenhardt & Brown, 1999; Robins & Wiersema, 2000).

OPPORTUNITIES

In the 20th century, media were often conceptualized as one of society's power systems. In line with that, Ball-Rokeach and DeFleur's (1976) media system dependency theory discusses variables that predict when the power of the media system in society will be the greatest. These include the extent to which media meet individuals' needs (information, functioning in society, or fantasy escape) and the degree of social or political instability. A particular medium (e.g., television) might be preferred over another (e.g., newspaper) due to its ability to meet one or more of those needs more effectively. The greater the dependency on a particular medium, the stronger its effects on users.

In the 21st century, people are living in a multimedia environment with an array of devices, platforms, and applications. Reflecting McLuhan's (1964) famous statement "the medium is the message," new media technologies profoundly shape how we interact with media messages. Increasingly, scholars are moving away from the term *audiences* and toward *users* in order to emphasize individuals' ability to engage in two-way communication with media organizations. More important, the nature of users' dependency on media is likely more technologically determined.

Griffiths (1996; 1999) introduced the concept of technological dependency, defining it as a nonchemical addiction to a media technology (e.g., Internet). Mobile devices are an example of a technology argued to produce strong dependency. Some users report feeling anxious when they are away from their phones (Anshari, Alas, & Sulaiman, 2019). In addition, most feel the need to immediately respond to messages received on their phones (Robb, 2019). It is clear that mobile devices have changed the patterns of audience content consumption. For instance, Molyneux (2018) found that mobile news consumption takes on a "snacking" pattern, with users checking in briefly multiple times a day and switching between mobile and desktop devices to consume content. The ease of switching between apps, devices, and content products means that media organizations cannot count on users to keep coming back regularly the way they did for the nine o'clock news. Vukanovic (2018) predicts that media systems will continue moving toward cloud-based, hypermedia, on-demand, personalized content models that maximize audience reach.

INNOVATING ACROSS PRODUCTS AND PLATFORMS

For years, media companies operated in a stable marketplace. Newspapers released their daily issues, and evening news aired their segments. Movie studios churned out various movie genres, but fundamentally they were all films with a predictable length that could be watched in a movie theater or on home video. That is no longer the case.

Küng (2016) points to one major change in the form of digital disruption by large technology companies like Facebook, Google, and Apple. Some of those companies straddle more than one field. For example, Amazon started out as a book retailer, then diversified into general retail, media production, and, recently, even food distribution (see table 3.1).

Mierzejewska (2011) points to two key challenges faced by media companies in today's changing media landscape: getting noticed by audiences and monetizing content. Convergent/deconvergent media dynamics and intense competition are leading media companies, both legacy and pure play, to continue developing and testing new media products. Given this velocity and intensity, it is helpful to use concepts from new product development (NPD) research to examine how new products are created. Mierzejewska (2018) notes that such theories have not been widely used by media managers before. Yet, NPD models are useful frameworks both for developing media innovations and understanding what distinguishes successful ideas from failed ones.

General NPD models may be a good starting point. The consulting firm Booz Allen Hamilton (1982) divides the NPD process into seven stages. During new product strategy, a media company needs to consider its organizational goals and develop goals and objectives for the new product. Next, specific product ideas are brainstormed and

TABLE 3.1. Timeline of Amazon's Diversification

Date	*Event*
1994	Amazon is founded
1997	The company goes public
1998	Product line expanded to music
2002	Amazon begins selling clothing
2003	Amazon Web Services launched
2007	Kindle introduced
2008	Audiobooks company Audible acquired
2009	Shoe seller Zappos acquired
2012	Robotics company Kiva Systems acquired
2013	*Washington Post* is acquired
2014	Amazon Fire phone launched; social gaming site Twitch acquired
2015	Amazon Echo launched
2017	Whole Foods acquired

Source: DePillis & Sherman, 2018.

generated. These ideas are then screened to determine which merit further evaluation. During the business analysis stage, profitability of the potential products is determined. The product ideas that pass this step are then developed into products. A series of tests will follow in order for the company to refine and officially launch the product.

For instance, a local newspaper might desire to increase audience engagement and deliver more value through its content, to ultimately maximize profits. The brainstorming process might result in an idea to create a smartphone app with local news and weather delivered 24/7 to users' devices and opportunities for users to contribute stories and comments. The screening and analysis process allow the newspaper to critically examine this idea against its business strategy. The organization can then hire user experience developers to create a prototype of the app and deliver it to a small segment of its audience for user testing and refinement until the app is finally launched via the newspaper's website and app marketplaces.

CHALLENGES

An industry that went from several decades of relative stability to a reality where change is constant faces considerable leadership challenges in areas like encouraging creativity, achieving shared vision, managing projects, and resolving conflicts. Many of these challenges are shaped by the industry's unique characteristics (Deslandes, 2016).

For example, journalists and news editors can have potentially conflicting goals and motivations. Achtenhagen and Mierzejewska (2016) propose that journalists typically show intrinsic motivation and are guided by professional values as well as ego rewards (e.g., public respect). Understanding the motivation of key actors within media organizations can be helpful in leading employees through ongoing strategic pivots.

The complexity and fluidity of the media environment means that future media managers have to be prepared to wear many hats in their organization. Küng (2017a) discusses four roles of an effective future media leader. First, leaders must build strategies to navigate industry changes. Second, they need to be able to promote creativity in order to achieve a steady stream of competitive products. Third, they need to develop expertise in technology and an understanding of how technology impacts their business. Finally, they must act as stewards of the public interest and ensure that their organization ethically and morally fulfills its role in society.

In addition to being technologically determined, media creative processes have increasingly become project based (Lundin & Norbäck, 2016). Project teams are often made up of diverse professionals selected for their individual expertise of value to the project. For example, a branded content team may include writers, video editors, data analysts, web developers, and marketing specialists, each with their own expertise, professional identity, and values. Media managers, therefore, face the challenge of defining best leadership practices in such contexts. Murphy and Ensher (2008) introduce the concept of shared charismatic leadership, which bridges the ideas of leader personality and charisma and the need to share leadership with various team members. A leader may use their personal influence to set the initial vision for the project but then take turns with other team members in leading the group through different project stages. Who gets to lead at any given time will be determined by the project goals and expertise required by each project stage.

A major aspect of media leadership for the foreseeable future is managing changes. Studies of media leaders' approach to change reveal that their own response to disruption predicts their organization's ability to successfully navigate changes (Killebrew, 2003; Pérez-Latre & Sánchez-Tabernero, 2003). Küng's (2017b) extensive road map for media organizations offers a number of strategic recommendations. These are listed in the action plan below.

ACTION PLAN

1. Media organizations need clear long-term strategies focused on the company's identity and vision.
2. Media managers have to be ready to make changes to strategies quickly as the environment changes.
3. Any innovations, no matter how attractive, must be screened against the business model and core goals of the organization.
4. Although strategy and innovation are the purview of organization leaders, they should delegate some of their responsibilities to other competent team members.
5. Organizations need to focus on hiring and retaining quality staff as well as promoting lifelong learning of the workforce at all levels. Since much ongoing innovation is technologically driven, leaders must make efforts to merge the engineering and content aspects of media work into their organizational culture.

KEY TAKEAWAYS

1. Media management research is a vast field, but it lacks its own theoretical perspectives, relying instead on theories from business, media studies, communication, and psychology.
2. Rational theories of management dominated the field early on, with the assumption of a stable industry and focused strategies that would maintain a stable competitive advantage over a firm's rivals.
3. Media industries have undergone major disruptive transformations, and media managers face constant changes.
4. Some media management theories have reflected the changes by adopting more emergent strategy approaches.
5. Recent research suggests that media management should center on building long-term strategies grounded in audience research and organizational identities and cultures, with the assumption that frequent pivot adjustments to the strategies will be made as necessary.

CONCLUSION

This chapter discussed theoretical work relevant to media management in convergent/deconvergent media contexts. Media organizations are unique in that many have operated for decades in a dual-product marketplace (Napoli, 2001; 2003). This means that audiences are both the consumers of media content and the products delivered to advertisers. More recently, audience members have also become content producers through platforms like YouTube, Snapchat, Facebook, Instagram, and WordPress. In addition to their bottom line, many media organizations also carry the mission of contributing to the social good (e.g., by informing the public about the country's governing process).

Given the unique perspective of media management contexts, researchers rely on theories from business management, psychology, marketing, and communication studies (Mierzejewska, 2018). As the field emerges in today's convergent environment, it is important for future scholars to work toward a more cohesive theoretical framework that continues to prioritize interdisciplinary and hybrid scholarship.

Early theories of media management were grounded in the industrial era and assumed that media organizations operate in a stable technological and business environment. The concepts of market structures, external forces, internal resources, and value chains apply well to the postindustrial world. However, media organizations must adapt to the transitional nature of today's ever-evolving media environments. Theories of technological diffusion are central to understanding how the media environment changes, and theories of organizational adaptation and leadership help researchers and practitioners identify the best ways to adapt to the changes.

Media management is a vast field of research, reflecting the magnitude of the global media industry. The industry has been revolutionized by emerging technologies, such as the Internet, mobile devices, and social media. New technologies, such as artificial intelligence, machine learning, and computer visualization, are continuing to diffuse, empowering consumers to do more and expect more from media companies. These advancements are forcing the many players in the crowded media field to reassess their management strategies.

Given this, dedicated theories of media management focusing in particular on emergent strategy, change management, and audience behavior will be central to whether media organizations can successfully navigate their environments and fulfill their complex missions.

Media practitioners must engage in multidimensional thinking about strategy. On one hand, it is a good idea to learn from tech start-ups in developing long-term, multiyear strategies for growth and clear vision of the future in 10, 20, or 30 years. On the other hand, media managers need to be aware that major changes do not happen overnight, but quick strategic pivots can and should occur in response to environmental changes (Küng, 2017b). Innovation is key in this context, but any new ideas should be consistent with the organization's business objectives. Following new product development processes in developing media content will help. Investing in employee expertise and lifelong learning in a variety of specializations, sharing leadership with team members, and collaborating with external experts are essential for the ongoing success of media organizations.

Future media practitioners need to be ready to reinvent their professional identities and prepare for jobs that don't yet exist. Based on extensive interviews with media industry leaders, Küng (2017b) recommends a number of transformations media organizations, especially legacy players, have to undergo in order to thrive in this new environment. Particularly, a key recommendation for media theorists is to center their efforts on developing management theories specific to mass media (Achtenhagen & Mierzejewska, 2016; Picard & Lowe, 2016). To do so, it is critical that media theorists and researchers step beyond academia and build stronger ties to industry practitioners. Collaborating with practitioners will allow researchers to keep up with rapid changes (Küng, 2016) and develop theoretical perspectives that will unify the field and help guide ongoing changes in the industry.

Despite the rapid changes in the media landscape, theory is still key to developing effective and successful strategy in media industries. Practitioners must continue to be trained in multiple perspectives and historical case studies that will serve as the foundation for future strategic decisions. Perhaps more than in any other discipline, the intersection between theory, scholarship, and applied industry training is critical to success in media management.

The next chapter extends the exploration of media management scholarship by discussing the plethora of scholarly research methods that have been used to examine media management. Media management theoretical perspectives outlined in this chapter should be used to drive media management research. Thus, it is critical for media practitioners to understand the connections between media management theories, research, and practices. The next chapter will discuss some of the popular research methods used in media management research.

REFERENCES

Achtenhagen, L., & Mierzejewska, B. (2016). The development of media management as an academic field: Tracing the contents and impact of its three leading journals. In G. F. Lowe & C. Brown (Eds.), *Managing media firms and industries* (pp. 23–42). Springer.

Anshari, M., Alas, Y., & Sulaiman, E. (2019). Smartphone addictions and nomophobia among youth. *Vulnerable Children and Youth Studies, 14*(3), 242–247. doi: 10.1080/17450128.2019.1614709

Ball-Rokeach, S. J., & DeFleur, M. L. (1976). A dependency model of mass-media effects. *Communication Research, 3*, 3–21.

Barnato, K. (2015, August 14). *Here's why we sold the* FT, Economist*: Pearson CEO*. CNBC. https://www.cnbc.com/2015/08/14/heres-why-we-sold-the-ft-economist-pearson-ceo.html

Barney, J. (1991). Firm resources and sustained competitive advantage. *Journal of Management, 17*, 99–120.

Bauman, Z. (2000). *Liquid modernity*. Polity Press.

Bloor, G., & Dawson, P. (1994). Understanding professional culture in organizational context. *Organization Studies, 15*, 275–295.

Booz Allen Hamilton. (1982). *New product management for the 1980's*. Booz Allen Hamilton, Inc.

Bradley, S. P., & Nolan, R. L. (1998). *Sense & respond: Capturing value in the network era*. Harvard Business Review Press.

Busterna, J. C., & Hansen, K. A. (1990). Presidential endorsement patterns by chain-owned papers, 1976–84. *Journalism Quarterly, 67*, 286–294.

Chakravarthy, B. S., & Doz, Y. (1992). Strategy process research—focusing on corporate self-renewal. *Strategic Management Journal, 13*, 5–14.

Davies, J. (2018a, January). *"We're at the foothills of what we can do": How* The Guardian *improbably put itself on the path to profits*. Digiday. https://digiday.com/media/guardian-improbably-put-way-path-profits

Davies, J. (2018b, September). *How* The Guardian *overhauled its content studio to make it more efficient*. Digiday. https://digiday.com/media/guardian-overhauled-content-studio-make-efficient

Davis, F. D. (1989). Perceived usefulness, perceived ease of use, and user acceptance of information technology. *MIS Quarterly, 13*, 319–339.

DePillis, L., & Sherman, I. (2018, October 4). *Amazon's extraordinary evolution: A timeline*. CNN Business. https://www.cnn.com/interactive/2018/10/business/amazon-history-timeline/index.html

Deslandes, G. (2016). Leadership in media organisations: Past trends and challenges ahead. In G. F. Lowe, & C. Brown (Eds.), *Managing media firms and industries* (pp. 311–327). Springer.

Dimmick, J. (2003). *Media competition and coexistence: The theory of the niche*. Lawrence Erlbaum Associates.

Dimmick, J., Feaster, J. C., & Hoplamazian, G. J. (2011). News in the interstices: The niches of mobile media in space and time. *New Media & Society, 13*, 23–39.

Dimmick, J., & Rothenbuhler, E. W. (1984). Competitive displacement in the communication industries: New media in old environments. In R. Rice (Ed.), *The new media* (pp. 287–304). Sage.

Dixon, S., Meyer, K., & Day, M. (2014). Building dynamic capabilities of adaptation and innovation: A study of micro-foundations in a transition economy. *Long Range Planning, 47*, 186–205. doi: 10.1016/j.irp.2013.08.011

Donaldson, L. (1996). The normal science of structural contingency theory. In S. R. Clegg, C. Hardy, & W. R. Nord (Eds.), *Handbook of organizational studies* (pp. 57–76). Sage.

Eisenhardt, K. M., & Brown, S. L. (1999). Patching: Restitching business portfolios in dynamic markets. *Harvard Business Review, 77*, 72–82.

Evans, P., & Wurster, T. S. (2000). *Blown to bits: How the new economics of information transforms strategy*. Harvard Business School Press.

Ferguson, D. A., & Greer, C. F. (2011). Local radio and microblogging: How radio stations in the US are using Twitter. *Journal of Radio & Audio Media, 18*, 33–46.

Fu, W. (2003). Applying the structure–conduct–performance framework in the media industry analysis. *International Journal on Media Management, 5*, 275–284.

Fulmer, W. E. (2000). *Shaping the adaptive organization: Landscape, learning, and leadership in volatile times*. Amacom.

Glasser, T. L., Allen, D. S., & Blanks, S. E. (1989). The influence of chain ownership on news play: A case study. *Journalism Quarterly, 66*, 607–614.

Griffiths, M. (1996). Gambling on the Internet: A brief note. *Journal of Gambling Studies, 12*, 471–473.

Griffiths, M. (1999). Internet addiction: Fact or fiction? *The Psychologist, 12*, 246–250.

Hensmans, M., Johnson, G., & Yip, G. (2013). *Strategic transformation: Changing while winning*. Palgrave Macmillan.

Hirsch, P. M. (1977). Occupational, organizational and institutional models in mass media research: Toward an integrated framework. In P. M. Hirsch, P. V. Miller, & F. G. Kline (Eds.), *Strategies for communication research* (pp. 13–42). Sage.

History of *The Guardian*. (2017, December 11). *The Guardian*. https://www.theguardian.com/gnm-archive/2002/jun/06/1

Killebrew, K. C. (2003). Culture, creativity and convergence: Managing journalists in a changing information workplace. *International Journal on Media Management, 5*, 39–46.

Kroman, D. (April 11, 2018). *More layoffs at the already depleted Seattle P-I*. Crosscut. https://crosscut.com/2018/04/more-layoffs-already-depleted-seattle-p-i

Küng, L. (2007). Does media management matter? Establishing the scope, rationale and future research agenda for the discipline. *Journal of Media Business Studies, 4*, 21–39.

Küng, L. (2016). Why is media management research so difficult—and what can scholars do to overcome the field's intrinsic challenges. *Journal of Media Business Studies, 13*, 276–282.

Küng, L. (2017a). *Strategic management in the media: Theory to practice*. Sage.

Küng, L. (2017b). *Going digital: A roadmap for organisational transformation*. Reuters Institute. https://reutersinstitute.politics.ox.ac.uk/our-research/going-digital-roadmap-organisational-transformation
Küng, L. (2018). Excess sensitivity of high-income consumers. *The Quarterly Journal of Economics, 133*, 1693–1751.
Lawson-Borders, G., & Kirk, R. (2005). Blogs in campaign communication. *American Behavioral Scientist, 49*, 548–559.
Lowe, G. F. (2016). Introduction: What's so special about media management. In G. F. Lowe & C. Brown (Eds.), *Managing media firms and industries* (pp. 1–20). Springer.
Lundin, R. A., & Norbäck, M. (2016). Projectification in the media industries. In G. F. Lowe & C. Brown (Eds.), *Managing media firms and industries* (pp. 367–382). Springer.
Lynch, R. (2015). *Strategic management*. FT Prentice Hall.
Maijanen, P., & Virta, S. (2017). Managing exploration and exploitation in a media organisation: A capability-based approach to ambidexterity. *Journal of Media Business Studies, 14*, 146–165.
McLuhan, M. (1964). *Understanding media: The extensions of man*. McGraw-Hill.
Merikivi, J., Bragge, J., Scornavacca, E., & Verhagen, T. (2019). Binge-watching serialized video content: A transdisciplinary review. *Television & New Media*. doi: 10.1177/1527476419848578
Mierzejewska, B. I. (2011). Media management in theory and practice. In M. Deuze (Ed.), *Managing media work* (pp. 13–30). Sage.
Mierzejewska, B. I. (2018). Theoretical approaches in media management research. In A. Albarran, B. I. Mierzejewska, & J. Jung (Eds.), *Handbook of media management and economics* (pp. 17–35). Routledge.
Mintzberg, H., Lampel, J., Quinn, J. B., & Ghoshal, S. (2003). *The strategy process: Concepts, contexts, cases* (global 4th ed.). Prentice Hall.
Molyneux, L. (2018). Mobile news consumption: A habit of snacking. *Digital Journalism, 6*, 634–650.
Murphy, S. E., & Ensher, E. (2008). A qualitative analysis of charismatic leadership in creative teams: The case of television directors. *The Leadership Quarterly, 19*, 335–352.
Napoli, P. M. (2001). The audience product and the new media environment: Implications for the economics of media industries. *International Journal on Media Management, 3*, 66–73.
Napoli, P. M. (2003). *Audience economics: Media institutions and the audience marketplace*. Columbia University Press.
Net Marketshare. (2019, January). *Search engine market share*. https://www.netmarketshare.com/search-engine-market-share.aspx
Nielsen. (2018). *The Nielsen total audience report: Q1 2018*. https://www.nielsen.com/us/en/insights/reports/2018/q1-2018-total-audience-report.html
Oliver, J. J. (2018). Strategic transformations in the media. *Journal of Media Business Studies, 15*, 1–22.
Olson, D. (2018, January 29). Meet the woman building Facebook's Ebay killer. *Forbes*. https://www.forbes.com/sites/parmyolson/2018/01/29/facebook-marketplace-ebay-craigslist
Penrose, E. (1959). *The theory of the growth of the firm*. Oxford University Press.
Pérez-Latre, F. J., & Sánchez-Tabernero, A. (2003). Leadership, an essential requirement for effecting change in media companies: An analysis of the Spanish market. *International Journal on Media Management, 5*, 199–208.
Perrott, B. E. (2008). Managing strategy in turbulent environments. *Journal of General Management, 33*, 21–30.
Picard, R. G., & Lowe, G. F. (2016). Questioning media management scholarship: Four parables about how to better develop the field. *Journal of Media Business Studies, 13*, 61–72. doi: 10.1080/16522354.2016.1176781
Picard, R. G., & Van Weezel, A. (2008). Capital and control: Consequences of different forms of newspaper ownership. *The International Journal on Media Management, 10*, 22–31.
Porter, M. E. (1979). How competitive forces shape strategy. In D. Asch & C. Bowman (Eds.), *Readings in strategic management* (pp. 133–143). Palgrave.
Porter, M. E. (1985). *Competitive advantage: Creating and sustaining superior performance*. Free Press.
Postman, N. (1985). *Amusing ourselves to death: Public discourse in the age of show business*. Viking.

Pulkinnen, L. (July 18, 2018). Lessons on going online-only on Seattle PI. *Columbia Journalism Review*. https://www.cjr.org/business_of_news/seattle-pi-online-only.php
Robb, M. (2019). *Screens and sleep. The new normal: Parents, teens, screens, and sleep in the United States*. Common Sense Media. https://www.commonsensemedia.org/sites/default/files/uploads/research/2019-new-normal-parents-teens-screens-and-sleep-united-states.pdf
Robins, J. A., & Wiersema, M. F. (2000). Strategies for unstructured competitive environments: Using scarce resources to create new markets. In R. K. F. Bressler, M. A. Hitt, R. D. Nixon, & D. Heuskel (Eds.), *Winning strategies in a deconstructing world* (pp. 201–220). John Wiley & Sons.
Rogers, E. M. (1962). *Diffusion of innovations*. Free Press.
Rusbridger, A. (2018). *Breaking news: The remaking of journalism and why it matters now*. Farrar, Straus & Giroux.
Scott, D. M. (2015). *The new rules of marketing and PR: How to use social media, online video, mobile applications, blogs, news releases, and viral marketing to reach buyers directly*. John Wiley & Sons.
Similarweb. (2018). *Top website ranking*. https://www.similarweb.com/top-websites/category/news-and-media
Tate, C. (2009). Seattle Post-Intelligencer *(1863–2009)*. History Link. https://www.historylink.org/File/8956
Teece, D. J. (2007). Explicating dynamic capabilities: The nature and microfoundations of (sustainable) enterprise performance. *Strategic Management Journal, 28*(13), 1319–1350.
Teece, D., & Pisano, G. (1994). The dynamic capabilities of firms: An introduction. *Industrial and Corporate Change, 3*, 537–556.
Vukanovic, Z. (2018, September). The influence of digital convergence/divergence on digital media business models. *International Conference on Entertainment Computing* (pp. 152–163). Springer.
Watkins, A. (2014, February 13). The launch of Guardian Labs: How *The Guardian* is approaching content marketing. *The Guardian*. https://www.theguardian.com/media-network/media-network-blog/2014/feb/13/launch-guardian-labs-content-marketing
Wei, L. Q., & Lau, C. M. (2010). High performance work systems and performance: The role of adaptive capability. *Human Relations, 63*, 1487–1511.

CHAPTER 4

Academic Research Methods in Media Management

Brandon T. Sweitzer, Kent State University

LEARNING OBJECTIVES

1. Define media management as an academic discipline.
2. Identify traditional academic research approaches in the field.
3. Explore emerging methodologies for future scholars entering the field.
4. Identify key opportunities and challenges of academic research in the field of media management.

The field of media management studies is a comparatively young discipline that has experienced some growing pains over the past several decades (Picard & Lowe, 2016). Providing a concise, consensus definition of the discipline is challenging due to its relative youth as well as its unique position among other media studies strands. The aim of media management research is to "cover all the goal-oriented activities of planning, organization and control within the framework of the creation and distribution process for information and entertainment content" (Wirtz, 2013, p. 15). Scholarship seeks to bridge the gap between the "goal-oriented activities" of the media industry and the theoretical concepts of business and media studies (Doyle & Frith, 2004; Küng, 2016; Murschetz & Friedrichsen, 2017). The seeming inability to meet this goal has led many of the leading scholars in the field to be critical of its approach, suggesting that the field of media management lacks organization and cohesion (Albarran, 2016; Küng, 2007; Mierzejewska & Hollifield, 2006; Murschetz & Friedrichsen, 2017). Let's explore a snapshot of time in media management research to better understand why the topic is so difficult to study and illustrate the tenuous relationship between the industry and academia.

CASE STUDY

Throughout the 20th century, most of the research surrounding the business of media was applied in nature rather than being conducted to satisfy the curiosity of researchers (Küng, 2016). Industry practitioners were concerned not with the growth of theoretical understandings of the industry but rather with the search for answers to questions that could directly benefit their corporation (Doyle & Frith, 2004). This relationship is not unique to media management scholarship; for better or worse, there is often a disconnection between academics and the industry or group they study. Academics rely on empirical data to draw conclusions about phenomena and determine proper interpretations, while practitioners rely on their industry experiences and use a "best practices" approach to fuel its application and financial gain.

In the field of media management research, this distance is exacerbated by the attitude the industry holds toward academics. Scholars suggest media managers do not trust research that is not "industry focused," and they tend not to value the input of scholars (Bryman, 1995; Küng, 2010; Murschetz & Friedrichsen, 2017). This perspective makes it difficult to establish direct communication with media practitioners, leading academic researchers to often abandon primary data collection methods and rely on secondary data. Additionally, media managers are atypical in the business world because they rely more heavily on irrationalities (such as "gut feelings," "star power," and the "it factor") rather than empirical evidence that has been gathered and interpreted by academics (Picard, 2005). While some progress has been made in theoretical development, its growth has been stunted by the industry's ability to hold sway over the research process (Albarran, 2016).

According to Küng (2016), "Media management seeks to apply a set of theoretical constructs from a specific, yet at the same time exceedingly wide set of academic disciplines, to a specific and also extremely diverse set of industries, industries that—and this is very significant for research design—are undergoing extreme change" (p. 276). Academics in this field must find a way to reconcile two seemingly mutually exclusive theoretical fields. They must master management theories that are fragmented, sometimes competing, and often based on the organization being studied (large versus small, profit versus nonprofit, curation versus production, etc.). They must also master media theories that are just as complicated and demanding, containing theoretical inconsistencies and holding theories that depend on the medium being studied (print, broadcast, Internet, film, etc.).

In addition, there is also a conflict in the theoretical fields based on the application of theory in the research process. Küng (2017) suggests that management scholars maintain a constant theoretical lens to answer research questions in order to develop theory, while media theorists determine the unit of measurement and search for theories that may be used to explain phenomena within media. These contradictions often lead researchers to use outdated or improper theoretical arguments.

These tenuous relationships and theoretical challenges have shaped the way academics approach media management studies, narrowing the focus of research and stunting the growth of theory unique to the discipline. While the past three decades have not been as fruitful as desired, most scholars agree that positive trends are emerging in the field (Albarran, 2006; Mierzejewska & Shaver, 2014; Picard & Lowe, 2016). The current media ecosystem provides new opportunities for scholars to embrace industry convergence to fuel stronger research. Additionally, these convergent disruptions have industry practitioners turning to academic research for guidance. This chapter aims to explore how traditional media management scholarship can be shaped in a convergent environment to identify opportunities and challenges in further improving the relationship between industry and scholarship.

Something Old

It is not within the scope of this chapter to outline specific methodological procedures (sampling, scale creation, analytic techniques, etc.) used in the research process. There are many formative established research method textbooks that can guide these questions (Berger, 2019; Creswell, 2014; Davis & Lachlan, 2017; Keyton, 2015). The same techniques used by researchers in social sciences are also implemented by academic researchers of media management, so illustrating them here would be redundant (Doyle & Frith, 2006; Dupagne, 2018). Instead, this chapter will consider three key components of the research process: the unit of analysis, methodological approach, and data collection methods. Following the changes in these research facets allows us to track the progression of media management research and evolution within the constraints of industry and theory.

UNIT OF ANALYSIS

The unit of analysis used most often by media management researchers has changed over the past three decades as the media ecosystem has evolved. According to a meta-analysis of articles published in the two leading journals in the field of media management studies (*Journal of Media Economics* and *International Journal on Media Management*) conducted by Beam (2006), the unit of analysis predominantly focused on the media firm (37%) in the years following the digital revolution (1990–2006). Other units of analysis for academic media management research at that time include market (18%), individual (12%), and industry (9%). Researchers were interested in how organizations cope with the changes to the landscape and their strategy for adapting to increased globalization and convergence (Albarran, 2006). The media marketplace and individual employees within media corporations were sparingly examined, but research involving the firm was greater than the two combined.

As media firms began adopting new strategies to answer demands of the new media ecosystem, academic research interests also changed. A meta-analysis conducted by Dupagne (2018) provides insights into these changes. From 2004 to 2009, while the firm was still the most common unit of analysis (27.8%), interest in individuals (27.3%) increased dramatically, with more than twice the percentage of earlier studies exploring individual members of the industry. Additionally, during this time, the content/product created by a media outlet became more popular (15.9%), while interest in the industry (10.8%) and the marketplace (10.8%) waned slightly. Between 2010 and 2016, the individual (37.5%) and the content/product produced by the corporation (29.4%)

continued to emerge as topics of interest (content almost doubled in percentage), while interest in the firm (15.6%) dropped dramatically, and focus on the marketplace (6.9%) and industry (5.6%) continued to decline.

These percentages suggest that as the media industry has evolved over the past three decades, the focus of researchers has changed as well. Research focused on the individual member of the organization has more than tripled in percentage, suggesting the characteristics of the individual (adaptability, creativity, ingenuity, etc.) are more impactful (if not just more worthy of study) in the modern digital media landscape than the media firm itself. As the media industry continues to be fragmented and diversified, the focus on individuals may become even more important moving forward.

METHODOLOGICAL APPROACH

One great challenge for media management researchers is the task of conducting comprehensive scholarship on an industry that strongly favors profit margins, costs, audience sizes, and revenues. Institutional decisions are established through quantitative mentions based on deductive reasoning. Properly executed quantitative methodologies rely on existing knowledge to provide raw data that is analyzed to offer valuable insights into audiences, trends, patterns, and processes (Doyle & Frith, 2006). While there are times when a more qualitative approach may be of interest to scholars, it is unlikely that these inductive findings will be useful to media managers.

Verhoeven, von Rimscha, Krebs, Siegert, and Sommer (2018) explored existing studies on media success and found that traditional media management scholarship is often inconsistent and incohesive. Through deductive reasoning, the authors were able to create a more holistic approach to measure these variables, finding four factors predicting success: good distribution, environmental orientation, form/design, and human resources. These findings can be used in subsequent studies to establish a more nuanced approach to media management scholarship.

Quantitative data helps provide comparative empirical evidence, but as aspects of the media industry continue to be fragmented and favor niche audiences and distribution outlets, generalizing results and making comparisons becomes difficult (Wirth & Bloch, 1995). With practitioners' tedious relationship with scholars, it is often difficult for researchers to establish representative and generalizable samples for quantitative study (Doyle & Frith, 2006). Samples of existing research are inconsistent across sectors of the industry due to the reliance of researchers on convenient sampling approaches. Additionally, it is easier for quantitative researchers to get more time and attention from the practitioner. Taking 15 minutes to complete a web-based survey is much more appealing to a busy media manager than sitting down for a 45-minute in-depth interview. Qualitative research can be time consuming and quite possibly seen as a nuisance to media managers.

Nonetheless, an integration of qualitative methodologies would strengthen the field, as they would better uncover the complexity of the industry and audience experience (Doyle & Frith, 2006). Rather than relying on deductive reasoning, qualitative methods gain insights directly from audiences and industry practitioners (Bryman, 1995). For example, Chan-Olmsted and Wolter (2018) employed a qualitative method to better understand how media managers engage audiences. Results help media managers better understand nuanced strategies for capturing the cognitive, affective, and behavioral needs of their audiences and the difficulties media managers face in integrating engaging content across multiple platforms. By using qualitative methods, researchers were able to uncover new insights that could not be revealed via the deductive approach and survey method.

As with quantitative methods, qualitative techniques have to face their own challenges. Qualitative methods are often very time consuming and require the ability to detect commonly occurring codes and themes across many pages of transcripts. Qualitative software must be taught with the same reverence as quantitative programs. Additionally, qualitative researchers need to have excellent "people skills" (active listening, prodding, adapting, building rapport, etc.) if they are to extract effective data from their participants. These soft skills must be integrated into media management training, something we will discuss more in chapter 24, "Looking Forward."

Trends across the methodological approaches are consistent with these claims. Over the years 1990 to 2016, we see the dominating use of quantitative methodologies in the field as well as its steady increase (1990–2006: 60% of the research; Beam, 2006; 2004–2009: 64.8%; 2010–2016: 75.6%; see Dupagne, 2018). Qualitative research accounts for 24% from 1990 to 2006, to 30.1% from 2004 to 2009, and 18.8% from 2010 to 2016 (Beam, 2006; Dupagne, 2018). With the emergence of social media analytics, big data, and other large-scale numerical approaches, it is not expected that this reliance on quantitative data across the industry will waiver. However, we did see the emergence of the application of mixed research methods (2004–2009: 5.1%; 2010–2016: 5.6%; Dupagne, 2018). There is certainly a need for more uses of mixed methods and a more balanced approach in academic media management research moving forward.

DATA COLLECTION METHODS

Traditionally, media management researchers have relied quite heavily on secondary data (corporation reports, governmental documents, industry databases) to answer their research questions. Dupagne (2018) suggests today's academics must become "data retrieval experts," acquiring topical, timely information from governmental, commercial, academic, and industry data sources throughout the world. With quantitative approaches most often guiding media management research, it is no surprise that data collection favors more numeric collection tools, such as responses to surveys and analysis of secondary data (Beam, 2006; Dupagne, 2018). Over the years 1990 to 2016, secondary data analysis remained the most common data collection method for media management research (1990–2006: 57%; Beam, 2006; 2004–2009: 28.4%; 2010–2016: 35.6%; Dupagne, 2018), followed by survey (1990–2006: 24%; Beam, 2006; 2004–2009: 22.7%; 2010–2016: 36.9%; Dupagne, 2018). Content analysis (13%) and experiment (2%) were other data collection methods for academic media management research from 1990 to 2006. In the years that follow, we see more diverse data collection methods. Meta-analysis (2004–2009: 18.8%; 2010–2016: 9.4%; see Dupagne, 2018) and interview (2004–2009: 9.1%; 2010–2016: 8.8%; see Dupagne, 2018) became more popular data collection methods for media management research than content analysis (2004–2009:

5.7%; 2010–2016: 7.5%; see Dupagne, 2018) and experiment (2004–2009: 2.3%; 2010–2016: 1.9%; see Dupagne, 2018).

Although quantitative data is appealing due to its low cost and high quality (Beam, 2006), it can be harmful to the quality of scholarly research for several reasons. The first and most important concern is the validity of secondary data. When a researcher relies on secondary data, they are relying on methods that researchers or programs have used to answer questions that may not be relevant to the current study. Additionally, secondary research is not always acquired accurately and can be misleading (Doyle & Frith, 2006). Media corporations may intentionally or unintentionally inflate numbers that are reported to government databases or stakeholders, which leads to concerns about data accuracy. When researchers inherit secondary data, they also inherit the problems of the data. The dominant use of secondary data analysis further illustrates the one-sided relationship between the industry and academia mentioned above. Many times, researchers who attempt to answer questions based on their own curiosity (rather than client-driven questions) are unable to directly study members of the media industry and thus have to rely on secondary data.

One important trend in media management research is the limited range of data collection methods. Except for secondary data and surveys, other quantitative methods such as content analyses and experimental designs used in academic media management research are exceedingly rare. Additionally, while there have been some examples of interviews, qualitative methods such as focus groups and participant observation are essentially nonexistent. Let's explore some emerging "new" changes to the field that may help address this gap.

Something New

Tracing the evolution of media management research over the past three decades, its lack of cohesion and holistic thinking is evident. The field has allowed its tenuous relationship with the media industry to stall its progress. Relying on a macro-level approach with heavy reliance on quantitative methods and secondary data has led to a disjointed, weak field (Albarran, 2016). However, dynamic convergent advances in the field over the past several years suggest this trend may be changing. Scholars are relying more on new paradigms and employing a wider range of methodological approaches.

One of the greatest advantages of digital media platforms is their ability to harvest vast amounts of consumer data. When properly harnessed, this information can provide unprecedented insights into the cognitive, affective, and behavioral aspects of audiences. Media corporations are in a great position to tap into big data and constantly investigate new ways to utilize it (Napoli & Roepnack, 2018). Traditional media firms (particularly print-based and music-recording corporations) are increasingly relying on the profit potential of big data to recoup the major losses they have endured since the digital revolution (Bell, 2012). Other corporations, such as Netflix, Hulu, and Amazon Prime, have used big data as the foundation for their business model and have thus grown exponentially (Bulger, Taylor, & Schroder, 2014; Carr, 2013; Napoli & Roepnack, 2018).

The potential for revenue generation via big data has made it an essential aspect of the business of media. Regardless of its potential for profit, personalized advertising, and audience measurement, both the media industry and academe lack a clear understanding of big data. Napoli and Roepnack (2018) suggest scholars should use big data to gain a better understanding of audience behavior in the modern media landscape. They suggest these efforts will allow scholars to measure the utility of traditional media theories to a digital environment and develop theories specific to the contemporary ecosystem.

Conversely, Neef (2014) is hesitant to accept a reliance on big data because it has the potential to undermine the epistemological nature of research. He argues that relying on enormous data sets will lead to an approach that relies less on age-old facets of research, such as significance, correlation, and causation, and replace them with an "analyze everything and see what turns up" approach (p. 183). Regarding these aspects of validity, Athique (2018) suggests "in many respects, it is starting to look like we are coming full circle to a world of 'mass effects' research driven by *a priori* assumptions and tested on sophisticated correlations of dirty data garnered from a reasonably unethical trawling operation" (p. 72). As seen by this statement, there are not only validity concerns but also ethical issues involved in big data research.

As illustrated in the previous section, rather than focus on media firms for much of their research, today's media management scholars are more often studying individual employees within corporations and smaller niche audiences. This approach has allowed scholars to delve more deeply into multiple levels of the industry, creating a more holistic understanding of the field. The macro-level approach of previous researchers caused them to rely heavily on the input of senior-level managers and concern themselves less with members of middle-level management (Picard & Lowe, 2016). This perspective is beginning to change as more media management researchers are seeking the input of middle-level managers to answer their research questions.

For example, Horst and Moisander (2015) intentionally sought the input of middle-level managers when attempting to discover how print-oriented media organizations are addressing the need for convergence in the industry. Specifically, they were interested in better understanding how these managers overcome the challenge of finding the balance between well-established business practices (often championed by members of senior management) and the need for innovative tactics. Interview results suggest middle-level managers have needs and responsibilities that differ greatly from previous studies that only involved senior management. These differences were found in both the decision-making process and the strategies used in the implementation of business plans. Studies taking similar approaches will help broaden the discipline's understanding of the industry and allow for a more holistic view of the decision-making process needed to respond to a convergent media environment.

In addition to changing their perspective concerning research subjects, media management scholars have been employing a wider range of data collection methods. For some, this means employing a ground qualitative approach, which allows the results of their study to generate new understandings of media management and business. Lee (2015) employed a ground approach when attempting to understand how modern journalists are interacting with Twitter. In order to better understand how social media is perceived as both a concern and a tool for journalists, Lee (2015) interviewed journalists from national, metropolitan, and local newspapers. The results of the interviews suggest that journalists today recognize the many nuances in how Twitter can be used as a tool for news dissemination and as a source of revenue for a news organization. Utilizing a qualitative approach allowed Lee to gather information about a subject and media platform not often explored and also provided a framework for future research and theory development. This method fills a gap by providing a shift from an over-reliance on quantitative methods to adding a wide range of techniques to study a media management phenomenon (Achtenhagen & Mierzejewska, 2016; Doyle & Frith, 2004; Mierzejewska & Shaver, 2014; Picard & Lowe, 2016). Utilizing multiple, hybrid methodological approaches is essential to the field of media management moving forward. Let's explore additional "new" examples of these methodological approaches below.

Malmelin and Virta (2017) used a diary method when answering questions about the "irrational" concept of serendipity, often credited for success in the media industry, and how it impacts decisions and creativity. The authors conducted the study among members of a print-based media firm that was attempting to find new avenues for convergence. The diary method provided researchers with an in-depth look at the everyday events of the firm and demonstrated that the presence of strategic, structural, and cultural elements can provide an environment for serendipitous development.

Chen, Yang, and Smith (2016) employed an experimental design when exploring the effects of content in television advertisements. They were particularly interested in the relationship between ad creativity and ad repetition. To answer their research questions, participants were subjected to participate in varying conditions, manipulating the amount of creativity and repetition found within the ads. After comparing the responses to the stimuli, researchers concluded that ads that were both divergent (novel and unique) and relevant (important to consumers) had more staying power with their participants. While they could not speak to the long-term effects of ads, the authors were able to provide empirical evidence regarding the initial reaction audiences express toward formatted ads.

Ladson and Lee (2017) conducted a content analysis to explore the strategies utilized by print-based media corporations in a digital ecosystem. The digital revolution has led to a worldwide decline in print-based news media, which has forced media managers to pursue new business models to generate revenue. One such avenue is crowdfunding, which relies on small contributions from individual web page visitors to generate large amounts of revenue. To gain an understanding of this tactic, researchers examined the techniques used by journalists on the international crowdfunded site Byline. By integrating concepts from media effects studies, media economics, and Cialdini's rule of reciprocity, the authors created a sound theoretical framework that allowed them to empirically examine the phenomenon. They coded the publication time, column topic, author location, and rewards offered by the site in relationship to the likelihood that a column would reach its funding goal. Results of the study help provide a road map for future crowdsourcing efforts as well as future theoretical development. The reciprocity found in offering rewards in return for financial contributions may lead to overall financial success for crowdfunded sites.

The trend toward broadening methodological approaches to answer research questions in media management research is certainly encouraging. Relying on a wider range of data-gathering techniques provides a more accurate and holistic view of the industry. As evolution within the media ecosystem perpetuates, corporations inside the industry will be forced to adapt to these changes. Scholars studying media management also need to find new approaches to keep stride across media platforms and industries. Advances in media technology have given unprecedented power to the audience and have asked us to reconceptualize the relationship between the audience and the industry as well as within the industry itself. All these changes provide exciting opportunities for media management scholars but also present difficult challenges.

Opportunities and Challenges

In addition to the sweeping changes to the audience-industry dynamic, the modern media ecosystem is truly a global market for consumers and practitioners alike. Albarran (2016) explores how the globalization of media opens many new avenues for media management research. It is important to pay attention to not only the corporations that dominate globally but also how the definition and composition of "global domination" changes over time.

OPPORTUNITIES

Media management researchers should look closely at how much sway major media corporations hold over a country's gross domestic product and how the rise of the "FANG" companies (Facebook, Apple, Netflix, and Google) impact these changes on a global level (Albarran, 2016). Modern changes in the media ecosystem call for new conceptualizations and research methodologies. While these new avenues of research are certainly vast and challenging, they provide an exciting opportunity for the field of media management research.

Scholars suggest implementing a systematic approach to the study of media firms that employs a wide range of methods and scientific rigor (Küng, 2007; 2016; Murschetz & Friedrichsen, 2017; Picard & Lowe, 2016). This process allows researchers to provide clearer definitions and objectives for their studies. Questions such as "What aspect of the industry is being studied?" "How can it be defined?" "What theories explain the phenomenon in question?" and "What theoretical framework can be used to study it?" provide structure to their research that can be built on by future researchers. Answering these questions will add to the literature in media management and lead to a broader spectrum of theories unique to the discipline.

While media management theories certainly exist (see chapter 3), there is an overall lack of unification and application of them in empirical research (Doyle & Frith, 2004). In addition, many media management studies are essays about the state of the field rather than empirical research (Küng, 2016; Picard & Lowe, 2016; Wirtz, Pistoia, & Mory, 2015). The lack of heuristic research may be attributed to the fact that it is a multidisciplinary field that has historically borrowed from other disciplines to develop theoretical frameworks (Küng, 2016). Media management scholars must delve deeper into research to meet their objectives and use its interdisciplinary nature to strengthen the field. Additional theory-based and ground approaches to research media management must be conducted.

In addition to theoretical frameworks, scholars must reconceptualize which methodological approaches are best for studying the media industry. Picard and Lowe (2016) suggest a mixed-methodological approach that employs quantitative (surveys, experimental designs, etc.) and qualitative (interviews, observations, etc.) methods will provide a more holistic understanding of the field. As the media landscape continues to evolve, the need for fresh paradigms, such as mixed-methods approaches, is greater than ever. As seen in the previous section, the application of mixed methods has remained steady over the past three decades but has not been implemented enough. Tashakkori and Creswell (2008) suggest that mixed methods provide flexibility for researchers that allows them to utilize all potential methods they may need to answer a question or provide a multidimensional look at a phenomenon that a single methodology could not examine on its own. As the field of media management research moves forward and attempts to stay relevant in a convergent media environment, the implementation of mixed methods will become even more important. Simply put, an industry that is becoming more complex requires more complex research strategies to study it.

Olsen and Solvoll (2018) conducted a mixed-methods study when exploring the effectiveness of paywalls among print-based media companies. Paywalls (or paid subscriptions) have been used more frequently by print media companies that are attempting to recoup some of the revenue they have lost in the wake of the digital revolution. The authors aimed to test if the success of paywalls was predicated on the ability to create content that is valuable enough for consumers to opt in. When considering the new industry-audience relationship, the authors wondered if there was compatibility between the media managers and audience members regarding "quality content." To answer this question, they used a mixed-methods approach through in-depth interviews with managers at print-based media firms and a national survey of newspaper audiences. Results point to a distinct disconnection between media managers and their audiences, especially among younger, lower-income, and lower-news-interest audience members. Through the implementation of a more complex and nuanced methodological approach, the scholars were able to gain valuable insights into a multifaceted issue that has been difficult to examine empirically.

CHALLENGES

Academic researchers are under obligations to conduct ethical research that provides certain protections to their participants that media practitioners are not. Boyd and Crawford (2012) suggest the big data era makes ethical research more difficult to conduct. Ethical research requires researchers to explain why research is being conducted and to preserve the anonymity of their participants. The gathering of big data has made this exceedingly difficult (Athique, 2018).

Determining methods that allow researchers to harness big data in a manner that is both valid and ethical is arguably the biggest challenge faced by media management researchers today. Studies that maintain scientific rigor and consider the ethical concerns of respondents can provide understandings into audiences that have never been possible before. As Athique (2018) suggests, "Staking a claim to big data may well prove critical for understanding the dynamics and potentials of media in the twenty-first century. As long as we remember that audiences are not data, then everything should be fine" (p. 72).

Defining the relationship between academe and members of the media industry is challenging. The central issue of the relationship involves answering the question "Who is the research for?" (Doyle & Frith, 2004). Essentially, is the research being conducted to solve a problem for a media firm or to satisfy the curiosity of the researcher?

Research that is conducted for media firms certainly has its advantages. Scholars can gain access to information (sales figures, business plans, organizational flow charts, etc.) that they could not access on their own. Additionally, working directly for a firm allows researchers to have direct access to senior managers of the organization (production managers, CEOs, etc.) that would not normally be available if researchers were conducting research for personal curiosity. Gaining access to relevant data, however, is not without its drawbacks.

Client-driven research often leads organizations to dictate research questions to researchers, and clients sometimes want the results of the research to be presented in a light that is beneficial to the company (Doyle & Frith, 2004). To overcome this issue, media researchers must carefully consider the relationships they have with members of the media industry. Küng (2016) suggests researchers should develop relationships with practitioners that lead to inside information rather than relying on them to fund the research. By working with key industry players, scholars can stay up to date with the latest trends and practices and not have to "report the obvious and no longer relevant" (p. 280). Timely and relevant research is of particular importance in a field that is evolving as rapidly as the media industry. Additionally, more communication between academics and industry members will help bridge the gap between theory and practice. By conducting more research that holds mutual benefit for researchers and industry practitioners alike, scholars can develop theories and conduct research that can advance the field and serve as valuable tools for media firms. The following action plan can be used as a guide.

ACTION PLAN

1. Take time to understand changes in the media ecosystem, especially regarding how much sway major media corporations hold over time.
2. Before embarking on new research, take a systematic approach that better builds on the methods and scientific rigor of previous research in the field.
3. Consider utilizing a mixed-method approach to provide a more holistic understanding of the field.
4. Utilize big data in a manner that is both valid and ethical to answer your research questions as well as protect the privacy of your research subjects.
5. Continue to improve communication between academic and industry members to help bridge the gap between theory and practice.

KEY TAKEAWAYS

1. Although academic research in media management has existed for more than three decades, it is still a disjointed and comparatively weak field.
2. Much of the weaknesses in the field stem from the tenuous relationship scholars have with the parent disciplines they draw their theories from (management and media studies).
3. While early efforts centered mostly on quantitative methods using secondary data, scholars have recently made great strides by considering new research methods and using primary data collection techniques.
4. Academic research in media management is a growing field that is very rewarding and needs aspiring researchers to join existing scholars to carry it into the new decade.
5. In order to ensure development in the field, future media management researchers must employ scientific rigor, develop more theories unique to the discipline, learn to effectively use technology, and develop stronger relationships with industry practitioners.

CONCLUSION

This chapter provides a brief introduction to academic media management research by considering its evolution over the past three decades. Scholars in the field have the seemingly impossible challenge of keeping up with an industry that is dynamic, fluid, and unpredictable. During its early years, this task manifested in literature that was very applied and allowed media industries to direct research questions and data interpretation. This approach made theory development unique to the discipline quite difficult and stunted the field's overall growth. While scholars have been critical of these shortcomings, there are challenges that the discipline has to face to make it unique among other media studies.

Research in the field of media management will always present challenges due to a reliance on a theoretical hybrid framework that is very difficult to reconcile. Studying media management requires expertise in both management theories and media studies theories—two disciplines that often contradict one another in substance and application. Despite these challenges, today's media management scholars are dedicated to conducting research that is beneficial to both academe and practitioners. As Küng (2016) suggests, "A healthy media industry is central to healthy democratic processes. Media management researchers can help ensure that the sector survives, and hopefully thrives, and continues to fulfil its important societal role" (p. 281). As the media ecosystem continues to evolve and hold sway over public opinion and sociological discourse, this task becomes more important.

While the discipline may have had a slow start, the last decade has shown great promise. Scholars have kept up with significant changes in the media industry by turning more toward theoretical foundations and shifting their research approach. The digital revolution of the late 20th century dismantled the medium-based silos that defined the industry and created an ecosystem of convergence and globalization that has given increasing power to consumers. To respond to these drastic changes, academics shifted their focus from the macro-level unit of analysis to a consideration of the individual members of the industry. Additionally, a discipline that was dominated by quantitative methodologies and secondary data is broadening its scope by implementing new methods and paradigms. It is imperative for current and future media management scholars to continue this trend of innovation and paradigmatic flexibility in order to advance the field.

The next decade holds the potential to dramatically impact academic research in media management. While the aspects discussed earlier in the chapter (the need for a unified, theoretical approach; application of complex methodologies such as mixed methods; and tackling big data) provide research opportunities for academics, there are structural and conceptual changes occurring that media management scholars must also consider.

Advances in digital technology and its use by both practitioners and consumers continue to shape the industry and pose challenges to scholars. Structurally, while digital media has led to convergence in the sector, fragmentation and specialization are leading to differences among corporations that distribute on the same medium (compare the business model of the online version of the *New York Times* to an online news platform like Byline that uses crowdsourcing to pay its authors). Conceptually, the new "digital disruptors" (Facebook, Amazon, Netflix, Google, etc.) are so broad, multifaceted, and diverse they are virtually impossible to classify (many of them could be considered tech companies, media outlets, networking sites, etc.). This makes empirical aspects of media management quite difficult, such as defining a unit of analysis, operationalizing variables, and collecting data.

While there are many opportunities, academics will find it difficult to grow the field if they are unable to build a better relationship with the practitioners they study. Since the early days of the discipline, the relationship between academics and practitioners has been essentially one sided. If strides are to be made in media management research, this relationship must be repaired.

There are several ways to reconcile the relationship between academe and the industry. Academics must conduct more studies that provide valuable insights to both academe and the industry. Providing practitioners with an empirical "road map to success" that simultaneously builds academic knowledge of the subject benefits both parties. Media management researchers can also approach creative individuals who are forward thinking. Küng (2016) suggests, "Such early adopters are always happy to talk, in my experience" (p. 280). Lastly, academics can develop relationships with media managers by including them in more aspects of the research process (e.g., while formulating research questions, while interpreting results, and following up with them to see how valid the results are in the sector). Bridging the gap between theory and practice will lead to a symbiotic relationship between the academe and industry, with academics "keeping in the loop" and gaining access to up-to-date information and practitioners receiving empirical insights into the factors that impact success in their industry.

The field of media management is both challenging and rewarding and needs current and aspiring scholars to carry it into the next decade. The insights provided by media management research are able to stabilize and drive the media industry, an industry that informs public opinion and allows for democratic discourse. As the next chapter will show, the industry's approach to research is quite different from the academe's. Hopefully by understanding both academic and industry research methods, you will be able to apply the knowledge to your own research and build a stronger bridge between the academe and industry.

REFERENCES

Achtenhagen, L., & Mierzejewska, B. (2016). The development of media management as an academic field: Tracing the contents and impact of its three leading journals. In G. L. Lowe & C. Brown (Eds.), *Managing media firms and industries: What's so special about media management?* (pp. 23–42). Springer.

Albarran, A. B. (2006). Historical trends and patterns in media management research. In A. B. Albarran, S. M. Chan-Olmsted, & M. O. Wirth (Eds.), *Handbook of media management and economics* (pp. 3–22). Lawrence Erlbaum.

Albarran, A. B. (2016). *Management of electronic and digital media* (6th ed.). Cengage Learning.

Athique, A. (2018). The dynamics and potentials of big data for audience research. *Media, Culture & Society, 40*, 59–74.

Beam, R. A. (2006). Quantitative methods in media management and economics. In A. B. Albarran, S. M. Chan-Olmsted, & M. O. Wirth (Eds.), *Handbook of media management and economics* (pp. 523–551). Lawrence Erlbaum.

Bell, E. (2012). Journalism by numbers. *Columbia Journalism Review, 51*(3), 48–49.

Berger, A. A. (2019). *Media and communication research methods: An introduction to qualitative and quantitative approaches*. Sage.

Boyd, D., & Crawford, K. (2012). Critical questions for big data: Provocations for a cultural, technological and scholarly phenomenon. *Information, Communication & Society, 15*, 662–679.

Bryman, A. (1995). *Research methods and organization studies*. Routledge.

Bulger, M., Taylor, G., & Schroeder, R. (2014). *Data-driven business models: Challenges and opportunities of big data*. Research Councils UK. http://www.nemode.ac.uk/wp-content/uploads/2014/09/nemode_business_models_for_bigdata_2014_oxford.pdf

Carr, D. (2013, February 24). Giving viewers what they want. *New York Times*. https://www.nytimes.com/2013/02/25/business/media/for-house-of-cards-using-big-data-to-guarantee-its-popularity.html

Chan-Olmsted, S. M., & Wolter, L. C. (2018). Perceptions and practices of media engagement: A global perspective. *International Journal on Media Management, 20*(1), 1–24.

Chen, J., Yang, X., & Smith, R. E. (2016). The effects of creativity on advertising wear-in and wear-out. *Journal of the Academy of Marketing Science, 44*, 334–349.

Creswell, J. W. (2014). *Research design: Qualitative, quantitative, and mixed methods approach* (4th ed.). Sage.

Davis, C. S., & Lachlan, K. A. (2017). *Straight talk about communication research methods* (3rd ed.). Kendall Hunt Publishing Company.

Doyle, G., & Frith, S. (2004, May). Researching media management and media economics: Methodological approaches and issues. Paper presented at the 6th Annual World Media Economics Conference, Montreal, Canada.

Doyle, G. & Frith, S. (2006). Methodological approaches in media management and media economics research. In A. B. Albarran, S. M. Chan-Olmsted, & M. O. Wirth (Eds.), *Handbook of media management and economics* (pp. 553–572). Lawrence Erlbaum.

Dupagne, M. (2018). Methodological approaches in media management and economics. In A. B. Albarran, B. I. Mierzejewska, & J. Jung (Eds.), *Handbook of media management and economics* (pp. 363–378). Routledge.

Horst, S. O., & Moisander, J. (2015). Paradoxes of strategic renewal in traditional print-oriented media firms. *International Journal on Media Management, 17*, 157–174.

Keyton, J. (2015). *Communication research: Asking questions, finding answers* (4th ed.). McGraw-Hill Education.
Küng, L. (2007). Does media management matter? Establishing the scope, rationale, and future research agenda for the discipline. *Journal of Media Business Studies, 4*, 21–39.
Küng, L. (2010). Why media managers are not interested in media management and what we could do about it. *The International Journal on Media Management, 12*, 55–57.
Küng, L. (2016). Why is media management research so difficult—and what can scholars do to overcome the field's intrinsic challenges? *Journal of Media Business Studies, 13*, 276–282.
Küng, L. (2017). Reflection on the ascendancy of technology in the media and its implications for organisations and their lenders. *Journal of Media Innovation, 4*, 77–81.
Ladson, N., & Lee, A. M. (2017). Persuading to pay: Exploring the what and why in crowdfunded journalism. *International Journal on Media Management, 19*, 144–163.
Lee, A. M. (2015). Social media and speed-driven journalism: Expectations and practices. *The International Journal on Media Management, 17*, 217–239.
Malmelin, N., & Virta, S. (2017). Managing for serendipity: Exploring the organizational prerequisites for emergent creativity. *The International Journal on Media Management, 19*, 222–239.
Mierzejewska, B., & Hollifield, C. A. (2006). Theoretical approaches in media management research. In A. Albarran, S. Chan-Olmsted, & M. O. Wirth (Eds.), *Handbook of media management and economics* (pp. 37–65). Erlbaum.
Mierzejewska, B., & Shaver, D. (2014). Key changes impacting media management research. *The International Journal of Media Management, 16*, 47–54.
Murschetz, P., & Friedrichsen, M. (2017). Making media management research matter. In M. Friedrichsen & Y. Kamalipour (Eds.), *Digital transformation in journalism and news media: Media management, media convergence and globalization* (pp. 17–28). Springer.
Napoli, P. M., & Roepnack, A. (2018). Big data and media management. In A. B. Albarran, B. I. Mierzejewska, & J. Jung (Eds.), *Handbook of media management and economics* (pp. 410–421). Routledge.
Neef, D. (2014). *Digital exhaust: What everyone should know about big data, digitization and digitally driven innovation*. Pearson FT Press.
Olsen, R. K., & Solvoll, M. K. (2018). Reinventing the business model for local newspapers by building walls. *Journal of Media Business Studies, 15*, 24–41.
Picard, R. G. (2005). Unique characteristics and business dynamics of media products. *Journal of Media Business Studies, 2*, 61–69.
Picard, R. G., & Lowe, G. F. (2016). Questioning media management scholarship: Four parables about how to better develop the field. *Journal of Media Business Studies, 2*, 61–72.
Tashakkori, A., & Creswell, J. W. (2008). Mixed methods across disciplines. *Journal of Mixed Methods Research, 2*(1), 3–6.
Verhoeven, M., von Rimscha, M. B., Krebs, I., Siegert, G., & Sommer, C. (2018). Identifying paths to audience success of media products: The media decision-makers' perspective. *International Journal on Media Management, 20*, 51–77.
Wirth, M. O., & Bloch, H. (1995). Industrial organization theory and media industry analysis. *Journal of Media Economics, 8*(2), 15–26.
Wirtz, B. W. (2013). *Media and Internet management*. Gabler Verlag.
Wirtz, B. W., Pistoia, A., & Mory, L. (2015). Current state and development perspectives of media economics / media management research. *Journal of Media Business Studies, 10*, 63–91.

CHAPTER 5

Industry Research Methods in Media Management

Ronen Shay, Fordham University

LEARNING OBJECTIVES

1. Understand Nielsen ratings and shares, and discuss their relevance to broadcast and cable networks.
2. Interpret bounce rates, conversion rates, and other fundamental web analytics used when assessing the performance of online and mobile media products and services.
3. Apply academic research methods to industry research in order to facilitate greater understanding of media audiences today.
4. Discuss recent developments in audience analytics and how research methods have shifted from capturing audience size to measuring audience engagement.

There are many similarities between industry and academic research methods in media management in regard to their forms but great variety in their functions. As mentioned in the previous chapter, academic research may use surveys to examine newspaper readability, aiming to explain a widespread latent media phenomenon (e.g., length of time reading, length of time looking) (Birt, Consterdine, & Robinson, 1999; Ipsos, 2015; Thurman & Fletcher, 2019), while industry research uses surveys for a more applied purpose, aiming to improve the media product and service. The industry application of experiments also proves critical. For example, clutter tests emulate an experimental research design by surrounding the tested commercials with control commercials (Pandey, Pandey, & Kumar, 2016). The video stimulus is then shown to an audience to measure the effectiveness of the ads in gaining audience attention with distraction from other competing advertisements. Often the function of an industry experiment is to assess the quality of experience-based products, instead of suggesting causal relationships supported by academic theories.

One of the unique characteristics of industry research in media management is that the quality of media content often cannot be assessed until after audience consumption. Accordingly, many traditional research methods are used in the pursuit of feedback, by either pretesting content before it is released to consumers or post-testing after audience consumption.

Focus groups are often used by broadcasters for these functions. For example, in summer 2017, CBS decided to kill off actress Erinn Hayes's character on the television series *Kevin Can Wait* after focus groups stated that participants preferred actress Leah Remini, who guest starred in the finale of season one (CBS Television City, 2018; Wagmeister, 2017). Remini had previously worked with the lead actor, Kevin James, on *King of Queens*, an award-winning sitcom. This feedback-driven application of focus group research was used to deductively test an existing hypothesis suggesting the need for a change. Alternatively, in academic settings, focus groups may have been used in an exploratory capacity to inductively identify themes and variables. This is another example of how academic and industry application of research methods are similar in form but differ greatly in function. It is these differences in function that ultimately led practitioners to create their own original, and sometimes proprietary, research methods.

Traditionally, industry research in media management has focused on techniques measuring audience size. This was based on the commodification of an audience's time through the dual product business model (i.e., sell media products to audiences and sell audiences to advertisers) that dominated legacy media, including radio, print, and television (Napoli, 2009). Essentially, the larger the audience, the more legacy media could charge for advertising. As Internet-based media platforms become a viable alternative to advertising on legacy media, the focus of industry research has shifted from measuring audience size to measuring audience engagement and conversion. Let's explore one of the largest audiences in U.S. media, those who watch the Super Bowl, as a case study.

CASE STUDY

In 2018, advertisers paid NBC an average of $5 million for a 30-second advertising spot during the Super Bowl (Lombardo, 2017). For example, Procter & Gamble, the company that makes the famous laundry detergent Tide, spent $15 million to air an ad in every quarter of the game, for a cumulative run time of 90 seconds (AdAge, 2018). The decision to do so was based on Nielsen audience metrics, a staple of industry research used by media managers to communicate the value of their audiences to potential advertisers. Nielsen estimated that 115.6 million total viewers watched the NBC Super Bowl broadcast alone and that the total audience delivery across all platforms was 118.2 million (NBCUniversal, 2018). How Nielsen determined these metrics will be an important topic of discussion in this chapter.

While many sponsors, including Doritos, M&M's, and Pepsi, continue to purchase Super Bowl ads, others have raised questions regarding the degree to which audiences are actually engaged with Super Bowl ads (AdAge, 2018; Lombardo, 2017). For example, it is possible for a viewer not to be sitting in front of the TV during a commercial break. This challenge is not exclusive to Super Bowl advertising, as the lack of a feedback loop on legacy media can prevent industry researchers from capturing any real-time measures of audience engagement.

Accordingly, the feedback loop presented by online media creates a paradigm shift in industry research, as it is now possible to assess the degree to which an audience member has interacted with an advertisement or other media content in real time. Examples of research methods that allow for this include clickstream data, social media analytics, and e-commerce conversion rates. While Nielsen remains relevant in this area of research (e.g., Twitter TV), new players like Google, Facebook, and Twitter have developed powerful analytics tools that diversify the research methods available to practitioners (Facebook, 2019; Google, 2019a; Twitter, 2019). This chapter will explore developments and best practices in measuring audience size on legacy media that are still being used for industry research today as well as measuring audience engagement and conversion in a new media environment. Finally, it will conclude with a discussion of new developments in industry research methods as well as an overview of the opportunities and challenges faced by media managers and industry researchers in today's convergent media environments.

Something Old

One of the oldest audience measurement tools is television ratings. As mentioned previously, $5 million for a 30-second Super Bowl ad spot is dependent on the acceptance of a standardized audience metric by both advertisers and broadcasters. Nielsen is the accepted provider of this metric, and its television ratings and shares act as a common currency between advertisers and broadcasters. Ratings are defined as the percentage of households who own a television and are tuned in to a specific program. Accordingly, a rating is the measure of a program's audience relative to the total potential audience that could be universally reached, as it includes all households who own a television regardless of whether it is on or not (Wimmer & Dominick, 2014). It is calculated by dividing the number of households (HH) tuned in to a specific channel by the total number of television households (TVHH):

$$Rating = \#\ of\ HH\ tuned\ in / total\ \#\ of\ TVHH$$

In the example shown in figure 5.1, there are a total of 16 TVHHs, with 6 watching NBC, 5 watching CW, 3 watching Fox, and 2 that have their televisions off (represented by the houses in black). Using the formula given above, let's calculate each network's rating:

$$NBC's\ rating = 6/16 = 0.375 = 37.5\% = 37.5$$
$$CW's\ rating = 5/16 = 0.3125 = 31.3\% = 31.3$$
$$Fox's\ rating = 3/16 = 0.1875 = 18.8\% = 18.8$$

FIGURE 5.1. Distribution of TVHHs

Another "old" concept still being used to measure audience size is television share, or the percentage of households whose television is on and tuned in to a specific program. A share is the measure of a program's audience relative to the active audience that was consuming television at the time and therefore is less concerned with the potential audience size but is more commonly used to understand market competition. It is calculated by dividing the number of households (HH) tuned in to a specific channel by the total number of households using television (HUT):

$$Share = \#\ of\ HH\ tuned\ in / total\ \#\ of\ HUT$$

In the example shown in figure 5.1, there are a total of 14 HUTs (2 out of the 16 households were not using TV), with 6 watching NBC, 5 watching CW, and 3 watching Fox. Using the formula given above, let's calculate each network's share:

$$NBC's\ share = 6/14 = 0.429 = 42.9\% = 42.9$$
$$CW's\ share = 5/14 = 0.357 = 35.7\% = 35.7$$
$$Fox's\ share = 3/14 = 0.214 = 21.4\% = 21.4$$

You may notice that shares for all three networks are larger than the ratings. Shares are always larger than ratings, as the denominator HUT will always be smaller than the denominator TVHH. In addition, the percentage sign is dropped when reporting both shares and ratings. It is also a common practice to round to one decimal place (Kantar, 2019). It should be noted that the numbers included in the examples above are simply made up for training purposes. Due to audience fragmentation, contemporary television ratings are significantly lower. Table 5.1 shows the prime-time (8:00 p.m.–11:00 p.m.) broadcast network television ratings in the United States from the week of January 7, 2019 (Nielsen, 2019a).

As you can see, most serialized programs today have a rating below 10, whereas live sports still achieve appointment viewing that results in double-digit ratings numbers. Yet, in the 1990s (before the increased use of digital technologies and the ensuing audience fragmentation), it was common for a popular show to receive a double-digit

TABLE 5.1. Prime-Time U.S. Broadcast Network Television, January 7, 2019

Rank	*Program*	*Network*	*Rating*	*Viewers (000s)*
1	Fox NFC Playoff-Sat	FOX	17.9	33,352
2	Fox NFC Playoff-Kick-Sat	FOX	13.0	24,085
3	Fox NFC Playoff-PST-Sun	FOX	12.6	22,797
4	Big Bang Theory, The	CBS	8.1	13,535
5	NCIS	CBS	7.4	12,083
6	Young Sheldon	CBS	7.2	12,057
7	AGT Champions	NBC	5.9	9,966
8	Mom	CBS	5.7	9,358
9	Blue Bloods	CBS	5.7	9,052
10	Chicago Med	NBC	5.5	8,558

Source: Nielsen, 2019a.

rating. For example, in 1981–1982, *60 Minutes* (CBS) had an average rating of 27.7, but in the 2017–2018 season, the show had an average rating of 1.37 (Brooks & Marsh, 2007; Nielsen, 2018a). Regardless, the program was renewed for the 51st season and at the time of this writing still airs on Sundays at 7:00 p.m. (CBS, 2019). Clearly, CBS understands how digital technologies influence industry measurements of audience size.

Today, Nielsen data continues to drive many industry decisions. However, it is important for industry practitioners to understand how they secure their data, what adjustments they've made to factor in audience time-shifting behavior, including DVR/PVRs and multiplatform consumption, as well as how radio and print media capture comparable audience metrics.

The data that Nielsen uses to derive its proprietary ratings and shares comes from a representative sample of the general population in the United States (Nielsen, 2019b). In order to ensure generalizability, Nielsen uses national census data to ensure the sample correctly reflects the demographic distribution of the United States (Nielsen, 2011a). For example, during the 2010 census, the gender distribution in the United States was 50.8% female and 49.2% male (U.S. Census Bureau, 2011) As such, Nielsen would recruit a sample with 50.8% female and 49.2% male participants. In addition to gender, Nielsen would take other factors into consideration, including age, race, income, and heavy versus light television consumption habits (Wimmer & Dominick, 2014).

Moreover, the participants are recruited using a multistage probability sampling method that aims to match the geographic population distribution of TVHHs in the United States. For example, during the 2016–2017 television season, New York City accounted for 6.407% of TVHHs (Lyons Public Relations, 2017). Accordingly, 6.407% of Nielsen's sample would be recruited from New York City. It should be noted that New York City is the number-one market in the United States of the 210 designated market areas (DMAs). A DMA is a geographical region where audiences receive the same broadcast television programming (Nielsen, 2013). Using these geographic segmentations, Nielsen is able to provide both local television viewing metrics as well as national prime-time ratings (Lyons Public Relations, 2017).

Prime time is the period between 8:00 p.m. and 11:00 p.m. (ET/PT in the United States), Monday through Friday, when all network affiliates agree to air the same programming in order to reach a national advertising audience (Nielsen, 2011b). For example, Gainesville, Florida, is an entirely different DMA than Rochester, New York. However, they both aired the television sitcom *The Big Bang Theory* at 8:00 p.m. on Thursdays, allowing CBS to sell national advertising spots to sponsors. The same McDonald's advertisement can air during the first commercial break of *The Big Bang Theory* in Gainesville and Rochester. Outside of prime time, an ad is likely to run at different times and during different programs depending on the DMA and what is arranged with the broadcaster. As advertising rates for local and national audiences differ, the DMA system affords Nielsen the ability to report ratings/shares on both. Prime-time television ratings were first recorded by Nielsen in 1950, and DMAs were established in 1955, yet despite being "old," they remain relevant today (Nielsen, 2018b). Other examples of "older" concepts that remain relevant today include Nielsen households, local people meters, set meters, and Nielsen television viewing diaries.

NIELSEN HOUSEHOLDS

When a TVHH is recruited into Nielsen's sample, it is referred to as a Nielsen household. The method by which data is collected from each Nielsen household varies depending on the DMA. There are 56 DMAs (out of the 210 DMAs in the United States) where ratings and shares are measured in real time, using either local people meters or set meters (Nielsen, 2019c). The remaining 154 DMAs are captured using Nielsen television viewing diaries (Nielsen, 2019c). Before explaining the differences between methodologies, it is important to note that diary-based markets are only measured four months a year due to the high volume of work involved for participants. These four months are colloquially referred to by broadcasters as "sweeps" and are often when programmers plan to air their best content as they know these are the four times a year when Nielsen is measuring national viewership and corresponding advertising rates are determined (Nielsen, 2009a). While the start and end dates of "sweeps" fluctuates from year to year, they are always held in November, February, May, and July (Nielsen, 2009a). During other points in the year, it is only the top 56 DMAs that are being actively measured. The aforementioned data collection methods are discussed below (Nielsen, 2019c).

LOCAL PEOPLE METERS (LPMs)

LPMs are set-top boxes accompanied by a remote control that allow Nielsen to determine both the program being consumed as well as the demographics of the viewer (Nielsen, 2019c; Wimmer & Dominick, 2014). While the set-top box automatically tracks what channel is tuned in to and when, the determination of demographics is facilitated through personal viewing buttons; each member of the household is expected to press their unique button prior to commencing their television consumption. LPMs allow Nielsen to report tuning and viewership demographics 24 hours a day, 365 days per year in the top 25 DMAs, which accounts for approximately 50% of TVHHs in the United States (Lyons Public Relations, 2017; Nielsen, 2019c; Wimmer & Dominick, 2014).

SET METERS (SMs)

SMs are similar to LPMs; however, without the personal viewing buttons, they cannot measure demographic information (Nielsen, 2019c; Wimmer & Dominick, 2014). SMs only report when and which channel/program is being consumed. Demographic information is obtained through handwritten diaries completed during sweeps by a separate sample of people within the same DMA. Accordingly, SMs allow Nielsen to report tuning-only data 24 hours a day, 365 days per year in DMAs 26–56, which accounts for approximately 21% of TVHHs in the United States, whereas viewership demographics in these DMAs are only available four times a year (Lyons Public Relations, 2017; Nielsen, 2019c; Wimmer & Dominick, 2014).

NIELSEN TELEVISION VIEWING DIARIES

As mentioned previously, Nielsen uses television viewing diaries to measure audience size in DMAs 57–210. Nielsen diaries are completed in five steps. The first step requires respondents to answer questions about their household (Nielsen, 2015). Examples include:

- How many TV sets are in your home?
- How many of these are in working order?
- Is your TV connected to a satellite dish?

Respondents are also asked to list the local channels they receive. This includes the channel number, the station's call letters, and where in the city the respondent is located (Nielsen, 2015). Step three requires respondents to designate a number for each member of the household as well as list their first name, age, gender, and number of hours they work per week. Visitors are also indicated by listing first name as "Visitor" and answering the remaining demographic questions (Nielsen, 2015). Step four is the actual handwritten form documenting every household member's television viewing. This includes the time, name of the show, channel information, how the show was watched (live TV, DVR, other), and which member of the household consumed the program (Nielsen, 2015). Step five requires the respondent to mail the diary back to Nielsen.

It is important to note that DVR viewing is captured automatically by LPMs and SMs and manually recorded in step four of the diary process (Nielsen, 2009b; 2015). DVR viewing has been factored in to ratings and shares by creating different subcategories to denote the viewing type being described. For example, Nielsen provides ratings and shares for live consumption, live-plus-same-day DVR consumption, live-plus-three (i.e., live plus DVR consumption within three days of the live broadcast), and live-plus-seven (Nielsen, 2009b). Internet viewing was not traditionally factored into Nielsen ratings and shares, as they were predominantly used to determine television-specific advertising rates. However, Nielsen started to report a total audience delivery metric (NBCUniversal, 2018), which estimates the total audience size of a video program across all media platforms on which it was available (as mentioned in the Super Bowl example above).

While much of what is described above relates to the research methodologies widely used in the television industry, there is clearly a need for a common currency in audience size measurement shared by all media platforms. Much like television shares, *radio shares* refer to the percentage of listeners whose radio is on and tuned in to a specific program. Radio broadcasters also use average-quarter-hour persons (AQH persons), which measures the share of listeners who tune in to a specific station for at least 5 minutes during a 15-minute period (Wimmer & Dominick, 2014). Similarly, publishers are interested in the number of readers (i.e., readership) relative to the total size of the population (Wimmer & Dominick, 2014). Notice that the fundamental methodological formula for audience measurement remains the same regardless of platform:

ratings/share/readership = number of viewers
OR listeners OR readers / the population of interest

Ultimately, future audience measurements must employ a convergent media approach. This demonstrates that much like academic research methods, there are traditional industry practices that continue to remain relevant today, regardless of specific media platform. The fundamental concepts in audience measurement outlined above will drive the discussion of the Internet's feedback loop in the following section.

Something New

While legacy media audience metrics like ratings, shares, AQH, and readership remain the industry standard used by media managers, it is important to acknowledge their shared limitation—they measure audience size, not audience engagement. *Audience engagement* is an umbrella term for an array of industry metrics and research methods that attempt to quantify the degree to which an audience is involved and connected with the content they are consuming (Napoli, 2011). Examples of engagement metrics include the average time spent in a branded experience, a positive consumer attitude resulting from a communication, and the net effect of attentiveness to a program and an ad that brings about a measurable impact (Napoli, 2011).

Audience engagement is of "new" interest to advertisers given the growing attention economy of audiences. Measuring audience engagement in legacy media is challenging due to the lack of a feedback loop by which audiences can share their involvement with the content they are consuming. New media does not suffer from this limitation due to its interactive nature. Accordingly, the "click" has developed into a common currency for measuring audience engagement in online media.

The rationale behind using a consumer's click of a mouse to indicate engagement (or tapping on a link/app on a smartphone) is that if a consumer is disengaged, they can simply scroll through the content that is irrelevant to them. Alternatively, if a consumer is interested and paying attention to the content on their screen, they will engage in pull communication by "clicking" on the interactive elements of the content in order to pursue additional information or entertainment.

For example, imagine a user scrolling through their Twitter timeline. Each time a tweet is displayed on their screen, it is tallied as an impression metric (Twitter, 2019). An *impression* refers to the possible exposure of content to one audience member (Arens & Weigold, 2017). This term is a legacy media holdover, as it is a metric of audience size, not audience engagement. Alternatively, should a user be scrolling through their Twitter timeline and click on a tweet, this counts as engagement (Twitter, 2019). This first click and every ensuing click they make is then logged in a data file for future analysis by practitioners to facilitate more advanced measurement metrics, like engagement rate (i.e., engagement/impressions). This, of course, is not limited to social media, as should the user have clicked on a tweet that took them to Nike.com, Nike would track their entry click and every ensuing click until they exited Nike.com. These data sets are known as clickstream data, a widely used industry research method in today's new media management (Kaushik, 2009). It is important to note that while clickstream data was popularized as a method to demonstrate to advertisers that their audiences are indeed paying attention, its relevance for nonadvertising-based business models should not be understated.

For example, Nike, having an e-commerce business model, could track the number of transactions per visit (i.e., conversion rate). Whereas Netflix, having a subscription-based business model, could track which genre of films viewers consume the most (i.e., genre engagement rate). This could help Netflix establish a competitive advantage through product differentiation by providing better recommendations than their competitors. Ultimately, objective-based rates, like conversion and engagement rates, can be customized to meet the company's research needs. They are generally reported as a percentage of the outcomes desired relative to the number of visitors or visits (Kaushik, 2009).

CONVERSION RATE EXAMPLE

$$\textit{Conversion rate} = (\#\ \textit{of transactions} / \#\ \textit{of visitors or visits}) \times 100$$

If in January 2019 Nike had 108,238 visits, of which 1,248 resulted in a purchase transaction, the conversion rate = (1,248 / 108,238) × 100 =1.15% (see figure 5.2).

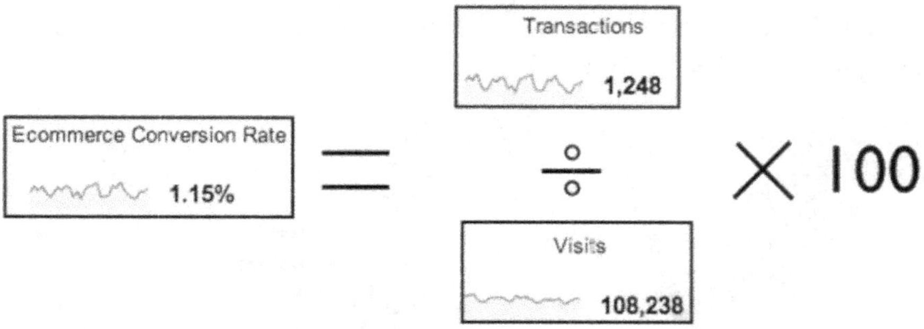

FIGURE 5.2. Conversion Rate Example

ENGAGEMENT RATE EXAMPLE

$$\textit{Engagement rate} = (\#\ \textit{of engagement} / \#\ \textit{of impressions}) \times 100$$

If in January 2019 Hulu posted two tweets, and the first tweet had 474 impressions, resulting in 14 likes, comments, or retweets, the engagement rate for the first tweet would be (14/474) × 100 = 2.95%. If the second tweet had 132 impressions, resulting in 33 likes, comments, or retweets, the engagement rate for the second tweet would be (33/132) × 100 = 25% (see figure 5.3).

FIGURE 5.3. Engagement Rate Example—Twitter Analytics (2019)
Source: Retrieved from https://analytics.twitter.com

CUSTOMIZED OBJECTIVE RATE EXAMPLE

Customized objective rate = (# of desired outcomes / # of possible outcomes) × 100

Perhaps Netflix is interested in determining how successful their free trial promotion in January 2019 was. With this in mind, they could create their own conversion metric where the numerator is the number of people who subscribed to Netflix after their free trial concluded and the denominator is the total number of users who were on a free trial during January 2019 (see figure 5.4).

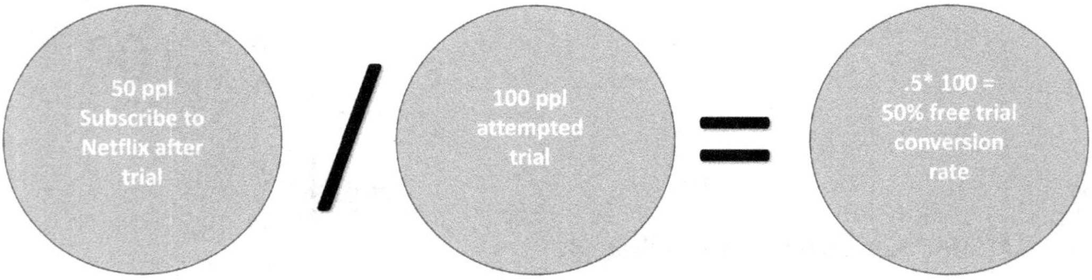

FIGURE 5.4. Netflix Free Trial Promotion Success Example

While engagement and conversion rates are often favored by media managers, due to their close relationship with a company's outcomes (e.g., ad revenue, transactions, or number of subscribers), there are a variety of different web analytics used by media managers in practice. It is important to note that the metrics discussed do not discriminate based on the device used to access the content and therefore are inclusive of broadband and mobile Internet users across all devices.

VISITS AND VISITORS

Visits report the fact that a user came to a website/app and spent some time browsing the site before leaving (Kaushik, 2009). Visit count is not unique, meaning that a single person can count for more than one visit. This is different from visitors, which counts each user one time only. The visitor count represents the number of unique individuals who visited a site/app.

For example, should a user visit Amazon.com five times in a single day, they would contribute to the visit count five times and the visitor count once. A visitor is determined by a device's IP address (Matomo, 2019). While it is possible for a single user to own multiple devices, or have a device that is shared by multiple people, industry practitioners have achieved consensus that this is the best research method currently available for estimating unique visitor counts (Google, 2019a; Matomo, 2019). Visits and visitors are the clickstream data versions of audience size metrics, such as ratings and shares. Time on page and time on site are two examples of commonly used engagement metrics.

TIME ON PAGE AND TIME ON SITE

Time on page refers to the amount of time a user spends on a single page contained within a larger website. It provides managers with a granular level of understanding of each piece of content's performance on a website as opposed to the macro-level measure provided by time on site. *Time on site* refers to the amount of time cumulatively spent across all pages by a single user in a single visit. For example, if a user's time on page for page 1 is 11 seconds and time on page for page 2 is 20 seconds, after which they exit the website, their time on site would be 31 seconds.

When interpreting time on page and time on site, it is important to account for outliers. Extremely low measures have low utility for practitioners, as a visit of a few milliseconds says little about whether the user enjoyed the content or not, as pragmatically there was not enough time for them to view the content before they exited. Alternatively, extremely high measures of multiple hours can be a result of a user leaving their device on with the website still open in the browser. Removing outliers is recommended before average time on site is calculated (Webtrends, 2019). Media managers tend to prefer high measures for time on page and time on site, but the opposite can be said for bounce rate and exit rate.

BOUNCE RATE AND EXIT RATE

Bounce rate is the percentage of visits that ended as a result of a user navigating away after only looking at a single page (Google, 2019b). In order to be eligible to be counted as part of the bounce rate, a visit must start and end on the same page without generating any additional clickstream data. Exit rate, often confused with bounce rate, is the percentage of visits that conclude on a specific page, regardless of how many pages were visited (Google, 2019c). Essentially, every time a user leaves a website, they are contributing to an increased exit rate for the last page viewed. To better illustrate the difference between bounce rate and exit rate, let's examine Google Analytics, a free analytics service that tracks and reports clickstream data (Google, 2019c):

Visit A: Page 1 > Page 2 > Exit
Visit B: Page 1 > Exit
Visit C: Page 2 > Page 1 > Exit
Visit D: Page 1 > Page 2 > Exit
Page 1 exit rate = 2 exits at page 1 / 4 visits of page 1 = 50%
Page 1 bounce rate = 1 visit starts and exits at page 1 /
3 visits that start with page 1 = 33%

Notice that the denominator of exit rate includes all visits of a page regardless of their starting point, whereas the denominator of bounce rate only includes the visits that had the page in question as the starting point. Exit rates are used to identify weak pages within a site that may be contributing to users leaving. Bounce rates are perceived to be measures of engagement, and practitioners argue the lower the bounce rate, the more engaged the audience is. While a bounce rate of less than 40% is desirable, many marketers report that average industry performance is about 50%, assuming the site in question is not a social media site (Peyton, 2019). Social media sites tend to have higher bounce rates, as they are content aggregators designed to link users to other content online (Morrison, 2014).

While clickstream data represents a research method that has the potential to measure both audience size and engagement, it too has limitations. Ultimately, the data tells media managers what somebody clicked on, when they clicked on it, and how often they clicked on it, but it doesn't tell them why (Kaushik, 2009). This leaves a lot of unanswered questions for media managers.

For example, did a news article receive a lot of clicks because it was an important piece of journalism or because the headline was enticing? When a practitioner sees an underperforming section of their website, would it be better to invest more in that section to improve the content, or is it better to discontinue that content? When Netflix reported that *Birdbox* generated 45 million views in its first week (Spangler, 2018), does that mean 45 million people enjoyed the film, and if so, what was so enjoyable about the film? The limitations of clickstream data and how academic research methods present opportunities to resolve these challenges will be discussed in the following section.

Opportunities and Challenges

Media convergence has brought many opportunities and challenges to industry research. By understanding each, we can better establish how to address the unanswered questions raised in the previous section. Throughout history, each new media industry challenge created an opportunity to improve industry research methods in media management. For example, in 1949, NBC launched and subsequently canceled *Twenty Questions*, a game show that later was revived by ABC in the 1950–1951 season, and then again by the DuMont Television Network for 1951–1954, and then again by ABC in the 1954–1955 season (Brooks & Marsh, 2007). The volume of cancelations and revivals of *Twenty Questions* highlights an early challenge faced by media managers who were forced to make business decisions based on their own intuition until metrics like ratings, shares, AQH, and readership became widely available.

Traditional metrics also present many new opportunities and challenges in today's convergent media environment, specifically in understanding the degree of audience engagement relative to audience size. This is well illustrated by the cancelation of *Freaks and Geeks* in 2000. The network canceled the show after 12 episodes, despite 18 episodes being produced; incredibly high reviews from critics; numerous award nominations; and an engaged, albeit smaller than anticipated, audience (Schneider, 2014). At the time, NBC executive Garth Ancier, who was responsible for the cancelation of the program, cited low ratings as the show had 6.77 million viewers on average throughout its run (Bartleet, 2018).

Interestingly, these numbers are considered successful in today's fragmented media environment. Shows with audiences of comparable size—*Young Sheldon* (7.20 million), *Modern Family* (7.10 million), and *How to Get Away with Murder* (6.42 million)—all continue to be renewed (Nielsen, 2019a). *Freaks and Geeks* executive producer Judd Apatow argued that the ratings did not tell the whole story and that the show was given a time slot that was known to be weaker performing. In addition, the relatively low ratings may be because NBC refused to promote the show online due to fear of audience cannibalization.

Since its cancelation, *Freaks and Geeks* has generated a high volume of revenue through DVD sales and aftermarket sales to content aggregators like Netflix (Bartleet, 2018; Schneider, 2014). This has led to numerous post-cancelation accolades. In 2006, *Rolling Stone* ranked *Freaks and Geeks* in the top 100 shows of all time; in 2013, *TV Guide* ranked it as number one of shows that were canceled too soon; and in 2014, Garth Ancier acknowledged that he regretted canceling such a well-written show (Roush, 2013; Sheffield, 2016; Schneider, 2014; TV Guide, 2019).

This example demonstrates the challenges faced by media managers who choose to rely solely on audience size instead of embracing new developments in audience engagement research methods. Thankfully, the ever-complex and dynamic media environment provides many new opportunities for industry research in media management.

OPPORTUNITIES

When reflecting on the *20 Questions* and *Freaks and Geeks* cases, it is easy to empathize with network executives who have limited data to make an informed decision. However, both examples represent missed opportunities to supply in-demand programming to an engaged audience. This highlights the lack of actionable data faced by industry researchers and media managers before Web 2.0. The proliferation of Web 2.0 technologies, services that allow audiences to post on the Internet without learning how to code a website (e.g., Facebook), and the introduction of automated capturing of clickstream data (e.g., Google Analytics) provide media managers with an abundance of market intelligence. As a result, there are various opportunities to make informed business decisions that capitalize on niche audiences that may have otherwise been ignored. This is well illustrated by Netflix's tendency to revive shows previously canceled by other media firms. By identifying that engaged audiences still exist for *Full House*, *Gilmore Girls*, and *Arrested Development*, Netflix has created opportunities for new enterprise using content rejected by other firms (Acevedo, 2019). While the benefits of extracting market intelligence from audience analytics are clear, the key is how to translate such a high volume of data into actionable business insights.

Avinash Kaushik, author of *Web Analytics 2.0* and winner of the University of British Columbia Award of Achievement in Web Analytics, refers to this challenge as the "paradox of data" (Kaushik, 2009). Ultimately, if a media manager has too little data, they are increasing the likelihood of making the wrong decision. On the contrary, if a media manager is faced with too much data, it obscures their interpretation of what the correct decision is. Understandably, this leads to a variety of unanswered questions, such as "Why did an online article, section of a website, or a Netflix film generate more or fewer clicks?"

Kaushik (2009) argues that actionable insights are derived from a combination of clickstream data, multiple outcomes analysis, experimentation and testing, the voice of the customer, and competitive intelligence. Practitioners should be strategic in how they procure, store, and analyze their clickstream data. For example, a small-town retailer may need to rely on free services like Google Analytics, whereas a company like Apple could likely design and implement its own vertically integrated tracking software. The small-town retailer may also need to hire an intern or entry-level analyst to assist with data interpretation, whereas Apple has probably already employed individuals with the requisite skill set.

In an environment focused on clickstream data, *multiple outcomes analysis* refers to understanding the relationships between a firm's clickstream data and its revenue, costs, and customer loyalty (Kaushik, 2009). Practitioners often use descriptive statistics, correlation analysis, and regressions to test for these relationships (Gallo, 2015). This presents an organic research opportunity for collaborations between academics and practitioners, which could enhance a company's multiple outcome analysis through the use of multivariate statistical approaches, including discriminant analysis, multivariate analysis of variance, factor analysis, and structural equation modeling. This additional experimentation and testing would better incorporate latent consumer thoughts and feelings, as well as the actions of competitors, into industry analyses. Yet, the complexity of the data presents new challenges for media managers.

CHALLENGES

While Kaushik's *Web Analytics 2.0* framework (2009) speaks to the strengths of a mixed-methods industry approach, it does provide challenges to future industry researchers hoping to integrate both relevant media management theories and academic research methods. The triangulation of the clickstream data with any revenue, costs, and customer loyalty relationships forecasts is difficult. *Triangulation* refers to testing the data using a variety of different research methods to fully understand what is being observed while simultaneously ensuring high degrees of reliability and validity (Wimmer & Dominick, 2014). Ultimately, practitioners are faced with the challenge of avoiding making business decisions based on faulty data, as the costs associated with bad data can potentially account for 15–25% of a company's revenue (Redman, 2017). Employing media management theories and academic research methods outlined in previous chapters (i.e., chapter 3, "Theories of Media Management," chapter 4, "Academic Research Methods in Media Management") has the potential to help mitigate these risks.

Unfortunately, as was the case in the *Freaks and Geeks* example, choosing a course of action without first addressing the deficiency in the available data can lead to an inappropriate decision. It is recommended that practitioners go beyond their spreadsheets and engage in research methods that require a sample of actual audience members. This often takes the form of focus groups, guided AB testing, or eye-tracking experiments. These methodologies are expensive and often require funding, which can present a challenge to media management researchers.

In Kaushik's (2009) framework, the voice of the customer is the outcome of the experimentation and testing phase and should be analyzed to answer previously unaddressed questions regarding the clickstream data (e.g., why a user clicked on some items and not others). Theoretical support for justifying the need to secure the consumer's voice can be found in Latour's (2005) actor-network theory. Latour argues that actors within a society should be allowed to speak for themselves, as a researcher's interpretation of their statements can be subject to bias (Latour, 2005). As such, combining clickstream data with the voice and opinions of customers provides media managers with a more holistic assessment of performance than clickstream data alone.

Kaushik (2009) also argues for the inclusion of competitive intelligence. *Competitive intelligence* refers to macro data regarding industry performance baselines as well as micro data regarding the performance of specific competitors. Using television audience sizes as an example, a manager without competitive intelligence may look at *Young Sheldon*'s 7.2 million audience as small, especially considering pre-Internet audiences were sometimes upward of 70 million. In reality, *Young Sheldon*'s 7.2 million is among the top 10 performing prime-time broadcast shows today (Nielsen, 2019a).

Notice how easy it would be to make the wrong decision regarding keeping or canceling *Young Sheldon* without competitive intelligence. Theoretical support for justifying the inclusion of competitive intelligence in industry research can be drawn from Keller's (2012) consumer-based brand equity model, which suggests that perceived quality cannot be accurately assessed without using a competitor as a frame of reference. Securing competitive intelligence is another challenge faced by industry researchers and media managers in today's ever-evolving media environment.

Challenges in industry research in media management have evolved from dataless decisions made by subject matter experts to debates regarding the degree of value of audience size relative to audience engagement, to questions regarding why audiences are more engaged in some instances than others. Ultimately, Kaushik's framework (2009) presents a new and promising growth area for industry research in media management. It is important for future practitioners to consider a mixed-methods approach, as this allows for data-driven decisions that consider both audience size and engagement while enabling audiences to speak for themselves. The following action plan can be utilized in this pursuit.

ACTION PLAN

1. Increase the objectivity and accuracy of business decisions by utilizing the cost-effective market intelligence provided by Web 2.0 technologies, including clickstream data and user-generated content.
2. Triangulate data using a variety of different research methods to ensure validity, reliability, and accurate interpretation. This will help avoid the costs associated with business decisions based on faulty data.
3. Resolve inconsistencies in the interpretation of clickstream data through research methods that allow audiences to speak for themselves (e.g., focus groups). Ultimately, remember to ask audiences, "Why?"

KEY TAKEAWAYS

1. Historically, industry research methods in media management have focused on techniques for measuring audience size, but the feedback loop presented by online

media created a paradigm shift as contemporary research methods focus on measuring audience engagement. More recent developments have attempted to address why audiences are more engaged during certain consumption experience scenarios.
2. The fundamental methodological formula for audience measurement on legacy media is audience size divided by population of interest (e.g., ratings, shares, readership).
3. New media measurements include conversion rates, engagement rates, and customized objective rates.
4. Kaushik's (2009) *Web Analytics 2.0* model argues that actionable business insights are best achieved through a combination of (1) clickstream data, (2) multiple outcomes analysis, (3) experimentation and testing, (4) the voice of the customer, and (5) competitive intelligence.

CONCLUSION

The value of industry research methods in media management lies in the balance of three conflicting needs. First, there is the economic feasibility of the undertaking. As legacy media business models continue to be challenged by digital technologies, industry research methods like ratings, shares, AQH, and readership provide a mechanism by which practitioners can empirically demonstrate their continued value to advertisers. As Jenkins (2006) points out, while the role of legacy media may change and even diminish in magnitude, any communication platform that continues to fill a relevant need will never be obsolete. Second, there are the needs of audiences. Netflix, Steam, Apple Music, NYTimes.com, and other new media enterprises have empowered consumers, creating an audience that wants a wide variety of content on their own schedule and on any device (Jenkins, 2006). Given that audiences are fragmented across an ever-growing number of platforms, it is through industry research methods that media managers can reassemble the fragmented audience and gain an accurate understanding of cumulative audience size and engagement (Jenkins, 2006). Finally, media managers must consider the quality of the content itself. Notice that facing convergence, practitioners can no longer just follow a dual product model of economic feasibility and content quality, as the audience is not regulated to consuming content on the platform selected by the practitioner.

For example, a person may like the quality of Marvel films and be willing to pay to watch, but this only addresses two of the three aforementioned priorities (i.e., economic feasibility and content quality). Perhaps another person is only willing to watch Marvel films in theaters, as they are generally large-scale special effects spectacles (i.e., audience needs). Alternatively, perhaps another person is not a fan of the superhero genre but does enjoy watching the films with their significant other because of the kinship it creates; therefore, that person may only consume Marvel films with another person, regardless of the platform.

Notice that platform choice splits audience needs into consumption experience needs and content quality needs. This highlights the increasing importance of industry research that assesses reasons why audiences are more engaged in certain scenarios as opposed to measuring only to what degree they are engaged. Kinepolis, a Belgian cinema chain, expanded beyond data-driven research methods and captured the true voice of the consumer, as audiences identified the lack of adequate babysitting options as the reason for not attending the cinema (Bekefi, Epstein, & Yuthas, 2009; Pitta & Pitta, 2012). Kinepolis then began offering a daycare service where moviegoers would know their children were well cared for and could check them in for the duration of a movie. This introduced a new revenue stream while simultaneously improving box office performance (Bekefi et al., 2009; Pitta & Pitta, 2012). Such an insight was not something they could have learned through quantitative audience metrics and clickstream data alone.

While mixed-methods approaches combine measures such as ratings and shares with clickstream data, face-to-face consumer research, and competitive intelligence, researchers have the opportunity to further customize the frameworks reviewed in this chapter to better fit their needs. This could include the integration of relevant media management theories and academic research methods is likely to continue to be developed over time. Ultimately, the newest and most promising areas for growth in industry research methods are often to address a need / limitation that is present within the existing method.

Given the pattern of new research methods being developed to address the limitations of previous tools, it is likely that through the use of mixed-methods approaches, like Kaushik's (2009), new limitations will be revealed, which in turn will lead to the development of new industry research methods. Ultimately, industry research methods have the potential to enhance audience size and engagement metrics through improved understanding of consumers. This invaluable knowledge has the potential to facilitate an increased willingness to pay from viewers while also establishing common currencies between advertisers and content providers.

The trend of hiring practitioners well versed in industry research is growing as the number of jobs in 2015 that involved big data reached 1.9 million in the United States and 4.4 million worldwide (Gartner, 2019). In 2019, the highest-paid entry-level job in the tech industry in the United States was data scientist, with an average annual salary of $113,254 (Liu, 2019). In addition to the research methods outlined in this chapter, practitioners looking to make a career as industry researchers should ensure they are critical thinkers that can debunk faulty data, are comfortable with visually displaying their results in an engaging fashion (i.e., data visualization), and are strong communicators during both informal discussions and formal presentations (Northeastern, 2019). Ultimately, results from an analysis may be correct, but if you are unable to convince anyone of the value of such insights, there will be few opportunities to showcase your industry research skill set.

Clearly, navigating media convergence requires a diverse array of expertise from practitioners. As media managers will likely work with industry researchers and analysts, ensuring those onboarded have the requisite data literacy skill sets outlined above is crucial to a company's success. While the inclusion of industry research methods in business decisions likely falls under the purview of management, hiring and evaluating these industry researchers need to start with a media company's human resource department. The next chapter will identify human resource management trends in the media industries as well as the opportunities and challenges.

REFERENCES

Acevedo, A. (2019, August 10). 11 shows Netflix saved from cancellation. *Business Insider*. https://www.insider.com/shows-netflix-saved-from-cancellation-2019-8

AdAge. (2018). *Super Bowl LII*. https://adage.com/series/2018-super-bowl-lii/92

Arens, W., & Weigold, M. F. (2017). *M: Advertising*. McGraw-Hill Education.

Bartleet, L. (2018). *Why was there never a second season of "Freaks and Geeks," the cult show that's now on Netflix?* NME. https://www.nme.com/blogs/tv-blogs/freaks-and-geeks-season-2-1969369

Bekefi, T., Epstein, M. J., & Yuthas, K. (2009). *Creating growth from effective opportunity risk management*. CMA Management. http://daedalusadvising.com/Bekefi_managementmag_09.pdf

Birt, H., Consterdine, G., & Robinson, L. (1999). The quality of reading survey: An instrument for change. Paper presented at Worldwide Research Symposium, Florence, Italy.

Brooks, T., & Marsh, E. (2007). *The complete directory to prime time network and cable TV shows 1946–present*. Ballantine Books.

CBS. (2019). *"60 Minutes."* https://www.cbsnews.com/60-minutes

CBS Television City. (2018, April). *"Kevin Can Wait" focus group*. CBS Television City.

Facebook. (2019). *Facebook analytics*. https://analytics.facebook.com

Gallo, A. (2015). A refresher on regression analysis. *Harvard Business Review*. https://hbr.org/2015/11/a-refresher-on-regression-analysis

Gartner. (2019). *Number of big data jobs in the United States and globally in 2015 (in millions)*. Statista. https://www.statista.com/statistics/255952/number-of-big-data-jobs-in-us-and-globally

Google. (2019a). *Google analytics*. https://analytics.google.com

Google. (2019b). *Bounce rate*. https://support.google.com/analytics/answer/1009409?hl=en

Google. (2019c). *Exit rate vs. bounce rate*. https://support.google.com/analytics/answer/2525491?hl=en

Ipsos. (2015, July). *National readership survey DS-CAPI protocol*. http://www.nrs.co.uk/wp-content/uploads/2013/08/External-DS-CAPI-protocol_-July-2015.pdf

Jenkins, H. (2006). *Convergence culture: Where old and new media collide*. New York University Press.

Kantar. (2019). *SRDS*. https://www.srds.com/frontMatter/sup_serv/calculator/hut_put/huts_puts.html

Kaushik, A. (2009). *Web analytics 2.0*. Wiley Publishing.

Keller, K. L. (2012). *Strategic brand management: Building, measuring, and managing brand equity*. Pearson.

Latour, B. (2005). *Reassembling the social: An introduction to actor-network-theory*. Oxford University Press.

Liu, S. (2019). *Highest paying entry-level jobs in the technology industry in the United States as of 2019 (in U.S. dollars)*. Statista. https://www.statista.com/statistics/1012267/united-states-highest-paying-tech-jobs-entry-level

Lombardo, T. (2017, February 1). *This is what happened when we tried to spend a $5 million Super Bowl budget on Facebook*. AdAge. https://adage.com/article/special-report-super-bowl/happened-spend-a-5-million-super-bowl-budget-facebook/307709

Lyons Public Relations. (2017). *2017 Nielsen DMA rankings: Full list*. https://www.lyonspr.com/latest-nielsen-dma-rankings

Matomo. (2019). *How is a unique visitor counted in Matomo?* https://matomo.org/faq/general/faq_43

Morrison, K. (2014). *Social referrals result in a 65% bounce rate after first page*. AdWeek. https://www.adweek.com/digital/addthis-engagement-report-social-referrals

Napoli, P. M. (2009). Environment cognitions in a dual-product marketplace: A participant-observation perspective on the U.S. broadcast television industry. *International Journal on Media Management, 5*, 100–108. doi: 10.1080/14241270309390024

Napoli, P. M. (2011). *Audience evolution: New technologies and the transformation of media audiences*. Columbia University Press.

NBCUniversal. (2018). *NBC's Super Bowl LII gains more than 12 million Nielsen "out of home" viewers: Increasing total audience delivery to 118.2 million viewers*. https://nbcsportsgrouppressbox

.com/2018/02/08/nbcs-super-bowl-lii-gains-more-than-12-million-nielsen-out-of-home-viewers-increasing-total-audience-delivery-to-118-2-million-viewers
Nielsen. (2009a). *Sweeps*. https://www.nielsen.com/content/dam/nielsen/en_us/documents/pdf/Misc/Nielsen%20Sweeps%20Dates.pdf
Nielsen. (2009b). *How DVRs are changing the television landscape*. https://www.nielsen.com/us/en/insights/article/2009/how-dvrs-are-changing-the-television-landscape
Nielsen. (2011a). *Incorporating census 2010 data in Nielsen pop-facts*. http://www.tetrad.com/pub/documents/nielsencensus2010.pdf
Nielsen. (2011b). *What time is really prime time*. https://www.nielsen.com/us/en/insights/news/2011/what-time-is-really-primetime.html
Nielsen. (2013). *DMA regions*. https://www.nielsen.com/intl-campaigns/us/dma-maps.html
Nielsen. (2015). *Completing your TV diary*. https://www.nielsen.com/content/panel/tvdiary8b-en-feb2014/instructions.html
Nielsen. (2018a). *"60 Minutes": Season 50 ratings (2017–18)*. https://tvseriesfinale.com/tv-show/60-minutes-season-50-ratings-2017-18
Nielsen. (2018b). *Celebrating 95 years of innovation*. http://sites.nielsen.com/timelines/our-history
Nielsen. (2019a). *Top ten*. https://www.nielsen.com/us/en/top10s.html
Nielsen. (2019b). *About Nielsen measurement*. https://www.nielsen.com/eu/en/about-us/public-affairs/about-nielsen-measurement.html
Nielsen. (2019c). *Local measurement methodology*. http://en-us.nielsen.com/sitelets/cls/documents/nielsen/Local-Measurement-Methodology-Ex.pdf
Northeastern. (2019). *6 must-have skills for data analysts*. https://www.northeastern.edu/graduate/blog/must-have-data-analyst-skills
Pandey, B., Pandey, P. K., & Kumar, M. (2016). Effectives of advertising clutter: A comparative analysis. *International Journal on Transformations of Media, Journalism & Mass Communication, 1*(2), 6–13.
Peyton, J. (2019). *What's the average bounce rate for a website?* RocketFuel. https://www.gorocketfuel.com/the-rocket-blog/whats-the-average-bounce-rate-in-google-analytics
Pitta, D., & Pitta, E. (2012). Transforming the nature and scope of new product development. *Journal of Product & Brand Management, 21*(2), 35–46.
Redman, T. C. (2017). *Seizing opportunity in data quality*. MIT Sloan. https://sloanreview.mit.edu/article/seizing-opportunity-in-data-quality
Roush, M. (2013). The 60 best shows that got cut short. *TV Guide*. http://www.sitcomsonline.com/boards/showthread.php?t=313034
Schneider, M. (2014). Former NBC exec Garth Ancier responds to Seth Rogen about *Freaks and Geeks'* cancellation. *TV Guide*. https://www.tvguide.com/news/freaks-geeks-seth-rogen-cancellation-nbc-garth-ancier-1088062/
Sheffield, R. (2016). 100 greatest TV shows of all time. *Rolling Stone*. https://www.rollingstone.com/tv/tv-lists/100-greatest-tv-shows-of-all-time-105998/freaks-and-geeks-102385/
Spangler, T. (2018). *Bird Box* viewed by 45 million Netflix members in first week company says. *Variety*. https://variety.com/2018/digital/news/bird-box-netflix-45-million-views-first-week-1203096379
Thurman, N., & Fletcher, R. (2019). Has digital distribution rejuvenated readership? *Journalism Studies, 20*, 542–562. doi: 10.1080/1461670X.2017.1397532
TV Guide. (2019). *21 shows that should have never been canceled*. https://www.tvguide.com/galleries/21-shows-that-shouldve-never-been-canceled
Twitter. (2019). *Twitter analytics*. https://analytics.twitter.com
U.S. Census Bureau. (2011). *Age and sex composition: 2010*. https://www.census.gov/prod/cen2010/briefs/c2010br-03.pdf
Wagmeister, E. (2017). Erinn Hayes' character to be killed off *Kevin Can Wait* to make room for Leah Remini. *Variety*. https://variety.com/2017/tv/news/erinn-hayes-kevin-can-wait-donna-killed-off-leah-remini-1202512614
Webtrends. (2019). *Difference between median visit length and average visit length*. https://kb.webtrends.com/articles/Information/Difference-between-Median-Visit-Length-and-Average-Visit-Length
Wimmer, R. D., & Dominick, J. R. (2014). *Mass media research*. Wadsworth.

PART II

FUNDAMENTAL ISSUES IN CONVERGENT MEDIA MANAGEMENT

CHAPTER 6

Human Resource Management

Heather L. Walter, The University of Akron
Andrea L. Meluch, The University of Akron

LEARNING OBJECTIVES

1. Define human resource management (HRM) and provide examples of HRM functions in a media organization.
2. Describe the differences between theory X, theory Y, theory Z, and total quality management and how they influenced the development of HRM.
3. Explain human capital theory and resource-based theory.
4. Identify HRM trends in media industries.
5. Consider the opportunities and challenges for HRM in a convergent media environment.

Now that we understand the many ways in which media convergence has impacted the theories and research of media management, it is important to turn our attention to more specific fundamental issues in convergent media management. We will begin by focusing on the field of human resource management. *HRM* refers to the process by which people are recruited, employed, managed, and developed for an organization. Specifically, HRM describes the approach of an organization toward the employment and development of people. Under the umbrella of HRM are the multiple functions that provide a framework for developing and implementing an organizational plan that values the contributions of well-prepared workers.

As you can see in figure 6.1, *human resource management* is an umbrella term that includes key practices such as finding, recruiting, and selecting the right people for an organization; training and developing those people to match the needs of the organization; setting up structures for performance and reward that match the organization's goals; managing employee relations in a way that motivates and engages workers; and developing a human resource (HR) plan to embrace policies and practices that support

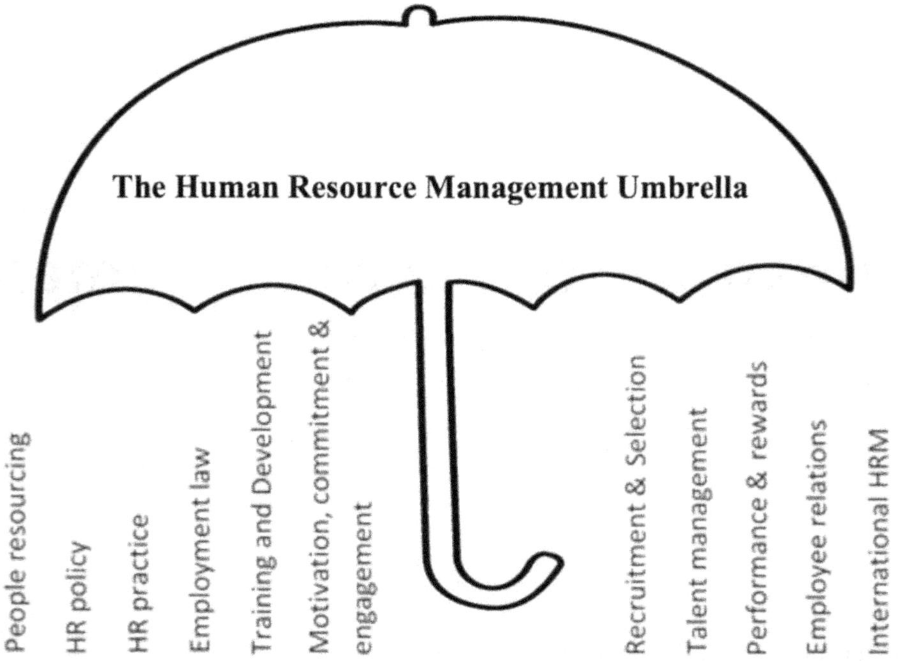

FIGURE 6.1. Human Resource Management Umbrella

HRM efforts. Together, these functions provide a stable workforce that is flexible and informed enough to meet a company's goals.

Media organizations develop in all different sizes, with great variety of duties and functions, requiring various levels of staff and resources. Regardless of these differences, human resource management plays a critical role in the overall strategic operation of a company. In media industries specifically, there is a great need for HRM to serve a proactive function, meeting and addressing needs before they arise. With the rapidly changing convergent environment of increased technology for HRM functions, coupled with the convergence of media personnel across platforms, media industries are specifically in need of robust HR policies. Let us begin with a case study that explains how a typical human resource professional operates in a small community media company, Fusions, Inc.

CASE STUDY

Fusions, Inc. is a small community media company that houses production for cross-platform media content. There are many employees and departments within Fusions, Inc. that are critical to its success. Consider Jeff, a human resource professional within the company. Jeff's responsibilities include recruiting on-air talent and workers for all the other off-air responsibilities. Recruitment might require placing ads, developing social media outreach to potential employees, conducting background checks, wading through résumés, listening to sizzle reels, and igniting interview processes. However, his job does not just stop when he has completed hiring a new person. Jeff must also participate in the development of all workers to keep them growing to meet the company's needs. Jeff routinely prepares and offers trainings essential to the growth of the workers. Recently, Jeff needed to hold a mandatory two-day training to ensure all workers were prepared for the roll-out of a new software. Next month Jeff will hold an optional training for the new Adobe Premiere upgrade.

Beyond hiring and training, Jeff must also operate within the confines of employment law, so issues of hiring, firing, abuse, and harassment must be navigated through his office. Employees come to him when there are personnel issues or conflicts that cannot be resolved. Knowing how much time and money it costs to recruit and train new employees, Jeff actively focuses on programs that will support and motivate good workers so that they do not seek employment elsewhere.

The low turnover at Fusions, Inc. is attributed to Jeff's efforts to improve engagement and satisfaction. Keeping excellent employees is essential to maintaining stability and consistency. Finding ways to meet employees' needs and to help them balance their home and work lives creates challenges for Jeff. For example, one of Jeff's producers, Cheryl, is about to have a baby. Jeff does not want to lose Cheryl, so he is working with her to build a plan that will enable her to work from home and have a flexible schedule while Cheryl is adapting to the newborn. This type of maternity plan will mean Cheryl can continue to be a highly productive member of the team while feeling supported enough that she will not feel frustrated or quit.

As you can see, Jeff's role in managing HR for the company is varied and complex. He is tasked not only with seeking and hiring appropriate employees but also with developing a culture that encourages participation and meets employees' needs so that they don't seek employment elsewhere. All the tasks that Jeff performs fall under the title of human resource management. While this role fluctuates depending on the size of a media company, this case illustrates how crucial the role of HRM is to the successful operation of media companies. Understanding traditional "old" approaches to HRM can guide future practitioners in any media climate.

Something Old

Today's human resource management environment is quite different from the classical approaches that organizations used in the early 20th century. However, despite these notable differences, understanding the historical foundations of HRM provides insight into the organizational management structures we use today. The following sections provide a brief review of the history and theories of HRM. In particular, the section follows the chronological development of HRM to highlight important changes and turns that have shaped how we manage media organizations.

A BRIEF HISTORY AND THEORIES OF HUMAN RESOURCE MANAGEMENT

HRM began as an approach to organizational management that ran counter to many of the earlier approaches. At the turn of the 20th century, as the industrial revolution took hold, manufacturing became prevalent, and business owners and academics began grappling with the best practices for ensuring company success. Early theories for management were derived from the longest and largest existing organizations: the church, the government, and the military. These highly hierarchical examples of organizations in existence for hundreds of years provided a model of management that focused on formal structure and autocratic leadership. The earliest modern managerial theories concentrated on organizing workers and increasing productivity, which necessitated formulating an approach reliant on workers' subservience to the organization's leadership. These approaches focused on finding the right ways to hire employees and create their work in order to optimize output and productivity. Nevertheless, these approaches lacked a focus on the human aspect of work, minimalizing the process to a scientific equation that did not consider employee interest, satisfaction, or motivation processes.

The earliest focus on the human part of management is traceable to the Hawthorne studies of the 1920s (Roethlisberger, 1947). In this series of studies, researcher Elton Mayo (1933) examined the impact of environmental changes (such as varying lighting levels) on the performance of repetitive tasks. The surprising results of the studies included an increase in productivity regardless of the manipulation. Even when lighting was very low, productivity increased. Mayo (1933) argues that these performance improvements were a result of workers being flattered and motivated by the attention received during the study.

Rice (1982) suggests that the Hawthorne effect represents the improvement of any performance or behavior as a result of increased attention. Other researchers interpret these findings differently. For example, Parsons (1974) claims that the changes were better attributed to feedback and learning issues in the study. Ultimately, the Hawthorne effect became the subject of great debate and dozens of interpretations (Macefield, 2007). While the validity of the interpretations surrounding these studies is still a point of contention, it is important to recognize that findings from these studies propelled an interest in the study of human resources and how humans change their work behavior based on controlling or changing external stimuli.

HR managers must understand the impact of the Hawthorne studies on industry practice today. Researchers used these debates as a foundation for considering worker motivations and behaviors. By the 1950s, managerial theory began to shift toward participative leadership. Over time, the emphasis on worker participation helped build much more informal work environments. This trend continues to transform successful businesses even in today's convergent media environment. For example, the online retailer Zappos has regularly earned the distinction of being named in *Fortune* magazine's list of "100 Best Companies to Work For," attributing much of its success to its positive corporate culture that values a work environment where employees can have a sense of fun, meaningful work, and incentives to minimize monotony (Heathfield, 2019). Here, you can see how findings of traditional HRM influence industry practices today. Some of the most substantial roots include McGregor's theory X and Y, human capital theory, and resource-based theory.

THEORY X AND THEORY Y (AND EVENTUALLY THEORY Z)

Douglas McGregor introduced *The Human Side of Enterprise* in 1960. In this work, he highlighted the extreme contrast between prevailing managerial approaches (McGregor, 1960). He identified two differing managerial mindsets. The first he called theory X and described a conventional managerial viewpoint based on a vision of workers as focusing on rewards (i.e., money), lacking in self-motivation, and requiring a leader for direction. The second managerial mindset, theory Y, focused on a vision of workers motivated by responsibility and autonomy in addition to rewards and who were capable of self-motivation if given the proper tools for success. McGregor (1960) questioned the usefulness of the theory X approach, claiming that this view of people was cynical and minimized the potential that workers brought to the workplace. According to Cunningham (2011), the theory X perspective views workers as untrustworthy and likely to avoid work when a manager is not looking. McGregor (1960) further argues that theory Y would be more advantageous for helping to meet workers' social, ego, and self-fulfillment needs, thus improving morale and productivity. Additionally, he also claimed that while theory X propels a manager whose objective is to gain worker compliance in exchange for rewards, theory Y would integrate individual and organizational goals to find alternative ways to motivate and maintain employee participation.

McGregor's theory X and theory Y highlight two different ways of viewing workers, though later research implores us not to assume either is a perfect solution for worker management. The assumptions of each are highlighted in table 6.1. Managers in today's media organizations tend to continue to subscribe to one of these theories or seek to find some middle ground.

Before he died in 1969, McGregor began working on an extension to theory X and theory Y, which would address the criticisms made about the lack of mutual exclusivity between these two approaches. He proposed a theory Z, which included a focus on

TABLE 6.1. Explanation of McGregor's (1960) Theories X and Y

Theory X Is Based on Assumptions That	*Theory Y Is Based on Assumptions That*
1. Most people inherently dislike work and will avoid it if at all possible. 2. Most people prefer to be directed in that work and lack self-motivation. 3. Most people seek to avoid responsibility and lack ambition. 4. Most people are motivated only by financial gain.	1. For most people work is as natural as play. If workers are unhappy in their jobs, it is probably because of the managerial approach. 2. Most people have the capacity to be self-motivated. 3. Most people seek responsibility and are ambitious by nature. 4. Most people are motivated by multiple factors including autonomy, achievement, and financial gain.
As a result of these assumptions, a theory X managerial style requires close, firm supervision with a clear sense of expectations and tasks. A manager working under these types of assumptions might weigh out the benefit of using rewards and/or punishments to get workers to stay motivated. McGregor referred to this as a hard managerial approach.	As a result of these assumptions, a theory Y managerial style would focus on a cooperative relationship between managers and workers. A manager working under these types of assumptions might focus on building a working environment where the personal needs and objectives of a worker can exist in harmony with the organization's goals. McGregor referred to this as a soft managerial approach.

lifetime employment, concern for employees and their work-life balance, and a commitment to quality (Cunningham, 2011). Theory Z was an answer to the critics of theories X and Y. Critics claimed that the dichotomy between the two was unrealistic and that most organizations do not subscribe to only one approach or the other, nor should they. Theory Z was an attempt to find the realistic middle ground and a way to implement the findings of his previous theoretical explorations.

After his premature death, McGregor's work on theory Z was extended in the 1970s and 1980s by William Ouchi (1981). Ouchi focused on the differences between Japanese and American management. At the time, Japanese companies were booming, while American companies in similar industries (steel, automobiles, and consumer electronics) were struggling in comparison. As a result of observing the impact of culture (national and organizational) on management, Ouchi (1981) noted that type A (achievement-based Americans) idealized short-term employment, rapid evaluation and promotion, specialized career paths, and individual functions (such as responsibilities and decision making). These individuals contrasted with the type J (Japanese), who focused on lifetime employment, slower promotion cycles, and support for team decision making and responsibility. While Ouchi (1981) recognized that the culture within each of these countries heavily influences these managerial approaches, he also argued in defense of a theory Z, which aimed to find a middle ground where workers were valued and developed in a way that would encourage longer-term employment and supported to participate in team/organizational decision making and commitment. Theory Z later became known as human resource management.

While Ouchi was studying theory Z, another influencer to the HRM approach was working with organizations to shape the future. According to Knouse et al. (2009), W. Edwards Deming was a statistician and consultant who pioneered the idea of quality in organizations, which later birthed the term *total quality management* (TQM). TQM was an approach to organizational management that aimed to engage employees in work teams focused on quality improvements. While never standardized, the essential TQM elements included a commitment by management to involve all employees in a proactive, customer-focused approach. Deming and his work on quality were highly regarded in Japanese industry and elicited great interest from the American corporate world in the 1980s, but the high investment of time and money to implement TQM was a difficult fit in a culture where the "if it's not broke, don't fix it" motto prevails (Curry & Kadasah, 2002). TQM still persists in small pockets today but has largely given way to a broader interpretation seen in general HRM approaches. However, while TQM had slightly different objectives than HRM, the long-lasting impact was a solidifying focus on employee satisfaction as essential to lowering turnover.

HUMAN CAPITAL THEORY

As part of the development of HRM, several theories emerged as meaningful to understanding and implementing HRM in the workplace. The primary theory of interest is human capital theory. Based on the works of Schultz (1971), human capital theory recognizes that investing in education, training, and experiential learning can yield both individual and organizational benefits. Within this theory, researchers such as Gattiker

(1995) and Garavan, Morley, Gunningle, and Collins (2001) articulate that cultivating human competencies creates resources available to organizations. Thus, investment in human capital provides justification for expenditures on training and developing workers in both company-specific skills that are not likely transferable and in general training that has career-enhancing value. Proponents of this theory emphasize that proper training and employee development increase productivity and efficiency of workers while improving satisfaction that encourages longer-term employment and lower turnover.

RESOURCE-BASED THEORY

Another meaningful theory to HRM is the resource-based theory, which considers human resources as strategic assets. Research in this area suggests that a set of universal and strategic HRM practices might include job training, leadership development, technical competency development, and social networking strategies (Garavan, Carbery, & Rock, 2012). Essentially, these best practices of human development can be associated with improved organizational and individual performance.

Given key theoretical shifts, HRM was predicated on the idea that workers are more productive when they have the tools they need to succeed and when their well-being and considerations are supported. In today's media environment where technology is ever evolving, the foundations of HRM in media companies are evident in the way that workers are recruited and employees are developed. HRM focuses on the day-to-day functions within the media organization to hire, develop, and support workers. Strategically speaking, organizations that value the development of human resources are better able to manage the transformation of technology and maintain a competitive advantage. Therefore, it is important for future media practitioners and managers to identify new trends in HRM.

Something New

The shifting media landscape has influenced the structure of media organizations at almost every level. Although HRM remains a field onto itself with new trends affecting HR professionals working in all sectors of the economy, several elements of HRM intersect in important ways with issues in media management. The following section provides an overview of the trends affecting HR professionals working in media industries. These areas include the expansion and use of social media, big data, and self-service technology.

SOCIAL MEDIA

Social media has evolved drastically over the past decade, changing not only the way media interacts with audiences but also how media industries manage employees. Research on the use of social media by HR professionals has grown exponentially and indicates that human resource professionals are increasingly using social media in their everyday work (e.g., Davison, Maraist, & Bing, 2011; Iddekinge, Lanivich, Roth, & Junco, 2016; Madia, 2011; Stopfer & Gosling, 2013). Specifically, HR professionals have incorporated the use of social media into their recruitment strategies and monitoring of employee productivity.

SOCIAL MEDIA AND RECRUITMENT

Recruitment for the organization is one of the many functions that HR professionals provide to media organizations. In particular, HR professionals often serve the critical function of promoting the media organization, attracting talent, and identifying potential employees who meet the needs of the organization (Noe, Hollenbeck, Gerhart, & Wright, 2015). From a media management perspective, recruitment of new media talent is a critical aspect of human resources. That is, media professionals, such as broadcast journalists, producers, camera operators, and digital media specialists, perform many of the key functions of media organizations and, thus, hiring quality individuals is critical. HR professionals are increasingly relying on social media to both promote jobs and to screen potential employees.

Although organizations commonly rely on their company websites as a main online presence, the social media presence of an organization can have important implications for attracting potential talent. Traditional job board websites, such as CareerBuilder and Indeed.com, are still popular among both job seekers and recruiters. However, HR professionals today commonly promote open positions through social media sites, such as LinkedIn (Stopfer & Gosling, 2013).

When used properly, social media can provide recruiters with increased visibility of the company and open positions (Madia, 2011). For example, media companies can use their Twitter accounts to update their followers and the public about new content produced, organizational initiatives the company is undertaking, and open positions. Researchers have found that using social media for recruiting purposes is quite economical and useful for reaching candidates who are not actively seeking a job (e.g., individuals who are currently employed but open to changing organizations if the right position is available) (e.g., Nikolaou, 2014). Furthermore, HR professionals who use social media for the promotion of their company are not limited by geography or skills-based searches that some websites use.

Social media has provided human resource professionals with the ability to interact at a closer level with job candidates and reach many more individuals than traditional recruitment practices once allowed. That is, social media has created opportunities for job candidates to interact with HR professionals beyond submitting a résumé. Candidates can now connect with additional resources about the company and receive information about upcoming hiring events (Lagunas, 2018). Furthermore, advances in artificial intelligence technology have led some companies to employ "chatbots" to answer common job seeker questions related to the position and the company (Lagunas, 2018).

For some time, researchers have documented the relationship between social capital and access to occupational opportunities (Flap & Boxman, 2017). Today, the use of social media is changing the nature of social capital by granting quicker access to vast professional and personal networks (Ellison & Vitak, 2015). Through social media, individuals are able to share job postings with their networks, and these shares have an important impact on whether individuals will consider applying for the job. For example, Monster.com found that 65% of individuals would consider applying for a job if a personal connection had shared the job via social media (Budzienski, 2019). As such, HR professionals cannot ignore the impact that social networking sites have on access to quality talents. Looking ahead, as social media use increases and social media platforms evolve, HR professionals need to be increasingly aware of the utility of social media for recruitment and company promotion purposes. In addition, HR professionals need to master social media skills (see the Media Convergence section below) as part of the process of effectively utilizing these platforms.

SOCIAL MEDIA AND APPLICANT SCREENING

HR departments often secure background information on job candidates during the hiring process. Background information on job candidates may include contacting references directly (in contrast to solely relying on recommendation letters) and validating educational background, credentials, and employment history (Noe et al., 2015). In addition, employers will often check criminal records and credit reports. Today, employers are screening job candidates' online presence (e.g., social media, blogs) in addition to the traditional background information. According to Brown and Vaughn (2011), "Social networking sites provide a readily available public forum to research candidates while incurring minimal cost, allowing even small businesses to engage in such practices" (p. 220). Although the practice of screening applicants' online presence, or "Googling" the individual, has increased substantially in recent years, researchers have questioned the utility of the practice and the validity of the information that is found online (Davison et al., 2011; Iddekinge et al., 2016). That is, personal social media pages may not be current or even accurate, and thus relying on them for screening purposes is not always the best option for HR professionals.

Beyond the issues of dated and inaccurate social media pages, individuals often carefully control their social media presence and information that they share online (Picone, 2015). Although impression management is not isolated to online contexts (see Goffman, 1959), researchers have found that our increasing use of technology has paralleled implications concerning our presentation of self to the world (Picone, 2015). In other words, individuals are often aware of potential perceptions of their information posted online (e.g., pictures, dating profiles, tweets) and try to present a positive version of themselves. As such, assessing personality and organizational fit by examining individuals' social media presence alone may be difficult (Davison et al., 2011). Further, research has indicated that social media screening may adversely affect people of color (Iddekinge et al., 2016). Iddekinge et al. (2016) found that HR professionals were more likely to rate white candidates' social media profiles more favorably than those of candidates of color (e.g., Hispanic, African American). Thus, managers and HR professionals need to carefully consider the drawbacks of screening candidates' social media profiles and the potential implications of relying heavily on applicants' social media presence as a key indicator of organizational fit.

SOCIAL MEDIA AND PERFORMANCE MANAGEMENT

In media management, the intersections of employees' social media usage and HRM are unique. Unlike other employment sectors, many employees in the media industry use social media to connect with their audiences, promote digital content (e.g., videos, articles), and manage their public image. The necessity of social media usage across the media industry can create unique challenges for HR managers who may monitor employee use of social media to determine employee productivity and professionalism.

The practice of performance management, or monitoring employee activities and outputs to ensure individuals are meeting job-related objectives, is common among HR professionals (Noe et al., 2015). Performance management often includes evaluating the quality of an individual's work and ensuring that employees are conducting themselves in a professional manner. In media contexts, employees' use of social media may directly contribute to their daily work (e.g., creating digital content) and thus may be incorporated into employee reviews. However, the use of social media among media professionals can identify inappropriate behaviors exhibited by employees. For example, in 2017, BuzzFeed White House reporter Adrian Carrasquillo was named on a social media website as allegedly sexually harassing coworkers and was subsequently fired (Shapiro, 2017). HR professionals may need to evaluate negative claims about employees made on social media sites and / or the appropriateness of content that employees post to their professional and even personal social media accounts. More information about how social media impacts media management in today's convergent environment will be discussed in chapter 18, "Social Media."

BIG DATA

HR professionals are increasingly relying on "big data" to assist them in using evidence for decision making (Rasmussen & Ulrich, 2015). *Big data* refers to the large-scale collection of information examined through data analytics. Big data for HR professionals is often composed of information stored in HR databases, such as employee tenure, employee satisfaction surveys, and job applicant information collected through electronic hiring websites, such as CareerBuilder.com. Although big data is generally applied in media contexts for marketing and consumer engagement purposes (Napoli, 2016; Stone, 2014), HRM has used big data to analyze employee traits (Cappelli, 2017) and health care usage (Noe et al., 2015) and for more strategic applicant recruitment (Marr, 2018) among other applications.

Big data may be especially beneficial for HR professionals working in media industries who are in charge of recruiting and screening job candidates. Specifically, HR professionals who need to recruit and screen applicants with exclusive skills, such as digital content expertise, are able to utilize data analytics to determine whether batches of applicants fit the organization's needs. The ability to use big data to better screen candidates in the media professions is especially useful in the changing media landscape (Bartosova, 2011). That is, employees in the media environment are often lacking key skills related to new technologies. Thus, identifying and then hiring individuals with these skill sets is of the utmost importance (Bartosova, 2011). Big data also has important implications for HRM in terms of the number of applicants viewing and applying for jobs (Spina et al., 2017). Specifically, Spina et al. (2017) examined applicant behaviors and whether "clicks" on job postings influenced the likelihood of potential candidates applying for jobs and the quality of those candidates. They found that more clicks on job advertisements did not always mean more applicants; however, these findings do not detract from the overall increases in job applicant pools.

The ability to easily apply for jobs online has increased the number of applicants per job for many employment sectors (Workopolis, 2016). However, greater quantity does not always mean greater quality. In fact, one of the disadvantages of using big data in HRM today is the fact that very few applicants are actually interviewed because key word searches used by organizations may not pick up a candidate's qualifications (Workopolis, 2016). For media industries, this drawback to big data can have important implications due to the necessity of identifying candidates who possess the requisite skills. Thus, HR professionals must carefully consider the benefits and drawbacks of using big data in their work. More about big data can be found in chapter 22, "Big Data and Entrepreneurship."

SELF-SERVICE TECHNOLOGY

Employees have gradually become more able to obtain their HR data (e.g., pay stubs, health care benefits) through websites and apps or self-service portals (Noe et al., 2015). For HR professionals, the increasing use of self-service technology provides greater opportunities for employee access to HR information and online training programs. In media companies, the use of self-service technology may be especially beneficial as employees (e.g., journalists) often work in distant locations from their HR department. Research has indicated that HR professionals play a key role in educating employees about the company's self-service technology (Huang & Martin-Taylor, 2013). That is, to ensure that employees are able to effectively utilize self-service portals, HR professionals need to actively promote the use of this technology within their organizations. As the media industry increasingly operates on a global scale, self-service technology can provide employees and HR professionals with important information via these portals (Beulen, 2009). Many opportunities and challenges emerge for future HR managers in a convergent environment.

Opportunities and Challenges

Today, HR professionals are finding new opportunities to support their organizations as well as challenges that they are uniquely suited to address. Media industries are particularly susceptible to some of these opportunities and challenges because of technological advances, shifting organizational structures, and ever-evolving work arrangements. The following section provides an overview of the opportunities and challenges HR professionals are facing in the media industry. In addition, each section provides a brief action plan that helps HR professionals respond to these issues.

OPPORTUNITIES

According to the Bureau of Labor Statistics (2018a), employment in media industries is projected to experience a 6% growth between 2016 and 2026. Specifically, demand for digital media professionals is projected to increase as technology increases access to and desire for high-quality digital content. Despite increased demand for digital media professionals, demand in other traditional media professions (e.g., print journalists, radio announcers) is expected to continue to decline over the next decade (Bureau of Labor Statistics, 2018b). As the media industry evolves alongside technology, there are both increased needs for certain skills and declining employment opportunities for individuals with outdated qualifications.

HR professionals typically assist their media organizations by forecasting, or determining, the future needs of the company and the supply of individuals who meet those needs (Noe et al., 2015). Although the evolution of technology is changing the job outlook for many sectors, media industries have been impacted deeply by the changing media landscape. For example, print newspapers were once a robust industry but have experienced decreased advertising and subscription revenues with the advent of online access to media content (Brock, 2013; McLennan & Miles, 2018). Similarly, the radio and music industries have seen massive shifts in their business models with the increased availability and usage of streaming services, such as Spotify and Amazon Music (Sisario & Russell, 2016). As media industries continue to change, HR professionals will play an important role in tracking desirable digital media skills and projecting future staffing needs.

MEDIA CONVERGENCE

Convergence, or the blending of media technologies, has emerged over the past two decades in the media industry (Huang et al., 2006; Quandt & Singer, 2009). As new media technologies have emerged and media professionals are required to be able to work across media platforms, hiring individuals who possess the variety of skills necessary to navigate these platforms has become a critical function of HR professionals working in the media industry. According to the Society for Human Resource Management (2016), "68% of human resource professionals are experiencing difficulty recruiting candidates for full-time positions in their organizations" (p. 5). These difficulties across employment sectors are due to many individuals lacking both specialized skills and sometimes even basic skills, such as writing, oral communication, and computer abilities (Society for Human Resource Management, 2016). However, because of the varied, numerous, and often changing skills that media professionals need to stay competitive in the industry today, some media companies are finding it more difficult to recruit qualified talent for their organizations (Society for Human Resource Management, 2016). Clearly, convergent media provides many challenges for future HR managers.

CHALLENGES

Although the media industry is experiencing opportunities for growth, it is also facing new challenges that HR professionals are particularly well suited to address. Specifically, changing workforce demographics, relying on a contingent workforce, and the onset of globalization all present unique obstacles in terms of attracting and retaining employees who can readily meet the demands of the media industry. The following section describes these challenges more specifically and provides suggestions to media managers and HR professionals.

ADDRESSING WORKFORCE SHIFTS IN MEDIA MANAGEMENT

As HR professionals work to address the shifts in the workforce, some steps can provide direction to manage the challenges media organizations are facing. First, employee turnover increases may mean media companies losing quality employees. HR professionals can play an important role in preventing employees from leaving the company. For example, HR professionals can identify potential causes of job dissatisfaction among employees and work with media managers to address these issues before employees decide to leave the organization (Noe et al., 2015). HR professionals also monitor employee pay and benefits packages. Thus, tracking job dissatisfaction and working with the organization to keep pay and benefits packages competitive help retain top talent.

The second way that HR professionals can help address challenges affecting media companies is by providing ongoing training and educational opportunities to employees. HR professionals are often in charge of the training and development initiatives in their organizations. Thus, determining the skills that employees need to succeed in their work and developing training programs and/or identifying continuing education programs that can help employees develop these skills is an important role of HR professionals. Furthermore, as employees increasingly work remotely from a traditional office space, HR professionals can ensure that they are keeping all employees, even remote employees, up to date on the newest online training programs, digital media skills, and organization initiatives.

CONTINGENT WORKFORCE

One of the emerging changes that has affected media organizations over the past several decades is increasing reliance on a contingent workforce. Contingent employees are those individuals who are hired to be short-term temporary employees, consultants, or individuals who complete work on a freelance basis for their organizations. Freelancing, also known today as the "gig economy," is on the rise across employment sectors (Pofeldt, 2017). Emerging media industries in particular employ many freelance professionals for a variety of positions (e.g., journalists, web developers). Some projections are showing that nearly half of the workforce may be composed of individuals contributing some degree of freelance work in the next decade (Pofeldt, 2017).

According to CNBC (2018), Google, Facebook, Amazon, Uber, and other Silicon Valley companies increasingly rely on contracted employees to sustain their business models. Lower cost is one of the primary factors driving this gig economy. Contract workers rarely earn health insurance, retirement packages, or other benefits. The lack of commitment to permanent employment provides companies with flexibility to add or subtract workers to meet in-demand skills in an increasingly tight labor market.

Working with contingent employees presents many challenges to HR professionals in the media industry. For example, contingent employees may not experience the same training as traditional employees. In addition, many freelance employees may work remotely, thus preventing HR professionals from evaluating employee performance and job satisfaction using established methods. Further, temporary employees have little motivation to be committed to the company's long-term goals. As such, HR professionals must be open to overcome the challenges, develop new ways of interacting with a contingent workforce, and provide the necessary resources to ensure these contracted employees are successful.

DIVERSITY AND GLOBALIZATION

Perhaps the most positive change to the convergent workforce is an increase in diversity. Media organizations are experiencing diversification of their workforce and hiring more individuals from countries all over the world. Diversity and a global economy afford media companies many benefits, such as generating a multitude of perspectives that can better meet different audiences. However, monitoring workplace diversity and the influences of globalization within an organization can be a challenge for HR professionals.

Race, ethnicity, gender, sexual orientation, age, religion, and educational background are just some of the differences among employees working in any given organization. Today, the workplace is facing unique challenges related to diversity. For example, as individuals are living longer lives, some are choosing to postpone retirement and work to more advanced ages (Noe et al., 2015). As such, there are more generations in the workplace today and more generational differences that can affect interpersonal communication and use of technology among employees (Miller-Merrell, 2012). HR professionals need to be able to work with individuals from different generations who have distinctive worldviews and skill sets.

The changing gender and racial composition of the workforce is another diversity-related challenge encountered by HR professionals. These changes to the makeup of the workforce affect organizations at every level. HR professionals must help create a welcoming organizational culture that is free of bias (Noe et al., 2015). It is important for HR professionals to be aware of laws and policies that may impact hiring decisions (e.g., equal opportunity laws, affirmative action).

In today's global media environment, HR professionals working in media organizations must increasingly work with international employees. However, working with individuals from different countries and cultures can be challenging. Research has indicated that HR practices that are ethnocentric, or based on the same belief systems in which the organization is headquartered, can cause frustrations among international employees who do not share the same background (Kopp, 1994). In addition, the country in which the media organization is headquartered may contribute to the policies that HR professionals need to follow (Ferner, 1997).

Today, many media organizations employ individuals from diverse countries and may have organizational structures that place the organization in several countries simultaneously. For example, the Associated Press operates out of more than 100 countries at any given time (Associated Press, 2019). This type of global environment that many media organizations, especially news organizations, function in requires HR professionals to be competent in communicating across cultural backgrounds. HR professionals may be especially challenged in working across cultural backgrounds when they develop training programs that are designed to address communication issues within the organization (Noe et al., 2015). Thus, cross-cultural communication competencies are critical for today's HR professionals in media industries.

ADDRESSING DIVERSITY AND GLOBALIZATION IN MEDIA MANAGEMENT

Although diversity and globalization present unique challenges for HR practices in media organizations, there are specific and measurable ways that HR professionals can get involved to ensure their organizations are responding effectively. First, HR professionals have the ability to shape the organizational culture of media companies through training initiatives. HR professionals should work to create training programs that teach employees, especially those in managerial positions, how to interact with individuals from different backgrounds. HR professionals can work to help individuals from diverse backgrounds by offering leadership programs that encourage individuals who may otherwise be intimidated by increased involvement in their organizations. Second, HR professionals may be able to help their organizations with company-wide initiatives aimed at combating bias and encouraging a diverse workplace. These types of initiatives may include crafting and distributing diversity statements, developing educational materials and programs, and closely monitoring employee engagement and disenfranchisement. Finally, HR professionals experiencing changing organizational structures because of globalization need to be increasingly aware of the promises and pitfalls of employing an international workforce. Ensuring that one's organization is culturally sensitive to international employees' perspectives and needs is extremely important if media organizations are to retain top talent from across the globe. It is important for HR professionals and media managers to consider each of these initiatives using the action plan below.

ACTION PLAN

1. Identify potential causes of job dissatisfaction among employees, and work to address these issues in order to avoid high turnover.
2. Provide training and educational opportunities to employees, especially online programs to keep employees in media organizations up to date.
3. Be cognizant of cross-cultural communication competencies and any laws and policies that may impact hiring decisions.

KEY TAKEAWAYS

1. *Human resource management* is an umbrella term for the functions in an organization that focus on hiring, training, and developing employees.
2. Theory X and theory Y helped to identify two different managerial mindsets based on assumptions about how people do work. These approaches led to a more moderated theory Z, eventually renamed as *human resource management*.

3. Human capital theory and resource-based theory served as a foundation for how we understand investing in training and developing employees so that they are greater assets to media organizations.
4. Trends in social media have impacted HRM in media organizations by improving opportunities for recruitment, screening, and performance management.
5. Big data and self-service technology have helped media organizations expand their HRM capacities in multiple ways, including forecasting trends and attracting applicants globally.
6. HRM can help address shifts in the workforce while managing diversity and globalization concerns.

CONCLUSION

This chapter provides an overview and contextual history of HRM, explains how HRM is of importance to the media industry, and describes the opportunities and challenges that individuals working in HRM in the media industry are experiencing. By better understanding how HRM functions within an organization, and the influence of theory X, theory Y, theory Z, and TQM, future HR practitioners and media managers will be able to adapt in today's convergent environment.

Additionally, this chapter explores the impact of human capital theory and resource-based theory and how these theories are applied to help us better understand and adapt to technological trends. Organizations today recognize the importance of hiring, retaining, and developing quality employees who contribute to their goals. Media organizations, in particular, need to recruit and maintain talented individuals who help make their organizations grow and adapt to ever-changing technological advances. Media technologies can both aid and hinder this quest. Some key adaptations include social media, big data, and self-service technology.

As evidenced throughout the chapter, HR professionals facilitate the functioning of organizational work in myriad ways. Specifically, HR professionals are often one of the first organizational members that job candidates interact with, and they continue to be important organizational problem solvers who contribute to day-to-day operations. Media industries, in particular, rely heavily on the contributions of HR professionals. Across the globe, HR professionals ensure that media organizations have the staff to meet their changing needs and that their employees can access the levels of training and resources needed to succeed.

Over the course of the 20th century, the field of HRM evolved to become an integral component of organizational life. Today, HRM is turning out to be even more imperative to the success of organizations. Specifically, HR professionals are particularly well suited to help media organizations respond to shifting employee demographics and a global economy and are essential for managing the challenges of big data and contingent employees. While media organizations consistently face new challenges when adapting to new technologies and new approaches to work, HR professionals are on the front line, ensuring that employees can thrive and contribute during these changing times.

These changes have influenced media industries in countless ways. Perhaps the most important shift is the increased diversity in the workforce. Diversity of race, ethnicity, gender, sexual orientation, age, religion, and educational background are providing media companies a multitude of perspectives that can be used to better serve the audience and organizational goals. While a global market does bring some unique HR challenges, it is an important, refreshing, and long overdue change to media industries.

Scholarship in the intersecting areas of convergent media and HRM is increasing in volume because of the growing complexity of the media industry today. In years past, organizations could rely on using traditional approaches to HRM. However, the fast-paced changes of the global economy and the media industry require organizations to continue to keep up. These challenges force HR professionals working in media organizations to consider new organizational structures to meet these demands.

Research suggests that media convergence will only continue to change the way HRM exists within media organizations. In other words, as media converges, HR professionals must recognize the need to recruit talent with skills that can meet the demands of multiple platforms. The media landscape continues to evolve in ways that we are only beginning to understand. As the needs of the media industry continually change with technology and globalization, it may seem to HR professionals that it is impossible to keep up. However, the core purpose of HRM—to identify, hire, and develop quality organizational members—continues to be imperative to the well-being of the industry. The next chapter will focus on issues of marketing and branding in the media industry. Much like HRM, marketers of media organizations contribute in a variety of ways to overall organizational well-being. It is important to consider how effective HRM helps media organizations develop a successful brand image.

REFERENCES

Associated Press. (2019). *Our story*. https://www.ap.org/about/our-story

Bartosova, D. (2011). The future of the media professions: Current issues in media management practice. *International Journal on Media Management, 13*, 195–203. doi: 10.1080/14241277.2011.576963

Beulen, E. (2009). The contribution of a global service provider's human resources information system (HRIS) to staff retention in emerging markets: Comparing issues and implication in six developing countries. *Information Technology & People, 22*, 270–288.

Brock, G. (2013). *Out of print: Newspapers, journalism and the business of news in the digital age*. Kogan Page.

Brown, V. R., & Vaughn, E. D. (2011). The writing on the (Facebook) wall: The use of social networking sites in hiring decisions. *Journal of Business and Psychology, 26*, 219–225.

Budzienski, J. (2019). *3 ways to be constantly recruiting star talent through social media*. Monster. https://hiring.monster.ca/hr/hr-best-practices/recruiting-hiring-advice/attracting-job-candidates/recruit-talent-through-social-media-ca.aspx

Bureau of Labor Statistics. (2018a). Media and communication occupations. *Occupational outlook handbook, 2017–2018*. https://www.bls.gov/ooh/media-and-communication/home.htm

Bureau of Labor Statistics. (2018b). Reporters, correspondents, and broadcast news analysts. *Occupational outlook handbook, 2017–2018*. https://www.bls.gov/ooh/media-and-communication/reporters-correspondents-and-broadcast-news-analysts.htm

Cappelli, P. (2017, June 2). There's no such thing as big data in HR. *Harvard Business Review*. https://hbr.org/2017/06/theres-no-such-thing-as-big-data-in-hr

CNBC. (2018, October 22). *Silicon Valley's dirty secret: Using a shadow workforce of contract employees to drive profit.* https://www.cnbc.com/2018/10/22/silicon-valley-using-contract-employees-to-drive-profits.html

Cunningham, R. A. (2011). Douglas McGregor—A lasting impression. *Ivey Business Journal, 75*(5), 5–7.

Curry, A., & Kadasah, N. (2002). Focusing on key elements of TQM—evaluation for sustainability. *The TQM Magazine, 14*, 207–216. doi: 10.1108/09544780210429816

Davison, H. K., Maraist, C., & Bing, M. N. (2011). Friend or foe? The promise and pitfalls of using social networking sites for HR decisions. *Journal of Business Psychology, 26*, 153–159.

Ellison, N., & Vitak, J. (2015). Social media affordances and their relationship to social capital processes. In S. Sundar (Ed.), *The handbook of psychology of communication technology* (pp. 205–227). Wiley-Blackwell.

Ferner, A. (1997). Country of origin effects and HRM in multinational companies. *Human Resource Management Journal, 7*, 19–37.

Flap, H., & Boxman, E. (2017). Getting started: The influence of social capital on the start of the occupational career. In N. Lin, K. S. Cook, & R. S. Burt (Eds.), *Social capital: Theory and research* (pp. 159–184). Routledge.

Garavan, T. N., Carbery, R., & Rock, A. (2012). Mapping talent development: Definition, scope and architecture. *European Journal of Training and Development, 36*, 5–24.

Garavan, T. N., Morley, M., Gunningle, P., & Collins, E. (2001). Human capital accumulation: The role of human resource development. *Journal of European Industrial Training, 25*, 48–68.

Gattiker, U. E. (1995). Firm and taxpayer returns from training of semiskilled employees. *Academy of Management Journal, 28*, 1152–1173.

Goffman, E. (1959). *The presentation of self in everyday life.* Anchor Books.

Heathfield, S. (2019). *Find out how Zappos reinforces its company culture.* Human Resources Culture. https://www.thebalancecareers.com/zappos-company-culture-1918813

Huang, E., Davison, K., Shreve, S., Davis, T., Bettendorf, E., & Nair, A. (2006). Facing the challenges of convergence. *The International Journal of Research into New Media Technologies, 12*, 83–98.

Huang, J., & Martin-Taylor, M. (2013). Turnaround user acceptance in the context of HR self-service technology adoption: An action research approach. *The International Journal of Human Resource Management, 3*, 621–642. doi: 10.1080/09585192.2012.677460

Iddekinge, C. H. V., Lanivich, S. E., Roth, P. L., & Junco, E. (2016). Social media for selection? Validity and adverse impact potential of a Facebook-based assessment. *Journal of Management, 42*, 1811–1835.

Knouse, S. B., Carson, P. P., Carson, K. D., & Heady, R. B. (2009). Improve constantly and forever: The influence of W. Edwards Deming into the twenty-first century. *The TQM Journal, 21*, 449–461.

Kopp, R. (1994). International human resource policies and practices in Japanese, European, and United States multinationals. *Human Resource Management, 33*, 581–599.

Lagunas, K. (2018, August). *Talent acquisition: Emerging trends.* IDC Custom Solutions. https://www.jobvite.com/wp-content/uploads/2018/09/Jobvite_IDC-AnalystConnections_August_2018.pdf

Macefield, R. (2007). Usability studies and the Hawthorne effect. *Journal of Usability Studies, 2*, 145–154.

Madia, S. A. (2011). Best practices for using social media as a recruitment strategy. *Strategic HR Review, 10*, 19–24.

Marr, B. (2018, May 4). Data-driven HR: How big data and analytics are transforming recruitment. *Forbes.* https://www.forbes.com/sites/bernardmarr/2018/05/04/data-driven-hr-how-big-data-and-analytics-are-transforming-recruitment

Mayo, E. (1933). *The human problems of an industrial civilization.* Macmillan.

McGregor, D. (1960). *The human side of enterprise.* McGraw-Hill.

McLennan, D., & Miles, J. (2018, March 21). A once unimaginable scenario: No more newspapers. *The Washington Post.* https://www.washingtonpost.com/news/theworldpost/wp/2018/03/21/newspapers

Miller-Merrell, J. (2012). The workplace engagement economy where HR, social, mobile, and tech collide. *Employment Relations Today, 39*, 1–9.
Napoli, P. M. (2016). Special issue introduction: Big data and media management. *International Journal on Media Management, 18*, 1–7.
Nikolaou, I. (2014). Social networking web sites in job search and employee recruitment. *International Journal of Selection and Assessment, 22*, 179–189.
Noe, R. A., Hollenbeck, J. R., Gerhart, B., & Wright, P. M. (2015). *Human resource management: Gaining a competitive advantage* (9th ed.). McGraw-Hill Education.
Ouchi, W. (1981). Theory Z: How American business can meet the Japanese challenge. *Business Horizons, 24*(6), 82–83.
Parsons, H. M. (1974). What happened at Hawthorne? *Science, 183*, 922–932.
Picone, I. (2015). Impression management in social media. In R. Mansell & P. H. Ang (Eds.), *The digital encyclopedia of digital communication and society* (pp. 1–7). Wiley-Blackwell.
Pofeldt, E. (2017, October 17). Are we ready for a workforce that is 50% freelance? *Forbes*. https://www.forbes.com/sites/elainepofeldt/2017/10/17/are-we-ready-for-a-workforce-that-is-50-freelance
Quandt, T., & Singer, J. B. (2009). Convergence and cross-platform journalism. In K. Wahl-Jorgensen & T. Hanitszch (Eds.), *The handbook of journalism studies* (pp. 130–140). Routledge.
Rasmussen, T., & Ulrich, D. (2015). Learning from practice: How HR analytics avoids being a management fad. *Organizational Dynamics, 44*, 236–242.
Rice, B. (1982). The Hawthorne defect: Persistence of a flawed theory. *Psychology Today, 16*, 70–74.
Roethlisberger, F. J. (1947). *Management and morale*. Harvard University Press.
Schultz, T. W. (1971). *Investment in human capital*. The Free Press.
Shapiro, R. (2017, December 28). *BuzzFeed fires White House correspondent Adrian Carrasquillo over "inappropriate message."* Huffington Post. https://www.huffingtonpost.com/entry/buzzfeed-adrian-carrasquillo-fired_us_5a449eaae4b06d1621b6ded5
Sisario, B., & Russell, K. (2016, March 24). In shift to streaming, music business has lost billions. *New York Times*. https://www.nytimes.com/2016/03/25/business/media/music-sales-remain-steady-but-lucrative-cd-sales-decline.html
Society for Human Resource Management. (2016). *The new talent landscape: Recruiting difficulty and skills shortages*. SHRM Headquarters.
Spina, D., Maistro, M., Ren, Y., Sadeghi, S., Wong, W., Badwin, T., . . ., & Zobel, J. (2017, August). Understanding user behavior in job and talent search: An initial investigation. Paper presented at SIGIR eCom, Tokyo, Japan. http://ceur-ws.org/Vol-2311/paper_2.pdf
Stone, M. L. (2014). Big data for media: Report from the Reuters Institute for the study of journalism. https://reutersinstitute.politics.ox.ac.uk/sites/default/files/2017-04/Big%20Data%20For%20Media_0.pdf
Stopfer, J. M., & Gosling, S. D. (2013). Online social networks in the work context. In D. Derks & A. Bakker (Eds.), *The psychology of digital media at work* (pp. 39–59). Psychology Press.
Workopolis. (2016, November 10). *Why only 2% of applicants actually get interviews*. https://careers.workopolis.com/advice/only-2-of-applicants-actually-get-interviews-heres-how-to-be-one-of-them/

CHAPTER 7

Marketing and Branding

Todd Holmes, California State University Northridge

LEARNING OBJECTIVES

1. Understand fundamental marketing concepts of segmentation, positioning, and branding, and recognize their importance to media managers.
2. Identify how changes in technology and consumer trends are presenting unique opportunities and challenges for today's media marketing manager.
3. Apply strategic marketing concepts in order to effectively compete in an increasingly fragmented media landscape.

Due to the influence of new technologies and the wide range of content providers that compete for audiences today, understanding marketing concepts is essential to media managers. The opportunities provided by new technological innovations and changing consumer trends are resulting in an unprecedented ability for companies to access potential and existing customers through an array of media. These opportunities, however, are certainly wrought with challenges, as there are plenty of available channels and competitive offerings (Smith & Taylor, 2004).

As defined by the American Marketing Association (2019), marketing is "the activity, set of institutions, and processes for creating, communicating, delivering, and exchanging offerings that have value for customers, clients, partners, and society at large." Media enterprises need to have managers in place who fully understand marketing concepts and are willing to ensure that the necessary internal structure is in place so that consumers' changing needs can be met (Warner & Buchman, 2004). To be more consumer oriented, a number of media firms, such as CBS Corporation (2019), have developed their organizational structure based on product category (e.g., CBS Television Network, CBS Television Stations, CBS Television Distribution, CBS Consumer Products) as opposed to function (e.g., operations, research and development, finance, distribution).

In addition, the success of a new product hinges on marketing. When effective strategies are developed and implemented, strong sales of the product can be expected. However, inappropriate marketing decisions can be detrimental to the successful launch of a new product. An example of this can be found in the case of the videotape format war that ensued between Sony's Betamax and JVC's VHS in the 1970s (Ochoa, 2016; Owen, 2005). The marketing team at Sony felt that the superior resolution and sound of their format would outweigh the higher costs and shorter recording times of Betamax. Unfortunately, Sony had not properly accounted for consumers' needs and preferences. Their marketing message was weak and vague. What consumers wanted was a format allowing for longer recording times, at a low price, and compatible with other machines (i.e., features provided by JVC's VHS technology). As such, after owning 100% of the market in 1975, Sony's Betamax only had a 25% market share by 1981 (Moulding, 1996; Ochoa, 2016). The importance of successful marketing and branding initiatives and strategies cannot be overstated.

This chapter aims to explore the significant role of marketing and branding in media management. Media marketing management entails what enterprises do, and ought to do, in order to deliver value to audiences and advertisers. These tasks typically include four primary stages: developing marketing plans and strategies, understanding customers and defining target markets, establishing marketing mixes, and implementing and evaluating marketing activities (Churchill & Peter, 1998). Let's now take a look at how recent technological developments pertaining to distribution, a key component of the marketing mix, are impacting strategic marketing decisions at two prominent media conglomerates, the Walt Disney Company and AT&T.

CASE STUDY

Media distribution is currently experiencing a massive shift from the wholesale delivery of content via multichannel video program distributors (MVPDs), such as cable and satellite companies, to direct-to-consumer (DTC) distribution of content through over-the-top (OTT) streaming services. According to the Video Advertising Bureau, the proportion of households using only OTT streaming services has tripled since 2013, rising to 14.1 million homes or 11% of all U.S. households with TVs in 2018 (Grines, 2018). As consumers increasingly rely on OTT streaming services, revenues in this sector are expected to grow from $64 billion in 2017 to $120 billion in 2022 (Pegus, 2018).

Disney launched the Disney+ streaming service in 2019. In launching their own DTC platform, the company had to forgo an estimated $300 million in annual revenue that it was receiving from Netflix for rights to its theatrical releases (Littleton, 2018). Although this development will result in financial challenges for Disney, it will lead to unique opportunities for product differentiation from competitive offerings.

Today, Disney has purchased many of Fox's assets for $71.3 billion. As a result, Disney will have a majority stake in Hulu, allowing the media conglomerate to thrive in the DTC market (Littleton, 2018). This considerable debt load will put more pressure on Disney executives as the company seeks favorable performance on Wall Street. Disney believes that the key to its success with the new DTC service is its exclusive content from selected Marvel, Star Wars, Pixar, and Disney-branded properties. Nonetheless, Todd Juenger, an analyst at Bernstein Research, believes that "the single worst thing Disney could do is launch a DTC service that is underwhelming" (Littleton, 2018, p. 40).

AT&T finds itself in a similar conundrum as Disney with its recent purchase of Time Warner for $85.4 billion. The DTC strategy employed by AT&T must consider the influence of DTC services on DirecTV, an MVPD service that the conglomerate purchased prior to the acquisition of Time Warner. It is hoped that AT&T will be able to leverage its DirecTV and international telecommunication services to lure subscribers to the new services. The strong brand equity of HBO can be leveraged to reach new and profitable market segments, such as consumers who have an interest in high-end services (Littleton, 2018). For example, HBO Go, a predecessor to HBO Max, launched in 2015, had been a streaming service for consumers without a traditional MVPD subscription. Within three years, the DTC service had acquired more than five million subscribers (Littleton, 2018).

The major media conglomerates are following along a similar trajectory to Disney and AT&T by launching their own streaming services to carry exclusive content. It is believed that while profits may be lost in the near term, over the long haul, a focus on DTC services will benefit the media conglomerates. Yet, developing effective marketing and branding strategies to address consumer concerns related to product, pricing, distribution, and promotion becomes rather essential.

Something Old

Marketing efforts hinge on decisions made concerning the marketing mix or four Ps: product, price, place (distribution), and promotion. The product pertains to the actual goods and services produced for customers, while the price element concerns the amount of money or other resources marketers ask for their offerings (Churchill & Peter, 1998). In the case of media, the product could be the content itself, whether it is a film or a television program in a physical (a DVD or CD) or digital form. When determining price, it is necessary to consider the price of other competing products.

Distribution of media products can be accomplished through a variety of means, such as through legacy distribution channels via windowing beginning with theaters for film or over the air in the case of broadcast television, or through wired and wireless digital platforms, including digital cable television and wireless Internet. When determining distribution strategies for marketing messages, marketers have to consider which platform or advertising vehicle can best reach the product's target consumers. Will the product target local, national, or international audiences? While a local TV station may want to cross-promote its new Sunday sports show via local radio, an international media conglomerate like Disney may not use local radio stations to market its new Disney+ streaming service, unless it wants to target audiences living in a particular geographic area.

Due to the tremendous influence of social media on business strategy, it is necessary to add a fifth P of marketing: participation (Tuten & Solomon, 2015). Social media has transformed how media firms and brands pursue their target audiences and maintain their relationships with their customers, competitors, and partners because of the ability to interact and exchange ideas with media audiences.

A fundamental role of media managers, thus, is to understand what audiences and advertisers want and need and then to develop and execute strategies that will fulfill these needs. Because the media industry has operated as a dual-product market, and audiences and advertisers have different and sometimes contradictory needs, developing and rolling out solid marketing strategy has always been essential to the lifeblood of any media organization. Three key marketing strategies include segmentation, positioning, and branding.

SEGMENTATION

Media firms divide their total market into moderately homogenous segments. This process is called market segmentation. The individuals or organizations within each group have comparable needs and wants, value perceptions, and purchasing behavior; thus, they will respond similarly to certain marketing strategies (Churchill & Peter, 1998). Segmentation is an important part of marketing, as it is often included in a media firm's situation analysis, objectives, strategies, and tactics. Segments can be identified through the use of a variety of methods. One of the most popular methods is to examine purchasing behavior of existing customers. Companies are now using database marketing to identify target consumers who watch certain channels and use certain products, websites, and apps (Albarran, 2017).

Regardless of the source or method for gathering the data, to be viable, a segment must be measurable, substantial enough to be profitable, reachable, and relevant (Smith & Taylor, 2004). There are four major approaches that marketers use for segmenting an audience: demographics, geographics, geodemographics, and psychographics (Churchill & Peter, 1998).

Demographics provide media organizations (e.g., broadcasters, networks) with an estimate of the number of viewers/listeners in a variety of age and sex categories in a particular market. Popular demographic segments in television include people, men, and women 18–34, 18–49, and 25–54. While age and sex are the most commonly used demographic variables, other factors, such as race/ethnicity, education level, and household income, are also utilized in demographic segmentation.

Geographic segmentation is used for dividing potential viewers by location. In local broadcast television, designated market areas (DMAs) are used. There are 210 DMAs within the United States, and they are rank ordered by the number of television households served in the areas (Nielsen, 2018). Geodemographics links demographic data with geographic information. For example, in the United States, media organizations often use the data collected by the U.S. Census Bureau to identify local neighborhoods based on zip codes that share similar demographic traits. One such group, Young Digerati, is composed of people who are highly educated, tech savvy, and live in fashionable neighborhoods on the urban fringe (Claritas, 2018). Furthermore, psychographic segmentation is needed as a means of understanding consumer lifestyles, which includes activities, hobbies, interests, opinions, and personality characteristics (Albarran, 2017). A variety of qualitative research methods like focus groups, program testing, and in-depth interviews are used to generate psychographic data.

POSITIONING

In addition to considering which segments to target, media marketers must also consider product positioning. Positioning encompasses creating a favorable perception of one's product, brand, or service related to competing brands in the minds of target consumers (O'Guinn, Allen, & Semenik, 2009). There are two major types of positioning: positioning by competitors and positioning by the audience. Nonetheless, the positioning should be unique and have a definable competitive advantage that noticeably stands out from competitive offerings (Warner, 2009).

When the Walt Disney Company positions ESPN as a global leader in sports, it considers other competing sports brands, such as CBS Sports, Fox Sports, and the regional sports networks. Similarly, Lifetime Television says that "it's television for women," while Spike TV (now Paramount Network) marketed itself as television for men. One tool that helps in conceptualizing your brand's unique position is the positioning map. These maps include depictions of consumer perceptions of various brands typically on two dimensions (e.g., originality / value, product differentiation). These dimensions are determinant attributes that a consumer considers in their purchasing decisions (McCarthy, McGuiggan, Perreault, & Quester, 2007). Figure 7.1 illustrates a hypothetical example of a positioning map. In this example, the two dimensions are originality / value and product differentiation. The four dots represent four different brands, with Brand D occupying the ideal position relative to the other three brands as consumers perceive it to be high in both originality / value and product differentiation.

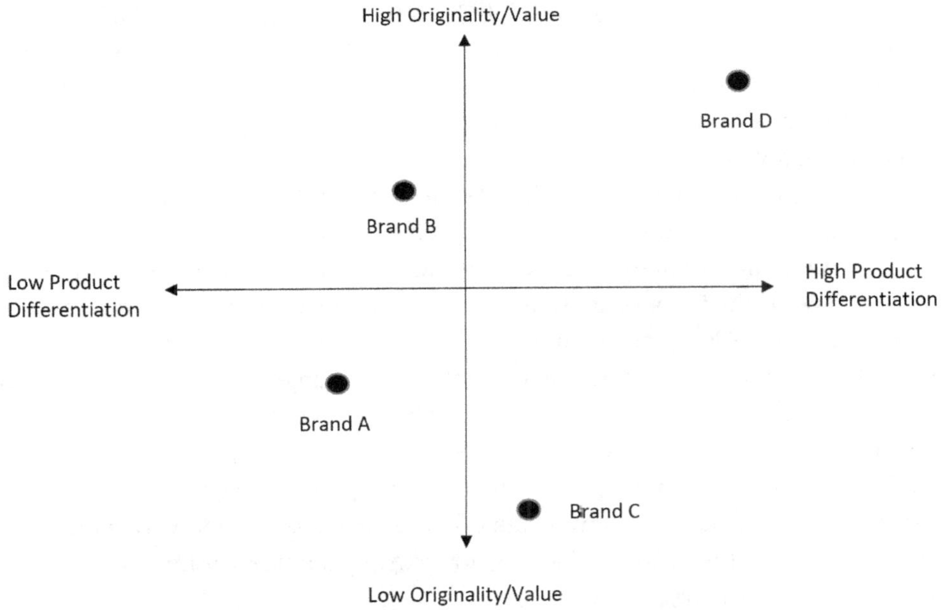

FIGURE 7.1. Positioning Map Example for Four Different Brands

BRANDING

A brand is "a name, term, design, symbol, or any other feature that identifies one seller's good or service as distinct from those of other sellers" (Bennett, 1995, p. 27). The branding process involves capitalizing on both tangible and intangible characteristics to create a favorable image of the product or service in consumer minds (Albarran, 2017). These characteristics include packaging, name, price, the advertising campaign, and the method of distribution (D'Alessandro, 2001). To effectively establish and maintain a brand's image, marketers need to ensure that these characteristics are properly coordinated.

In media industries, the content itself or an actor can be the brand (Van Tassel & Poe-Howfield, 2010). People may go to see a film just because George Clooney is in the movie even if other aspects of the content (at least from what they know going in to see the film) do not sufficiently draw their interest. As a matter of fact, in the early days of film, studios offered long-term contracts to specific actors in an effort to build the film studios' brands and generate revenues (Van Tassel & Poe-Howfield, 2010). In addition to talent, networks, digital distributors, and individual programs are each considered to be brands. While the successes of programming and the actors starring in the program may have an enriching or reducing effect on the brand image of a network/distributor, a collaborative relationship needs to exist between the two (Drinkwater & Uncles, 1992).

Regardless of the brand's form, one key challenge to media marketing managers has been maintaining synergy across different media platforms while maximizing the exclusive characteristics of each media channel (Chan-Olmsted & Shay, 2015). The current state of the media marketing environment provides media firms with the opportunity to respond better to consumer needs given the array of potential brand touch points while at the same time increasing the potential for diluted brand associations. This may occur, for instance, when ABC airs a show on Hulu, which diminishes the brand associations viewers make with ABC's network identity (Chan-Olmsted, 2011). Even though there are concerns about the impact of newer platforms on legacy outlets, media enterprises need to meet consumer needs through the complementary use of various forms of content distribution, which can positively contribute to financial rewards (NBCUniversal, 2014).

In addition to using various media platforms for optimally connecting with consumers, other branding strategies are being employed by both traditional and new media firms. One such strategy is brand extension, which is the use of an existing brand name for a new product. There are two types of brand extensions: horizontal and vertical (Kim & Lavack, 1996). A horizontal brand extension is when an existing brand name is applied to a new product, which can be related to the same category as the focal brand or entirely new. A vertical brand extension is when a new product is introduced in the same category as the core brand, but it differs in some ways. Brand extensions allow media firms to capitalize on the positive associations people have with existing brands. One of the primary means for showcasing brand extensions is via advertisements. Let's now take a look into the process of selling advertising, a long-standing business model used in the media industry.

TRADITIONAL ADVERTISING SALES

There are three major categories of advertising sales: national spot, local, and network. National advertisers work with advertising agencies to create and place advertising. Advertising agencies' creative departments are mainly responsible for writing and producing ads. For national spot advertising, ad time is sold to clients at the national level to air on a local television affiliate or a radio station or group of stations. Many major brands are interested in buying national spot advertising, as it can reach all 210 local markets in the United States. The brands that buy national spot advertising include some of the biggest advertisers in the ad categories of cars, fast food, airlines, soft drinks, insurance, and consumer products (such as Procter & Gamble).

Local advertising sales can be either direct or through an agency. Direct sales are when an account executive for a media outlet works directly with business owners in developing an advertising schedule and campaign. Agency sales are when a media salesperson works with an advertising agency that represents the clients. Sometimes the ad agency serves the town in which the retailer is located, but oftentimes the agency is located elsewhere. Whether a media salesperson is dealing with a direct client or an agency, it is suggested that a consultative sales approach be employed. This requires the media salesperson to conduct an interview with a potential client or agency representative to learn everything possible about the business and its advertising goals prior to developing an advertising solution or schedule. When dealing with agencies, the agency will want a particular percentage of the ad buy, which has historically been 15% of the gross cost of the ad buy. Agencies are most concerned with ratings, shares, CPM (cost per thousand), CPP (cost per rating point), reach, and frequency, while direct sales focus more on revenues generated and return on investment (Warner, 2009). In local advertising, the salesperson is often responsible for creating ads themselves in addition to securing the advertising contract. Given that traditional radio serves more as a local medium, radio advertisements tend to be created at the local level. It is estimated that 77% of total radio revenues, 33% of broadcast television revenues, and 22% of cable television revenues are derived from local ad sales (Albarran, 2017).

Network advertising is sold by account executives at the network level. These spots are sold in two different markets. One is known as the upfront market, while the other is the scatter market. The upfront market is when advertising spots are sold in advance, such as in late May and early June, when networks are holding their annual affiliates meetings. At these meetings, trailers for new and returning programs for the upcoming fall season are shown to various media buyers from a plethora of advertising agencies. Ad prices for new programs are based on estimated ratings within different demographic groups calculated by ad agencies and minimal ratings guaranteed by networks. Ordinarily, around 70% or 75% of network advertising inventory is sold in the upfront market (Friedman, 2019). The scatter market is when television ad time is sold closer to the actual air date, and it involves the selling of ad inventory that was not sold during the upfront market. The scatter market tends to break in late August or September, and agencies purchase schedules for the upcoming fourth quarter. There are also scatter markets for the other three quarters of the year. Scatter market prices tend to be higher than the upfront market, and there tends to be less guesswork and more stable prices.

Advertising agencies are also tasked with placing the marketing messages (i.e., ads) on the right medium, at the right times, and in the appropriate positions. As stated by media consultant Erwin Ephron, "The purpose of media planning and buying is to enhance advertising's positive effects on sales" (as cited in Warner, 2009, p. 361). These critical agency functions focus on selecting which media to buy, how much from each individual media provider, and the actual process of purchasing the available advertising inventory. The goal of media buyers and planners is to accomplish these tasks in the most effective and efficient way that reaches an advertiser's target audience (Warner, 2009).

Now that we understand traditional approaches used in marketing, advertising, and branding, it is important to consider how a convergent media environment changes the field of marketing. Practitioners must adapt to these new technological trends and consumer behaviors to stay relevant in a saturated and competitive media environment.

Something New

Although demographic, geographic, and geodemographic research have been commonplace in traditional marketing practices, big data, discussed more in chapter 22, allows marketing researchers and managers to achieve a more comprehensive understanding of audience consumption behaviors. In addition, new media technologies are revolutionizing how media firms target and deliver content to potential audiences as well as the approach they take in order to attain high levels of brand equity or value in consumers' minds.

MEDIA BRANDING 3.0 AND PERSONALIZATION

Today, audiences wield a significant amount of power as media firms grapple with developing and maintaining brand associations (Chan-Olmsted, 2011; Napoli, 2011). Accordingly, Chan-Olmsted and Shay (2015) identified five key changes that have ushered in what they refer to as the media branding 3.0 era.

The first change is the introduction of new business models given the influx of new competition in stages of the value chain, including content creation, packaging, and distribution. The second change is that consumers anticipate that they will be engaged across all media touch points with which they come into contact. Therefore, media marketing managers need to consider user engagement during each phase of media products from concept development to product consumption (Chan-Olmsted & Shay, 2015). The third key change pertains to the rise of brand messages integrated into professionally produced content as opposed to those delivered in the form of interruptive ads often 15 or 30 seconds in duration. This form of engagement with consumers, which is often referred to as *branded entertainment* or *brand integration*, is deemed to be especially valuable if there is an appropriate fit between the program's subject matter and the sponsor's message. The fourth and fifth changes refer to the development of connected, networked, and intelligent media access and the availability of big data (Chan-Olmsted & Shay, 2015). As stated by Jenkins (2006), media content needs to be offered in the best possible format for consumption on a particular platform or mix of platforms. The rapid spread of artificial intelligence (AI) is driving a shift from traditional networks to intelligent networks. In fact, social networking sites, such as Facebook and LinkedIn, are relying on AI technology to deliver news, profiles, and events with high levels of relevancy, indicating added value over and above their impressive growth in the number of users. Other prominent examples of intelligent networks include Amazon's and Netflix's recommendation systems, which rely on big data to personalize recommendations of products, films, and television programs for consumers (Breakstone, 2019).

Personalization is likely the most visible application of big data. At its core, "personalization is about moving from mass creative to a place closer to individualized creative" (Lau, 2018, p. 38). The direct access to consumers allows Netflix to implement a user-generated ranking system, which asks subscribers to rate films they have watched. This system generates crowdsourcing data so that recommendations are more aligned with what similar users crave (Shih, Kaufman, & Spinola, 2009). The data gathered from recommendation systems has then directed viewership to a wide range of content, which has helped Netflix become a successful disrupter in the media distribution and content creation business segments.

Recently, Netflix has begun changing the cover art used for movies based on which actor a subscriber viewed or liked in the past. It is believed that media marketing managers should begin creating consumer profiles through their partners with registration data (e.g., email, phone numbers). Studios and other partners can then build permanent customer relationship management marketing databases that can be utilized for people-based ad targeting and personalization akin to Netflix (Lau, 2018).

NEW ADVERTISING FORMATS

Due to these new technologies, increased use of data analytics, and the influence of the subscription video-on-demand services, a variety of new ad formats and approaches are being initiated. For example, CBS and AMC networks recently announced that they are moving toward addressable TV advertising on Internet-connected TV devices. In the fourth quarter of 2018, CBS proceeded with a plan with Nielsen that allows advertisers to add tailored messages to national commercials seen by viewers using certain connected TVs. This would allow, for instance, a franchise restaurant to tout its delivery service in a certain city or town or for a retailer to add a message for viewers living close by (Steinberg, 2018). Given the targeted advertising afforded by addressable TV, it is expected that many other networks will soon be introducing their own versions of targeted advertising to advertisers.

According to media research firm Magna, television networks are attempting to blend commercials with programming (Steinberg, 2018). They are doing so in three major ways: reducing the advertising load, incorporating ad pods that tie directly into content, and sponsoring product placement. 21st Century Fox offered shortened commercial pods during the second season of *The Orville* as well as throughout their prime-time schedule on three Sundays in 2018. Fox Networks Group is also running just two minutes of advertising per hour in its digital streams. In addition, NBCUniversal cut the fourth-quarter 2018 prime-time ad inventory by 10% during the original airing of its programs. Mark Marshal, executive vice president of entertainment advertising sales at NBCUniversal, stated that viewers were not likely to see an ad until 20 minutes into an hour-long drama and 8 minutes into a half-hour comedy (Steinberg, 2018). Furthermore, NBCUniversal is introducing what they are referring to as a "prime pod," a first break that will feature advertising that directly plays off of the program or contains a timely element (Steinberg, 2018).

Other networks have turned to product placement or have continued to expand their brand integration strategies, a trend associated with the media branding 3.0 era. While product placement—"the location or, more accurately, the integration of a product or a brand into a film or televised series" (Lehu, 2007)—is no longer a new concept/

practice, we see an increased use of "branded entertainment" campaigns by media companies. For example, advertising giant Procter & Gamble was provided the opportunity to insert a cause-related message into an episode of ABC's *Black-ish*, aligning a commercial pitch with a plot line in the script and dialogue spoken by the show's characters (Steinberg, 2018).

Coordinated brand-building efforts, or integrated marketing communication (IMC), have also risen as a key marketing strategy for media brands. IMC is defined as all aspects of marketing communication working together across all available media platforms and speaking with one cohesive voice (Churchill & Peter, 1998). Such a strategy requires media managers to take all channels, platforms, and strategies into consideration, including advertising, sales promotion, public relations, and direct marketing.

TRANSMEDIA STORYTELLING

Storytelling does not have to be confined to a narrative played out on screen or in an audial form. Today, there are many opportunities for transmedia storytelling. Henry Jenkins (2006) defines transmedia storytelling as a process where integral elements of a fiction get dispersed systematically across multiple delivery channels for the purpose of creating a unified and coordinated entertainment experience. Jenkins (2006) cited the Matrix franchise as an ideal example of transmedia storytelling. While various pieces of information are presented through three live-action films, to fully comprehend the Matrix universe, one must also reference information from a series of animated shorts, several video games, and two collections of comic book stories. While the concept has been around for some time, it is increasingly incorporated into marketing strategy by media firms today. According to Jim Marsh, vice president of digital and social media at HBO, "transmedia gives us an opportunity to reach consumers in a way that is compelling and interesting" (Turchiano, 2018, p. 10).

Transmedia campaigns can be very labor intensive, so there needs to be a clear goal set at the beginning. These aims must be agreed on by both corporate marketing teams and associated production studios. In successfully coordinating these efforts, additional brand messaging and demographics must be taken into consideration.

Recently, HBO has encouraged its creators to pursue intensive transmedia campaigns for comedies such as *Silicon Valley* and the sci-fi western epic *Westworld*. For *Silicon Valley*, HBO launched websites for each character, which were then updated weekly when the shows were in season. Moreover, a virtual reality experience was created in which fans could unlock Easter eggs inside a room-scale rendering of the house, and real-life apps were created that coincided with the apps that characters on the show mentioned (Turchiano, 2018). Another example of a successful transmedia campaign is one that was launched midway through the second season of CW's *Riverdale*. An Instagram account was launched for the character of Kevin Keller, and then several months later, AT&T began running ads that directed people to the social media page. While the content was sponsored, it was launched in a more organic way that provided viewers with a perspective into Kevin's point of view that would not be possible to ascertain from just watching episodes of the program (Turchiano, 2018). Clearly, converged media brings many opportunities and challenges to media marketers.

Opportunities and Challenges

This chapter has investigated the ways in which marketing and branding principles are being utilized in today's convergent media environment. While the marketing principles of segmentation, positioning, and branding have remained steadfast, new technologies allow media firms to pursue marketing goals with improved efficiency and effectiveness. While these clear advantages exist, there are challenges that must be overcome so that media managers are able to maximize the benefits of new technologies.

OPPORTUNITIES

New technologies and consumer trends are the driving forces in media marketing and branding. These trends require media managers to consider new paradigms for developing marketing plans and strategies, understanding customers and identifying target audiences, establishing marketing mixes, and implementing and evaluating marketing activities.

Given the rapid growth of OTT streaming services and the expected cord cutting for MVPDs, media managers need to urgently develop and launch new options for distributing their content directly to consumers. The delivery format of this content has to be nonlinear and on-demand. It should also be developed and prepared with the intention that much of the content will be viewed on mobile devices by many consumers. This DTC distribution strategy will greatly benefit the relationship between media firms and consumers.

Managers need to consider not only the ad content but also the platforms used for delivering these messages. Creativity and detailed planning are essential when it comes to generating the largest return on investment possible for the ad campaigns. Another way in which media management teams can benefit from multiplatform capabilities is through branding initiatives and transmedia storytelling. Since consumers now expect to be engaged across all potential product touch points, it is imperative that media brand managers develop and implement campaigns at each stage of the value chain (Chan-Olmsted & Shay, 2015). Assuming an ideal fit between content and an advertiser's message exists, branded entertainment has a strong potential to immerse audiences to an extent that eclipses that of traditional ads delivered in either commercial pods or as stand-alone spots (Steinberg, 2018).

Media managers ought to consider a variety of new metrics that are now made available through big data analytics, such as new users or followers, time spent on a platform, location of users, content viewed on the platform, and how users found a website. In addition, when sharing audience metrics with potential advertisers and business partners, third-party analytics platforms, such as Google Analytics or Hootsuite, should be used whenever possible. Third-party data is a necessity in acquiring potential new business partners, since it is perceived as more legitimate due to its impartiality (Albarran, 2017).

Database marketing, big data, and AI-driven intelligent networks can provide an enormous quantity of individual-level consumer data regarding media consumption and purchasing behaviors. These technological advancements aid media content creators, distributors, and marketers to understand their target consumers at a much deeper level than ever before. While having access to this data is allowing media companies to more efficiently reach consumers who will likely have an interest in viewing or purchasing their products, demographic, geographic, geodemographic, and psychographic research should not be abandoned. Demographic and geographic segmentation information, in the form of ratings and share data for various media markets, will continue to be important metrics provided through research firms such as Nielsen. While there are a number of opportunities made possible by new technologies and consumer trends, many new challenges have also arisen for today's media managers.

CHALLENGES

The single biggest challenge in this realm is the financial loss resulting from traditional distributors being cut out of the value chain. Carriage fees, which studios have typically received from television networks, will be nonexistent (Littleton, 2018). While the possibility still exists to make up for these losses, the initial implementation will be a major obstacle. One area of infrastructure that may require substantial resources is database management (Regal, 2015). For a DTC streaming service to succeed, it is critical that firms have a thorough understanding of their customers, which includes having databases available to media managers (Lau, 2018).

These databases will assist efforts to bridge a closer connection with consumers, one that will enable media firms to provide content and services that are appealing to their customers. Media managers also need to look for ways to maximize the effectiveness of these databases by ensuring that registration data is inserted into their own unique media content as opposed to what is licensed (Lau, 2018). Nonetheless, media conglomerates and smaller media firms will feel compelled to offer more DTC services as the trend for cord cutting increases. The best path forward, therefore, is to launch DTC services in an incremental fashion instead of releasing multiple services at any one point in time. This will help keep the infrastructure costs manageable while giving the marketing and marketing research departments opportunities to examine the operation of each new service. In addition, by taking this approach, much of the content produced by studios will continue to be channeled through distributors, which will ensure a substantial revenue stream from carriage fees in the meantime (Littleton, 2018).

In conjunction with database marketing, media managers must be prepared for the challenges of implementing IMC campaigns. This is primarily a branding issue as the content offered on each media channel needs to complement that which is delivered through other channels. In other words, each branding touch point needs to provide content that ideally matches consumer needs at the moment while simultaneously communicating a message that is cohesive across all touch points (Chan-Olmsted & Shay, 2015). To accomplish this, additional branding personnel and content creators/producers will need to be hired and trained. In addition, time will need to be allotted to creating new branding messages and subsequently having marketing researchers test them with potential audiences before launching them across their platforms.

Another major set of challenges linked to the development of marketing plans and strategies relate to the expenses and infrastructure necessary to roll out addressable television services. There are surely considerable expenses that must be incurred as television networks, and soon perhaps local stations, look into launching these services providing targeted advertising. Therefore, it is important that media managers seek out appropriate partners, such as data providers, that can assist them with their addressability efforts (Steinberg, 2018). Sales managers and advertising account executives must educate ad agencies and advertisers on addressable television and data analytics. This is where investments in training and development can really pay dividends for media companies. Once the sales departments see and believe in these benefits, it is their responsibility to communicate these advantages with their clients so that they become equally enthusiastic about reaping the benefits of more precise consumer targeting.

Finally, the introduction of numerous new streaming services can bring additional challenges to media managers. Because it is expected that many media providers will begin to launch competing OTT streaming services in which they will offer exclusive access to their unique programming, it is imperative for media managers to develop positioning statements that cut to the essence of what makes their particular streaming service unique and valuable. This can be accomplished first by the type of content provided, naturally, but also by the business model to be employed.

It can be difficult for media practitioners and managers to balance the opportunities and challenges new media has brought to marketing practices. Since audiences are using multiple platforms to access unique branded content, the vast amount of creative decisions may seem overwhelming. The following action plan may help practitioners balance how each new technology aids in the process.

ACTION PLAN

1. Employ market testing of DTC services and methods of developing customer relationship management databases before and after launching new DTC platforms.
2. Identify potential partners, such as data and software providers, for the development of addressable TV advertising. Advertising account executives at both the local and national levels will need to be trained in the full suite of options available to advertisers so that maximum revenue can be generated.
3. Develop goals and detailed strategies before launching new IMC campaigns. Remember to consider the importance of delivering a cohesive message across all branding touch points while also providing content on a particular platform that best matches consumer expectations.
4. Implement cross-functional training and development programs that facilitate the effective collaboration of studio creatives and marketing personnel for the roll out of IMC, branded integration, and transmedia campaigns.

KEY TAKEAWAYS

1. Media distribution is shifting from the wholesale delivery of content via multichannel video program distributors to direct-to-consumer distribution through over-the-top streaming services.

2. The use of database marketing and digital platforms together now allow media companies to target consumers who watch certain television networks and OTT streaming platforms. These databases facilitate the move from mass to individualized creativeness, a fundamental aspect of personalization.
3. Audience fragmentation and the plethora of platforms and devices available today for consumers to view content at any time and place have led to a substantial increase in the use of integrated marketing communication and brand integration campaigns by content creators and distributors.
4. A crowded competitive media landscape has escalated the importance of strong positioning and branding. Therefore, positioning must clearly encapsulate how your media brand differs from a multitude of competitive offerings.

CONCLUSION

This chapter examined the significant role of marketing and branding in the media management field. Media marketing managers are challenged to deliver value to two entities with differing needs: audiences and advertisers. While this is a substantial challenge for media managers today, many are rising to the occasion, assisted by new technologies, consumer trends, and ideas.

Technological changes have resulted in the need to add a fifth P of marketing, participation, to the long-held four-P model of product, price, place (distribution), and promotion. Participation is made possible through the shift to Web 2.0 in that now consumers can interact with brands online and create their own value-added content. The impact of the major changes of the media branding 3.0 era results in new business models and approaches for deeper engagement with audiences and advertisers. The use of demographics, geographics, geodemographics, and psychographics will remain vital to the segmentation efforts of media firms. However, new technologies are providing media marketers with an array of techniques and resources that can be harnessed for developing increasingly detailed segmentation clusters.

Due to the prevalence of big data, intelligent networks, analytics, and AI, many media managers are able to examine the success of content and marketing campaigns by looking directly at individual consumers instead of through a sample of the population. These technologies provide marketing managers at Amazon and Netflix with unprecedented opportunities to drive engagement and revenues through personalization. The capabilities of AI and intelligent networks are also assisting media companies in the development of more detailed customer relationship management databases. As a result, database management will become even more important for media marketing and branding managers in the years ahead as the sheer volume of data available on each consumer increases.

Audience fragmentation has resulted in increased use by content creators and distributors of IMC, brand integration, and transmedia storytelling campaigns. These approaches rely on the use of multiple media platforms to carry individually important and unique content to audiences. The key for the success of these campaigns is to have the platforms and content work together synergistically. In addition, audience fragmentation and increased competition have underscored the significance of brand extensions as well as brand positioning utilizing positioning maps. Brand extensions allow media companies to exploit favorable consumer attitudes toward their existing brands by attaching current popular brand names to new media products that are being launched. Brand positioning maps provide marketing managers with a tool for solidifying a niche audience that will prefer their brands over competitive offerings.

Moreover, national spot, local, and network advertising sales have continued to be the principal engine for generating revenues for broadcast stations and networks. The symbiotic relationship between media firms, ad agencies, and advertisers has always been and will continue to be central to the functioning of the industry. However, the format of the ad messages is now diversified beyond the traditional interruptive ads, often 15 or 30 seconds in length, that have been a mainstay in television and radio over the years. For instance, several television networks are now offering addressable television ads to advertisers, allowing them to target specific segments of consumers with tailored messages. Furthermore, media firms are increasingly integrating brands into programming through such practices as shortening ad pods, matching advertisements directly to content, product placement, and branded entertainment initiatives.

No matter the extent to which new technologies and consumer trends impact the media industry, the four primary stages of marketing management and their aims should always be central in the minds of media managers and marketing professionals. The stages include developing marketing plans and strategies, understanding customers and defining target audiences, establishing marketing mixes, and implementing and evaluating marketing activities.

While technology brings many new changes to marketing, traditional marketing research techniques, including concept testing, focus groups, and surveys, should still drive practitioner decisions in the field. New research measurements, including big data and consumer insights, can subsidize these efforts. With multiple media platforms and an increasingly demanding audience, marketing professionals are able to facilitate a more personalized design, placement, and implementation of branding campaigns to optimally engage consumers both cognitively and affectively. Thus, it is an exciting time for content creators and distributors.

In closing, marketing and branding have evolved significantly since the days in which marketing emerged as a focus of media firms. While today's media managers are clearly aware of remarkable technological advances and shifting consumer trends, many are hesitant to introduce new approaches into their existing operations. It is evident that media disrupters are reaping rewards in terms of audience engagement and revenues, and these companies can be looked at as shining examples of success. Nevertheless, it will be prudent for managers at legacy media companies to be willing to take risks by implementing new technologies and relentlessly responding to customer needs while also being careful to develop explicit and detailed strategies for propelling their firms to the next level in the months and years ahead. Whether media firms are long-standing multinational corporations or innovative small start-ups, they will each be required to operate within the domain of an increasingly complex set of laws and regulations. The next chapter explains how laws and regulations shape managerial decisions about strategy and operations at media firms.

REFERENCES

Albarran, A. B. (2017). *Management of electronic and digital media* (6th ed.). Cengage Learning.

American Marketing Association. (2019). *Definition of marketing*. https://www.ama.org/AboutAMA/Pages/Definition-of-Marketing

Bennett, P. D. (1995). *Dictionary of marketing terms* (2nd ed.). NTC Business Books.

Breakstone, M. (2019, January 23). The rise of intelligent networks: Where do they fit into our lives and work? *Forbes*. https://www.forbes.com/sites/forbestechcouncil/2019/01/23/the-rise-of-intelligent-networks-where-do-they-fit-into-our-lives-and-our-work

CBS Corporation. (2019). *Our businesses*. https://www.cbscorporation.com

Chan-Olmsted, S. (2011). Media branding in a changing world: Challenges and opportunities 2.0. *The International Journal on Media Management, 13*(1), 3–19.

Chan-Olmsted, S., & Shay, R. (2015). Media branding 3.0: From media brands to branded entertainment and information. In G. Siegert, K. Forster, S. Chan-Olmsted, & M. Ots (Eds.), *Handbook of media branding* (pp. 11–29). Springer International Publishing.

Churchill, G. A., & Peter, J. P. (1998). *Marketing: Creating value for customers* (2nd ed.). Irwin McGraw-Hill.

Claritas. (2018). *04-young digerati*. https://claritas360.claritas.com/mybestsegments/#segDetail/PZP/04

D'Alessandro, D. F. (2001). *Brand warfare: 10 rules for building the killer brand*. McGraw-Hill.

Drinkwater, P., & Uncles, M. (1992). The impact of program brands on consumer evaluations of television and radio broadcast brands. *The Journal of Product & Brand Management, 16*, 178–187.

Friedman, W. (2019). *CBS completes upfront, estimates prime-time revenues could hit $2.7 billion*. Television News Daily. https://www.mediapost.com/publications/article/337323/cbs-completes-upfront-estimates-prime-time-revenu.html

Grines, K. (2018). What programmers can learn from the fall of Toys 'R' Us: Working with aggregators helps, but that should not come at the expense of their own brands and apps. *Multichannel News, 39*, 29.

Jenkins, H. (2006). *Convergence culture: Where old and new media collide*. New York University Press.

Kim, C. K., & Lavack, A. M. (1996). Vertical brand extensions: Current research and managerial implications. *Journal of Product & Brand Management, 5*(6), 24–37.

Lau, K. M. (2018). What Netflix recommends for entertainment marketing: Achieving a people-based approach that has competitors playing catch-up. *Broadcasting & Cable, 148*(6), 38.

Lehu, J. (2007). *Branded entertainment: Product placement & brand strategy in the entertainment business*. Kogan Page.

Littleton, C. (2018). Media wars go over the top. *Variety, 341*(6), 36–42.

McCarthy, J., McGuiggan, R., Perreault, W., & Quester, P. (2007). *Marketing creating and delivering value* (5th ed.). McGraw-Hill Irwin.

Moulding, H. S. (1996). *AFU white paper: The decline and fall of Betamax*. Internet Archive Wayback Machine. https://web.archive.org/web/20081002042948/http://tafkac.org/products/beta_vs_vhs.html

Napoli, P. M. (2011). *Audience evolution: New technologies and the transformation of media audiences*. Columbia University Press.

NBCUniversal. (2014). *NBCUniversal unveils original video programming initiative for digital platforms & video on demand*. TV by the Numbers. https://tvbythenumbers.zap2it.com/press-releases/nbcuniversal-unveils-original-video-programming-initiative-for-digital-platforms-video-on-demand/

Nielsen. (2018). *Local television market universe estimates*. https://www.nielsen.com/content/dam/corporate/us/en/public%20factsheets/tv/2018-19-dma-ranker.pdf

Ochoa, C. (2016). *Legendary products: VHS vs. BETA*. https://www.netquest.com/blog/en/blog/en/legendary-products-vhs-vs-beta

O'Guinn, T. C., Allen, C. T., & Semenik, R. J. (2009). *Advertising and integrated brand promotion* (5th ed.). South-Western Cengage Learning.

Owen, D. (2005). *The Betamax vs VHS format war*. https://www.mediacollege.com/video/format/compare/betamax-vhs.html
Pegus, M. (2018). How to stand out from the OTT crowd: Content is as important as ever, but players should take cues from digital marketers. *Broadcasting & Cable, 148*(3), 24.
Regal, M. (2015). *Five steps for choosing and implementing a database*. The Nonprofit Technology Enterprise Network. https://www.nten.org/article/five-steps-for-choosing-and-implementing-a-database/
Shih, W., Kaufman, S., & Spinola, D. (2009). *Netflix: Harvard Business School Case*. Harvard Business School Publishing.
Steinberg, B. (2018). Commercial breakdown. *Variety, 341*(6), 45–47.
Smith, P. R., & Taylor, J. (2004). *Marketing communications* (4th ed.). Kogan Page.
Turchiano, D. (2018). So much story it spills out of the screen. *Variety, 341*(2), 10.
Tuten, T. L., & Solomon, M. R. (2015). *Social media marketing* (2nd ed.). Sage.
Van Tassel, J., & Poe-Howfield, L. (2010). *Managing electronic media: Making, marketing, and moving digital content*. Burlington, MA: Focal Press.
Warner, C. (2009). *Media selling: Television, print, Internet, radio* (4th ed.). Wiley-Blackwell.
Warner, C., & Buchman, J. (2004). *Broadcast and cable selling* (3rd ed.). Iowa State Press/Blackwell.

CHAPTER 8

Law and Policy

Gregory Newton, Ohio University

LEARNING OBJECTIVES

1. Describe philosophical principles that support specific goals and strategies of media policy makers.
2. Explain how specific laws and regulations have evolved to implement those goals in the United States and other regions.
3. Describe how courts have analyzed challenges to laws relating to media.
4. Explain how laws and regulations shape managerial decisions about strategy and operations at media firms.

Legal considerations are among the numerous factors affecting media business strategy and managerial decisions. Laws directly affecting media content and media business structures along with those more generally applying to any business (or nonprofit) organization create a framework within which media enterprises operate. A complete, detailed discussion of media law and policy is far beyond the reach of a single book chapter. Rather, the goals here are to outline some of the significant ways that federal, state, local, and international legal factors can affect a media business; introduce some of the key regulatory actors; and discuss the role of legal issues in management decisions. An understanding of these basic elements will prepare practitioners for more detailed and complex discussions likely to happen with the legal professionals representing a media company's interests and to more effectively incorporate legal factors into decision making.

Many of the terms you will encounter in this chapter are often treated interchangeably in colloquial usage but have very specific meanings that should not be confused when we are in a legal context. *Laws* include statutes or constitutional provisions passed by a legislative body—or sometimes via citizen initiatives—as well as rules developed as common law. *Regulations* (also known as administrative law) are rules with the force of statutory law, developed and primarily enforced by a government agency. *Policy* covers foundational principles and related guidelines describing how something should operate. It often provides the basis for laws and regulations. Policy, laws, and regulations work together to articulate societal goals, the means for implementing strategies to achieve those goals, and enforcement of requirements intended to further those goals.

The legal framework in which that process operates includes legislative, executive, and judicial elements. A legislature's primary function is to create laws; executives enforce laws and have policy responsibilities; and judicial bodies interpret laws. In the United States, Congress (made up of the Senate and House of Representatives) is the national legislative body; most states have a similar bicameral structure. The executive branch is widely referred to as the *administration* and includes the president along with various cabinet departments and other agencies and offices at the federal level; at the state level, the executive branch is headed by a governor and includes various other statewide offices similar to the federal cabinet-level departments and agencies. The federal judicial branch consists of trial courts in 94 geographic districts, which feed into 12 regional appellate courts plus the court of appeals for the federal circuit (commonly referred to as the D.C. circuit court), and the Supreme Court (United States Courts, n.d.). This structure is also largely mirrored within each state.

Each part of the government has powers that enable it to serve as a check on the power of the others. For example, the executive has the power to veto a law passed by the legislative body (United States Constitution, 1992, art. I, § 7, cl. 2) and also has some authority to decide how enacted laws are enforced (United States Constitution, 1992, art. II, §1). Congress has the ability to override a veto if there is enough support (United States Constitution, 1992, art. I, § 7, cl. 2), and—through its control of the federal budget (United States Constitution, 1992, art. I, § 9, cl. 7) as well as the "advice and consent" confirmation process for executive agency and judicial nominations (United States Constitution, 1992, art. II, § 2, cl. 2)—can shape activity in the other branches. The judiciary is empowered to pass judgment on enforcement actions as well as to review and overrule actions by the other branches as unconstitutional or in violation of procedural legal requirements (United States Constitution, 1992, art. III, §2).

It is worth noting the somewhat unique status of the "independent regulatory agency" in the U.S. federal structure. These agencies are created by Congress, nominally operate within the administration, and are typically given explicit statutory authority to set standards and regulate a specific field of activity. Rather than a single executive, their leadership is typically a group—a commission or board. Commissioners are appointed by the president, subject to Senate confirmation. Beneath the commissioners in the agency hierarchy are several groups of professional staff organized by function—known as bureaus, offices, groups, or task forces—that carry out the day-to-day activities of the agency (e.g., https://www.fcc.gov/about-fcc/organizational-charts-fcc; https://www.ftc.gov/about-ftc/bureaus-offices with descriptions and chart). Regulatory agencies include all three functions (legislative, executive, judicial) within their structure. They are considered "independent" because they are structured to operate largely outside concerns of political influence,* and the president has limited authority to remove an appointee and generally has no control over independent agencies' day-to-day activity. Congress generally retains some degree of oversight responsibility,

*This is the theoretical conception of the agency; their independence in practice, or whether they even should be free from politics, has long been subject to study and debate. See, e.g., Miller, 1988; Humphries & Songer, 1999; Selin, 2015.

exercised primarily through funding directions in the budget process and the ability to amend the agency's statutory authority.

Examples of independent regulatory agencies with broad responsibility directly related to media include the Federal Communications Commission (FCC), which regulates radio, television—including satellite and cable TV—and other communication services such as mobile phones, and the Federal Trade Commission (FTC), which has broad responsibilities for protecting consumers and market competition, giving them oversight of advertising content and business mergers among other things. Each has five commissioners, no more than three of whom may be from one political party. One of the three will serve as the chairperson of the commission, a position that has significant ability to drive the agency's agenda. Commissioners are officially appointed for lengthy terms (five years for the FCC, seven years for the FTC), but it is common for many to resign before their appointment is up, either to pursue other opportunities or because of a change in administration, providing a new president the opportunity to shape the agency's agenda.

There are many other agencies whose actions touch on media operations, although media businesses are not their primary concern. For example, media managers in large firms with publicly traded stock may also need to be aware of the Securities Exchange Commission, which governs the trade of equities and protects investors; or, at the other end of the size continuum, they may make use of the services of the Small Business Administration, which provides various forms of assistance to owners starting and trying to grow small businesses.

Media firms engage with these various branches and offices in different ways. They will frequently engage in lobbying a position on an issue before Congress or the FCC and may also suggest statutory or rule changes. They may appeal FCC or legislative action through the courts or file briefs arguing some element of a court case brought by another party when it affects them in some way. They can also be the subject of enforcement actions by executive branch offices or a regulatory agency if one of those believes that a business has run afoul of the law.

Law and policy is a constantly evolving landscape, with legislative activity, other regulatory actions, and court decisions altering the rules of the game for media in ways big and small. Something that may have been illegal for a media firm last year (or last month) may now be allowed—or something once permitted may no longer be legal or may require additional safeguards or processes for your company. Advertising is one area where this sometimes suddenly shifting ground can be easily seen. Let's explore one such case study by examining the impact of new hemp laws and policy in the United States.

CASE STUDY

The 2018 farm bill (formally known as the Agriculture Improvement Act of 2018) was a successful legislative process to legalize hemp* in the United States that impacted many

*Beginning in 1937, federal law did not distinguish between marijuana and hemp versions of the cannabis plant. The distinction is now based on levels of tetrahydrocannabinol, which for hemp must be below 0.3%—too low to produce any psychoactive effect (Yoakum, 2019; Agriculture Improvement Act, §10113 and 12619).

individuals, policies, and businesses, including media advertising. There are still some elements that are unknown (and thus will continue to change), but the basic process for implementing many of these changes requires each state to set up rules governing production, processing, distribution, and sale of manufactured hemp products. Those rules must then be approved by the federal Food and Drug Administration (Agriculture Improvement Act, § 10113 HEMP PRODUCTION); that process is ongoing as of this writing. In addition, 33 states and the District of Columbia have also passed laws legalizing marijuana in some form (10 of those allow recreational use), nearly all of those in the past few years, although marijuana is still classified as an illegal drug at the federal level (Yoakum, 2019).

Given that set of recent legal changes, and with more hemp-derived products coming to market (and, in states where there is no longer state prohibition, marijuana products coming to market), companies selling those products want to advertise them to consumers. But are there potential liabilities for media companies who carry such advertising messages? The answer, right now, is different in every state and also depends on a number of other factors related to the specific product advertised, the content of the ad, and the medium carrying the ad, such as whether the product is intended to be ingested as a food additive or dietary supplement, or if there is any health claim made, or whether the medium is under direct federal oversight as in the case of broadcasting, or if there would likely be significant numbers of children in the audience in the case of marijuana products (Oxenford, 2019). As a result, broadcasters, newspapers, podcasters, websites, or any other media outlets wishing to carry advertising for CBD oil, medical marijuana edibles, or any of these products should engage in careful analysis with their attorney regarding what is permissible in their location for any particular product. Practitioners must have a strong understanding of old and new policies that impact these decisions.

Something Old

It is important to understand that the goals of media policy, and of media laws and regulations, can broadly be grouped into categories of encouraging things of social value or of trying to prevent harm that might come from media activity. Despite the dynamic nature of a convergent media landscape, this fundamental goal remains the same. There are many specific goals and ways to achieve them within each category, which then find expression in specific policy statements, constitutions and statutes, regulations and other agency actions, and court decisions. For example, one overarching and widely accepted social value goal is the need in a democracy for a functioning "marketplace of ideas," where citizens can speak and hear competing information and claims about issues facing society. The underlying philosophy is typically traced back to John Milton's *Aeropagitica* of 1644 and was amplified by John Stuart Mill two centuries later in *On Liberty*. There are various legal structures intended to move us toward that policy goal. For example, the First Amendment to the U.S. Constitution protects freedom of speech and press, enabling citizens to freely and openly communicate with each other and with the government. Congress has passed laws intended to encourage wide open and robust debate, such as the laws covering political candidates' access to television and radio* that help ensure that all legally qualified candidates for office have the opportunity to make their case to voters before an election.

Although the FCC has generally adopted a more hands-off approach in recent years, even many of the deregulatory actions they have taken, such as repealing the Fairness Doctrine (which required broadcasters to present programming to address issues of importance to their community and to include diverse perspectives on the issues), were premised on the idea that removing old rules would encourage a free marketplace of ideas in a changing media environment (Federal Communications Commission, 1987). It's interesting to note that in other media contexts, such as newspapers, the courts had long held that requirements such as those in the Fairness Doctrine (and the corollary political editorializing and personal attack rules) were impermissible because a "government-enforced right of access inescapably 'dampens the vigor and limits the variety of public debate.'"†

This is just one example of differing opinions as the best means of achieving a policy goal; sometimes, the prevailing opinion comes around to choosing one, while other times the debate rages on even as various options are tried. The vigorous marketplace concept has been frequently cited by courts (and also in minority opinions) as a factor that tips the scales as they balance competing concerns, from Justice Holmes's dissent in *Abrams v. United States* in 1919 right up through Justice Kennedy's majority opinion in *Citizens United v. Federal Elections Commission* in 2010.

There are also many attempts to prevent harm. For example, state laws punish defamation (making a false statement that harms somebody's reputation). Other rules are designed to protect vulnerable populations, such as children, by limiting their potential exposure to certain types of advertising or requiring explicit parental consent for access to certain content. It's important to note here that there have been several efforts by media industries to head off restrictive laws and regulations by adopting guidelines for their companies to follow that address concerns about potential harm. You're probably familiar with the rating systems that are intended to provide information to parents about the content of movies (Motion Picture Association, n.d.), video games (Entertainment Software Rating Board, n.d.), and television programs (TV Parental Guidelines Monitoring Board, 2019). All of those grew out of industry perceptions that government restrictions were likely unless companies in the industry did something themselves and that government restrictions would be less desirable. There are several statutes and a few elements in the Constitution governing media and dating to much earlier eras but that endure to this day. Let's start with three elements of the Constitution that provide the broad foundations for media businesses themselves and guide what media laws or regulations might try to accomplish.

---

*There are several elements to the political broadcasting rules in addition to candidate access. For a summary and analysis, see Oxenford and O'Connor (2019).

†For example, *Miami Herald Publishing Co. v. Tornillo*, 418 U.S. 241, 257 (1974) quoting *New York Times v. Sullivan*, 376 U.S.254, at 279 (1964).

CONSTITUTIONAL FOUNDATIONS

The First Amendment is actually a collection of limits on legislative authority to restrict citizens' freedoms of belief and expression: "Congress* shall make no law respecting an establishment of religion, or prohibiting the free exercise thereof; or abridging the freedom of speech, or of the press; or the right of the people peaceably to assemble, and to petition the Government for a redress of grievances."

Like every element of the Constitution, the First Amendment does not create an absolute right; rights guaranteed in some places may come into conflict with rights guaranteed in another. Thus, the courts have developed processes over time for balancing various competing interests and determining whether a law passed by Congress or another legislative body that might restrict speech in some way is still acceptable because the competing interest being served outweighs any potential harm to speech rights.

Article I, Section 8 of the Constitution (National Archives, n.d.) has two clauses that help create the foundation for laws and rules that apply to media businesses: the Commerce Clause (clause 3) and the Intellectual Property Clause—sometimes called the Copyright and Patent Clause (clause 8). The Commerce Clause is very broad and grants Congress legislative authority to "regulate Commerce with foreign Nations, and among the several States, and with the Indian Tribes" (United States Constitution, 1992, art. I, § 8, cl. 3). In other words, any transaction that takes place across a state or national border is potentially subject to federal authority. As a practical matter, that has come to include just about any business, including media, because nearly any product or service has some sort of activity or transaction (supply chain, marketing, distribution, etc.) that crosses (or potentially crosses) one or more of those boundaries.

There are many statutes and regulations justified at least in part by the Commerce Clause. One primary example would be the provisions within the Communication Act of 1934 as well as subsequent amendments of that law, such as the 1996 Telecommunications Act and, therefore, all regulations promulgated by the Federal Communications Commission, which was established by that legislation. Because telephone service and broadcasting—and later, cable and satellite TV and satellite radio—are enterprises that cross over state lines, Congress has authority to regulate the activity (and they have delegated some of that authority to the FCC).

NOT ALL MEDIA ARE THE SAME IN LAW

As new technologies of media creation and distribution have emerged, along with various business models sustaining the enterprises in those different spaces, policy makers and courts have frequently drawn distinctions among them based on technological or economic considerations (e.g., use of the electromagnetic spectrum, whether access is

*The First Amendment explicitly refers to "Congress" and through the 19th century was understood to apply only to the federal government. However, beginning in the 1920s, the Supreme Court began to interpret the Due Process Clause of the 14th Amendment as meaning that the Bill of Rights also applies to state legislatures. In *Gitlow v. New York*, 268 U.S. 652 (1925), the court explicitly held that the First Amendment applied to the states.

limited to audiences who directly pay for a product) and chosen to weight those various forms differently in terms of the protection afforded by the First Amendment. The forms given the greatest weight in legal balances are printed books, magazines, and newspapers along with individual speech in recognized public spaces—the forms of communication and media that were familiar to the framers of the Constitution. At the other end, subject to more regulation, are the broadcast media that emerged in the first half of the 20th century—radio and television. In between are later media forms, from cable TV and satellite radio to various Internet-delivered media (websites, streaming audio and video services, etc.). Thus, laws and regulations governing ownership of media enterprises and the kinds of content permitted (or limited in some way) on different media platforms find greater or lesser favor. Limits restricting the number of properties that an owner can control have been strictly enforced (and changed multiple times) for radio and television but would not be allowed in most cases for publishers of books or newspapers. Content requirements—such as the political broadcasting rules (Federal Communications Commission, 2015)—or restrictions such as the prohibition on indecent content (Federal Communications Commission, n.d.; Federal Communications Commission v. Pacifica, 1978; but also see Federal Communications Commission v. Fox, 2012) that were deemed permissible when applied to radio and television have been ruled unconstitutional infringements of First Amendment rights when attempts were made to address print media or the Internet in similar ways (e.g., Reno v. ACLU, 1997). Congress and the courts justify these different regulatory approaches based on differences in the distribution technology (broadcasting uses a "scarce" public resource of electromagnetic spectrum, while paper and Internet capacity are less limited) and economics (broadcasting is freely available to anybody with a receiver, while newspapers or Internet access generally requires a purchase). Whether these distinctions are logical and supported by empirical evidence has been the focus of decades of legal debates in classrooms, boardrooms, cloakrooms, and courtrooms.

INTELLECTUAL PROPERTY LAW

Article I, Section 8 of the Constitution grants Congress several enumerated powers, including the authority to "promote the Progress of Science and useful Arts, by securing for limited Times to Authors and Inventors the exclusive Right to their respective Writings and Discoveries" (Copyright Clause, Art. I, §8, Clause 8). There are a couple of important things to note here. The framers of the Constitution chose to explicitly provide a basis for subsequent laws addressing copyright (covering authors) and patent (covering inventors); however, the Constitution does not mention trademarks. Instead, Congressional authority for trademark regulation is found in the broader authority of the Commerce Clause (Art. I, §8, Clause 3).

Copyright and trademark protections for creators provide the basis for the business of media—the ability to generate revenue from media content for which you control the rights and block unauthorized distribution or other uses by others. The right of a creator to control and profit from their intellectual work has long been recognized in law. This protection is intended to encourage people to continue to create. Broad intellectual property rights are the legal foundation for the business of media.

Intellectual property rights are protected under three different structures, each with its own purposes and elements: copyright, trademark, and patent. Copyright covers forms of original authorship (expression) including artistic, literary, musical, and dramatic works as well as computer software. Some things are not subject to copyright, including ideas or concepts (the expression of an idea can be protected but not the idea itself), names (although the name of a creative work like a movie or book may be eligible for trademark protection), and processes or methods (those things may be eligible for patent protection). Trademark covers words, symbols, designs, and other recognizable elements (which might include a sound such as the NBC chimes or the 20th Century Fox fanfare or a shape like the classic Coca-Cola bottle) that distinguish a business and the product or service* they provide from competitors. Patents cover inventions, including both the man-made objects themselves and the processes of manufacturing an object. For most media businesses, copyright and trademark are the areas of primary concern and are the focus in this chapter.

Basic copyright protection applies as soon as a work is "fixed in tangible medium of expression" (17 U.S.C. §102). It grants the right holder exclusive rights over:

- making copies of the work
- distributing copies of the work
- public performance of the work
- public display of the work
- producing derivative works (17 U.S.C. §106)

Registering a work with the U.S. Copyright Office is a simple and affordable process (https://www.copyright.gov/registration/), although it can take several months for the office to process and approve the registration, and the registration is not official until that approval is granted (Fourth Estate Public Benefit Corp. v. Wall-Street.com, 2019). You might wonder why anybody would bother going through even the modest effort required if copyright automatically applies once a work is fixed in tangible form. The answer is that registration provides several additional benefits beyond basic protection (see 17 U.S.C. §411, §501 et seq.), most notably the ability to claim statutory damages as well as collect attorneys' fees against an infringer. It is also considered prima facie evidence of authorship in court, making the case against an infringer much simpler to prove. Finally, there is also a preregistration option for classes of works that the Registrar of Copyrights has determined to be frequently infringed before their publication, which can help rights holders enforce their copyright. These include motion pictures, sound recordings, books, and computer software among others. There is an additional fee for preregistration, and the Copyright Office will typically process those applications within a week (Smith, 2019).

The term of U.S. copyright protection has grown over time. The last extension came in 1998 (Sonny Bono Copyright Term Extension Act, 1998) and added 20 years so that U.S. copyright can now be enforced for the author's life plus 70 years for works created after 1978 and 95 years total for works created prior to 1978 if all renewals of the

*Although designs intended to distinguish services are officially known as service marks, *trademark* is frequently used broadly to encompass both goods and services.

original copyright were completed. Thus, classic works produced in the late 1920s will soon be entering the *public domain* (no longer protected and available for anybody to use), including George Gershwin's *Rhapsody in Blue* (2020), F. Scott Fitzgerald's *The Great Gatsby* (2021), and Walt Disney's classic cartoon *Steamboat Willie*, which introduced the world to Mickey Mouse (2024). Over the following decade, early versions of Superman, Batman, and several Looney Tunes characters will also fall into public domain unless Congress once again extends the copyright term (something now widely considered to be unlikely) (Lee, 2019). There are also many works, some of them quite famous (e.g., *Night of the Living Dead* [1968] and *It's a Wonderful Life**), where copyrights lapsed earlier because they were not renewed under the copyright statutes that existed prior to 1978.

There can be dozens of intellectual property rights in a single media product. A movie, for example, would likely involve not only the copyright in the finished film along with trademarks covering the characters, film name, producer, and studio but also copyright covering the original story, the screenplay, the music (which would involve separate rights to each composition and each sound recording), trailers and TV advertising (and again separate music rights for these distinct products along with perhaps voice-over performances by a narrator), and marketing photos or other visual art. The core concern around intellectual property for most media businesses is thus "What can I use?" (or "How can I acquire the right to use that?"). If you created something yourself, or somebody you employ created something for you as part of their assigned duties ("work for hire"), you are the copyright holder and can use the work as you see fit—assuming you have not assigned the rights to somebody else. It is frequently possible to acquire permission to use somebody else's work, although it commonly requires paying a rights fee. For example, this is how movies, television programs, video games, and advertisements incorporate popular songs. Finally, if a work is no longer protected by copyright because it has entered the public domain, one may use it without securing any permission—but this needs to be checked very carefully. Using any creative expression without clearly owning or securing the rights potentially puts you at risk of infringing the rights of an author, and the penalties for infringement can be substantial. Many individuals as well as media organizations have discovered at great cost that the existence of a photo or a song or some text on the Internet does not mean you can share or publish that material on your own website or use it in other ways without permission (Oxenford, 2016, 2018; Peters, 2018).

Under some circumstances, fair use may be available as a defense against an infringement claim. This is most common when the use is for one of the recognized fair use examples mentioned in statutory law: criticism, comment, news reporting, teaching (including multiple copies for classroom use), scholarship, or research. However, it is critical to understand several factors affecting when and how fair use applies. The considerations articulated by the Supreme Court (Campbell v. Acuff-Rose Music, Inc., 1994) are:

---

*The story of *It's a Wonderful Life* illustrates the complexity of rights in many media products. Although television stations began showing the film at Christmastime in the 1970s in part because they believed there were no royalties owed, it wasn't so simple. Rights to underlying elements in the film, such as the original story ("The Greatest Gift") as well as the music in the film, had been renewed, and that became the basis for the current licensing arrangement granting public performance rights to NBCUniversal (Kosarzycki, 2017).

- *the purpose and character of the use*—have you used the original to build something new so that the work has been transformed in some way that added value, or did you merely copy the original verbatim?
- *the nature of the copyrighted work*—fair use is more likely if the original work was factual (rather than fiction) and was published
- *the amount and substantiality of the portion taken*—there is again no bright-line rule here, but in general, the less you use, and especially the less that material is "the heart" of the original, the more likely it is that the use might be fair
- *the effect of the use on the potential market for the copyrighted work*—is your use likely to deprive the author of income?

A court will weigh all four factors when assessing an infringement claim and the validity of a fair use defense. No individual factor is always going to be dispositive, and different sets of facts lead courts to different balancing acts. Parodies, for example, lead to a very different analysis than you might find in other situations. A very successful parody might use the entire "heart" of the original as necessary for conjuring the original, and may significantly damage the potential revenue for the author by denigrating the work, but courts have often found that transformative use of parody (and the recognition by Congress of comment or criticism as examples of desirable fair use) as more important in their analysis than the other three factors under those circumstances. Courts have also drawn a distinction between uses for parody and satire. A parody must criticize, or comment on, the original work in some way (along with, perhaps, commenting on other social issues), while satire is focused on attacking societies' stupidities or vices and does not require the use of another original work to comment on those shortcomings. Compare the facts and the analyses, for example, in *Campbell v. Acuff-Rose Music, Inc.* (1994) and *Rogers v. Koons* (1992), where both used large, core portions of the original work in question, but the parody use in the former was judged to be fair and the satirical use in the latter case was not granted fair use. The U.S. Copyright Office maintains a searchable database of fair use cases (https://www.copyright.gov/fair-use) intended to help make the principles and application of fair use more understandable.

Something New

While there are many foundational elements of the Constitution as well as statutory laws and agency regulations designed to govern that still endure to this day, there are many new alternatives for media businesses interested in expanding creative work across digital distribution platforms.

ALTERNATIVES

Not everybody agrees that the traditional intellectual property protection structures are the best way to encourage the growth of creative work or to capitalize on the possibilities created by various digital distribution platforms. Alternative copyright schemes have emerged in recent years, most notably Creative Commons, that are intended to be more flexible and cognizant of digital realities. Creative Commons offers a set of legal tools that enable creators to easily tailor permissions for potential uses of their work through six different copyright license types plus an "all rights" public domain placement (Creative Commons, n.d.). Several digital platforms distribute Creative Commons–licensed content, including YouTube, Vimeo, Bandcamp, Flickr, Public Library of Science, Wikipedia, and European Collections.

INTERNATIONAL COPYRIGHT

There is no global copyright (or trademark) protection, but nearly every country recognizes intellectual property rights to some extent. There are various treaties and other agreements in place that afford rights holders some ability to enforce copyright internationally,* although registrations in multiple jurisdictions may be necessary in some cases. These include:

- *The Berne Convention* (1886; most recently amended in 1979): this agreement establishes minimum standards for the types of works protected, the duration of copyright, certain limitations and exceptions, and basic principles such as "automatic protection" (copyright applies as soon as a qualified work is fixed in a tangible medium). The United States is among 177 signatory countries.
- *World Intellectual Property Organization (WIPO) Copyright Treaty* (1996): this special agreement under the Berne Convention deals with the digital environment, protecting computer programs and databases, and recognizes that Internet transmission is among the exclusive rights within the scope of copyright. The United States is among slightly more than 100 signatories.
- *Agreement on Trade Related Aspects of Intellectual Property Rights* (1996): commonly known by the acronym TRIPS and administered by the World Trade Organization, this requires that national laws make effective enforcement of intellectual property rights possible and describe in detail how enforcement should operate.

TRADEMARK

Trademarks and service marks cover identifying symbols (including but not limited to words, images, and graphics) that serve to distinguish goods or services provided by a business from those offered by competitors. Trademarks provide protection against competing uses that could cause confusion in the public's mind (infringement), that might tend to cause deterioration of the distinctiveness of the mark (dilution), and against anyone making misrepresentations about a protected product (disparagement). The term of trademark protection is 10 years. Although this is much shorter than the term covered by copyright, trademarks can be repeatedly renewed as long as they remain in use, and they can be registered up to three years in advance of use.

Applying for trademark protection is far more difficult than registering a copyright, primarily because searching for existing, potentially competing marks is complicated,

*The U.S. Copyright Office maintains a listing and description of bilateral and multilateral agreements with other countries around the world, https://www.copyright.gov/circs/circ38a.pdf.

and making judgments about possibly confusing marks requires detailed knowledge and experience. It is possible to perform basic searches using the U.S. Patent and Trademark Office's (PTO) online tool if you have some conception of what you would like to protect (https://www.uspto.gov/trademarks-application-process/search-trademark-database); however, it is wise to engage a licensed U.S. attorney with substantial trademark expertise to conduct a thorough analysis of your proposed mark and help you move forward through filing an application. An attorney is required by law if you are not a U.S.-domiciled individual or company. In addition, once you have successfully registered your trademark, your attorney is likely to be very helpful in protecting and enforcing your rights, including providing advice on monitoring for potential infringing, diluting, or disparaging uses and making sure renewals are filed in a timely manner.

Like other long-standing legal factors, trademark law continues to evolve and thus has new aspects, such as types of marks, that must be refused or that may be granted. The trademark statutes list several categories for which registration shall be refused, including any mark that "consists of or comprises immoral, deceptive, or scandalous matter; or matter which may disparage or falsely suggest a connection with persons, living or dead, institutions, beliefs, or national symbols, or bring them into contempt, or disrepute" (15 U.S.C §1052(a)).

Native Americans had been pressing to revoke the trademark protection for the Washington Redskins team in the National Football League based on that statutory requirement since 1992, winning an appeal with the PTO in 1999 that then led to years of subsequent rounds in federal court before it looked like the team was going to finally lose protection in 2014 (Shapira & Marimow, 2017). However, two other cases working their way through the courts at approximately the same time seem to have eliminated most, if not all, enforcement of the immoral, scandalous, and disparagement portions of that section and effectively restored the team's marks along with those that had been denied in the other cases. In each of these cases, the Supreme Court held that denying a trademark violated the Free Speech Clause of the First Amendment because the asserted government interest in preventing an alleged harm under §1052 constituted viewpoint discrimination and violated the expressive interests of the parties attempting to register a mark.

In the first case, Simon Tam sought registration for the name of his band, The Slants. The examining staff attorney at the PTO denied the application under §1052 because *slants* is a derogatory term for persons of Asian heritage, falling under "disparaging" in the law. Tam appealed, arguing that taking the word as the name of his band was an attempt to diminish its denigrating power by reclaiming the word and that he and his band had a First Amendment right to the name. A unanimous Supreme Court agreed (8–0) that the denial of trademark registration violated Tam's constitutional rights, although the justices had varying approaches to reaching that conclusion (Matal v. Tam, 2017).

The second case focused on the immoral or scandalous block, and the court once again found that the decision to deny a registration violated the First Amendment by disfavoring a particular expression. Erik Brunetti is the creator of a clothing line he branded FUCT. According to Brunetti, the name is pronounced as a series of letters (F-U-C-T), but as Justice Kagan's majority opinion recognized, you would not be alone if you read it as "the past participle of a well-known word of profanity." After walking through multiple examples where the PTO had accepted registrations for marks conveying a socially approved position on issues from religion to drug use while denying marks conveying less widely held or mostly unacceptable positions on those or similar subjects under the provisions of the statute, the court found that the law obviously discriminated based on viewpoint and thus was unconstitutional (Iancu v. Brunetti, 2019).* For now, it would appear that there are few, if any, blocks to registering and protecting trademarks featuring offensive symbolism.

SOCIAL MEDIA MARKETING

Rules prohibiting deceptive or fraudulent advertising have long been in place, so the basic principles are well established. It should be transparent to the audience when something is a commercial message, the sponsor of the message must be identified, and advertising must be truthful in making any factual claims. Because we have lengthy history with traditional broadcast and print media, adult audiences easily recognize what is an ad, while television content targeted to children has additional restrictions to account for their less developed ability to analyze the commercial messaging (Federal Communications Commission, 2019b). However, those principles are finding new applications as they are employed to regulate marketing within media like Instagram or Snapchat posts, blogs, or YouTube videos, particularly when it comes to "influencers." If somebody you know tells you how much they enjoy a particular beverage or how they loved staying at a certain hotel on vacation or that the service at a restaurant was fantastic, you might be inclined to check it out yourself. However, if you knew they had been paid to tout the beverage or their hotel stay was comped or the chef at the restaurant was catering a dinner at their house the next night for free, you might view their recommendation differently. That is the heart of the concern about the use of endorsements in advertising.

The Federal Trade Commission has taken the position that advertisers are obligated to train and monitor what is said about them by people with whom they have a material connection, which can be money or other valuable consideration such as a free product (Federal Trade Commission, 2017). Disclosures of a material relationship need to be clear and conspicuous, even if they have to use valuable and limited space in social media (Federal Trade Commission, 2017). The FTC has published (and regularly updates) useful guidelines for marketers and advertising media, including case examples (Federal Trade Commission, 2019b) that can be found on their website.

Opportunities and Challenges

There are many changes to law and policy that have taken on greater importance in the 21st century, where audiences are more individualized with access to more content and more control of when, where, and how that access occurs in a digital media

*Although the court was unanimous that *immoral* represented unconstitutional viewpoint suppression, and six justices felt that the statute could not be saved by a more narrow interpretation of either word, Justices Sotomayor and Breyer and Chief Justice Roberts felt that *scandalous* could be more narrowly construed to only include "obscenity, vulgarity, and profanity." Because words meeting those legal definitions can sometimes be legally proscribed, this may leave an opening for a future Congress to attempt to redraft this section of the law.

environment. This dynamic media landscape provides many opportunities and challenges for future media practitioners.

OPPORTUNITIES

Regulators have faced many challenges in staying current with evolving marketing practices taking place across digital media and especially via social media platforms. In the United States, the FTC is the independent regulatory agency that Congress has charged with protecting consumers against fraudulent, unfair, or deceptive practices (Federal Trade Commission, 2019a). The FTC also works to educate consumers and businesses about their rights and responsibilities in the marketplace. As such, they have a significant role where digital technologies have given rise to new media issues—digital media marketing, particularly the use of influencers in social media, and the collection of personal (private) information online, particularly that of children.

REGULATION OF OWNERSHIP AND ANTITRUST

Regulations governing media ownership have been a hotly debated topic throughout the past 100 years, starting in radio's infancy with who should control the means of broadcasting and continuing to today. In most other countries, ownership of broadcasting was originally reserved to the government, but in the United States, a private and mainly commercial system was developed right away, with some limits on ownership as well as some content requirements. For a long time, there were explicit numerical caps on the number of radio (and later television) stations one entity could own. These national maximums grew over time, from 7 to 14 to 20 stations in a service, with limits also on the number of outlets one could control in a local market. That bright-line structure was largely overhauled by the 1996 Telecommunications Act (§202) along with subsequent actions by the FCC that responded to a mandate in the 1996 act to periodically review all ownership rules and discard or change those found to be no longer in the public interest (§402). Although a few aspects of the old system remain in place, particularly a cap on national TV ownership along with sliding-scale limits based on market size governing the number of properties one owner can have in a market as well as various combinations of media in a local market (Federal Communications Commission, 2019), the 1996 act moved broadcast ownership into an era where the size and reach of a company were limited primarily not by statute and FCC rule but by their available capital and the guidance of antitrust law. As large media companies (or large companies with significant media involvement, like Amazon or Facebook) have dramatically grown in the past 20 years, and grown not just in the United States but globally, various antitrust regulators have become significant.

The foundation of antitrust law is much like the premise of the First Amendment—a free and robust marketplace benefits society, in this case economically. Competition in a marketplace encourages lower prices, better quality, and service and product innovation. Antitrust regulation has existed for more than a century in the United States. The Sherman Act (1890) together with the Federal Trade Commission Act and the Clayton Act (1914) still form the basis for federal antitrust regulation (Department of Justice, n.d.).

In addition to the statutory authority for enforcing these laws delegated to the Department of Justice and to the FTC, the FCC also engages in antitrust oversight when mergers or acquisitions involve firms under their regulation, and many states have antitrust laws as well. It is now common for very large mergers or acquisitions to face review on several levels before a transaction is approved. Several proposed mergers involving media and telecommunication companies at the time this chapter was written faced inquiries on multiple federal and state fronts, including Nexstar/Tribune and T-Mobile/Sprint.

Provisions of the Clayton Act (and subsequent legislation amending it) form the basis of many antitrust issues faced by media firms. The Clayton Act prohibits mergers and acquisitions where the effect "may be substantially to lessen competition, or to tend to create a monopoly" (§7). An amendment in 1936 prohibited certain discriminatory prices, services, and allowances in dealings between merchants. For example, a cable or satellite TV company acquiring the operator of several major television channels might raise concerns among competitors that the new company would either provide the channels to their own service at a lower price or refuse to sell popular offerings to them outright. The Clayton Act was amended again in 1976 to require companies planning large mergers or acquisitions to provide advance notification to the government of their plans (Federal Trade Commission, 2019c). Several recent large combinations would have required notification under this provision, including Comcast's acquisition of NBCUniversal from GE in 2011 (originally a 51% stake, Comcast assumed 100% control in 2013), Universal Music's purchase of EMI's recorded music operations in 2012, and AT&T's merger with Time Warner in 2019. The advance notice allows regulatory staff and company representatives to identify major issues with the deal early in the process and to begin working on remedies.

Enforcement of the Clayton Act requires complex analyses of a company's market power and the potential effects on competition that would result from a merger. Analysts at the FTC and the antitrust division of the Department of Justice, as well as the FCC, employ various economic tools (e.g., Pittman, 2017) to define the relevant market (based on geography, product, relationships with customers and suppliers) and consider whether the proposed combination would allow the new firm to leverage excessive market power resulting in harm to consumers or causing unfair competitive situations for other market participants. It is a very different way of regulating ownership of media than bright-line, number-of-outlets rules. The regulators have a number of options available to them when a deal poses potential problems, including setting additional terms and conditions or blocking the combination entirely. The FCC's analysis is slightly different, as they not only look at competition and market effects but also inquire as to whether the combined firm will be likely to create positive public interest benefits for audiences.

The recent acquisition of Tribune's television stations by Nexstar is a good example of how this analysis functions. Both the Department of Justice and the FCC analyzed the deal, along with attorneys general in three states, looking at various markets that would be impacted. The Department of Justice's antitrust division was focused on television advertising in the markets where the companies had stations and on the retransmission consent deals between the station owners and pay TV providers in those markets. The issue was whether permitting the combined company to retain multiple stations in many markets would allow them to leverage that combination in ways that harmed other market participants. Justice ultimately approved the deal (and the state attorneys general also signed on) but required Nexstar to sell a station in 13 markets to address concerns that, absent those divestitures, Nexstar would be able to "'charge cable and satellite companies higher retransmission consent fees to carry the combined company's broadcast stations, resulting in higher monthly cable and satellite bills for millions of Americans,' as well as higher spot prices in the divestiture markets," which would harm local businesses (Eggerton, 2019, quoting Department of Justice). The FCC concluded their analysis two months later, approving the deal as structured in the consent agreement with the Department of Justice. In the FCC's analysis, following the merger "viewers would benefit from their local stations having increased access to Nexstar's Washington, DC, news bureau and state news bureaus. Additionally, Nexstar demonstrated that it would invest savings resulting from the merger into its stations, including investments in ATSC 3.0, the next-generation television broadcast standard" (Federal Communications Commission, 2019c). It's worth noting that each regulatory body allowed Nexstar to retain multiple stations among the top four stations in several markets, so divestiture was not required everywhere.

Antitrust rules in the European Union (EU) are similar in structure to those in the United States, prohibiting agreements between two or more firms that serve to restrict competition in a market (the classic example here would be a cartel structure) and prohibiting any firm holding a "dominant" position in a market from abusing that position, for example, by charging unfair prices, limiting production, or refusing to innovate to the detriment of consumers (European Commission, 2014). Interpretation of those rules, however, has been widely perceived to be more consumer friendly (or more restrictive of business) than in the United States, although authorities there have cleared large mergers including 21st Century Fox's 2017 acquisition of Sky. That combination joined the leading pay-television operator in several EU member countries, including Germany, Italy, and the United Kingdom, with one of the six major film and TV studios in Hollywood that is also the operator of several TV channels, including Fox and National Geographic. Analyzing the proposal in the context of affected member states, the regulators concluded that the combination would produce only a limited increase in Sky's existing share of the markets for the acquisition of video programming as well as in the market for the wholesale supply of television channels (European Commission, 2019). Overall, there is a clear trend toward permitting media firms to grow in scope and reach. Media managers face questions about how to best position their companies for these opportunities as well as deal with convergent challenges, whether it is by adding to their portfolio or looking for potential suitors who may wish to acquire them.

CHALLENGES

One of the most challenging concerns for tomorrow's media practitioners is the changing regulations regarding audience privacy across media platforms. Failure to understand and comply with these regulations could be detrimental to success in tomorrow's convergent environment.

PRIVACY

As the commercial Internet rolled out in the 1990s, some citizens and legal experts began to raise concerns about the ability of digital platforms to gather information about audiences engaging with websites and other online platforms. Although privacy is potentially a concern for anybody online, this was particularly a concern regarding young children, who likely would not have the knowledge to understand how personal information they provided in order to watch something online might be used. Responding to those concerns, Congress passed the Children's Online Privacy Protection Act (COPPA) in 1998 in an effort to give parents control over what information could be collected from their children online. The legislation tasked the FTC with developing specific regulations and enforcing them. The FTC issued the initial rule in 2000; the most recent amendments took effect in 2013.

Under COPPA, children are defined as under 13 (§1302), so the law does not apply to teenagers. Affected online services include

- commercial websites and online services (including mobile apps) that are directed to children that collect, use, or disclose personal information from children;
- general audience websites or online services if they know they are collecting, using, or disclosing personal information from children; and
- websites or online services that have actual knowledge that they are collecting personal information directly from users of another website or online service directed to children. (Federal Trade Commission, 2015)

Covered services are required to meet several standards for parental notification and consent, along with maintaining data security. Specifically, online services subject to COPPA must

- post a clear and comprehensive online privacy policy describing their information practices for personal information collected online from children;
- provide direct notice to parents and obtain verifiable parental consent, with limited exceptions, before collecting personal information online from children;
- give parents the choice of consenting to the operator's collection and internal use of a child's information, but prohibiting the operator from disclosing that information to third parties (unless disclosure is integral to the site or service, in which case, this must be made clear to parents);
- provide parents access to their child's personal information to review and/or have the information deleted;
- give parents the opportunity to prevent further use or online collection of a child's personal information;
- maintain the confidentiality, security, and integrity of information they collect from children, including by taking reasonable steps to release such information only to parties capable of maintaining its confidentiality and security; and

- retain personal information collected online from a child for only as long as is necessary to fulfill the purpose for which it was collected and delete the information using reasonable measures to protect against its unauthorized access or use. (Federal Trade Commission, 2015)

Failing to comply with the rule can be a costly mistake. The FTC levied a $5.7 million fine against Musical.ly, the operator of short-form video app TikTok, for knowingly collecting personal information from children and failing to meet COPPA's requirements for parental notification (Burstein, 2019).

The FTC was in the process of reviewing the rule at the time this chapter was written, seeking public comment on the rule's application to the educational technology sector, to voice-enabled connected devices, and to general audience platforms that host third-party child-directed content (Request for Public Comment, 2019), so it is quite possible there will soon be new amendments.

Probably the most significant change to privacy law in at least a few decades took place in 2018, when the European Union passed the EU General Data Privacy Regulation with detailed requirements affecting how organizations collect, use, disclose, or process personal information. The law obviously affects media businesses primarily located in the EU but can also potentially reach any media firm doing business with a customer in the EU (de Lozier et al., 2018), for example, a company in the United States streaming video or delivering a podcast to somebody in Germany. It applies to the use of "cookies" for tracking and profiling behavior as well as to information directly provided by an individual (de Lozier et al., 2018)—perhaps you've seen the pop-ups asking for your consent to use cookies that many websites began employing after the rule took effect. The General Data Protection Regulation takes a very broad view of personal information, including online usernames and identifiers that have not typically been considered "identifiable" in the United States. Another substantial requirement is that privacy policies and consent requests must be clearly and intelligibly written (de Lozier et al., 2018)—the intent is to force online services to stay away from the type of lengthy, dense, jargon-filled legal documents that most people regularly ignore. As with other rules, failing to comply can be costly with fines of up to €20 million or 4% of a company's annual revenue (whichever is higher) possible for the most egregious violations (de Lozier et al., 2018).

DYNAMIC MEDIA LANDSCAPE

Not only are privacy laws and regulations ever-changing; technologies and audiences are transforming almost every culture. The single greatest challenge facing media industry managers from a legal perspective is simply keeping up with the changes in areas of the law and regions of the world that affect their business.

Although change is a constant in most aspects of media, and as this chapter pointed out there are many underlying principles that have remained steady, significant and detailed shifts in the legal landscape seem to happen almost weekly as policy makers, legislators, and regulatory agencies struggle to keep up. For media managers, this can mean repeated cycles of strategy adjustment as they respond to (and try to anticipate) market shifts and legal changes. Several sections of this chapter, including discussions of trademark, privacy, and antitrust, would be significantly different if they had been written just a year or two earlier. It would be surprising by the time you're reading this if there were not at least a few things that have either changed or newly emerged since this chapter was written. Facing this ever-evolving media marketplace, managers may follow the action plan below.

ACTION PLAN

1. Research the key legal aspects related to your work and your company's strategies and operations.
2. Understand nuances between intellectual property rights, advertising regulations, and privacy regulations for media corporations.
3. Consult legal professionals for guidance on long-term strategic planning initiatives.
4. Integrate legal resources into the daily planning and everyday rituals in your organization.

KEY TAKEAWAYS

1. Media managers need to be able to incorporate legal factors into strategic planning and daily decision making.
2. The possibly relevant legal factors include statutes, regulations, and case law. What might be legally important is determined by the geographic and product markets in which a company operates. Media businesses are affected by both general business legal factors as well as industry-specific laws and regulations. Those laws may be local, state, or national in their coverage. Businesses may also need to take laws in multiple countries and various international agreements into consideration.
3. The laws affecting media businesses are complex. Statutes, regulations, court precedents, and international agreements are constantly evolving. The risks posed by costly legal mistakes need to be mitigated by incorporating expert legal advice in planning and decision-making processes.

CONCLUSION

Legal considerations affect nearly every aspect of media business strategy and managerial decision making. Constitutional guarantees of freedom of speech and of the press enable journalists to report on issues of public concern and enable society to hold institutions accountable. Intellectual property statutes and treaties provide a framework that makes it possible for media creators and distributors to profit from their efforts, while fair use and public domain ensure that society benefits from other opportunities to build on those works. Some legal structures are intended to prevent harm to the public, so there are agency regulations that prohibit false or misleading marketing practices and limit the ways advertisers can target vulnerable children. Privacy rules enable individuals to determine if and how information about them can be collected, used, and shared by advertisers and others.

Although this chapter has discussed some of the most significant aspects of the law related to media, practitioners will encounter many more issues. These may stem from legal elements generally applicable to all businesses, such as labor or tax law, or things that are very specific to a particular media niche, such as the requirements and processes that come with a broadcast license for radio or television or the Federal Aviation Administration rules governing the use of drones that might be used for aerial photography by journalists. Media firms must also be constantly aware of issues that may drive additional regulation and adopt strategies to address those situations. Those may include adopting self-regulation approaches intended to preempt formal laws, lobbying legislative bodies considering statutes or regulations, and business shifts to remain competitive if the legal landscape changes.

This chapter outlined some of the significant ways that global, national, and local legal factors can affect a media business; introduced some of the key regulatory actors; and discussed examples of how legal issues can inform management decisions. An understanding of these basic elements will prepare you for more detailed and complex discussions on these topics and other legal matters that you will have with legal professionals representing your company's interests along with the other members of your team and will enable you to effectively incorporate legal factors in your decision making. While the law provides a framework, a series of guideposts that set boundaries around what media can do, or in some cases direct what must be done, the law is generally silent on the question of what should be done. In making decisions about strategy or day-to-day operations, managers must incorporate additional factors in their decision making. Those factors are the subject of other chapters in this book, including the next one. Ethical principles are important considerations for media managers making decisions that meet their fiduciary responsibilities to their companies, their employees, and their audiences. The next chapter will discuss ethical issues faced by media managers in today's convergent environment, particularly in the news media.

REFERENCES

Abrams v. United States, 250 U.S. 616 (1919).

Agriculture Improvement Act of 2018, Pub. L. 115-334, codified at 7 U.S.C. §§178, 1508, 1518, 1639.

Burstein, A. (2019, March 5). *FTC obtains record $5.7 million fine for children's privacy protection act violation*. Broadcast Law Blog. https://www.broadcastlawblog.com/2019/03/articles/ftc-obtains-record-5-7-million-fine-for-childrens-privacy-protection-act-violation

Campbell v. Acuff-Rose Music, Inc. 510 U.S. 569 (1994).

Children's Online Privacy Protection Act of 1998, Pub. L. 105-277, codified at 15 U.S.C. §§6501–6505.

Citizens United v. Federal Elections Commission, 558 U.S. 310 (2010).

Creative Commons. (n.d.). *Creative commons licenses*. https://creativecommons.org/about/cclicenses

De Lozier, E., Burstein, A., & Bercu, J. (2018, June 15). *What do broadcasters and media companies need to know about the GDPR?* Broadcast Law Blog. https://www.broadcastlawblog.com/2018/06/articles/what-do-broadcasters-and-media-companies-need-to-know-about-the-gdpr

Department of Justice. (n.d.). *Antitrust enforcement and the consumer*. https://www.justice.gov/atr/file/800691/download
Eggerton, J. (2019, July 31). *Justice OKs Nexstar-Tribune merger with divestitures*. Broadcasting & Cable. https://www.broadcastingcable.com/news/justice-oks-nexstar-tribune-merger-with-divestitures
Entertainment Software Rating Board. (n.d.). *Ratings*. https://www.esrb.org/ratings
European Commission. (2014, November 11). *Antitrust overview*. https://ec.europa.eu/competition/antitrust/overview_en.html
European Commission. (2019, July 25). *Mergers: Commission clears 21st Century Fox's proposed acquisition of Sky under EU merger rules*. https://europa.eu/rapid/press-release_IP-17-902_en.htm
Federal Communications Commission. (n.d.). *Organizational charts of the FCC*. https://www.fcc.gov/about-fcc/organizational-charts-fcc
Federal Communications Commission. (1987). *In re* Complaint of Syracuse Peach Council against Television Station WTVH Syracuse, New York, 2 FCC Rcd 5043.
Federal Communications Commission. (2015, December 10). *Statutes and rules on candidate appearances and advertising*. https://www.fcc.gov/media/policy/statutes-and-rules-candidate-appearances-advertising
Federal Communications Commission. (2019a, May 15). *FCC broadcast ownership rules*. https://www.fcc.gov/consumers/guides/fccs-review-broadcast-ownership-rules
Federal Communications Commission. (2019b, July 19). *Children's educational television*. https://www.fcc.gov/consumers/guides/childrens-educational-television
Federal Communications Commission. (2019c, September 16). *FCC grants approval of Nexstar-Tribune merger*. https://www.fcc.gov/document/fcc-grants-approval-nexstar-tribune-merger
Federal Communications Commission. (2019d, December 30). *Obscene, indecent and profane broadcasts*. https://www.fcc.gov/consumers/guides/obscene-indecent-and-profane-broadcasts
Federal Communications Commission v. Fox Television Stations, 567 U.S. 239 (2012).
Federal Communications Commission v. Pacifica, 438 U.S. 726 (1978).
Federal Trade Commission. (2015). *Complying with COPPA: Frequently asked questions*. https://www.ftc.gov/tips-advice/business-center/guidance/complying-coppa-frequently-asked-questions
Federal Trade Commission. (2017). *The FTC's endorsement guides*. https://www.ftc.gov/tips-advice/business-center/guidance/ftcs-endorsement-guides
Federal Trade Commission. (2019a). *About the FTC*. https://www.ftc.gov/about-ftc
Federal Trade Commission. (2019b). *Advertisement endorsements*. https://www.ftc.gov/news-events/media-resources/truth-advertising/advertisement-endorsements
Federal Trade Commission. (2019c). *The antitrust laws*. https://www.ftc.gov/tips-advice/competition-guidance/guide-antitrust-laws/antitrust-laws
Federal Trade Commission. (2019d). *What we do*. https://www.ftc.gov/about-ftc/what-we-do
Fourth Estate Public Benefit Corp. v. Wall-Street.com, 139 S. Ct. 881 (2019).
Humphries, M. A., & Songer, D. R. (1999). Law and politics in judicial oversight of Federal Administrative Agencies. *The Journal of Politics, 61*, 207–220.
Iancu v. Brunetti, 588 U. S. ____; 139 S. Ct. 2294 (2019).
Kosarzycki, S. (2017, December 22). *It's a wonderful life*. Library of Congress. https://blogs.loc.gov/copyright/2017/12/its-a-wonderful-life
Lee, T. B. (2019, January 1). *Mickey Mouse will be public domain soon—here's what that means*. https://arstechnica.com/tech-policy/2019/01/a-whole-years-worth-of-works-just-fell-into-the-public-domain
Matal v. Tam, 582 U.S. ___; 137 S. Ct. 1744 (2017).
Miami Herald Publishing Co. v. Tornillo, 418 U.S. 241 (1974).
Miller, G. P. (1988). The debate over independent agencies in light of empirical evidence. *Duke Law Journal, 1988*, 215–222.
Motion Picture Association. (n.d.). *The film rating system*. https://www.filmratings.com
National Archives. (n.d.). *The Bill of Rights: A transcription*. https://www.archives.gov/founding-docs/bill-of-rights-transcript

National Archives. (n.d.). *The Constitution of the United States: A transcription.* https://www.archives.gov/founding-docs/constitution-transcript
Oxenford, D. (2016, October 20). *More lawsuits for unauthorized use of photos—even on social media sites.* Broadcast Law Blog. https://www.broadcastlawblog.com/2016/10/articles/more-lawsuits-for-unauthorized-use-of-photos-even-on-social-media-sites
Oxenford, D. (2018, February 22). *Court finds that embedded Twitter photo on website may subject website owner to copyright liability.* Broadcast Law Blog. https://www.broadcastlawblog.com/2018/02/articles/court-finds-that-embedded-twitter-photo-on-website-may-subject-website-owner-to-copyright-liability-be-careful-what-you-post
Oxenford, D. (2019, March 25). *Advertising for CBD—Safe for broadcasters?* Broadcast Law Blog. https://www.broadcastlawblog.com/2019/03/articles/advertising-for-cbd-safe-for-broadcasters
Oxenford, D. D., & O'Connor, D. A. (2019, June). *Political broadcasting 2020.* Wilkinson Barker Knauer, LLP. https://www.wbklaw.com/uploads/file/Articles-%20News/Political%20Broadcasting(2).pdf
Peters, J. (2018, May 24). Why every media company fears Richard Liebowitz. *Slate.* https://slate.com/news-and-politics/2018/05/richard-liebowitz-why-media-companies-fear-and-photographers-love-this-guy.html
Pittman, R. (2017). *Three economist's tools for antitrust analysis: Economic analysis group discussion paper.* https://www.justice.gov/atr/page/file/925641/download
Reno v. American Civil Liberties Union, 521 U.S. 844 (1997).
Request for Public Comment on the Federal Trade Commission's implementation of the children's online privacy protection rule—proposed rule. 84 FR 35842 (2019). https://www.federalregister.gov/documents/2019/07/25/2019-15754/request-for-public-comment-on-the-federal-trade-commissions-implementation-of-the-childrens-online
Selin, J. L. (2015). What makes an agency independent? *American Journal of Political Science, 59,* 971–987. doi: 10.1111/ajps.12161
Shapira, I., & Marimow, A. E. (2017, July 29). Washington Redskins win trade fight over team's name. *Washington Post.* https://www.washingtonpost.com/local/public-safety/2017/06/29/a26f52f0-5cf6-11e7-9fc6-c7ef4bc58d13_story.html
Smith, R. A. (2019, March 14). *The fourth estate decision and copyright registration.* Library of Congress. https://blogs.loc.gov/copyright/2019/03/the-fourth-estate-decision-and-copyright-registration/
Sonny Bono Copyright Term Extension Act. (1998). Pub.L. 105–298, codified at 17 U.S.C.
TV Parental Guidelines Monitoring Board. (2019). *TV parental guidelines.* http://www.tvguidelines.org
United States Constitution. (1992). https://www.govinfo.gov/content/pkg/GPO-CONAN-1992/pdf/GPO-CONAN-1992-6.pdf
United States Copyright Office. (2019). *International copyright relations of the United States.* https://www.copyright.gov/circs/circ38a.pdf
United States Courts. (n.d.). *Court role and structure.* https://www.uscourts.gov/about-federal-courts/court-role-and-structure
United States Patent and Trademark Office. (2019). *Search trademark database.* https://www.uspto.gov/trademarks-application-process/search-trademark-database
Yoakum, K. (2019, May 6). *Do's and don'ts: Advertising CBD products.* Thought Leadership. https://thoughtleadership.oaaa.org/dos-and-donts-advertising-cbd-products

CHAPTER 9

Making Ethical Choices in the News Media

Jenn Burleson Mackay, Virginia Tech

LEARNING OBJECTIVES

1. Understand complex ethical issues in the news media in today's convergent environment.
2. Apply research-developed concepts to enact a plan for addressing ethical challenges in the news media.
3. Identify and address potential ethical dilemmas in the news media.

Technology and media convergence have transformed the ways that the news media collect and share news and information. Journalists affiliated with newsrooms are no longer the only people sharing updated content to the world. They are competing with and, in some cases, collecting information from nonprofessional journalists—those people who post updated content to their own social media pages throughout the day. Technology has given media the ability to sift through massive amounts of data in the pursuit of news. Sometimes that data might be loaded with information about unsuspecting individuals who had no idea that their personal information was so readily available. Media managers must ensure that their staff recognizes those ethical issues and considers how to best serve their audiences without causing harm. As Black and Roberts (2011) state, "A society that expects its citizens to be informed and its consumers to be discriminating must be served by moral media" (p. 1).

This chapter will delve into the complex issues that surround the news media, which is loaded with technological tools but also faces financial challenges and concerns from a public that decreasingly trusts journalists (Ingram, 2018). It will consider tried-and-true ethical concepts such as conflicts of interest and accuracy, which continue to be important to the modern news media. Finally, it will examine technologies that are creating new concerns and opportunities for journalists, such as public data and drones. It will suggest that the public be given a voice in evaluating the media's approach to ethics.

The Society of Professional Journalists (2014) proclaims that "ethical journalism should be accurate and fair." The organization's code of ethics explains that "ethical journalism treats sources, subjects, colleagues, and members of the public as human beings deserving of respect," and "journalists should balance the public's need for information against potential harm or discomfort." Often, media technologies challenge traditional assumptions of audience privacy, right to information, and news coverage. Let's explore one such new media function, autoplay, and the case study of the 2015 shooting in Roanoke, Virginia.

CASE STUDY

Reporter Alison Parker was on air when the shooting started. Audiences watching the station's morning show heard eight shots and the reporter's screams before Roanoke's WDBJ-7 news crew cut away from the live video feed. Television screens reverted back to a stunned anchor sitting at a news desk. Both Alison Parker and photojournalist Adam Ward died from wounds sustained during the August 2015 gun attack (Shear, Pérez-Peña, & Blinder, 2015). The live shooting was covered heavily by the national news media. Many news organizations linked to video of the shooting or even embedded video that had aired live on the morning show. That video often began playing on users' screens through an autoplay function, forcing unsuspecting viewers to watch the live attacks whether they wanted to see them or not (Abbruzzese, 2015). Those audience members who came across autoplay content had no opportunity to decide whether they wanted to press the Play button on the video. The video simply sprang to action as viewers looked at the screen.

Police soon learned that the shooter was a disgruntled former colleague from the news station. He took video of himself waiting for and watching the journalists. He recorded himself firing at the reporters and posted videos taken from his perspective to Twitter and Facebook (Shear et al., 2015). One of the videos was shared more than 800 times before it was removed by the social media provider. Many audiences encountered the video through the autoplay function integrated across multiple social media platforms. The idea of autoplay video was still relatively new when the shooting took place. There was no law in place to determine how journalists should handle the content. That left journalists across the country to decide for themselves how to handle disturbing but prolific media content.

Current law provides journalists some guidance as to what they can and cannot do. They know that they can be sued for revealing private facts about an individual, such as someone's mental health status or sexual orientation. Journalists know that they can be sued for publishing erroneous information that ruins an individual's reputation. The law, however, fails to address one critical issue—what *should* journalists do? For example, there was no law to prevent journalists from posting disturbing videos of the shootings of Parker and Ward. There was no law that required the news media to turn off the autoplay feature for the videos. The lack of legal ramifications may protect news managers in a court of law, but that doesn't ensure that the media will do the *right* thing.

One might argue that newsrooms made a mistake in judgment when they embedded or aired the video of the shootings of the two Roanoke journalists, particularly since audiences often had no choice in whether they wanted to see the content. The news media might have caused harm to audience members who had no interest in seeing the content as well as to the families of the two shooting victims. Yet, this was new terrain for the news media. Never had a journalist shot two of his own colleagues during a live broadcast. The on-air deaths of Parker and Ward illustrate the complex world that journalists face as technology rapidly transforms. Nonetheless, technology has not eliminated the tried-and-true boundaries of ethical journalism. Concepts such as conflict of interest and accuracy still lie at the heart of journalism.

Something Old

Technology has transformed how news gathering takes place and how information is shared. Many of the fundamental aspects of ethical journalism, however, have remained consistent, even in a convergent era. Concerns about conflicts of interest still linger throughout the profession, whether one considers an overt conflict such as a reporter covering a business where they own stock or merely something that might be perceived as a conflict of interest, such as a journalist expressing an opinion about a political figure on a personal social media site. Though the concept may not immediately seem to be directly related to ethics, the need for accurate information remains ever-present in journalism, particularly as political figures, pundits, and audiences shout taunts about "fake news." This section will explore how both of these issues continue to be important to journalists and their audiences.

CONFLICTS OF INTEREST

The Society of Professional Journalists' Code of Ethics proclaims that journalists should "act independently" and "avoid conflicts of interest, real or perceived. Disclose unavoidable conflicts" (Society of Professional Journalists, 2014). There are two important aspects to that statement. The emphasis is on both actual and *perceived* conflicts of interest. This indicates that journalists should disclose information that audiences might perceive as a bias even if the journalists do not feel that the issue is a conflict of interest. One might think of this as being transparent with the audience. Conflicts of interest might take several forms. Wasserman (2009) explains, "Broadly, conflict of interest comprises a variety of instances where undeclared obligations or loyalties exist that might plausibly intervene between journalists or journalism organizations and the public they principally serve" (p. 229). Wasserman suggests that conflicts of interest must be avoided because they can damage the trust between the audience and the news organization. He argues that trust matters because it demonstrates that the journalist has good intentions (Wasserman, 2009).

In 1999, the *Los Angeles Times* made a deal with the Staples Center in downtown Los Angeles. The paper published a 168-page special issue and devoted all the content to the Staples Center. The newspaper shared the advertising profits from the publication with the Staples Center. Readers called and wrote to the paper to complain that the agreement damaged their trust in the publication (Shaw, 1999). Research has shown that advertising does influence news content, particularly if a news organization is reliant on advertising from a specific industry, such as fashion (Rinallo & Basuroy, 2009). Advertising directors who work at smaller news organizations tend to be more likely to support decisions that please advertisers despite risking damage to the credibility of the news organization (An & Bergen, 2007). Reports show that advertisers do try to influence content in various ways. They may threaten to withdraw advertising if they don't see the content that they prefer in a publication (Hays & Reisner, 1990). Sometimes, news organizations admit that they give in to the demands of their advertisers (Soley & Craig, 1992). By giving in to the advertisers, the news media may withdraw content that could be damaging to the advertiser, even if that story is true and important to their audience. If news managers are unable to prevent advertisers from influencing content, the public has little reason to trust the news organization. If the public does not trust the media provider, they have little reason to continue viewing its content.

Politics is another sensitive area where conflicts of interest can arise. The *New York Times* specifies in their lengthy ethics code that employees cannot do anything that would damage "*Time*'s reputation for strict neutrality in reporting on politics and government; in particular, no one may wear campaign buttons or display any other form of political partisanship while on the job" (New York Times, 2020). Many news organizations don't allow employees to hold political office. At the very least, news organizations frequently prohibit employees from holding political positions if those positions conflict with the employee's obligations to the news organization (Davenport & Izard, 1985).

NPR faced criticism after it fired Lisa Simeone, a freelance music host. Simeone was fired for participating in an Occupy D.C. protest group, an offshoot of the Occupy Wall Street movement. NPR employees are not allowed to participate in political protests. Simeone, however, was allowed to keep her job after the organization was criticized for the firing (Folkenflik, 2011). Similarly, multimedia journalist James Bunner was fired from a local television station when management discovered that he had worn a "Make America Great Again" hat to a Trump rally that he covered. The station's news director said that staff members were not permitted to wear political gear while covering stories (AP News, 2018). There are cases where journalists have left the news industry to work in politics. Then, those same journalists make a return to the newsrooms. When this has happened, one study suggests that journalists tend to return to the newsroom through one of four methods: (1) the journalist chooses to avoid covering politics; (2) the journalist is not allowed by the editors to go straight back into covering news; (3) the journalist takes time off between the political role and returning to news; (4) the journalist goes straight back into political reporting but addresses conflicts of interest as they develop (Fisher, 2016).

The long-standing boundary between politics and journalism has been met with challenges as social media has spread into newsrooms. Research suggests that political journalists typically don't feel comfortable sharing their opinions online (Rogstad, 2014). Many news organizations, such as the *New York Times* and BBC, have policies that recommend that journalists keep their company's reputation in mind as they interact online (Bedei, 2018).

Former *Quill* editor Joe Skeel argued that it is impossible for journalists to avoid every potential conflict of interest. He suggests following these two rules: "If you feel like you might be too close to a source, you probably are. The only protection you have as a journalist is to always write with the complete truth, even if it puts your source in a bad light. If you aren't prepared to do that, it's time to step back from the relationship or get out of the job" (Skeel, 2005, p. 3).

ACCURACY

Accuracy lies at the foundation of good journalism. The news media must have it in order to maintain an audience. Yet, one might ask, "How is accuracy an ethical issue?" For example, what if a journalist gets a number wrong in a story and then someone calls them to tell them to correct it? Then, what if that journalist chooses to ignore that phone call and the inaccurate information continues to linger on web pages? The reporter who chooses to not make that change has made an ethical decision, which left unchecked could harm the credibility of the news organization. Consider the firing of NBC anchor Brian Williams. The anchor was leading the number-one evening broadcast, NBC *Nightly News*, when he publicly acknowledged that he had misled viewers when he said that he had been shot down in a helicopter while covering a story in Iraq. Soldiers who knew what had happened during his visit to Iraq had challenged his embellished version of the story. Williams was initially suspended from his position for six months. Then he was permanently removed from his position. The anchor later moved to MSNBC and quickly rose through the ranks again (Steinberg, 2017).

Williams's removal from a top-ranked news show, however, demonstrates the importance that news organizations place on accuracy, even if the accuracy is reflected by the statements that one makes about oneself. Fabrication can take other forms. One might argue that the master of fabrication was the *New York Times*'s Jayson Blair. One ethicist used the work of Mahatma Gandhi to emphasize the importance of truth to journalism. He argued that truth can only be achieved by the moral journalist (Merrill, 1997).

Photography is another place where accuracy continues to be important. Digital technology has made it easy to remove insignificant details from photos. One might blur out a distracting element that is taking the viewer's eye away from the primary focus. On the other hand, one might add a little something to the photograph to make the image more appealing. That's exactly what Allan Dietrich did when he worked for the *Toledo Blade*. Dietrich resigned from his job after editors discovered that he had altered a sports photo. Following an investigation, the news organization discovered that the award-winning photographer had submitted 947 photos to the news organization during a three-month period. Of those, 79 had been altered. He had removed people, tree limbs, and other elements from photos. Sometimes he added shrubbery or branches to a photograph. After making this discovery, the news organization removed all the photographer's work from the news website. They explained the importance of not manipulating photographs this way: "Journalism, whether by using words or pictures, must be an accurate representation of the truth" (Royhab, 2007). Both professional photographers and citizen photographers tend to view digital manipulation of photographs as unacceptable (Mortensen, 2014). Manipulation of an image, even in the slightest way, distorts a moment in time. When viewers realize that the image isn't an accurate representation, they might question other content in the publication. After all, if one journalist is willing to distort an image to make it more appealing, what other facts might that news organization change to their own liking?

Something New

Lukis Anderson's DNA nearly got him convicted of murder (Worth, 2018). *Frontline*, in a partnership with the Marshall Project and *Wired*, published a story explaining how DNA contamination could have cost Anderson his life. In addition to describing Anderson's history and the science of DNA testing, the 2018 story delved into the original homicide. The publication included a photograph of the 2012 murder scene. It also described the location and the body of the victim. It briefly described the marital status of the victim and discussed his relationship with sex workers (Worth, 2018).

While that story may have opened the public's eyes to the problems with an over-reliance on DNA evidence in crime cases, it opened up old wounds for the victim's family. Daughter Raina Kumra described the experience in a piece published in the *Columbia Journalism Review*. She acknowledged that the *Frontline* piece was newsworthy, but she questioned the way that organizations handled the story. She described the publication as a revictimization of her family. "For me, the promotional teasers on social media were worse than the piece itself: They featured an audio recording of my mother, frantic and distraught in the worst moments of her life, calling 9-1-1 to report the crime. The audio is played over police body camera footage of the first responders arriving on the scene, with my father's dead body clearly visible on the floor," (Kumra, 2018). In the same publication, Kumra describes her horror in learning that the organizations were also planning to create a virtual reality experience of the murder scene.

New technology has given journalists access to unprecedented amounts of information and new ways to share that information to wider audiences than ever before. A 9-1-1 tape that might have only been featured a single time on a nightly news broadcast can now be shared over and over again on social media. Journalistic virtual reality is in its infancy but still offers a new opportunity to news organizations that are hungry for audiences in a competitive news market. It's easy to get lost in the technological wonder and to forget about the real people who can be affected by every part of our storytelling process.

Journalists are able to create massive databases to search for trends, making interactive graphics to make data easy to digest. Everyone has the ability to share their own opinions of news stories or even their own videos of events through social media sites such as Twitter and YouTube. The news media then has the opportunity to incorporate that information into their own news stories. Journalists even have the ability to launch drones in the sky in pursuit of news. It's like living in a journalistic labyrinth surrounded by technological marvels, but at every turn we face an ethical dilemma. A wrong decision could cause irreparable damage to victims, communities, the journalism profession, or the news organization. The following section will explore some of the ethical challenges that journalists face in light of these new opportunities.

BIG DATA AND ETHICS

New technology has provided journalists with the ability to get easy access to troves of information. It has also given them new tools for analyzing and displaying that information for audiences. Shortly after the 2012 shootings at Sandy Hook Elementary, the White Plains *Journal News* used public records to create an interactive map that showed the names and addresses of gun owners in its readership area. The public responded with angry phone calls and letters. The newspaper hired a security guard to keep employees safe. Eventually, it removed the map (Goodman, 2013). That didn't happen until after a local blogger published his own clickable map that showed the names and addresses of employees of the *Journal News* (Trotter, 2012). The publisher of the newspaper stated that the purpose of the map was to educate parents so they could keep their children safe. The map, however, sparked arguments about privacy and the rights of gun owners.

While the newspaper relied on public information that anyone could have obtained, it organized the data in a way that made it easy for audiences to understand, even if viewers had otherwise never needed that information. Al Tompkins of the Poynter Institute argues that the newspaper's mistake was that it failed to provide enough depth to justify the decision to violate the privacy of gun owners. "When we publish private information, we should weigh the public's right to know against the potential harm publishing could cause" (Tompkins, 2012). Tompkins suggests that if privacy must be compromised, a news story should provide important insight into an issue. In other words, just because the data is accessible does not justify its use, particularly where issues of privacy are concerned.

Andrew Seaman of the Society of Professional Journalists' ethics committee responded to the gun map fiasco by suggesting a set of guidelines for journalists to use in dealing with public information. His first step is to question the relevancy of the information. There's no need to confuse the audience with data they don't need. His second step is to ask whether the data might cause harm. He suggests asking colleagues for advice and emphasizes the importance of minimizing harm as much as possible. The final step is to be prepared to defend the use of the information. He also suggests including an explanation for why the material was used within the news story that uses the information.

One of the major issues brought by big data is the sheer volume of data that individuals can access. While the information may be publicly accessible, it is possible that people who contributed that information are not aware of how their information is being used. Some groups of people will inevitably feel singled out by the use of the data. Discretion should be used when one chooses to work with a data set. There is value in journalists talking with the community before they choose to release big data sets. This can help them understand the potential harms related to that information. One might think of these steps as a way for social science scholars and journalists to learn from one another the best ways to use data ethically (Fairfield & Shtein, 2014).

REPORTING WITH DRONES

The news media is still relatively new to the use of drones as a reporting tool. There is inevitably potential for these flying robots to provide photography or video that can enhance news stories. They might be used to provide aerial imagery of storm damage or analytic data such as wind speed during a hurricane. There are Federal Aviation Administration guidelines that govern the legal use of drones. Still, there are other ethical concerns, which are outlined by Culver (2014). One issue is securing the safety of people who are in the vicinity of the drone. Is the use of the drone worth the risk of the vehicle malfunctioning and hurting a bystander? It may be important to weigh the public interest in the information that can be provided by the drone against the potential risk. Culver notes the importance of providing context with the images that are provided by the drone. An image without context might confuse or mislead the audience.

Journalists who use drones must have preset guidelines that determine how information collected by these tools should be managed. News organizations should have a plan in place that prevents them surrendering their drone data to authorities on request. This is to prevent the government using the media as its own tool. "News media cannot allow themselves to be used by authorities as a means to circumvent civil liberties" (Culver, 2014, p. 60). Drones should be used by journalists only when they will not infringe on the rights of other people (Culver, 2014).

Newsrooms that intend to use drones should prepare their communities for that technology before they insert them into coverage. There is a possibility that people will not be comfortable when they first notice drones flying above them. Newsrooms should also develop their own plans to govern the use of the technology and make sure that the community knows about those rules. It will be valuable for residents to understand how the use of drones will benefit the community (Kadado, 2016).

SOCIAL MEDIA

For years, journalists have been told that they can't have bumper stickers supporting a particular political candidate on their cars. They have been instructed to keep their personal political preferences out of news stories and to avoid participation in political protests. The goal has always been to avoid the appearance of bias inside and outside the newsroom. Now, social media has created a new platform for everyone to share their thoughts and experiences. It's often a minefield of political debate. News organizations have been struggling to figure out exactly how social media should feed into the work and personal lives of journalists. Many newsrooms inevitably tackle this issue within their ethics codes. Still, mistakes can be made.

Consider the issue of gay marriage. After the U.S. Supreme Court struck down parts of the Defense of Marriage Act in 2013, a barrage of people flooded social media either to show their support for biblical interpretations of marriage or to show their support for gay rights. Even journalists dived into the fray. Some apparently felt that the Supreme Court's ruling was so historic that traditional journalistic rules didn't apply. Radio and Television News Directors Association chairman Vincent Duffy bemoans journalistic reaction to the case: "For the same reason we as journalists should not participate in protest marches, sign petitions, or donate money to candidates, we should not be celebrating or criticizing Supreme Court decisions in social media," he argues (Duffy, 2013). One way or another, management needs to ensure journalists have guidance as to where the line should be drawn between their own right to freedom of expression and the news industry's need to protect its credibility (Rector, 2008).

Opportunities and Challenges

New technology has given audiences a variety of ways to dissect and publicly criticize the work of journalists. Audiences have been empowered and given the opportunity to publish their own news stories to mass audiences. Yet the technology has created new ethical challenges as journalists incorporate new tools into their work. It has given journalists the ability to work collaboratively on stories with global importance and has created new storytelling methods that couldn't have been imagined a few years ago. Leaked documents have become an important storytelling opportunity for the industry, but it can be difficult for journalists to confirm the details of the leaks. This raises questions as to whether unverified information should be published. These new tools offer a promising new future to news employees and an opportunity to communicate directly with their audiences. At the same time, new technology has led to job losses and funding concerns for the news media. Layoffs have plagued the industry, and news organizations have searched for alternative funding sources. The industry is at a crossroads.

OPPORTUNITIES

New technology offers journalists new ways to approach the news. While social media provides its share of challenges, it offers journalists a new way to gather and verify information. It is irresponsible for journalists to write stories solely based on the information that is gathered from social media sites. Yet, social media posts can serve as a starting point that guides journalists to particular stories or news sources. For journalists who are open to engaging with an audience as part of the reporting process, social media can allow the public to be collaborators in the reporting process (García de Torres & Hermida, 2017). One might consider the online conversations between journalists and the public as a benefit of two-way communication. By looking at social media conversations as a sort of collaboration, it may be possible for journalists to strengthen their credibility with the audience.

Feighery (2011) suggests that one way for journalists to maintain their credibility in the world of new technology is by engaging in a two-way symmetrical communication that's similar to the work done by public relations practitioners. He offers four steps in this communication process. First, he suggests that journalists must publicly justify their decisions. They need to explain why a specific source was included in a news story. Second, media practitioners must be prepared to contextualize their decisions. They need to help the public understand why decisions are made. That may mean publicly publishing ethics codes. Next, the news media should ask their audience to provide feedback about the standards and practices that the newsroom is using. Allow the public to say if they disagree with a particular practice and have a conversation about the issue. Finally, he suggests that journalists should have conversations with the public regularly. The media tends to have a habit of engaging the public in conversations only when a reporting crisis has occurred (Feighery, 2011).

If used regularly, this model could empower journalists to use new technology to strengthen their relationship with the audience. It could help the media at a time when rumors of "fake news" run rampant on the Internet. New technology has aided journalists in developing new investigative journalism techniques. Rather than a single reporter or a small group of reporters in a single newsroom working on investigative stories, newsrooms are collaborating on large-scale projects, such as the Panama Papers project, a global investigation into tax evasion, which was completed by 300 journalists working internationally on a single project. Collaborative projects existed previously, but they have increased in recent years along with technological advances (Carson & Farhall, 2018). This gives newsrooms that may have strapped budgets the opportunity to be involved in important stories that might have otherwise never been covered.

CHALLENGES

Perhaps the biggest challenge that journalists face today is money. The old tried-and-true method of relying on advertisers to pay the bills is obsolete. Newsroom employee staffing dropped by 23% between 2009 and 2017. Most of those losses were in the newspaper industry (Grieco, 2019). During one week in January 2019, roughly 1,000 media jobs were lost through layoffs at BuzzFeed, HuffPost, and Gannett (Darcy & Kludt, 2019). CareerCast (2018) named newspaper reporter the sixth most stressful job of 2018, followed by broadcaster. The company creates its annual career ranks by looking at categories such as career growth potential, competition, meeting the public, hazards encountered, and deadlines.

Ekdale, Tully, Harmsen, and Singer (2015) considered how journalists have responded to concerns about job security. They found that journalists tended to respond in one of three ways. Hopeful journalists, often those in management, tended to feel secure in their jobs. They tended to support new company goals and propose innovative ideas. Obliging employees, on the other hand, tried to maintain their own job satisfaction while not delving into new company initiatives. Fearful and cynical journalists felt that they could not risk failure. They feared the consequences that would follow making a mistake. They felt that the company was making the wrong decisions (Ekdale et al., 2015). Findings illustrate the importance of helping employees to feel secure in their work if management hopes for them to support new newsroom initiatives.

The crisis in the industry has led many news organizations to experiment with new funding concepts. Several organizations have attempted crowdfunding, in which organizations rely on supporters to finance the coverage of news stories. The model has been used with several online news start-ups. In these cases, journalists often act as both reporters and fundraisers. The relationship can cause concern about journalists maintaining their independence from their audiences (Porlezza & Splendore, 2016).

Research suggests that donors tend to be well educated and young and feel that there isn't enough local news coverage. Donors have reported that their primary motivations for supporting crowdfunding journalism are their belief in freedom of content, altruism, and supporting the community. Having fun and supporting reporters that they know were additional motivations, but there is some question as to whether these two motivations are enough to sustain crowdfunded reporting (Jian & Shin, 2015). There are also concerns about the workload involved in raising money for crowdfunded journalism. The amount of work involved in raising funds is the equivalent of a journalist having a second full-time job. Some journalists are uncomfortable with the idea of raising their own funds for stories. The process comes into conflict with traditional journalistic news-gathering routines. There are journalists, however, who feel empowered by the opportunities offered to work outside of the traditional news model. Some see it as an opportunity to change the practice of journalism (Hunter, 2016).

Crowdfunded journalism is an interesting option in terms of sustaining journalism. News organizations that decide to experiment with this method need to consider the ethical concerns associated with this use. It may be worthwhile to consider publishing a list of donors to ensure that crowdfunding is not being used as a means to control or manipulate content. It's also useful to be transparent throughout the reporting process to show the audience how the information for the story was gathered and why some details were included in the story while others were left out.

Another challenge is dealing with leaked information. Leaks are not new to the world of journalism, but as technology has improved, more leaked information has flooded the Internet. Journalists have had to decide how to handle that information. What happens if they cannot confirm the details in the leaked information? Should they go ahead and publish it and risk someone beating them to the story, or do they take their time to confirm the facts? For example, a 35-page dossier alleging that the Russian government had compromising information about Donald Trump floated around Washington for several weeks before BuzzFeed decided to publish all of the unconfirmed details. Traditional news organizations avoided publishing the unverified dossier, but after BuzzFeed published the story, everyone started talking about the details, whether they were fact or fiction. The situation is further complicated by sources who refuse to talk to journalists unless they are promised anonymity. These sources may be able to verify leaked information, but audiences question the credibility of anonymous sources. This puts journalists in a difficult situation (Marcus, 2017). Navigating the information age in a new media environment presents journalists and managers in news organizations with many opportunities and challenges. Journalists should use the action plan below to help guide moral and ethical decision making in the field.

ACTION PLAN

1. Pay attention to potential conflicts of interest for both the overall organization as well as for individual news workers. Determine whether posting political content or opinions on private social media accounts will be permitted. Provide guidelines to staff members that explain what content is not acceptable on social media.
2. Follow the guidelines of two-step communication, and help the public understand how new technologies will be used and how they will be beneficial to the community. Provide context in terms of news decisions as well as technological adoption. Talk with the public regularly about news decisions and use of new technologies.

If attempts at crowdfunding are made, explain those decisions and opportunities to the public. Make transparency a goal.

3. Consider the people who are likely to be affected by content before you publish. Avoid publishing content just because you can. Likewise, weigh the benefits of using invasive technology before it is used. Consider the harm that a story or a news-gathering tool might cause before a story is published.
4. Pay attention to the morale of news workers as the industry continues to evolve. Strive to keep morale high and to help employees see the potential of new initiatives. Help them feel secure in their jobs.

KEY TAKEAWAYS

1. The traditional expectations of conflicts of interest are still important to the news media. Managers need to give employees guidance as to what that means in terms of their personal social media accounts.
2. The news media is still the historical record for society. Accuracy should be maintained whether that means correcting errors as they are recognized or ensuring that photos depict the truth.
3. News workers should be careful to avoid unnecessary harm to victims or the public in general. Consider the individuals who could be affected by a story before content is published.
4. Consider the implications of using new technology before it is used. Have a plan in place ensuring that the public is protected and that the news media is not treated as an arm of law enforcement.
5. Engage the public in discussion about the decisions being made by the media. Allow them to discuss areas where they feel the news media has made an error in judgment.
6. Be transparent. Allow the public to see how news decisions are being made. Explain why a particular story is written. Provide context to help the community understand the purpose of a story.
7. When dealing with funding problems and new initiatives to boost viewership, pay attention to the morale of employees. Help them see the potential for their own successes in new ventures.

CONCLUSION

Ethics are important to sustaining the credibility of the news media. While journalism is a business institution, it is also an ethical service to the public. Research suggests that only 21% of adults in the United States have a lot of trust in the news media; compare that with 49% who have some trust and 29% who have very little or no trust in the news media (Mitchell, Gottfried, Barthel, & Sumida, 2018). The popularity of the phrase *fake news* in modern rhetoric means the news media is dealing with a problem of public trust. If audiences don't trust journalists, they have little reason to view news content. A misinformed public is a great detriment to society.

Technology offers new opportunities for the media to involve the public in the news-gathering process. Yet, technology needs to be used responsibly to ensure that it doesn't add to trust problems that the public already has with the news media. For example, the media has access to troves of data that can be analyzed and published to illustrate trends. Before that data is used, however, the media need to consider whether publication might cause harm to the public. Journalists should consider the fact that people likely did not realize that the information they provided to various organizations would be eventually analyzed by the news media. Their data should be treated with care. Just because data is available does not mean that the news media should incorporate it into their business strategy. Similarly, the public might feel as though the media is intruding on their privacy while using technology such as drones. An effort should be made to educate the public on these tools before they become part of the news-gathering routine. Similarly, classic concepts such as conflicts of interest are important to maintaining public trust. Audiences need to feel that they can trust journalists to be honest with their reporting. They need to feel that outside forces, or personal biases, are not influencing the coverage. It's important to address the perception of conflicts of interest as well as actual conflicts. Policies should be in place to provide news workers with guidance on handling potential conflicts.

Transparency is key to maintaining a credible relationship with the public. While technology provides a variety of ways of gathering information, it also offers the possibility for providing more context to the public. It can be used to help the public understand how content for stories was gathered and why journalists believed that a particular technology was necessary for developing a story. It also offers the public a way of contacting the newsroom when they are concerned about particular news-gathering methods or stories. Employing the two-way communication method as described by Feighery (2011) can help managers consider ways to involve the public in news discussions. However, this additional stream of communication increases workload for a working environment that is minimizing employees. It is important that journalists are respected and treated with care, while some may be doing the work previously completed by two or three employees. Additionally, journalists must be compensated for all required elements of their job, including required professional social media communication. Issues of ownership and copyright in a digital age must be the focus of future research in this field.

While the public should have some voice in the modern news media, managers need to decide how much involvement audiences should have. If the public is invited to invest in news stories through crowdfunding projects, a line must be drawn that allows reporters some degree of independence from those who financially support the product. Journalists need to be trained in the tried-and-true rules of ethics that have been fundamental to the industry for years, such as telling the truth, serving as a watchdog, and being a voice for the disadvantaged. They also need to be prepared to deal with the ethical questions that can arise from new technology. Future practitioners need to see that while technology provides access to treasure troves of information, journalists have a responsibility to consider the consequences of using technology and the harm that some news stories can cause.

The modern news media is facing a number of financial challenges as people have become accustomed to free news and information. Technology has shifted how the news is gathered and shared. It has also changed what the public expects from journalists and how audiences consume content. Jobs in the industry have been lost, and some employees worry about the financial well-being of the industry around the globe. Nonetheless, news and information industries are important to maintaining a democracy. The next chapters will explore the importance and the unique opportunities and challenges of media management in a global age.

REFERENCES

Abbruzzese, J. (2015, August 26). *Harrowing video of WDBJ7 news crew shooting ignites debate about autoplay*. Mashable. https://mashable.com/2015/08/26/video-shooting-controversy

An, S., & Bergen, L. (2007). Advertiser pressure on daily newspapers: A survey of advertising sales executives. *Journal of Advertising, 36*, 111–121.

AP News. (2018, October 5). *Minnesota TV reporter fired for wearing Trump hat at rally*. https://apnews.com/8e92405dba1f4d429427fb9da0931bf6/Minnesota-TV-reporter-fired-for-wearing-Trump-hat-at-rally

Bedei, C. (2018, September 13). *How can journalists engage with politics on social media?* International Journalists Network. https://ijnet.org/en/story/how-can-journalists-engage-politics-social-media

Black, J., & Roberts, C. (2011). *Doing ethics in media: Theories and practical applications*. Routledge.

CareerCast. (2018). *The most stressful jobs of 2018*. https://www.careercast.com/jobs-rated/2018-most-stressful-jobs

Carson, A., & Farhall, K. (2018). Understanding collaborative investigative journalism in a "post-truth" age. *Journalism Studies, 19*, 1899–1911.

Culver, K. B. (2014). From battlefield to newsroom: Ethical implications of drone technology in journalism. *Journal of Mass Media Ethics, 29*, 52–64.

Darcy, O., & Kludt, T. (2019, January 24). *Media industry loses about 1,000 jobs as layoffs hit news organizations*. CNN Business. https://www.cnn.com/2019/01/24/media/media-layoffs-buzzfeed-huffpost-gannett/index.html

Davenport, L. D., & Izard, R. S. (1985). Restrictive policies of the mass media. *Journal of Mass Media Ethics, 1*(1), 4–9.

Duffy, V. (2013, July 11). *Journalism ethics apply to social media*. RTDNA. https://www.rtdna.org/article/journalism_ethics_apply_to_social_media

Ekdale, B., Tully, M., Harmsen, S., & Singer, J. B. (2015). Newswork within a culture of job insecurity: Producing news amidst organizational and industry uncertainty. *Journalism Practice, 9*, 383–398.

Fairfield, J., & Shtein, H. (2014). Big data, big problems: Emerging issues in the ethics of data science and journalism. *Journal of Mass Media Ethics, 29*, 38–51.

Feighery, G. (2011). Conversation and credibility: Broadening journalism criticism through public engagement. *Journal of Mass Media Ethics, 26*, 158–175.

Fisher, C. (2016). Managing conflict of interest: Shifting between political PR and journalism. *Journalism Practice, 10*, 373–386.

Folkenflik, D. (2011, October 20). *Protest role does not cost public radio host her job on opera program*. NPR. https://www.npr.org/sections/thetwo-way/2011/10/20/141560182/protest-role-does-not-cost-public-radio-host-her-job-on-opera-program

García de Torres, E., & Hermida, A. (2017). The social reporter in action: An analysis of the practice and discourse of Andy Carvin. *Journalism Practice, 11*, 177–194.

Goodman, J. D. (2013, January 2). Journal news hires armed guards after outcry over map. *New York Times*. https://www.nytimes.com/2013/01/03/nyregion/putnam-officials-keep-gun-permit-records-from-journal-news.html

Grieco, E. (2019, July 9). *U.S. newsroom employment has dropped by a quarter since 2008, with greatest decline at newspapers*. Pew Research Center. https://www.pewresearch.org/fact-tank/2019/07/09/u-s-newsroom-employment-has-dropped-by-a-quarter-since-2008

Hays, R., & Reisner, A. (1990). Feeling the heat from advertisers: Farm magazine writers and ethical pressures. *Journalism Quarterly*, 40, 42.

Hunter, A. (2016). "It's like having a second full-time job": Crowdfunding, journalism and labour. *Journalism Practice, 10*, 217–232.

Ingram, M. (2018, September 12). Most Americans say they have lost trust in the media. *Columbia Journalism Review*. https://www.cjr.org/the_media_today/trust-in-media-down.php

Jian, L., & Shin, J. (2015). Motivations behind donors' contributions to crowdfunded journalism. *Mass Communication and Society, 18*, 165–185.

Kadado, C. (2016). *FAA clarifies use of drones for newsgathering*. The EIJ News. https://eijnews.org/2016/09/19/faa-clarifies-use-of-drones-for-newsgathering

Kumra, R. (2018). Even ethical journalism can have collateral damage. *Columbia Journalism Review*. https://www.cjr.org/first_person/frontline.php

Marcus, J. (2017). The ethics of leaks: The increasing use of anonymous sources and leaks has intensified the debate over how to vet information and sources. *Nieman Reports, 71*(3), 14–23.

Merrill, J. C. (1997). *Journalism ethics: Philosophical foundations for news media*. St. Martin's Press.

Mitchell, A., Gottfried, J., Barthel, M., & Sumida, N. (2018, June 18). *Can Americans tell factual from opinion statements in the news*. Pew Research Center. https://www.journalism.org/2018/06/18/distinguishing-between-factual-and-opinion-statements-in-the-news

Mortensen, T. M. (2014). Blurry and centered or clear and balanced? Citizen photojournalists and professional photojournalists' understanding of each other's visual values. *Journalism Practice, 8*, 704–725.

New York Times. (2020). *Ethical journalism*. https://www.nytimes.com/editorial-standards/ethical-journalism.html

Porlezza, C., & Splendore, S. (2016). Accountability and transparency of entrepreneurial journalism: Unresolved ethical issues in crowdfunded journalism projects. *Journalism Practice, 10*, 196–216.

Rector, K. (2008). Murky boundaries: What are the guidelines for the personal blogs of journalists who work for mainstream news organizations. *American Journalism Review, 30*(3), 40–48.

Rinallo, D., & Basuroy, S. (2009). Does advertising spending influence media coverage of the advertiser? *Journal of Marketing, 73*(6), 33–46.

Rogstad, I. D. (2014). Political news journalists in social media: Transforming political reporters into political pundits. *Journalism Practice, 8*, 688–703.

Royhab. (2007, April 15). A basic rule: Newspaper photos must tell the truth. *The Blade*. https://www.toledoblade.com/frontpage/2007/04/15/A-basic-rule-Newspaper-photos-must-tell-the-truth.html

Shaw, D. (1999, December 20). Crossing the line. *Los Angeles Times*. https://www.latimes.com/archives/la-xpm-1999-dec-20-ss-46240-story.html

Shear, M., Pérez-Peña, R., & Blinder, A. (2015, August 27). Ex-broadcaster kills 2 on air in Virginia Shooting: Takes own life. *New York Times*. https://www.nytimes.com/2015/08/27/us/wdbj7-virginia-journalists-shot-during-live-broadcast.html

Skeel, J. (2005, April 1). For many journalists, life is a conflict of interest. *Quill Magazine*. https://www.quillmag.com/2005/04/01/for-many-journalists-life-is-a-conflict-of-interest

Society of Professional Journalists. (2014). *Code of ethics*. https://www.spj.org/ethicscode.asp

Soley, L. C., & Craig, R. L. (1992). Advertising pressures on newspapers: A survey. *Journal of Advertising, 21*(4), 1–10.

Steinberg, B. (2017, October 24). Brian Williams opens up about regaining viewers' trust after scandal. *Variety*. https://variety.com/2017/tv/news/brian-williams-msnbc-11th-hour-trust-trump-1202597588

Tompkins, J. (2012, December 27). *Where the journal news went wrong in publishing names, addresses of gun owners*. Poynter. https://www.poynter.org/reporting-editing/2012/where-the-journal-news-went-wrong-in-publishing-names-addresses-of-gun-owners
Trotter, J. (2012, December 27). Newspaper that published gun-owner addresses gets its staff's info outed. *The Atlantic*. https://www.theatlantic.com/politics/archive/2012/12/newspaper-published-gun-owner-addresses-gets-its-staffs-info-outed/320128
Wasserman, E. (2009). Conflict of interest enters a new age. In L. Wilkins & C. G. Christinas (Eds.), *The handbook of mass media ethics* (pp. 229–241). Routledge.
Worth, K. (2018, April 19). *Framed for a murder by his own DNA*. The Marshall Project. https://www.themarshallproject.org/2018/04/19/framed-for-murder-by-his-own-dna

PART III

GLOBALIZATION

CHAPTER 10

Transnational Media and Business Strategy

Global Messages in the Digital Age

Richard A. Gershon, Western Michigan University

LEARNING OBJECTIVES

1. Describe three reasons why media companies engage in foreign direct investment.
2. Understand how over-the-top video streaming services have transformed the international delivery of television and film programs.
3. Understand the purpose of a mergers and acquisitions strategy.
4. Describe the business model and delivery systems that underlie electronic commerce with a special emphasis given to the principle of exchange efficiency.
5. Recognize the changing nature of global message design, specifically as it pertains to electronic commerce and social networking.

A transnational corporation (TNC) is a nationally based company with overseas operations in two or more countries. One distinctive feature of TNCs is that strategic decision making and the allocation of resources are based on economic goals and efficiencies with little regard to national boundaries. The transnational media corporation (TNMC) is the most powerful economic force for global media activity in the world today. Through a process of foreign direct investment, TNMCs actively promote the use of advanced media and information technology on a worldwide basis. This has become a salient feature of our present-day global economic landscape (Athique, 2016; Bartlett & Beamish, 2014; Gershon, 1997, 2013; Strube, 2010). This chapter will consider some of the important business strategies now being employed by a new generation of transnational media corporations.

We begin with the argument that the study of transnational media management has changed in light of three significant business and technology shifts. The first shift is the importance of the Internet and broadband delivery (Zang, 2018). During the 21st century, the Internet has been steadily woven into all aspects of business and leisure. The Internet, specifically electronic commerce (EC), has created a new business model that maximizes the potential for instantaneous communication to a worldwide customer base (Albarran, 2013; Amit & Zott, 2001; Gershon, 2014, 2017; Kung, 2008). The second business/technology shift is the importance of digital media, which represents the artistic convergence of various kinds of hardware and software design elements to create entirely new forms of communication and expression (Dogruel, 2014; Gershon, 2017; Levinson, 2013; Wong, 2009). From social media sites like Facebook to over-the-top video streaming services like Netflix and YouTube, digital media has proven to be the seminal 21st-century game changer in terms of worldwide message delivery and storytelling (Athique, 2016; Lambert, 2012).

The third business/technology shift is the very transnational media companies themselves. In the past, the term *transnational media* was most often associated with media enterprises like the Walt Disney Company, Time Warner Inc., and the Sony Corporation, to name only a few. Today, transnational media has come to include such companies as Amazon, Facebook, Google, and Netflix. The new generation of TNMCs represents a solid blending of media, technology, and electronic commerce. Each relies heavily on the Internet and the power of intelligent networking and algorithmic functioning. This is clearly evident in the following case study.

CASE STUDY

Amazon is a transnational media and electronic commerce company headquartered in Seattle, Washington. Company founder, Jeff Bezos, incorporated the company in July 1994. Today, Amazon is the largest EC retailer in the world. In 1994, Bezos resigned his position as vice president at D. E. Shaw, a Wall Street firm, and moved to Seattle. He began to work on a business plan that would serve as the blueprint for what would become Amazon. The basic idea was to create a mail-order catalog using the Internet and the power of intelligent networking.

Amazon started with online books, given the large worldwide demand for literature, the low price points for books, and the large number of titles available in print. At the time, there were no significant mail-order book catalogs. To build a substantial mail-order catalog covering books in all areas of arts, sciences, and humanities would require an encyclopedia-like publication. The cost for publication and distribution would be prohibitive. The solution, of course, is the Internet, which is ideally suited to organizing and displaying a limitless amount of information. Bezos reasoned that such information could be organized and put online. Within its first two months of operation, the company was selling and distributing books in all 50 states in the United States as well as in 45 other countries (Brandt, 2011). While the largest bookstore chains in the United States might carry 200,000-plus titles, an online bookstore can offer several times that, since it does not require the same level of warehouse space when compared to a traditional retailer.

From the beginning, Bezos took a careful and long-term view of his business. He did not expect to make a profit for several years. Two decades later, Bezos presides over an EC company that has redefined online shopping for billions of people worldwide. The value proposition for all would-be Amazon customers is exchange efficiency, which can be translated in one of three ways: selection, convenience, or low prices, factors that are central to the Amazon business model and philosophy (Gershon, 2017).

Amazon employs a multilevel e-commerce strategy. In its formative years, Amazon focused on business-to-customer electronic commerce. The challenge was to become more fully diversified in terms of product and service offerings. In time, they incorporated customer reviews and leveraged such information as a way to sell more products and services as well as improve the customer experience. Amazon is a highly innovative company and has adopted the principle of boundary spanning in three specific ways. Each area is a natural extension of what Amazon already does (Stone, 2013).

Amazon Web Services is a collection of cloud computing services offered via the Internet. The expression "putting something on the cloud" refers to the idea of storing information and data on a remote host site. Amazon's most daring strategy is its foray into business-to-business services. In recent years, Amazon has greatly expanded its cloud computing services by leasing out server capacity in its large data centers around the world so that small businesses do not have to make large upfront investments in computing infrastructure. One such client happens to be Netflix.

Amazon has also greatly expanded its third-party marketplace, where merchants all over the world can set up their own virtual stores on Amazon and sell their products alongside Amazon's—all while leveraging Amazon's large customer base and credit-card-processing capability. Both retailers and individual sellers alike use Amazon to sell goods. Large retailers like Target and Nordstrom use Amazon to sell their products in addition to selling them via their own websites.

In November 2007, Amazon launched its Amazon Kindle—an e-book reader. Most analysts agree that Amazon probably sold its original Kindle hardware at breakeven or a small loss to subsidize media sales. With the original Kindle, Amazon pioneered the sale of digital books and as a result owns more than 90% of their distribution. By July 2010, Amazon e-book sales for its Kindle reader outnumbered sales of hardcover books for the first time ever. The Amazon Kindle is much more than an e-reader and computer tablet. It represents the foundation of an entire media ecosystem. Specifically, the Kindle Fire is a computer tablet, media store, platform for digital media sales, and publishing imprint. The goal is to make all of Amazon's digital media product offerings part of the company's digital ecosystem, which includes (1) Amazon EC, (2) digital books, (3) Amazon Prime video streaming, (4) Amazon Prime music, and (5) Amazon EC software applications. This is media convergence in its most essential form.

Something Old

For many years, scholars used the term *transborder data flow* to describe the international flow of voice, data, and video communication across national borders (Fair, 1987). Through a process of foreign direct investment (FDI), TNMCs actively sell and distribute television/film entertainment, news, and EC goods on a regular basis. At issue is the fact that TNMCs possess a level of power and influence that is second only to nation-states. It is not surprising, therefore, that the globalization of media activity poses a unique dilemma for many host nations.

For some, the instantaneous flow of information across geographic borders presents a direct challenge to national sovereignty. On one hand, there are the clear benefits of international free trade and the specific advantages that TNMCs offer, including jobs, investment capital, technology resources, and so forth. On the other hand, there are the problems associated with media imports, including cultural trespass, challenges to political sovereignty, privacy invasion, and possible economic control. In this next section, we consider the importance of FDI from a business strategy perspective.

FOREIGN DIRECT INVESTMENT

Foreign direct investment refers to the ownership of a company in a foreign country. This includes the control of assets. As part of its commitment, the investing company will transfer some of its managerial, financial, and technical expertise to the foreign-owned company. The decision to engage in FDI is based on the profitability of the market, growth potential, regulatory climate, and existing competitive situation (Blaine, 2009). TNMCs are arguably better able to invest in the development of new media products and services than are smaller, nationally based companies or government-supported industries. There are three primary reasons that help explain why a company engages in FDI: proprietary assets and natural resources, foreign market penetration, as well as production and distribution efficiencies.

PROPRIETARY ASSETS AND NATURAL RESOURCES

Some TNCs invest abroad for the purpose of obtaining specific proprietary assets and natural resources. The ownership of talent or specialized expertise can be considered a type of proprietary asset. Sony Corporation's purchase of Columbia Pictures in 1989 enabled the company to become a formidable player in the field of television and film entertainment. The company would undergo a name change to Sony Pictures Entertainment. Rather than trying to create an altogether new company, Sony purchased proprietary assets in the form of exclusive contracts with some of the world's leading film producers and directors as well as acquiring a dedicated film library. Sony was then well positioned to combine the company's technology expertise with its newly acquired television / film capability.

FOREIGN MARKET PENETRATION

A second consideration is the recognized need to expand into new markets. Some TNMCs invest abroad for the purpose of entering a foreign market and serving it from that location. The market may exist or may have to be developed. While TNMCs are indeed highly global in their approach to business, few companies operate in all markets of the world. Instead, TNMCs tend to operate in preferred markets with a decided preference (and familiarity) toward one's home market (Gershon, 1997, 2000). Buying an existing media or telecommunication property is the easiest and most direct method of market entry. This was the strategy employed by Japan-based Softbank Group when it acquired Sprint-Nextel in 2013 for $21.6 billion. The acquisition has given Softbank a presence in the United States by acquiring a well-respected telecommunications company. In the process, Softbank has infused Sprint (now T-Mobile) with needed cash to compete with media / telecommunication giants like AT&T and Verizon.

RESEARCH, PRODUCTION, AND DISTRIBUTION EFFICIENCIES

The costs of research, labor, and production are important factors in the selection of foreign locations. Some countries offer select advantages, such as a well-trained workforce, lower labor costs, tax relief, and technology infrastructure. Depending on the country and / or technical facility, products and services can be produced for less cost with greater efficiency. One such example is the Foxconn Technology Group located in Taiwan (Republic of China), which is one of the largest consumer electronics manufacturing facilities in the world. The sprawling factory compound blends seamlessly into the outskirts of the city of Shenzhen in China (Merchant, 2017). Foxconn serves as the primary manufacturing site for Apple, where it produces the Apple iPhone, iPod, and iPad devices.

THE RISKS ASSOCIATED WITH FDI

The decision to invest in a foreign country is not without its risks. TNCs are subject to the laws and regulations of the host nation. TNCs can sometimes find themselves vulnerable to the host nation's politics and business policies. It is not uncommon for a host nation to engage in various protectionist policies designed to protect local industry. Host nations will sometimes impose tariffs on product imports, change currency convertibility rules, revise tax laws, and / or impose requirements involving technology transfer as part of the requirements for doing business. The decision to impose import tariffs, as an example, can prove highly destabilizing for both the host country and the investing company. Nowhere is this more evident than in the 2018 / 2019 trade war between the United States and China. The Trump administration's tariffs on China and China's retaliatory tariffs set into motion a number of unintended consequences. At the most basic level, tariffs increase the price for goods and services while temporarily making the foreign exporter less competitive. A trade war can destabilize a company's FDI strategy in terms of manufacturing and sales as well as its willingness to make future resource commitments (Lawson, 2018).

Another type of risk occurs when a country (or set of countries) creates laws designed to address specific business practices resulting from the direct presence of the foreign direct investor. One such example can be seen with the passage of the Europe-based General Data Protection Act (GDPA) on May 25, 2018. The GDPA places restrictions on how media and information technology companies handle their customers' private information. The imposition of these rules is targeting the perceived threat of such companies as Google and Facebook.

Google, for one, has been engaged in a long-standing regulatory battle with the European Union. In July 2018, European authorities fined Google a record $5.1 billion for abusing its power in the mobile phone market in one of the most aggressive regulatory actions ever taken against an American company. Google has also been accused of favoring its own services (i.e., Google Search and Maps) when compared to Europe-based services in terms of listing priority (Stone & Silver, 2015). Google, however, remains the most popular search engine in Europe. The GDPA strengthens the rights of individuals by giving them greater control over their personal information and what is said and stored about them.

A third risk relates to the issue of technology transfer. The decision to enter a foreign market may require the investing media or technology enterprise to partner with a domestic firm in order to gain entry into that country. At issue is the fact that the domestic firm will sometimes use that relationship in order to obtain proprietary information. A growing number of nations rely on forced technology transfer, requiring the establishment of research and development labs as well as advanced production facilities as part of the cost of doing business (Atkinson & Ezell, 2012). This has proven to be a special problem for U.S. and European companies doing business in China. The challenge, of course, is that today's business partner can often become tomorrow's competitor. In sum, FDI can only occur if the host nation is perceived to be politically stable, provides sufficient economic investment opportunities, and maintains reasonable business regulations (Breznitz & Murphree, 2011).

Something New

The main roles of strategy are to plan for the future and to react to changes in the marketplace. Strategic planning is the set of managerial decisions and actions that determine the long-term performance of a company or organization. A competitive business strategy is the master plan, including specific product lines and approaches to be used by the organization in order to reach a stated set of goals and objectives. A firm's competitive business strategy needs to be understood in terms of scope—that is, the breadth of the company's product line as well as the markets it is prepared to serve (Gershon, 2013; Hitt, Ireland, & Hoskisson, 2013; Kung, 2008). Competitive strategy assumes a willingness to enlarge and improve the flow of a company's products and services internationally when and if the time is appropriate.

THE PURPOSE OF A GLOBAL BUSINESS STRATEGY

Most companies do not set out with an established plan for becoming a major international company. Rather, as a company's exports steadily increase, it establishes a foreign office to handle the sales and services of its products. In the beginning stages, the foreign office tends to be flexible and highly independent. As the firm gains experience, it may get involved in other facets of international business, such as licensing and manufacturing abroad. Later, as pressures arise from various international operations, the company begins to recognize the need for a more comprehensive global strategy (Bartlett & Beamish, 2014; Blaine, 2009; Gershon, 1997, 2000). In sum, most companies develop a global business strategy through a process of gradual evolution rather than by deliberate choice.

VERTICAL INTEGRATION AND COMPLEMENTARY ASSETS

There are several ways that a major corporation can strategically plan for its future. One common growth strategy is vertical integration, whereby a company will control most or all of its operational phases. In principle, the TNMC can control an idea from its appearance in a book or magazine to its debut in domestic and foreign movie theaters as well as later distribution via cable, satellite, DVD, or video streaming service (Albarran, 2013, 2017). The rationale is that vertical integration will allow a large company to be more efficient and creative by promoting combined synergies between its various operating divisions. Accordingly, many of today's TNMCs engage in a variety of cross-media ownership strategies that include owning a combination of news, entertainment, and enhanced information services. Cross-media ownership allows for a variety of efficiencies, such as news gathering as well as cross-licensing and marketing opportunities between company-owned properties.

THE STRATEGIC NECESSITY OF OWNING BOTH SOFTWARE AND DISTRIBUTION LINKS

Today's TNMC wants to own both media content and the means of distribution into people's homes—hence the reason for companies like Comcast owning the NBC television network as well as multiple cable television program services. Similarly, AT&T acquired Time Warner Inc. in 2018 at a cost of $85 billion. For AT&T, the purchase of Time Warner represents an opportunity to obtain one of the single best-known media companies in the world, with such established brands as HBO, CNN, and TBS. The purchase of Time Warner (now called WarnerMedia) provides AT&T with a ready-made distribution outlet for various kinds of media entertainment and information while offering numerous cross-licensing and marketing opportunities.

MERGERS AND ACQUISITIONS STRATEGY

Mergers and acquisitions represent two of the most direct ways that companies can join (or partner together) to achieve increased market share, to diversify product lines, and/or to create greater efficiency of operations. In a *merger* transaction, two companies are combined into one company. The newly formed company assumes the assets and liabilities of both companies. By contrast, an *acquisition* involves the purchase of one company by another company for the purpose of adding (or enhancing) the acquiring firm's productive capacity (Albarran, 2017; Van Kranenberg & Ziggers, 2018). This can be seen with such examples as Microsoft's 2016 acquisition of LinkedIn at a cost of $26.2 billion and Google's 2006 acquisition of YouTube for $1.65 billion. During an acquisition, one company acquires the operating assets of another company in exchange for cash, securities, or a combination of both. Table 10.1 identifies several high-profile media mergers and acquisitions both completed and pending for the years 2006 to 2019.

WHEN MERGERS AND ACQUISITIONS FAIL

Not all mergers and acquisitions are successful. The question is whether the proposed merger or acquisition accomplishes what it sets out to create. As companies feel the

TABLE 10.1. Select Media and Telecommunications Mergers and Acquisitions, 2006–2020

Walt Disney	2019	$71.3 billion acquisition of 21st Century Fox
AT&T	2018	$85.4 billion acquisition of Time Warner
Qualcomm	2016	$47.0 billion acquisition of NXP Semiconductors
Microsoft	2016	$26.2 billion acquisition of LinkedIn
AT&T	2015	$48.5 billion acquisition of DirecTV
Axel Springer SE	2015	$450 million acquisition of Business Insider
Dell	2015	$66.0 billion acquisition of EMC
Comcast	2014	$46.2 billion acquisition of Time Warner Cable
Facebook	2014	$19.5 billion acquisition of WhatsApp
Google	2013	$966 million acquisition of Waze
Softbank	2013	$21.6 billion acquisition of Sprint
Facebook	2012	$1.0 billion acquisition of Instagram
Comcast	2011	$30.0 billion acquisition of NBC/Universal
Walt Disney	2009	$4.0 billion acquisition of Marvel Entertainment
News Corp.	2007	$5.6 billion acquisition of Dow Jones (*Wall Street Journal*)
Google	2006	$1.6 billion acquisition of YouTube

Sources: Company reports.

pressures of increased competition, they embrace a somewhat faulty assumption that increased size makes a better company. Yet, on closer examination, it becomes clear that a merger agreement is not always the best strategy. It sometimes happens that the combining of two major companies creates problems that no one could foresee. A failed merger or acquisition can be highly disruptive to both organizations in terms of lost revenue, increased capital debt, and a possible decrease in job performance. The inevitable result is the elimination of staff and operations as well as the potential for bankruptcy. There are several reasons that help explain why mergers and acquisitions can sometimes fail: (1) lack of a compelling strategic rationale, (2) failure to perform due diligence, (3) post-merger planning and integration failures, and (4) financing and the problems of excessive debt (Gershon, 2013, 2000).

In the desire to be globally competitive, both companies go into the proposed merger (or acquisition) with unrealistic expectations of presumed strengths and synergies. Once a target company has been identified, a price level must be established. At issue is the question of how to properly value the target company. Once negotiations are underway, there is sometimes undue pressure brought to bear to complete the deal. Unwarranted optimism regarding future performance can sometimes cloud critical judgment.

In the highly charged atmosphere of intense negotiations, the merging parties sometimes fail to perform due diligence prior to the merger agreement. The acquiring company may only later discover that the intended merger or acquisition may not accomplish the desired objectives. Often the lack of due diligence results in the acquiring company paying too much for the acquisition. One of the best examples of this can be seen with America Online's purchase of Time Warner for $163 billion in 2001, resulting in one of the most catastrophic failed mergers in U.S. corporate history.

Another important reason that mergers sometimes fail is due to bad post-merger planning and integration. If the proposed merger does not include an effective plan for combining divisions with similar products, the duplication can be a source of friction rather than synergy. Turf wars can erupt, and reporting functions among managers can become divisive. The problem becomes further complicated when there are significant differences in corporate culture.

In order to finance the proposed merger or acquisition, some companies will assume major amounts of debt through short-term loans. If or when performance does not meet expectations, such companies may be unable to meet their loan obligations. If a company is perceived to be highly leveraged, both lending institutions and product suppliers, which are critical to the enterprise's day-to-day operations, will scale back their commitment for fear that they may not be paid back. The newly formed merged company may be forced to sell off entire divisions in order to raise capital, or worse, may default on its payments altogether.

Opportunities

Digital media represents the artistic convergence of various kinds of hardware and software design elements to create entirely new forms of communication and expression (Gershon, 2017). From well-constructed website displays to Facebook and YouTube video postings, digital media has proven to be the seminal 21st-century game changer in terms of global message design—specifically, how we communicate, receive, and store information (Levinson, 2013; Wong, 2009). Central to this discussion is the importance of intelligent networking that provides the technology and electronic pathways that make global communication possible for both business and individual users alike. As noted earlier, ideas such as foreign market penetration and transborder data flow mean something very different given the proliferation of international EC sites, social media, and over-the-top video streaming services (Berger & Milkman, 2012; Friedrichsen & Mühl-Benninghaus, 2013; Tabernero, Villanueva, & Orihuela, 2013; Wirth & Rizutto, 2013).

TRANSNATIONAL MEDIA AND ELECTRONIC COMMERCE

The term *electronic commerce* represents the ability to sell goods and services electronically via the Internet. The strength and delivery reach of EC has created a vast global playing field where buyers and sellers from around the world are free to participate. The principle of *exchange efficiency* is an important concept found in management theory (Gershon, 2013). It has to do with creating the optimum conditions through which a consumer can obtain a product or service. Traditional examples of exchange efficiency can be seen in speed lanes in a supermarket, which allow customers to move quickly through the checkout line. Today, EC has taken the principle of exchange efficiency to a whole new level in terms of retail trade and distribution. This is especially important for TNMCs like Apple, Amazon, and Netflix, who regularly fill customer orders on a global basis and whose business is time sensitive. EC and the power of intelligent networking have made such companies transnational in scope and operations, in turn globalizing the shopping experience.

TRANSNATIONAL MEDIA AND INFORMATION SEARCH

Searching for information represents the most essential reason why someone uses the Internet—namely, to gather information about topics and issues that are important to the user. The success of the Internet today is due in large measure to a combination of factors, including hypertext linking, improved website design, and powerful search engines. A search engine is a software tool that helps a user perform key word searches and locate specific information available on the Internet. The search engine is responsible for organizing information resources on the Internet. This can include general information search engines like Google, Baidu, and Yahoo. Today, Google is the single largest Internet search engine in the world. From its very beginning, one of Google's stated missions was to organize the world's information. Since 2008, Google has indexed trillions of URL links.

Less understood by the general public, however, is the importance of specialized search engine websites like WebMD (health care), Tripadvisor (travel), and Kelley Blue Book (automobile comparison shopping) that offer the user a more dedicated focus. The specialized search engine provides structure and makes the Internet far more accessible to navigate. What is important to remember about these specialized search engines is their ability to leverage user information for the purpose of engaging in worldwide EC activity. Tripadvisor, for example, has enabled the company to cross a whole host of geographic and virtual boundaries with its recommendations on hotels, places to visit, and special travel promotions. Companies like Tripadvisor have transformed the business of international travel.

TRANSNATIONAL MEDIA AND SOCIAL NETWORKING

Social media represents a category of Internet-based activity where a virtual community of users share information through the use of individual profiles, contact information, personal messages, blogs and commentary, and videos. Simply put, social media is about relationship building (Friedrichsen & Mühl-Benninghaus, 2013). Social media gives its users a public voice that bypasses the traditional media intermediaries, including the traditional news outlets as well as corporate and political communication specialists. Social media disrupts the one-way information flow by giving the general public an opportunity to comment and react in a more direct way. In addition, social media provides business marketers with an altogether new tool for engaging one's audience in a more personalized way.

The broad reach and immediacy of social media make it possible to communicate in real time regardless of time zones, geographical borders, and physical space. It allows for instantaneous communication between one's friends, colleagues, and peers. Social media is able to achieve several important communication goals. First and foremost, social media allows individuals to meet new people and strengthen existing relationships (Piskorski, 2011). From personal friendships to professional contacts, social media utilizes the power of intelligent networking to make communication easy and accessible. Both Facebook and LinkedIn use a specialized algorithm that generates a list of potential friends (or contacts) that's built on a friend-of a-friend reference matrix algorithm (i.e., common index naming points) based on two or more name listings.

Second, social media aids in the diffusion of new ideas when individuals comment on stories and/or share a news item for general distribution. With the emergence of Internet news and social media, readers now go through the additional step of commenting on and/or passing along a news item that is of particular interest to them. In journalism parlance, that means keeping the story alive. Researchers found that two features predictably determine an article's success: how positive the message is and how much it excites the reader (Berger & Milkman, 2012). Facebook, in particular, encourages the uploading and distribution of unique specialty news items that are of interest to the user. All this points to the fact that users are especially interested in the news items shared by friends (Urban & Bodoky, 2013).

OVER-THE-TOP VIDEO STREAMING SERVICES

Video streaming involves sending information and entertainment content via the Internet in a digitally compressed format. The programming can be displayed on high-definition television sets, laptop and tablet computers, and smartphones. Video streaming has become a major force for television viewing with the success of Netflix, Amazon Prime, and YouTube, which demonstrated the possibility of streaming movies (and video clips) via a broadband connection directly to the end user's HDTV set or mobile device. Central to this discussion is the future of over-the-top (OTT) video streaming services—that is, television programming that can be video streamed via the Internet to both smart homes and various kinds of mobile devices, including smartphones, computer tablets, and laptop computers. More and more subscribers are dropping cable, telephone, and satellite services than ever before. This is especially true for younger viewers, who have switched exclusively to watching OTT video or watching it in combination with free TV (Evens, 2013; Wirth & Rizzuto, 2013). The provision of OTT services is expanding internationally as well. Broadcasters and other television/film producers are looking to expand globally in search of new opportunities by capitalizing on the Internet and the power of intelligent networking (Ooyla, 2018).

Becoming increasingly clear is the fact that the traditional (or linear) television program schedule with viewers watching television in real time has become less the norm. Instead, digital video recorders in combination with OTT streaming video are creating a library approach to TV watching among younger viewers. OTT will forever change how we watch television and give new meaning to the term *video on demand*.

The OTT marketplace is competitive, dynamic, and even a bit chaotic. Some market analysts suggest that, within the next five years, viewership hours of online OTT video will surpass those of traditional broadcast TV. The provision of OTT services is expanding internationally as well. Broadcasters and other television/film producers are looking to expand globally in search of new opportunities by capitalizing on the Internet and the power of intelligent networking (Ooyla, 2018). An international market study performed by Ampere Analysis shows that the commitment to OTT services is fast becoming a worldwide phenomenon with countries like Denmark and Sweden providing a close second and third to the United States.

TABLE 10.2. Select Examples of Transnational Media Corporations

Company	*World Hdq.*	*Principal Business Operations*
Alibaba	China	Electronic commerce
Alphabet (Google)	USA	Internet search, YouTube video
Amazon	USA	Electronic commerce, digital books, e-readers
Apple	USA	Smartphones, Macintosh computers, iTunes music
AT&T/Time Warner	USA	Magazine publishing, HBO film, entertainment, CNN, AT&T wireless, DirecTV, U-verse service
Axel Springer	Germany	Television stations, newspapers, radio
Baidu	China	Social networking, electronic commerce, and mobile services
Bertelsmann AG	Germany	Television stations, radio, magazines, publishing music and film
Comcast	USA	Cable television operations, NBCUniversal television
Facebook	USA	Social networking, Instagram
Grupo Globo	Brazil	Television stations, newspapers, radio
Huawei	China	Consumer electronics
Lenovo	China	Consumer electronics
Microsoft	USA	Business office software, Xbox videogame system
Netflix	USA	Television/film EC video streaming service, television/film production
News Corp. Ltd.	Australia/USA	Newspapers, magazines, television, and film
Samsung	South Korea	Consumer electronics, smartphones
Sony	Japan	Consumer electronics, video game consoles and software, music and film, entertainment
Walt Disney	USA	Theme parks, broadcast and cable television, film entertainment, consumer merchandising

Table 10.2 lists some of today's best-known transnational media corporations in terms of their work in information search, electronic commerce, social media, and over-the-top video streaming services.

Challenges

Given the power and influence of TNMCs, various researchers have argued that a small set of dominant media corporations exercises a disproportionate effect over the marketplace of ideas. Implicit in such arguments is that TNMCs should be treated differently from other TNCs because of their unique ability to influence public opinion. Corporate size is presumed to limit the diversity and availability of new media products and ideas in favor of promoting a type of corporate agenda. There is also a public perception that such companies exercise an undue influence over the marketplace of ideas, especially when it comes to various political and social issues (McChesney, 2008, 2013). This has been further aided by the power of the Internet. Thus, any new or announced media merger is often met with public skepticism. As Noam (2016) points out, the general public seems more willing to accept the power and success of large-scale companies as they pertain to general business, but they are much less tolerant when it involves media ownership. People recognize that media is a powerful instrument of influence over their hearts, minds, wallets, and votes. They attribute to the media—and therefore to their owners—responsibility for what they dislike in their society (Noam, 2016, p. 5).

Therefore, the question is whether TNMCs are susceptible to anticompetitive behavior. From Facebook's failure to protect consumer privacy to China-based Huawei being accused of corporate espionage, there are indeed examples of such companies engaging in anticompetitive behavior. Do such companies contribute to a decline in the marketplace of ideas? Not exactly. It would be more accurate to say that most TNMCs are market leaders in very specific areas of media and information technology (see table 10.2).

At issue is the problem of market concentration. The term *market concentration* can be used to describe the number of sellers within a given market. A market is said to be highly concentrated if it is dominated by a limited number of firms. There are two ways to examine the problem of media concentration. The first way is to look at media concentration in terms of single-industry dominance—specifically, a monopoly situation. How much does a single company dominate a specific area of media or telecommunication? The second way to look at media concentration is in terms of cross-media ownership (Noam, 2009). How many related kinds of industries does the media company engage in? Consider, for example, the case study of Amazon cited earlier. Media managers looking to navigate this complex environment may use the following action plan as a reference.

ACTION PLAN

1. Attention to detail is important when undertaking major initiatives like foreign direct investment and / or engaging in a mergers and acquisitions strategy.
2. Utilize the tools of media convergence, specifically electronic commerce, specialized search engines, social media, and video streaming services, to guide your business strategy.
3. At a very core level, ask yourself what business you are really in. Be able to identify your competitors' opportunities for collaboration while recognizing those portions of the market that are presently being underserved.
4. Recognize the power of social media and digital media opinion leaders when launching a new product or service.

KEY TAKEAWAYS

1. From electronic commerce to over-the-top video streaming services, the Internet provides a level of immediate access to global information, business, and entertainment that is unparalleled in the history of media and communication.
2. Digital media, and by extension digital storytelling, has proven to be the seminal 21st-century game changer in terms of global message design. All companies, both large and small, require a digital presence in order to fully engage the public whether it be one's organizational website display, social media activity, or sales and distribution via an EC site.

3. The broad reach and immediacy of social media make it possible to communicate in real time regardless of time zones, geographical borders, and physical space. It allows for instantaneous communication between one's friends, colleagues, and peers. All companies, both large and small, need to have a social media strategy.
4. Today's TNMCs, like Comcast, AT&T, and Verizon, want to own both media content and the means of distribution into people's homes.
5. Companies like Google, Facebook, Amazon, and Netflix represent the new face of transnational media. They have proven to be major game changers by redefining foreign market penetration and transborder data flow in the 21st century.

CONCLUSION

We are living in a transitional time in the fields of media and telecommunication where the business of information and entertainment is being redefined. The term *transnational media* has come to mean something very different in the digital age given the rapid emergence of the Internet and the power of intelligent networking. The study of transnational media management has changed in light of three significant business and technology shifts.

The first shift is the importance of the Internet and broadband delivery. From electronic commerce to over-the-top video streaming services, the Internet provides a level of immediate access to global information, business, and entertainment that is unparalleled in the history of media and communication.

The second business/technology shift is the importance of digital media. Digital media, and by extension digital storytelling, has proven to be the seminal 21st-century game changer in terms of global message design. All companies, both large and small, require a digital presence in order to fully engage the public, whether it be one's organizational website display, social media activity, or sales and distribution via an EC site. The Internet in combination with digital media has leveled the electronic playing field, thus enabling both large and small companies alike to compete internationally. More to the point, an innovative start-up company with good ideas can often rise to the top and bypass traditional market barriers.

The third business/technology shift is the TNMC players themselves, including the emergence of such companies as Google, Facebook, Amazon, and Netflix. These companies represent the new face of transnational media. They have proven to be major game changers by redefining foreign market penetration and transborder data flow.

Media managers hoping to compete in a TNMC must pay attention to details when engaging in potential mergers or major acquisitions. New media technologies provide many opportunities to guide business strategy, particularly electronic commerce, search engines, social media, and video streaming services. Each of these provide opportunities to engage and foster relationships with new audiences not possible in a local marketplace. It is also important to know when to say no. Be able to identify opportunities for collaboration, but remember that not every deal is a good deal. Perhaps the most important question in a TNMC is "What business are you really in?" It is an exciting time with great opportunities for enthusiastic and skilled media managers wanting to understand the global dimension to media and communication.

The 21st-century TNMC is transitioning into a new class of hybrid media company capable of designing highly engaging media products while simultaneously relying on the Internet and broadband delivery as the basic platform for EC services to the general public. Taken together, these three business/technology shifts have redefined the size, scope, and delivery of transnational media products and services. In the next chapter, we will discuss media management in Africa in detail.

REFERENCES

Albarran, A. (2013). *Management of electronic and digital media* (5th ed.). Wadsworth.

Albarran, A. (2017). *The media economy* (2nd ed.). Routledge.

Amit, R., & Zott, C. (2001). Value creation in e-business. *Strategic Management Journal, 22*, 493–520.

Athique, A. (2016). *Transnational audiences: Media reception on a global scale*. Polity Press.

Atkinson, R., & Ezell, S. (2012). *Innovation economics: The race for global advantage*. Yale University Press.

Bartlett, C., & Beamish, P. (2014). *Transnational management: Text, cases and readings in cross-border management*. McGraw-Hill Education.

Berger, J., & Milkman, K. (2012). What makes online content viral? *Journal of Marketing Research, 49*, 192–205.

Blaine, H. (2009). *Foreign direct investment*. Nova Science Publishers.

Brandt, R. (2011). *One click: Jeff Bezos and the rise of Amazon.com*. Penguin Books.

Breznitz, D., & Murphree, M. (2011). *Run of the red queen: Government, innovation, globalization and economic growth in China*. Yale University Press.

Dogruel, L. (2014). What is so special about media innovations? A characterization of the field. *The Journal of Media Innovations, 1*(1), 52–69.

Evens, T. (2013). Platform leadership in online broadcasting markets. In M. Friedrichsen & W. Mühl-Benninghaus (Eds.), *Handbook of social media* (pp. 477–492). Humboldt Media Business, Springer.

Fair, J. (1987). The regulation of transborder data flows: An international law perspective. *Gazette–Leiden Netherlands, 40*, 21–38.

Friedrichsen, M., & Mühl-Benninghaus, W. (2013). *Handbook of social media*. Humboldt Media Business, Springer.

Gershon, R. (1997). *The transnational media corporation: Global messages and free market competition*. Erlbaum.

Gershon, R. (2000). The transnational media corporation: Environmental scanning and strategy formulation. *Journal of Media Economics, 13*, 81–101.

Gershon, R. (2013). *Media, telecommunications and business strategy* (2nd ed.). Routledge.

Gershon, R. (2014). Digital media, electronic commerce and business model innovation. In Y.-L. Liu & R. Picard (Eds.), *Policy and marketing strategies for digital and new media* (pp. 202–217). Routledge.

Gershon, R. (2017). *Digital media and innovation: Management and design strategies in communication*. Sage.

Hitt, M., Ireland, R., & Hoskisson, R. (2013). *Strategic management: Competitiveness and globalization* (10th ed.). Cengage.

Kung, L. (2008). *Strategic management in the media*. Sage.

Lambert, J. (2012). *Digital storytelling: Capturing lives, creating community* (4th ed.). Routledge.

Lawson, G. (2018, November 28). The American casualties of Trump's trade war. *New York Times*. https://www.nytimes.com/2018/11/28/magazine/trade-war-tariffs-small-business.html

Levinson, P. (2013). *New new media* (2nd ed). Pearson.

McChesney, R. (2008). *The political economy of media*. Monthly Review Press.

McChesney, R. (2013). *Digital disconnect: How capitalism is turning the Internet against democracy*. The New Press.

Merchant, B. (2017, June 17). Life and death in Apple's forbidden city. *The Guardian.* https://www.theguardian.com/technology/2017/jun/18/foxconn-life-death-forbidden-city-longhua-suicide-apple-iphone-brian-merchant-one-device-extract
Noam, E. (2009). *Media ownership and concentration in the U.S.* Oxford University Press.
Noam, E. (2016). *Who owns the world's media?* Oxford University Press.
Ooyla. (2018). *State of the broadcast industry report.* Ooyla Reports.
Piskorski, H. (2011, November). Social strategies that work. *Harvard Business Review,* 117–122.
Stone, B. (2013). *The everything store: Jeff Bezos and the age of Amazon.* Little, Brown.
Stone, B., & Silver, V. (2015, August 6). Google's $6 billion miscalculation on the EU. *Bloomberg Businessweek.* https://www.bloomberg.com/news/features/2015-08-06/google-s-6-billion-miscalculation-on-the-eu
Strube, M. (2010). Development of transnational media management research from 1974–2009: A propositional inventory. *International Journal on Media Management, 12,* 115–140.
Tabernero, A. S., Villanueva, J., & Orihuela, J. L. (2013). Social networks as marketing tools for media companies. In M. Friedrichsen & W. Mühl-Benninghaus (Eds.), *Handbook of social media* (pp. 161–178). Springer.
Urban, A., & Bodoky, T. (2013). The impact of Facebook on news consumption. In M. Friedrichsen & W. Mühl-Benninghaus (Eds.), *Handbook of social media* (pp. 805–818). Springer.
Van Kranenberg, H., & Ziggers, G. (2018). Mergers and acquisitions and their performance. In A. Albarran, B. Mierzejewska, & J. Jung (Eds.), *Handbook of media management and economics* (pp. 201–218). Routledge.
Wirth, M., & Rizutto, R. (2013). Future prospects for cable telecommunications in an over-the-top world. In A. Albarran (Ed.), *Media management and economics research in a transmedia environment* (pp. 18–45). Routledge.
Wong, Y. L. (2009). *Digital media primer.* Prentice Hall.
Zang, X. (2018). Media globalization. In A. Albarran, B. Mierzejewska, and J. Jung (Eds.), *Handbook of media management and economics* (pp. 333–346). Routledge.

CHAPTER 11

Media Management in Africa

Rasha Allam, The American University in Cairo

LEARNING OBJECTIVES

1. Demonstrate the main technological changes in today's African media landscape.
2. Highlight the deficiencies of the business models of African mainstream media organizations by addressing managerial challenges for future African media managers.
3. Identify internal and external factors that affect the performance of African media outlets.
4. Understand barriers to achieving good governance and advancing democratic developments in Africa.
5. Identify opportunities for media investments that increase value capture in African media.

Technological, political, and economic changes have significantly influenced the African media marketplace, but perhaps no change has proved greater than media convergence. The field of media management research has a long trajectory in examining organizational structure, programming, market structures, and business models by geographic location. Unique cultural indicators of the media marketplace influence the ways in which media products are created and distributed. The aim of this chapter is to examine media management issues faced by traditional media organizations in Africa, highlight the main challenges in media management within the African context, and discuss foreseen growth in the region and in the global marketplace.

Africa, the second-largest continent, has adapted to media convergence in unique and important ways. The changing media use patterns in Africa provide many opportunities for monetizing media products that have been used in other societies as well as capitalizing on locally produced programming. In a region known historically for tightly government-controlled media, especially in print forms, new media outlets are a refreshing change. Many African citizens strongly distrust government-controlled media, regardless of the content, and have turned to the Internet as a source for reliable information—though it is often fraught with misinformation.

The popularity of mobile media has brought many exciting changes to the region, especially to the exchange of goods and services. Given the lack of a universal banking system, cellular services are heavily relied on for transferring funds. The intersection of money and media should be exciting to media managers in Africa, especially when other regional markets with established banking systems show high levels of distrust of these types of mobile ventures.

Several factors contribute to the increasing popularity of mobile technologies across Africa. First, many private mobile networks have entered the market with creative and unique marketing tactics. Second, competing networks have attempted to offer packages and services at a lower cost than their rivals. Third, mobile networks have shifted from offering only telephone services to now offering services such as transferring rich media, video files, and mobile TV (Susman-Pena, 2012; Wirtz, 2011).

All African countries today have access to the Internet and mobile networks. The number of mobile subscribers is on the rise, and fierce competition between mobile companies has encouraged a faster spread of mobile Internet. Steep costs are projected to go down and will no longer be a barrier for those who are eager to access public goods. New technologies have impacted almost every facet of the African media marketplace. Perhaps none is as dramatic as its influence on official governance. Specifically, the Egyptian and Tunisian media have witnessed a management change after the African digital revolution, as illustrated by the case study below.

CASE STUDY

The African digital revolution was brought on by many changes related to social media use patterns. The digital revolution can be traced back to the introduction of the Internet, but it grew tremendously with the adoption of mobile phones. Just 30 years ago, there were almost no mobile networks on the African continent, as Africa was almost the last continent to obtain telephone connectivity.

Mobile technology was a main tool that facilitated communication through the Egyptian and Tunisian revolutions. Many have even dubbed the political changes *digital revolutions* given the importance of technology in the process. Egypt and Tunisia have witnessed tremendous political changes since 2011 and have made considerable progress when compared to other African countries. However, press in both countries still lack the diversity of opinion necessary to assert themselves and emerge from the patronizing tutelage of the government (Allam, 2018; Webb, 2014).

Almost all the African countries have undergone some level of upheaval influenced by political and economic systems. Countries that used to perform under a total authoritarian system have been challenged by new technologies, where media professionals, citizens, and politicians seek to utilize technologies to affect political freedom and to monetize media products and services. Yet, until today, informing, educating, and entertaining remain the primary roles of media throughout Africa.

The region has entered an era of low-cost mobile network adoption. As in most media marketplaces, private, creative storytellers are attracting the widest attention from audiences. Strong content will spread quickly, especially if it includes rich media, audio, and video files. Given the recent decline in entry costs, now is the time to engage this understudied market.

Changes in media management have mainly taken place in the press and private sector. Since 2010 and early 2011, we have seen several major changes in the media industry in Egypt and Tunisia. After the revolutions, the newspaper industry in both countries was shaken as distribution and circulation rates went down (Allam, 2019). At the same time, most of the newspapers gave increasing attention to the development of effective, user-friendly websites that update audiences with news all the time. Private newspapers adopted media analytics software, such as Google Analytics and Chart Beats. These audience analytics tools enable editors and managers to track real-time audience engagement with specific pieces of content and get new forms of data about consumers. The news itself has become a measured product for the first time in Africa (Carlson, 2015).

Such development of back-end technologies helped many newspapers boost their revenue models as they started to understand their audiences' interests and tailor content to satisfy their needs. This kind of adaption to new technologies is not the same in the state-owned news organizations, where bureaucracy and hierarchies still dominate the work process, increasing the difficulty of implementing change. The flexible organizational structure helped most of the private news organizations make changes by integrating print with online newsrooms. This combination of "old" and "new" practices is outlined further below.

Something Old

Traditional broadcast media remains the primary platform to reach a wide range of audiences in Africa. This "old" technology still guides many of the new technology advancements even in today's convergent media environment. According to UNESCO (2018), 83% of Tanzanians said they get news and information from radio, making it the most prominent information source in Africa. Comparing radio and television dependency between rural and urban areas, research finds that access to radio and television in urban areas is about equal (85% for radio and 79% for TV), while in rural areas the difference is significant (68% for radio and 26% for TV; see UNESCO, 2018).

Newer forms of media, such as social media and podcasts, have been used to supplement traditional media in Africa. Media managers are utilizing new media platforms to engage audiences by getting their feedback on programs. Perhaps more than any other marketplace, African media program-specific social networks allow content producers to cultivate a virtual target audience (Olorunnisola, 2000).

TRADITIONAL MEDIA

Radio remains the information leader in several African countries (Ogoso, 2004) and is dominant largely due to its reliability and affordability. For example, radio is still the most accessible and used medium in Zambia. Community radio is also viewed as an important platform for small communities to voice their concerns. However, often community radio succumbs to tight regulation and control from government. Though it is a strong outlet for niche, local issues, even NGO outlets have been faced with citizen scrutiny. As long as programming is dependent on external resources, some citizens in Africa may feel uncomfortable fully participating and engaging with the content.

Dependency on television varies among different African countries (Jenson & Oster, 2009). The first terrestrial television broadcast signals in Africa were sent on October 31, 1959, and belonged to the Western Nigeria Television Service. The South African Broadcasting Corporation was introduced in 1971 for audiences in Southern Africa. In Northern African countries, especially in Arabic-speaking countries, such as Egypt, Morocco, and Tunisia, television services are more developed, sophisticated, and reliable. For example, the television market in Egypt (with an estimated population of 97 million citizens) is quite robust and is still the most popular medium today. Free-to-air television is still the most watched in Africa with only 14% of households subscribing to pay TV services in 2016 (Allam, 2018). Even in an era of media convergence, traditional media still hold power in Africa.

Governments in most of the African countries still control national television broadcasters. Some countries have taken further steps toward the conversion of national/state-owned television into public broadcasters, such as Tunisia, where public television started to pay more attention to local news compared to the amount of government news it used to produce (Webb, 2014).

Working with existing institutions is essential to media managers in Africa. In 2017, the South African regional children's television program *Takalani Sesame* was looking for a new director of media. The top skills sought for the position included (1) developing a business plan for long-term strategic growth; (2) nurturing key partner and stakeholder relations in South Africa; and (3) cultivating new strategic partnerships with government, corporations, and NGOs (NGO Pulse, 2017). Here, you can see the emphasis placed on new programming that works within traditional regimes.

Most of the African countries maintain a centralized broadcasting system out of their desire to use the broadcasting sector as an arm to guide and mobilize the public and keep it out of hostile hands. This is particularly true as radio and television have the ability to overcome or bypass the illiteracy problem in some African countries. Most private-sector stations are dealing with an unstable financial situation, and their independence is always questionable due to the media laws that allow room for interference (Jensen & Oster, 2009; Mdlongwa, 2009; Olken, 2009).

Print media face many of the same challenges as broadcast media in Africa, such as lack of access to information, deficient media laws, and dependency on governments for funding. Giving attention to these challenges is crucial for achieving a sustainable media system in countries in Africa and in enforcing government accountability (Jones, 2010; Monga, 2009). Often, media managers must go through existing institutions and systems in order to enter the marketplace. Thus, this region may have more oversight and regulations than others.

Access to information is not yet attainable in most of the developing countries in Africa. Changes require advocacy and are directly correlated with the role of journalism in monitoring government performance and quality of public goods. These factors are important for good governance and democratic development (Olken, 2009).

POLITICAL SYSTEMS, ECONOMIC FACTORS, AND MEDIA PERFORMANCE

Media businesses in Africa are shaped by many economic factors that can impact the quality of content. While Hallin and Mancini's (2011) three media system models—the polarized pluralist model, democratic corporatist model, and liberal model—are important guides for future media professionals, it is difficult to apply them within the complexity of most of the African countries. There is a common belief that diversifying platforms is a desirable goal. However, in developing countries in Africa, without a strong economic base, this is not usually the case. Here, too many platforms produce a chaotic scene that can lead to a low-quality journalism industry.

For example, the high number of newspapers in some African countries does not reflect a strong state of the industry. They face many difficulties, such as lack of financial independence, irregularity in publication, the absence of a fourth state concept, and the exercise of commercial and regime pressure (Allam, 2019; Becker, Hollifield, Jacobsson, Jacobsson, & Vlad, 2009). In the Democratic Republic of Congo, for instance, while there were close to 700 registered publications in 2012, fewer than 250 published on a regular basis (Greenberg, 2012). All these publications tend to have a small circulation. The newspaper with the largest circulation, *Le Soft*, a private weekly newspaper, has a circulation of only 2,500 copies. Chad's only daily newspaper, *Le Progrès*, prints 3,000 copies a day, while Chad's weekly and twice-weekly newspapers have never sold more than 4,000 copies per edition (Greenberg, 2012). In Cote d'Ivoire, the government daily *Fraternité Matin* has the largest circulation with 13,000 to 16,000 copies sold per day, but most newspapers sell between 2,000 and 10,000 copies per day. Ethiopia's biggest daily newspaper, the government daily *AddisZemen*, has a print run of less than 13,000 copies. The privately owned weekly *Addis Admas* has an average print run of 21,000 to 25,000 copies, yet most titles in Ethiopia have small print runs of about 3,000 copies (Greenberg, 2012).

Almost all the African governments have a monopoly on national radio and television stations. For instance, in Angola, the government has a monopoly on all TV and national radio; in fact all terrestrial channels are owned by the state (Moehler & Singh, 2011). In Botswana, the government owns and runs the two major radio stations and has a monopoly on television. In Cameroon, the state-run Cameroon Radio Television is the only station with a wide reach. Similarly, in Chad, the only radio station with nationwide reach is the government-run Radio Nationale du Tchad, and the only TV station, TlTchad, is also state run. In Cote d'Ivoire, the state-run radio and television authority Ivoirienne has an official monopoly on free-to-air television broadcasting and broadcast media and is tightly controlled by the government. In Ethiopia, nearly all radio and TV stations are owned by the government (Moehler & Singh, 2011).

In other parts of Africa, such as Egypt, Morocco, and Tunisia, the government still owns the terrestrial channels, yet they allow many private channels to be launched via satellite only. It is important to note that the presence of private channels does not necessarily correlate with freedom of expression, as media laws in Africa permit government interference in different ways (Allam, 2019; Jensen & Oster, 2009; Ogoso, 2004).

Compared to some developed countries, newspaper penetration in African countries is very low. While some countries are doing better than others, most of the African newspapers are facing challenges in their production and circulation. This is mostly due to affordability, accessibility, and low literacy rate. According to the 2005 Afrobarometer survey, on average, only 33% of the individuals surveyed read a newspaper at least once a month (while 86% listen to news on radio and 45% watch news on TV) in sub-Saharan Africa. A recent survey made by the Lumina Foundation in southern and middle-belt Nigeria found that 13% of the individuals read a national newspaper every day (Cage, 2014). The order of magnitude is the same for Ethiopia: 13% of the respondents in Ethiopia said that they receive information from newspapers (Scribd, 2011). In South Africa, the sub-Saharan African country with the highest newspaper penetration, 40% of the population read a newspaper at least once a week. In Nigeria, depending on the survey cited, newspapers achieved 20% to 40% penetration among the adult population. The same is seen in Egypt and Tunisia, where newspaper circulation is very low compared to the citizens' usage of radio and television. As such, business models for print media must be revamped in many African countries.

All newspapers, whether state run or private, are facing a remarkable drop in terms of circulation due to the shift in readership from traditional print copies toward online news websites. This has also led to a drop in the number of advertisements. State-run national newspapers suffer from bigger problems, as they still perform under a very centralized organizational structure where the management decisions come from the top down to serve the government's agenda. In addition, state-run newspapers are overstaffed with employees who lack the required multimedia skills for today's news environment; consequently, these papers often lack a user-friendly interactive website.

Legacy media undoubtedly still dominate the African media marketplace. These various examples illustrate how traditional "old" media continue to guide business strategy in countries across Africa. While it may seem like an impossible terrain to enter as a new media manager, there are many opportunities for growth. Let us turn our attention toward "new" business models that can guide future media practices in Africa.

Something New

Long-term strategic growth is the most sought-after skill in today's African media. Developing a business plan that includes strong partnerships, media relations, and revenue sources is imperative for success. Today's media environment is fast changing and unpredictable. In many African regions, technology can also be unreliable, with service inexplicably being disrupted. With a heavy integration of commerce exchange apps, this technological unreliability can be detrimental to the lives of citizens in Africa. However, new technologies also show a lot of promise for disrupting existing structures.

Media entities that have noticed the importance of revisiting their business models to adapt to audience needs and market changes are ahead in the marketplace. Revisiting business models might require a shift in the value chain, such as in formatting, packaging, or distribution. One great new technology influencing the media market in Africa is the use of social media analytics (which will be discussed in detail in chapter 22, "Big Data and Entrepreneurship").

Often, government-controlled media outlets keep ratings and audience information a secret. They may push content onto producers due to their own agenda, not necessarily because it works the best for a network. Paying attention to new audience measurements can provide a transparent and clear understanding of audience behavior and needs. These audience analytics tools measure audience behavior and examine consumer needs in order for media managers to develop customized content. Newer measurement tools based on data analytics should be directly incorporated into future media business models in Africa.

BUSINESS MODEL EFFICACY

Traditional media business models are drastically changed by emerging technologies. As such, new strategic thinking is necessary in order to succeed in any African media landscape. Traditionally, newspapers have garnished funding through government subsidy, advertising revenues, sales, and so on, each influencing their degree of independency. Today, in addition to the factors mentioned above, media businesses need to consider audience access to media technologies and different kinds of institutional or structural barriers when launching a new platform (Mdlongwa, 2009; Purdy, Wong, & Harris, 2017).

Similar to most countries in the world, media convergence has brought a rapid merger and acquisition process (as we discussed in the previous chapter) to parts of Africa. Some barriers exist in the online media sector—namely, structural and strategic barriers, such as first copy cost, network effects, and branding. Facing convergence, all media organizations go through similar value creation steps until they reach the end user. The process is much more niche and personalized. The packaging stage is considered the core, as this process is used to tailor content to satisfy audience needs (Bock & George, 2018; Wirtz, 2011). With consideration of the fact that Africa is a region with so many distinct languages, cultures, and geographic nuances, a niche media strategy will be the most effective.

There is a great opportunity in African countries for low-cost access through digital news. Closed captions and video on demand may also help address the illiteracy challenges. However, a clear revenue model has not yet been determined. In other words, if an individual is unwilling to pay for a print subscription, they probably will not be open to paying for a digital subscription. Instead, media managers must rely on alternative revenue options such as digital advertising.

Unlike in other regions, business models across African countries require more collaboration between different institutions. There are many political ties that exist between newspapers and governments, especially when considering newspapers' reliance on government subsidy. These ties often make media subordinate to the government's agenda. As a result, newspapers must follow specific protocols that mainly consist of reporting news about government officials' activities while ignoring important domestic issues (Abdulla, 2014; Webb, 2014). One example is seen in Egypt, where the Egyptian print media have been facing a severe budget deficit and mainly depend on the government for financial support of 2 billion Egyptian pounds a year to cover running costs and salaries (Supreme Council Media Regulation, 2017). This gives the government controlling stocks, which again influences the news agenda. Nonetheless, this challenge opens opportunities for news media through alternative new media channels in Africa. For example, the Internet, and associated technological developments, have enabled the establishment of several websites that bypass the structural barriers. The Internet has made room for establishing digital natives' websites that depend solely on advertisements. Such websites are called "digital natives" as they were born on the digital platform, and they neither have hard copies nor depend on distribution or circulation rates.

PODCASTS

Podcasts have emerged as a popular and effective technology for citizen journalists to share stories with their community. Most notably, the podcast *Talking Heads* is an independently produced program that invites African thought leaders to come together and talk about various issues. *Loose Talk*, a smaller, more niche podcast has garnished much success as well. Three influential Nigerian journalists, Steve Dede, Ayomide Tayo, and Osagie Alonge, created the podcast to discuss trending issues around the world without the same regulation and control that they face through traditional media (Lunga, 2019). As discussed in chapter 17, "Podcasting," podcasts are a growing new media form everywhere, and they are offering fresh, new content previously unavailable in African media.

WEB SERIES

Young African citizens have always gravitated more toward visual media, especially television. Thus, web series have emerged as a promising new space to share eclectic and authentic African stories (Mosiuoa, 2016). Popular web series come in many different forms. *Reconnecting Pangaea* is a longer-form four-part documentary series that explores the influence of the Internet on modern African society. *Africa on a Plate* is a shorter format and incorporates cooking, culture, and travel with popular chef Lentswe Bhengu. *Kronikles of Hip Hop* is an animated comedy website designed to poke fun at major events in the music industry. These web series attract young adults' attention in African countries and show promise to media managers in Africa.

MUSIC INDUSTRY

One interesting emerging market in Africa is the rise of digital music streaming services. What is most unique to this region is the reliance on Chinese technologies, such as ZTE and Hikvision (Pilling, 2019). American tech giants, particularly in the music industry, have yet to capitalize on the African market. For example, Spotify only serves South Africa and has not yet expanded to other countries in Africa, while Apple Music has not offered affordable pricing for the 12 African countries that it serves, limiting its growth (Lunden, 2019). This has provided an opportunity for smaller media companies to take over.

Spinlet and Boomplay have taken over as the premiere media platforms to stream music in Africa. Boomplay, a Chinese software company, is the largest streaming music service in Africa, serving 56 million users with a catalog of more than five million videos and songs (Salaudeen, 2019). The technology is particularly appealing to young citizens in the region. With long commutes and a passion for music among African young adults, the venture is only projected to grow.

Clearly, there is room for growth across African media, in both news and entertainment industries. It is important for media managers to have a nuanced understanding of cultural and political relationships before entering the market. Let us explore many of the opportunities and challenges for future media practitioners and managers in the African region, particularly in the news sector.

Opportunities and Challenges

Media sustainability is a precondition for good journalism. Lack of sustainability poses a threat to resources and freedom. Media convergence has made it difficult to operate media organizations within the constraints of the conventional business model, especially through the reliance on the traditional advertising-supported business model (Hamilton, 2004; Schizer, 2011; Svensson & Yanagizawa, 2009). The Media Sustainability Index has recently found that the degree of media sustainability in the African continent is weak. Furthermore, the prevailing funding sources and management approaches are to blame for decreased sustainability and impact the role of media in enhancing democracy (IREX, 2005).

One may assume that the African media market is in the infancy stage and will follow the developed model toward growth and consumption. However, this may not be the case. The recent financial crisis across Africa, and other parts of the world, has drastically affected advertising revenues in media. Clearly, there is much to be uncovered about how to manage a successful media business in Africa.

OPPORTUNITIES

In today's convergent media environment, African media managers must take advantage of some unique opportunities in order to succeed. These include changing the degree of ownership concentration through a balance between the number of outlets and the quality of journalism, reforming the organizational structure so that it depends more on delegation of authority instead of a centralized system, and developing more locally tailored content.

OWNERSHIP CONCENTRATION

In sub-Saharan African countries over the last decades, media outlets have often been very short lived. The increase in media competition can lead to a decrease in both the quantity and quality of news provided (Cage, 2014), particularly with tight advertising markets and low consumer purchasing power in some African countries. However, it is important to highlight that the functionality of the business model is largely affected and related to the PESTEL (political, economic, social, technical, educational, legal) model, where these variables affect a media organization's performance to different degrees. Thus, in developing countries, a high level of competition in markets may lead to poor journalistic performance as advertising revenues are always limited, and moderate competition levels lead to higher-quality journalism (Becker et al., 2009).

ORGANIZATIONAL STRUCTURE REFORM

Media organizations in Africa have to work on reforming their organizational structure. In the old bureaucratic authoritative structure, there are several levels of hierarchies and a highly functional division of labor where the work is highly specialized, and everyone is concerned with their own specialization area. There is evidence that such a bureaucratic structure in African media affects the decision-making process and the efficacy of the media organization because the slow managerial system cannot adapt to the ever-changing media environment. Such a structure defines management as a "top-down" process: communication and movement within the organization happen vertically. There's a strong hierarchy and rigid demarcation between functions. Divisions, departments, and units develop their own "tribal" cultures and are fiercely defensive of their territory (Allam, 2018; Thomas, 2009).

It is understandable that one would find such hierarchies in the African countries where media organizations do not enjoy political independence. Such a structure that lacks editorial independence affects the degree of content diversity. In addition, the government's strict control of media organizations affects the kind of programming offered in African countries. For example, the Sudanese government always sets the agenda of the newscasts to focus on government achievements. Programs are also politicized by promoting the government's acts and always monitored by the government to ensure that they do not cross the red line. Many Egyptian programs, mainly in the public media and some in the private media, mobilize citizens toward governmental policies. Tunisia also suffers from a total monopoly over public media organizations (Cage, 2014; Mdlongwa, 2009).

On the other hand, systems that aim to provide innovative media products follow a different structure, described as organic and based on an innovative strategy the target of which is to introduce new and creative products and programs. While such systems are not large, they allow flexibility, leading to high performance and satisfaction. The African continent is the only one that has shown sustained population growth over the last century (World Bank, 2018). Media organizations in Africa should use this opportunity to invent a novel model for offering information to new generations of readers, viewers, and citizens.

Providing telephony services to this population has historically been an expensive affair, until the rise of mobile phone technology. This means that there are people who may be cut off from traditional media channels but could have access to the Internet and mobile media. Media organizations in Africa could widen their reach by using mobile channels to target this group (Cherubini & Nielsen, 2016; Susman-Pena, 2012).

Digital media platforms are seen as an important avenue not only for providing more access to information but also for enhancing audience engagement. Many media organizations in Africa now have a strong presence on social media and welcome audiences to share opinions, ideas, and stories. Encouraging audience interaction is one important step toward promoting democracy and building a successful business model for media organizations in Africa. In addition, the African media market lacks independent and consistent market research about audience behavior. More data-driven empirical audience research is needed for developing media businesses in African countries.

LOCALLY TAILORED CONTENT

Tailoring content toward audience interests and needs provides an opportunity in African media. Localizing and personalizing media content is an effective way to increase the reach of a media outlet and enhance efficacy (Purdy et al., 2017). Just as in other regions, the increasing supply of media products and services has led to audience fragmentation. Young audiences today use diverse services to satisfy their needs for information and entertainment. At the same time, a change in user preferences toward increased application of personal information and communication tools is taking place. Audiences, particularly the younger generation in Africa, now ask for more personalization in media content. As such, media organizations should use tools through which they can identify user interests and create integrated information and communication services that would satisfy their individual needs (Bock & George, 2018). In addition, business models should guarantee viability and independence. It should be noted that the solution for media organizations in Africa should not be costly media service reserved for the elite.

CHALLENGES

While the convergent media environment and changes in many African countries point to a promising media marketplace, there are many challenges that should be considered. Media organizations across the continent still lack an independent funding source and have struggled with financing shortfalls. This is partly due to their dependency on capricious government funding to stay afloat. Any small criticism toward the government could result in losing funding. In many countries, the government or its agencies are still the biggest advertisers. This presents the greatest challenge to African media managers.

The traditional media (newspapers, TV, radio) in Africa and worldwide are also losing revenue as readers and listeners increasingly shift to free digital content. As audiences migrate to other media venues, traditional media's influence and, by extension, advertising revenues diminish. In the traditional media business model, subscriptions and advertising are the main revenue sources that pay for production costs. Subscription revenue has proved very difficult to obtain and exists only in very few platforms that target high-end audiences who are capable of paying a monthly subscription fee (e.g., OSN in Egypt).

It is clear that advertising takes slower steps to migrate from the mainstream to the online platform when compared to other global audiences. In today's convergent environment, online audiences are more fragmented and geographically dispersed. It is difficult for advertisers to target them with the same advertising concepts that are used in traditional media (Petrova, 2011). Innovative approaches and better measurement tools are needed for media managers to see improved returns on investment.

One of the main challenges that traditional African media is currently facing is the shift in how audiences access their news. Mobile technology and social media have grown exponentially by providing an extraordinary amount of news content. Most of the news organizations have had a strong digital presence, and the media consumption pattern in Africa has begun leaning more toward online platforms, which will impact the traditional media outlets. Yet, digital media will still need to face the political and economic pressures in Africa. For example, in some countries, governments expand diagonally in order to have an arm in digital platforms. In other words, media outlets that are owned by the government can have a strong presence on digital platforms and influence public opinion by competing with other digital media.

Although technological development is taking a slower pace in Africa compared to the rest of the world, Africa has witnessed several positive steps toward digital revolution, such as the rapid spread of mobile companies to enhance the free flow of information. For example, Egypt has recently introduced 4G and is on its way to introducing 5G technology, enabling a better quality of Internet service and easier access to online content with almost uninterrupted service. We clearly see the opportunities and challenges in the African media marketplace. Media practitioners and managers looking to enter the African marketplace should consider the following action plan.

ACTION PLAN

1. Media organizations in Africa should invest in reevaluating their business models and content/services offered in order to better adapt to audience and advertiser expectations.
2. African media outlets should develop strong digital platforms and implement an integrated strategy between mainstream and digital platforms that encourages interactivity and engagement.
3. New formats for content should be adapted, taking advantage of new measurement tools.
4. Media marketing and promotional strategies in African media should emphasize localized and customized content according to behavior and consumption patterns detected on analytics.

KEY TAKEAWAYS

1. Broadcast media is still a dominant media platform in all African countries.
2. The print media sector is challenged by the sharp drop of advertising revenues and audiences' migration to other platforms.
3. Political systems still control most of the public media, which affects news coverage and always puts its credibility in question.
4. The African continent has an asset as it is the only continent that has seen sustained population growth in the century underway.

CONCLUSION

The African media industry has experienced tremendous growth and upheaval with the rise of mobile technology. The changing market structures, new technologies, regulatory environment, and fragmented audience have drastically changed media management practices in the region. It is important for media managers in Africa to consider restructuring their hierarchies. Ensuring that organizational structures remain oriented toward market demands must be a priority for all the strategies planned ahead. Creating a flat structure and clear demarcation of responsibilities is essential to adapt to the fast-changing media environment. Only when African media organizations have a more efficient decision-making process can they better react to unexpected and changing circumstances. Highly motivated and satisfied employees become a crucial factor in affecting any African media organization's performance by directly impacting the quality of production.

The media ecology in Africa is changing fast, and there are a few things that managers need to be aware of. How audiences seek information has greatly changed during the past 20 years. Consumers today have become more interactive with content creation and distribution. The Internet has largely removed institutional barriers to entry and opened the forum for anyone to publish or broadcast in a few minutes. More policies and regulations will be issued to regulate the spread of fake news and misinformation in Africa.

It should be noted that many media organizations in African countries still either operate under authoritarian systems or exist in transitional stages. Media managers in such organizations should be aware of the new technical changes and proliferation of alternative sources of information as well as how these alternative sources would put their media organizations' credibility in question. This is due to the fact that audiences now are exposed to infinite sources of news, and the structural boundaries are getting blurrier. Consequently, media organizations in Africa should change their traditional one-voice, top-down communication approach and start looking for audience interactivity and engagement as a means of maintaining audience consumption.

Audiences in African countries tend to be enthusiastic about new media content. In some ways, they find alternative platforms more trustworthy and accessible. This is especially true when content is cheaply accessed and locally produced. Emerging media platforms such as podcasts, web series, and streaming music are especially popular.

Changes that are taking place in Africa in terms of media usage and reach are mostly positive. Perhaps the most significant and positive innovation is the rapid proliferation of mobile phones and the extension of mobile phone network coverage, which has greatly enhanced the free flow of information. Thus, traditional media managers should ensure a strong presence on mobile platforms to increase the reach of their content and enhance audience engagement as citizens start to heavily use these technologies.

The responsibility of managing media organizations in Africa is more crucial than ever. Media managers must understand that development is now an ongoing task due to the rapid technological changes that are always present in the media field and that the volume and velocity of the changes have created a peculiarly challenging environment for the media. Practitioners must shape their business models according to the predicted changes. Such responsibility does not require a new managerial mindset but instead well-trained and multiskilled employees who will help navigate the latest tools and technological advancements necessary to create appealing content for a target audience.

Africa is certainly a region where a "backpack" skill set would prove useful for future practitioners. Much media content is being produced locally and on the go. There are different expectations for quality and professionalism, and in some ways, the more authentic and amateur the production, the more audiences may trust the source. Future media managers in Africa need to be technologically savvy and research oriented. However, interpersonal relationships and connections may be the key to entering such a tightly controlled market. It is important to make connections and form relationships with the right institutions.

Some of the changes discussed in this chapter are widespread around the world. Other nuances are unique to this region. Given the heavy reliance on Chinese technology companies, African media has many similarities to that in some Asian regions. Next, we will explore media management in Asia and how this influences the global marketplace.

REFERENCES

Abdulla, R. (2014). *Egypt's media in the midst of revolution: Carnegie endowment for international peace.* Carnegie Endowment. http://carnegieendowment.org/files/egypt_media_revolution.pdf

Allam, R. (2018). The bureaucratic broadcasting governing structure and content diversity: The case of the Egyptian national television system. *Global Media Journal, 16,* 30–99.

Allam, R. (2019). Constructive journalism in Arab transitional democracies: Perceptions, attitudes and performance. *Journalism Practice.* doi: 10.1080/17512786.2019.1588145

Becker, L., Hollifield, C., Jacobsson, A., Jacobsson, E., & Vlad, T. (2009). Is more always better? *Journalism Studies, 10,* 368–385.

Bock, A., & George, G. (2018). *The business model book: Design, build and adapt business models that drive business growth.* FT Press.

Cage, J. (2014). The economics of the Africa media. In C. Monga & J. Y. Lin (Eds.), *The Oxford handbook of Africa and economics: Policies and practices* (pp. 605–625). Oxford University Press.

Carlson, M. (2015). The many boundaries of journalism. In M. Carlson & S. C. Lewis (Eds.), *Boundaries of journalism: Professionalism, practices and participation* (pp. 1–18). Routledge.

Cherubini, F., & Nielsen, R. (2016). *Editorial analytics: How news media are developing and using audience data and metrics.* Reuters Institute for the Study of Journalism. https://reutersinstitute.politics.ox.ac.uk/our-research/editorial-analytics-how-news-media-are-developing-and-using-audience-data-and-metrics

Greenberg, B. A. (2012). A public press?: Evaluating the viability of government subsidies for the newspaper industry. *UCLA Entertainment Law Review, 19,* 189–244.

Hallin, D. C., & Mancini, P. (2011). *Comparing media systems beyond the western world.* Cambridge University Press.

Hamilton, J. (2004). *All the news that's fit to sell: How the market transforms information into news.* Princeton University Press.

IREX. (2005). *Media sustainability index (MSI).* https://www.irex.org/resource/media-sustainability-index-msi

Jensen, R., & Oster, E. (2009). The power of TV: Cable television and women's status in India. *The Quarterly Journal of Economics, 124,* 1057–1094.

Jones, A. S. (2010). *Losing the news: The uncertain future of the news that feeds democracy.* Oxford University Press.

Lunden, I. (2019, April 5). *Boomplay, a Spotify-style music and video streaming service for African music and Africa, raises $20M*. Tech Crunch. https://techcrunch.com/2019/04/05/boomplay-a-spotify-style-music-and-video-streaming-service-for-african-music-and-africa-raises-20m

Lunga, N. (2019). *9 African podcasts that you are certainly going to enjoy*. Africa. https://www.africa.com/top-african-podcasts

Mdlongwa, F. (2009). *Doing digital media in Africa: Prospects, promises and problems*. https://www.ru.ac.za/jms/archivednewsfeed/newsarchive/2009/2009-06-172304.html

Moehler, D., & Singh, N. (2011). Whose news do you trust? Explaining trust in private versus public media in Africa. *Political Research Quarterly, 64*, 276–292. doi: 10.1177/1065912909349624

Monga, C. (2009). *Uncivil societies: A theory of sociopolitical change*. World Bank. http://documents.worldbank.org/curated/en/228941468162850862/pdf/WPS4942.pdf

Mosiuoa, T. (2016, May 25). *5 South African web series you should be watching*. Okay Africa. https://www.okayafrica.com/south-african-web-series

NGO Pulse. (2017, January 17). *Takalani Sesame: Director*. http://www.ngopulse.org/opportunity/2017/01/17/takalani-sesame

Ogoso, O. (2004). *Talk radio and public debate: A case study of three Ugandan radio stations*. Rhodes University Thesis.

Olken, B. A. (2009). Do television and radio destroy social capital? Evidence from Indonesian villages. *Applied Economics, 1*(4), 1–33.

Olorunnisola, A. A. (2000). African media, information providers and emigrants as collaborative nodes in virtual social networks. *African Sociological Review, 4*, 46–71.

Petrova, M. (2011). Newspapers and parties: How advertising revenues created an independent press. *The American Political Science Review, 105*, 790–808.

Pilling, D. (2019). The fight to control Africa's digital revolution. *Financial Times*. https://www.ft.com/content/24b8b7b2-9272-11e9-aea1-2b1d33ac3271

Purdy, S., Wong, F., & Harris, P. (2017). *Stop the presses: Newspapers are struggling. Can all digital strategy be the path to profitability?* KPMG. https://home.kpmg.com/content/dam/kpmg/co/pdf/co-17-01-08-tmt-stop-the-presses.pdf

Salaudeen, A. (2019, June 6). *How China's Boomplay beat Spotify and Apple to corner Africa's streaming market*. CNN. https://www.cnn.com/2019/06/05/africa/boomplay-music-africa-intl/index.html

Schizer, D. M. (2011). Subsidizing the press. *Journal of Legal Analysis, 3*(1), 1–64.

Scribd. (2011). *ERIS audience survey: Ethiopia 2011*. https://www.scribd.com/document/62811336/Audience-Survey

Supreme Council Media Regulation. (2017). *Annual report*. https://www.almasryalyoum.com/news/details/1292556

Susman-Pena, T. (2012). *Making media development more effective: A special report to the Center for International Media Assistance*. Center for International Media Assistance. https://www.internews.org/sites/default/files/resources/CIMA_MediaDevelopment_2012-10.pdf

Svensson, J., & Yanagizawa, D. (2009). Getting prices right: The impact of the market information service in Uganda. *Journal of the European Economic Association, 7*, 435–445.

Thomas, J. P. (2009). *Media management manual: A handbook for television and radio practitioners in countries-in-transition*. UNESCO Office New Delhi. https://unesdoc.unesco.org/ark:/48223/pf0000187966

UNESCO. (2018). *Media sustainability report in the Middle East and North Africa*. https://unesdoc.unesco.org/ark:/48223/pf0000152010

Webb, E. (2014). *Media in Egypt and Tunisia: From control to transition?* Palgrave Macmillan.

Wirtz, B. W. (2011). *Media and Internet management*. Springer Gabler.

World Bank. (2018). *The future of the world's population in 4 charts*. https://blogs.worldbank.org/opendata/future-world-s-population-4-charts

CHAPTER 12

Media Management in Asia

Quan Xie, Southern Methodist University
Drew McDaniel, Ohio University

LEARNING OBJECTIVES

1. Understand the basic sociocultural and macroeconomic environment in Asia.
2. Describe media convergence theory and its implications in media management in Asia.
3. Understand media censorship and its influence on media management in Asia.
4. Review the emerging trends in Asia's media management practices.
5. Analyze how digital media technologies have disrupted Asia's media industries and revamped the business models in regional media management practices.

Asia is the world's largest and most populous continent, its expanse amounting to roughly 30% of the Earth's land area, and its residents total more than 60% of the entire world population (National Geographic Society, 2018). Asia is known as the cradle of human civilization, where, according to Haque (2004), "Asians founded the first cities, started agriculture and trading, set up the first systems of law, invented writing, paper, and moveable type, and created the earliest literatures" (p. 247).

At the same time, Asia presents great diversity of cultures, political systems, market sizes, economic power, and technological infrastructure (Jung & Kim, 2018). Asia has also been influenced by "traditions as varied as Buddhism, Hinduism, Confucianism, Islam, and Christianity, with economic structures ranging from capitalism to communism and governments ranging from democracies to dictatorships" (Alaimo, 2017, p. 214). Asia is home to some of the most densely populated countries, such as China and Singapore, but also countries with thinly scattered populations, such as Mongolia and Turkmenistan. While wealthy residents of Japan have one of the world's highest standards of living, children in North Korea struggle with malnutrition.

Asia accounts for two-thirds of global growth in the world economy (International Monetary Fund, 2018). India, the location of one of the world's youngest workforces, is the fastest-growing economy in Asia (Inquirer, 2018). Several Southeast Asian countries, including Cambodia, Philippines, and Myanmar, have also been top performers in the region (World Bank, 2018). Most notably, China has maintained a remarkably rapid growth since the country-initiated market reforms in 1978 (International Monetary Fund, 2018). For these reasons, Asia has become the most dynamic region in the global economy.

Additionally, Asian media has evolved from diverse historical roots—former colonial nations have tended to replicate features from their ties to European colonial powers—but across the entire region there tends to be careful government oversight of day-to-day operations. Managers of Asian media thus are often placed in an intermediary role, striving to accommodate the political interests of government authorities while simultaneously serving the country's public interests and needs.

Despite the sustained growth, Asia's economy also faces heightened global uncertainties such as trade tensions, a sharp tightening of global financial conditions, geopolitical tensions, and inflation (International Monetary Fund, 2018; World Bank, 2018). These factors, coupled with disparities arising from the economic gains from globalization, have not been equally shared across the region. Population aging, slowing productivity growth, and the rise of the digital economy are major challenges for media organizations in Asia (International Monetary Fund, 2018). Most important perhaps, Asian media have eagerly embraced the digital revolution, something that has fundamentally reshaped the region's media management outlook.

This chapter aims to provide a review of media management practices in Asia, as seen through the lens of media convergence and disruptive innovation theories. In the following sections, we first review media convergence theory, its implications in Asian media, and the impact of media convergence on media management practices. Next, we discuss the intervention of sophisticated political systems in the management of media across the region. We then review emerging trends in Asia's media markets during recent years to provide a glimpse of the region's changing media landscape. We specifically focus on the disruption of media industries caused by emerging digital technologies, looking particularly at the way business models have altered regional media management practices. We also propose opportunities for the region's media practitioners as well as challenging hurdles that managers need to overcome in order to be successful.

It should be noted that huge differences across Asian media ecosystems exist, not to mention political and cultural contexts. These produce highly varied forms of media convergence, which, in turn, fundamentally affect each country's media management practices. In this chapter, we employ Jung and Kim's (2018) approach in defining Asia's scope, one that follows the customary division of Asia into the South, the Southeast, and the East regions. Excluded are Oceania, countries in the Asian continent that are part of the Middle East, and Asian portions of the former Soviet Union. The remaining area includes 23 countries.*

*The 23 countries are as follows: 5 countries in East Asia (China, Japan, South Korea, North Korea, Mongolia); 7 countries in South Asia (India, Pakistan, Bangladesh, Nepal, Sri Lanka, Bhutan, and Maldives) belong to the South Asian Association for Regional Cooperation; and 11 countries in Southeast Asia (Indonesia, Philippines, Vietnam, Thailand, Myanmar, Malaysia, Cambodia, Laos, Singapore, Timor-Leste, and Brunei Darussalam). Among them, 10 countries, except for Timor-Leste, which separated from Indonesia in 1999, belong to the Association of Southeast Asian Nations.

Let's first explore how one Asian country, China, has dealt with the unique issues of media convergence. Later in the chapter, we will explore regional differences in other countries, including Japan, Singapore, and India—each representing a unique national setting.

CASE STUDY

Media convergence in China is mostly government driven. With consideration to the increasing popularity of digital media since 2000 in China, the government has come to view these new media platforms as an emerging ideological battleground. "The traditional media, particularly those incorporated in press groups, should be at the force in not only increasing the online voice of the party-state but also in keeping the orientation of online opinion in line with the Party" (Yin & Liu, 2014, p. 563). Media convergence is consequently considered a necessary approach to these challenges.

In August 2014, the concept of media convergence was brought forward as a national strategy by China's president, Xi Jinping. China's traditional press adopted four ways of convergence through digital media—online versions of print media, e-newspapers, digital platforms, and all-media strategies. For example, South Daily Media Group (SDMG), one of the most influential press groups in China, thoroughly implemented digital media strategies. It not only publishes online versions of the group's newspapers and mobile newspapers but also has developed news websites for each affiliated newspaper. In addition, SDMG reoriented itself as an all-media information provider, with an ambition to establish "a comprehensive system involving print media, digital media, mobile media, broadcasting, outside LED and e-bulletins" (Yin & Liu, 2014).

Although the convergence of traditional and digital media has been performed on a national scale under the supervision of China's central government, availability of state funding has been limited, and the converged media has had difficulty in gaining profitability (Yin & Liu, 2014). Yin and Liu (2014) conducted in-depth interviews with the staff at Shenzhen Press Group, another pioneer in China's media convergence, and found that its response to the government's push for media convergence was nothing more than "a gesture of compliance" (p. 561). In other words, although the press managers wished to move toward an emphasis on digital media, feeling a great urgency to match the trend and meet the new demands, rank-and-file staff responded to convergence with little commitment or engagement.

In China's case, media management is aligned with common Asian practices, especially in terms of media regulations and censorship. The following sections review various historical perspectives regarding the way the media system has been regulated and managed by national governments.

SOMETHING OLD

One thing that hasn't changed in today's convergent media environment is the strict oversight of media managers on their outlet's content by Asian governments and governmental agencies. This has been much criticized by Western scholars who view this control as an infringement of freedom of information. Negotiating the restrictions imposed by regulators is an important aspect of the job of media managers at every level, all the way down to the individuals who make content decisions across the organization. Reporters and editors in newsrooms, of course, are engaged in selectively choosing which stories to report and how stories within newscasts are framed. However, even in entertainment divisions, there are rules that must be observed about religious references, appropriate dress, references to sexuality, and so on.

Two broad types of censorship are related to content. One type is based on the wholesomeness of the subject matter. Media presentations tend to be evaluated by regulators on the basis of perceived conformity with social norms and more specifically on avoidance of social taboos. Obviously, there is great variation among Asian nations in their acceptance, for instance, of content involving portrayals of nudity and sexual acts. This is true even among nations that appear superficially similar in culture. Violent media content, especially in entertainment programs, also falls within this category of censorship. The other type of censorship concerns political and ideological content. It is within this category that the potential for the greatest controversy exists. In theory, democratic principles require an open political dialogue, and for this reason, restrictions in political content are a particular issue for Western observers. Nevertheless, there are few if any countries anywhere in the world without limitations on political discourse in the media.

Government engagement with media organizations and the content they produce have been understood in several different ways, including through historical, political, and cultural lenses. This still holds true today. Most nations of Asia have a colonial history, and in many of these colonies censoring practices can be traced to their origins decades ago. Rigorous censorship by colonial governments was often considered necessary to suppress independence movements. Generally, in these countries, any message supporting a break away from colonial rule was blocked. Paradoxically, upon gaining independence, these nations often continued the practice of censorship they resisted under colonial governance. Frequently, the very same regulations and rules imposed during colonial times were employed. In many countries across Asia, these inherited rules protecting the interests of government and political leaders remain to the present. Malaysia, like Brunei and Singapore, has a system of law and jurisprudence adapted from a British model. For many years, Malaysia's Broadcasting Act and Printing Presses Act provided the government with a high degree of control, similar to laws in place when Malaysia was a British colony.

Typically, justification for restrictions in political media content is that inflammatory materials could undermine governments, leading to political instability. In fact, upon gaining independence, nations were in a delicate state, often facing conflict created by separatist movements. Unification was an urgent, ongoing need. In Southeast Asia, there were insurgencies in the post-independence period. Malaysia faced a protracted Communist uprising known as the "Emergency," and in the Philippines the Huk Resistance arose. Consequently, nation building was required, and governments used whatever means they possessed to enlist media in that effort. At that time, radio tended to be preferred because it could reach citizens who lacked access to television and print media, including those living in remote areas and those unable to read.

To heal the social and ethnic divisions left behind by colonialism, radio was given the responsibility of fostering a sense of belonging and commitment to shared political ideals. The effectiveness of those early radio broadcasts is uncertain, and the programs were filled with heavy-handed heroic nationalistic themes. Messages conveyed through these transmissions were meant to encourage stability, especially by building support for the new political systems and their leaders.

Arguably, however, media in some countries became politicized through this engagement in nation building. As post-independence political leaders turned to broadcasting and print media as tools in national integration, these tools also promoted the personal and political interests of those leaders. In both Indonesia and the Philippines, media supported national integration and unification while also protecting the welfare of national figures such as Sukarno, Suharto, and Marcos. Therein lies the core problem for nation building and national unification as justification for strict media control. Such unification implies the need to support uncritically the government of the day.

In order to maintain firm control, regulatory agencies in most countries provide guidelines for media operators, and this is usually supported by some sort of monitoring process. Indeed, there may be direct involvement in reviewing content prior to broadcasting or other means of dissemination. In some countries, media functions are taken on by the government itself. In Malaysia, for example, Radio Television Malaysia is a department within the Ministry of Communication and Multimedia. In this organization, there is never any doubt about the content reflecting official viewpoints as it is effectively a government voice (McDaniel, 1994).

An unfortunate by-product of top-down pressures to manage information flow is the creation of an impulse among professional media staff to exert self-censorship. When confronted with content choices, editors, program executives, and others with decision-making power tended to opt for choices unlikely to cause problems with regulatory officials. These personnel reasoned there was no advantage in permitting content that might cause them professional difficulties. For less-motivated staff members, the ease of doing their job without fighting the system was the preferred way. As a result of these conditions, self-censorship quite often produced choices that were more conservative than ones that officials might have tolerated. The result was a more restricted diet of information achieved without formal censorship. Managers find it difficult to address this problem because they, too, will be held accountable for controversies that arise because of media content.

Controlling information flow to and within Asian nations was manageable when the primary sources of information were a few radio and television channels and a collection of newspapers and magazines, but there was always a desire among many in the public for alternatives that were less filtered by censorship. Long before the Internet boom in the 1980s, communication satellites brought foreign channels to viewers in many parts of the continent. In Singapore and Malaysia, home satellite receiving equipment was banned for a while, even though illegal home satellite systems were common in the hinterlands of East Malaysia. Such efforts to block technology by regulation and by law proved not to be fully effective. Technology cannot be blocked easily unless the country is able to cut itself off from the rest of the world. This was amply demonstrated with the arrival of Internet technologies.

Public resistance to government control of information increased as time went on. Growing access to news from foreign sources and increasing educational levels undercut the argument that societies needed protection from harmful information. Media managers were forced to accept their inability to exert absolute control over information circulating in the societies and to cope with the resulting diversity of thoughts and opinions.

Nevertheless, many Asian countries sought to regulate new technologies because they threatened political leaders' control of information. This has worked at times in some parts of Asia, but on the whole regulations of this sort have had only a moderate effect. China and Singapore are two countries whose regulatory efforts have been generally effective, largely because both nations have made information management a high priority and have invested heavily in monitoring and controlling technologies. Elsewhere, government officials have carried on with censoring practices even though new media channels spawned by advancing technologies have made them decreasingly effective. Traditional approaches to content management cannot really respond to the ever-proliferating alternative sources of information.

The primary reason that traditional methods of information control cannot be effective is that new technologies have utterly transformed the media environment. Every smartphone has the power to capture, edit, and distribute an individual's media messages. These messages are often relayed by Facebook, Instagram, or YouTube and sometimes by local mainstream media as user-generated content. If the subject matter is important and arresting, users need little production expertise in order to create materials that can sometimes reach millions of viewers. It is important to understand new Asian influences in today's global media marketplace.

Something New

In recent decades, Asian countries have had a growing presence in media content disseminated around the world. For example, China's news media is busily expanding its international influence. China's state-run press agency, Xinhua, now has more than 180 news bureaus around the world, publishing news around the clock in eight languages. China Radio International broadcasts its programs in 64 languages from 32 foreign bureaus, thus making it the world's second-largest international radio service after the BBC (Zhang, 2015). South Korea has also emerged as a vital pop culture exporter due to the global popularity of K-pop music and K-dramas. In 2012, South Korean singer Psy released his super hit "Gangnam Style," which had been viewed more than 3.2 billion times on YouTube as of January 2019. Since its emergence as a phenomenon within Korea, K-pop spread first to neighboring Asian countries and then farther afield to Europe, the Americas, and the Middle East, becoming a true global popular culture expression (Lie, 2012).

On the other hand, Asia has also become an increasingly profitable market for global media companies outside the region due to its sustained growth in media consumption. According to the Motion Picture Association of America, China will soon become the largest film market in the world. In 2018, for the first time, the Chinese movie market overtook North America in box office revenues (Associated Press, 2018).

Big-budget Hollywood productions sometimes had bigger debuts in China than in the United States. Even in advertising spending, Asia-Pacific now ranks second in regional media ad spending with $210.43 billion, which amounts to roughly one-third of the global ad business (eMarketer, 2018). Today, China and Japan are the world's first- and third-largest ad markets, respectively, and eMarketer projected that Asia-Pacific will surpass North America to become the leading ad-spending market in 2022.

The growing impact of Asian media markets will require global enterprises to develop a thorough understanding of Asian societies and audiences in order to produce content tailored to meet their needs and tastes. Meanwhile, Asian media are playing an increasingly critical role in conveying their political ideology and cultural values to global audiences. Let's explore how Asian media markets have taken advantage of unprecedented growth and digital disruptors.

BOOMING DIGITAL GROWTH

Throughout Asia, technological developments and rising ownership of Internet-enabled devices have resulted in fundamental shifts in the way individuals consume media. Internet users in the Asia-Pacific region total at least 2.2 billion people (Kemp, 2019). The Internet penetration level in the region is estimated at 52%, slightly lower than the global rate of 57% (Kemp, 2019).

Mobile Internet usage is a radical driver of digital growth in Asia. In 2019, mobile subscriptions in Asia-Pacific reached 4.4 billion, which equates to 104% of the region's total population (Kemp, 2019), much higher than the comparable global level of 67%. In addition, the monthly smartphone data traffic in Asia-Pacific was 19.43 billion gigabytes as of January 2019, which is almost five times the mobile data traffic in North America and four times that of Europe (Kemp, 2019). Mobile connectivity rates are high for the entire continent across Eastern Asia, Southern Asia, Central Asia, and Western Asia (Kemp, 2019). According to a report by Deloitte (2018), China is likely to own the world's largest 4G network, and only India can rival China's billion-plus subscribers. Southeast Asia also has exhibited a particularly strong growth in digital adoption due to its young population and high mobile penetration (Lacy, 2018).

However, digital connectivity is not evenly distributed across the region. East Asia is most developed in terms of Internet penetration, broadband mobile connectivity, social media penetration, and mobile social media penetration (Kemp, 2019). Central Asia and Southern Asia are much less developed in all four dimensions. Even within the same geographic area, differences still exist. For instance, within the 11 countries in Southeast Asia, Brunei leads the region in terms of Internet penetration at 86%, with Singapore closely behind at 82% (Kemp, 2017). Yet, in Laos and Myanmar, only less than one-third of the local residents are Internet users, and Cambodia and Timor-Leste were also at the lower end of the regional rankings (Kemp, 2017). The same pattern applies to social media usage within this region as well.

The variability in digital adoption inevitably poses a predicament for global media managers who intend to enter the pan-Asian market. Each Asian country is at a different stage of implementing digital media technologies due to their differing development of infrastructures and media systems. As a result, a single universal approach to media digitalization will not function for the whole region. Global media managers will be forced to implement a localized strategy that carefully considers the availability of technology providers and skilled human resources in individual countries. Their strategies must take the extent of local audiences' digital media engagement into account.

IMPACT OF DISRUPTED TECHNOLOGIES ON MEDIA MANAGEMENT

The Internet has been an important technological force, but changes in other areas also produce a powerful push forward in Asia's media industries. This region's media markets are experiencing the emergence of what have been called disruptive technologies. These are defined as "science-based innovations that have the potential to create a new industry or transform an existing one" (Day & Schoemaker, 2000, p. 2). Artificial intelligence (AI) and 5G are just two examples of technologies that have revolutionized Asian media industries and media management practices.

ARTIFICIAL INTELLIGENCE

Many Asian countries, including China, Japan, and South Korea, have pioneered the use of AI in the media, where the technology assists practitioners in content production, audience engagement, and monetization (OSA_DC, 2018; Walch, 2018).

Media managers engaged in content production can utilize AI for in-depth analyses on factors that determine which content brings the best return on investment. By doing this, AI allows producers to optimize creative decision making. AI also allows for automating content generation, such as producing movie trailers or creating different text versions of a news story. For example, China's state-run Xinhua News Agency launched the world's first AI anchor. The AI anchor was modeled on one of the agency's human presenters, but this artificial anchor can work 24 hours a day. The AI anchor learns from live broadcasting videos and can read texts as naturally as a professional news anchor. He reports through social media and on the agency's website (Handley, 2018).

AI technology also aids in developing media publishing strategies, such as translating content and monitoring different aspects of a live event. Furthermore, AI can improve the management and delivery of content and automate these operations by analyzing big data generated by content consumption. For social media content distribution, AI can generate automated and tailored content for different platforms, thus avoiding the redundancy of posting identical content on every platform.

Perhaps most important, AI technology has been widely used in advertising to target consumers with personalized ads and to provide dynamic content marketing strategies. For instance, Cyber-Agent, a leader in Japan's AI-empowered Internet ad business, widely supports promotion and advertising activities to clients (OSA_DC, 2018). Recently, advertisers have begun to use AI technology to identify various specific points in media content to enhance placement of advertising. AI therefore opens up a new realm of advertising delivery where highly powerful targeting can occur (Bragg, 2018).

In Asia, AI will undoubtedly continue to improve efficiency in content production, distribution, and audience engagement. The future will be very much as the Chinese

AI anchor described in his first broadcast: "The development of the media industry calls for continuous innovation and deep integration with international advanced technologies" (Handley, 2018).

FIFTH-GENERATION WIDE-AREA WIRELESS NETWORKS

Like AI, fifth-generation (5G) wide-area wireless networks present another disruption in global media industries. 5G wireless networks are expected to offer superior connectivity and data speed. Key advantages of 5G include high transmission speeds and low latency rates. In particular, the fastest-ever 5G lab transmission is 1 terabit per second (Storm, 2015). Download speeds of true 5G are bound to increase up to a hundredfold compared to 4G. 5G also enables close to zero latency between a streaming source and the audience (Granados, 2017). This means it only takes a few seconds to download an HD movie with the 5G network. Also, with latency at a negligible level, online real-time streaming of live events will enter a new era.

Asia has been a pioneer in the race to implement 5G infrastructure. Asian countries like China, South Korea, and Japan are outpacing the United States in 5G infrastructure development. Most notably, China is leading the way toward the 5G era by spending $24 billion more than U.S. firms on wireless communications infrastructure since 2015 (Deloitte, 2018). China now significantly exceeds the United States in terms of both the number of wireless communication sites and tower density per square mile (Deloitte, 2018). Chinese telecom firm Huawei—considered a leader in the technology—is already in the process of rolling out 5G service. According to Susan Crawford, a professor at Harvard Law School whose work focuses on technology policy, "The implication is that new industries of the future, the new ways of making a living, will be in China and not here. They'll have this huge sandbox to play with and a lot of control over the market" (McCausland, 2019).

The significant technical improvements brought by 5G will inevitably shift audiences' media demands and behavior, which, in turn, will lead to transformational changes in media management. The changes will focus on media content innovation and value chain effects (Granados, 2017). First, 5G reduces the trade-off effect between transmission speed and quality by allowing audiences to get HD-quality media on a high-speed stream. This trend calls for innovations in premium media content and high-resolution digital content and a move to live streaming, such as multiplayer mobile games and virtual reality–enabled real-time streaming of live events. 5G will also change the value chain in media industries in Asia. Currently, the industry believes "content is king" and positions the content creators/owners in the most profitable role because distribution costs are quite low. However, in the 5G era, the network providers will gain in market power due to their ability to distribute content of a superior technical quality. Content providers will then need to partner with 5G network providers and pay the price for their distribution network in order to deliver premium content.

The new changes in digital technology, such as AI and 5G wireless networks, have brought revolutionary opportunities and challenges for media managers in Asia. Several major trends are reviewed in the following section.

Opportunities and Challenges

Technology changes are a global reality, but they are amplified by the parallel economic changes that have taken place and are still underway. The Internet, communication satellites, and smartphones, along with many other technologies, diminished the power of governments to control media content. One reason for this change was due to regulators being overwhelmed by the sheer number of new media outlets available through various technologies. It became nearly impossible to monitor and supervise them all. But the proliferation of channels also disrupted the operations of existing media by shrinking the size of their viewing, listening, and reading audiences. Whereas in the 1980s a television station in a capital city of Asia might have only a dozen competing channels, within two decades the number of new competitors numbered in the dozens or hundreds (McDaniel, 2002).

OPPORTUNITIES

As noted in the introduction, huge differences exist between Asian media ecosystems. Over the course of the last few decades, media management practices in Asia, as in much of the world, have been utterly reshaped by media convergence. It is important to note that the particular contexts within nations significantly impact the culture of convergence and media management in a convergent environment because media products are produced and circulated within and across national borders. As Jenkins (2006) points out,

> The rate of convergence will be uneven within a given culture, with those who are most affluent and most technologically literate becoming the early adopters and other segments of the population struggling to catch up. Insofar as these trends extend beyond a specifically American context, the rate of convergence will be uneven across national borders, resulting in the consolidations of power and wealth within the "have" nations and some shift in the relative status and prominence of developing nations. (p. 35)

This is particularly true in Asian countries. To best understand how media managers have taken advantage of regional opportunities, we will summarize the opportunities in media management by analyzing media management practices in three Asian countries—Japan, Singapore, and India—each representing a unique national setting. Note the differences among them as well as how they differ from the Chinese case study introduced earlier in this chapter.

JAPAN

Japan's media market assumed its modern form in the late 19th century. But today the Japanese media industry is facing unprecedented opportunities and difficulties posed by the Internet's expansion and drastic social changes brought about by a population decline and a rapidly aging society.

Newspapers remain the nation's most significant print media. The largest national newspaper, the *Yomiuri Shimbun*, has the world's highest daily circulation at 8.73 million copies (Dentsu Media Innovation Lab, 2018). In addition, most regional papers, operated mainly by their original owners, have a circulation share of more than half of Japanese households. The business models generally rely on circulation revenue instead of advertising (Dentsu Media Innovation Lab, 2018). TV is another vital mass medium, especially as a source for breaking news and as an advertising vehicle. The major players in TV broadcasting are a public broadcaster—NHK (a.k.a., Japan Broadcasting Corporation) and five national commercial broadcast networks (Nippon Television Network, Tokyo Broadcasting System Television, TV Asahi, TV Tokyo, and Fuji Television Network), each operating a flagship station in a major city and sharing content with its affiliates.

The Internet has brought structural shifts to the nation's media industries, and newspaper revenues have been declining in recent years, mainly attributed to a fall in ad sales. The overall telecommunication infrastructure in Japan has shifted from fixed to mobile. In 2011, mobile communication revenues for the first time surpassed revenues from fixed-line services, and they have kept growing. As in other industrialized countries, in Japan TV audiences are increasingly watching content online, and this has forced TV broadcasters to experiment with new ways to maintain their traditional viewership while leveraging digital opportunities.

In responding to such structural shifts, Japan's media industries have undergone management changes. Newspapers increasingly cope with digital technologies via streamlined staffing, outsourced printing, and eliminating evening editions with the introduction of digital editions. Broadcasters are increasingly incorporating the Internet as part of their business strategy. For instance, NHK started a trial to simultaneously stream programs online and offer 4K/8K Super Hi-Vision Satellite Broadcasting for its regular services (Tarr, 2018). The five major commercial TV networks also jointly started TVer, which is an ad-supported and free streaming video service (Nikkei, 2017). TVer provides more than 170 programs on a weekly basis via a mobile app. Clearly, Japan's newspaper and broadcasting industries have adopted technological and structural convergences to exploit opportunities presented by digital technologies.

Unique, yet significant, pop cultural presences in Japan are maintained by manga and animation, industries that highlight a media-mix strategy in order to maximize content impact (Dentsu Media Innovation Lab, 2018). Typically, a manga product is first serialized in a manga magazine, then published in comic book format. If the manga accumulates a large fan base, it will then be adapted as an animated TV program or film. During a production's life cycle, many different forms of content are spun off based on the manga work, such as books, TV programs, animated films, live-action movies, theater plays, video actor concerts, animation song concerts, original key drawing exhibitions, and toys (Galbraith & Karlin, 2016). To pursue a media-mix strategy and commercial successes such as merchandising opportunities, companies from various media sectors, such as TV stations, book publishers, ad agencies, film companies, and music studios, work closely together as a "production cooperative committee" to produce animation-related content (Galbraith & Karlin, 2016). In this process, convergence occurs at the tactical and presentation levels for the animated content production.

Japan's audiences have followed the global trend of using multiple devices for seamless access to a wide variety of digital media content. Media industries have generally recognized the importance of Internet engagement to meet audience demands and to maintain business viability. However, in the past, traditional media industries in Japan have been developed around multiple platforms, "each with its own monopolized transmission and distribution channels" (Dentsu Media Innovation Lab, 2018, p. 9). According to a white paper released by Dentsu (2018), "this multi-platform model does not suit an emerging networked society, where electronic transfers no longer rely on specific channels and devices" (p. 9). Thus, media managers in Japan must adapt to convergence at the platform level while also pursuing innovation and efficient practices through the deployment of digital technologies. We will discuss the challenges faced by the Asian media organizations in the following section.

SINGAPORE

Media practices in Singapore have tended to keep the government in absolute power and control. Since the nation's independence in 1965, an ideology of control has been the dominant force behind the government's management of mass media (Lee & Willnat, 2009). Media management in Singapore is therefore understood as the government seeking to "control, manipulate or influence media organizations in ways which correspond to their political objectives" (McNair, 1995, p. 135).

Like most other Asian countries, Singapore's media landscape can be divided into broadcast media, print media, and the Internet. By far the leading player in the broadcast sector is the Media Corporation of Singapore (MediaCorp), which is a private company wholly owned by the Singapore government through its state investment agency Temasek Holdings (Lee & Willnat, 2009). Similarly, Singapore Press Holdings (SPH) dominates the print media industry, leading to a government-linked print media monopoly. According to Lee and Willnat (2009), the formation of SPH resulted in "a reduction in alternative voices and venues" because "domestic news about Singaporean political affairs became more and more centralized and mainstreamed" (p. 100). Beyond these two big corporations, a wide range of global media publications and broadcasters also exist, showcasing a contrasting open and vibrant media marketplace in Singapore.

Singapore offers users some of the fastest Internet speeds in the world, both on mobile and broadband (*ASEAN Post*, 2018). Singaporeans are also considered more tech-savvy than Americans or Britons (Lee, 2005). With relatively fewer regulatory constraints compared to broadcast and print media, the Internet remains the platform most open to alternative voices in the country (Freedom House, 2017). However, monitored by the Media Development Authority, the Internet in Singapore is protected from threats to the People's Action Party (PAP) that controls government (Freedom House, 2017).

In this government-driven media ecosystem, media convergence in Singapore is also orchestrated by the PAP government and required to serve the nation's economic development effort. In September 2004, the government publicly announced that an adjustment to the television and newspaper operations would be needed for the purpose of stemming losses and enhancing shareholder value (Lee & Willnat, 2009; Teo, 2004). Using this rationale, a quasi-merger between MediaCorp and SPH was launched to solidify Singapore's duopolistic media structure, even though the government denied that it had directed the merger (Lee, 2003; Teo, 2004).

In sum, the media management model employed in Singapore has been designed to serve the interests of the PAP government while restraining political expression in the nation (Lee & Willnat, 2009). At the same time, this model has also weakened domestic media's efforts to compete in the global media market and imposed inefficiency in preparing the nation's media sector for global expansion. In short, media managers in Singapore gain a competitive edge by aligning their strategies with the national development plan and with the government's positions on media-related issues. Also, in striving to be a world-class Asian technology hub, Singapore has developed an advanced technology infrastructure and therefore can provide deep technical resources and talents to media players overseas wishing to enter the Singapore market.

INDIA

The largest newspaper market in the world is in India, where there are more than 70,000 newspapers (Biswas, 2012), and print advertising constitutes around half of overall media ad revenues (Vaidyanathan, 2011). There are more than 500 satellite channels and over 250 FM radio stations competing for India's broadcasting audience (Biswas, 2012; Thakurta, 2012). Television has surpassed newspapers to become the primary information source for Indian audiences due to its instant availability and frequent news breaks, live-ins, and voice-overs (Chishti, 2017).

Even though robust, traditional media must share audiences with digital media, which have become an increasingly important platform of communication. India is the world's fastest-growing smartphone market with an estimated 435 million Internet-enabled mobile phones (Chishti, 2017), and this has encouraged India's digital marketers to shift to "mobile-first" branding and consumer engagement strategies. A few large media conglomerates (e.g., the ABP Group, The Hindu Group, HT Media Limited, NDTV Group, The Times Group, Zee Entertainment Enterprises) dominate the Indian media market both vertically and horizontally (Thakurta, 2012). Cross-media ownership like this naturally plays a deciding role in controlling the information available to audiences.

In India, media convergence is not an immediate concern, primarily because of the dominance of print media, even though convergence has occurred at a tactical level, such as cross-promotion and cloning of content on different media platforms. India's media organizations commonly cross-promote content produced by partner outlets or subsidiaries. A good example of such cross-media coordination is the Alive app launched by *Times of India*. This app allows *Times of India* readers to use a mobile phone's video camera to capture selected images published in the newspaper and from those to produce a video or other digital content on the device (Mishra, 2016).

Social media use among Indian media organizations and professionals is more top-down than bottom-up (Mishra, 2016). Upper-level managers/editors, well-known television personalities, and famous journalists frequently interact with audiences on Twitter, and some build large fan bases. Editors in some media organizations even direct reporters to make use of Twitter for professional purposes (Mishra, 2016). However, most reporters seem not to take social media seriously for coverage of hard news

(Belair-Gagnon & Agur, 2013; Mishra, 2016). Many news organizations still need significant investments in social media.

While tactical convergence is a marked feature of many Indian media organizations, structural convergence is hardly visible. Mishra (2016) identified four barriers facing media convergence in India. First, traditional media do not yet view digitization as profitable because of print media's hold on readers. Second, traditional journalists have not yet accepted the benefits of convergence and have only considered it as a cost-cutting tool for media enterprises. Third, media organizations lack organizational policies on convergence that support incentives and remuneration for reporters with multimedia skills. Lastly, media organizations in India have largely failed to provide sufficient investments in technological resources and training required for convergence. For these reasons, opportunities in the television and digital realms are particularly attractive for media managers in India. Considering that practitioners in India are slowly moving toward media convergence, incremental strategies could be applied to evolving business models without cannibalizing current ones.

CHALLENGES

Clearly, media managers in Asia must grapple with the challenges of media convergence in different ways depending on regional nuances. However, one main challenge for all managers in Asia is an increase in channels and segmentation.

INCREASED CHANNEL GROWTH

While the Internet was the main factor in the growing number of media outlets, other technologies played a role as well. In broadcasting, a major change occurred because of the shift from analog to digital transmissions. By 2015, many Asian countries had begun the digital conversion or at least had a plan in place. Accomplishing this changeover was not an easy task.

Broadcasters and viewers alike had to adapt or replace their equipment to make the digital transition, and the added costs were particularly painful in developing nations. Moreover, the analog to digital conversion actually increased the number of channels on the air in some nations. For example, in Thailand's digital transformation, 48 digital channels were allocated, greatly expanding the number of licensed domestic channels from just six. This large expansion in channels introduced many new media enterprises that were forced to compete within the Thailand market, thus intensifying competition for market share. In Thailand, as in most of Asia, broadcast outlets—even those operated by governments or public corporations—are dependent on advertising to finance their operations (Magpanthong & McDaniel, 2015).

INCREASED MARKET SEGMENTATION

The net result of the growth in channels was increasing market segmentation. Channels that provided a broad mix of content found it increasingly difficult to maintain their audiences against competing channels that offered greater specialization, such as action movies, food channels, or sports. The problem posed by specialization was that the channels with narrower program types would draw smaller audiences. In countries like India, Indonesia, or China with large populations, specialized channels could attract an audience sufficient to sustain themselves through advertising, but in markets with smaller populations, this programming strategy would not be successful.

Print media faces similar technological challenges, accompanied by a general decline in print readership across the region. Smartphones and tablets became the growth opportunities in most parts of Asia, and as print circulations have declined, publishers have concentrated their attention on delivering digital versions online. Between 2015 and 2020, Asian readership was projected to shrink by 5.4% with smaller but substantial drops forecast in Korea and Japan (Kikuchi, 2016).

Despite these challenges, the Asian media market offers many opportunities for future practitioners. Use the following action plan as a guide to implement future business strategies.

ACTION PLAN

1. Take advantage of unique regional differences of your media market to adapt to media convergence.
2. Utilize new technology, specifically AI and 5G networks, to engage audiences in the process.
3. Plan for the challenges of channel growth and market segmentation.

KEY TAKEAWAYS

1. Asia presents a high level of heterogeneity in terms of culture, political system, market size, economic power, and technological infrastructure. Asia is the most dynamic part of the global economy.
2. Media management practices in Asia have been remade by convergence. Media convergence can occur at the ownership, tactic, structure, information-sharing, and presentation levels. National contexts significantly impact the culture of convergence.
3. Managers of Asian media are subject to strict oversight of their outlet's content by government and governmental agencies. Many Asian countries also seek to regulate new technologies because they threaten political leaders' control of information.
4. Asian countries have an evolving influence on media content creation and dissemination in the global media marketplace. Asia has also become an increasingly profitable media market.
5. Asia is embracing digital revolution, which has fundamentally influenced the region's media management practices. Mobile Internet usage is a radical driver of digital growth in Asia. However, digital connectivity is not evenly distributed across the region.

6. Asia's media markets are facing the emergence of disruptive technologies. Artificial intelligence and 5G are the two technologies that have revolutionized the Asian media industry and media management practices.

CONCLUSION

Asia is an extremely complex region, with its nations ranging from the most highly developed industrial countries to some of the world's least developed. Political systems within the region are equally varied, running the gamut from highly open democracies to closed hierarchies. For this reason, making generalizations about Asia is a risky business, but this chapter has sought to capture key themes that are broadly important within the region.

Asian governments and governmental agencies mostly apply strict censorship on media content and practices. The types of censorship imposed differ from nation to nation, as each has its own historical and cultural context. It is not uncommon for Asian countries to regulate new technologies for political and economic purposes. For example, in little more than a generation, China has gone from a tightly controlled command economy to a semi-capitalist system that has produced long-term growth in wealth. Chinese families that a few decades ago would not have had any kind of telephone now have multiple smartphones that connect owners with global media. These conditions have simultaneously spawned convergence while diminishing controls exercised by governments over information flows within national borders.

On the flip side, media practices are experiencing radical growth due to the impact of revolutionary digital technologies such as AI and 5G wireless networks. In terms of the number of mobile Internet users and Internet penetration rate, Asia has become one of the world's most connected regions. This alone has enabled Asian nations to move from merely consuming media products to producing media content that is distributed worldwide. The most important task faced by media managers in Asia is to stay ahead of these swiftly evolving trends while adopting successful strategies to cope with intensifying global competition.

Both opportunities and challenges exist in the region's media management environment, in large part because media convergence has reshaped the industry. In Japan, a multiplatform model does not suit audiences' needs for seamless access to various digital content. In Singapore, media practices must be consistent with the national development plan, and media are tightly monitored by the government to ensure compliance. Of course, this type of close oversight could weaken Singapore media's competitive edge in the global marketplace. In India, traditional media industries such as TV and print are still robust, but opportunities for growth also can be found in the digital realm thanks to the world's fastest growth in smartphone usage. Across the region, however, media managers are being forced to accommodate the demands imposed by channel growth and market segmentation.

Rapid changes in technology are placing new pressures on Asian media practitioners. Xie, Schauster, and Neill (2018) studied expectations for higher education among advertising executives in China and found that skills in communication, creativity, storytelling, digital/social media, and business, and a facility in the English language, are highly valued for those entering the job market. Also, soft skills such as adaptability, critical thinking, continuous learning, teamwork, and a deep understanding of the domestic cultures and audiences are also needed by media professionals who work in diverse Asian social settings. Furthermore, an ability to make use of expanded AI capabilities is needed by Asian media managers. Increasingly, they have to be capable of generating consumer insights from big consumer data sets and developing successful media strategies through those insights.

The next chapter will focus on media management practices in Latin America. Since the late 16th century, businessmen, artisans, and sailors from Asian countries such as China and Korea have traveled through the Maritime Silk Road to Latin America for trade purposes. In the 19th century, Western colonialists recruited millions of contracted labor workers from Eastern and Southeastern Asia and sent them to Latin American countries such as Peru and Mexico for infrastructure construction, work that dramatically contributed to contemporary economic and social development there. Considering this historical bond between the two regions, it is interesting to compare their media management practices and to review the latest trends in Latin America's media industries.

REFERENCES

Alaimo, K. (2017). *Pitch, tweet, or engage on the street.* Routledge.

ASEAN Post (2018, August 24). Singapore wins Internet speed race. https://theaseanpost.com/article/singapore-wins-internet-speed-race

Associated Press. (2018, April 5). Hollywood says China will soon be world's top film market, as ticket sales overtake US-Canada in 2018. *South China Morning Post.* https://www.scmp.com/culture/film-tv/article/2140381/china-will-soon-be-worlds-top-film-market-having-over taken-us-canada

Belair-Gagnon, V., & Agur, C. (2013, January 14). *When print is thriving, where does social media fit in? A look at practices at India's* The Hindu. Nieman Journalism Lab. http://www.nieman lab.org/2013/01/when-print-is-thriving-where-does-social-media-fit-a-look-at-practices-at-indias-the-hindu

Biswas, S. (2012, January 12). *Why are India's media under fire?* BBC News. https://www.bbc.com/news/world-asia-india-16524711

Bragg, T. (2018, January 18). *AI is helping media and entertainment do more with less.* Tech Wire Asia. https://techwireasia.com/2018/01/arti%EF%AC%81cial-intelligence-helping-media-enter tainment

Chishti, A. H. (2017). *India's changing media landscape: Cross media ownership, FDI and broadcast bill.* Partridge India.

Day, G. S., & Schoemaker, P. J. H. (2000). *Wharton on managing emerging technologies.* Wiley.

Deloitte. (2018, December 11). *China, by design: World-leading connectivity nurtures new digital business models.* https://www2.deloitte.com/us/en/insights/industry/technology/technology-media-and-telecom-predictions/china-communications-infrastructure.html

Dentsu Media Innovation Lab. (2018, August 27). *Information media trends in Japan 2018: Information media white paper.* Dentsu Inc. http://www.dentsu.com/news/release/2018/0827-009593.html

eMarketer. (2018, May 7). *eMarketer releases new global media ad spending estimates.* https://www.emarketer.com/content/emarketer-total-media-ad-spending-worldwide-will-rise-7-4-in-2018

Freedom House. (2017). *Singapore: Freedom on the net 2017*. https://freedomhouse.org/sites/default/files/FOTN%202017_Singapore.pdf
Galbraith, P. W., & Karlin, J. G. (2016). *Media convergence in Japan*. Kinema Club.
Granados, N. (2017, July 17). 5G: The next tech disruption in media and entertainment is coming. *Forbes*. https://www.forbes.com/sites/nelsongranados/2017/07/17/5g-the-next-tech-disruption-in-media-and-entertainment-is-coming
Handley, L. (2018, November 9). *The "world's first" A.I. news anchor has gone live in China*. CNBC. https://www.cnbc.com/2018/11/09/the-worlds-first-ai-news-anchor-has-gone-live-in-china.html
Haque, M. (2004). Overview of public relations in Asia. In D. J. Tilson & E. C. Alozie (Eds.), *Toward the common good: Perspectives in international public relations* (pp. 346–362). Pearson.
Inquirer. (2018, May 30). *GDP growth projection for Asia, 2018*. https://business.inquirer.net/251677/gdp-growth-projection-asia-2018
International Monetary Fund. (2018, May). *Regional economic outlook: Asia Pacific*. https://www.imf.org/en/Publications/REO/APAC/Issues/2018/04/16/areo0509
Jenkins, H. (2006). *Convergence culture: Where old and new media collide*. New York University Press.
Jung, J., & Kim, Y. (2018). Media management and economics research in Asia. In A. B. Albarran, B. I. Mierzejewska, & J. Jung (Eds.), *Handbook of media management and economics* (pp. 61–77). Routledge.
Kemp, S. (2017, February 16). *Digital in Southeast Asia in 2017*. We are social. https://wearesocial.com/special-reports/digital-southeast-asia-2017
Kemp, S. (2019, January 30). *Digital 2019: Global Internet use accelerates*. We are social. https://wearesocial.com/blog/2019/01/digital-2019-global-internet-use-accelerates
Kikuchi, T. (2016, October 20). Asia's print media are on the ropes. *Financial Times*. https://www.ft.com/content/068095bc-9d24-11e6-8324-be63473ce146
Lacy, L. (2018, December 3). *Why 2018 was the "year of ecommerce" in Southeast Asia*. AdWeek. https://www.adweek.com/digital/why-2018-was-the-year-of-ecommerce-in-southeast-asia
Lee, T. (2003). Internet use in Singapore: Politics and policy implications. *Media International Australia Incorporating Culture and Policy, 107*, 75–88.
Lee, T. (2005). Internet control and auto-regulation in Singapore. *Surveillance & Society, 3*, 74–95.
Lee, T., & Willnat, L. (2009). Media management and political communication in Singapore. In L. Willnat & A. J. Aw (Eds.), *Political communication in Asia* (pp. 93–111). Routledge.
Lie, J. (2012). What is the K in K-pop? South Korean popular music, the culture industry, and national identity. *Korea Observer, 43*, 339–363.
Magpanthong, C., & McDaniel, D. O. (2015). The audience for Thailand's booming community radio system. *Journal of Radio & Audio Media, 22*, 60–76. doi: 10.1080/19376529.2015.1015863
McCausland, P. (2019, February 22). *Race is on for global 5G dominance—and Trump is cheering from the sidelines*. NBC News. https://www.nbcnews.com/tech/mobile/race-global-5g-dominance-trump-s-it-n974156
McDaniel, D. O. (1994). *Broadcasting in the Malay world: Culture, conflict, and accommodation*. Ablex.
McDaniel, D. O. (2002). *Electronic tigers of Southeast Asia: The politics of media, technology, and national development*. Iowa State University Press.
McNair, B. (1995). *An introduction to political communication*. Routledge.
Mishra, S. (2016). Media convergence: Indian journalists' perceptions of its challenges and implications. *Convergence, 22*, 102–112.
National Geographic Society. (2018). *Asia: Physical geography*. https://www.nationalgeographic.org/encyclopedia/asia
Nikkei. (2017, April 1). *Japan's key TV networks to band together on online streaming*. Nikkei Asian Review. https://asia.nikkei.com/Business/Japan-s-key-TV-networks-to-band-together-on-online-streaming
OSA_DC. (2018, April 4). *Artificial intelligence in Japan*. Medium. https://medium.com/osadc/artificial-intelligence-in-japan-r-d-market-and-industry-analysis-a738c3295b16
Storm, D. (2015, February 25). *UK researchers shatter world record by hitting 5G speeds of 1Tb per second*. Computer World. https://www.computerworld.com/article/2889154/uk-researchers-shatter-world-record-by-hitting-5g-speeds-of-1tb-per-second.html

Tarr, G. (2018, November 29). *NHK to begin 1st 8K satellite broadcast channel.* HD Guru. https://hdguru.com/nhk-to-begin-1st-8k-satellite-broadcast-channel-dec-1

Teo, L. (2004, September 19). PM Lee: No u-turn in opening up of media. *The Sunday Times* (Singapore), p. 8.

Thakurta, P. (2012, July 30). *Media ownership trends in India.* The Hoot. http://asu.thehoot.org/resources/media-ownership/media-ownership-in-india-an-overview-6048

Vaidyanathan, R. (2011, August). *Newspapers: Why India's newspaper industry is booming.* BBC. https://www.bbc.com/news/business-14362723

Walch, K. (2018, September 7). Is South Korea poised to be a leader in AI? *Forbes.* https://www.forbes.com/sites/cognitiveworld/2018/09/07/is-south-korea-poised-to-be-a-leader-in-ai

World Bank. (2018, October 4). *East Asia and Pacific growth remains resilient despite heightened global uncertainty, World Bank says.* https://www.worldbank.org/en/news/press-release/2018/10/04/east-asia-and-pacific-growth-remains-resilient-despite-heightened-global-uncertainty-world-bank-says

Xie, Q., Schauster, E., & Neill, M. S. (2018). Expectations for advertising and public relations education from agency executives: A comparative study between China and the United States. *Journal of Current Issues & Research in Advertising, 39,* 289–307.

Yin, L., & Liu, X. (2014). A gesture of compliance: Media convergence in China. *Media, Culture & Society, 36,* 561–577.

Zhang, V. (2015, August 10). *How Chinese media is going global.* World Economic Forum. https://www.weforum.org/agenda/2015/08/how-chinese-media-is-going-global

CHAPTER 13

Media Management in Latin America

María Elena Gutiérrez-Rentería, Universidad Panamericana
Carlos López-Hernández, Universidad Panamericana

LEARNING OBJECTIVES

1. Understand the macroeconomic environment in which media companies in Latin America operate.
2. Describe the structure of the media market in Latin America, mainly represented by Argentina, Brazil, Mexico, and Chile, the leaders in the media business of this region.
3. Identify the opportunities and challenges of the media industry brought by the era of digital convergence in Latin America.

Media companies, like others, operate to obtain profits and have an economic, political, and social responsibility. These companies produce and distribute information and entertainment content to attract audiences and advertisers. Historically, advertisers have been the main revenue source for traditional media organizations in Latin America. Today, some media managers seek to expand the revenue model through subscriptions and monetization of the database.

The five most influential multimedia firms in Latin America are América Móvil and Grupo Televisa (Mexico), Grupo Globo (Brazil), Grupo Cisneros (Venezuela), and Grupo Clarín (Argentina). The majority of these companies, considered traditional media, have adapted to the era of digital convergence. The business strategies of these groups have been to consolidate and expand their business models to continue to attract audiences and advertisers. All these exist in a context where the globalization of markets and the liberalization of industries have allowed international media with a global presence, such as Walt Disney, Netflix, Amazon, Facebook, and Google, to participate more actively in the Latin American market.

Latin America and the Caribbean have more than 600 million inhabitants (ECLAC–United Nations, 2016), in which Brazil and Mexico account for more than 50% of the population. The media market is ripe, as the society is represented by an active, young audience. Specifically, 35% of the population in Latin America is between 15 and 34 years, and 28% are children (ECLAC–United Nations, 2016).

The field of media management and economics examines how media companies operate through different levels of activities (e.g., global, national, household, and individual) and how they interact with other market forces, such as globalization, technology, and social aspects (Albarran, 2017). One of the main objectives of media management research is to identify how media companies use different business models to take advantage of scarce resources to satisfy the needs and desires of media consumers.

Beginning in the 2000s, technology companies, mainly focused on software, started to participate in the traditional media marketplace in Latin America. Firms such as Netflix, Amazon, and YouTube, and social media like Facebook, Twitter, and Instagram, began offering video streaming services. In addition, telecommunication companies, such as Comcast, Cablevisión, AT&T, and Sky, entered the Latin American media market. All these companies use strategies to gain more audiences and advertisers while dealing with different economic, political, and social challenges depending on their level of influence in the marketplace.

The objective of this chapter is to introduce the media marketplace in Latin America, mainly represented by Argentina, Brazil, Mexico, and Chile, as the leaders of this region's media business. In the following sections, we will first discuss the traditional "old" macroeconomic environment of the media industry in Latin America and then present the structure of the marketplace in the region. In addition, we will describe the new characteristics of the Latin American media business environment in the era of convergence. Finally, we will identify the opportunities and challenges for media entrepreneurs and managers who want to enter the Latin American market. Let's explore the case study of the consolidated companies América Móvil and Grupo Televisa to see how they have adapted and made media history in the region.

CASE STUDY

The media industry in Latin America presents a new competitive environment resulting from digital media convergence and the liberalization of the telecommunication market since the 1990s. In the Mexican telecommunication and media market, there are two leading companies, América Móvil and Grupo Televisa, that have a significant influence on the national economy, politics, and society.

América Móvil and Grupo Televisa both compete for the same national and regional markets (Gutiérrez-Rentería & López, 2014). In addition, these Mexican companies also offer video streaming through the digital platforms Claro Video (América Móvil) and Blim (Grupo Televisa) that compete with the U.S. company Netflix in Latin America. Facing different macro- and microeconomic challenges in the national market, América Móvil and Grupo Televisa have stood out for adapting to media convergence and making strategic decisions. As such, these two Mexican companies are still leaders in Latin America's communication, information, and entertainment industry today.

América Móvil started its business by offering fixed telephony and later the Internet in Mexico in the 1990s. Today, this company has taken the opportunities offered by digital convergence to expand its business in the news media industry. For example, UnoTV, a news company owned by América Móvil, is the largest news creator and distributor in Mexico (Gutiérrez-Rentería, 2018). It should be noted that America Móvil started its business in the telecommunications industry. Its network-based business was unrelated to the information and entertainment industry. Regardless, due to its strategic business decisions and adapting to the convergent environment, the company is still one of the leaders in the Latin American media market, offering information and entertainment to large audiences today.

On the other hand, Grupo Televisa has continued to be faithful to its initial business model. Yet, it has also taken advantage of digital convergence to find new niches in the Mexican media market by adapting its digital platforms to the new electronic devices. Grupo Televisa is unique in offering all its news programs via Alexa, Google Assistant, Siri, and Apple TV. In addition, these news programs can be viewed through social networks and mobile devices. Digital convergence has allowed Grupo Televisa to expand its offerings through Blim, the digital platform from which it obtains new revenues based on subscriptions. Here you see how media giants in Latin America have adapted to media convergence. This dynamic and adaptable nature is critical to media managers who want to enter the Latin American marketplace. Let us explore how traditional regional nuances of Latin America continue to drive future business strategies.

Something Old

Latin America can be studied as a regional block because there are shared social and cultural values in the Ibero-America region. However, it is a reality that the economic, political, and social circumstances of each country have been different during the media industry development in the region. Many of the media companies hold strong roots in Latin American culture. These "old" stories are important for any future practitioner to understand before entering the market.

Media practitioners must visualize the marketplace and contextualize the media and telecommunication companies in Latin America by comparing them with larger media companies within a global scope (López Hernández, 2013). The media and telecommunication industry in the region can also be understood with respect to the current participation of leading companies in the convergent environment (Gutiérrez-Rentería & López, 2014).

According to *América Economía* (2018), 30 of the top 50 companies in Latin America are linked to the media industry. They are divided into the telecommunication (25 firms), media (3), and entertainment (2) sectors. América Móvil appears in first place among the companies in the region and ranks third on the overall list. In addition, IO company from Brazil is in fourth place in the telecommunication industry and ranks 64th among all companies. The Mexican Grupo Televisa is in seventh place, and Telecom of Argentina places 10th in the industry. Given that América Móvil and Grupo Televisa are the two Latin American companies with greater economic and social weight in the media industry at the regional level, it is pertinent to understand their "old" strategic successes.

ORIGIN OF AMÉRICA MÓVIL

América Móvil Teléfonos de México (Telmex) was created in 1947 as the outcome of the merger between Ericsson, a Swedish company, and the International Telephone and Telegraph Company (AT&T), a U.S. company, becoming the only telephone service operator in the country. In 1958, the Mexican government decided to grant facilities for national private capital to acquire the shares of Telmex. Three decades later, the government decided to take control of the company and left only 49% of shares in the hands of private investors in 1973. In 1990, the government decided to privatize the company, and it was acquired by businessman Carlos Slim. Due to government control and support, no other companies in Mexico could offer telephone service from 1947 to 1990. Telmex grew as a monopoly under state protection.

The strategic success of Carlos Slim and América Móvil were largely due to the purchase of Telmex, a landline telephone monopoly. The purchase was made from the government when there were macro- and microeconomic opportunities for Mexican industry development (Gutiérrez-Rentería, 2011). This entrepreneur strengthened the telecommunication industry in the domestic market and initiated further movements for international expansion. Beginning in the late 1990s, América Móvil led the triple and quadruple play market in Latin American countries. The economic and political environment in the domestic market led to the international expansion and consolidation of other companies within the group.

Currently, América Móvil's affiliated companies offer fixed and mobile telephony services, Internet, and information and entertainment content through the digital platform Claro Video. The company also offers telephone services in the United States and triple and quadruple play in other Latin American countries (América Móvil, 2017). Yet, it should be noted that América Móvil's main revenue does not come from fixed telephony today. It has expanded from its monopoly position of this sector to many other businesses in Mexico. In addition, América Móvil has a presence in 18 countries and competes in the international market with U.S. companies such as AT&T and Verizon Communications, China Mobile of Hong Kong, and Telefónica de España (Gutiérrez-Rentería & López, 2014).

ORIGIN OF GRUPO TELEVISA

Grupo Televisa, owned by the Azcárraga family and Televisa, has predominated over other media companies in Mexico with its production and distribution of audiovisual content (Gutiérrez-Rentería, 2011). This private capital company, during the period 1973–1993, was exempt from competitors of the same nature. The country only allowed two other television alternatives: public and university. Therefore, it can be considered a monopolistic commercial company in the market.

The content strategy of Grupo Televisa resulted in loyal audiences and advertisers. Its flagship products were soap operas and music programs. In addition, Emilio Azcárraga Vidaurreta, of the Azcárraga family, was the first Latin American entrepreneur who entered the audiovisual market targeting a Spanish-speaking audience in the United States in 1962.

In the 1980s, the three most important channels targeted to the Hispanic population in the United States were Galavisión, Telemundo, and Univisión. These channels gained 50% of their content from Grupo Televisa. In addition to the U.S. market, Televisa's participation in Europe led to establishing companies such as Galavisión in the Netherlands and Spain. Furthermore, in the first three years of the 1990s, Televisa joined in the Mexican Stock Exchange and the New York Stock Exchange.

Grupo Televisa is one of the leaders in the entertainment industry in Mexico due to its audiovisual content production and distribution, both in open commercial television and in pay TV through cable and satellite. It is also an important player of the international media marketplace. Through the years, Televisa has diversified its business model to include games and raffles.

As mentioned in the case study earlier in this chapter, Grupo Televisa and América Móvil are the leading media companies in Mexico. There is much to learn from both companies' business strategies. Both companies have directly influenced the development and penetration of the Internet in Mexico and in what today is known as the "network economy." The media products created by América Móvil and Grupo Televisa, like most other Mexican companies in these convergent industries, have benefited from Mexicans' 5.5-hour daily consumption of digital media, information, and entertainment. These companies, along with foreign companies AT&T, Telefónica, and Oi de Brazil, are the most influential companies in the media marketplace in Latin America.

It is always important for media companies to understand the macro- and microenvironment of an industry. In this case, the companies that have excelled in the media industry in Latin America have raffled different economic, political, and social environments to succeed in the marketplace. Digital convergence now allows them to be present in multiple regional markets, with the opportunity to expand their business models to attract new consumers.

Something New

The use of digital technologies and Internet penetration in Latin America are increasing. The percentage of households connected to the Internet in the region was 50.2% in 2017 (ECLAC–United Nations, 2019). These new media adaptations have transformed many of the "old" assumptions of media businesses.

The 10 most competitive countries in the region are Chile, Panama, Costa Rica, Mexico, Colombia, Peru, Uruguay, Brazil, Ecuador, and Guatemala (World Economic Forum, 2015). However, the growth of Latin American companies is low according to the Global Innovation Index (GII) report (Dutta, Lanvin, & Wunsch-Vincent, 2018). This report considered factors such as the level of competitiveness, technological innovation, the development of new business models and the ease of doing business with other companies. Of the total 126 countries analyzed by the GII, there are only 16 countries from the region.

The top countries in the region by their level of competitiveness are Chile (37.79), Costa Rica (35.72), Mexico (35.34), Uruguay (34.2), Colombia (33.78), and Brazil (33.44).

THE STRUCTURE OF THE MEDIA MARKET IN LATIN AMERICA

While the macro- and microeconomic circumstances of each country influence regional media industries (Albarran & Hutton, 2009), there are similar characteristics that may be important to understanding the current competitive media environment and telecommunication industry. Regional leading companies, as well as concentrated structures of the market, have maintained dominant positions due to their ability to adapt to changes (Gutiérrez-Rentería, 2011; Moreira, 2016; Noam, 2016). In addition, some communication and telecommunication companies are of family origin, actively competing in capital markets with global penetration. Since the 2000s, the participation of global media companies in Latin America has grown.

For example, in Argentina, the government has passed legislation that exempts media firms from a national bankruptcy law that allows foreign investors to purchase their assets, extends their licensing arrangements, and grants them tax exemptions (Mastrini, Bizberge, & Becerra, 2016). The liberalization of the industry has attracted large investments in telecommunication. Regarding this, Noam and Mutter (2016) point out that the penetration level of the cable television market made it attractive for "foreign video industries."

Some foreign companies that have a stake in the Argentine market include Telefónica and Prisa (Spain), Telecom (Italy), DirecTV and Murdoch Interests (United States), and Grupo Televisa and América Móvil (Mexico). In Argentina, Grupo Clarín is the media group of Argentine origin with a high market share. This company was founded by Roberto Noble in 1945 and became a media conglomerate in 1999. It owns the newspaper *Diario Clarín*, one broadcast television station, and several cable and radio stations; it also offers Internet service. Grupo Clarín merged with a telecom company, which enabled it to provide broadband Internet connections to more than half of the market and made it the first company to offer "quadruple play" (Mitchelstein & Boczkowski, 2018).

Brazil also deals with saturated and competitive markets due to high levels of participation from foreign companies, such as Telefónica (Spain), América Móvil (Mexico), and Telcom (Italy) (Noam & Mutter, 2016). The Brazilian media company with the highest market penetration is Telemar, which belongs to the Telecomunicaciones Oi company. The second most important company in this country is Grupo Globo, founded in 1925. This multimedia group has the largest market share in broadcast television and more than 50% in the digital and newspaper markets. Another leading group in the press sector is Folhapar. Moreover, Grupo Abril leads the magazine market in Brazil.

Chile is a small market compared to Brazil, Mexico, and Argentina. This marketplace also has strong participation of Ibero-American companies, such as Telefónica (Spain) and América Móvil (Mexico). The newspapers of Chilean origin with a high market share are *El Mercurio* and *Copesa*. The latter company is also the owner of radio, broadcast TV, and cable stations. Currently, the Chilean media market is represented by traditional media as well as digital native media companies. Vernier, Cárcamo-Ulloa, and Scheihing-García (2017) found that traditional media, in addition to putting their content in web formats, have constantly adapted to technological evolutions like social media, mobile platforms, and other digital broadcasting resources. Some examples of Chilean media firms that have taken advantage of digital convergence are El Mercurio Online, La Tercera, Mega, and TVN. Digital native media that stand out in the region are El Mostrador, El Desconcierto, and Pulse.

Furthermore, Mexico has also been a country characterized by the concentration of media companies (Gutiérrez-Rentería, 2014). The competitive structure of the audiovisual market is represented by Grupo Televisa, TV Azteca, Multimedios, Grupo Imagen, and MVS. The telecommunication industry is dominated by América Móvil, which leads the cable, Internet, and fixed and mobile phone sectors. Megacable also participates in this sector. In addition, the press is dominated by publishing companies such as Grupo Reforma, Organización Editorial Mexicana, and Grupo Milenio. Foreign investment in media companies has also been allowed in Mexico since 2014 (Gutiérrez-Rentería, 2014). Currently, AT&T (of U.S. origin) is the main telecommunication company that competes directly with América Móvil in Mexico.

Traditional media companies continue to be the top choices for news and information among Mexicans (Gutiérrez-Rentería, 2018). TV Azteca and Televisa are generally considered to be the brands with the highest level of political, economic, and social influence in the country. Companies such as Grupo Imagen, Grupo Milenio, and Radio Fórmula have also built brands with loyal audiences and advertisers. Though public broadcasting did not develop in the same way as in Europe, Channel 22, a university television station operated by the National Polytechnic Institute (Instituto Politécnico Nacional), is one of the most popular offline news brands. The Mexican press, represented by some traditional media firms like El Universal, Grupo Reforma, Excelsior, El Economista, and El Financiero, also continues to be consumed online by audiences. However, Proceso is the only news magazine that retains a paper product. All of these brands are followed by the public through their digital platforms.

TV Azteca and Televisa continue to be the leading commercial TV companies, with their news programs reaching the largest Mexican audiences. The newspaper *El Universal*, founded in 1916, leads the online news market and is also the second-most popular among traditional media. The most popular digital native news media are Aristegui Noticias, UnoTV, and Animal Político. They have very different characteristics and strategies from one another.

The business model of Latin American media companies is traditionally based on obtaining large audiences for advertisers where the distribution channel was guaranteed. Most of the leading companies in the audiovisual sector in the region had opted for a low-risk content strategy (e.g., soap operas, sports programs, and some movies and series from the United States). As of the 2000s, some traditional media have adapted their business model as a result of the opportunities brought by digital convergence. Some examples of these companies are Grupo Clarín (Argentina); Grupo Globo (Brazil); and Grupo Televisa, Grupo Imagen, and Multimedios (Mexico). The leaders continue with the strategy of low risk and also generate revenues with content offered and distributed through digital platforms well adapted to mobile devices. In addition, there are companies that have also developed video streaming platforms to increase their revenues through the subscription model, like América Móvil and Grupo Televisa.

The implementation of digital technologies, mobile phone penetration, and social networks provided many opportunities for the new digital natives. In addition, information can be obtained from the cloud, which has changed consumer behavior in many Latin American countries. In Latin America, there are many opportunities for further developing the media companies in a convergent environment. Let us now discuss more opportunities and challenges in managing media organizations in Latin America.

Opportunities and Challenges

The majority of Latin American audiences are characterized by their higher content consumption of entertainment and information through radio, television, and social media (Godoy, 2016; Mazziotti, 1996; Noam, 2016; Totalmedios, 2017). Most of the advertising investment in the region is concentrated in Argentina, Brazil, Chile, and Mexico (eMarketer, 2016). Television continues to be the means of communication that represents the highest percentage of advertising dollars (Forbes, 2018; Totalmedios, 2017). Pay TV subscriptions in the region have been growing due to increasing affordability and the range of programs offered. The main advertisers of Latin American commercial television include Unilever, Genomma Lab, Procter & Gamble, Coca-Cola, Nestlé, Claro, Colgate Palmolive, and Johnson & Johnson. These relationships provide many opportunities for media managers in Latin America.

OPPORTUNITIES

Investments in digital advertising and electronic commerce seem promising in their first stage of development. Evans (2019) points out that digital consumers are characterized by being early adopters who tend to be both younger and more affluent. Digital consumers who participate in electronic commerce are characterized by their greater purchasing power and represent a younger group, between 25 and 34 years of age (Sprout, 2015). The majority of these consumers prefer social networks to email, and only one-third of this audience views targeted advertisements that are based on online searches and purchase history as an invasion of privacy (Evans, 2019). For this group, site navigation is a strong motivator to shop online.

Opportunities for advertising investment can be found in the high penetration of smartphones with Internet access as well as the heavy consumption of digital content and social networks by young people. In this regard, Sánchez (2016) points out that being in a region in which smartphones are considered a necessity, there is promise for brands to lead smart digital marketing. As such, advertising investment in digital media should mainly aim at search engines, social networks, and videos (Totalmedios, 2017). Katz (2015) suggests that easy access to social networks in local languages facilitates consumption. Showing interest in the culture and users of each country will be crucial to the success of media businesses in Latin America (Statista, 2019).

There are many opportunities to adapt to digital technologies, especially mobile technology and social media. Media management in Latin America has not been developed as an area of study as widely as it has been in the United States or Europe (Gutiérrez-Rentería, 2018). Most media managers do not have the business training required to start a media business in Latin America. As such, educational programs for communication and media professionals to learn about business models, revenue streams, marketing, and entrepreneurship present opportunities in Latin America.

Media entrepreneurs with the skills to work with professionals in journalism, communication, and marketing in the region are needed to provide a business vision with holistic thinking that considers sociocultural aspects of Latin America. The success of digital native media that offer local content and social networking sites demonstrates the crucial role of language and culture in an innovative media company in Latin America. Furthermore, there are opportunities for developing marketing companies that focus on carrying out research that explains Latin American audiences by socioeconomic segment, measures based on their civic participation, value given to national institutions, and the interactive connection they have with media regarding social and political issues.

There are numerous local markets in the region that have not been served by traditional media that still aim to address a more homogeneous audience. Yet, niche audiences represent a significant market share that has not been served by the existing media companies in the region. We can see opportunities for developing digital media businesses to serve niche markets and underrepresented audiences in Latin America. Furthermore, while most of the media businesses, advertisers, funding, and research have been focused on 4 of the 20 countries in the region (i.e., Argentina, Brazil, Chile, and Mexico), opportunities exist in developing and understanding other media marketplaces in the region. By taking advantage of the convergent media environment, more can be done to engage regional audiences. However, these changes also bring many challenges to future practitioners. Specifically, differences in development and unfamiliarity with the marketplace can be problematic.

CHALLENGES

One important challenge faced by media managers in Latin America is the ability to provide consulting services for traditional media companies that have not been able to adapt to the current convergent media environment. It would be necessary to identify the keys to success in order to help the local media companies and communities in this region. While many development opportunities exist in Latin America, there are also challenges that practitioners must consider in order to develop successful business models and strategies.

The macro- and microenvironments in the region themselves can become a main challenge for media entrepreneurs in Latin America. For example, insecurity, violence, corruption, and political polarization in some societies can affect the government, the economy, and thus the growth of media organizations.

On the other hand, trust in the journalistic system in some countries has been compromised as a result of the aggressive dynamics between the government and media. A similar situation has occurred recently in the United States (Newman and Reid, 2018). Other examples of distrust in the industry are found in Brazil and Mexico due to increasing fake news incidents and false social media accounts. Constant threats directed at members of the media industry in Venezuela have deterred many media professionals from entering the field. Likewise, there are numerous cases in which freedom of expression and the safety of journalists have been threatened.

Other challenges for media managers to consider are the issues of media concentration, legislation, and the sustainability of media companies in Latin America (Podesta, 2016). The market's concentrated structure still directly impacts pluralism and diversity of information. Regarding legislation and media regulation, Podesta (2016) points out that the main problems that still need to be overcome are censorship, lack of independence of public media, and lack of autonomy and independence of regulators. In the digital age, this region still lacks regulations or limits that must exist in order for the companies to commercialize the large consumer databases. For sustainability, media companies should address the challenges that characterize the industry in the disruptive phase of the business model.

Finally, an enormous challenge for entrepreneurs who want to venture into the industry is the presence of leaders who have historically stood out in the region. In the digital age, entry barriers are lower than in the time of traditional media. However, the industry is being run by only a few companies that participate in almost all sectors of the industry. They know their domestic markets very well and, at the same time, suffer the same disruptive stage that globally distinguishes the media industry. Examples are América Móvil and Grupo Televisa from Mexico, Oi and Grupo Globo from Brazil, Grupo Clarín from Argentina, and Copesa and El Mercurio from Chile. Based on these understandings, it is suggested that future practitioners consider the following action plan.

ACTION PLAN

1. Develop a market strategy based on the market segmentation and target market in the Latin American country in which you hope to participate. Subsequently, identify unique behaviors of media consumers in the market that was selected.
2. Develop a business model based on the main characteristics of Latin American digital media consumers. The business plan must include digital strategies regarding the content, distribution, marketing, and revenue model.
3. Analyze the structure of the competitive market, and identify differentiation points of your product compared to existing media firms within the same market.
4. Consult a financial analyst to evaluate the profitability of your project.

KEY TAKEAWAYS

1. This region is an attractive market in terms of audience and advertisers due to high levels of media consumption in the digital age. There are small and medium companies belonging to different sectors that have not been able to access the traditional media marketplace due to high entry prices. The strategy of market segmentation presents opportunities for media entrepreneurs.
2. Established Latin American companies have taken advantage of digital convergence to expand their offerings to different audiences in the region. These com-

panies offer easy access to a variety of media platforms that serve to generate new ways to consume content and create new experiences for their audiences. These companies are still facing the disruptive environment of the industry. Some media firms have strategic alliances with other multimedia companies that lead them to the global market.

3. Digital native media entrepreneurs have adopted attractive strategies of business media models related to content production and distribution within the digital ecosystem.
4. Some of the main barriers to entry in the Latin American media market, such as high investment costs, are no longer an obstacle in the digital age in Latin America, where people consume information and entertainment through digital platforms.
5. Digital technologies, such as smartphone penetration and social networks, provide opportunities for media entrepreneurs. Digital media consumers in Latin America are characterized by being early adopters who tend to be both younger and more affluent. Digital consumers who participate in electronic commerce are characterized by their greater purchasing power.

CONCLUSION

Latin American countries share many social and cultural values. However, the economic, political, and social circumstances of the countries differentiate themselves during the development of convergent media in the region. The 10 most competitive countries in the region are Chile, Panama, Costa Rica, Mexico, Colombia, Peru, Uruguay, Brazil, Ecuador, and Guatemala, while the main media markets are Chile, Mexico, Colombia, and Brazil.

According to the level of competitiveness, technological innovation, development of new business models, and ease of doing business with other companies, the growth of Latin American companies proves low. These distinguishing characteristics could be unique cultural and economic factors of the Latin American firms. As such, it is important for media entrepreneurs who want to participate in the Latin American media sector to pay attention to these cultural characteristics. Future practitioners must ensure that new media businesses take advantage of these cultural weaknesses in developing the digital economy in the region, especially given that the investment in digital advertising and electronic commerce shows promise in the first stage of development in Latin America.

In this era characterized by convergence between industries and a growing digital economy, the media industry in Latin America presents opportunities for those who wish to venture into the media marketplace. Latin America is an attractive and fertile market to develop competitive strategies through disruptive business models in the information and entertainment industries. Entry barriers to the Latin American market exist, mostly due to the excessive concentration of the sector. However, there are few limits in the digital sector with globalized and deregulated markets. Although the competitive structure of the media market in the region continues to have high levels of concentration, the leading companies face the same challenges as the global brands and digital natives of the region.

The region has a large, young population compared to that of the United States and Europe. This audience has been heavy consumers of information and entertainment, mainly focused on video streaming and social networks accessed through smartphones. Media content that reflects the language and culture of this population will generate large audiences on this continent. It should be noted that, in Latin America, there are still market segments that have not been served by existing media companies. This presents great opportunities to entrepreneurs and digital natives who may overcome the high entry barriers of the sector by being aware of brand positioning and creating new digital-first business strategies.

There are many opportunities for entrepreneurs and managers when a market is in its beginning and developing stages. This is the case of electronic commerce and digital native media in Latin America. Digital consumers have great purchasing power in Latin America, representing a young group between 25 and 34 years of age. Understanding their media consumption behavior, habits, and spending, as well as their brand engagement, will aid in developing marketing and communication strategies if international brands hope to enter the Latin American market.

Another focus for future media companies in Latin America is video streaming that reflects the duality of the content. Likewise, the distribution strategy matters, as does the effective development of various revenue and marketing models, which are typical in a digital economy. One main challenge for these companies is to take the characteristics of the market in this region into consideration when developing their business models.

Regional players include large global companies as well as leading regional companies that have adapted to the digital era, such as Walt Disney and Apple (United States), Grupo Clarín (Argentina), El Mercurio (Chile), and América Móvil and Grupo Televisa (Mexico). There are also growing digital native companies in the marketplace, such as Netflix and Amazon (United States); Claro Video, Blim, Carmen Aristegui News, and UnoTV (Mexico); and Emol, Lun, and BioBioChile Online (Chile). It will be interesting to see which new players stand out with so many macro- and microeconomic opportunities in the region.

Latin America represents a young region that has been characterized by a high level of media consumption thanks to the offer made by domestic firms and by those global media companies that have taken advantage of the liberalization of the industry and the digital economy. In this region, a large market becomes fertile ground for those entrepreneurs who want to face the challenge of the political environment. The next section will discuss media management in a dynamic landscape, with special emphasis on convergent forms of media platforms, which are critical to help media managers achieve a better understanding of the current global media marketplace.

REFERENCES

Albarran, A. (2017). *The media economy* (2nd ed.). Routledge.

Albarran, A., & Hutton, B. (2009). Young Latinos use of mobile phones: A cross-cultural study. *Revista de Comunicacion, 8*, 95–108.

América Economía. (2018, November). *Conozca las 500 Empresas más Grandes de Latinoamérica 2018*. https://www.americaeconomia.com/negocios-industrias/conozca-las-500-empresas-mas-grandes-de-latinoamerica-2018
América Móvil. (2017). *2017 annual report form 20-F*. https://s22.q4cdn.com/604986553/files/doc_financials/annual/2017/2017-annual-report-on-form-20-f.pdf
Dutta, S., Lanvin, B., & Wunsch-Vincent, S. (2018). *The global innovation index 2018: Energizing the world with innovation*. INSEAD and World Intellectual Property. https://www.wipo.int/publications/en/details.jsp?id=4330
ECLAC–United Nations. (2016). *Anuario estadístico para América Latina y el Caribe*. https://estadisticas.cepal.org/cepalstat/web_cepalstat/estadisticasIndicadores.asp?idioma=e
ECLAC–United Nations. (2019). *Estado de la banda ancha en América Latina y el Caribe 2016*. https://cepalstat-prod.cepal.org/cepalstat/tabulador/ConsultaIntegrada.asp?idIndicador=1877&idioma=e
eMarketer. (2016). *Digital ad spending in Latin America: Trends and insights for Argentina, Brazil, Chile and Mexico*. https://www.emarketer.com/Report/Digital-Ad-Spending-Latin-America-Trends-Insights-Argentina-Brazil-Chile-Mexico/2001887
Evans, M. (2019, August 10). 3 things you need to know about Latin American digital consumers. *Forbes*. https://www.forbes.com/sites/michelleevans1/2017/08/10/3-things-you-need-to-know-about-latin-american-digital-consumers
Forbes. (2018). *The world's largest public companies*. https://www.forbes.com/global2000
Godoy, S. (2016). Media ownership and concentration in Chile. In E. M. Noam (Ed.), *Who owns the world's media? Media concentration and ownership around the world* (pp. 641–674). Oxford University Press.
Grupo Televisa. (2017). *Big challenges, bigger opportunities: 2017 annual report*. http://www.televisair.com/~/media/Files/T/TelevisaIR/documents/annual/2017/Televisa2017eng.pdf
Gutiérrez-Rentería, M. E. (2007). Media concentration in the Hispanic market: A case study of TV Azteca vs. Televisa. *International Journal on Media Management, 9*, 70–76.
Gutiérrez-Rentería, M. E. (2011). *Estrategias de Grupo Televisa: Del Monopolio Audiovisual a la Competencia*. Editorial Académica Española.
Gutiérrez-Rentería, M. (2014). Market components to understand the dynamics of the Mexican communications media. *Palabra Clave, 17*, 1194–1212.
Gutiérrez-Rentería, M. (2018). México. In N. Newman, R. Fletcher, A. Kalogeropoulos, D. Levy, & R. Kleis-Nielsen (Eds.), *Reuters Institute digital news report 2018* (p. 122). Reuters Institute–Oxford University.
Gutiérrez-Rentería, M. E., & López, C. (2014). Digital convergence propitious convergence between industries: Main companies are involved in the capital market and concentrate higher revenues in 2013. *Revista de Comunicación, 13*, 144–162.
Katz, R. (2015). *El ecosistema y la economía digital en América Latina*. http://www.fundaciontelefonica.com/arte_cultura/publicaciones-listado/pagina-item-publicaciones/itempubli/430
López Hernández, C. (2013). *Comercio, clusters internacionales y grandes firmas*. UPAEP.
Mastrini, G., Bizberge, A., & Becerra, M. (2016). Ownership and concentration in Argentina. In E. M. Noam (Ed.), *Who owns the world's media? Media concentration and ownership around the world* (pp. 575–605). Oxford University Press.
Mazziotti, N. (1996). *La industria de la telenovela la producción de ficción en América Latina*. Paidós Estudios de Comunicación.
Mitchelstein, E., & Boczkowski, P. (2018). Argentina. In N. Newman, R. Fletcher, A. Kalogeropoulos, D. Levy, & R. Kleis-Nielsen (Eds.), *Reuters Institute digital news report 2018* (p. 116). Reuters Institute–Oxford University.
Moreira, S. (2016). Media ownership and concentration in Brazil. In E. M. Noam (Ed.), *Who owns the world's media? Media concentration and ownership around the world* (pp. 606–633). Oxford University Press.
Newman, N., & Reid, A. (2018). *Journalism, media and technology trends and predictions 2018* (pp. 1–50). Reuters Institute for the Study of Journalism.
Noam, E. M. (2016). *Who owns the world's media? Media concentration and ownership around the world*. Oxford University Press.

Noam, E., & Mutter, P. (2016). Brazil-data summaries. In E. M. Noam (Ed.), *Who owns the world's media? Media concentration and ownership around the world* (pp. 634–640). Oxford University Press.
Podesta, D. (2016). *Media in Latin America: A path forward.* Center for International Media Assistance. https://www.cima.ned.org/wp-content/uploads/2016/01/CIMA-Media-in-Latin-America_the-Path-Forward.pdf
Sánchez, M. (2016, July 26). The digital opportunity in Latin America: A connected region needs connected brands. *The Branding Journal.* https://www.thebrandingjournal.com/2016/07/digital-opportunity-latin-america
Statista. (2019). *Penetración de las redes sociales en América Latina entre 2013 y 2018.* https://es.statista.com/estadisticas/598526/america-latina-penetracion-redes-sociales—2018
Totalmedios. (2017, May 12). *La inversión publicitaria global crecerá 5% en 2018 (En América Latina 9.3%).* https://www.totalmedios.com/nota/33622/la-inversion-publicitaria-global-crecera-5-en-2018-en-america-latina-93
Vernier, M., Cárcamo-Ulloa, L., & Scheihing-García, E. (2017). Diagnóstico de la estrategia editorial de medios informativos chilenos en Twitter mediante un clasificador de noticias automatizado. *Revista Austral de Ciencias Sociales, 30,* 183–201.
World Economic Forum. (2015, September 30). *Las 10 economías más competitivas de América Latina el mundo.* https://www.weforum.org/es/agenda/2015/09/10-economias-mas-competitivas-de-america-latina-y-el-mundo

PART IV

MANAGEMENT IN A DYNAMIC LANDSCAPE

CHAPTER 14

News and Information Industry

Kelly Kaufhold, Texas State University

LEARNING OBJECTIVES

1. Learn about current trends among legacy news outlets regarding ownership and news delivery.
2. Understand how social and mobile media are dramatically changing the news business.

Think critically about what changes in the business of journalism mean for society. Half a century ago, news managers did not think much about the age of their audience members. Starting in the 1960s, younger adults began a long but steady drift away from traditional news channels—especially the metro daily newspaper and local television newscast (Putnam, 2000). Even a decade ago, many journalists pointed to the demographics showing that Americans over 40 followed the news twice as much as those under 30. The assumption was as people age, move up in their careers, get married, buy homes—as they become more integrated in society—they'll become more reliant on journalism (Mindich, 2004). Perhaps, in the predigital era, that assumption held some merit. But today, in the era of free mobile media, traditional news consumption by younger adults is plummeting. Nielsen reported that viewership of local TV news by those under 35 is down from 15% to 45%, depending on the newscast—double the decline among older viewers (Schoettle, 2019). Millennials do report being interested in news; in fact, 85% self-report that they stay current with news. However, their media consumption behaviors do not mean consuming newspapers or television. In fact, nearly half of American adults aged 45 and younger consume *no* traditional TV (broadcast, cable, or satellite news or entertainment) (Schoettle, 2019).

These trends mirror the reality among print newspapers. Pew (2018a) reports that print newspapers are the least-consumed news source among Americans under 30, at 2%. For perspective, among Americans 65 and older, four out of five still read print newspapers, and four out of five watch television news—*five times* higher than those under 30 (Pew, 2018a). Young people must be getting news from social media, though, right? Wrong. The oldest Americans, those over 65, are three times as likely to get news via social media (30%) as those under 30 (13%) (Pew, 2018a). People are migrating to new platforms but exhibiting old behaviors. Older Americans read and share news online, while younger adults are consuming more media online, but increasingly it's entertainment, not news. A lack of a replacement cohort for legacy media is not only bad for business—it may be bad for society. That dwindling audience is at the center of a decline in audience and advertising revenue, which is having an adverse impact on traditional economics. Let us explore one such case study of this impact on Gatehouse Media.

CASE STUDY

On Monday, April 2, 2018, Gatehouse Media closed on the purchase of "a flagship of Gatehouse"—the *Austin American-Statesman*, one of the largest-circulation newspapers in Gatehouse's rapidly growing portfolio of 142 daily newspapers at that time, 145 by the end of 2018 (Davis & Novak, 2018; Gatehouse Media, 2018). The purchase, one of seven daily papers bought in 2018, came with a Spanish-language weekly, the Austin Community Newspaper Group in a half dozen communities around metro Austin, and a legacy media building on 19 acres of lakefront, downtown—close enough to the state capitol to afford a nice view of it, just over the river (Davis & Novak, 2018; Gatehouse Media, 2018). Executive Jason Taylor, president of the publisher's western U.S. region, described it as "doubling down on Gatehouse's commitment in Austin," which has been home to the company's Center for News and Design since 2014 (Davis & Novak, 2018, B7).

Five months later, Gatehouse offered buyouts to every remaining employee (Austin Business Journal, 2018). The buyouts were entirely voluntary, and no employees were forced into layoffs, but by the end of 2018 the voluntary severance had brought the staff of the newsroom to near 100, just more than half the news staff of 190 from a decade earlier (Austin Business Journal, 2018). Two months later, in October, the Spanish-language weekly, *Ahora Si*, was gone (Associated Press, 2018).

Gatehouse paid nearly $100 million for three properties in 2018; the *American-Statesman*, the *Palm Beach Post*, and the *Palm Beach Daily News*. Yet, in an era of declining print revenues, layoffs and buyouts, and migration to online-only news production, Gatehouse's revenue went up 6.9% in 2017, to $1.34 billion (Davis & Novak, 2018). What's Gatehouse's secret to growing revenue at a time of dwindling newspaper readership? Centralization, elegantly described as "200 newspapers; 1 copy desk" (King, 2016).

Gatehouse did grow staff and expand operations in Austin in recent years, but at the Center for News and Design, not at any of its daily or weekly print publications. The center serves 296 print publications and their itinerant websites, all designed and edited from one office. By the way, the Center for News and Design has grown quickly since 2016, from 225 employees to more than 300 now, while the daily papers shed jobs (Gatehouse Media, 2018; King, 2016).

The parent company of Gatehouse, New Media Investment Group, started in 2015 and has spent nearly $1 billion buying newspapers since then (Boston Business Journal,

GATEHOUSE CENTER FOR NEWS AND DESIGN

Legacy journalists, especially the thousands who have been laid off, bought out, or left daily metro newspapers, cringe at the proliferation of aggregation hubs like Univision's weather hub, Sinclair Broadcast Group's weather and sports centralcasting, and Gatehouse Media's Center for News and Design, but these hubs do offer some meaningful benefits. Branding and design tend to be unified, which can help readers and viewers recognize and build a relationship with the brand, popular features and individuals can be leveraged across numerous papers or newscasts, and some features that would be out of the reach of smaller news outlets, like investigations, web interactives, or elaborate weather technology, are available for the first time. That is the vision behind the design innovation lab within Gatehouse Media's Center for News and Design.

"When we speak a common language, we create more powerful work" is how digital designer Mara Corbett described the role of the design studio during a panel presentation at Texas State University in October 2018 (Yosko, 2018). Gatehouse designers have unified the use of certain colors across many of the chain's 142 daily newspapers and, in deference to the inexorably increasing age of print readers, have increased the size of the type. Designers consult on and help craft print news packages on national stories, like sports playoffs, politics, and holidays. They've also worked closely with journalists at the various newspapers to create richer web packages from existing print journalism, including investigative journalism on the aftermath of Hurricane Maria in Puerto Rico, the expansion of wind-generated power, and a data interactive showcasing of the 20 finalists for Amazon's HQ2 expansion. The designers not only create web content but also teach journalists how to analyze and maximize its impact once it's published on the local news sites. And they manage an active social media presence that includes regular promotion of content in various Gatehouse papers (http://www.centerfornewsanddesign.com).

2017). Gatehouse started in 2017 with $200 million cash on hand and freed up another $27 million by wringing efficiencies out of newspapers already in its portfolio in order to buy more (Boston Business Journal, 2017).

Chapter 13 discussed the ethics of convergent media management. Is it ethical for a Boston-based investment group with $1 billion in revenue to collect local newspapers then wring more profit out of them so as to buy more? Or for Advance Publications, with $2 billion in revenue, to cease daily printing of the only daily newspaper in New Orleans (Forbes, 2018)? For billionaire publishing novices like Jeff Bezos (Amazon), John Henry (financial services), Sheldon Adelson (Sands Casino), Carlos Helu Slim (cellular telephones), and Warren Buffett (Berkshire Hathaway) to buy newspapers? The argument in this chapter is not so much that change is good or that it's bad for legacy news outlets—it's that change is inevitable.

Something Old

Fears of the demise of newspapers date to the radio era, nearly a century ago, and to the proliferation of television starting in the 1950s. Yet circulation grew steadily through the 20th century until the early 1970s, when it peaked above 60 million daily newspapers in circulation, where it held until 1990 (Edge, 2014; Lacy, Stamm, & Martin, 2014; Putnam, 2000). However, even during the peak years, publishers noted that their core readers were aging, and newspaper readership among younger Americans was dwindling in the 1960s (Tolley, 1999). As conglomerate ownership grew, aggressive chain competition in multipaper markets was initially seen as good for the industry and democracy, forcing both newspapers in a market to be better and leaner; but 30 years later, that seems quaint (Busterna, 1988). Newspapers' inability to cultivate replacement readers for their traditional audience raised red flags among publishers and scholars; television news was also not immune. As Putnam notes, "Daily newspaper readership among people under thirty-five dropped from two-thirds in 1965 to one-third in 1990, at the same time that TV news viewership in this same age group fell from 52 percent to 41 percent" (Putnam, 2000, p. 36).

Consequently, the 1990s were the decade in which news outlets, especially daily newspapers, committed what critics have called three original sins: migrated their content online, for free; failed to aggressively compete with early online advertisers, like Craigslist; and cut content offerings and staff in a way that limited circulation but reached a broader advertising base (Gorman, 2015; Lacy et al., 2014; Mutter, 2009). There were, indeed, circulation declines in the decade after the proliferation of the Internet, to 52.3 million by 2006, but reader decline predates the web by decades. In fact, daily circulation fell 8.2% from 1996 to 2006—the first Internet decade—but fell even more, 10%, from 1984 to 1996 (Lacy et al., 2014).

Four other contributors were likely responsible for declining circulation over the last 30 years. First, a decision by publishers to consolidate holdings in a metro area, as in buying or merging with competing newspapers, reduced total circulation. Second, eliminating distant deliveries at the edges of metro areas, which were often growing suburbs, addressed the costliest circulation regions but simultaneously eliminated advertising monopolies with clients in hyperlocal communities and reduced circulation in a self-inflicted way. Third, companies reduced investment in both staff and reporting, with a commensurate reduction in the amount and quality of content, and fourth, they arrogantly assumed that a 150-year-old business model could migrate seamlessly into a new platform without disruption (Ingram, 2012; Lacy et al., 2014).

In fact, more than a decade into the Internet era, the newspaper industry was among the hardest hit in the great recession of 2007, with a catastrophic loss of nearly two-thirds of advertising revenue in eight years, beginning in 2006 (Edge, 2014). Given that U.S. newspapers were the world's most dependent on advertising for revenue, this was a serious decline (Edge, 2014). A random aside for old-school newspaper journalists—in a $20 million irony, the City University of New York renamed its graduate school of journalism for benefactor Craig Newmark, founder of Craigslist—an online entity that helped devastate newspaper classified advertising nationwide (Newmark J-School Staff, 2018).

Does economic pressure affect content? After all, media management is not only about ownership—it also heartily affects how newsrooms are run. Some scholars have argued that editors at independent papers might be more concerned about revenue than those working within a chain conglomerate (Demers & Wackman, 1988). Early evidence suggested the opposite—that those in management at chains were more, not less, concerned with revenue, presumably because of pressure ordained from above (Demers & Wackman, 1988). After all, some of the ownership entities are investment firms, not traditional media companies (Busterna, 1988). Concerns over the impact of ownership on content date back a century (Picard & Dal Zotto, 2015). But there are substantial market forces ensuring that editors do not behave in such a way as to alienate audiences, and, in fact, different ownership models don't necessarily predict content behaviors (Picard & Dal Zotto, 2015). There are obvious exceptions to this, especially news outlets with ideological owners, like Sinclair Broadcasting and Rupert Murdoch's News Corporation (Fortin & Bromwich, 2018; McKinnon, 2016).

The argument that newspapers could have preserved their economic model by charging for online content from the start has been rightly chastised. Critics reduced this argument to an assumption that, by charging for news content online at the beginning, in the 1990s, newspapers would have preserved "something close to a monopoly on the news, and also controlled one of the primary platforms through which it was distributed"—both are assumptions that can be roundly disputed (Ingram, 2012). The Internet, especially with the interactivity of Web 2.0, broadband, always-on access, and mobile smartphone technology, "democratized" the tools of both production and distribution (Malik, 2011). Fairly suddenly, a provocative YouTube personality or insightful blogger could reach audiences larger than legacy media outlets (Malik, 2011). At the same time, the long tail of production and consumption atomized the audience so that revenue, and especially profit, became increasingly concentrated among brand names and scarce among everyone else (Anderson, 2004; Huang & Wang, 2014).

Concern about the effects of conglomeration, such as chain ownership, on editorial content date back more than 40 years (Wagenberg & Soderlund, 1975). Baker (2006) argued that the public sphere was essential to how members of a populace arrive at informed policy positions and that traditional mainstream news media were essential to the quality of information in the public sphere. But his assertions came at the dawn of the eras of social and mobile media, along with dramatically expanded broadband Internet access—a new era of unimaginable choices and fragmentation (Küng et al., 2008). The one-stop-shop nature of legacy media (breaking news, local news, national politics, weather, sports, entertainment, etc.) is now wildly diffused and respecialized by content—it is "unbundled" from limited legacy sources and resorted by topic (Ala-Fossi et al., 2008, p. 150).

In the midst of the decline of legacy consumers and revenue, two more recent (although well-established) entries have enjoyed episodic success: cable television news and news satire. Starting with CNN in 1980, cable news offered competition to legacy outlets that was unique in two important ways: first, it disrupted appointment news consumption with a 24-hour schedule; second, it benefited from a robust secondary revenue stream in addition to advertising—cable subscription fees (Baldwin, Barett, & Bates, 1992). Cable news really earned its wings with CNN's extended coverage of the first Gulf War in 1991, which not only drew record-high viewers but also showed the possibility of a global political influence driven by worldwide television news (Gilboa, 2005). The debut of Fox News Channel in 1996 brought another kind of disruption—the opportunity for ideologues in the audience to select agreeable news. Fox quickly surpassed CNN in ratings and was actually shown to bolster Republican voter turnout in cable TV markets where it appeared in the 1990s—and to fuel a hostile media perception of legacy news sources (Coe et al., 2008; DellaVigna & Kaplan, 2007). As broadcast news networks suffered steady declines in viewership, cable news consumption more than doubled from 1997 to 2005 (Coe et al., 2008). MSNBC languished behind Fox and CNN during its early, objective years but found that going partisan in the leadup to the 2008 election was good for business. Cable news revenue doubled from 2007 to 2016, with MSNBC surpassing CNN in viewers (Pew, 2018b). Also, the panel-of-guests format popular during prime time on MSNBC, CNN, and Fox is cheaper than actual correspondents reporting from around the world (Economist, 2012). The obvious implication for society is that many more Americans are exposed to far fewer points of view; empathy declines, and adversarialism grows.

Despite the contemporary eruption in the hyperbolic use of the term *fake news*, *real* fake news—misinformation—has actually been around for a while and is growing in popularity. Satirical mainstay *The Onion* just marked its 30th year of publishing; Comedy Central's *The Daily Show* has aired for more than 20 years; *The Onion* surpassed 10 million unique visitors, and Comedy Central's two top performers, *The Daily Show* and *The Colbert Report*, were the most-watched nighttime talk shows among viewers under 50 (Becker, 2015; Thai, 2014). In fact, satirical television news was linked with an increase in political engagement among young adults (Becker, 2015), who cited *The Colbert Report* as among their most trusted news sources (Gottfried & Anderson, 2014), although audiences for both print and broadcast satire have waned since the 2016 election.

Contemporary consumers can reach for their phone and choose objective legacy news, partisan broadcast news, news satire, local or global sources—or no news at all. As an example of the power of endless selectivity, fans of the Miami Dolphins don't rely on coverage from one of two local newspapers in South Florida—they can get immersive articles, statistics, and commentary from a specialty sports outlet, like ESPN, which may be richer and more robust than any local coverage (ESPN, 2018). At the same time, global members of the diaspora from South Florida, or anywhere in the world, can retain ties to distant communities and cultures by patronizing local media; or they can form new communities around similar interests, shared with complete strangers (as in video game communities or celebrity fan sites) with both pro- and antisocial effects (Karim, 2003; Kowert & Oldmeadow, 2015).

The point is that we do not have "the" Internet—we have "our" Internet. Personal perspective is everything. That atomization applies not only to the audience; it's also impacting ownership. Owning a news outlet used to give a publisher or broadcaster access to a discrete geographic audience of tens of thousands of people. Now, aggregation means single owners may have access—theoretically—to hundreds of thousands, spread across the country. The personalization of the Internet and news is just one of the many ways that new technology is impacting the information industry.

Something New

Media aggregation—more news outlets in the hands of fewer owners—certainly appears to be the future of media ownership, at least in the short term. In the years immediately after the great recession, starting in 2007, McClatchy, Gatehouse, Lee Enterprises, and A. H. Belo Corporation recorded fairly stable revenues year to year

(Edge, 2014). There were exceptions: Gannett, Media General, and News Corp newspaper revenue fell by half; E. W. Scripps and the *Washington Post* saw revenue fall by two-thirds (Edge, 2014). The nation's largest owner of television stations, Sinclair Broadcasting with 173 stations, saw enough revenue to bid $3.9 billion to buy 42 more from Tribune (Finley, 2018). That deal fell through, including accusations of impropriety lodged against Sinclair, which denied any wrongdoing (Finley, 2018). But months later, Nexstar—owner of 170 stations—made a $4.1 billion bid to Tribune, which would make it the largest TV owner in the United States (Nexstar, 2018). Newspapers and TV station owner groups, by eliminating redundancy and maximizing shared resources, such as design, copyediting, and weather forecasting, have managed to capitalize on the new economy of scale.

The radio industry—which saw, by far, the largest single media owner by numbers—yielded a very different outcome. Both Cumulus, with 445 stations, the nation's second-largest radio owner, and iHeartMedia—the largest with 850 stations—filed for bankruptcy in 2018. Both struggled with the debt required to buy so many radio stations—in the case of iHeartMedia, more than $20 billion (Pix11, 2018; Valinsky, 2018). In fact, the predecessor of iHeartMedia, Clear Channel, owned more than 1,200 radio stations a decade earlier (Baker, 2006).

One strategy to wring more revenue out of ownership conglomeration was the use of technology to aggregate some tasks across multiple stations, both radio and TV, which allowed owners to cut staff at numerous outlets. Radio stations increasingly use prevoiced introductions to songs or segments, which lets owners run a popular host on numerous stations—sometimes at the same time on multiple stations in a market (Jacobson, 2018). This "voice-tracking" and other syndicated programming have virtually eliminated overnight radio hosts and newscasters across the country (Crider, 2012; Jacobson, 2018). In addition to the obvious loss of local job opportunities in radio and, to a lesser extent, television news, scholars argue that syndication and centralization are bad for society, diminishing local programming and social capital (Crider, 2012).

Television news hubs were hugely aided by the advent of high-definition digital television a decade ago. The added bandwidth and more elegant networking ability allowed local TV station ownership groups to aggregate certain tasks under one roof with minimal staff, which quickly led to layoffs at numerous local television stations (Lawrence, 2015; Pierce, 2012; Winslow, 2011). Nexstar, for example, operates hubs in Salt Lake City, Utah; Little Rock, Arkansas; Memphis, Tennessee; and Indianapolis, Indiana, with each hub responsible for master control operations (airing programs, keeping logs, etc.) of a dozen stations or more, all managed by just one employee at a time (NewscastStudio, 2013; Winslow, 2011). Years earlier, Meredith Broadcasting Group aggregated some technical and business operations from Tennessee, South Carolina, and Georgia to a single hub in Atlanta while considering other potential hubs in Phoenix, Las Vegas, and Portland (Malone, 2009).

Newsrooms aren't immune from this cost-cutting hub aggregation, also called "centralcasting." Spanish-language network Univision centralized its weather broadcasting in a single Houston-based hub, which will serve all affiliated radio and television stations nationwide (NewscastStudio, 2017). IBM, the legacy business service company, took that a big step further by buying the Weather Company, a suburban Atlanta company oriented around providing all things weather related to a variety of businesses, including "agriculture, aviation . . . chemical & petroleum . . . energy & utilities, government, ground transportation" and, at the time of the purchase in 2015, broadcast journalism, offering complete weather segments to subscribers all day long in English and Spanish (Weather, 2018). The Weather Company under IBM recently stopped weather centralcasting to local TV news stations, citing cost, but numerous broadcasters embraced centralcasting early and often, beginning in 2001 and maturing rapidly (Van Tassel, 2001). Sinclair Broadcast Group was especially aggressive early on, centralizing weather and sports and eliminating local jobs all around the country (Bracht, 2003; Trigoboff, 2003). The practice obviously saves owners money, a revenue gain that is replicable across each new station purchased. Critics, though, say it's bad for news outlets and their local communities because it can dramatically slow coverage of breaking news, and it reduces resources for other important local coverage, like investigative journalism (Van Tassel, 2001). Sinclair endured special criticism for using its wide reach to promote a politically conservative agenda, which was roundly met with derision in other media (Fortin & Bromwich, 2018).

While the *New York Times* and *Washington Post* enjoy special notoriety among media brands, both also found themselves facing dwindling print audiences, and, in the case of the *Post*, an 82% drop in advertising revenue between 2006 and 2013, which led directly to the purchase by Amazon founder Jeff Bezos (Edge, 2014). While revenue at the *New York*

THE WEATHER COMPANY

The Weather Company is a fascinating entity that has capitalized on three contemporary realities in recent decades: the birth and growth of cable television and Internet specialty news, a commensurate growth in knowledge about and interest in weather, and fears about and/or the reality of global climate change and its impact on severe weather. The Weather Company began as The Weather Channel, a cable TV outlet that debuted in 1982 (Moore, 2012; Stelter, 2012). The "channel" started humbly enough, taking advantage of the specializing nature of cable television to offer forecasting and explanations of weather events 24 hours a day, evolving over time to offer regular local forecasts then partnering with numerous business and news entities to spread the brand (Stelter, 2012). The Weather Channel has more than 100 million subscribers, a robust web presence, and a nearly ubiquitous weather app on hundreds of millions of smartphones; 10% or more of its business now comes from providing weather services to business subscribers, which drove IBM to buy The Weather Channel in 2015 for $2 billion (Stelter, 2012; Weber, 2015). The weather app on your phone, by the way, is a two-way street—the Weather Company collects data from sensors in millions of phones to help localize and improve the accuracy of weather data (Hardy, 2015). The Weather Channel cable TV network was sold again in 2018, to Entertainment Studios, but the business services arm, with 900 employees, stayed with IBM (Albiniak, 2018; Hardy, 2015). In 2016, after the sale to IBM, the Weather Company ceased what had been a big part of business services—supplanting local weathercasters with subscription meteorologists, who provided "local" forecasts for any newscast throughout the day (Hardy, 2015). Across all industries, the company reports more than 5,000 subscribers who benefit from the company's hyper-local weather data, but the Weather Company found that revenue from serving television stations with on-camera weather anchors wasn't as successful as providing them with data and technological support (Weber, 2015; IBM, 2018).

Times actually held fairly steady during the same period, its owners spent $600 million on a new Manhattan building that opened just at the start of the great recession, leaving the paper more than $1 billion in debt (Edge, 2014; Perez-Peña, 2009). The *Times* company leased space in its new building and borrowed $250 million from Mexican telecom billionaire Carlos Helu Slim to literally buy time to manage the debt (Perez-Peña, 2009).

Recent years have continued to challenge newspapers with the inevitable migration from print to online, for both audiences and advertising, yet, even that shows some troubling signs. Across the top 50 circulation papers in the United States, online readership was down 9% in 2017 (although, again, top brands like the *Wall Street Journal*—26%, and the *New York Times*—42%, saw substantial growth) (Pew, 2018c). Total circulation of all U.S. daily newspapers is half what it was in 1990, and, perhaps even more important, advertising revenue is less than half what it was in 2000 (Pew, 2018c). The share of ad revenue from digital ads has nearly doubled since 2011—from 17% to 31% in 2017—but that's a less optimistic metric than it seems at first blush (Pew, 2018c). It actually reflects a more dramatic loss of print revenue than a commensurate increase in online ad revenue, and some 80 million Americans now use ad blockers (Tzuo, 2017).

Total nationwide newspaper circulation is about half (30 million) what it was at its peak 30 years ago, and while digital subscriptions are up, they mostly apply to just three brands, who account for perhaps half of all digital newspaper subscriptions (6.6 million) in the United States: the *New York Times* (3.4 million), the *Wall Street Journal* (1.7 million), and the *Washington Post* (1.5 million) (Hagey, Alpert, & Serkez, 2019; Pew, 2017a). For perspective, Hulu just reached 28 million subscribers and Netflix 139 million (Jarvey, 2019a; 2019b), and the number of people working in newspaper newsrooms in the United States is half what it was just a decade ago (Pew, 2018c).

Local television news is still the top news source cited by Americans, but viewers are increasingly grabbing the remote to change the channel or turn it off. For the last two decades, morning newscasts were the top area of growth for local TV newsrooms, which responded by growing those newscasts from one hour to two and a half hours—even more for Fox or nonaffiliated stations (Stelter, 2010). Morning show expansion dramatically increased local ad opportunities, and viewership commensurately doubled, until recently. Local newscasts in all dayparts declined, including morning shows (Bark, 2008; Pew, 2018b; Stelter, 2010). Network morning newscasts, like ABC's *Good Morning America* and NBC's *Today Show* also added hours but lost viewers over the last year (Ariens, 2018). Local TV ad revenue is slowly migrating online; 2017 saw local TV digital sales nationwide climb to "about $1 billion," but this coincided with total revenue falling, from about $18 billion to $17.4 billion (Pew, 2018d). Interestingly, the one area of revenue growth for local TV, retransmission fees, is expected to nearly double in coming years. Retransmission fees—income from cable and satellite TV providers to content providers, or "cable channels"—grew from $8 billion to $9 billion in just one year in 2017, which is especially interesting as younger media consumers increasingly "cut the cord" on subscribing TV services (Mullin, 2018; Pew, 2018d). Video viewers migrating away from traditional cable and TV subscriptions to online streaming services seems to have moved robustly from early adopters, largely young males, into Rogers's category of early majority (Lin, 2004; Mullin, 2018; Rogers, 1962). One forecast said cord cutting would grow by a third in 2018, to more than 30 million Americans (Mullin, 2018).

Network television news has endured decades of slowly dwindling viewership, while cable television news enjoyed sporadic but tenacious growth (Baldwin et al., 1992; Bowman, 2009; Pew, 2017b). In the 1970s, Walter Cronkite alone drew nearly 30 million viewers; now the three legacy networks share about 20 million viewers (Bowman, 2009; Pew, 2017b). While the last decade has seen stable viewership of just over 20 million viewers split three ways among ABC, CBS, and NBC, the network newscasts haven't seen growth in 20 years. Cable TV news, on the other hand, has seen its shared audience double in 10 years (Pew, 2017b). Note, this cable ratings growth occurred well into a mature cable TV news era, so novelty cannot explain the growth—after all, CNN debuted in 1980. Another important consideration is the nature of cable versus broadcast television news. The legacy network newscasts still practice objectivity. Cable outlets, starting with Fox News Channel in 1996, have aggressively pursued partisan audiences, and, in the case of Fox and MSNBC, an ideological perspective has been very good for business (Dana, 2008; Katz, 2018; King, 2016; Reals, 2008). When MSNBC became more ideologically Left starting late in 2008, it rose to second in cable news audience; Fox News Channel sat atop the cable news ratings with steady growth for 16 years (Dana, 2008; Joyella, 2018; Reals, 2008). Elections—especially when there are changes in which political party has power—are especially good for the business of cable TV news (Schneider, 2017). Critics decry the insularity of ideological news, and there is substantial evidence that partisans, especially conservatives, tend to isolate themselves to sycophantic news sources (McKinnon, 2016; Muller & Kaufhold, 2019).

Opportunities and Challenges

Just because many legacy news outlets are struggling to monetize their Internet presence doesn't mean there's no advertising revenue online—in fact, it's an enormous and rapidly growing slice of the advertising pie, presenting many opportunities for future practitioners. Let us explore some new media business opportunities and challenges for various news industries below.

OPPORTUNITIES

Online advertising in the United States alone amounts to $111 billion; it grew 21% in just the last year; digital advertising surpassed all TV ad spending in 2017; and mobile ads now account for more than half of all digital advertising revenue (Swant, 2018; Tran, 2017). There is a catch, which we will discuss next in the section on challenges. The short version is that upward of $40 billion in digital advertising is up for grabs.

Earlier, this chapter broached the touchy topic of finding a replacement cohort for dwindling legacy news audiences. There are two broad strategies to try: capture young adults into legacy platforms—as newspaper readers, radio listeners, television news viewers, even online news consumers—or increase news presence where young adults already engage. Previous research has found that young adults are the most likely to *be* online but that their parents—folks in their 40s and 50s—are the most likely to be *consuming news* online (Kaufhold, 2015). The same study found that existing habits tend to migrate into online behavior, including in social media; people who are into games and entertainment tend to engage in that behavior online and in social media, while news seekers tend to bring those information habits into digital domains (Kaufhold, 2015).

So, while young adults are still the most likely to be in social media, and to be the most active there, they are the least likely to be encountering and sharing traditional journalism while there (Perrin, 2015). Still, social and mobile media seem the most-ripe sources for reaching the audience most missing from legacy media—young adults.

Research has found that social media users, especially younger users, are more likely to be incidentally exposed to news via social media, but there are dueling hierarchies. Facebook is the world's dominant social media channel with more than 2.3 billion *active* users (on the platform at least once a month) (Zephoria, 2019). But young users of Facebook are less likely to seek and use news sources than users of Twitter and YouTube are. Still, young adults who are incidentally exposed to news through social media are more likely than others to seek out more news (Fletcher & Kleis, 2017). When young adults do encounter news via social media, it's largely under two defined circumstances: in the context of ubiquitous mobile media consumption (of all kinds) and as part of a constant effort to stay *socially* connected but not necessarily *informed* (Boczkowski, Mitchelstein, & Matassi, 2018). In other words, among young adults in social media and on their phones, news does not hold an elevated position in the information hierarchy—it's largely equal to information about celebrities, friends, or happy hour, and it's stumbled upon while checking on friends, if at all.

CHALLENGES

While many opportunities exist in a convergent news era, there is also a catch. That substantial and growing advertising pie is largely already cut into three big slices, with Google capturing about one-third of total online advertising, Facebook one-fourth, and Amazon one-tenth (Bary, 2020). That means $83 billion in online ad revenue is being siphoned off by three companies, with about $50 billion left for everyone else to fight over. Again, the total digital ad pie grows every year.

News exposure and sharing on social media have influenced the industry in two substantial ways—ideological sorting and the proliferation of fake news (Newman, Fletcher, Kalogeropoulos, Levy, & Kleis, 2017). Because social media algorithms respond to users' behavior, connections with the most interactions, reactions, comments, views, shares, retweets, and so on rise in importance and frequency in users' social media circles (Bakshy, Messing, & Adamic, 2015). The problem, from a political perspective, is that this contributes to society's ideological fragmentation and tribalism, reducing exposure to opposing viewpoints and creating a false sense of ideological support and agreement (Bakshy et al., 2015; Newman et al., 2017). Those who are not active news seekers, especially young adults, do get exposed to some news on social media, and this accidental exposure can fill some gaps, although they tend to be less informed than those who seek news (Fletcher & Kleis, 2017; Gil de Zuñiga, Weeks, & Ardèvol-Abreu, 2017; Kaufhold, 2015).

Those who are less media literate can be highly susceptible to accepting and sharing "fake news," which is now being actively generated and disseminated more aggressively, and successfully, than at any time in history (Wendling, 2018). Organized content producers in Eastern Europe preyed on both the ubiquity and insularity of social media "tunnels" to create a vortex of partisan falsehoods, which spread with abandon (Allcott & Gentzkow, 2017; Doshi, Raghavan, Petitt, & Weiss, 2018; Wendling, 2018). Due to a lack of media literacy, or a sycophantic rejection of it, some 140 websites peddling falsehoods earned heavy traffic because they were being so widely shared (Wendling, 2018).

Users were shown to be far more likely to believe and share consonant information: supporters of Democrat nominee Hillary Clinton shared this intentional fake news 8 million times on Facebook in 2016, and Republican nominee Donald Trump's supporters did it 30 million times (Allcott & Gentzkow, 2017). Fake news was found to be about as effective and persuasive as more familiar online ads (Doshi et al., 2018). One consolation is that mainstream news sources were more dominant among people who were actually looking for political news (Allcott & Gentzkow, 2017). Social media can play a prosocial role, allowing easier civic organizing and offering less restricted information sharing than highly regulated mainstream media (Valenzuela, Correa, & Gil de Zuñiga, 2017).

What about emerging social media platforms? After all, Snapchat attracts a substantially younger audience than legacy news outlets, and Snapchat Discover offers a platform for those outlets to make their pitch to a younger demographic. While legacy outlets retain their identities in Snapchat Discover (i.e., the *Wall Street Journal* still emphasizes business news; the *Washington Post* is still primarily about politics), there is not much evidence showing that young adults active on Snapchat ever set foot into Snapchat Discover (Lee & Kaufhold, 2018). Rather, the prevailing opinion among active Snapchat users is that it's a platform for socializing and entertainment, not for news (Lee & Kaufhold, 2018). As social media use matures, with growth leveling off and use now ubiquitous, it's vital to understand what gets consumed and shared, and why, in these spaces. We will further discuss the role of social media in media management and business in chapter 18. The following action plan may help news businesses and managers make strategic decisions in this dynamic, ever-evolving media environment.

ACTION PLAN

1. Study entrepreneurial techniques and strategies for reaching a niche audience (such as the *Texas Tribune*).
2. Use transparency and data to fight fake news, and work to increase media literacy in audiences.
3. When it comes to revenue, be both agnostic and aggressive: consider events, memberships, subscriptions, sponsors, partnerships, donations, foundation support, and ways you can repurpose (resell) your existing content.

KEY TAKEAWAYS

1. Aggregation is the future of *profitable* legacy media, with fewer entities owning more news outlets, both traditional print and broadcast; most of those owners will be established traditional media conglomerates, such as Advance Publications, Media Investment Group, iHeartMedia, Nexstar, and Sinclair Broadcasting. However, investment funds and wealthy individuals seem likely to acquire more news outlets.
2. Legacy consumers (print readers, broadcast listeners and viewers) will continue to atrophy, and legacy advertising revenue will dwindle faster than digital advertising can replace it.
3. Audience and ad migration to digital powerhouses—especially the new "big three" of Google, Facebook, and Amazon—will continue, and news businesses will increasingly find themselves in those spaces: online, in social media, and especially via mobile; and millions of online advertisers will compete and, in some cases, lose an existential fight over the roughly $40 billion, or one-third, of digital advertising revenue left after the big three subsume the rest.
4. Among existing media companies, expect growth in centralized media delivery, such as data interactives, investigative journalism, issue analysis, and centralcasting—especially of features, weather, and sports.
5. Brands will be increasingly important and dominant—both institutional, like the *New York Times* and *Washington Post*, and individual, like popular weather- and sportscasters and social media influencers.

CONCLUSION

This chapter aimed to explore news and information industries in a converged media environment. While many traditional perspectives still advance much of the discipline today, three trends seem inevitable in current news ownership, operations, management, and delivery: (1) Most legacy news outlets will continue to see declines in both consumers and advertising revenue, which will not be matched by growth in digital spaces. (2) News production, distribution, and consumption will increasingly migrate to the biggest new media players, especially Google and Facebook, although newer social media, like Instagram and Snapchat, *may* become more relevant to news distribution and consumption in coming years, especially as Facebook struggles to retain younger users. (3) Aggregation of ownership and resource allocation mean more properties in the hands of fewer owners and more content wrought from fewer individuals.

It is likely that brands will become increasingly important in coming years. Since we can all choose our own channels and content, it can become less important to get sports coverage from a local outlet than to get it from a favorite sports specialist, such as a famous former athlete, or to choose to watch an eSports tournament live on YouTube, ignoring traditional sports altogether. Popular news anchors, meteorologists, columnists, and investigative journalists may find themselves leveraged across multiple channels owned by a conglomerate. The bigger legacy brands, including the *New*

York Times, Washington Post, USA Today, and the *Wall Street Journal*, will enjoy their widespread familiarity and niche specialties covering politics, international news, entertainment, and business and be able to capitalize, literally, on growth in digital, which will far outpace what less-famous brands will enjoy. The star power of celebrity may eclipse demand for quality.

Expect nonprofit and foundation-supported journalism to grow slowly and to mature in the news ecosystem. ProPublica, with millions of dollars in annual support from three dozen foundations, is now a decade into its mission of providing high-quality, expensive, investigative journalism (ProPublica, 2018). A host of online non-profits, including MinnPost, the St. Louis Beacon, Voice of San Diego, and the *Texas Tribune*, are all still viable but all depend heavily on philanthropy and foundation support. ChiTownDailyNews failed just a couple of years after it launched. In the same way that retail and restaurants are becoming more experiential in the era of Amazon and Favor, the *Texas Tribune* hosts more than 50 events a year. Yes, they often connect lawmakers with citizens in virtuously unique opportunities. "If I'm a public official and I'm extensively quoted in a story, extensively quoted, I maybe get 150 words," said Ross Ramsey, executive editor and cofounder of the *Texas Tribune*. "If I see somebody on stage, I can see them in a contextual sense. What you really learn from that is, what is she like?" But events are also a vital source of revenue for the successful Austin-based nonprofit news outlet they started within a year of the site's launch and account for more than 20% of revenue now.

Finally, and perhaps most troubling, the average age of news consumers continues its inexorable march upward. Intriguingly, the era of President Donald Trump rallies against traditional news organizations has actually been good for legacy political news outlets, especially the *Washington Post* and *New York Times*, and young adults are among the growing audiences, even among the growing ranks of paid subscribers (Schwartz, 2017). That is good for the economics of these outlets, especially if these new subscribers stick around, but it's also good for society because exposure to objective legacy outlets comes with a serving of media literacy (Fields, 2017).

Importantly, adults over age 65 were by far the most likely to share fake news via social media, in fact seven times more likely than younger adults (Guess, Nagler, & Tucker, 2019). Conservatives and those with ideologically sycophantic social media networks were much more likely to share (and believe) fake news if it agreed with their personal political leanings (Allcott & Gentzkow, 2017; Guess et al., 2019).

Likely no one has embraced the term *fake news* more than President Donald J. Trump. His attacks have been described as "so persistent . . . over-the-top . . . deranged . . . crude . . . impulsive, and indiscriminate" that they must have some effect, on the public and the press, and data bear that out (Greenberg, 2017, p. 52; Sullivan, 2017). Republican criticism of a perceived left-leaning media dates to Richard Nixon in 1962, a seed that found fertile ground in the ensuing decades (Greenberg, 2017), exacerbated by more contemporary media trends. Modern reporters are more likely to take sides, in print, on cable television, and in social media. Us-versus-them adversarial reporting has grown since the Pentagon Papers and Watergate in the 1970s and Sam Donaldson in the 1980s; media fragmentation and the growth in ideological media since the national debut of Rush Limbaugh in 1988, and Fox News in 1996, allowed for selective exposure

TEXAS TRIBUNE

The *Texas Tribune* is approaching its 10-year anniversary and it has served as an absolute lodestar for subsequent nonprofit news start-ups. The *Tribune* went live in November 2009 with just a handful of staff and $4 million in seed funding. Some of the structure and content of the *Tribune* felt very familiar, including beat reporting (education, health care, immigration, transportation, environment . . . although all oriented around state politics) and some old political journalism hands on the original staff. CEO Evan Smith edited *Texas Monthly* for 15 years before launching the *Tribune*; cofounder Ross Ramsey edited *Texas Weekly* and had previously worked at the state capitol. It was no accident that the *Tribune* launched on election day in 2009 because its singular mission is state politics. "This is, in some measure, the class everybody ditched in high school," Ramsey said. "We're covering civics and politics and history. But there is an audience for it and the question is, how do you pay for it?"

Because this is a web-only entity, information and data play an outsized role compared to legacy news outlets. TexasTribune.org maintains enormous data repositories and directories on law makers, state budgets, and legislation. Users can track the status of bills from proposal to passage and can check the salary of every employee of the state of Texas—it's all online, searchable, and free. "You put on everybody's desk in the middle of the night, in Amarillo or wherever, the same stuff that's on a reporter's desk all the time," Ramsey said. The *Texas Tribune* is essentially agnostic about two things—information and revenue. From the perspective of a business model, the *Tribune* borrowed from all available predecessors: display advertising from legacy media; memberships à la public broadcasting; foundation support, akin to the *Christian Science Monitor*; philanthropic gifts, like in academia; collaborations with other news outlets, especially on investigations; and events, including an enormous, yearly, heavily sponsored Texas Tribune Festival each fall in downtown Austin. Any one of them wouldn't be adequate to support the mission and steady growth of the *Tribune*. Growth has been cautious, from 2010 expenses of $4.1 million to $8.3 million in 2017, matched by a commensurate growth in revenue (Texas Tribune, 2018). Evan Smith has argued that Texas is uniquely positioned to support nonprofit journalism because of the substantial population to serve as both consumers and event participants, numerous foundations and venture capital entities, and a diverse population with many complex issues and constituencies to cover. At a time of dwindling subscriber and advertiser support for daily print newspapers, the *Tribune* has been able to capitalize on a remaining demand for political news and information. Perhaps the most telling symbol of success is that Smith often hosts visitors who are interested in launching other nonprofit news outlets, with a necessary early step being a pilgrimage to the *Texas Tribune* (https://www.texastribune.org).

and amplification of a hostile media effect (Greenberg, 2017; Kornblut, 2005; Priest, 2016; Sullivan, 2017). Trust in national news outlets has fallen steadily since the 1970s, with half of Democrats and Independents viewing the media negatively and Republicans viewing national news negatively by an *eight-to-one margin* (85% negative, 10% positive) (Pew, 2017c). President Trump must know this, and he circumvents legacy media via social media and partisan outlets to feed this as red meat to his base. Punditry among mainstream media contributes to hostile media perception, selective exposure increases partisan divides, and both further erode trust in legacy media.

So, young adults are slightly more likely to be online but increasingly choose entertainment over news, while the oldest adults are the most likely to consume news online (Kaufhold, 2015). Yet, the oldest adults are also, by far, the most likely to accept and share fake news and the least likely to trust legacy media (Allcott & Gentzkow, 2017; Guess et al., 2019; Pew, 2017c). The most objective news sources struggle financially, while the most partisan ones prosper. We are all steeped in a milieu of ubiquitous information but seemingly more "sorted," less informed, and less empathetic than in the era before cable, digital, social, and mobile media. In fact, self-selected media consumption via the web and untethered power of smartphones is leading to all kinds of self-sorting: by ideology (Fox versus MSNBC; Huffington Post versus Drudge Report; NPR versus Rush Limbaugh); news versus entertainment (Netflix versus the *New York Times*); digital news subscription aggregation (the *New York Times, Washington Post, Wall Street Journal* account for much of U.S. digital news subscriptions); digital ad absorption (Google, Facebook, and Amazon versus everyone else). Having endless choices does not mean we choose wisely.

Now that we understand the current trends among legacy news outlets regarding ownership and news delivery, how dramatically social and mobile media are changing the business of news, and what these changes in the business of journalism mean for society, it is important to understand how these changes are consistent with and different from transformations within the entertainment industry. The same trends seen in news—disruption from channel fragmentation, the ubiquitous eruption of mobile media, consolidating ownership, less risk-taking—can also be seen in play in sport media. In the next chapter, we will talk about the changing media consumption trends of sport fans and identify opportunities and challenges faced by the sport media industry.

REFERENCES

Ala-Fossi, M., Bakker, P., Ellonen, H.-K., Küng, L., Lax, S., Sadaba, C., & van der Wurff, R. (2008). The impact of the Internet on business models in the media industries: A sector-by-sector analy sis. In L. Küng, R. G. Picard, & R. Towse (Eds.), *The Internet and mass media* (pp. 149–169). Sage.

Albiniak, P. (2018, March 22). *Byron Allen acquires the weather group in $300 million deal*. Broadcasting + Cable. https://www.broadcastingcable.com/news/byron-allen-acquires-weather-group-300-million-deal

Allcott, H., & Gentzkow, M. (2017). Social media and fake news in the 2016 election. *Journal of Economic Perspectives, 31*, 311–236.

Anderson, C. (2004, October 1). The long tail. *Wired*. https://www.wired.com/2004/10/tail

Ariens, C. (2018, May 25). *In 2 years the 3 network morning shows have lost 1.8M viewers*. Adweek. https://www.adweek.com/tvnewser/in-2-years-the-3-network-morning-shows-have-lost-1-8m-viewers/365698

Associated Press. (2018, August 9). *Austin American-Statesman to shut Spanish weekly, cut jobs*. APNews. https://apnews.com/article/f18b661aac714dd1ac92bb2bdfdadc47

Austin Business Journal. (2018, August 10). *Statesman offers buyouts to all 200-plus employees*. https://www.bizjournals.com/austin/news/2018/08/10/statesman-offers-buyouts-to-all-200-plus-employees.html

Baker, C. E. (2006). *Media concentration and democracy: Why ownership matters*. Cambridge University Press.

Bakshy, E., Messing, S., & Adamic, L. A. (2015). Exposure to ideologically diverse news and opinion on Facebook. *Science, 348*, 1130–1132.

Baldwin, T. F., Barett, M., & Bates, B. (1992). Influence of cable on television news audiences. *Journalism & Mass Communication Quarterly, 69*, 651–658.

Bark, E. (2008, April). Local TV revenue shifts to early-morning news shows. *D Magazine*. https://www.dmagazine.com/publications/d-ceo/2008/april/local-tv-revenue-shifts-to-early-morning-news-shows

Becker, B. (2015, April 3). *Political satire makes young people more likely to participate in politics: Trevor Noah's "The Daily Show" is likely to continue that trend.* LSE US Centre. https://blogs.lse.ac.uk/usappblog/2015/04/03/political-satire-makes-young-people-more-likely-to-participate-in-politics-trevor-noahs-the-daily-show-is-likely-to-continue-that-trend

Boczkowski, P. J., Mitchelstein, E., & Matassi, M. (2018). "News comes across when I'm in a moment of leisure": Understanding the practices of incidental news consumption on social media. *New Media & Society, 29*, 3523–3539. doi: 10.1177/1461444817750396

Boston Business Journal. (2017, February 21). GateHouse media parent signals cuts as it preps to buy more newspapers. *Boston Business Journal*. https://www.bizjournals.com/boston/news/2017/02/21/gatehouse-media-parent-signals-cuts-as-it-preps-to.html

Bowman, K. (2009, July 26). The decline of the major networks. *Forbes*. https://www.forbes.com/2009/07/25/media-network-news-audience-opinions-columnists-walter-cronkite.html

Bracht, M. (2003, March 27). Klein loses spot, Sinclair goes to "centralcasting." *Oklahoma City Oklahoman*. https://newsok.com/article/1921644/klein-loses-spot-sinclair-goes-to-centralcasting

Busterna, J. C. (1988). Commentary: Competitive effects of newspaper chain "deep pockets." *Newspaper Research Journal, 10*, 61–72.

Coe, K., Tewksbury, D., Bond, B. J., Drogos, K. L., Porter, R. W., Yahn, A., & Zhang, Y. (2008). Hostile news: Partisan use and perceptions of cable news programming. *Journal of Communication, 58*, 201–219. doi: 10.1111/j.1460-2466.2008.00381.x

Crider, D. (2012). A public sphere in decline: The state of localism in talk radio. *Journal of Broadcasting & Electronic Media, 56*, 225–244.

Dana, R. (2008, August 28). MSNBC anchors' fights go live. *Wall Street Journal*. https://www.wsj.com/articles/SB121989105850778775

Davis, B., & Novak, S. (2018, April 4). *Statesman*'s new owner says Austin will be a "flagship" for media group. *Austin American-Statesman*. https://www.statesman.com/business/20180404/statesmans-new-owner-says-austin-will-be-a-flagship-for-media-group

DellaVigna, S., & Kaplan, E. (2007). The Fox News effect: Media bias and voting. *The Quarterly Journal of Economics, 122*, 1187–1234. doi: 10.1162/qjec.122.3.1187

Demers, D. P., & Wackman, D. B. (1988). Effect of chain ownership on newspaper management goals. *Newspaper Research Journal, 9*, 59–68.

Doshi, A., Raghavan, S., Petitt, E., & Weiss, R. (2018, June 15). The economics of fake news: Consumer behavior during the 2016 election. *Academy of Management Global Proceedings*. https://journals.aom.org/doi/abs/10.5465/amgblproc.surrey.2018.0061.abs

Economist. (2012, September 22). Unbiased and unloved. *The Economist*. https://www.economist.com/node/21563298/all-comments?page=3

Edge, M. (2014). Newspapers' annual reports show chains profitable. *Newspaper Research Journal, 35*(4), 66–82.

ESPN. (2018). *Miami Dolphins*. http://www.espn.com/nfl/team/_/name/mia/miami-dolphins

Fields, S. (2017, July 12). "Digitally savvy" and at the mercy of fakers. *Washington Times*. https://www.washingtontimes.com/news/2017/jul/12/fake-news-particularly-dangerous-to-young-consumer

Finley, K. (2018, August 9). The Sinclair/Tribune merger is dead. *Wired*. https://www.wired.com/story/the-sinclairtribune-merger-is-dead

Fletcher, R., & Kleis N. R. (2017). Are people incidentally exposed to news on social media? A comparative analysis. *New Media & Society, 20*, 2450–2468.

Forbes. (2018). *#204 advance publications*. https://www.forbes.com/companies/advance-publications

Fortin, J., & Bromwich, J. E. (2018, April 2). Sinclair made dozens of local news anchors recite the same script. *New York Times*. https://www.nytimes.com/2018/04/02/business/media/sinclair-news-anchors-script.html

Gatehouse Media. (2018). *About us*. http://www.gatehousemedia.com/about-us

Gil de Zuñiga, H., Weeks, B., & Ardèvol-Abreu, A. (2017). Effects of the news-finds-me perception in communication: Social media use implications for news seeking and learning about politics. *Journal of Computer-Mediated Communication, 22,* 105–123.

Gilboa, E. (2005). Global television news and foreign policy: Debating the CNN effect. *International Studies Perspectives, 6,* 325–341. doi: 10.1111/j.1528-3577.2005.00211.x

Gorman, B. (2015). *Crash to paywall: Canadian newspapers and the great disruption.* McGill-Queen's University Press.

Gottfried, J., & Anderson, M. (2014, December 12). *For some, the satiric "Colbert Report" is a trusted source of political news.* Pew Research Center Journalism & Media. https://www.pewresearch.org/fact-tank/2014/12/12/for-some-the-satiric-colbert-report-is-a-trusted-source-of-political-news

Greenberg, D. (2017, April 28). *Trump's media war: Trump goes after the news media not because he thinks they're strong, but because he thinks they're weak and he can diminish them further.* The American Prospect. https://prospect.org/article/there%E2%80%99s-logic-trump%E2%80%99s-war-media

Guess, A., Nagler, J., & Tucker, J. (2019). Less than you think: Prevalence and predictors of fake news dissemination on Facebook. *Science Advances, 5*(1), 1–8. doi: 10.1126/sciadv.aau4586

Hagey, K., Alpert, L. I., & Serkez, Y. (2019, May 4). In news industry, a stark divide between haves and have-nots. *Wall Street Journal.* https://www.wsj.com/graphics/local-newspapers-stark-divide

Hardy, Q. (2015, October 29). IBM to acquire the Weather Company. *New York Times.* https://www.nytimes.com/2015/10/29/technology/ibm-to-acquire-the-weather-company.html

Huang, J. S., & Wang, W.-C. (2014). Application of the long tail economy to the online news market: Examining predictors of market performance. *Journal of Media Economics, 3,* 158–176.

IBM. (2018). *How round-the-clock weather reports help VTV keep citizens informed.* https://www.ibm.com/weather/industries/broadcast-media

Ingram, M. (2012, February 6). *Debunking the "original sin" of online newspapers.* GigaOm. https://gigaom.com/2012/02/06/debunking-the-original-sin-of-online-newspapers

Jacobson, A. (2018, November 28). *"Big money" success, yet year-end layoffs.* Radio + Television Business Report. https://www.rbr.com/big-money-success-yet-year-end-layoffs

Jarvey, N. (2019a, May 1). Hulu grows to 28 million subscribers. *Hollywood Reporter.* https://www.hollywoodreporter.com/live-feed/hulu-grows-28-million-subscribers-1206322

Jarvey, N. (2019b, January 17). Netflix grows subscriber base to 139 million worldwide. *Hollywood Reporter.* https://www.hollywoodreporter.com/news/netflix-grows-subscriber-base-139-million-worldwide-1176934

Joyella, M. (2018, August 28). Unstoppable: Fox News hits 200 months at no. 1. *Forbes.* https://www.forbes.com/sites/markjoyella/2018/08/28/unstoppable-fox-news-hits-200-months-at-number-one

Karim, K. (2003). *The media of diaspora.* Routledge.

Katz, A. J. (2018, July 31). *July 2018 ratings: Fox News marks 25 consecutive months as most-watched cable network in total day.* Adweek. https://www.adweek.com/tvnewser/july-2018-ratings-fox-news-marks-25-consecutive-months-as-most-watched-cable-network-in-total-day/372050

Kaufhold, K. (2015). Seriously social: Young adults, social media and news. *International Journal of Interactive Communication Systems and Technology, 4,* 1–13.

King, D. (2016, January 26). 200 newspapers; 1 copy desk: Gatehouse Media expands its centralized news hub in Austin. *Realty News Report.* https://realtynewsreport.com/200-newspapers-1-copy-desk-gatehouse-media-expands-its-centralized-news-hub-in-austin

Kornblut, A. (2005, June 5). The news media is still recovering from Watergate. *New York Times.* https://www.nytimes.com/2005/06/05/weekinreview/the-news-media-is-still-recovering-from-watergate.html

Kowert, R., & Oldmeadow, J. A. (2015). Playing for social comfort: Online video game play as a social accommodator for the insecurely attached. *Computers in Human Behavior, 53,* 556–566.

Küng, L., Picard, R. G., & Towse, R. (2008). *The Internet and mass media.* Sage.

Lacy, S., Stamm, M., & Martin, H. (2014). Short-run decisions threaten papers' long-run viability. *Newspaper Research Journal, 35*(4), 6–20.

Lawrence, C. (2015, June 4). Layoffs hit Las Vegas's KLAS-TV. *Las Vegas Review Journal*. https://www.reviewjournal.com/business/layoffs-hit-las-vegass-klas-tv

Lee, E. J., & Kaufhold, K. (2018). Journalistic professionalism and motivations for Snapchat video. *International Journal of Interactive Communication Systems and Technologies, 8*(1), 1–19.

Lin, C. (2004). Webcasting adoption: Technology fluidity, user innovativeness, and media substitution. *Journal of Broadcasting and Electronic Media, 49*, 446–465.

Malik, O. (2011, May 10). *The distribution democracy and the future of media*. GigaOm. https://gigaom.com/2011/05/10/the-distribution-democracy-and-the-future-of-media

Malone, M. (2009, March 4). *Meredith sets up Atlanta hub*. Broadcasting & Cable. https://www.broadcastingcable.com/news/meredith-sets-atlanta-hub-41583

McKinnon, A. (2016, July 26). Rupert Murdoch's influence in the US could be much worse: Just ask Australians. *QZ*. https://qz.com/741420/rupert-murdochs-influence-in-the-us-could-be-much-worse-just-ask-australians

Mindich, D. T. Z. (2004). *Tuned out: Why Americans under 40 don't follow the news*. Oxford University Press.

Moore, T. (2012, May 2). 30 years at The Weather Channel: Insiders perspective. The Weather Channel. https://weather.com/news/news/tom-moore-anniversary-blog-201204

Muller, P. D., & Kaufhold, K. (2019). *Bordering on hysteria: The effect of selective exposure on immigration attitudes*. Broadcast Education Association.

Mullin, B. (2018, July 24). Viewers cut the cable TV cord faster than expected. *Wall Street Journal*. https://www.wsj.com/articles/viewers-cut-the-cable-tv-cord-faster-than-expected-1532452053

Mutter, A. D. (2009, February 8). *Mission possible? Charging for web content*. Reflections of a Newsosaur. http://newsosaur.blogspot.com/2009/02/mission-possible-charging-for-content.html

Newman, N., Fletcher, R., Kalogeropoulos, A., Levy, D., & Kleis, N. R. (2017, August 28). *Reuters Institute digital news report 2017*. Social Science Research Network. https://papers.ssrn.com/sol3/papers.cfm?abstract_id=3026082

Newmark J-School Staff. (2018, June 11). *Craig Newmark endows the CUNY Graduate School of Journalism with a $20 million gift*. City University of New York. https://www.journalism.cuny.edu/2018/06/now-craig-newmark-graduate-school-journalism-city-university-new-york

NewscastStudio. (2013, May 6). *Nexstar opening HD hub in Memphis*. https://www.newscaststudio.com/2013/05/06/nexstar-opening-hd-hub-in-memphis

NewscastStudio. (2017, May 8). *Univision hubbing weather for news and radio operations*. https://www.newscaststudio.com/2017/05/08/univision-hubbing-weather-news-radio-operations

Nexstar. (2018). *Stations*. https://www.nexstar.tv/stations

Perez-Peña, R. (2009, March 9). Times go: Building deal raises cash. *New York Times*. https://www.nytimes.com/2009/03/10/business/media/10paper.html

Perrin, A. (2015, October 8). *Social media usage*. Pew Research Center. http://www.pewInternet.org/2015/10/08/social-networking-usage-2005-2015

Pew. (2017a, June 1). *Despite subscription surges for largest U.S. newspapers, circulation and revenue fall for industry overall*. https://www.pewresearch.org/fact-tank/2017/06/01/circulation-and-revenue-fall-for-newspaper-industry

Pew. (2017b). *Fact sheet*. http://www.pewresearch.org/wp-content/uploads/sites/8/2018/07/State-of-the-News-Media_2017-Archive.pdf#page=38

Pew. (2017c, July 10). *Sharp partisan divisions in view of national institutions*. https://www.people-press.org/2017/07/10/sharp-partisan-divisions-in-views-of-national-institutions

Pew. (2018a, December 10). *Social media outpaces print newspapers in the U.S. as a news source*. https://www.pewresearch.org/fact-tank/2018/12/10/social-media-outpaces-print-newspapers-in-the-u-s-as-a-news-source

Pew. (2018b). *Cable news fact sheet*. https://www.journalism.org/fact-sheet/cable-news

Pew. (2018c). *Newspapers fact sheet*. http://www.journalism.org/fact-sheet/newspapers

Pew. (2018d). *Local TV news fact sheet*. http://www.journalism.org/fact-sheet/local-tv-news

Picard, R. G., & Dal Zotto, C. (2015). The dimension of ownership and control of media. In P. Valcke, M. Sukosd, & R. Picard (Eds.), *Media pluralism and diversity* (pp. 54–66). Palgrave Macmillan.

Pierce, S. (2012, December 19). New owners lay off KTVX and KUCW staffers. *Salt Lake Tribune*. http://archive.sltrib.com/article.php?id=55491871&itype=CMSID
Pix11. (2018, March 15). *iHeartMedia, one of the biggest radio station owners, files for bankruptcy*. https://pix11.com/2018/03/15/iheartmedia-files-for-bankruptcy
Priest, D. (2016, Spring). Did the Pentagon Papers matter? *Columbia Journalism Review*. https://www.cjr.org/the_feature/did_the_pentagon_papers_matter.php
ProPublica. (2018). *ProPublica.com, about and supporters*. https://www.propublica.org
Putnam, R. D. (2000). *Bowling alone: The collapse and revival of American community*. Simon & Schuster.
Reals, T. (2008, November 24). At MSNBC, the "M" is for (Rachel) Maddow. *CBS News*. https://www.cbsnews.com/news/at-msnbc-the-m-is-for-rachel-maddow
Rogers, E. (1962). *Diffusion of innovations*. Free Press.
Schneider, M. (2017, December 28). *Ranking 2017's winners and losers*. Indiewire. https://www.indiewire.com/2017/12/highest-network-ratings-2017-most-watched-hbo-cbs-espn-fx-msnbc-fox-news-1201911363
Schoettle, A. (2019, May 24). Young viewers skip local TV news, consume info online. *Indianapolis Business Journal*. https://www.ibj.com/articles/73902-young-viewers-skip-local-tv-news-consume-info-online
Schwartz, J. (2017, October 21). Young subscribers flock to old media. *Politico*. https://www.politico.com/story/2017/10/21/millennials-trump-paying-for-news-244001
Stelter, B. (2010, August 31). TV news for early risers (or late-to-bedders). *New York Times*. https://www.nytimes.com/2010/09/01/business/media/01morning.html
Stelter, B. (2012, October 22). Weather Channel's parent company is renamed. *New York Times*. https://www.nytimes.com/2012/10/22/business/media/weather-channels-parent-company-is-renamed.html
Sullivan, M. (2017, July 10). Are Americans moved by Trump's media-as-enemy war cry? The opposite may be true. *Washington Post*. https://www.washingtonpost.com/lifestyle/style/are-americans-moved-by-trumps-media-as-enemy-war-cry-the-opposite-may-be-true/2017/07/10/c3d082ea-658c-11e7-9928-22d00a47778f_story.html
Swant, M. (2018, May 10). *Digital advertising revenue grew 21% and surpassed TV ad spend last year*. Adweek. https://www.adweek.com/digital/digital-advertising-revenue-grew-21-and-surpassed-tv-ad-spend-last-year
Texas Tribune. (2018). *About us*. https://www.texastribune.org/about
Thai, A. (2014, February 6). Political satire: Beyond the humor. *The Harvard Crimson*. https://www.thecrimson.com/article/2014/2/6/harvard-political-satire
Tolley, S. (1999). *The abyss that is destroying daily newspaper reading*. Newspaper Association of America.
Tran, K. (2017, December 26). Digital ad revenue growth is accelerating. *Business Insider*. https://www.businessinsider.com/digital-ad-revenue-growth-is-accelerating-2017-12
Trigoboff, D. (2003, January 6). *Sinclair speeds central casting*. Broadcasting + Cable. https://www.broadcastingcable.com/news/sinclair-speeds-centralcasting-97321
Tzuo, T. (2017, March 4). *Why newspaper subscriptions are on the rise*. TechCrunch. https://techcrunch.com/2017/03/04/why-newspaper-subscriptions-are-on-the-rise
Valenzuela, S., Correa, T., & Gil de Zuñiga, H. (2017). Ties, likes, and tweets: Using strong and weak ties to explain differences in protest participation across Facebook and Twitter use. *Political Communication, 35*, 117–143.
Valinsky, J. (2018, December 3). Nexstar buys Tribune in $4.1 billion deal. *CNN Business*. https://www.cnn.com/2018/12/03/media/tribune-nexstar-merger/index.html
Van Tassel, J. (2001, April 23). *Centralcasting: From a single location, major groups can manage all their stations*. Broadcasting + Cable. https://www.broadcastingcable.com/news/centralcasting-96943
Wagenberg, R. H., & Soderlund, W. C. (1975). The influence of chain-ownership on editorial comment in Canada. *Journalism Quarterly, 52*, 93–98.
Weather. (2018). *About us*. The Weather Company. https://business.weather.com/about-us

Weber, J. (2015, October 28). *Why IBM buys The Weather Channel.* Seeking Alpha, Jonathan Weber's Blog. https://seekingalpha.com/instablog/28873105-jonathan-weber/4478896-ibm-buys-weather-company

Wendling, M. (2018, January 22). *The (almost) complete history of "fake news."* BBC Trending. https://www.bbc.com/news/blogs-trending-42724320

Winslow, G. (2011, May 16). *Nextar expands Little Rock hub.* Broadcasting + Cable. https://www.broadcastingcable.com/news/nexstar-expandslittle-rock-hub-42889

Yosko, A. (2018). *Innovation at Gatehouse media's design space.* Texas State University Mass Communication Week. https://www.txstatemcweek.com/innovation-at-gatehcuse-medias-design-space/

Zephoria. (2019). *The top 20 valuable Facebook statistics.* https://zephoria.com/top-15-valuable-facebook-statistics

CHAPTER 15

Sports Industry

Michael Devlin, Texas State University

LEARNING OBJECTIVES

1. Describe how sport is both a commodity and a vehicle for additional commodities.
2. Identify the importance of relationship marketing in convergent sport media.
3. Understand how highly identified fans shape media consumption trends.
4. Understand how social TV functions in the modern sport media mix.
5. Recognize opportunities for growth, primarily related to eSport and virtual reality.

While the concept of sport is commonly accepted and has remained unchanged over time, the vast impact of sport on the economy coupled with technological advancements have certainly changed the discussion about sport as an industry. An apparent shift is not only occurring where one consumes sport media but also *how* and *when* it is consumed. Overall, sport mostly benefits from convergent media, whereby it occurs in one locale at one time, only to be simultaneously disseminated via radio or television broadcast while concurrently being discussed on ancillary devices by fans and traditional media, such as the sport section of a newspaper and on sport broadcast channels. The sport media landscape is ripe with demand for digital and social media engagement, allowing for new methods of consuming and sharing sport to naturally occur. As technology evolves, so do consumer expectations. Tape delay, for example, is no longer acceptable, evident by the criticism NBC received for its decision to tape delay the 2016 Olympic Games Opening Ceremony in order to fill its prime-time slots, which was described as "absurd at best, and shallowly profit minded at worst" (McNear, 2016, para. 5). It is hard to understate the influence of advertising on sport media managerial decisions; however, striking the balance between providing fans on-demand entertainment and maximizing profit is an ever-growing challenge in the convergent media environment.

The immediacy and demand for access to sport media has major implications with both economic and social outcomes. The influence of technologies on communication now provides an impetus for change—especially as sport media respond to new opportunities to commodify spectating opportunities, resulting in the proliferation of commercialization and causing "a conflict [that] has developed between sports as a business and sports as a game" (Rein, Kotler, & Shields, 2006, p. 14). Decades ago, sport revenue was largely dependent on audiences filling stadiums, but improvements in technology and media channels has shifted the way audiences consume sport, thus presenting new opportunities for revenue streams. Today, not only are teams and leagues seeking to profit from the on-field product, so too are media conglomerates, networks, and commercial sponsors.

Sport media professionals should feel optimistic, as there is no indication that an attenuation in demand or revenue exists. Sport is a $1.3 trillion industry with the top five sports in the United States accounting for $180 billion in total revenue (Plunkett Research, 2018). Sport still dominates television ratings over scripted shows, garnering 44 of the top 50 most-watched programs in the United States in 2017 (Crupi, 2018), and earns $62.7 billion worldwide from sponsorship spending (IEG, 2018). Therefore, this chapter seeks to explicate how sport media has shifted from a passive form of entertainment to an active, and potentially immersive, commodity. Doing so addresses the need to delineate how media managers can reach desired target audiences using technology, convergent media, and relationship marketing tactics.

Nuances between sport and other entertainment sources must be operationalized in order to properly address convergent media in sport. First, one must accept that sport is a commodified product, not just defined by the audience size it is able to garner but also by the number of ways it is commodified through corporate partnerships (Devlin, 2016). Second, rather than strictly examine convergent media, aspiring media professionals may be better suited to focus on the target audience—the highly identified sport fan. Third, marketing paradigm shifts require professionals to understand the role of digital and social media; however, when examining sport media, it would be prudent to understand how fans are using what once was dubbed a "second screen" by preparing to challenge the notion that devices ancillary to the television may now be the *primary screen*. Lastly, strategies and tactics to reach the fans on behalf of interested stakeholders have moved beyond simple transactional approaches and now require increased levels of engagement to stand out from the cluttered sport economy. Leveraging key insights about sport fans and reaching them through engagement marketing strategies is certain to yield positive results, particularly for sponsoring partners, as demonstrated by the case study below.

CASE STUDY

Every 12 years, the British and Irish Lions rugby team, composed of the best rugby players from England, Scotland, Wales, and Ireland, tour New Zealand for scheduled matches against New Zealand's professional rugby teams and senior national teams. A 10-match schedule occurring between June 3 and July 8, 2017, featured three separate matches between British and Irish Lions and New Zealand All-Blacks. In an attempt to reach fans participating in this historic event, Steinlager, New Zealand's top-selling beer company and official sponsor of the All-Blacks, sought new ways to reach and engage fans and better promote its product.

Rather than compete against brands in the stadium, where fans only spend approximately 80 minutes per game and would arguably be more focused on the event rather than sponsors, Steinlager turned its attention to the airport. Realizing nearly 2.5 million people would pass through a single airport during the six-week period, and with very few competing distractions, they could authentically engage fans of both teams in a novel manner. Steinlager's advertising agency, DDB, purchased every digital display in both the national and international terminals at the Auckland Airport, resulting in the purchase of 65 digital displays and eight static billboards. Boldly, Steinlager offered a challenge to Guinness, the official beer sponsor of the British and Irish Lions, proposing they could have all the signs to advertise on for free if they "fight us for them" in a fan-centric marketing campaign known as "Fight for Territory."

Each of the 65 digital screens were retrofitted with a camera and microprocessors that were linked together and programed to recognize supporting fans of either of the two teams based on team colors and logos. All fans had to do was find a sign and stand in front of it to change the sign from one team's beer-sponsored sign to their team's sign. As a result, fans from both sides blanketed the airport to keep territory for their team and show their support as they traveled through each airport. The result was 96,000 turnovers, indicating 96,000 purposeful interactions with an advertisement over a six-week span. While impressive, what is more notable was how this benefited the sponsor—Guinness reported a sales increase of 18%, while Steinlager, which was already New Zealand's top-selling beer, increased its sales by 5.1%. Furthermore, this campaign received recognition and several international advertising awards in addition to helping earn revenue for the teams' sponsors.

This campaign worked because rather than rely on an archaic transactional approach or compete for attention in a space where brands would most likely be ignored, Steinlager engaged highly identified fans at an unexpected place and provided them an opportunity to showcase their allegiance to their team. In their quest to compete and represent their team, fans were willing to interact with a display billboard 96,000 times. Naturally, fans were inclined to share their experience through their own social channels, increasing exposure for the brands. In this case, we witnessed how sport provides an opportunity to promote an ancillary product outside the stadium by utilizing traditional media (billboard display), but it worked only because marketers and managers understood the predictable behaviors of fans—resulting in success for the teams and the sponsoring brands. Perhaps what is most important to acknowledge is how effectively technology was interwoven with fan-centric consumer insights to garner interaction with potential consumers. The execution was authentic and purposeful in a way that was neither gimmicky nor distracting, thus demonstrating the importance of relationship marketing over transactional marketing tactics.

Something Old

Sport is multifaceted, providing opportunities to transmit messages through traditional media (television, radio, newspaper) and digital media (social and online). Sport media then provides "a statement of culture, lifestyle, locality, social group, nationality, socio-economic class, political orientation, history, and much more" (Thrassou, Vrontis,

Kartakoullis, & Kriemadis, 2012, p. 295), enabling it to be many things to a variety of stakeholders—fans, cities, sponsors, and so on.

Like most media, sport generates a reasonably predictable and reliable audience, resulting in year-over-year increasing broadcast rights fees and ticket prices. This may be in addition to the idea that sport is a key television exemplar, leaving some to suggest sport should be perceived as necessary to the growth of television (Bellamy, 2006). Sport uniquely provides real-time suspense, has minimal barriers of language and literacy proficiency for viewers, is ingrained into our cities and communities, and remains one of the few zap-proof programming choices in an era of on-demand media selection since people regularly schedule viewing major sport events live (Bellamy, 2006). Arguably, some networks have overvalued sport's capabilities, resulting in pursuit of high-dollar media rights for leagues and events all while simultaneous cord cutting is occurring among younger generations. For example, in 2018, Disney's annual earnings report shows that ESPN lost 2 million subscribers as a result of cord cutting (Shah, 2018).

Despite the potential overvaluation, sport has shown the ability to withstand changes brought by emerging technologies by embracing them to reach and engage with vast audiences. To counter cord cutting, ESPN quickly introduced its own digital subscription service, ESPN+, which allows subscribers to stream select ESPN content for $5 a month. Whether sport media is being consumed on television or a mobile device, sport media will remain profitable because of its ability to draw a predictable audience and to provide space for ancillary stakeholders to commoditize sport for their organization's gain. The commodification extends beyond media companies and sponsors, as sport leagues and teams no longer see themselves as just producing an on-the-field product but rather as media businesses producing content across their own websites, creating specialized television networks (i.e., Longhorn Network and University of Texas; NBA-TV), and engaging with fans in the digital space to better promote themselves and partners.

SPORT MEDIA AS A BUSINESS AND RELATIONSHIP MARKETING

Sport generates revenues from a variety of sources—ticket sales, media rights, endorsements and sponsorships, and merchandise to name a few—leaving sport purists to question the authenticity of sport as a game over sport as a business. As Wenner (1989) notes, sport "is a vertical integration strategy aimed at maximizing the ways the complementary holdings can strengthen each other through cross-promotion and marketing to make the corporate whole stronger than the sum of its parts" (p. 316), which is further marked by soaring television contracts and expensive broadcasting rights. In 1951, DuMont paid $75,000 for the television rights to broadcast the National Football League championship game between the Cleveland Browns and Los Angeles Rams—a stark contrast to the approximately $1 billion broadcast rights just for the regular season games currently being paid by television networks (NBC, CBS, and Fox) (Crupi, 2011). The rationale for paying these excessive costs rests in the opportunities for reaching large, expected audiences, which provides an attractive marketing vehicle for the networks who own the media rights.

Sport has a unique duality in that networks help promote the sport event, which then provides a vehicle for other brands and media companies to promote themselves. Therefore, sport is both a commodity and commodifier, and aspiring media managers would be wise to recognize this duality when navigating the current convergent media landscape. Media managers should acknowledge the need for increased relationship marketing tactics over traditional, transactional tactics to reach audiences, which will be likely to create lasting bonds and yield greater results among sport fans (Gladden & Sutton, 2009).

The traditional four Ps of marketing (price, product, promotion, and place) (Stanton, Etzel, & Walker, 1994) are fairly antiquated in respect to the sport media environment due to their inability to fully address the complexity of convergent media coupled with associated behaviors related to sport fans. Convergent media has muddied traditional sport media offerings, making it unclear as to what is being offered (product) and by whom (Devlin, 2017), and where it is being consumed (place), all while gaps between pricing models exist. As these key factors become less controllable, promotion becomes less reliable. Sport occurs in the stadium, but television and radio are simultaneously broadcasting the game, while several competing sport apps offer updates, highlights, and box scores. This all occurs while sport fans (both attending the event and consuming away from the stadium via television) are sharing insights, images, and opinions related to the game through social media channels. Furthermore, ballooning prices for entry into stadiums (Mullin, Hardy, & Sutton, 2007), contrasting with the free-television or people streaming pay-per-view events, make pricing difficult to control.

Sport organizations, among other businesses, have slowly shifted from a transactional paradigm toward one focusing on cooperation and engaging with an active audience (Bee & Kahle, 2006; Gladden & Sutton, 2009) known as relationship marketing. Research suggests "sports organizations should strive to develop this deeper level of relationship with target consumers" (Bee & Kahle, 2006, p. 103) to decrease marketing costs, enhance loyalty (Gladden & Funk, 2001), increase product familiarity, and reduce risk (Bee & Kahle, 2006; Dwyer, Schurr, & Oh, 1987; Sheth & Parvatiyar, 2000). Relationship marketing's two-way relationship is mutually beneficial as it encourages active participation by both parties (Sheth & Parvatiyar, 2000) and ultimately helps attract and maintain positive customer relationships (Berry, 1983). The goal should be to move fans from compliance (merely tuning in to the event) toward identification (feeling the team represents the viewer) and ultimately internalization (ingrained shared behaviors between the organization and the audience) (Bee & Kahle, 2006).

Sport media and sport organizations should develop strategies that permit interaction (Underwood, Bond, & Baer, 2001). Fortunately, advances in technology allow for constant two-way communication all while the multiplexity of the sport bundle and its ancillary offerings provide numerous platforms to reach fans. Rather than simply supply content, media managers must participate in community conversations themselves and encourage dialogue between the organization and its consumers, which "conveys confidence, accessibility, respect, and authenticity to people both inside and outside the brand community" (Hanlon & Hawkins, 2008, p. 15).

UNDERSTANDING THE TARGET AUDIENCE

Despite the technological advances and digital trends that rapidly change, media managers would benefit by first understanding a more stable variable—the target audience, or the modern sport fan, in order to practice relationship marketing. Fan identity (interchangeably referred to as *team identity* in the literature) is best described as "the extent to which a fan feels a psychological connection to a team and the team's performances are viewed as self-relevant" (Wann, 2006, p. 322).

Various terms like *identification* (Donavan, Carlson, & Zimmerman, 2005; Wann & Branscombe, 1990), *attachment, allegiance* (Funk & James, 2001), and *loyalty* (Gladden & Funk, 2001) are used to describe the relationship between a specialized audience and the specific sport, league, and/or team. Aspiring media managers should be aware of these terminologies, noting "any effort to review the literature becomes an exercise in untangling semantic differences" (Funk & James, 2001, p. 120). Research ultimately highlighting cross-sectional acceptance of sport fans and notable behaviors serves as a foundational base that media managers can leverage for research and practical application, as multidisciplinary research finds predictable subsequent behaviors among sport fans as they relate to marketing (Donavan et al., 2005; Funk & James, 2001; Madrigal, 2001), consumer behavior (Wakefield, 2016; Wann, Grieve, Partridge, Zapalac, & Parker, 2013), sociology, and psychology (Devlin, 2016; Donavan et al., 2005; Funk & James, 2001).

Sport fans are often thought of as an unpredictable audience, yet studying sport fans reveals quite the opposite, unsurprisingly demonstrating that as fan identity increases, so too does the amount of media consumed and merchandise purchased (Trail & James, 2001; Wakefield, 2016). What is surprising, however, is that fans will often purchase sponsors' products or engage in team-related activities presumably due to normative pressure from others in the in-group (Madrigal, 2000, 2001). This should inform media managers that it is more important to convince the *group* to act rather than convince them *why* they should prefer one brand, product, or event over another.

The theoretical underpinnings of team identity are easily recognizable in the aforementioned case study. First, sport fandom encourages vicarious group participation (Katz & Kahn, 1978), where interactions with members of the in-group bolster identification with a sport team (see Funk & James, 2001; Gwinner & Swanson, 2003). Unlike music or art, which arguably features a high degree of fan identification as well, sport team identification is based not only on shared connections between the fans and the team (Wann, 1994) but also on perceived incongruencies with opposing/rival teams (Smith & Schwarz, 2003), creating an us-versus-them dichotomy that further enhances one's identity with one's team. In the case study, fans were willing to actively show their commitment to a team (Mahony, Madrigal, & Howard, 2000) by interacting with digital advertisements in an effort to oppose their rival's presence. Taken one step further, research suggests increased team identification positively influences sponsorship evaluation (Cornwell, Weeks, & Roy, 2005), similar to the outcomes demonstrated for each of the beer brands' increased sales following the "Fight for Territory" campaign.

Aside from marketing and sponsorship opportunities, media professionals would also benefit by recognizing the various entries for sport fandom, emphasizing numerous opportunities in a convergent media mix to reach and entice potential or highly identified fans. Aesthetics of the game (Wann, 1995), the need to fulfill entertainment desires, and the need for escapism (Bryant, 1989) indicate passive media may be sufficient for reaching and garnering fans. However, other research signals the importance of watching in a social environment, as it enhances self-esteem by belonging to a group (Wann & Branscombe, 1993; Greenwood, Kanters, & Casper, 2006).

Sport media must also offer opportunities for entertainment and escapism and be aware of opportunities to garner connectivity and build relationships. Researchers have pointed toward the economic interests (i.e., sport wagering) (Gantz & Wenner, 1995) associated with sport media, suggesting information gathering and instant feedback are necessary components for being a sport fan; therefore, media managers must maintain diligence and accuracy when providing information to fans. In an era of social media, it is more important to be correct than it is to be first.

While much of the early research signaled evidence for uses and gratifications approaches for sport fandom and sport media, other scholars have looked at psychological personality profiles of sport fans (Devlin, 2016), finding that traits such as increased extraversion and sociability coupled with lowered modesty lead to increased fandom, again signaling the importance of sport media as a communal gathering. As this relates to convergent media, the paths and associations between fans and media provide multiple opportunities for gratification, which will undoubtedly lead to increased consumption. Media managers should be aware of both old and new ways to reach this coveted audience. Despite the attractiveness of social and digital media brought by media convergence, one should not ignore the core audience and the many opportunities to develop meaningful relationships with fans.

Something New

As previously noted, it is necessary to understand the behaviors of highly identified fans and the maturing marketing tactics used by sport to promote its product and permitted by sport to promote ancillary partner products. However, as paradigms in media convergence shift, so too should the manner in which media managers reach specialized audiences. In the era of social media, one of the failed assumptions is that users of new media are active consumers, when in fact it is estimated that less than one-third of Twitter users are active. Despite the ubiquity of active users on social media, sport media still provides a passive source of entertainment; and although television amply suffices for many of our passive viewing needs, as technology improves, so too might the way we consume sport media in a convergent market. As Devlin (2017) notes, we must better understand relationship marketing in the digital and social spaces, which are increasingly important as habits like social TV watching and capabilities like virtual reality continue to grow.

SOCIAL TV

The mobile phone and apps have gradually changed the way sport media is disseminated and consumed. In 2014, 51% of television viewers surveyed said they used their smartphone while watching television (Henderson, 2017), with users likely to be young, female, and less educated (Gil de Zúñiga, Garcia-Perdomo, & McGregor, 2015). This rate of screen usage has increased dramatically to include 88% of U.S. adults in 2017 (Henderson, 2017).

Wang (2013) provides underlying support for these numbers, proclaiming that "it is no longer a question of which screen users will view at what times—it's a matter of delivering television programming everywhere, across all screens" (para. 7), asserting one's attention is balanced among multiple devices by alternating between television screens, mobile phones, tablets, or computers to fulfill sought gratifications. Recent trends recognize that viewers are simultaneously on more than one device when consuming media (Henderson, 2017), and while many of these findings point to the media audience at large, sport fans and their viewing habits are not distinctively different (Tang & Cooper, 2017).

There are a number of reasons why this growth is occurring and expected to continually increase. Platforms such as Twitter and Facebook allow every team, league, and athlete to have a virtual presence in consumers' daily lives. Journalists and sport broadcasters alike are able to circumvent gatekeepers and disseminate breaking news, while fans explore a "virtual sport bar" to discuss the game in a mediated environment. Social network analysis reveals that subnetworks largely exist between fans and traditional media, signaling fans are fully utilizing computer-mediated communication to consume sport while still relying on traditional media to guide their ancillary viewing preferences.

While television has been the predominant choice for media consumption for several decades, social media platforms and smartphone devices are increasingly folded into the sport media mix after slightly less than two decades of existence. As other chapters in this book explain, convergent media enables various aspects of sport media to be accessed concurrently. While met with initial skepticism, it has been found that the use of multiscreen *sport* viewing was something the "majority of the participants, in our evaluation . . . [believed was] . . . a welcome addition to their television viewing experience" (Anstead, Benford, & Houghton, 2014, p. 108). The term *second screen* was coined to describe the simultaneous use of television and an ancillary device, although there was friction in the literature regarding ancillary screen usage, noting that "the two media's (first and second screen) diverse functions are able to *complement* each other and coexist during the viewing experience" (Cunningham & Eastin, 2017, p. 302). Second screen operationalization is largely accepted as the use of a second screen that interrupts or complements the primary device's usage, but it is becoming less certain which device is the primary device and which is complementary.

Some scholars still point to an existing hierarchy when comparing traditional television to ancillary devices (e.g., mobile phones) (Tang & Cooper, 2017), but the term *second screen* is still problematic when describing the multiscreen habits of sport fans because it designates a hierarchy whereby one screen is a primary device receiving a majority of the user's cognitive attention, and a concurrently used second device either interrupts or complements the user experience (Vaccari, Chadwick, & O'Loughlin, 2015). Typically, it is assumed the hierarchy is television first, all other devices second. Gantz and Lewis (2014) suggest that sport fans consume live-game content on large screens, fulfilling a desire for an immersive experience, whereas mobile content is utilized during in-game lulls or to consume postgame content, maintaining that sport fans have become their "own media manager—creating a specific and unique experience through their media choice and consumption patterns" (p. 767).

As media professionals seek to describe and recommend using multiplatform media in their product offerings, they are advised to take a "social TV" approach, which more accurately describes the real-time, primary-screen-related backchannel communication occurring during a television broadcast, which subsequently bolsters channel loyalty (Lim, Hwang, Kim, & Biocca, 2015). Social TV is not linked to one specific architecture, such as television or radio, but can occur across several competing devices, such as computer, tablet, or mobile phone (Harboe et al., 2008). To illustrate this, in 2015, sport events only comprised 1.4% of all television programming but nearly 50% of all Twitter TV-related conversations (Casey, 2017), suggesting a cognitive demand directed at something other than a television screen. This accurately illustrates how sport fans are able to engage with an ancillary device (e.g., mobile phone or tablet) across several platforms (e.g., Twitter, group text message) while watching a televised sporting event (Highfield, Harrington, & Bruns, 2013) in either the background or foreground. As fans engage in a more narrowly focused, mediated coviewing social TV experience, users may be transported back and forth from a passive form of entertainment to a communal, active form of media entertainment. This is partly done through televised sporting events by offering a collective hashtag and inviting viewers to share and discuss events happening in real time (Hwang & Lim, 2015).

Media professionals seeking to improve ratings and loyalty among audiences would also benefit from understanding *why* social TV works from the fan perspective and designing concrete tactics that can be replicated through a process. As previously discussed, one of the primary antecedents and motivations for fan identity is the increased self-esteem provided to sport fans when belonging to an in-group (Wann & Branscombe, 1993) and engaging in discourse with members of the in-group. With increased second-screen use, televised sport channels and networks must find opportunities for engagement as fans appear insatiable in their desire to search for information, share feelings, and connect with other fans during events (Proulx & Shepatin, 2012). Access to televised events is commonplace, and fans can access content from around the world from the comfort of their home, but they may still be looking for opportunities to have a shared, immersive fan experience.

Interweaving the underpinnings of fan identity helps explain why the social TV phenomenon is likely to occur among sport fans. Fandom is contingent on the development of a structured social identity (Tajfel & Turner, 1986). Awareness of others and their social existence is a prerequisite for social identity (Prasolova-Forland, 2003). Advancements in technology and the emergence of social TV, coupled with increased usage of social network sites, allow users to participate in social TV and experience what is known as *social presence* (Biocca, Harms, & Burgoon, 2003; Short, Williams, & Christie, 1976), the perception of being socially present with others as a result of increased second-screen use (Lin & Chiang, 2017). Social presence may be enhanced through social media and online forums allowing fans to connect with defined social groups without being physically present; the more social one's network becomes, the larger social capital they ascribe, which is important for shaping identities and group formation (Kietzmann, Silvestre, McCarthy, & Pitt, 2012).

Fans seeking out one another facilitate emotional bonds, positive social interactions, and increased sharing; make the second-screen environment crucial for social TV; and allow for the experience of group viewing without being physically present (Ellison, Steinfield, & Lampe, 2007). This process increases user interaction (Kruikemeier, van Noort, Vliegenthart, & de Vreese, 2013) and reinforces aspects of one's identity.

Sport fans primarily engage in social TV behaviors to BIRG (bask in reflected glory) (see Cialdini et al., 1976), allowing fans to celebrate the prestige shared by other fans who are also consuming the game, to engage in social broadcasting (which allows them to share notable sport content with their social network), and to discuss the game in their virtual environment based on stats and facts about the game they are able to find due to search capabilities (Greenwood & Yorke, 2014). For modern sport fans, any type of backchannel communication results in increased interactivity, feelings of immediacy, and belonging (Gantz & Lewis, 2014). Social TV engagement provides the technical medium for sport fans' virtual sport bar and the simulated feeling that other fans are present. The convenience and capability to attract and interact with vast user networks increases the resources available to individuals and improves one's social capital (Lin, 2001). The desire to increase social capital then becomes a predictor for dual-screen use (Lin & Chiang, 2017). The evidence is overwhelmingly supportive for incorporating aspects of social TV into the viewing experience for the sport fan. This book will discuss second screening in detail in chapter 21.

VIRTUAL REALITY

In contrast to the previously discussed social TV aspects is the prevalent interest and rise in incorporating virtual reality into the media fold. This immersive experience is just that—*immersive*—and may consequently interfere with the collective, social nature routinely sought by sport fans and provided through social TV. Therefore, in the years to come, audiences, content creators, and business managers may be at an impasse when determining where to invest funds to provide fans (and consumers at large) opportunities to fulfill each motivation for sport consumption. Virtual reality (VR) is a computer-generated environment that typically showcases a user-controlled 360-degree view of a computer-mediated environment with the purpose of providing a completely immersive experience. Technological capabilities coupled with natural curiosity helped introduce the plausibility of incorporating VR (Cooley, 2014) by offering widespread uses such as helping athletes train by visualizing competitive environments (Miles, Pop, Watt, Lawrence, & John, 2012) and allowing fans of the Atlantic Coast Conference to watch highlights from football and basketball (Rettig, 2017).

There is an optimism among sport stakeholders that a VR experience will be a profitable channel offering. Keith Pelley, CEO of the PGA European Tour, acknowledged the biggest change in media consumption in 2017 was people watching the tour on multiple devices, particularly among generation Z, but predicts the future of sport media may be in virtual reality (Pelley, 2018). In 2018, virtual reality was used for the Ryder Cup for the first time to help put the fan "inside the ropes," and it was optimistically received by fans (Cronin, 2019). Other leagues are taking advantage of this emerging media by incorporating a virtual reality experience as an add-on package or as incentive for buying season passes. For example, the National Basketball Association allows subscribers of *NBA League Pass* to watch one game a week in virtual reality from home. Although the preceding sections discussed the importance of social relationships and sport, the virtual reality experience may pose as many challenges as opportunities; nevertheless, it would be ill advised for sport media professionals to ignore virtual reality as a new channel offering for sport fans. There is a lack of research citing whether sport fans would be willing to adopt VR technology, which would seemingly interrupt the social rewards that sport offers, but to what degree is largely unknown and will require more attention in the coming years.

Opportunities and Challenges

Sport media professionals should feel comfort in knowing that sport itself is not hard to sell—but the ever-growing competition for fans' attention, particularly as ever more information and offerings are provided, presents as many challenges as opportunities. There is solace, however, in knowing that sport remains one of the few zap-proof, must-watch live offerings (Bellamy, 2006). Paying attention to what the next generation considers sport and how they choose to consume sport may present several new opportunities.

OPPORTUNITIES

We have witnessed the rise of several niche sports slowly becoming more mainstream, primarily due to the fact that (1) gatekeepers have been eliminated due to Internet access and user-generated content streaming, and (2) an increase in specialty sport-related cable and satellite channels is now permitting would-be fans to access a plethora of sport media. Perhaps one of the biggest opportunities for media managers to focus their attention on is eSport—organized video game competitions encompassing a variety of platforms, including personal computers and gaming consoles, featuring everything from sport-themed games (e.g., NBA2K, FIFA) to real-time strategy games.

Investing in, marketing of, and developing relationships with eSport organizations and fans may be one of the biggest opportunities in the coming decade, largely due to the demographics of eSport consumers. eSport players and spectators are primarily in their teens and early 20s, creating a large potential for revenue growth, which is expected to generate $1.5 billion in annual revenues in 2020 (Deloitte, 2020) and attracts more than $500 million in sponsorships annually from companies like Microsoft, Red Bull, and Intel (Casselman, 2015). While initially seen as subversive to sport by some in 2010 (Jonasson & Thiborg, 2010), eSport has since become seemingly impossible to ignore due to its establishment of national and international governing bodies and development of teams, sanctioned tournaments, and endorsement deals, securing eSport as a recognizable form of sport (Funk, Pizzo, & Baker, 2018). As a result, its audience size has recently increased, with a global audience of 600 million fans (Deloitte, 2020) who will watch an event once a week and, in some cases, up to as much as four hours weekly (Westcott, Loucks, Ciampa, & Srivastava, 2019). In comparison to mainstream sport, the most recent Super Bowl, often referred to as the premiere sport event each year, only had 98.2 million viewers in 2019, a notable decline from 2018's 111.3 million viewers (Handley, 2019).

Twitch, YouTube Gaming, and Ustream are the most common platforms for eSport viewing; however, mainstream cable stations would be prudent to dedicate future resources to investing in and broadcasting tournaments. Like traditional sport, research has also identified social interaction as a primary motivation for consuming eSport (Brenda, 2017). Dovetailing with earlier sections in this chapter, the social aspect of eSport should help media managers seek opportunities for securing the media rights to such events and providing complementary platforms for social TV and relationship marketing.

Researchers have identified several factors as the underpinnings of eSport's success. Advancements in Internet speed and connectivity coupled with more realistic games provide improved real-time feedback and reliance on teamwork, which ultimately create a skill gap between regular competitors and novice recreational gamers (Jenny et al., 2018). Interestingly enough, this heightened level of skill has encouraged consumers to watch others play the game rather than play themselves. On its surface, that seemed like an unlikely turn of events, but it is no less logical than someone who once played basketball at the amateur level who now enjoys watching the professional level with heightened appreciation and satisfaction. Currently, the number of people watching eSport without ever having played the game has nearly equalized, with 42% of eSport viewers admitting to watching games they themselves have not played (Newzoo, 2017). Collectively, this demonstrates two prominent considerations: (1) eSport is a growing opportunity for media managers to expand their portfolio, and (2) creating an atmosphere for social interactions (i.e., social TV) is as necessary in eSport as it is in traditional sport.

Virtual reality is another significant opportunity for sport media managers. As diffusion of innovation theory would suggest (Rogers, 1962), adoption of VR technology will be more commonplace as fans start to desire it as an option for consumption. If social TV enables one to transform their home into a virtual sport bar, then if the infrastructure is done correctly, VR could enable one to transform their home into the virtual stadium with 100,000 fellow fans and to avoid the hassles often associated with attending large events, such as parking and lines at concessions or bathrooms. Media managers need to look no further than to the development and infrastructure of online gaming to potentially create an area where fans can consume sport media from their home and authentically feel they are present with other fans. The media companies that can best develop, streamline, and implement access to the largest number of sporting events and offer VR service may be best prepared to capitalize on cord cutting, provide a new source of revenue, and lessen the risk associated with securing high-dollar media rights.

CHALLENGES

While the future of sport media remains profitable and attractive, there are a number of challenges media managers may encounter in the coming years. As previously mentioned, technology has enabled fans to access content across a variety of platforms from around the globe. In the 2000s, media corporations invested at unprecedented levels to secure media rights to mega sporting events such as the Olympics and World Cup and leagues like the National Football League in the United States and the English Premiere League in England. Soon after, media companies were no longer buying just the rights to events and games but also engaging in direct media ownership of clubs, franchises, and leagues (Zhang, Pitts, & Kim, 2017), thus overly inflating the cost of entry for competing companies. This may present an extraordinary challenge to media managers as costs for entry and cord cutting among audiences simultaneously increase.

Increasing digital disruption may also present a challenge to sport media managers looking to reach generation Z, individuals born between 1995 and 2012, who are predominantly mobile-first when consuming media (Sutton, 2017). Traditional sport telecasts are witnessing a decline in television ratings, but this trend does not indicate fewer people are watching—they are simply viewing content differently than previous generations. Media managers will now need to account for the viewing habits of a mobile-first generation. Generation Z only watches 13.2 hours of television a week (Kleinschmit, 2015) but claims to watch 3.5 hours of video daily, much of which is consumed in snippets and shared through influencers (Evans, 2019). It is not enough for media companies to secure the television rights to a sport broadcast; they must now consider the digital infrastructure to appeal to and engage with the growing mobile-first generation.

Nonbroadcast media outlets also allow users to cultivate their viewing experience, resulting in a saturated field competing for attention. Jeff Toney, Dude Perfect's chief branding officer, correctly summarized generation Z's sentiment toward media: "Entertain me now, if I don't like it, I have 1,000 other options to be distracted with" (Evans, 2019, para 3). Sport media managers today must determine how to stand out from the rest in a cluttered field while keeping a fickle generation's attention throughout the course of a game or event. The risk of inattention is effervescent and may continue to push would-be advertisers and sponsors away from investing in traditional sport media and its televised advertising partners. The result would be catastrophic for media companies, many of whom have already invested large sums in securing media rights in hopes of bringing in advertising dollars.

Lastly, improvements in technology and the changing digital landscape have loosened would-be regional restrictions on gaining access to sport media events. However, media managers looking to protect their investments should also be aware of the unintended effects of globalization—lack of trademark enforcement, piracy, and unenforced copyright protections in developing countries (Zhang, Kim, Mastromartino, Qian, & Nauright, 2018). Both burgeoning intellectual properties advanced by technology as well as physical copyrights belonging to teams and leagues are increasingly susceptible to being stolen and/or misused, heightening the need for better electronic security and monitoring existing copyright usage abroad. Following the action plan below can help guide sport media management practices.

ACTION PLAN

1. Highlight increased areas of collaboration between traditional sport and the emerging eSport market.
2. Develop further engagement opportunities for sport fans at home to feel authentically present with other sport fans and players.
3. Implement digital engagement opportunities for mobile-first users during slow or inactive parts of a sporting event.

KEY TAKEAWAYS

1. Sport is uniquely a commodity and a vehicle to promote other commodities and should be recognized as such.
2. Sport media managers need to completely understand the antecedents and outcomes associated with being a highly identified fan.
3. Relationship marketing strategies must be developed over traditional, transactional strategies in order to attract, maintain, and enhance participation among highly identified fans.
4. Technology has allowed for new opportunities to reach fans, and media managers should consider the role social TV plays in the consumer media mix during live sport events and develop ways to communicate with the fans during events.
5. Virtual reality may present future revenue streams for leagues and media companies, and its uses and gratifications in conjunction with sport require further investigation by both the academic and professional community.
6. eSports may be one of the best investment opportunities on the horizon for media companies wishing to enter the realm of sport media.

CONCLUSION

Sport media is a business, evident by both the growing audience size and economic impact. As it grows and matures as a business, so too must media managers in the way they reach, attract, and maintain fans. This chapter provided several areas to consider: (1) the importance of highly identified fans, (2) the need to shift from traditional/transactional marketing to relationship marketing, and (3) the interwoven aspects of technology, ancillary devices, and social TV in the convergent sport media mix. Each aspect, to some degree, is identified in the case study, highlighting the fact that when fans are given an opportunity to showcase their loyalty and engage with the team and sponsoring brands, opportunities for recognition and revenue increase. Research in social identity acknowledges the effect that distinctiveness has on developing one's sense of fandom (Ashforth & Mael, 1989); therefore, if leveraged as an opportunity to make one's league or team distinct, it may help move potential audiences closer to fandom, which subsequently will affect future consumption (Raney, 2006), thus building brand loyalty.

Several opportunities lie ahead for sport media professionals, but they do require accepting new ways of speaking with sport fans and adopting new platforms. Coupling the technology capabilities permitting social TV viewing while relying on the theoretical blueprint for relationship marketing should yield opportunities that excite aspiring professionals and sport teams, as highly identified fans are more likely to participate in dialogue with other fans and fulfill a desire to have a meaningful connection to the team they most closely identify with. As technology and acceptance both improve and increase, so too do opportunities for increasing involvement, enhancing team identity, and ultimately providing new revenue streams by engaging fans who want more access.

Despite optimism from stakeholders, it is still unclear if VR should be leveraged as a complementary feature to attract new fans or if it will become yet another alternative offering that may have no impact on increasing viewership or attendance. Some studies suggest that if a newly introduced channel offers a unique or diversified experience, then it is unlikely to cannibalize the current audience (Deleersnyder, Geyskens, Gielens, & Dekimpe, 2002), thus assuaging some of the concerns media managers may currently have about diverting current audiences. While much of this chapter has focused on developing relationships and acknowledging how technology has given rise to social TV and VR opportunities, it is not meant to overlook the fact that time is finite, and as more offerings and experiences are made available, each portion of the audience may be divided. Furthermore, as each device and platform offers increased entertainment opportunities, an already divided audience is likely to shift from a traditional television "channel-surfing" audience to a more diverse and convoluted "content-surfing" media audience, which will further dilute dwindling audience sizes. As such, media managers should consider whether the immediacy of watching one game live will suffice or if we will see a time-shifting effect that permits users to watch or rewatch their favorite events. Additionally, motivations for consumption may change as generational gaps widen, as discussed in the challenges section of this chapter. For example, the ability to engage with social TV may be seen as a distraction from the experience for older generations but may be a mandatory addition for enjoyment fulfillment for younger generations who have never known life without a mobile screen.

As media ownership costs for traditional sport increase, savvy media managers may want to look toward new opportunities, one such being eSport. Evidence has been provided that it is growing annually, thus making an attractive opportunity for investment. The following chapter, "Gaming Industry," will further acknowledge the growth and integration of gaming in the media mix. Recognizing opportunities to treat gaming as sport may provide aspiring media managers with additional tools to reach an ever-shifting viewing audience.

REFERENCES

Anstead, E., Benford, S., & Houghton, R. J. (2014, June). Many-screen viewing: Evaluating an Olympics companion application. In *Proceedings of the ACM International Conference on Interactive Experiences for TV and Online Video* (pp. 103–110).

Ashforth, B. E., & Mael, F. (1989). Social identity theory and the organization. *The Academy of Management Review, 14*(1), 20–39. doi: 10.2307/258189

Bee, C. C., & Kahle, L. R. (2006). Relationship marketing in sports: A functional approach. *Sport Marketing Quarterly, 15*, 102–110.

Bellamy, R. V. (2006). Sports media: A modern institution. In J. Bryant & A. Raney (Eds.), *Handbook of sports and media* (pp. 331–352). Lawrence Erlbaum Associates.

Berry, L. L. (1983). Relationship marketing. In L. L. Berry, G. L. Shostack, & G. Upah (Eds.), *Emerging perspectives on services marketing* (pp. 25–28). American Marketing Association.

Biocca, F., Harms, C., & Burgoon, J. K. (2003). Toward a more robust theory and measure of social presence: Review and suggested criteria. *Presence: Teleoperators and Virtual Environments, 12*, 456–480.

Branscombe, N. R., & Wann, D. L. (1991). The positive social and self-concept consequences of sport team identification. *Journal of Sport & Social Issues, 15,* 115–127.
Brenda, H. K. S. (2017). Spectating the rift: A study into eSports spectatorship. In J. Hiltscher, & T. M. Scholz (Eds.), *eSports Yearbook 2015/16* (pp. 9–35). Books on Demand.
Bryant, J. (1989). Viewers' enjoyment of televised sports violence. In L. A. Wenner (Ed.), *Media, sports, and society* (pp. 270–289). Sage.
Casey, S. (2017, January 17). *2016 Nielsen social media report.* Nielsen. https://www.nielsen.com/us/en/insights/report/2017/2016-nielsen-social-media-report
Casselman, B. (2015, May 22). *Resistance is futile: eSports is massive . . . and growing.* ESPN. http://www.espn.com/espn/story/_/id/13059210/esports-massive-industry-growing
Cialdini, R. B., Borden, R. J., Thorne, A., Walker, M. R., Freeman, S., & Sloan, L. R. (1976). Basking in reflected glory: Three (football) field studies. *Journal of Personality and Social Psychology, 34,* 366–375. doi: 10.1037/00223514.34.3.366
Cooley, B. (2014). *Virtual reality: No longer niche.* CNET. https://www.cnet.com/videos/virtual-reality-no-longer-niche
Cornwell, T. B., Weeks, C. S., & Roy, D. P. (2005). Sponsorship-linked marketing: Opening the black box. *Journal of Advertising, 34,* 21–42.
Cronin, B. (2019, November 12). "We can no longer rely on the Ryder Cup, and in this cycle we will not." Sport Business. https://www.sportbusiness.com/2019/11/__keithpelley-4
Crupi, A. (2011, August 18). *Fox sports lands UFC rights.* Adweek. http://www.adweek.com/news/ television/fox-sports-lands-ufc-rights-134224
Crupi, A. (2018, January 2). Despite another ratings slump, the NFL remains TV's top dog. Ad Age. https://adage.com/article/media/ratings-slum/311777/
Cunningham, N. R., & Eastin, M. S. (2017). Second screen and sports: A structural investigation into team identification and efficacy. *Communication & Sport, 5,* 288–310.
Deleersnyder, B., Geyskens, I., Gielens, K., & Dekimpe, M. (2002). How cannibalistic is the Internet channel? A study of the newspaper industry in the United Kingdom and the Netherlands. *International Journal of Research in Marketing, 19,* 337–348.
Deloitte (2020). *2020 Sports industry outlook: Breaking down the latest sports market trends.* https://www2.deloitte.com/us/en/pages/technology-media-and-telecommunications/articles/sports-business-trends-disruption.html
Devlin, M. (2016). Sport and advertising. In A. C. Billings (Ed.), *Defining sport communication* (pp. 312–325). Routledge.
Devlin, M. (2017). Highly identified sports fans' personality traits. In A. C. Billings & K. A. Brown (Eds.), *The evolution of the modern sports fan* (pp. 9–28). Lexington Books.
Donavan, D., Carlson, B. D., & Zimmerman, M. (2005). The influence of personality traits on sports fan identification. *Sport Marketing Quarterly, 14,* 31–42.
Dwyer, F. R., Schurr, P. H., & Oh, S. (1987). Developing buyer-seller relationships. *Journal of Marketing, 51*(2), 11–27.
Ellison, N. B., Steinfield, C., & Lampe, C. (2007). The benefits of Facebook "friends": Social capital and college students' use of online social network sites. *Journal of Computer-Mediated Communication, 12,* 1143–1168.
Evans, P. (2019, March 14). *Here to stay: Generation Z's impact on sports content strategy.* Front Office Sports. https://frntofficesport.com/generation-z-sports
Funk, D. C., & James, J. D. (2001). The psychological continuum model: A conceptual framework for understanding an individual's psychological connection to sport. *Sport Management Review, 4,* 119–150.
Funk, D. C., Pizzo, A. D., & Baker, B. J. (2018). eSport management: Embracing eSport education and research opportunities. *Sport Management Review, 21,* 7–13.
Gantz, W., & Lewis, N. (2014). Sports on traditional and newer digital media: Is there really a fight for fans? *Television & New Media, 15,* 760–768.
Gantz, W., & Wenner, L. A. (1995). Fanship and the television sports viewing experience. *Sociology of Sport Journal, 12,* 56–74.

Gil de Zúñiga, H., Garcia-Perdomo, V., & McGregor, S. C. (2015). What is second screening? Exploring motivations of second screen use and its effect on online political participation. *Journal of Communication, 65*, 793–815.
Gladden, J. M., & Funk, D. C. (2001). Understanding brand loyalty in professional sport: Examining the link between brand association and brand loyalty. *International Journal of Sports Marketing & Sponsorship, 3*, 67–94.
Gladden, J. M., & Sutton, W. A. (2009). Marketing principles applied to sport management. In H. P. Masteralexis, C. A. Barr, & M. A. Hums (Eds.), *Principles and practices of sport management* (pp. 42–59). Jones and Bartlett.
Greenwood, J. G., & Yorke, Z. (2014, June). *Sports fans and the second screen*. Think with Google. https://www.thinkwithgoogle.com/consumer-insights/sports-fans-and-the-second-screen
Greenwood, P. B., Kanters, M. A., & Casper, J. M. (2006). Sport fan team identification formation in mid-level professional sport. *European Sport Management Quarterly, 6*, 253–265.
Gwinner, K. P., & Swanson, S. (2003). A model of fan identification: Antecedents and sponsorship outcomes. *Journal of Services Marketing, 17*, 275–292.
Handley, L. (2019, February 5). *Super Bowl draws lowest TV audience in more than a decade, early data show*. CNBC. https://www.cnbc.com/2019/02/05/super-bowl-draws-lowest-tv-audience-in-more-than-a-decade-nielsen.html
Hanlon, P., & Hawkins, J. (2008). Expand your brand community online. *Advertising Age, 79*, 14–15.
Harboe, G., Metcalf, C., Bentley, F., Tullio, J., Massey, N., & Romano, G. (2008). Ambient social TV: Drawing people into a shared experience. In *Proceedings of the ACM conference on Human Factors I, Computing Systems*.
Henderson, R. (2017). *Sports and the second screen*. Stats, LLC. https://www.stats.com/industry-analysis-articles/sports-second-screen
Highfield, T., Harrington, S., & Bruns, A. (2013). Twitter as a technology for audiencing and fandom: The Eurovision phenomenon. *Information, Communication & Society, 16*, 315–339.
Hwang, Y., & Lim, J. S. (2015). The impact of engagement motives for social TV on social presence and sports channel commitment. *Telematics and Informatics, 32*, 755–765.
IEG. (2018, January 8). *Signs point to healthy sponsorship spending in 2018*. Sponsorship.com. https://www.sponsorship.com/Report/2018/01/08/Signs-Point-To-Healthy-Sponsorship-Spending-In-201.aspx
Jenny, S. E., Keiper, M. C., Taylor, B., Williams, D. P., Gawrysiak, J., Manning, R. D., & Tutka, P. M. (2018). eSports venues: A new sport business opportunity. *Journal of Applied Sport Management, 10*, 34–49. doi: 10.18666/JASM-2018-V10-11-8469
Jonasson, K., & Thiborg, J. (2010). Electronic sport and its impact on future sport. *Sport in Society, 13*, 287–299.
Katz, D., & Kahn, R. L. (1978). *The social psychology of organizations*. Wiley.
Kietzmann, J. H., Silvestre, B. S., McCarthy, I. P., & Pitt, L. F. (2012). Unpacking the social media phenomenon. *Journal of Public Affairs, 12*, 109–119.
Kleinschmit, M. (2015). *Generation Z characteristics: 5 infographics on the gen Z lifestyle*. Business 2 Community. https://www.business2community.com/infographics/generation-z-characteristics-5-infographics-gen-z-lifestyle-01394477
Kruikemeier, S., van Noort, G., Vliegenthart, R., & de Vreese, C. H. (2013). Getting closer: The effects of personalized and interactive online political communication. *European Journal of Communication, 28*, 53–66.
Lim, J. S., Hwang, Y., Kim, S., & Biocca, F. A. (2015). How social media engagement leads to sports channel loyalty: Mediating roles of social presence and channel commitment. *Computers in Human Behavior, 46*, 158–167.
Lin, N. (2001). *Social capital: A theory of social structure and action*. Cambridge University Press.
Lin, T., & Chiang, Y. (2017). Dual screening: Examining social predictors and impact on online and offline political participation among Taiwanese Internet users. *Journal of Broadcasting & Electronic Media, 61*, 240–263.

Madrigal, R. (2000). The influence of social alliances with sports teams on intentions to purchase corporate sponsors' products. *Journal of Advertising, 29*(4), 13–27.

Madrigal, R. (2001). Social identity effects in a belief-attitude-intentions hierarchy: Implications for corporate sponsorship. *Psychology & Marketing, 18*, 145–165.

Mahony, D. F., Madrigal, R., & Howard, D. (2000). Using the psychological commitment to team (PCT) scale to segment sport consumers based on loyalty. *Sport Marketing Quarterly, 9*, 131–139.

McNear, C. (2016, August 4). *NBC's Olympics tape delay is absurd*. The Ringer. https://www.theringer.com/2016/8/4/16036352/nbcs-olympics-tape-delay-is-absurd-81efc2dd349

Miles, H. C., Pop, S. R., Watt, S. J., Lawrence, G. P., & John, N. W. (2012). A review of virtual environment for training in ball sports. *Computers & Graphics, 36*, 714–726. doi: 10.1016/j.cag2012.04.007

Mullin, B. J., Hardy, S., & Sutton, W. A. (2007). *Sport marketing*. Human Kinetics.

Pelley, K. (2018, March 19). What is the future of sports consumption? *The Telegraph*. https://www.telegraph.co.uk/business/events/business-of-sport/what-is-the-future-of-sports-consumption

Plunkett Research. (2018). *Sports industry, teams, leagues & recreation market research*. https://www.plunkettresearch.com/industries/sports-recreation-leisure-market-research

Prasolova-Forland, E., & Divitini M. (2003). *Collaborative virtual enviornments for supporting learning communities: An experience of use*. Proceedings of the 2003 International ACM SIGGROUP Conference, 58–67.

Proulx, M., & Shepatin, S. (2012). *Social TV: How marketers can reach and engage audiences by connecting television to the web, social media, and mobile*. Wiley.

Raney, A. (2006). Why we watch and enjoy mediated sports. In A. Raney & J. Bryant (Eds.), *Handbook of sport and media* (pp. 313–352). Lawrence Erlbaum Associates.

Rein, I., Kotler, P., & Shields, B. (2006). *The elusive fan: Reinventing sports in a crowded marketplace*. McGraw-Hill.

Rettig, M. (2017). *ACC fans get virtual reality football, basketball experiences with app*. SportTechie. https://www.sporttechie.com/acc-fans-basketball-football-virtual-reality-app

Rogers, E. M. (1962). *Diffusion of innovations* (3rd ed.). The Free Press.

Shah, S. (2018, November 22). *ESPN lost 2 million subscribers to cord cutting this year*. Engadget. https://www.engadget.com/2018/11/22/espn-lost-two-million-subscribers

Sheth, J. N., & Parvatiyar, A. (2000). *Handbook of relationship marketing*. Sage.

Short, J., Williams, E., & Christie, B. (1976). *The social psychology of telecommunications*. Wiley.

Smith, R. A., & Schwarz, N. (2003). Language, social comparison, and college football: Is your school less similar to the rival school than the rival school is to your school? *Communication Monographs, 70*, 351–360.

Stanton, W. J., Etzel, M. J., & Walker, B. J. (1994). *Fundamentals of marketing* (10th ed.). McGraw-Hill.

Sutton, D. (2017, July 13). *5 mind-blowing insights into mobile-first mindset of Generation Z*. Think With Google. https://www.toprightpartners.com/insights/5-mind-blowing-insights-mobile-first-mindset-generation-z

Tajfel, H., & Turner, J. C. (1986). The social identity theory of intergroup behavior. *Psychology of Intergroup Relations, 5*, 7–24.

Tang, T., & Cooper, R. (2017). Predicting changing media use patterns via mega events: An examination of multi-screen viewing during the 2016 Rio Olympics. *International Journal of Sport Communication, 10*, 531–549.

Thrassou, A., Vrontis, D., Kartakoullis, N. L., & Kriemadis, T. (2012). Contemporary marketing communications framework for football clubs. *Journal of Promotion Management, 18*, 278–305.

Trail, G. T., & James, J. (2001). The motivation scale for sport consumption: Assessment of the scale's psychometric properties. *Journal of Sport Behavior, 24*, 108–127.

Underwood, R., Bond, E., & Baer, R. (2001). Building service brands via social identity: Lessons from the sports marketplace. *Journal of Marketing Theory and Practice, 9(1)*, 1–13.

Vaccari, C., Chadwick, A., & O'Loughlin, B. (2015). Dual screening the political: Events, social media, and citizen engagement. *Journal of Communication, 65*, 1041–1061.

Wakefield, K. L. (2016). Using fan passion to predict attendance, media consumption, and social media behaviors. *Journal of Sport Management, 30*, 229–247.

Wang, Y. (2013). Beyond the second screen. *Wired*. https://www.wired.com/insights/2013/07/beyond-the-second-screen

Wann, D. L. (1994). The "noble" sports fan: The relationships between team identification, self-esteem, and aggression. *Perceptual & Motor Skills, 78*, 864–866.
Wann, D. L. (1995). Preliminary validation of sport fan motivation scale. *Journal of Sport and Social Issues, 19*, 377–396.
Wann, D. L. (2006). The causes and consequences of sport team identification. In J. Bryant & A. Raney (Eds.), *Handbook of sports and media* (pp. 331–352). Lawrence Erlbaum Associates.
Wann, D. L., & Branscombe, N. R. (1990). Die-hard and fair-weather fans: Effects of identification on BIRGing and CORFing tendencies. *Journal of Sport and Social Issues, 14*, 103–117.
Wann, D. L., & Branscombe, N. R. (1993). Sports fans: Measuring degree of identification. *International Journal of Sport Psychology, 24*(1), 1–17.
Wann, D. L., Grieve, F. G., Partridge, J. A., Zapalac, R. K.,& Parker, P. M. (2013). An examination of predictors of watching televised sport programming. *North American Journal of Psychology, 15*, 179–194.
Wenner, L. (1989). *Media, sports and society*. Sage.
Westcott, K., Loucks, J., Ciampa, D., & Srivastava, S. (2019, June 10). Digital media trends: Video gaming goes mainstrem. Deloitte. https://www2.deloitte.com/us/en/insights/industry/technology/digital-media-trends-consumption-habits-survey/trends-in-gaming-esports.html
Zhang, J., Kim, E., Mastromartino, B., Qian, T., & Nauright, J. (2018). The sport industry in growing economies: Critical issues and challenges. *International Journal of Sports Marketing and Sponsorship, 19*, 110–126.
Zhang, J. J., Pitts, B. G., & Kim, E. (2017). Sport marketing in a globalized marketplace. In J. J. Zhang, & B. G. Pitts (Eds.), *Contemporary sport marketing* (pp. 3–22). Routledge.

CHAPTER 16

Gaming Industry

Anthony Palomba, Darden School of Business at University of Virginia

LEARNING OBJECTIVES

1. Understand the dynamic relationship between interactive and passive media and how video game consoles serve as entertainment hubs.
2. Learn how blue ocean strategy may be incorporated to create singular markets across all video game industry spheres.
3. Explore the management opportunities and challenges in the professional video game industry.

Similar to the sport industry, the gaming industry is predicated on its ability to fashion video games that unspool rules, boundaries, threats, obstacles, and goals in an all-immersive experience for video game players. Unlike the physical and even pugilistic doctrines within sports play, during video game play, there is little to no physical risk of injury for its patrons. Instead, video game play encourages exploration and risk taking, such as jumping over chasms, leading a football team to a Super Bowl victory, shooting aliens, and challenging entire legions of villains. Video game designers and marketers have tackled nearly every fictional genre available, including action, horror, fantasy, sports, and first-person shooter (Entertainment Software Association, 2019a).

Due to the accessibility, portability, and intuitive engagement of video games, the gaming industry continues to grow at an exponential rate. In 2019, the global video game industry was estimated to be worth nearly $152.1 billion (Wijman, 2019). According to the annual Entertainment Software Association report (2019a), video game play has become a staple activity for many consumers in the United States. Nearly 75% of households in the United States include at least one gamer. The average age of video game players is 33 years, and 65% of American adults play video games. On average, adult video game players spend 4.8 hours a week playing online and 3.5 hours a week playing in person with other gamers. This audience breakdown is vital for the video game industry, as consumer lifestyles, preferences for portable media, and interest in unpredictable experiences have promoted hyper competition among Nintendo, Sony, and Microsoft.

In each successive generation of video game console, Nintendo, Sony, and Microsoft have strived to meet their consumers' dreams and fantasies, devising artistic milieus and tighter connections between game players and virtual worlds. All three companies have expanded into digital subscription services, pushing brand extensions out to further rev up revenue streams. To maintain market share in the video game console industry, it has become increasingly pertinent to skillfully manage consumer expectations. These consumers are deeply passionate and prone to making excoriating comments or laudable affirmations about the quality of video games and overall experiences. Let us explore how Nintendo has met the demands of media convergence over the years to stay a relevant leader in the video game industry.

CASE STUDY

For Nintendo, the last decade has been interspersed with consumer satisfaction and confusion stemming from its ability to properly deliver strategic communication to consumers about its branded products and services. The Nintendo Wii was the best-selling video game console during the seventh-generation video game console product life cycle, as it empowered its players to be further immersed in game play through its motion capture controllers (VG Chartz, 2018). This success pushed Nintendo to double down on novelty controllers. Marketed on the digital coattails of Wii, the Wii U was introduced as a video game play experience that allowed players to use a tablet controller. However, Wii U commercials created outright confusion and angst among some consumers, who could not tell if this was a video game console that incorporated motion capture or if it was a singular tablet that could connect with the Wii.

Despite possessing both product attributes, the release of Nintendo Wii U in 2012 was underwhelming and caused many to prognosticate that the demise of Nintendo was underway (Parkin, 2017). However, research found that Nintendo's brand equity largely remained untarnished despite dismal Wii U sales (Shay & Palomba, 2018). After the unexpected death of Nintendo's president Satoru Iwata in 2015, its business strategy went through a stringent internal examination. Unencumbered by antiquated business orthodoxies about protecting Nintendo's intellectual property, executives ramped up strategic marketing plans to exploit its stable of intellectual property with precision and a keen eye toward mobile and digital consumption trends (Kharpal, 2018).

Today, Nintendo leads the charge in offering interactive and unprecedented entertainment experiences unparalleled to experiences offered by stationary video game consoles. In December 2016, it entered into digital mobile gaming with *Super Mario Run*, an endless runner mobile game that has been downloaded more than 200 million times (Makuch, 2017). A Super Nintendo World within Universal Japan is set to open by 2021, as it has been delayed by COVID-19 (Peters, 2020). Additional construction on a Super Nintendo World at Universal Studios Hollywood began in August 2020 (Ward, 2020). In addition, Nintendo is working with Illumination Entertainment to develop a full-length movie that incorporates the Super Mario Bros. franchise, which is slated for a 2022 release (Gillette, 2018; Martinez, 2018). Aside from capitalizing on other media and entertainment platforms, Nintendo has successfully employed blue ocean strategy (which will be discussed in detail later in this chapter) with the Nintendo Wii as well as its current Nintendo Switch, offering a lower-cost video game console ($299.99 compared to initial prices of $499.99 for Xbox One and $399.99 for PlayStation 4) (Lawler, 2013; Loveridge, 2019; Peckham, 2017). Nintendo's online gaming subscription, Nintendo Switch Online, offers an array of classic Nintendo video games. It is also priced lower than its competitors, as a month-to-month subscription is priced at $3.99, and a yearly subscription is priced at $19.99 (Nintendo Switch Online, 2019).

Nintendo was able to forward media convergence through customization of controllers, video game console experiences, and game play settings. It has successfully innovated the video game play control from traditional physical video game controllers through enlisting video game players as controllers. Currently, the Nintendo Switch allows its users to access apps such as YouTube and Hulu, providing access to video, television, music, and movies via the gaming console (Welch, 2018). Furthermore, Nintendo was able to innovate the first mainstream video game console that was setting agnostic. The Nintendo Switch allows consumers to experience high-quality video game play in any setting, be it in a living room, a park, on a train, or elsewhere. These features tie together unprecedented flexibility in video game play, allowing consumers to seamlessly transition between passive and interactive entertainment to control the experience themselves. This combination of passive and interactive entertainment is a strong testimony to the success one can have when integrating "old" with "new."

Something Old

Media management theories allow researchers and managers to understand consumer proclivities toward video game adoption and access. Conceptual frameworks such as blue ocean strategy, flow theory, and self-determination theory help demystify how video game play may serve to provide novelty, an escape, and self-esteem for video game players. Through each video game console generation, video game players are inclined to seek out video game consoles with new features, such as streaming apps, virtual reality, or portability. Since each video game console generation lasts from five to seven years, it is important for video game console companies to give consumers reasons to invest in them for that period of time. Let's first take a look at the blue ocean strategy, a framework through which video game developers and video game console engineers can create new products in uncontested market spaces.

BLUE OCEAN STRATEGY

Amid tempestuous video game console and mobile marketplaces, parent video game console companies jockeying for market share position, and anticipated video game console product life cycles, the video game marketplace has experienced technology disruption through precise implementation and use of blue ocean strategy. This business model is based on crafting low-cost products and services that help create unique submarkets within an industry (Kim & Mauborgne, 2005). The reference to ocean is used to isolate different levels of business competition. Red ocean may be replete with saturated markets, limited opportunities for innovation, and high cost barriers that may limit entrance into the market by new players. On the other hand, blue ocean offers a new market that a company may innovate within and strive to deliver a product that has been differentiated from perceived competitors at a low cost.

During the seventh generation of video game consoles, Nintendo used this strategy to deploy the Nintendo Wii. The other video game consoles in this generation, including Microsoft's Xbox 360 and Sony's PlayStation 3, competed very closely on nearly every product attribute, as both possessed highly sophisticated graphics, exclusive video game titles, complex video game play, connections to the Internet, and the ability to stream apps (Kain, 2012; Nielsen, 2015). Nintendo Wii carved out a niche market that it could dominate without directly competing against the other two video game consoles.

Nintendo is neither a hardware nor a software company, and, in understanding the hypercompetitive nature and superior resources of Microsoft and Sony, Nintendo chose to create a new marketplace over which it could place a stranglehold. While the Xbox 360 and PlayStation 3 offered sophisticated and progressive video game play experiences, both video game consoles were equipped with familiar controllers. Granted, this is a typical business decision through each generation of video game consoles, as video game console companies and designers want to retain video game players who are familiar with existing controllers. Many gamers have built up trust and skills from investing hundreds of hours into mastering controllers, so both companies typically maintain controller scheme designs from generation to generation.

Nintendo decided to flex on this product attribute and created the Nintendo Wii, which offered traditional video game controllers, but it also employed unprecedented motion capture technology, making video game players exist as controllers themselves. This offered an extremely fluid and immersive experience during video game play. It also meant that Nintendo could offer casual, easy-to-learn video games for casual gamers to exert an unprecedented amount of physical energy in playing these video games. To stay in line with this blue ocean strategy approach, Nintendo did not create strategic communication targeted toward hard-core video game players, who typically gravitated toward Xbox and PlayStation video game consoles. Instead, Nintendo focused on deviant audience niches, including casual gamers and nongamers, such as parents and grandparents. The Nintendo Wii was marketed as a novelty console, a product that could be purchased alongside an Xbox or a PlayStation console and used for a party or as a family activity (Chambers, 2012).

The rationale behind blue ocean strategy is to transcend the high-risk threshold of introducing a new concept into a marketplace by capitalizing on an under-addressed latent consumer need in the current marketplace. As stated earlier, Nintendo has also implemented this strategy in developing the Nintendo Switch, which allows video game players to play the video game console at home or as a mobile device. For Nintendo, this strategy worked in part based on how video game player experiences are altered through controllers and immersion.

Blue ocean strategy offers a strategic marketing lens that helps explain how novelty may be introduced into a saturated video game console marketplace. However, this is only the first hurdle that a video game console must jump over to gain interest and affection from video game consumers. Ultimately, video game players are interested in experiencing novelty in a state of flow, in which they are uninterrupted by other external influences as they play video games. Unlike passive media, interactive media like video game play attempts to mimic our own spatial cognition, which can enrich memory (Clemenson & Stark, 2015). Since video game play involves settings and characters that respond to our actions and movements, which is a similar construction to our own reality and daily lives, video game players seek out intense immersive experiences in which their own realities are supplemented by a virtual one.

PLAY AND FLOW THEORY

Video game play is stationed within predetermined and agreed-on rules, settings, and the consumer's ability to relinquish control of their reality to obtain some control within a digital reality. Biocca (1997) discusses human-computer interaction and the feeling of consumption that video game players experience. The more realistic video game play feels, such as using a plastic guitar, a tennis racket, or a steering wheel as controllers while playing a video game, the greater immersion will be experienced during video game play (McGloin, Farrar, & Krcmar, 2011). This is also known as natural mapping, which allows a system to map controllers over an environment. Controllers that organically replicate actual behaviors (e.g., a steering wheel for driving) are predictive of stronger enjoyment and presence within the video game. Controllers such as these pique video game players' knowledge structures and cues used for navigating reality (Skalski, Tamborini, Shelton, Buncher, & Lindmark, 2011).

Video game players connect to video game play in order to realize intrinsic well-being, but it is important to consider the level of immersion necessary for this experience. This is best explicated by flow theory, which was first introduced by Csikszentmihalyi (1975), who studied artists, surgeons, and others involved in intense activities. He found that a particular fixation or intense focus on an activity was positive and even desirable, and many of these people drew a sense of purpose and enjoyment from these experiences.

Flow is based on play, which involves performing actions to match or exceed requirements within an environment. If there are few requirements, and the consumer has numerous abilities, boredom may strike. If there are too many requirements, and the consumer has limited abilities, this may initiate a state of anxiety or panic within the consumer (Csikszentmihalyi & Bennett, 1971). Flow can be interpreted as a state of pure cognitive focus and immersion in which other ancillary and external factors do not distract the video game player from game play. In order to reach a state of flow, a consumer must experience immersion and presence, particularly during full engagement in a video game, and believe they are capable of making accurate consumption decisions about their game play.

This state of video game play immersion creates a space for advertisers to engage in uninterrupted communication with video game players. Consumers positively note that advertisements within video games help create a sense of reality during video game play (Nelson, Keum, & Yaros, 2004), though too much product placement can spoil a video game play experience. In-game advertisements have greater longevity inside the memories of video game players (Nelson, 2002). Moreover, the size of the advertisement, from a billboard to an actual branded product within a digital world, also influences brand recall (Chaney, Lin, & Chaney, 2004). This clearly provides advertisers an opportunity to have a high- or low-engagement experience with video game players, offering opportunities to play with interactive advertisements as well. Video game players who engage in advergames, a strategy that combines advertisements and gaming, are inclined to feel flow during video game play and are likely to positively assess advertised brands after game play (Steffen, Mau, & Schramm-Klein, 2013).

A video game player's state of flow is a fundamental aspect of immersive video game play. Submerged and entrenched in pixelated universes, video game players are still knowledgeable and aware of their own performances, which they reflect on during and after video game play. This means it is equally important that consumers are able to competently make singular decisions about which video games to play as well as share these experiences with others.

SELF-DETERMINATION THEORY

For many video game players, playing video games can help them reconcile particular emotions (Palomba, 2018). Self-determination theory is one way to explain how consumers achieve internal psychological well-being through video game play. Intrinsic motivation is one of the catalysts involved in this process. Consumers who seek intrinsic motivations may largely look for unique or challenging experiences, as this aids them in exploring and learning about the world around them but also about themselves. Differently, extrinsic motivation may spur consumers to perform an activity to obtain something that is indirectly related to the outcome. As first devised by Ryan and Deci (2000), this theory cites three particular levels that must be achieved for intrinsic motivation during an activity, which in turn impacts self-regulation and well-being.

First, a consumer must feel competent in selecting an activity that they know will aid them in regulating their own emotions. Second, there must be autonomy in this decision, as the consumer must feel as though they are the sole arbiter in the decision-making process. Finally, relatedness includes being able to share these activities and experiences with others. In one study conducted by Ryan, Rigby, and Przybylski (2006), it was found that the ability to learn video game controls and perception of immersion during video game play were linked to competency and autonomy.

Oliver et al. (2016) demonstrated that different types of video game experience outcomes were tied to different video game play experiences. Video games that were found to be meaningful elicited appreciation from video game players, who were sensitive to story characteristics. While all video game players experienced enjoyment across all conditions, it was most related to video game play elements. It should be noted that intrinsic well-being is not confined to playing video games, as Pei-Shan and Hsi-Peng (2014) found that consumers are inclined to use mobile social games because these video games are easy to play, with great time flexibility, and offer the ability to earn pleasure and socialize with others. These "old" theories aid managers in understanding how transportation into digital worlds can imprint unique experiences and highlight business opportunities in the video game industry. Some new practices and trends are discussed in the next section.

Something New

There is an innate plasticity and malleability within user experience as much, if not more so, than in content itself. Interactive entertainment affords its consumers opportunities to customize experiences. Sometimes they are required to handle complex control sequences. Other times, they may need to complete a level in several different manners. The ubiquity of cell phone use has propelled video game companies to create portable though less immersive experiences through mobile video games. In addition, media multitasking between passive and interactive entertainment has emboldened video game console companies to become a digital Silk Road, allowing myriad streaming apps to be downloaded that connect consumers to video, television, radio, social media, news, and movie viewing and engagement. The very same principles of customization and plasticity have been applied to allowing consumers to connect to these apps via their video game consoles. While video game console companies may not be privy to what exactly consumers are doing in these apps, they are able to collect data surrounding what types of apps consumers access as well as date and time of engagement. Collecting and harvesting this data allows for video game console companies to pull consumer profiles more naturally and organically, creating opportunities for further refinement and alignment of strategic marketing campaigns.

MOBILE VIDEO GAMES

Although mobile video games began as a supplementary market alongside console games, they have since come to dominate the largest piece of revenue in the gaming industry. In 2019, mobile video games commanded roughly $68.5 billion of the $152.1 billion video game industry, which is on pace for roughly 46% of the video game industry revenue share against console and PC games (Wijman, 2019). Mobile games have expanded not only to handheld products developed by parent video game console companies, such as Nintendo's 3DS, but also to cell phones, tablets, and other mobile devices. Mobile games on cell phones have allowed video game companies such as Zynga to expand further into a market that offers intuitive gaming with little to no learning curve (Zynga, 2018). Its growth in the marketplace over the last decade can be traced back to improved Wi-Fi connections; the increasing adoption of mobile phones, tablets, and similar devices; improved ability to download; and increased storage on these devices (Chan-Olmsted, 2006).

Mobile gaming reached new heights during summer 2016, as *Pokémon Go* became the most downloaded app in Apple's store (Passalacqua, 2017). This marked a new phase of mobile gaming, because this introduced consumers to the concept of location-based mobile games. Traditionally, mobile games such as *Candy Crush*, *Clash of Clans*, *Angry Birds*, and *League of Legends* thrive in part because of usability, low cost for purchase, simple rules, low risk, and low investment from consumers (Penttinen, Rossi, & Tuuaninen, 2010; Think Gaming, 2018). They also allow consumers to connect with friends or strangers during game play, creating a socially interactive experience for all patrons. Most mobile games employ a business strategy referred to as "freemium" or "pay to play" in which consumers are able to download a free version of the game app to play the game for a certain amount of time, through a set amount of levels, or only make progress at a predetermined speed (Christou, 2018). To acquire access to more levels, or to acquire more points, weapons, coins, or other items to help make the mobile game move along quicker, consumers are asked to make additional financial investments in the game.

Academic research has found that there are particular antecedents that influence attitude, intent to play, and engagement with mobile games. Park, Baek, Ohm, and Chang (2014) found that perceived behavior control, perceived connectedness, satisfaction, and perceived mobility explained why consumers adopt mobile social network games. Molinillo, Munoz-Levia, and Perez-Garcia (2018) demonstrated that up to 70% of consumer intention to play mobile casual games could be explained by perceived convenience, attitude, hedonic motivation, and relational motivation, which also explained 42% of the actual use of mobile casual games. Sung, Sigerson, and Cheng (2017) examined social benefits from engagement with location-based mobile video games, such as *Pokémon Go*. These types of mobile games require players to leave their homes and engage with the world around them, as it is incumbent on them to do so to further their progression in the video game. It was found that social capital may be accrued during location-based mobile gaming, which permitted consumers to connect to people different from themselves.

MULTIMEDIA VIDEO GAME CONSOLES

Video game consoles have evolved from interactive entertainment bastions to multimodal devices capable of serving consumers as a one-stop destination for interactive and passive forms of entertainment. The supply of available entertainment content has overreached and superseded consumer demand, as there were nearly 500 television programs that debuted in 2016 alone (Ryan, 2016). Streaming video-on-demand services have cut into the entertainment content marketplace, driving advertising costs up to develop and market television programs (Albarran, Chan-Olmsted, & Wirth, 2006). This has undermined the power traditionally held by entertainment media conglomerates such as Paramount, Warner Bros., NBCUniversal, and Disney as the only mainstays for all entertainment content. Consumers are now able to customize their own entertainment experiences on an exceptionally granular level. This means that they can customize their video game consoles by downloading popular apps including HBO Go, Starz, and CBS All Access (Tannert, 2019).

Video game console menus now aid consumers in not just being a destination for entertainment but also helping video gamers organize and curate their own media content and subscriptions. They can seamlessly play video games and connect to television, video, film, or radio as they desire through video game consoles. However, questions remain unanswered in this convergent media environment. For one, there may be numerous apps on a particular video game console, and from a brand management perspective, it would be helpful to understand if there may be a halo effect with any of these video game app brands against the parent video game console. For instance, would downloading HBO Go or an ESPN app onto a Nintendo Switch create any brand meaning transference between the app brand and parent video game console brand? Additionally, understanding how consumers switch between interactive media consumption and passive media consumption would help underscore inherent differences between activities and how consumers make decisions, set goals, and actively manage emotions.

Video game consoles offer actual data for researchers. Modern video game consoles from the eighth generation and beyond collect player data, which is accessible to video game players. Palomba (2019) data-mined and collected 30 Nintendo Wiis in an effort to better understand how temperature, daylight, and time of year impact video game play habits. Results indicate that consumers play video games more often during increased hours of daylight and in warmer temperatures. Additionally, sport video games among other genres possessed the highest replay value, meaning consumers replayed video games in this category more than most categories. Battle genre video games were played the most during the months of April through June, while fighting games were played from July through September. For media managers and researchers, this illustrates that external weather conditions may impact video game play. Additionally, there may be seasonal preferences toward video game genres, which may inform video game marketers and advertisers about primary roll-out dates for different video games. Clearly, understanding audience behaviors brings ample opportunities to the gaming industry.

Opportunities and Challenges

The video game industry faces numerous and evolving opportunities and challenges. The advent of each video game console generation yields high expectations not only from video game players but also video game console designers and managers themselves. Similarly, the introduction of a new video game in a series bears a similar burden to meet or exceed expectations. The video game industry is a technology-laden industry, and through each generation gestation period for every console or game, the collective advancement made by each product is assessed through not just incorporated technology but also content, user experience, aesthetics, and even controllers. Currently, there are a multitude of different advancement opportunities for the video game industry, as nostalgic video games, cloud-based gaming, and subscription-based gaming offer unique avenues to connect to consumers.

OPPORTUNITIES

Nintendo was the first distinct parent video game console company to resurrect an old video game console, outfit it with modern technology, and create a video game console nostalgia submarket. The definition of *nostalgia* may be traced back to its Latin origin, which denotes some sort of painful homecoming (Beck, 2013). The Nintendo Classic Edition was introduced into the marketplace in November 2016. It is furnished as a retro video game console with modern computer processing upgrades, a modern screen display, and 30 preloaded video games (Nintendo, 2019). Consumer demand for the retro video game console mushroomed and took advantage of an otherwise relaxed 2016 video game console holiday marketplace, inspiring Nintendo to release the Super Nintendo Entertainment System Classic Edition in September 2017 (Coldewey, 2017), Sony to release the PlayStation Classic in December 2018 (Webster, 2018), and Sega, a past titan in the video game industry, to offer the Sega Genesis Mini in September 2019 (Macy, 2019).

Numerous older video games have been refurbished and readapted for younger generations and serve as pixelated blasts-from-the-past for older generations. Many of the levels in the updated 2014 version of Sega's *Castle of Illusion* are reminiscent of the older version of the game from 1990 (Kollar, 2013). Engaging in and completing these levels serve as exercises in digital memory-jogging, as older video game players may recall how to play the video game and complete levels quickly. This type of game play typifies reliving the past, reimmersing oneself in the fantasy and amazement previously experienced as a child, and experiencing other related personal and historical nostalgic notes from that era.

The future of video game nostalgia is replete with more video game consoles coming down memory-laden roads. Sony introduced a PlayStation Classic that includes 20 preloaded video games in December 2018 (Webster, 2018). This is a subindustry for video game companies, as these video game consoles can serve as a way to satiate consumers who are waiting to purchase the latest video game consoles. Since the classic editions of video game consoles are novelty items and priced well below the pricing anchors for new video game consoles, this is largely helpful for parent video game console companies in cultivating and managing brand awareness among consumers while they are devising new video game consoles. It illustrates how far these parent companies have come in digitizing experiences and making heart-warming digital memories for consumers.

VIRTUAL REALITY AND AUGMENTED REALITY

Virtual reality has been experimented with in video games for much of the gaming industry's life span. Nintendo's Virtual Boy was introduced in 1995 as the first video game console that incorporated virtual reality into games. However, the technology had not caught up to the artistic vision of video game designers, and the console experienced dismal sales (Edwards, 2015). Despite growing pains within the industry, virtual reality is not only a desired attribute for many video game players but also allows for further immersion into video game play, helping video game designers realize their vision and truly give video game players an immersive experience. The level of innovation between each video game console generation is crucial, as consumers need to be able to justify their purchase of costly video game consoles, which most video game players use for five to seven years, a typical product life cycle of a video game console (Kent, 2001; Thang, 2016). Video game companies have leaned toward embracing and adopting virtual reality technology across games and platforms, offering consumers different experiences within the same video game. Since video game consoles are also connected to the Internet, this allows video game console companies to gain a better handle on the technology, its implementation, and how consumers embrace it. Recently, video game companies began offering virtual reality headsets that could help expand video game play, including Sony PlayStation VR and Nintendo Labo VR Kit (Greenwald, 2019).

Perhaps a conceptual cousin of virtual reality is augmented reality (AR). AR has emerged as a feasible and cost-effective compromise that allows consumers to learn how to embrace manipulated environments without the cost (e.g., time, learning) surrounding virtual reality engagement. Aside from *Pokémon Go*, augmented reality has surfaced as a way for companies to interact with consumers as well as for consumers to engage with other consumers. Several sources have estimated that the AR industry may expand to $222 billion to $284 billion by 2023 (PR Newswire, 2017). Moreover, while virtual reality relies on complex arrangements of technology and content, augmented reality allows for video game creators to leverage external settings to imbue their own digital worlds with meaning and immersion for consumers. In July 2018, users downloaded nearly 1.25 million AR apps from the top 500 AR iPhone apps (Roettgers, 2018). However, endowing video games with sterling graphics and thrilling aesthetics still requires better storage capabilities on the part of video game console companies.

CLOUD STORAGE

The overwhelming numbers of gamers and digital downloads across video game consoles, handheld devices, and elsewhere have led to a storage concern, leading some executives to look toward the digital storage skies for answers. The future of the video game industry, from PC to console to mobile, in part relies on the ability to store and stream video game content. While aforementioned streaming services do exist for video game players across Nintendo, Microsoft, and PlayStation video game consoles and devices, consumers have learned to travel with their content and to demand consistent access to it. This notion is not lost on any of the parent companies, which are hastily and fastidiously working on allowing consumers to have constant and consistent access to their video games across numerous devices in the future.

For video game designers and marketers, cloud and/or digital locker services aid them from a cost-effectiveness perspective. The cost to store a video game may vary with each generation, and although they may be fixed in the sense that the video game console is produced with limited drives, there are additional costs associated with adding storage units onto the video game console to maximize the product life cycle. Through the fourth generation of video game consoles, affectionately known as the 16-bit era, video game capacity ranged from 0.23 mega-bytes (MB) to 6 MB. In the eighth generation of video game consoles, the Xbox One is capable of storing upward of 500 gigabytes (GB), and the PlayStation 4 is capable of holding and maintaining a similar digital threshold. Differently, the Nintendo Switch possesses only 32 GB of built-in storage, requiring additional memory cards for video game players to save video game play progress, as *The Legend of Zelda: Breath of the Wild* alone requires 13.4 GB of space (Sarkar, 2017). Console video game prices have largely remained at $60 per unit over the last decade (Yan & Gilbert, 2018). Digital downloads of video games are up among consumers, as this allows for backward compatibility (e.g., playing old video games on new video game consoles) (Boyle, 2017). Digitally downloaded video games tend to be cheaper and allow consumers to own their own libraries. Additionally, game subscriptions, such as PlayStation Now, may cost up to $120 to $200 per year, which is the cost of three to four physical video game console units (Brandt, 2019).

The cost of building a video game console is remarkably expensive, lending itself to the traditional razor blade business model. It is common for video game consoles to lose money on video game console sales but hope to recoup losses through sold video games. For instance, the PlayStation 4 costs $381 to build, which is just $18 under its initial price tag of $399. It should be noted that the system's processor and memory alone cost $188 (Suszek, 2013). In order to clamp down on the growing cost of housing video game progress or entire video games on video game consoles, executives have pushed to create digital cloud lockers. The rise of virtual-reality-imbued video games translates into more GB needed to create surreal landscapes, in-depth excavations, majestic wildernesses, and other rich designs. Impressive graphics and Hollywood actors used as characters have also ballooned video game design costs (Economist, 2014). If distribution, maintenance, and video game streaming quality can be improved, this may remove the need for consumers to purchase separate video games or encourage them to purchase as many as they desire, as they will not be constricted or confined to GB limitations. This will also aid video game publishers in concentrating on delivering the best video game experience possible and investing more time seeking influencers and other marketing campaign strategies to bolster interest in video games.

LET'S PLAY VIDEOS

Let's Play videos have catalyzed the video game market and advertising sectors to procure the video game playing and hosting talents of online YouTube influencers. Most notably, Markiplier and PewDiePie are top influencers who have played a slew of video games, including *Five Nights at Freddie's* and *Resident Evil 7* (Fischbach, 2014; Kjellberg, 2017). Often, these videos capture a video game player's journey through a video game and have the player's commentary in the background. These videos have served as a way for parent video game companies to illustrate video game play for consumers and help consumers manage their own expectations in purchasing the games. These videos are also nuanced and framed around enjoyment and fun, which do not resemble typical video game commercials but combine a do-it-yourself appeal alongside entertainment, serving as a way to galvanize audiences toward purchasing or playing a video game or simply offering entertainment for others. Platforms such as YouTube and Twitch, a video game viewing website, have allowed for the rise of these host video game players.

Clearly, Let's Play videos provide an additional avenue for video game developers and marketers who are interested in nontraditional advertisements and strategic communication targeted toward video game players. This is another form of celebrity endorsement, although these hosts are viewed as experts and typically only hype and promote the video games they are able to play for their audiences (Armstrong, 2017). The interest and intrigue surrounding others playing video games has blossomed from a living room experience into full-fledged arenas, creating one of the fastest-growing sports in the world.

ESPORTS

eSports, or electronic-based sports, has proliferated from a subculture within the video game milieu into several legitimate sports leagues, replete with star athlete video games and arenas to hold digital competitions. eSports are ubiquitous around the world, recognized as the fastest-growing sport, and supported by Microsoft and Red Bull among other corporate partners (Microsoft, 2018; Summers, 2018). Take the example of Tencent, a Chinese global corporation; it is the parent company for *League of Legends* and is one of the largest video game companies in the world. Not only does it have investments in Epic Games (e.g., *Fortnite*), Bluehole (e.g., *PlayerUnknown's Battlegrounds*), and Activision Blizzard (e.g., *World of Warcraft*) (Messner, 2019), but it also hosts its own annual *League of Legends* global league competition (Dent, 2015; Messner, 2019).

The eSports industry went from earning $655 million in 2017 to bringing in nearly $1.1 billion in 2019. The total eSports audience consists of a little more than 450 million individuals (Pannekeet, 2019). In addition, eSports leagues have surged as video game players seek out arenas and other live events at which they can root for their favored video game playing gladiators who seek out competition and establish rivalries within gaming tournaments (Witkowski, 2012).

The remarkable growth of these leagues has blossomed in part due to financial investment from other professional sports leagues and athletes. For instance, the Staples Center in Los Angeles has regularly hosted eSports events. Moreover, professional sports team owners such as Dallas Cowboys owner Jerry Jones have made investments in these particular leagues (Wolf, 2017). In each gaming tournament, rules are established to help frame the narrative around competitive play, which also has secondary influences on creating and stirring drama during video game competition (Seo & Jung, 2014).

The existence of eSports is not just another path for video game play fanfare; it also legitimizes video game play as a household sport. The U.S. government now recognizes eSports as a professional sport league (Tassi, 2013). This is also the first time a sport league has been introduced and grown in the last 60 years, as the professional sport league industry in the United States is arguably saturated with the National Basketball Association, Major League Baseball, National Hockey League, and National Football League. In realizing how quickly the eSports industry has grown, it is key to consider how it has impacted the video game business and other relevant mechanisms.

CHALLENGES

The video game industry has experienced fewer panics than radio, television, and movie industries, as legacy firms in those respective media appear to be constantly at odds with new entrants into their respective markets. However, there are still challenges faced by the video game industry, even when most video game executives express effusive optimism. Video game players may be less inclined to purchase video game hardware in the future, opting for subscription-based services or the ability to store video games in the cloud. Given the portability of the Nintendo Switch, Microsoft and Sony must consider whether they want to push for their own platform-agnostic video game consoles or subscription services, allowing members to play purchased video games on mobile phones, tablets, laptops, and other devices.

Specifically, video game console companies will face challenges surrounding platform agnosticism, since designing a video game for multiple platforms (e.g., smartphones, desktops, laptops, and tablets) is a difficult proposition and may also risk displacing video game consoles. Platform agnosticism is a concept that has been discussed at great length by several video game console executives. Yet, the Nintendo Switch has illustrated that it is possible to preserve much of the video game playing experience on the go. In addition, Phil Spencer of Xbox has stated that platform-agnostic devices allow for more video game play and open up consumer bases that have not really played video games or had interest in investing in video game consoles. He has also discussed opening up the Xbox Game Pass, a video game subscription service, to not just tablets, desktops, and smartphones but also rival video game consoles produced by Sony and Nintendo (Makuch, 2018).

Mastery of video game console controllers not only imbues players with confidence but also helps abate the number of players who may wish to switch to another video game console with different controller designs. While the makeup of gross revenue of the video game console companies is less clear, these companies are all considering ways in which to offer their video games to the greatest number of consumers possible. The future of obtrusive, bulky video game consoles seems unavoidable. Will future video game console companies need to habitually create and put out new video game console devices? If more video games become platform agnostic, will fewer video game consoles be sold?

A second challenge rests on how to design and create video games for aging video gamers. This presents challenges in creating video games that may appeal to consumer segments that have not been considered before. Amid dwindling consumer purchases among younger generations, particularly those who purchased video game consoles, video game console and content companies need to consider what to innovate toward in the future. Video game graphics are now supported by 4K technology and are often beamed through powerful flat-screen television sets. Digital facial animations allow for remarkably realistic-looking characters (Morris, 2018a). It has been argued that while graphics will improve, they will only get incrementally better without significant technology present in a room. Among millennials, tiny homes and delayed home purchases are significant trends, meaning that living rooms and other living quarters are likely to become smaller for many consumers (Bahney, 2018). While human motion capture was a joyful novelty in the Nintendo Wii, it has not notably shifted the manner in which consumers play video games. Video game console and content companies will need to consider what constitutes innovation in the future and how to energize consumer bases to purchase new video game consoles.

Considering that an average video game player is in their early 30s, they may be likely to embrace minimalism, another trend among millennials, who are inclined to be conservative with their money against unyielding debt accrued from student loans and elsewhere (Petro, 2018; Weinswig, 2016). Additionally, adults with disposable income are likely to be raising children and paying off mortgages and have other financial responsibilities to meet. While it is not clear if this will be a transient trend or a permanent cultural shift, video game companies need to consider different video game story lines, subgenres, and other elements to appeal to an aging consumer base that has grown up playing video games.

Finally, current video game console companies face challenges from new technology entrants. Amazon Game Studios is working to develop live streaming gaming and more eSports experiences (Amazon Game Studios, 2019). In November 2019, Google launched Google Stadia, a cloud subscription-based service similar to Netflix, in which consumers have access to video games through any screen available (Nelius, 2019). Despite initial struggles with poor PC performance and latency difficulties, Google is working to quickly revitalize its Stadia experience for video game players (Royse, 2019). As referenced earlier, Tencent, a Chinese conglomerate, is arguably the largest video game company and currently owns *League of Legends*, 40% of *Fortnite*, 5% in Ubisoft, 5% in Activision-Blizzard, a majority stake in Supercell (e.g., *Clash of Clans)*, and a partnership with Take-Two entertainment (e.g., *Grand Theft Auto, NBA 2K*) (Morris, 2018b).

The contours of the familiar oligopolistic video game console marketplace, occupied by Nintendo, Sony, and Microsoft, are ostensibly opposed by these new competitors. Amazon and Google have access to consumer data from their other products and services, and they also have a robust research and development budget, as Amazon alone spent $23 billion in research and development in 2017 (Molla, 2018). Tencent has investments across multiple video game design studios and gleans insights into consumer behaviors from its impressive video game portfolio. To combat this, research and development, consumer flexibility, and close scrutiny of product life cycles across video games and video game consoles are vital to the continued success of Nintendo, Sony, and Microsoft. Future practitioners should utilize the action plan presented below as a guide for future video game management practices.

ACTION PLAN

1. Harness video game player opinion and player data for initial research and video game development.
2. Consider positioning your video game to be platform agnostic to maximize consumer exposure across generations.
3. Have a detailed blueprint in place for video game rollout, and understand product life cycles of video game consoles.

KEY TAKEAWAYS

1. The average video game player's age continues to rise, and this is a nod toward sustained interest in the medium among adults.
2. Video game nostalgia and eSports have flourished as submarketplaces within the video game industry.
3. Let's Play videos offer a new playing field for all video game publishers to raise awareness of new games.
4. Video game players continue to seek unique and unheralded game play experiences from every additional video game console generation.

CONCLUSION

For media managers in the gaming industry, there are several takeaways. First, video game consumers are highly educated on upcoming products and services. Many video game players, particularly hard-core video game players or those who wield marked brand affinity or brand loyalty, possess extreme awareness of the marketplace. Media managers should establish and maintain relationships with consumers who are interested in their upcoming products and services, as video game consumers are inclined to criticize video game products and services. Video game critiques may be gathered on social media, as video game developers may use Twitter to release beta version video clips or a playable video game console demo to collect consumer feedback.

Additionally, media managers should consider the level of immersion their video game offers, as this will dictate what type of controllers and platforms (e.g., video game console, mobile device, PC) the game should be played on. On the other hand, video game managers may also think about how they may exploit the same video game across platforms, as the flexibility of a video game to be imported and exported across digital clouds and lockers onto tangible platforms is an increasingly useful tactic in gaining more exposure in the video game marketplace.

Through Let's Play videos and other video game vloggers, it is feasible to have a video game host with numerous patrons play a video game. Consumers are interested in watching video game play experiences before making a video game purchase. Leveraging this experience as entertainment, a contest (in which fans post videos of themselves playing the video game), or other activity helps make video game players part of the video game production and distribution process. Allowing fans to interact during the video game design and marketing phases will aid game managers in accruing actionable insights that may help them improve the overall video game play experience.

There is a burgeoning indie video game market as well as other channels by which video game managers can create start-ups and bring their video games to the marketplace. According to the Entertainment Software Association (2019b), there are roughly 220,000 individuals who comprise the video game industry. Additionally, employees in this industry earn about $97,000, and 95% of all video game companies are currently based in the United States (Entertainment Software Association, 2019b). From 2016 through 2026, the demand for multimedia artists and animators, under which video game designers fall, is likely to grow at an 8% rate (Bureau of Labor Statistics, 2019). Indie video games have made leaps and bounds in quality, video game play, story line complexity, and other elements germane to gamers. Given the reduced cost in creating a video game, the availability of video game design software, and dozens of universities now teaching students how to design video games, it has become more feasible for video game aficionados to create their own video games and attempt to bring them into the marketplace. For aspiring video game practitioners, utilizing the indie video game market may be very practical, as it is easier to create a video game and offer demos to parent video game console companies such as Nintendo, Sony, and Microsoft. This will allow video game managers the ability to retain intellectual property rights to content and offer more freedom to the artists and designers at video game publishing firms.

A lasting challenge for video game managers is to extend the product life cycle or consistently exploit video game intellectual property. Nostalgia marketing has demonstrated that consumers will play video games from the past, drawing inquiries about how modern video games may fare in the future. Video game designers and managers should cull deep understandings about why consumers like popular video games today and consider core traits that may elongate the longevity of a video game or position it as a timeless experience that transcends generations.

Video game managers should never lose sight of what it is they are selling: video games. These experiences appeal to numerous consumers because they allow us a step further into enacting certain actions and abilities, such as flying or saving an entire town from destruction. These are actions most video game players are unlikely to undertake in reality. Video game play affords consumers opportunities to learn, take risks, challenge each other, transcend time and space, and record progress, which are experiences that few other media can offer. Its rise from a children's toy industry to simply an entertainment industry speaks volumes about its universality and mass appeal around the world.

As video game consoles continue to proliferate around the world, and video game consumers age, it is important to note that we will eventually be in a position in which all living generations grew up with video games in one respect or another. This means that the gaming market has yet to reach its plateau or zenith, and its limitations are only within the boundaries of the human mind. Gaming is not the only industry blending creativity, information, and expression together. The next chapter will examine the tenets of podcasting and the opportunities and challenges in media management strategies.

REFERENCES

Amazon Game Studios. (2019). *Amazon game studios: Come play with us.* https://www.amazongames.com

Armstrong, P. (2017, February 14). PewDiePie just showed every brand why influencers are dangerous. *Forbes.* https://www.forbes.com/sites/maddieberg/2017/12/07/how-youtubes-pewdiepie-made-12-million-this-year-despite-racist-videos

Bahney, A. (2018, November 2). Demand for tiny homes is getting bigger. CNN Business. https://www.cnn.com/2018/11/02/success/tiny-homes/index.html

Beck, J. (2013, August 14). When nostalgia was a disease. *The Atlantic.* https://www.theatlantic.com/health/archive/2013/08/when-nostalgia-was-a-disease/278648

Biocca, F. (1997). The cyborg's dilemma: Embodiment in virtual environments. In *Proceedings Second International Conference on Cognitive Technology Humanizing the Information Age*, 12–26.

Boyle, E. (2017, April 9). *Why your digital games collection isn't yours to own?* Techradar. https://www.techradar.com/news/the-double-edge-of-digital-games-and-changing-ownership

Brandt, E. (2019, November 29). *3 reasons Google Stadia could shake up the gaming industry.* The Motley Fool. https://www.fool.com/investing/2019/11/29/3-reasons-google-stadia-could-shake-up-the-gaming.aspx

Bureau of Labor Statistics. (2019, April 17). *Occupational outlook handbook: Multimedia artists and animators.* https://www.bls.gov/ooh/arts-and-design/multimedia-artists-and-animators.htm

Chambers, D. (2012). "Wii play as a family": The rise in family-centered video gaming. *Leisure Studies, 31*, 69–82.

Chaney, I., Lin, K., & Chaney, J. (2004). The effect of billboards within the gaming environment. *Journal of Interactive Advertising, 5*, 37–45.

Chan-Olmsted, S. (2006). Issues in media management and technology. In A. B. Albarran, S. Chan-Olmsted, & M. Wirth (Eds.), *Handbook of media management and economics* (pp. 251–273). Lawrence Erlbaum Associates.

Christou, L. (2018, January 31). *Mobile dominated digital video game sales in 2017, making more revenue than PC and console combined.* Verdict. https://www.verdict.co.uk/mobile-video-game-sales

Clemenson, G., & Stark, C. (2015). Virtual environmental enrichment through video games improves Hippocampal-associated memory. *The Journal of Neuroscience, 35,* 16116–16125.
Coldewey, D. (2017, September 28). *Review: The SNES classic edition and all 21 games on it.* TechCrunch. https://techcrunch.com/2017/09/28/review-the-snes-classic-edition-and-all-21-games-on-it
Csikszentmihalyi, M. (1975). *Beyond boredom and anxiety.* Jossey-Bass.
Csikszentmihalyi, M., & Bennett, S. (1971). An exploratory model of play. *American Anthropologist, 73,* 45–58.
Dent, S. (2015, December 17). *"League of Legends" is now fully owned by China's Tencent.* Engadget. https://www.engadget.com/2015/12/17/league-of-legends-fully-owned-by-tencent
Economist. (2014, September 25). *Why video games are so expensive to develop.* https://www.economist.com/the-economist-explains/2014/09/24/why-video-games-are-so-expensive-to-develop
Edwards, B. (2015, August 21). Unraveling the enigma of Nintendo's Virtual Boy 20 years later. *Fast Company.* https://www.fastcompany.com/3050016/unraveling-the-enigma-of-nintendos-virtual-boy-20-years-later
Entertainment Software Association. (2019a). *2019 essential facts about the computer and video game industry.* https://www.theesa.com/wp-content/uploads/2019/05/2019-Essential-Facts-About-the-Computer-and-Video-Game-Industry.pdf
Entertainment Software Association. (2019b). *U.S. video game industry expands to 50 states, supporting 220,000 jobs and $30.4 billion in revenue.* https://www.theesa.com/industry/economic-growth
Fischbach, M. E. (2014, August 12). *Scariest game in years: Five nights at Freddy's* [Video]. YouTube. https://www.youtube.com/watch?v=iOztnsBPrAA
Gillette, F. (2018, June 21). The legend of Nintendo. *Bloomberg Businessweek.* https://www.bloomberg.com/news/features/2018-06-21/how-nintendo-s-switch-helped-the-japanese-gaming-giant-win-again
Greenwald, W. (2019, December 20). The best VR headsets for 2020. *PC.* https://www.pcmag.com/article/342537/the-best-virtual-reality-vr-headsets
Kain, E. (2012, June 19). 6 reasons to buy a PlayStation 3 instead of an Xbox 360. *Forbes.* https://www.forbes.com/sites/erikkain/2012/06/19/6-reasons-to-buy-a-playstation-3-instead-of-an-xbox-360
Kent, S. (2001). *The ultimate history of video games.* Three Rivers Press.
Kharpal, A. (2018, March 7). *Games console market has had its best year since 2011 thanks to Nintendo's "record-breaking comeback."* CNBC. https://www.cnbc.com/2018/03/07/nintendo-comeback-sees-games-console-market-have-best-year-since-2011.html
Kim, W., & Mauborgne, R. (2005). *Blue ocean strategy: How to create uncontested market space and make competition irrelevant.* Harvard Business Review Press.
Kjellberg, F. (2017, January 23). *Resident Evil 7: Biohazard—Gameplay—Part 1—It's frickin' terrifying!* [Video]. YouTube. https://www.youtube.com/watch?v=HduaXmGiRTQ
Kollar, P. (2013, September 3). *"Castle of Illusion" review: Mouse in the mirror.* Polygon. https://www.polygon.com/2013/9/3/4687826/castle-of-illusion-review-mouse-in-the-mirror
Lawler, R. (2013, June 10). *Sony PlayStation 4 price: $399.* Engadget. https://www.engadget.com/2013/06/10/sony-playstation-4-price
Loveridge, S. (2019, December 13). *Xbox Series X: Everything you need to know from release date to specs, and more.* Gamesradar. https://www.gamesradar.com/xbox-series-x-release-date-games-cost-specs
Macy, S. (2019, September 16). *Everything you need to know about the SEGA Genesis Mini: Where to preorder, full game list, and what's in the box.* IGN. https://www.ign.com/articles/sega-genesis-mini-release-date-preorder-games
Makuch, E. (2017, October 31). *"Super Mario Run" hits 200 million downloads but Nintendo says its profit is still unacceptable.* Gamespot. https://www.gamespot.com/articles/super-mario-run-hits-200-million-downloads-but-nin/1100-6454506

Makuch, E. (2018, December 5). *Xbox game pass will eventually be on "every device," Phil Spencer says.* Gamespot. https://www.gamespot.com/articles/xbox-game-pass-will-eventually-be-on-every-device-/1100-6463693

Martinez, P. (2018, November 6). "Super Mario Bros." animated movie eyeing 2022 release. *Newsweek.* https://www.newsweek.com/super-mario-bros-movie-release-date-1204223

McGloin, R., Farrar, K., & Krcmar, M. (2011). The impact of controller naturalness on spatial presence, gamer enjoyment, and perceived realism in a tennis simulation video game. *Presence Teleoperators & Virtual Environments, 20,* 309–324.

Messner, S. (2019, October 4). Every game company that Tencent has invested in. *PC Gamer.* https://www.pcgamer.com/every-game-company-that-tencent-has-invested-in

Microsoft. (2018, November 2). *Transforming eSports through the innovative power of startups.* Microsoft News. https://news.microsoft.com/europe/2018/11/20/transforming-esports-through-the-innovative-power-of-startups

Molinillo, S., Munoz-Leiva, F., & Perez-Garcia, F. (2018). The effects of human-game interaction, network externalities, and motivations on players' use of mobile casual games. *Industrial Management & Data Systems, 118,* 1766–1786.

Molla, R. (2018, April 9). *Amazon spent nearly $23 billion on R&D last year—more than any other U.S. company.* Vox. https://www.vox.com/2018/4/9/17204004/amazon-research-development-rd

Morris, C. (2018a, March 22). Video games can now have hyper realistic characters thanks to new graphics tech. *Fortune.* http://fortune.com/2018/03/22/epic-games-siren-hyper-realistic-characters-video-games

Morris, C. (2018b, August 30). China's Tencent folds yet another video company into its empire. *Fortune.* http://fortune.com/2018/08/30/chinas-tencent-folds-yet-another-video-game-company-into-its-empire

Nelius, J. (2019, November 11). Everything we know about Google Stadia. *PC Gamer.* https://www.pcgamer.com/everything-we-know-about-google-stadia

Nelson, M. (2002). Recall of brand placements in computer/video games. *Journal of Advertising Research, 42,* 80–92.

Nelson, M., Keum, H., & Yaros, R. (2004). Advertainment or adcreep: Game players' attitudes toward advertising and product placements in computer games. *Journal of Interactive Advertising, 5,* 3–21.

Nielsen. (2015, April 9). *Game consoles in 2015: One stop shop for games and entertainment.* https://www.nielsen.com/us/en/insights/article/2015/game-consoles-in-2015-one-stop-shop-for-games-and-entertainment

Nintendo. (2019). *NES classic edition: Now you're playing with power.* https://www.nintendo.com/nes-classic

Nintendo Switch Online. (2019). *Nintendo Switch online.* https://www.nintendo.com/switch/online-service/?cid=A1005-01:ch=pdpd

Oliver, M., Bowman, N., Woolley, J., Rogers, R., Sherrick, B., & Chung, M. (2016). Video games as meaningful entertainment experiences. *Psychology of Popular Media Culture, 5,* 390–405.

Palomba, A. (2018). Virtual perceived emotional intelligence: How high brand loyalty video game players evaluate their own video game play experiences to repair or regulate emotions. *Computers in Human Behavior, 85,* 34–42.

Palomba, A. (2019). Digital seasons: How time of the year may shift video game play habits. *Entertainment Computing, 30,* 1–7.

Pannekeet, J. (2019, February 12). *Newzoo: Global Esports economy will top $1 billion for the first time in 2019.* NewZoo. https://newzoo.com/insights/articles/newzoo-global-esports-economy-will-top-1-billion-for-the-first-time-in-2019

Park, E., Baek, S., Ohm, J., & Chang, H. (2014). Determinants of player acceptance of mobile social network games: An application of extended technology acceptance model. *Telematics and Informatics, 31,* 3–15.

Parkin, S. (2017, December 29). Nintendo's Switch brings some magic back. *New York Times.* https://www.nytimes.com/2017/12/29/technology/nintendo-switch.html

Passalacqua, M. (2017, January 5). *"Pokémon Go" was most downloaded app in Apple's app store in 2016.* IGN. https://www.ign.com/articles/2017/01/05/pokemon-go-was-most-downloaded-app-in-apples-app-store-in-2016

Peckham, M. (2017, January 13). Nintendo Switch: Everything you need to know. *Time.* https://time.com/4632820/nintendo-switch-nx

Pei-Shan, W., & Hsi-Peng, L. (2014). Why do people play mobile social games? An examination of network externalities and of uses and gratifications. *Internet Research, 24,* 313–331.

Penttinen, E., Rossi, M., & Tuunainen, V. (2010). Mobile games: Analyzing the needs and values of consumers. *Journal of Information Technology Theory and Application, 11,* 5–22.

Peters, J. (2020, July 2). Super Nintendo World Japan looks like a Mario level dropped into reality. *The Verge.* https://www.theverge.com/2020/7/2/21311592/super-nintendo-world-japan-mario-level-real-world-universal-studios

Petro, G. (2018, August 19). More debt, less stuff: The millennial spending dilemma. *Forbes.* https://www.forbes.com/sites/gregpetro/2018/08/19/more-debt-less-stuff-the-millennial-spending-dilemma

PR Newswire. (2017, June 26). *Augmented reality (AR) gaming market to reach $284.9 billion by 2023—Key Players are Microsoft, Google, Apple, Sony, Nintendo, Niantic, Cast AR & Gamar.* Markets Insider. https://markets.businessinsider.com/news/stocks/research-and-markets-augmented-reality-ar-gaming-market-to-reach-284-9-billion-by-2023-key-players-are-microsoft-google-apple-sony-nintendo-niantic-cast-ar-gamar-1002124561#

Roettgers, J. (2018, November 7). A sense of wonder: How within is evolving storytelling in augmented reality. *Variety.* https://variety.com/2018/digital/features/within-wonderland-ar-storytelling-1203020435

Royse, D. (2019, December 23). *Google buys Typhoon Studios to bolster Stadia.* Yahoo! Finance. https://finance.yahoo.com/news/google-buys-typhoon-studios-bolster-200540895.html

Ryan, M. (2016, December 21). TV peaks again in 2016: Could it hit 500 shows in 2017? *Variety.* https://variety.com/2016/tv/news/peak-tv-2016-scripted-tv-programs-1201944237

Ryan, M., & Littleton, C. (2017, September 26). TV series budgets hit the breaking point as costs skyrocket in peak TV era. *Variety.* https://variety.com/2017/tv/news/tv-series-budgets-costs-rising-peak-tv-1202570158

Ryan, R., & Deci, E. (2000). Self-determination theory and the facilitation of intrinsic motivation, social development, and well-being. *American Psychologist, 55,* 68–78.

Ryan, R., Rigby, C., & Przybylski, A. (2006). The motivational pull of video games: A self-determination theory approach. *Motivation and Emotion, 30,* 344–360.

Sarkar, S. (2017, January 20). *Totaling the hidden costs of owning a Nintendo Switch.* Polygon. https://www.polygon.com/2017/1/20/14304242/nintendo-switch-price-must-buy-accessories

Seo, Y., & Jung, S. (2014). Beyond solitary play in computer games: The social practices of eSports. *Journal of Consumer Culture, 16,* 635–655.

Shay, R., & Palomba, A. (2018). First-party success or first-party failure? A case study on audience perceptions of the Nintendo brand during the Wii U's product life cycle. *Games and Culture, 15,* 1–26.

Skalski, P., Tamborini, R., Shelton, A., Buncher, M., & Lindmark, P. (2011). Mapping the road to fun: Natural video game controllers, presence, and game enjoyment. *New Media & Society, 13,* 224–242.

Steffen, C., Mau, G., & Schramm-Klein, H. (2013). Who is the loser when I lost the game? Does losing an Advergame have a negative impact on the perception of the brand? *Journal of Advertising, 42,* 183–195.

Stevens, C. (2018, July 9). *Miyamoto comments on Universal Studios' Nintendo theme park.* IGN. https://www.ign.com/articles/2018/07/09/miyamoto-comments-on-universal-studios-nintendo-theme-parks

Summers, N. (2018, March 23). *Red Bull built an underground eSports bar in London.* Engadget. https://www.engadget.com/2018/03/23/red-bull-gaming-sphere-esports-london

Sung, H., Sigerson, L., & Cheng, C. (2017, January 31). Social capital accumulation in location-based mobile game playing: A multiple-process approach. *Cyberpsychology, Behavior, and Social Networking, 20,* 486–493.

Suszek, M. (2013, November 19). *PS4 costs $381 to make, according to hardware teardown.* Engadget. https://www.engadget.com/2013/11/19/ps4-costs-381-to-make-according-to-hardware-teardown

Tannert, C. (2019, August 19). How to cut the cord: The best gaming consoles for streaming video. *Forbes.* https://www.forbes.com/sites/chucktannert/2019/08/19/how-to-cut-the-cord-the-best-gaming-consoles-for-streaming-video

Tassi, P. (2013, July 14). The U.S. now recognizes eSports players as professional athletes. *Forbes.* https://www.forbes.com/sites/insertcoin/2013/07/14/the-u-s-now-recognizes-esports-players-as-professional-athletes

Thang, J. (2016, July 27). *The traditional console life cycle is dying.* Gamespot. https://www.gamespot.com/articles/the-traditional-console-life-cycle-is-dying/1100-6442192

Think Gaming. (2018, November 12). *Top grossing iPhone games.* https://thinkgaming.com/app-sales-data

VG Chartz. (2018). *Platform totals.* http://www.vgchartz.com/analysis/platform_totals

Ward, A. (2020, August 26). Super Nintendo World in Universal Studios Hollywood is under construction. *LAD Bible.* https://www.ladbible.com/news/news-super-nintendo-world-in-universal-studios-hollywood-is-being-built-20200826

Webster, A. (2018, November 27). *PlayStation Classic review: A journey through the exciting, awkward days of early 3D games.* The Verge. https://www.theverge.com/2018/11/27/18112685/playstation-classic-review-3d-games

Weinswig, D. (2016, September 7). Millennials go minimal: The decluttering lifestyle trend that is taking over. *Forbes.* http://fortune.com/2018/03/22/epic-games-siren-hyper-realistic-characters-video-games

Welch, C. (2018, November 8). *YouTube arrives on Nintendo Switch today.* The Verge. https://www.theverge.com/2018/11/8/18064958/youtube-app-nintendo-switch-now-available-features

Wijman, T. (2019, June 18). *The global games market will generate $152.1 billion in 2019 as the U.S. overtakes China as the biggest market.* Newzoo. https://newzoo.com/insights/articles/the-global-games-market-will-generate-152-1-billion-in-2019-as-the-u-s-overtakes-china-as-the-biggest-market

Witkowski, E. (2012). On the digital playing field: How we "do sport" with networked computer games. *Games and Culture: A Journal of Interactive Media, 7,* 349–374.

Wolf, J. (2017, November 6). *Jerry Jones, John Goff buy majority stake in complexity gaming.* ESPN. http://www.espn.com/esports/story/_/id/21309068/dallas-cowboys-owner-jerry-jones-john-goff-buy-majority-stake-complexity-gaming

Yan, M., & Gilbert, B. (2018, October 29). Here's the reason most new console video games cost $60. *Business Insider.* https://www.businessinsider.com/why-video-games-always-cost-60-dollars-2018-10

Zynga. (2018). *Zynga's latest featured games.* https://www.zynga.com

CHAPTER 17

Podcasting

Kim Fox, The American University in Cairo

LEARNING OBJECTIVES

1. Introduce ways to utilize convergent new media technologies to create a strong podcast.
2. Create an effective promotional strategy to reach target podcast audiences.
3. Identify media business models to successfully monetize a podcast production.

Author Stephen King famously states, "Sooner or later, everything old is new again." At first glance, it may be difficult to tell what elements of a podcast make it so appealing in today's convergent media environment, as digital audiences can click, vote, share, curate, and participate across various platforms whenever and wherever they wish. Yet, in 2019, an estimated 86 million listeners accessed podcasts in the United States (Statista, 2019), and more than half of all U.S. households are fans of podcasts (Podcast Insights, 2020).

Podcasts prove a unique and interesting technology, as they consist of a prerecorded digital audio file that is made available on the Internet for download. The traditional elements of new media content (e.g., transactional media channels, where audiences interact, click, and engage text) are not structurally possible with podcasts. Instead, users download content and passively *listen*.

Sure, if users are dissatisfied or wish to communicate with podcast producers, they are able to utilize social media to share their concerns. However, the podcast itself offers no new media technological affordance other than portability and ease of interface. On the surface, media managers may not see the appeal of investing in such a traditional technology. Yet, the *New York Times* cites a sharp growth in podcasts, with advertising revenue exceeding $500 million in 2018 (Peiser, 2019a). Podcasts have proven a winning strategy for large institutional media conglomerates, including NPR, *The Times*, *Washington Post*, the *New York Times*, and *Slate* magazine. It is important for future media managers and practitioners to understand the evolution of the podcast and why it proves so appealing to users in today's digital climate.

There are people who probably think that podcasts are a "new" technology, something that's been around for just a few years. In fact, podcasts have been around since the early 2000s, with former MTV veejay Adam Curry often receiving credit for his early involvement. His current podcast, *No Agenda*, consists of 2.5-hour episodes designed to examine the state of various media outlets (Curry, 2019). While this is considered a long-form podcast, other popular hits, such as *Ted Talks Daily*, consist of episodes that last just 11 minutes. The variety of formats implies that there is something for everyone, regardless of the length of their commute or workout.

The podcasting community has grown exponentially in recent years. According to Edison Research (2019), 51% of those surveyed had listened to a podcast. The Pew Research Center (2018) also notes that weekly and monthly podcast listenership increased to double digits over the past few years. In addition, the topics of podcasting cover everything from talk shows to interviews to narrative nonfiction and audio dramas. There is likely a podcast that focuses on any hobby, subject, or topic you're interested in. Thus, podcasting is an ideal media choice for niche media topics. Producers are able to build on episodes to dissect specialized topics, making podcasts a strong sell for advertisers looking to reach more segmented audiences.

Although the field has some saturation, at least in the U.S. market, the future looks bright for the podcasting industry with its ability to be nimble and low barriers to entry. Virtually anyone with a recording device is able to make a podcast. Yet, there are concerns about the data accuracy related to monitoring podcasts, a challenge discussed further below. Future media managers and practitioners should focus on creating cohesive and accurate evaluation and monitoring efforts for podcasts. Let us explore one case study of the podcast *2 Dope Queens*, which was able to produce a unique, authentic podcast and cultivate success for an established media brand.

CASE STUDY

When *2 Dope Queens* entered the podcast community in 2016, it was a welcome addition. The podcast, produced by WNYC, a public radio station in New York City, provided new perspectives, diversities, and stories unlike public radio shows of the time. In the short history of podcasting, the popular hosts have been white men. Voices in podcasting mirrored traditional successful radio and television outlets. Producers Phoebe Robinson and Jessica Williams hoped to change this as a part of WNYC's initiative to demonstrate its commitment to diversity (Spanos, 2018).

Prior to the podcasts, Robinson and Williams did not have any podcasting experience. They did have strong chemistry as a duo and the ability to make people laugh. It was enough to get them started. The *2 Dope Queens* podcast went well as the podcast was at the top of the iTunes charts for a week after it launched (Wikipedia, 2019a). The podcast formula was a combination of chat fest and interviews with high-profile people, but the element that seemed to cement the show was the hosts being themselves.

The authentic look at Black women really connected with a broad audience, an audience that sometimes got to see the show as a live performance. The podcast went out with a bang in November 2018 with guest Michelle Obama, who had just released her memoir *Becoming*, a reflection of her time as the first lady of the United States. The success of the *2 Dope Queens* podcast set Robinson and Williams up for what seems like their lifetime. They segued to HBO with several specials using pretty much the same formula as the podcast and their podcast live shows. Both women continue to work in the entertainment industry in various roles. Here you can see how using the podcast format to reach niche, specialized audiences is a refreshing change to even the most established traditional media forms.

Something Old

Podcasts are perhaps most closely aligned with the radio and music industry. Though even radio has a long history of encouraging direct live audience engagement, live interaction is not possible with podcast technology. As we try to posit podcasting within the existing media environment, both traditional and new, it is important to turn toward media theory to understand how a media manager might make the most of a podcasting strategy. One theory that helps explain emergent and refashioned media forms is remediation theory (Bolter & Grusin, 2000).

REMEDIATION THEORY

Remediation theory emerged as a theoretical explanation of how media producers are able to refashion existing pieces of media through a process of repurposing. "No medium today, and certainly no single media event, seems to do its cultural work in isolation from other media" (Bolter & Grusin, 2000, p. 15). Digital media audiences access all content with the same expectations and assumptions of more traditional media forms. In short, media do not exist in isolation from one another. Therefore, a podcast user would be familiar with radio and television broadcast formats and would naturally adapt their previous consumption with the new technology.

Remediation theory suggests that all media in today's digital age consist of structural elements across two principal styles: transparent immediacy and hypermediacy (Bolter & Grusin, 2000). Media managers must create forms that integrate elements of both in order to be successful in today's convergent environment. Transparent immediacy includes holding an immediate relationship to media, giving an immersive first-person perspective to linear content (Bolter & Grusin, 2000). Hypermediacy provides a more fragmented and windowed style of media content, emphasizing process or performance rather than the finished product and having no physical beginning, middle, or end (Bolter & Grusin, 2000).

Based on remediation theory, if podcasts exist as a repurposed radio or music technology, they must not only include transparent and hypermediacy elements, but the medium itself must be constituted by a unique set of essential characteristics that will define the medium (Bolter & Grusin, 2000). These structural elements of a podcast will ensure that the genre is unique enough to attract users. Let us explore transparent and hypermediacy elements of the podcast.

TRANSPARENT ELEMENTS

Similar to radio, a traditional media platform, podcasting employs the traditional one-to-many communication approach, as podcasts can be downloaded or streamed by many people. Audiences have the opportunity to select various podcasts, listen on the go, but not own the content (much like radio). The lack of appointment listening also makes podcasts different than the ephemeralness of terrestrial radio, where if you miss the morning show, you have missed out until the next broadcast.

In today's convergent media environment, we see increasing uses of new technology, such as split screens, HD visuals, and virtual reality. These new media technologies can prove expensive and in need of constant updating. The rise in popularity of podcasting is partly due to their low cost of entry and ease of use. Thus, this technology proves appealing to many media managers and practitioners who are interested in reaching a niche audience with a reasonable amount of investment.

Similar to successful radio shows and entertainment hosts, podcasting is also beginning to experiment with television, but going beyond the previously mentioned *2 Dope Queens* format. At first, it seemed like a bit of a stretch: pitch a successful nonfiction podcast to a television or movie production company in the hopes of optioning the rights for a potential video or movie. But, according to the *New York Times*, Hernan Lopez, the founder of podcast network Wondery, had the foresight that podcasts could be a content sensation. In an article titled "In the Race for Content, Hollywood Is Buying Up Hit Podcasts," Lopez was quoted as saying, "I set out to create a company that could build on bringing to podcasting the skill set of television and movies, both in storytelling and production, as well as marketing" (see Peiser, 2019b). Clearly, linear storytelling is crucial to a good podcast, radio, or television program.

In addition, the format of many podcasts mirrors traditional radio content. They include interviews, roundtable discussions, and sponsored commercial breaks. There has even been a bit of a renaissance with audio dramas as podcasts mimic radio serial dramas of the 1940s. There is a popular podcast for almost every popular entertainment genre: murder mystery, celebrity entertainment, and game shows. Successful podcasters understand that with good content comes advertising and sponsorship opportunities.

It seems clear that podcasts are one of the fastest-growing addressable markets for media businesses (Kaufer, 2018). Advertisers now see the value of using podcasts as a main performance marketing campaign to attract new customers toward niche products. Given that, as with radio, most audiences access podcasts free of charge, producers tend to rely on these monetization approaches and/or sponsorships to finance programming. This is achieved through a multitude of advertising strategies, including formal endorsement, where podcast hosts provide a product testimonial that is interwoven into the episode; nonendorsed advertising, which includes a prerecorded pitch provided by the advertisers that is inserted into the show; baked-in advertising content, where the ad lives in the show's content permanently, such as titling a game show with an advertising sponsor; and dynamic insertion, where the episode has designated breaks to insert prerecorded ads (Kaufer, 2018). Podcast hosts have to rely on affiliate link and podcast ratings to sell these spots to prospective advertisers. Chapter 7, "Marketing and Branding," talks more about the opportunities and challenges of marketing in a convergent environment.

HYPERMEDIACY ELEMENTS

Linear media content can be expensive to produce. While community radio does offer access to difficult-to-reach populations, the majority of Americans will never own a radio station due to lack of availability, licensing, regulations, and costs associated with obtaining and maintaining a station. However, podcasting creates a new opportunity for diverse content with less financial input for the hobbyist. Some of the equipment that podcasting requires is consistent with traditional radio, including microphones and headphones.

Some podcasters actually produce their shows using a mobile device and an app like Anchor, which was purchased by Spotify in 2019 (Carman, 2019). The low cost of entering the podcasting field has made it attractive, with early podcasters setting up in their garage à la Marc Maron of the *WTF with Marc Maron Podcast* (Wikipedia, 2019c). Some podcasters have episodic content; others create one stand-alone episode about a topic of their choice. Minimal technology requirements have reduced the barrier to enter the field even more, with USB mics, quality laptops, and relatively inexpensive hosting platforms for content. Many podcasters today use common audio editing software programs, such as Adobe Audition and Audacity, to produce their shows. Producers may make the content as fragmented or linear as they wish.

Whether they work in a studio or a basement, podcasters are producing content for their audiences, no matter the size. Clearly, podcasts are disrupting and subsidizing many traditional media industries. Podcasts are even becoming a strong tool in academic settings. iTunes University, a website with downloadable educational podcasts, provides students with the opportunity to obtain professors' lectures through podcast technology (McKinney, Dyck, & Luber, 2009). The majority of students using the technology report using it to take notes from the podcasts. They listen to lectures multiple times, are able to rewind, check notes, complete an assignment, and continue with the podcast later. While we do not advocate that podcasts replace traditional education, they prove a great alternative to support existing media ventures. For example, podcasts are a great tool to augment traditional teaching material. Instead of reading a book, students could listen to a podcast. Instead of writing a chapter summary, students could write a listening report.

Perhaps the single most hypermediacy element of a podcast is its portability. Users are able to download or even subscribe to podcasts and listen in fragmented shifts of time. They can binge listen to a series or break the episodes up to listen to during their commutes. Though most individual podcast episodes are meant to be listened to in linear fashion, often, the chronological nature of episodes does not matter. For example, Buffer's hit podcast, *The Science of Social Media*, allows users to pick and choose topics of interest to them. They do not need to listen to episode 2 before proceeding to episode 3.

With today's convergent media environment, there is no such thing as media content that exists solely with transparent logic. Every user is able to turn to social media and transactional communication structures to discuss, share, or comment on their experiences with the medium. Thus, even a technology such as podcasting, which mostly consists of transparent structures, can thrive in the digital age. Despite the technology not actually being new, there are many new elements that make it a strong choice as media managers look to refresh their media marketing and product plans.

Something New

The reach of podcasts has always been as pervasive as the Internet, thus making a global audience just a click away. The podcast community in the United States is rich, but the global podcast community is growing, with vibrant communities in the United Kingdom, Australia, and Canada as well as growth in Spanish-language areas.

While community radio has always been a global initiative, podcasting removes many of the traditional gatekeeping structures that still exist within governmental agencies. Podcasts reach a global community and have very little censorship in the marketplace. That's not to say that each and every podcast will prove successful. It's important to note that podcasts require strong research and a careful business plan. Like many new media forms, podcasting works best if it is designed and built for a niche audience. Planning a podcast involves having a unique idea and a creative approach for podcast content. Most central to the development of a podcast is the authenticity of your idea.

AUTHENTICITY

The term *authenticity* is certainly a buzzword for today's media creators and marketers. Though many believe the term only deals with being "true to one's self," the definition is actually narrower. Authenticity is about determining what makes you different from your closest competitor (Stratten, 2012). In today's digital environment, there are unlimited podcasts. Whatever your niche or passion is, likely there is already a podcast that focuses on the topic. However, finding your authenticity means that you harness whatever is unique and special about your perspective, voice, and contribution to the field.

Here, please consider the authenticity of one idea. In Jessica Abel's (2015) book *Out on the Wire: The Storytelling Secrets of the New Masters of Radio*, there are many pieces of sage advice for future podcasters. This includes the advice on authenticity with the XY story formula: "I'm doing a story about X. And what's interesting about it is Y." This is a great way to easily know the main focus and authenticity of a podcast.

This content authenticity will lead you to your target audience. For example, imagine you are interested in creating a podcast about celebrity fashion. Yes, there may already be other podcasts that focus on your passion. However, maybe you are more interested in environmentally conscious fashion trends and use your podcast to discuss ways in which audiences can be fashion forward and eco-friendly. Now you are offering a unique perspective on an otherwise covered topic.

Unlike radio, niche marketing is important to the podcast industry because it's more akin to narrowcasting, which could be valuable in terms of seeking advertising and sponsorships. There is no bottleneck of expensive content distribution. Once you have a sense of the authenticity you wish to embed in your podcast, you can begin incorporating it into your niche marketing strategy.

NICHE MARKETING

In low-cost markets, such as podcast hosting, distribution possibilities exist where previous marketplaces did not. Products are no longer bound by the constraints of physical shelf space and other bottlenecks of distribution. Anderson (2006) explored this phenomenon through the theory of the long tail, which explains how a larger portion of the population exists in the niche tail of the probability distribution. Long tail explains how media managers are able to profit from niche products with low demand by using alternative low-cost distribution channels (Anderson, 2006).

While music media managers have historically had to appeal to a common denominator mass audience, podcasts thrive on niche "long tail" marketing. In fact, Dalgic and Leeuw (1994) identified five essential elements of products that would do well through niche marketing: (1) positioning, (2) profitability, (3) distinctive competencies, (4) small market segments, and (5) adherence to the marketing concept.

It is important for media managers to keep these elements in mind when creating podcasting concepts. Though many new technologies and features could be integrated into podcast design, sometimes less is really more. Niche marketing tends to be driven by building relationships with audiences, reaching niche markets to build a database of followers, delivering authentic and differentiated messages to target demographics, and using technology to track their loyalty to your brand (Dalgic & Leeuw, 1994).

Once a practitioner understands their niche market, it is time to utilize it to develop a strong business plan. What is the format of your podcast? Will it be a short-term podcast? Where will your podcast be hosted? The general consensus from podcast listeners is that they want consistency. For example, if you published your first podcast on a Tuesday at 2:00 p.m., that is when your audience will expect the podcast to go live on a weekly basis. Be strategic and mindful during the planning stage of your podcast. Typically, podcasters should complete three episodes of their podcast before publishing. This approach will minimize the pressure of immediate deadlines.

PRODUCTION

Producers must also determine whether the show will include a stand-alone host or multiple hosts and whether guests will be invited to contribute. Consider this when selecting a physical space for recording. While guests are able to join podcasts remotely, there is something special about an interpersonal podcast session. The dynamic and chemistry between participants may seem better if they are in a room together. However, external noise is not your friend. The larger the space, the more difficult it is to capture professional sound quality, especially if using small USB mics. Just as in traditional radio, when recording audio for a podcast, many podcasters must alter their environment for the sake of sound quality, including turning off air conditioning, closing doors, or sitting in cramped spaces. While traditional radio required a more elaborate space for broadcasting, podcasts can be recorded virtually anywhere. Don't be afraid to experiment until you've achieved the sound that meets your goal.

DISTRIBUTION

New media have also created a plethora of options when it comes time to post a podcast. Though it can be hosted on one platform like Libsyn or PodBean, many podcast audiences access podcasts via apps such as Podcatchers. Many of them are free to host, making podcasts very different from traditional forms of media.

Smart home media devices, such as the Google Assistant and the Amazon Echo, are proving to be popular mechanisms for listening to podcasts. Be sure to research what outlets your niche audiences are most likely to use, and be sure that your podcast is available through these outlets. For example, Amazon Echo pulls from the iHeartRadio app library to access requested podcasts from users. If this is a device that your niche audience is likely to use when listening, it is important to distribute your content on iHeartRadio, even if you prefer a different platform. Be sure to pay attention to cross-platform licensing and copyright criteria, which we covered in chapter 8, "Law and Policy," in this book. Nonetheless, podcasting is an emerging field, and many of the legal guidelines are still being developed.

It would be easy for an eager new media professional to have an idea and immediately begin producing a podcast. However, this chapter urges media producers and managers to consider a business strategy prior to content creation. What is your authenticity? Who is your audience? How can you best reach them? While podcasting requires a more niche audience and more planning than many traditional forms of media, the monetization opportunities are plenty, if executed well. Here you see how the field of podcasting is adapting to many of the opportunities of new media. Let us explore how the industry is monetizing these opportunities by exploring what is new about podcast business strategies. It is important to consider how media convergence has created many opportunities and challenges for future podcast creators and managers.

Opportunities and Challenges

As in most new media forms, effective marketing of podcasts stems from building trust and relationships with audiences. This is why most successful podcasts do not exist in isolation. They are part of a larger media distribution package that often includes websites, blogs, and social media accounts. These new media technologies provide many opportunities for bringing in new audiences, engaging existing fans, and allowing users to have some feedback on podcast content. All these advantages help maximize your investment. Additionally, they provide alternative metrics to pitch to advertisers when seeking sponsorship.

OPPORTUNITIES

Opportunities in the podcasting community mostly stem from good old-fashioned networking. Attending a conference like the annual Podcast Movement or the Third Coast

International Audio Festival can net potential collaborators, guests, and a great deal of motivation to be a part of the community. There are many U.S.-based podcast and audio-specific conferences, such as WerkIt Festival, designed by and for female podcasters and those identifying as genderqueer and gender nonbinary. Other options include OzPod and Audiocraft in Australia, the Vancouver Podcast Festival in Canada, and PodUK and Radiodays Europe in the United Kingdom. All offer a lot of programming for podcasters and show the support that is generated from a semi-cultivated community. As a result, sometimes podcasters are quick to call out those who lack authenticity. It's through this community that connections are made, and although podcast creation can be executed without collaboration, networking still holds some importance. This could open the door to opportunities for creating a strong team to help build, create, and market a podcast.

TRADITIONAL MEDIA STRATEGIES

Many traditional media organizations, such as traditional print media, have been quickly adapted to the financial opportunity created by podcasts. The additional ad revenue stream fills the void of not enough digital subscriptions. *The Daily*, a popular podcast created by the *New York Times*, released in 2017, takes a deep dive into current events and demonstrates the strength of the medium. Other print media have also followed the podcast trail, including the *Washington Post* and the *New Yorker*.

Though creating podcasts can also be just a fun hobby, there are great opportunities for monetization in today's convergent media environment. Podcasters in the ecosystem are plenty, and not everyone can afford to be a hobbyist on the platform. Most podcasters include social media in their marketing and promotion efforts. A strong podcast promotion strategy involves the platform(s) that work best for your niche audience.

A newer opportunity for promotion is through audiograms, which can be short teasers for your podcast that allow you to add an image or a short video. The concept of the audiogram is using visuals to make the audio shareable. This helps create more hypermediacy artifacts for an otherwise transparent medium. Users are encouraged to share audiograms on social media sites to bolster their own fandom as well as attract an outside audience.

Monetizing podcasts has been a slippery slope. Some traditional approaches, like inserting advertisements within the content of the podcasts, similar to traditional radio commercials, have been executed to produce results, but perhaps not enough to be considered profitable. That does not seem to be the case for the popular podcast *The Joe Rogan Experience*, which opens the show with six minutes of ads (Cridland, 2019). Monetizing your podcast in an increasingly saturated market is difficult. Not to mention, how does a homegrown podcast compete with some of the large companies producing podcasts, like NPR and Gimlet? Thankfully, new media provide many opportunities for creating revenue streams.

One newer hypermediacy approach is actually a throwback to the early days of radio. The "live read" is back, where the podcast host reads an advertisement live. It's usually loosely scripted, and in most cases, it is clear to the listener what is sponsored content and what is the actual programming. Live reads also allow advertisers to have control over the scripted spot, particularly what they want to be the focal point.

Another opportunity for funding a podcast is through crowdfunding platforms. Crowdfunding platforms allow audiences to harness their collective energy to raise money for the production of a podcast. For example, crowdfunding has been exceptionally successful for Radiotopia, a podcast network. Rather than seeking a small number of large donors, crowdfunding sites, such as GoFundMe and Kickstarter, allow a large number of people to donate just a small amount of money. These small donations can add up to make a big impact. Patreon is another fundraising platform that many podcasters are utilizing to generate some revenue by soliciting sponsors.

Other podcasters are finding monetization opportunities through live shows. Live shows create a revenue stream that has a relatively low financial investment barrier. Putting on a show in front of a niche fan base can be a win-win situation for everyone: fans get to see their favorite podcaster in person, while the podcasters sometimes use the paid opportunity to record their podcast and share the live performances at a later date as exclusive content for their subscribers. *The Read*, a podcast produced by two African American comedians about pop culture, has a dedicated website just for their live shows. The live shows also open the opportunity to sell merchandise, such as T-shirts, stickers, and buttons, for additional revenue. For tips on taking to the stage, see *Bello Collective*'s DIY Guide to Podcast Live Shows (Join the Party Podcast, 2018).

Creating a network of podcasts could be an effective model to save money and generate revenue. For example, by combining resources like recording space and equipment, in addition to providing bundled advertising packages to potential advertisers, a podcast network could save money while also increasing its members' chances of sealing a deal with a client by offering a competitive rate package and therefore more exposure. Examples of rising successful podcast networks include Loud Speakers Network, home of *The Read*, and Pineapple Street Media, which produced *Missing Richard Simmons*, a short series of investigative podcasts.

While there are many opportunities for monetizing podcasts, demonstrating their success to advertisers can be difficult. Without direct affiliate links or click-through ratings that other new media technologies automatically enable, it can be almost impossible to track how many listeners engage sponsorship. Some podcasts mitigate this by providing a unique podcast promotional code that users can add at checkout if they decide to purchase a sponsored good. Currently, there is no single podcast measurement that measures the number of people that access a podcast across multiple distribution channels. This, and other elements of the saturated podcast market, presents many additional challenges.

CHALLENGES

In recent years podcasts have exploded in popularity. Though the technology has been available for decades, audiences were not regularly accessing podcasts until the advent of smartphones. One of the greatest hindrances to the growth of podcasting is the inability to discover content. The abundance of podcast platforms, and podcast productions, along with the plethora of apps for listening to podcasts, not only segment audiences and make it cumbersome to track listenership with accuracy but also often prove arduous for listeners to unexpectedly find new podcasts. However, in 2019, Google made it easier to immediately play podcasts through the search results (Porter, 2019).

Podcasts have not caught up in terms of accessibility in the same way that more traditional forms of media have, like with closed captioning on television. Not enough podcasters include transcripts in their podcasts, which could increase their SEO results and make the podcast content accessible to the hearing impaired. More standardization and accessibility features should be incorporated into future podcasting software.

Perhaps the greatest challenge to podcasting today is the saturated market. While podcasting started out in a grassroots kind of way, today, diverse voices struggle to break away from niche audiences. There are a few groups that have formed to discover podcasts, listen to them, and offer commentary, like the Podcast Brunch Club and the *New York Times* Podcast Club. With more podcasts being produced, media coverage of the podcasting industry has also increased. Newsletters like Nick Quah's *Hot Pod* as well as *Podnews* manage to keep up with the fast-moving industry. From a company perspective, more professional media organizations are beginning to see the lucrative opportunity of implementing podcasts as part of their business strategies.

HIGH DISRUPTION

The development of podcasting over the past few years has shown a high level of disruption. Perhaps some of the growth in podcasting can be attributed to how the radio industry ignored the possibilities to capitalize on podcasts. Not only could radio stations repurpose their content, but they could rent out their studios and other resources to allow community members to produce audio content. The lack of foresight parallels how the television industry disregarded social media in the early days as opposed to experimenting with the second screen.

The surge in interest in podcasting as a media economy creates unique opportunities for careers in the industry and structuring of departments dedicated to podcast production, including distribution and promotion. The disquiet, however, also threatens to overshadow small podcasters as the field teeters into the mainstream.

The high visibility of large podcast networks erupted in early 2019, particularly when Spotify, a music streaming company, purchased Gimlet Media "for more than 200 million dollars" (Johnson, 2019). Gimlet was an independent podcast company originally "focused on producing narrative podcasts" (Wikipedia, 2019b). The move solidified Spotify's interest in elevating the profile of their audio content. Not long after that, Luminary Podcasts, backed with $100 million in venture capital funding, launched an app (Carman, 2019). Luminary's strategy to set itself apart from other podcast companies and networks was that subscribers could access "exclusive content" from high-profile personalities like *The Daily Show*'s Trevor Noah (Carman, 2019).

LACK OF INTERACTIVITY

As discussed, another major challenge of podcasting is that it does not provide the same Web 2.0 interactive features as other forms of converged media. For example, the opportunity for synchronous dialogue between producers and audiences is not always an option with podcasts. This lack of interactivity makes it difficult to engage with an audience. But podcasters welcome this kind of disruption and have taken to social media for real-time "broadcasts," often using Facebook Live. While this does not contribute to the ratings of the podcast itself, it does increase audience engagement, which can attract audiences to the podcast's previous or future episodes.

Voice commands are evolving and may be a useful communication method for podcasters. As consumers gradually test out smart speakers, industry insiders predict that more opportunities will grow from this platform (Amplifi Media, 2018). As a matter of fact, NPR produced tutorials to help their audiences utilize a "new way to experience public radio" (NPR, 2019). However, not much is known about how successful these commands have proven to be.

DIFFICULT MEASUREMENT

Perhaps one ongoing challenge to the podcasting industry, and the bane of the podcast community, is the difficulty of measuring metrics. The inability to obtain accurate data about a podcast prohibits potential revenue streams because producers cannot provide a prospective advertiser the metrics to ensure that the podcast is a good fit for their target consumers. There have been numerous issues with inaccuracies of the iTunes charts. In 2018, Miller (2018), a tech website editor, stated, "Both the iTunes Podcast Chart and the charts in the Podcasts app display[ed] inaccurate rankings." Moving forward, Apple will have three separate apps instead of iTunes: Apple Music, Apple TV, and Apple Podcasts (Tambini & Lynch, 2019). Efforts to create newer and more accurate measurements for podcasting are expected and needed.

There are great opportunities for future podcasting professionals as podcasts continue to grow in popularity. The following action plan may help podcast practitioners balance the opportunities and challenges they will face in today's convergent media marketplace.

ACTION PLAN

1. Use strategic research, including niche marketing, in the development of your podcast.
2. Create a consistent schedule for producing podcasts to ensure a steady stream of content for yourself and your target audience.
3. Use new media, such as websites, blogs, and social media, to promote your podcast and engage audiences.

KEY TAKEAWAYS

1. Radio and podcasting share some similarities, such as they both follow the one-to-many communication approach.

2. Podcasting presents an opportunity to tap in to a niche market.
3. The podcasting community is growing globally with increasing audiences outside of the United States.
4. Podcasting networks are further disrupting the field and pushing it into the mainstream.
5. While accurate analytics are important, a consistent formula for collecting data does not exist.

CONCLUSION

This chapter examined the growth of podcasting and its impact on today's convergent media environment. Podcasts are an "old" yet emerging media form that can be an important tool for media managers when developing business strategies. However, many of the structural elements of podcasts present challenges for practitioners to directly engage audiences. Therefore, podcasts work best packaged with a larger communication marketing strategy. The shift to linear "one-to-many" broadcasts makes podcasts a unique star in today's digital environment.

Remediation theory suggests that emerging media content combines both transparent and hypermediacy elements. While podcasts tend to be a one-to-many medium that follows a linear transparent style, alternative social media tools can help promote and distribute content through niche marketing. Producers should also take advantage of websites, social media platforms, and blogs as they search for niche, segmented audiences that may be interested in their podcast authenticity.

The low cost of entry and ease of use make podcasting a very attractive emerging technology for media practitioners and managers. Emerging media technologies can be utilized to create a quality podcast with limited equipment, such as USB mics, laptops, and relatively inexpensive hosting platforms for content. Podcasters can use common audio editing software programs such as Adobe Audition or Audacity to produce their shows. However, prior to production, practitioners should consider creating a business plan that includes strategic research into the software platforms that can aid in recording as well as the ideal distribution platforms so that the podcasts will potentially reach the desired target audiences. A thorough understanding of your brand authenticity and niche audiences should help drive these decisions.

Media managers are able to monetize a podcast through many different forms of sponsorship. These include formal endorsements, nonendorsed advertising, baked-in advertising content, dynamic insertion, and others. Each of these come with many opportunities and challenges. Newer forms of advertising, such as crowdfunding, merchandise, and live shows, have also proved to be successful revenue streams. However, no uniform ratings or measurement tools exist to provide accurate data for podcasting. As such, gaining potential sponsors may prove difficult. Future software practitioners should focus on establishing such a uniform measurement so that podcasting practitioners will be better able to focus and sell their craft.

Podcasting is at a pivotal point where diverse voices and content are a part of a global spectrum that caters to a variety of audiences. Both listeners and content creators are weathering the storm of disruption to the field, which consists of threats of commodification by large podcast networks like Spotify and Luminary Podcasts and segregating content based on subscriptions. Steps have been taken to make podcasts more discoverable with Google search, though more could be done, such as using artificial intelligence to generate transcripts for podcasts. The use of innovative approaches to creating niche content for audiences remains a reason for the growth of podcasting. It is clear that the public's fascination with podcasts is just getting started, and it is exciting to explore the future of the podcasting industry.

It is clear that not every new media tool has a place in every industry's business model. Practitioners should carefully evaluate every hot emerging technology to ensure that it is a right fit for their brand, workforce, and audience. There are many opportunities and challenges associated with each. Podcasts present a great opportunity but require constant attention and reevaluation. Perhaps the most important element for a successful podcast is passion. If producers are not passionate about talk media, audiences will likely see through their lack of authenticity. No one should create a podcast simply to keep up with their competitors.

Hopefully, one highlight from this section is that just because a technology is new does not mean that everything about media is reinvented. Traditional theoretical foundations should still guide decision making. Podcasts are a great choice for practitioners who have something to say and have time to regularly research topics, produce content, and engage audiences. While media managers may be able to pick and choose the technologies that they implement in their strategy, the same is not true for the overall environment in which the content will be distributed.

Now, let us turn our attention toward the role of social media in helping media practitioners and managers to interact with audiences. In the next chapter, we will explore how a more interactive technology, specifically social networking, provides many unique challenges and opportunities for creating and managing media content.

REFERENCES

Abel, J. (2015). *Out on the wire: The storytelling secrets of the new masters of radio.* Broadway Books.

Amplifi Media. (2018, July 31). *Why so few people listen to podcasts on smart speakers—and how to fix that.* https://www.amplifimedia.com/blogstein/2018/7/31/07uqbp5hnrfb90iveqxz5ijuf4oank

Anderson, C. (2006). *The long tail: Why the future of business is selling less of more.* Hyperion.

Bolter, J. D., & Grusin, R. (2000). *Remediation: Understanding new media.* MIT Press.

Carman, A. (2019, April 22). *Podcast wars: $100 million startup Luminary launches Tuesday without reply all or the daily.* The Verge. https://www.theverge.com/2019/4/22/18510897/luminary-podcast-app-launch-the-daily-gimlet-media-spotify

Cridland, J. (2019, January 3). *The Joe Rogan experience podcast starts with 6 minutes of advertising* [Tweet]. Twitter. https://twitter.com/JamesCridland/status/1080751865594167297

Curry, A. (2019). *Adam Curry.* www.curry.com

Dalgic, T., & Leeuw, M. (1994). Niche marketing revisited: Concept, applications and some European cases. *European Journal of Marketing, 28*(4), 39–55.

Edison Research. (2019, April 5). *The podcast consumer 2019.* https://www.edisonresearch.com/the-podcast-consumer-2019

Johnson, E. (2019, February 7). *Full Q&A: Alex Blumberg and Matt Lieber explain why they sold Gimlet to Spotify.* Vox. https://www.vox.com/2019/2/7/18214941/alex-blumberg-matt-lieber-gimlet-spotify-deal-acquisition-peter-kafka-media-podcast-audio-interview

Join the Party Podcast. (2018, November 19). *We'll do it live: A DIY guide to podcast live shows.* https://bellocollective.com/well-do-it-live-248d07957cd4

Kaufer, K. (2018, August 1). A survival guide for podcast advertising. *Forbes.* https://www.forbes.com/sites/forbesagencycouncil/2018/08/01/a-survival-guide-for-podcast-advertising

McKinney, D., Dyck, J. L., & Luber, E. S. (2009). iTunes University and the classroom: Can podcasts replace professors? *Computers & Education, 52,* 617–623.

Miller, C. (2018, October 9). *Apple resolves issue that caused inaccurate podcast charts, likely due to manipulation.* 9 to 5 Mac. https://9to5mac.com/2018/10/09/itunes-podcast-charts-manipulation/

NPR. (2019). *How to listen to NPR on your smart speaker.* https://www.npr.org/about-npr/560809304/how-to-listen-to-npr-on-your-smart-speaker

Peiser, J. (2019a, March 6). Podcast growth is popping up in the U.S., survey shows. *New York Times.* https://www.nytimes.com/2019/03/06/business/media/podcast-growth.html

Peiser, J. (2019b, January 1). In the race for content, Hollywood is buying up hit podcasts. *New York Times.* https://www.nytimes.com/2019/01/01/business/media/podcasts-hollywood-tv-shows.html

Pew Research Center. (2018, July 12). *Trends and facts on audio and podcasts: State of the news media.* http://www.journalism.org/fact-sheet/audio-and-podcasting

Podcast Insights. (2020). *2020 podcast stats & facts.* https://www.podcastinsights.com/podcast-statistics

Porter, J. (2019, May 10). *Google now lists playable podcasts in search results.* Verge. https://www.theverge.com/2019/5/10/18564035/google-search-podcasts-ios-desktop-web-player

Spanos, B. (2018, February 2). "2 Dope Queens" Jessica Williams, Phoebe Robinson on taking HBO by storm. *Rolling Stone.* https://www.rollingstone.com/tv/tv-features/2-dope-queens-jessica-williams-phoebe-robinson-talk-bringing-podcast-to-hbo-206277

Statista. (2019). *U.S. podcasting industry.* https://www.statista.com/topics/3170/podcasting

Stratten, S. (2012). *UnMarketing: Stop marketing. Start engaging.* Wiley.

Tambini, O., & Lynch, G. (2019, June 3). *iTunes is dead, long live Apple Music, Apple TV and Apple Podcasts.* TechRadar. https://www.techradar.com/news/itunes-is-dead-long-live-apple-music-apple-tv-apple-podcasts

Wikipedia. (2019a). *2 Dope Queens.* https://en.wikipedia.org/w/index.php?title=2_Dope_Queens&oldid=899920637

Wikipedia. (2019b). *Gimlet Media.* https://en.wikipedia.org/w/index.php?title=Gimlet_Media&oldid=885389142

Wikipedia. (2019c). *WTF with Marc Maron.* https://en.wikipedia.org/w/index.php?title=WTF_with_Marc_Maron&oldid=899101194

CHAPTER 18

Social Media

L. Meghan Mahoney, West Chester University

LEARNING OBJECTIVES

1. Understand how media businesses are utilizing social media to engage audiences through more synchronous, personalized, and service-oriented features.
2. Apply theoretical concepts to a clear social media business strategy that supports business goals.
3. Identify the opportunities and challenges brought by technological development (e.g., social media) in media management and business.

Social media is a pervasive technology. Built on the ideological and technological foundations of Web 2.0 (Kaplan & Haenlein, 2010; Mahoney & Tang, 2016), social media proves a great tool for interacting and exchanging ideas with audiences. Media industries understand that social media is imperative to their survival in today's digital media marketplace. Media entertainment industries account for 63.2% of all posts across Facebook (Carranza, 2015). Advertisers spent more than $14 billion on paid media to reach consumers on social networks in 2018, finally surpassing spending on television advertising, and spent more than $89 billion in 2019 with a projected annual growth rate of 8.7% (Burstein, 2015; Krasniak, 2016; Zote, 2020). Despite the widespread adoption of social media technologies, media businesses are slow to share transparent information regarding their specific social media strategies and budgets (Gerth, 2015). The purpose of this chapter is to explore the role of social media in media management, including the many ways it has been integrated into business strategy.

Today, almost no media content is produced for a traditional "one-to-many" model that appeals to a mass audience via a single platform. Web 2.0 allows any participant to be a content creator by tagging, commenting, linking, and creating user-generated content (Mahoney & Tang, 2016). While media industries were once institutionalized gatekeepers of the public sphere, today they must navigate minimal control over content. Media managers must make strategic decisions about how to integrate Web 2.0 features to help accomplish organizational objectives regarding their brand (Montalvo, 2011).

Specifically, social media can be utilized in endless ways to increase interaction orientation. The technology can help gather information about media audiences, provide useful tools for customers, promote dialogue between stakeholders, or disseminate key messages about the media business. In addition, social media can help in the areas of brand awareness, reputation, strategy development, analytics, creativity, and collaboration. Still, media managers struggle to monetize and measure these functions. Companies know they must participate in these conversations, because failure to do so puts them at a competitive disadvantage (Friedrichsen, 2013), even if the rewards are unknown. While millions of users utilize social media for conversation, no one-size-fits-all business model exists to increase a media organization's return on investment. Creating long-term business strategy is difficult, as technologies and audience preferences are constantly changing. Let's examine how one such media company, Time Warner Cable, has integrated social media with their traditional services.

CASE STUDY

Time Warner, a global media conglomerate, has navigated social media in a variety of ways over the past decade. Each attempt highlights a different function of social media, some engaging in more interaction orientation with audiences than others. While the return on investment of each of these initiatives is uncertain, it is clear that Time Warner Cable is devoted to consistently adapting to the changing demands and expectations of social media.

In 2012, Time Warner launched Social One, a free application that cable audiences could use to manage all their social networking sites and messaging services (Castaneda, 2012). Here we see the media giant embracing social media by creating a portal to help audiences manage their own social media use, including email, social networking sites, and news consumption. This function also helps Time Warner gain increased information about its audience while also providing a needed service in its time. Yet, as more and more users gain access to smartphone application technology, the usefulness of such a cable application changed, forcing the company to reevaluate their social media strategy and initiatives. In order to survive, Time Warner must adapt in a convergent environment.

Time Warner then began utilizing social media as part of its customer service strategy. Time Warner's home television, Internet, and voice service provider, now called Spectrum, has its own Twitter account (@Ask_Spectrum, previously @TWC_Help). Here, social media is being utilized as a tool to engage in Web 2.0 interactions with consumers to improve customer relations. This social media integration provides Time Warner increased feedback about programmatic choices and the overall experiences of customers. While many of the tweets direct users to Time Warner's more traditional customer service tools (telephone and website), the Twitter account is an attempt to meet customers more immediately where they already hang out in the social sphere.

In addition to utilizing new media to drive audiences to traditional content, it is important for media businesses to create new products that meet changing audience demands. Time Warner has announced the launch of its new independent storytelling brand, Great Big Story. The company has invested $40 million into this video start-up (Smith, 2017). Great Big Story creates original digital content that is different from the entertainment content that audiences are used to from Time Warner. It produces stories aimed at urban millennial audiences. The narratives are much more synchronous, some even live, and less than three minutes in length. While the traditional demographics for the company indicate that the average consumer is 58 years of age (Smith, 2017), this application is clearly aimed at younger cord-cutting audiences. Great Big Story content is only distributed through social media platforms, a distribution channel appropriate for this niche market, something we will discuss in further detail below. Here we see how social media both aids and alters traditional media content.

Time Warner continues to integrate social media into its business strategy through a variety of outlets. Some attempts are to gain access to more information, some aim to interact and solicit feedback from audiences, while others change the content of distribution altogether. These changes brought by social media help engage audiences through more synchronous, personalized, and service-oriented features. Clearly social media is serving as a disruptor to the media market. However, not all marketing strategies are unfamiliar to companies. There are many fundamental rules of media management that hold true, regardless of the era. Most noteworthy is the emphasis on media audiences. Let's explore these traditional industry takeaways.

Something Old

During its inception, everything about social media seemed new. Social networking platforms were providing new experiences and ways for audiences to access, share, and create media messages that were not possible in a broadcast media environment. Traditional business models were disrupted as everyday consumers became cocreators of content. An estimated 2.65 billion people used social media worldwide in 2018 (Statista, 2020). Today, the "newness" of the technology has begun to fade, and practitioners are finally able to make marketing decisions based on longitudinal case studies and scholarship. While social media technologies have dramatically transformed the way marketers engage audiences, we are beginning to see that many traditional foundations of advertising and marketing still hold true in a social media environment. Let's explore some of these "old" practices, converged with a new technological application, below.

Perhaps the most basic underlying principle of effective marketing is to provide opportunities for consumers to engage brands. Traditionally, this communication was fostered through print, phone, or in-person communication. Today social media (Web 2.0) provides even greater opportunities for this communication to occur. Media managers must learn to adapt business strategies to better communicate with audiences, establish social media as a mutually beneficial service, and give up some control of their marketing content to better engage users. Perhaps the most fundamental role of social media management is that social media technologies should be used to empower and support the business (Wollan, Smith, & Zhou, 2010). How to achieve this objective through a strategic business procedure remains difficult to ascertain, especially if the business still holds antiquated assumptions about its audience. Before creating a new business model or strategy, media companies must accept fundamental social media truths. Specifically, they must adapt to niche markets and prioritize audience engagement as a value-positive endeavor.

NICHE MARKETING

It is widely understood that the digital age brought along a change in business models. While previously businesses could make large profits by offering a small number of products to audiences, the digital world offers a lower cost of distribution. Anderson (2006) dubbed the digital business model "the long tail," where a larger portion of the population exists in the niche tail of the probability distribution. Rather than focusing marketing efforts on reaching the largest audience possible, Anderson (2006) illustrates how businesses are actually able to increase profits by creating niche products and content better suited to a specialized audience. Here you see how today's businesses are able to profit from niche products, much like the audience behind Time Warner's Great Big Story, through low demand by using alternative distribution channels. For the most part, this focus on niche marketing continues to remain profitable for online businesses. More specifically, social media brought a fundamental shift in audience priority, where media businesses began prioritizing long-term relationships with fewer audiences rather than providing content to appeal to a homogenous mass (Stratten, 2012). The overall focus of audience engagement remains the same, but the strategy for increasing revenue has changed.

Consistent with the long tail model, audience segmentation research finds that businesses can make a higher return on investment by using social media to develop relationships with current satisfied customers rather than focusing marketing efforts on reaching new customers through push media strategies, such as cold calls (Mahoney & Tang, 2016). Media managers must shift from pushing generic content out to mass audiences to pulling audiences in through specialized quality content that is consistent with the lifestyle and values of a niche audience. Today's consumers make purchasing decisions based on their own trusted personal network over push advertising or experts in the field. The convergent media environment allows more niches to be created, offering opportunity for media business owners to enjoy a larger profit margin on their products and services (Totka, 2019).

While traditional word-of-mouth marketing is still a strong vehicle for behavior change, media managers are realizing the impact and appeal of blogger and influencer endorsements. Rather than turning to celebrities to promote products, media companies are seeing a high return when everyday trusted sources, with a high number of social media followers, promote a product. Influencer marketing is the fastest-growing online customer-acquisition method (Digital Marketing Institute, 2020). In fact, 16% of all Internet users aged 16 to 24 discovered new brands through these types of endorsements (Statista, 2017), with the social networking platform Instagram showing the highest engagement. We also see businesses sponsor popular niche YouTubers and bloggers to rate and promote products (Wu, 2016). This type of endorsement marketing provides an additional revenue opportunity for media practitioners.

Niche marketing promotion is successful partly due to its ability to harness users' specialized passions and values. Users are naturally likely to utilize social media to build connections and community around those niche interests. They have chosen to "opt-in" to content from these specialized niche influencers. As 70% of teens said that they trust influencers more than traditional celebrities (Digital Marketing Institute, 2020), today's media audiences are more trusting of experts that they have found themselves. Rather than media businesses "pushing" messages out to audiences, they should trust that audiences opt-in to messages related to their own niche passions. By taking time to delve into these niche communities and understand key influencers, businesses are able to make a higher return than they would through traditional homogenous mass advertising.

AUDIENCE ENGAGEMENT

As previously discussed, social media hinges on the ideological functions of Web 2.0. It is different from traditional media due to the ability for participants to exchange user ideas and to tag, comment on, and link to content (Mahoney & Tang, 2016). Just as the social media revolution fundamentally shifted audience value to a niche audience, it also prioritized online interactivity and engagement. Regardless of what new technologies emerge, media managers' emphasis on audience engagement has not gone away. Today, tracking audience engagement is easier and less costly than ever thanks to social media insights and big data.

Though social media success has always been difficult to measure, businesses understand that participation is crucial. Online customer interaction creates audience engagement and develops intimate bonds in enduring relational exchanges between content creators and consumers through a cocreated value (Prahalad & Ramaswamy, 2004; Sashi, 2012). Social media interactions will always prove a valuable entity, as active social media management drives more user-generated content (Miller & Tucker, 2012). The value of dyadic communication between media businesses and audiences is critical to a brand's success. Though there is no social media theoretical strategy for engaging customers, media companies see the disadvantage of not participating in the conversations (Friedrichsen, 2013; Sashi, 2012). Research demonstrates how considerable investments to control direct forms of consumer feedback have not proven an optimal strategy on social media platforms (Chen, Fay, & Wang, 2011; Miller & Tucker, 2012). By actively trying to shape and direct social media presence in a top-down manner, media businesses risk undermining their natural organic social media reach. Social media practitioners should work to engage as many media audiences as they are equipped to handle.

Social media insights also allow practitioners to view audience response in real time and make faster, more synchronous decisions. While there are many benefits of this efficiency, it can also lead to crisis communication if social media marketers are too fast to react or publish content. Just because social media allows faster communication with audiences, it is not always in the best interest of a business to react quickly. Employees must be trained and skilled at making strategic decisions that are consistent with the values and business model of their organization. Integrating traditional social media concepts throughout every business objective and strategy will prove lucrative for media managers.

While much has changed about the way businesses utilize social media to increase profits, more personalized audience engagement is not going anywhere. Once media managers and practitioners are in place to understand these foundational pieces of social media strategies, they can begin the process of reaching business objectives. These traditional "old" lessons of media management should continue to be integrated into social media strategy, and there are many "new" ways in which social media tools are set to influence the field.

Something New

Social media provide opportunities for many emerging business strategies. With the constantly changing landscape of social media, it can be difficult to keep up, let alone stay ahead of the curve through a long-term strategy. No one really knows what's to come, but in the immediate future, it appears as though shifting to a more service-oriented logic and integrating mobile technologies into social media strategies can provide key opportunities for the future of media businesses (Albarran & Moellinger, 2013). Let's explore how each of these new strategies influence media management today.

SHIFT FROM G-D LOGIC TO A MORE SERVICE-ORIENTED LOGIC

Social media permeates the lives of today's media users. More than 70% of audiences have developed a social habit, meaning they use social media more than several times in any given day (Smith & Anderson, 2018). It makes sense for media managers to capitalize on a technology that is such an integral part of their audiences' lives. The question really becomes, how do you make a meaningful impact through a technology that offers so much?

Social media allows for more synchronous, customized, and immediate information, transforming boundaries of time and space (Mahoney & Tang, 2016). Given the changing role of technologies, businesses recognize that the traditional top-down approach, where media businesses stood as the gatekeepers of information for audiences, is over. Instead, a shift in thinking has occurred, where media managers utilize social media technologies to cocreate business systems to best integrate consumer need. This perspective is only possible through a shift in logic (Zhang, Lu, & Kizildag, 2017).

Specifically, today's media businesses must shift from G-D logic to a more service-oriented logic. G-D logic is a business perspective where value is manufactured by the company and distributed to the market by exchanging goods for money. Even the idea that businesses should be utilizing social media in order to maximize a higher return on investment is G-D logic. If media companies continue to operate through this lens, they will miss out on innovation and future opportunities. Thus, there is a need for traditional media companies to make a shift in operating logic.

Service logic allows media companies and consumers to create value jointly. Here, media companies utilize skills to produce goods, and consumers use these products to improve their lives, creating a reciprocal and mutually beneficial relationship (Zhang et al., 2017). Customers become a critical piece of the media content production process. Technological development, such as social media, makes it possible to see the everyday lives of audiences and really shape and change products in order to better serve their needs. Service logic argues that the customer is the center of the value creation process and that a positive experience should be created solely by the customers. Only social media makes this type of logic possible. However, it does require media managers to be more flexible and give up control.

Social media allow audiences to simultaneously engage with many different points of contact at once, including people, objects, and physical environments (Verhoef et al., 2017). How audiences interact with these three areas should be considered in every business model in order to capitalize on service logic. In a social media environment, users are able to select the information that they want to receive, and producers have a better sense of the individual, not mass audience, that their content is reaching (Mahoney & Tang, 2016). Thus, it makes a perfect tool for customizing and personalizing brand content.

One example of a media business shifting from a traditional perspective to a more service-oriented approach is News Corp's 2013 acquisition of the social media platform Storyful (Lunden, 2013). Storyful is a social media news aggregator where everyday social media users become the news storytellers. Users can utilize the social media platform to upload news stories and events happening around their communities. While News Corp operated under G-D logic as the storytellers of news for decades, it began to see the value in meeting media audiences where they were and creating news content together. Storyful also works by monitoring other social media sites, such as Instagram and Facebook, for user-generated news stories. Users are able to share experiences about the people in their lives, objects that they regularly interact with, and their immediate physical environments. Storyful then verifies user content for authenticity using location-based services to help prevent the spread of misinformation. Utilizing social media and service-oriented logic to create and disseminate news content helps News Corp share news stories that are most important to their audiences and to reach remote communities that were difficult to cover before.

Storyful is just one example of how media businesses are utilizing social media to shift to a more service-oriented logic. There are many other ways in which social media allow for more synchronized, personalized, and pervasive content. While this provides many opportunities to learn more about audiences and increase returns, managers must also reconsider assumptions about audience value. Rather than simply using the technology to serve audiences through the same top-down, profit-for-profit's-sake mechanisms, social media should be utilized to cocreate innovative business systems that integrate consumer needs and improve their everyday experiences.

RISE OF PROFESSIONAL VIDEO CONTENT

One key manner in which media audiences are utilizing social media is through mobile video. In fact, the statistics are remarkable: one-third of all online activities are watching video; more video content is uploaded in 30 days than the major U.S. television networks have created in 30 years; 87% of online marketers have utilized video content for their companies (Lister, 2018). Mobile videos allow for shorter, more authentic projections of video content (Elder, 2016). We see brands leverage this type of content to better connect with viewers through tutorials, product launches, and exclusive behind-the-scenes footage. Mobile video has undergone many changes over the past 10 years, resulting in great promise in the future of successful media management. While there are many opportunities for mobile video to impact the media business, this section specifically focuses on new revenue shifts in the social media video giant YouTube. We will explore the ways in which mobile video shifted its business model to increase revenue for media companies and media practitioners alike.

Since its introduction in 2005, YouTube topped the market as the leading service for hosting free user-generated video content. While YouTube users were previously bound by desktop computers to view and share content, today they can stream and share from virtually anywhere. Initially, the free user business model that YouTube was built on did not produce much content. However, it proved a great disruptor to traditional media industries. While many users flocked to the social media platform, they met many challenges foreign to traditional broadcast media.

One such critical area is compensation for talents. By the late 2000s, YouTube was experimenting with revenue sources through AdSense, with a portion of advertising profit going to the uploader, later to become the YouTube Partner Program (Mahoney, 2019; O'Neill, 2013). Once compensation was introduced, competition between viewers increased, naturally raising the quality of user-generated content. Initially, YouTube promoted content based on viewership numbers, highlighting videos with the largest audience. However, these weren't always the type of videos that YouTube wished to promote. By 2010, YouTube changed its algorithm to promote "featured" videos uploaded from preselected and established YouTube channels (Wedmore, 2012). This shift allows YouTube a little more control over the type of content that viewers receive. Specifically, it allows the social media platform to promote live streaming videos over heavily edited video submissions. While many established YouTube artists felt a decline in their viewership, they quickly adapted to the new opportunities, providing a very different type of video product.

YouTube has found great success in promoting user-generated live mobile broadcast videos as well as live videos from professional cable networks. In March 2010, the platform began competing with online streaming giants Hulu and Netflix (Weintraub, 2010). It became the first platform to stream a free worldwide sporting event of the Indian Premiere Cricket League. YouTube no longer exists as just a digital space for hosting user-generated content; it now competes with the most professional and popular content providers and distributors around the world. Today, this service hinges on mobile broadcast technology, as YouTube TV offers live, local broadcast feeds for media businesses and consumers alike (Mahoney, 2019; Shieber, 2017). Media managers must encourage audiences to create and share content suitable for mobile video distribution.

Social media integrating with mobile technologies will greatly influence today's and tomorrow's media management practices. We will talk more about mobile technologies in the next chapter. Specifically, social media users are looking for more authentic content that speaks to their everyday lives. The days of media managers curating carefully edited projections that have undergone a lengthy vetting system are over. Today's media managers must make immediate decisions about an increased number of pieces that are shorter in length, produced through an amateur synchronous production process. As our audiences have embraced and integrated social media as part of their lives, let us turn attention to the opportunities and challenges brought by the technology.

Opportunities and Challenges

This chapter has explored many ways in which social media has proven a great disruptor to media management in today's convergent environment. It has forced media companies to give up control of their position as all-knowing entities and prioritize a more service-logic approach to business. These fundamental shifts in perspective provide many opportunities and challenges to media management.

OPPORTUNITIES

Social media revolutionize the way businesses attempt to reach their objectives. If your business is still operating under the same business model and strategy as it did 20 years ago, it is time to implement new processes, specifically cross-organizational processes with better integration across major departments (Wollan, Smith, & Zhou, 2010). Using this strategy can help media practitioners manage standards, implement budgets, develop partnerships, and/or improve relationships. When integrating social media into traditional media business practices to hit on any of these goals, it is recommended to follow the business objective process.

First, media managers should identify, prioritize, and plan investments (Wollan, Smith, & Zhou, 2010). By focusing on investments in the early stages, media managers will be better able to track efforts and benefits. Second, media managers should focus on empowerment and support. Here, managers will establish and manage company standards, develop shared service budgets with great transparency, manage social media partners, and measure and improve the overall experience.

While the business objective process provides an important guideline for creating effective social media strategies, it will only prove effective if media businesses engage in fundamental shifts in the way they value their audience. Specifically, we see the importance of niche marketing and audience engagement. These two key concepts remain just as critical today as they were at the beginning of the social media revolution and should be integrated at every level of the business objective process.

By focusing on social media in terms of value creation in business, practitioners will be better able to serve audiences and satisfy their needs (Sashi, 2012). Substantial research illustrates the benefits of social media marketing on consumers' attitudes toward a brand. Specifically, social media marketers are able to leverage the interactive orientation of social media, and the data it creates, to find opportunities across three common functions: opinion mining, targeted advertising, and customer relations (Jacobson, Gruzd, & Hernández-García, 2019). It is important for media managers to leverage each.

Opinion mining, often referred to as sentiment analysis, involves a natural language processing task that aims to track the public's mood regarding a particular product or service (Qazi, Raj, Tahir, Cambria, & Syed, 2014). Marketers are able to use opinion mining to monitor and analyze customer-generated opinions about their business as well as their competitors. Integrating opinion mining into a company's business strategy results in substantial performance growth, especially as a means to compare performance across a genre of brands (He, Wu, Yan, Akula, & Shen, 2015). For example, researchers examined large pizza chains' use of social media to effectively integrate opinion mining into their social media strategy (He, Zha, & Li, 2013). Results illustrate how Domino's Pizza, with a significantly smaller market share than Pizza Hut, was able to more effectively utilize social media opinion mining to provide additional customer service and consumer communication. As a result, Domino's Pizza was able to listen to feedback regarding price change, tastes, and new recipes to increase profit. Here it is easy to see how social media creates competitive intelligence to provide useful information regarding brand promotion, sales data, and consumer sentiments.

Social media data also provide an opportunity for companies to engage in targeted advertising with customers. Targeted advertising allows marketers to self-select segmented criteria before disseminating messages across distinguished audiences. When users sign up for a social media platform, they are generally required to provide information such as their name, email, gender, date of birth, and geographic region. Through subsequent social media interactions, they also leave digital footprints regarding the type of content that they wish and do not wish to engage. Media managers are able to use this database of information to more effectively reach specialized segments of their target audience. Research indicates that narrowly targeted ads are clicked as much as 670% more than regular advertisements (Cohen, 2013). Using social media to engage in targeted advertising allows the opportunity for brands to speak more directly to the interests and preferences of their target audience.

Social media technologies have become the focal point of emerging customer relations strategies. Specifically, they are able to improve external communication with current and potential consumers. Social media should be utilized to help facilitate two-way interaction between individual customers and the company about every aspect of their business, including prepurchase, during purchase, and the postpurchase experience (Gordon, 2013). Harnessing social media in this capacity will not only help a company reduce the cost of customer interaction but also increase the effectiveness of the communication and improve the customer experience. Undoubtedly, social media technologies make the business process easier and more forward thinking and bring in a greater return. However, integrating social media into traditional media business practices is not without some key challenges.

CHALLENGES

It is amazing to think how just five years after the emergence of Facebook and Twitter, Citadel Broadcasting Corporation, the largest public radio company in the United States, was minimally involved in social media. Other major media companies, such as News Corporation, Disney, and Time Warner, were still experimenting with social media with revenue-producing success (Albarran & Moellinger, 2013). Though media industries are often thought of as early technological adapters, social media adoption has proven very challenging.

While it would prove impossible to list all the challenges that the social media revolution has brought to media management practices, there are consistencies that leaders must focus on in order to best move forward. Specifically, media managers must understand the ways in which audiences are changing and how these changes produce an increase in content expectations.

One key challenge brought by social media is the ways in which audiences have evolved (Chan-Olmsted, 2006). In the past, the opportunity to find, produce, and distribute media content was only open to a select few. As social media tools got smarter through focused and personalized tags, lists, and filters, individuals became empowered (Friedrichsen & Muhl-Benninghaus, 2013). This changes audience expectations. Today's media audiences expect to become cocreators in business narratives and processes. Thus, media practitioners must provide both an emotional and functional process for their audiences (Wollan et al., 2010). This shift automatically carries inherent risk for those media managers who wish to participate and hold tight controls.

As social media popularity grows and audiences become more empowered, content management can become overwhelming. The more a media practitioner can do to understand and market through audiences' existing media repertoire, the more success they will find (Mahoney & Tang, 2016). Previously, businesses were advised to meet audiences on their favorite social media sites rather than spend money developing new media content. However, today we are finding that social media audiences still seek specialized knowledge for digital products (Friedrichsen & Muhl-Benninghaus, 2013). It is not enough just to engage conversation on your target audience's favorite social networking sites. Providing digitized content through multiple distribution outlets is an integral piece of the new media value chain (Chan-Olmsted, 2006). Secondary specialized portals should also be developed to help audiences learn about and engage with your product. This creates an enormous amount of content and workload across multiple distribution channels.

Finally, and perhaps most pressing, the most difficult challenge of social media management is its unpredictable nature. There is no single effective business model that can be applied uniformly across all media businesses (Albarran & Moellinger, 2013). Research demonstrates that much of the monetization of social media is still happening through more traditional means, such as advertising, subscription, and purchase offers. While social media is more than 15 years old, academic study of the phenomenon is still in its infancy. The lack of theoretical grounding is a great challenge for practitioners. Without a solid educational grounding, the field will continue to guess until we can edify the core competencies of social media management to produce effective media managers (Montalvo, 2011). The action plan below is a starting point for media managers to examine audiences and engage content in today's convergent media environments.

ACTION PLAN

1. Use empirical research to determine the needs of a target, niche audience. This can be done utilizing social media analytical metrics or through more traditional market methods, such as survey or focus group research.
2. Integrate these findings into the business objective process. Remember to focus on investments first and the many ways in which social media can be utilized to empower and support the business and your niche audience.
3. Constantly engage in dyadic communication with audiences to keep a pulse on brand service. Consistent monitoring and evaluation are necessary, as the social

media field changes rapidly. Revolutionize products and customer service often, and don't be afraid to take risks.

KEY TAKEAWAYS

1. Social media hold many opportunities for media businesses to increase engagement and profits. However, little theoretical strategy or consistency exists across today's digital environment.
2. Social media is being used to interact with media audiences, solicit user-generated content, as well as disseminate key information to audiences.
3. The future of social media management is mobile, as audiences are interested in interacting with content that is more synchronous, personalized, and service oriented.
4. Media managers should continue to prioritize niche markets. Audiences opt-in to messages from smaller organizations with greater trust than they do from larger distribution channels.
5. Without a clear strategy for how to engage audiences, this process can become ineffective. The media organization's business strategies should be rewritten to meet the demands of a digital age. The focus on new strategies should include ways to empower and support the business and its audiences.
6. Social media management is still in its infancy. More proactive education is needed to edify the core competencies of social media management to produce effective media managers.

CONCLUSION

This chapter explored the role of social media in impacting the field of media management and business. Given its Web 2.0 foundation in structure, social media technologies can be utilized in many ways to increase interactions between media businesses and consumers. This increased communication results in better trust, experience, and results for marketing efforts. It is imperative that media managers effectively integrate social media into existing business strategies to better reach target audiences. While many businesses may have been slow to adapt to these changes, it would be hard to find a successful brand that does not utilize social media to engage customers today. This chapter serves as a resource in explaining the various ways in which niche markets and audience engagement have retained, and in some cases even surpassed, their value. Additionally, it aims to offer future practitioners theoretically based strategies for achieving success in a convergent era.

Social media have revamped the customer service experience. The technology has made it easier for media managers to engage in a service logic, where audiences become cocreators of innovative business systems rather than simply consumers of products. Today's consumers expect immediate access to customer service while researching, purchasing, and utilizing products. Flipping the business model from a top-down experience to a more collaborative participatory relationship reaps many benefits for consumers and businesses alike.

Media audiences are looking for more authentic and less edited content through various aspects of social media content today. Authentic consumer reviews and ratings prove more useful to audiences than select customer testimonies on corporate websites. Additionally, consumers are increasingly relying on location-based services and mobile video broadcasts in their decision-making process. Therefore, media managers must develop strategies for working with more synchronous, less edited, and a higher volume of production pieces.

We see this trend across much of the user-generated content of social media. Specifically, YouTube has found great success in promoting user-generated live mobile broadcast videos. Many social media influencers utilize the platform to create reviews of products. While these efforts served the platform for much of the past decade, many audience expectations and needs have changed. Today, in addition to hosting free user-generated amateur video, the platform also competes with more professional online streaming giants such as Hulu and Netflix. By constantly adapting to user expectations, needs, and competing businesses, YouTube has been able to remain a giant in the social media sector.

There are many benefits for businesses who engage audiences and give up some control over their business to better integrate audience experience. By shifting the focus of social media to adapt niche markets and prioritize audience engagement as a value-positive endeavor, managers will find greater success in today's ever-evolving media marketplace. This loss of control can be scary for media managers, but the result is a stronger return on investment when implemented effectively.

Foundational lessons of social media business models should be incorporated through the business objective process (Wollan et al., 2010). Here, media businesses redesign their strategies to achieve business objectives and empower and support the business. This requires research and strategic thinking at every stage of the business process. Media managers must use communication research to identify, prioritize, and plan investments. By focusing on empowerment to support and establish company standards, service budgets will be devised with greater transparency, new social media partnerships will be formed, and more participatory measurements will help improve the overall experience. A new social media business process helps guide media organizations through future technological changes.

These changes allow media managers to better leverage the interactive orientation of social media to find many new opportunities for increased revenue. Specifically, social media offer many affordances in the data they create across three common functions: opinion mining, targeted advertising, and customer relations. Opinion mining grants managers more real-time access to consumer opinions across every stage of the business process. It also allows brands to compare these sentiments with competitors. Marketers are able to use targeted advertising to better reach and engage customers based on demographic, psychographic, and digital engagement criteria. Social media should utilize the interaction-orientation nature of social media to serve customers more efficiently and effectively. Tips for harnessing big data and social media analytics will be discussed further in chapter 22, "Big Data and Entrepreneurship."

Though this chapter provides a framework for incorporating social media into media management, the process is not without challenges. Audiences and workloads are constantly changing. Digital communication exists in a global 24/7 universe, and it is necessary for businesses to integrate these consummate consumer expectations into their business strategy. It is impossible to predict the future of social media, but a redesigned service-logic business strategy should help. Additionally, a new framework for social media education will help guide future media managers and practitioners, something discussed more in chapter 24, "Looking Forward." Future practitioners must constantly evolve with the changing expectations of social media and the convergent media environment.

Overall, we have come a long way since the advent of social media. Media organizations may have been slow to embrace social media technologies, but the tool has proven beneficial to both businesses and audiences alike. Practitioners must make strategic decisions about how to integrate Web 2.0 features, but these decisions no longer need to be made without research and data. By accepting the service logic of a cocreating social media audience, the future of social media management is promising, particularly when integrated with mobile technologies. Increasingly, social media users are utilizing mobile media in order to access these platforms. Popular social media applications such as Instagram and Snapchat have even sustained themselves through mobile-only experiences. The rapid diffusion of mobile broadband has become the premiere platform for distributing social media content and is not expected to wane. In the next chapter, we will examine how mobile technologies influence media management and strategies for mobile content producers.

REFERENCES

Albarran, A., & Moellinger, T. (2013). Traditional media companies in the U.S. and social media: What's the strategy? In M. Friedrichsen & W. Muhl-Benninghaus (Eds.), *Handbook of social media management: Value chain and business models in changing media markets* (pp. 9–24). Springer.

Anderson, C. (2006). *The long tail: Why the future of business is selling less of more.* Hyperion.

Burstein, D. (2015, July 28). *Ecommerce chart.* Marketing Sherpa. https://www.marketingsherpa.com/article/chart/online-shopping-behaviors-based-on-age

Carranza, A. (2015, June 16). *7 industries that benefit most from social media.* Social Media Today. https://www.socialmediatoday.com/social-networks/anthonycarranza/2015-06-16/7-industries-benefit-most-social-media

Castaneda, J. (2012, October 24). *Time Warner Cable launches Social One, a new way to enjoy social networks and messages better.* AOL. https://www.aol.com/2012/10/24/time-warner-cable-launches-social-one-a-new-way-to

Chan-Olmsted, S. (2006). *Competitive strategy for media firms: Strategic and brand management in changing media markets.* Routledge.

Chen, Y., Fay, S., & Wang, Q. (2011). The role of marketing in social media: How online consumer reviews evolve. *Journal of Interactive Marketing, 25,* 85–94.

Cohen, N. (2013). Labor online: Social media, audiences, and advertising. In M. P. McAllister & E. West, *The Routledge companion to advertising and promotional culture* (177–191). Routledge.

Digital Marketing Institute. (2020). *20 influencer marketer statistics that will surprise you.* https://digitalmarketinginstitute.com/en-us/blog/20-influencer-marketing-statistics-that-will-surprise-you

Elder, R. (2016, December 29). YouTube stars experience a sharp drop in viewership. *Business Insider.* http://www.businessinsider.com/youtube-stars-viewership-is-dropping-2016-12

Friedrichsen, M. (2013). Social media in companies: Integrated approach for social media strategy. In M. Friedrichsen & W. Muhl-Benninghaus (Eds.), *Handbook of social media management: Value chain and business models in changing media markets* (pp. 25–47). Springer.

Friedrichsen, M., & Muhl-Benninghaus, W. (2013). *Handbook of social media management: Value chain and business models in changing media markets*. Springer.
Gerth, B. (2015, February 26). *How Comcast is leveraging social media*. Smart Insights. https://www.smartinsights.com/social-media-marketing/social-media-governance/socialmedia-tools-review
Gordon, I. (2013). *Managing the new customer relationship strategies to engage the social customer and build lasting value*. Wiley.
He, W., Wu, H., Yan, G., Akula, V., & Shen, J. (2015). A novel social media competitive analytics framework with sentiment benchmarks. *Information & Management, 52*, 801–812.
He, W., Zha, S., & Li, L. (2013). Social media competitive analysis and text mining: A case study in the pizza industry. *International Journal of Information Management, 33*, 464–472.
Jacobson, J., Gruzd, A., & Hernández-García, Á. (2019). Social media marketing: Who is watching the watchers? *Journal of Retailing and Consumer Services, 53*, 1–12.
Kaplan, A. M., & Haenlein, M. (2010). Users of the world, unite! The challenges and opportunities of social media. *Business Horizons, 53*, 59–68.
Krasniak, M. (2016, October 12). *Social ad spending surpasses television*. Social Media Examiner. https://www.socialmediaexaminer.com/social-ad-spend-surpasses-television-new-research
Lister, M. (2018). *37 staggering video marketing statistics for 2018*. Word Stream. https://www.wordstream.com/blog/ws/2017/03/08/video-marketing-statistics
Lunden, I. (2013, December 20). *News Corp pays $25M for Storyful, which digs up and verifies news from social sites like Twitter and Instagram*. TechCrunch. https://techcrunch.com/2013/12/20/news-corp-buys-storyful-for-25m-to-dig-up-verified-news-from-social-media-sites-like-twitter-and-instagram
Mahoney, L. M. (2019). YouTube and advertising. In *Pop culture universe: Icons, idols, ideas*. ABC-CLIO. https://popculture.abc-clio.com
Mahoney, L. M., & Tang, T. (2016). *Strategic social media: From marketing to social change*. Wiley.
Miller, A., & Tucker, C. (2012). Active social media management: The case of health care. *Information Systems Research, 24*, 52–70.
Montalvo, R. (2011). Social media management. *International Journal of Management & Information Systems, 15*, 91–96.
O'Neill, M. (2013, February 6). *Digital*. Ad Week. http://www.adweek.com/digital/infographic-timeline-youtube
Prahalad, C., & Ramaswamy, V. (2004). Co-creation experiences: The next practice in value creation. *Journal of Interactive Marketing, 18*(3), 5–14.
Qazi, A., Raj, R., Tahir, M., Cambria, E., & Syed, K. (2014). Enhancing business intelligence by means of suggestive reviews. *The Scientific World Journal, 2014*, 879323.
Sashi, C. (2012). Customer engagement, buyer-seller relationships, and social media. *Management Decision, 50*, 253–272.
Shieber, J. (2017, February 28). *YouTube unveils YouTube TV, its live TV streaming service*. TechCrunch. https://techcrunch.com/2017/02/28/youtube-launches-youtube-tv-its-live-tv-streaming-service
Smith, A., & Anderson, M. (2018, March 1). *Social media use in 2018*. Pew Research Center. http://www.pewinternet.org/2018/03/01/social-media-use-in-2018
Smith, G. (2017, June 20). CNN to invest $40 million dollars in its video startup. *Bloomberg Technology*. https://www.bloomberg.com/news/articles/2017-06-20/cnn-to-invest-40-million-in-its-video-startup-great-big-story
Statista. (2017, July 22). *Share of worldwide Internet users who find brands or products through celebrity endorsements as of 1st quarter 2017, by age group*. https://www.statista.com/statistics/407838/celebrity-endorsement-brand-discovery-online-age
Statista. (2020, July 15). *Number of social media users worldwide from 2010 to 2021*. https://www.statista.com/statistics/278414/number-of-worldwide-social-network-users
Stratten, S. (2012). *UnMarketing: Stop marketing. Start engaging*. Wiley.
Totka, M. (2019, February 9). There are more niche markets than ever and that's a great opportunity for your business. *Forbes*. https://www.forbes.com/sites/allbusiness/2019/02/09/niche-markets-small-business-opportunity

Verhoef, P. C., Stephen, A. T., Kannan, P. K., Luo, X., Abhishek, V., Andrews, M., . . . & Hu, M. M. (2017). Consumer connectivity in a complex, technology-enabled, and mobile-oriented world with smart products. *Journal of Interactive Marketing, 40,* 1–8.

Wedmore, J. (2012, January 3). *3 new YouTube changes and what they mean for business.* Social Media Examiner. https://www.socialmediaexaminer.com/3-new-youtube-changes-and-what-they-mean-for-businesses

Weintraub, S. (2010, September 13). Bye-bye TV? YouTube debuts live streaming. *Fortune.* http://fortune.com/2010/09/13/bye-bye-tv-youtube-debuts-live-streaming

Wollan, R., Smith, N., & Zhou, C. (2010). *The social media management handbook: Everything you need to know to get social media working in your business.* Wiley.

Wu, K. (2016). YouTube marketing: Legality of sponsorship and endorsements in advertising. *Journal of Business & Ethics, 22,* 1–59.

Zhang, T., Lu, C., & Kizildag, M. (2017). Engaging generation Y to co-create through mobile technology. *International Journal of Electronic Commerce, 21,* 489–516.

Zote, J. (2020). *55 critical social media statistics to fuel your 2020 strategy.* Sprout Social. https://sproutsocial.com/insights/social-media-statistics

CHAPTER 19

Mobile Media

Xiaoquan Zhang, University of North Texas
Rob Upchurch, University of North Texas
Buddy Love, University of North Texas

LEARNING OBJECTIVES

1. Identify the trends of mobile device use and mobile broadband diffusion across the world.
2. Provide a theoretical explanation for the diffusion of mobile devices and mobile broadband.
3. Understand the patterns of mobile media consumption and the characteristics of mobile media consumers.
4. Analyze mobile media consumption and mobile media consumers from a time budget perspective.
5. Develop strategies for mobile technology managers and mobile content providers.

Mobile media has been diffused rapidly across the world over the past decades, especially through mobile phones and tablets. There were 5.15 billion mobile phone users globally in 2019, constituting 66.6% of the world population (Bankmycell, n.d.). Smartphones, a new generation of the mobile phone, have diffused even faster than their predecessors. The number of smartphone users worldwide reached 3.3 billion in 2019, constituting 42.5% of the world population (Bankmycell, n.d.). Likewise, tablets, such as the iPad and Samsung Galaxy Tab, have also diffused rapidly across the world. Around 1.23 billion people in the world used a tablet in 2019 (Ejectejecteject, 2019). This number is expected to rise to 1.28 billion by 2021 (Statista, 2019a).

On the other hand, as figure 19.1 illustrates, mobile media penetrates differently across different countries. Developed countries have higher mobile phone penetration rates than developing countries. The gap in mobile media penetration rates between different countries is called the global mobile divide, which is one of the essential dimensions of the digital divide (Zhang, 2017). Since the adoption rate of mobile media has

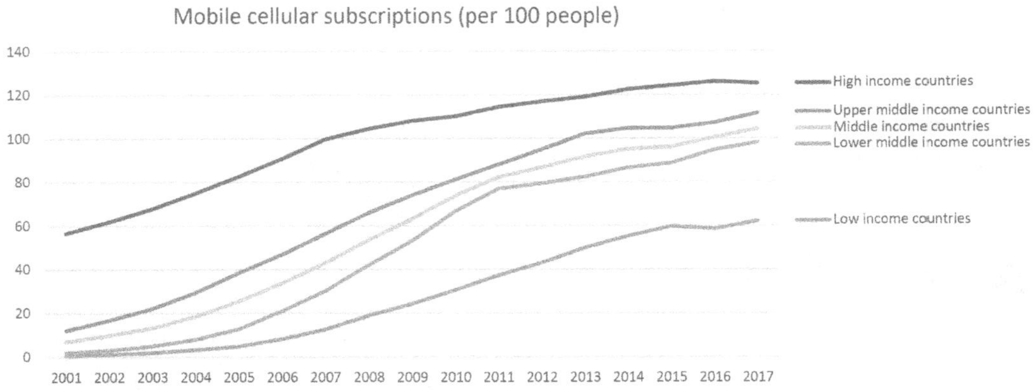

FIGURE 19.1. The Diffusion of Mobile Phones in Different Groups of Countries
Source: The World Bank, n.d.

accelerated quickly in many low-income countries, many scholars argue that mobile media has the potential to bridge the digital divide across the globe (e.g., Mir & Dangerfield, 2013; Srinuan, Srinuan, & Bohlin, 2012). The digital divide is coherently connected with media industries as digital media platforms, such as social media and streaming media, are based on broadband Internet services. Additionally, broadband drives various traditional media platforms, such as print and broadcast, to converge into digital media platforms. Media managers must be aware of these trends and understand how to manage various media assets in this convergent media environment. Moreover, there are many people around the world without access to these broadband services. Media managers, especially managers of transnational media corporations, should take note of the mobile divide when developing their mobile media strategies.

Recently, mobile media devices have become the primary devices for Internet access. People spend much more time on mobile Internet than desktop Internet. According to Zenith (2019), 71% of Internet use was via mobile in 2017. The average time spent on mobile Internet worldwide was around 122 minutes per day in 2019, while the average time spent on desktop Internet was only 35 minutes per day. These projections are expected to continue to rise.

The fast expansion of mobile Internet consumption is attributed to the rapid diffusion of mobile broadband around the world. Advanced Internet applications require high-speed Internet. For example, high-resolution video conferencing (5760×1080 resolution) needs 15 mbps for both downstream and upstream, and high-definition digital television (1440×1080 interlaced) requires 15 mbps for downstream speed (Ezell, Atkinson, Castro, & Ou, 2009). Papacharissi and Zaks (2006) define broadband as "all technologies that enable the high-speed transfer of multimedia and high bandwidth information" (p. 65). As an alternative to fixed broadband, mobile broadband has the advantages of low price, high mobility, compatibility, and quality of service (International Telecommunication Union, 2019; Molleryd, Markendahl, & Makitalo, 2009; Organisation for Economic Co-operation and Development, 2009).

Given these advantages, mobile broadband has diffused much faster than fixed broadband. According to the International Telecommunication Union (2019), the mobile broadband penetration rate worldwide reached 49.4% in 2016, while the fixed

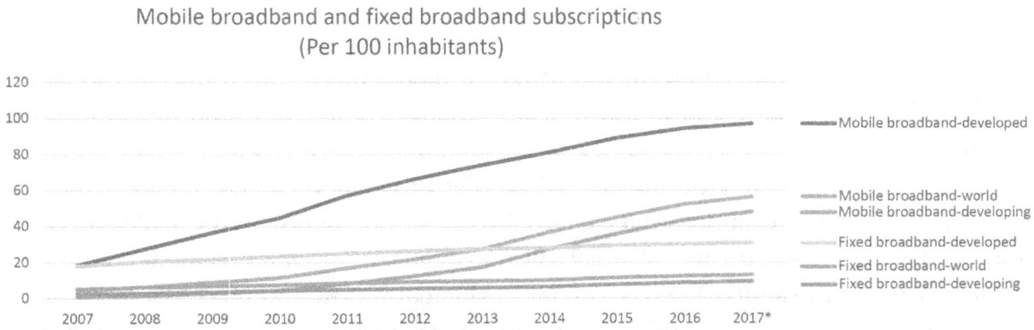

FIGURE 19.2. The Diffusion of Mobile Broadband and Fixed Broadband

Source: International Telecommunications Union, 2019.

*Estimate

broadband penetration rate worldwide was only 11.9%. It is important to note that the mobile divide also exists in the area of mobile broadband. The average mobile broadband penetration rate in developed countries was 90.3% in 2016, while the penetration rate was 40.9% in developing countries (International Telecommunication Union, 2019). Figure 19.2 illustrates the mobile broadband divide between developed countries and developing countries.

As such, it is important for mobile media companies to be aware of global and cultural nuances when developing marketing strategies across regions. Let's now explore how the next generation of mobile communication, the 5G network, developed differently in various locations.

CASE STUDY

Huawei, a mobile company based in China, launched the world's first 5G network with Deutche Telecom in Germany on September 1, 2017 (Lin, 2017). ZTE has also built its leading role in mobile communication and successfully completed tests with a speed of more than 1 gbps in Malaysia, Belgium, Hungary, and Austria (Zheng & Liu, 2019). 5G is 100 times faster than 4G technology and spurs a new wave of broadband innovation. The frugal innovations developed by Huawei and ZTE in 5G make this advanced technology affordable for many people in developing countries as well as in developed countries.

The development of 5G networks in these countries brings huge opportunities for developing and adopting new mobile applications in multiple industries/areas, such as automotive, data analytics, manufacture, health care, and smart cities (IEEE, 2017). Media industries will also see more opportunities in developing new media products and services based on 5G networks. Practitioners navigating these various mobile divides must critically assess traditional and new media markets.

This chapter discusses the theories that help explain the phenomenon of mobile media communication. Three traditional theories (diffusion of innovation, technology acceptance model, and consumption model) and two new theoretical approaches (frugal innovation and time budget) are discussed along with their implications for mobile media managers. Future trends in mobile communication and related opportunities and challenges are also identified.

Something Old

The diffusion of mobile media and mobile broadband has had a significant impact on digital media and telecommunication industries, with managerial implications for digital media and telecommunication companies. It is important to consider the many ways in which mobile media and mobile broadband diffuse within a society and the motivations for individuals to adopt these technologies. Traditional theoretical approaches, such as diffusion of innovation, technology acceptance model, and consumption model, examine the determinants of mobile media and mobile broadband diffusion. These foundational theories may aid media managers as they determine their future mobile strategies.

Diffusion of innovation theory (DIT) explains the diffusion process of new ideas, products, and technologies by providing a framework that consists of five major characteristics of innovations: relative advantage, compatibility, complexity, trialability, and observability (Rogers, 2003). DIT suggests that these characteristics determine the diffusion rates of innovations. Other factors such as communication channels and the characteristics of social systems are also believed to influence diffusion rates (Rogers, 2003).

As DIT explains how mobile media diffuses in a society and the different diffusion patterns in different societies, it helps media managers to understand the growth of mobile markets and different growth patterns in different societies. Mobile media has become the primary platform for Internet usage (Zenith, 2019), and, therefore, it has become the major distribution platform for digital media content and the major platform on which the business model of telecommunications companies is built. Understanding the patterns of mobile diffusions in different markets and their underlying driving forces is crucial for digital media and telecommunications managers to develop their product and marketing strategies.

The technology acceptance model (TAM), proposed by Davis (1989), is another theoretical approach that explains the diffusion process of mobile phones. TAM suggests that perceived ease of use and perceived usefulness influence the adoption intention for innovations. Perceived ease of use refers to the amount of effort required to use the innovations, while perceived usefulness identifies the subjective evaluation of the utility of the innovations. As TAM explains the psychological factors that drive people's mobile media adoption intention, it helps digital media and telecommunications managers understand why consumers accept or reject mobile media and thus develop their product and marketing strategies accordingly.

DIT and TAM have been applied to study mobile media diffusion in China, Thailand, India, Vietnam, and Peru, along with many other countries (see Gupta & Jain, 2012; Hwang, Cho, & Long, 2009; Loo & Ngan, 2012; Srinuan, Srinuan, & Bohlin, 2012; Yamakawa, Rees, Salas, & Alva, 2013). Many of these studies state that the mobile phone has become the platform for Internet access and hence has bridged the digital divide between developed countries and developing countries (e.g., Kalba, 2008; Loo & Ngan, 2012; Mir & Dangerfield, 2013; Prieger, 2013; Srinuan et al., 2012). DIT and TAM have also been used to investigate the adoption of tablets. For example, Kim and Sim (2012) found that playability, cost, functionality, and complexity significantly predict the adoption of tablets. Lee, Lee, and Chan-Olmsted (2017) also demonstrate that tablet price, income level, and social network penetration influence the tablet diffusion rate across countries.

While DIT and TAM provide important insights in understanding the diffusion of mobile media, they have both neglected, at least to some extent, the economic factors that influence the diffusion process. Mobile media devices are commodities that are sold in markets. Consumers need to pay for the mobile devices and data services to use them. It is important for media managers to be aware that mobile media adoption and use are consumption behaviors. The consumption model can help them achieve a more comprehensive understanding of mobile media consumption behaviors.

The consumption model suggests that consumers make rational choices so that they maximize their utility within their budgetary constraints. Zhang (2017) developed a new theoretical model that explains the adoption of mobile media in the marketplace. This model demonstrates that the perceived expenditure (i.e., the combination of the prices of mobile devices, data services, and apps) is determined by income budget, which is the constraint of people's consumption decisions. In addition, this model suggests that other factors, such as technological affordance, social influence, and substitutions, also influence the perceived usefulness of mobile media.

Globally, mobile phone penetration is positively correlated with income (e.g., Chu, Wu, Kao, & Yen, 2009; Frank, 2012; Kalba, 2008; Lee & Cho, 2007). Market size is another economic variable that has been investigated as it relates to network externality and economics of scale (e.g., Gruber & Koutroumpis, 2011; Thompson & Garbacz, 2007). Population and demographics are also considered as major determinants that can influence infrastructure cost, network externality, and adoption behaviors (e.g., Castells, Mdernandez-Ardevol, & Liu, 2007; Lee & Kim, 2014; Pearce & Rice, 2013). For example, education is believed to influence mobile phone penetration because higher education induces a higher demand for mobile phones (e.g., Okazaki, 2006; Pearce & Rice, 2013; Prieger, 2013; Srinuan et al., 2012). Overall, the consumption model explains how consumers make purchasing choices within the constraints of income budgets. Income level should be the primary factor that digital media and telecommunications managers take into account when creating their products and marketing strategies.

These traditional theories and concepts have important practical implications for digital media and telecommunication managers. Yet, over the past few years, new mobile communication technologies have emerged and diffused around the world. The following section discusses these new trends as well as the new theoretical perspectives that can guide mobile media management practices in today's convergent media environments.

Something New

One of the newest trends in mobile media is that many traditional media organizations use mobile media as their new content distribution platform. For example, CBS, one of the major broadcasters in the United States, created a mobile media strategy to expand its digital services. CBS has 15 owned-and-operated stations and affiliation agreements with 228 additional television stations in large and midsized markets. Its broadcast network has a national reach of 95.96% of households in the United States. As a traditional media company, CBS embraces mobile technologies quickly and has implemented mobile strategies by developing CBS Mobile, a new division that is specifically in charge of building CBS's mobile business (CBS, 2019). Such efforts include developing mobile sites, made-for-mobile videos on all major carriers, and a 24/7 mobile television network. CBS audiences can now watch thousands of episodes, live TV, and original series on their mobile devices through the mobile app (CBS—Full Episodes & Live TV). Sports content has been the focus of CBS Mobile from the very beginning. It has developed two iOS apps and streamed live events including 63 games of the NCAA tournament on mobile devices (CBS, 2019). CBS also uses mobile as a channel to effectively promote its original content. CBS Mobile creates a variety of mobile content, including mobile video alerts for CBS Mobile News, CBS Sports Mobile, and entertainment properties.

Other traditional media companies also use mobile media as a distribution channel for their media products. For example, the *New York Times* developed the NYTimes app for readers to access unlimited articles, which only costs one dollar a week. It also provides NYT Cooking and The Crossword subscription for additional charges. Print subscribers to the *New York Times* and the *International New York Times* get free access to the full range of NYTimes apps (New York Times, 2019).

Another new trend in the mobile communication world is the rapid diffusion of low-cost mobile devices and broadband infrastructure equipment that enable millions of people with limited incomes, especially those in developing countries, to purchase mobile media and use mobile broadband. This new phenomenon is referred to as frugal innovation.

Bhatti and Ventresca (2013) conceptualize frugal innovation as a type of innovation that aims at "leveraging limited resources or lackluster institutions and achieving the ends that serve more people who have less" (p. 16). Frugal innovation is a specific type of innovation that responds to limited resources and attempts to produce outcomes that address specific needs of the target populace (Bhatti & Ventresca, 2013). This type of innovation is different from high-end innovations that have been developed and mostly diffused in developed countries, where abundant resources, sufficient affordability, and mature infrastructure are available.

Carrying the common characteristics of innovations, such as novelty and improvement, frugal innovations have another crucial feature: they must be "significantly cheaper than competitive offerings and good enough to meet the basic needs of customers who would otherwise remain un(der)served" (Hossain, Simula, & Halme, 2016, p. 133). Thus, frugal innovations fit the needs of the vast majority of the population in developing countries, where there are significant societal resource constraints. The target consumers for frugal innovation often face very limited and incomplete means and social infrastructures.

The concept of frugal innovation has managerial implications for digital media and telecommunication industries because several high-end products, such as Apple's iPhone, do not meet the huge demand for frugal innovations in developing countries. Even in developed countries, there are a large number of underprivileged people who cannot afford expensive mobile devices and services. This huge demand is satisfied by the frugal innovations of mobile media devices and mobile broadband technologies developed in developing countries. For example, Shanzhai mobile phones, made in China, were produced at low costs and sold at low prices. Their prices are a fifth to a 10th of the cost of "real brands." The *Financial Times* estimated that the sale of Shanzhai phones accounted for about 20% of the global 2G mobile phone market in 2010 (Kwong, 2010). Since the end of 2012, Shanzhai mobile phone manufacturers have set up their own brand-name phones. For example, the Chinese brand Xiaomi has become a leading "clone" brand of iPhone. With similar features and functions, Xiaomi smartphones are sold at less than half the price of iPhones (International Data Corporation, 2019).

Frugal innovations in mobile broadband infrastructure and services have also lowered the mobile broadband price to a large extent in developing countries. Table 19.1 lists the 20 countries with the lowest broadband prices. The price of 1G mobile data in these 20 countries was less than $5 USD in 2017, and the price in five countries (Egypt, Sri Lanka, Myanmar, Pakistan, and Vietnam) is less than S2 USD (Worldwide Web Foundation, 2018). Comparatively, mobile broadband services in developed countries are much more expensive. For example, the average price for 1G mobile data in 28 European Union member states was 23.60 EUR ($26.70 USD) in 2017 (European Commission, 2018).

The decrease in mobile broadband data prices is one of the reasons for increasing mobile media consumption, which is a new trend in the mobile communication and

TABLE 19.1. The 20 Countries with the Lowest Mobile Broadband Data Prices (US$)

	Price 1GB Mobile Prepaid Data	*Price as % of Income*		
Country	*2017*	*2017*	*2016*	*2015*
Egypt	0.84	0.0033	0.0047	0.0235
Sri Lanka	1.29	0.0040	0.0043	0.0050
Myanmar	1.46	0.0147	n/a	0.0414
Pakistan	1.47	0.0112	0.0122	0.0167
Vietnam	1.60	0.0088	0.0104	0.0325
Cambodia	2.00	0.0195	0.0211	0.0235
India	2.32	0.0153	0.0269	0.0309
Rwanda	2.32	0.0387	0.0842	0.0477
Bangladesh	2.75	0.0224	0.0266	0.0311
Nigeria	2.76	0.0159	0.0157	0.0735
Indonesia	2.80	0.0095	0.0145	0.0136
Nepal	2.90	0.0441	0.0460	0.0995
Mozambique	3.30	0.0943	0.0685	0.1000
Haiti	3.89	0.0614	0.0590	0.1298
Tunisia	4.00	0.0137	0.0141	0.0130
Senegal	4.14	0.0523	0.0387	0.1140
Tanzania	4.40	0.0583	0.0625	0.0982
Ghana	4.42	0.0356	0.0411	0.0659
Kazakhstan	4.46	0.0068	0.0062	0.0045

Source: Worldwide Web Foundation (2018) from Alliance for Affordable Internet (A4AI).

digital media world. According to Zenith Media (2019), mobile media has become the second-largest platform for media consumption. The average mobile media consumption time worldwide is predicted to be 122 minutes per day, which is still less than TV (164 minutes per day) but much higher than other media platforms, such as radio (51 minutes per day) and newspapers (9 minutes per day).

Time is a limited resource, which constrains media consumption. Time budget is a specific perspective used to explore how time constrains media consumption. This concept was coined in an analogy to the term *income budget* mentioned in the previous section (Converse, 1968). The basic assumption of time budget is that "time" can be a quantitative resource, and people allocate time budget in the same manner as they do with income budget (Jackel & Wollscheid, 2007).

Time budget has been widely used in leisure studies (e.g., Larson & Shaikh, 2004; Rubin, Flowers, & Gross, 1986) and was recently used in media consumption studies (e.g., Jackel & Wollscheid, 2007; Zhang & Ha, 2016). Zhang and Ha (2016) explain how time budget is related to mobile news consumption. Specifically, people's time budget is divided into two categories: disposable time and work time. Disposable time is allocated between media activities and other activities. Media consumption faces a time constraint (time availability) and a space constraint (the space where media is accessible). These constraints along with media demand influence media consumption.

Researchers also used concepts related to time budget to explore mobile media consumption. For example, Dimmick, Feaster, and Hoplamazian (2010) suggest that mobile media enables people to employ the interstices, which was defined as the "intervening spaces between things or narrow or small spaces or, sometimes, an interval of time" (p. 25), and increase the time availability for media consumption. This proposition helps explain increasing mobile media consumption and the competitive advantage of mobile media over other media platforms. This competitive advantage makes mobile media one of the most-consumed media platforms.

Frugal innovation and time budget are two new concepts that help digital media managers understand new trends in mobile media communication. In an era when people use various approaches to save time and money, it is crucial to understand time budget and frugal innovation when determining mobile media strategies. Frugal innovations provide low-priced mobile devices and mobile broadband services to the majority of the population in developing countries as well as a large number of low-income people in developed countries. This huge population consists of audiences of many digital media products and the consumers of wireless telecommunications. As such, digital media managers should understand how low-priced mobile technologies and services are diffused in different markets and across the world, what kinds of consumers use these technologies and services, and other relevant characteristics of the marketplace in order to develop their mobile strategies. Time budget perspective helps digital media managers understand how consumers allocate their time among different media platforms and the unique characteristics of mobile media in terms of media consumption. It reveals the advantages of mobile media in increasing time availability for media consumption and encourages managers to take time spending into consideration when developing their mobile content and services.

Opportunities and Challenges

The rapid diffusion of mobile media across countries and the increase in media consumption in mobile media are the two prominent changes over the past decade. These changes have significant impacts on contemporary society and have transformed the global media landscape. They provide new opportunities for not only mobile communications industries but also other types of media industries.

OPPORTUNITIES

Frugal innovations have brought opportunities in the mobile industry, particularly in developing countries. There are still huge demands in developing countries for mobile broadband. The low-cost frugal innovations in mobile communications can satisfy these demands by providing low-priced mobile products and services.

In most developing countries, frugal smartphones occupy the biggest chunk of market share. China had more than 800 million smartphone users in 2018 and became the largest smartphone market in the world (McCarthy, 2018). In the third quarter of 2018, Chinese brands occupied a majority of the market: Huawei (23%), Vivo (21%), Oppo (21%), and Xiaomi (13%) (Counterpoint, 2018a). The number of smartphone users in India reached 337 million in 2018, making it the second smartphone market in the world (Tripathi, 2018). Three Chinese brands occupied the largest market share in India in the third quarter of 2018: Xiaomi (27%), Vivo (10%), and Oppo (8%). In Africa, three Chinese brands were among the top five: Huawei (17.6%), Tecno (6.8%), and Infinix (5%) (Statcounter, 2019). At the global level, frugal smartphones captured a significant chunk of the world marketplace. Huawei seized 14.6% of global market share in the third quarter of 2018. And two other Chinese brands, Xiaomi and Oppo, captured 9.7% and 8.4%, respectively, of the global market (Statista, 2019b).

In contrast, high-end brands occupy the biggest market share in developed countries. For example, Samsung captures the biggest market share in many of these countries and 31.5% of the market share worldwide (Statcounter, 2019). The market share of iPhone in the United States, Canada, Japan, and the United Kingdom were 63%, 61%, 72%, and 57%, respectively, in 2018, dwarfing all other brands using the Android system (DeviceAtlas, 2019).

Frugal mobile devices not only seize the biggest market share in many developing countries but also enter the markets in developed countries as there are many low-income people in these countries who have demands for these frugal innovations. For example, the Chinese brand ZTE boasted of its U.S. smartphone shipments growing 30%, reaching 15 million phones in 2015 (Cendrowski, 2016). Its shipment market share reached 11% in the first quarter of 2018, although it suffered a significant drop due to sanctions imposed by the U.S. government (Counterpoint, 2018b).

The rapid increase of mobile media consumption has substantially transformed media industries. As more people spend more time on mobile media, advertising revenues also move from traditional media platforms to mobile media. For example, mobile advertising spending in the United States has grown from 22% a decade ago to 75% of all digital advertising revenues in 2018, reaching more than $70 billion USD (Koetsier, 2018).

Streaming media constitutes a significant part of mobile media consumption. According to Statista, mobile media accounted for 58% of global online video views in the first quarter of 2018 (Statista, 2019c). The rapid diffusion of mobile media and mobile broadband provides new markets for streaming media services. Several giant media companies based on streaming media have emerged, such as Netflix and YouTube. The number of Netflix subscribers has grown from fewer than 23 million in 2011 to more than 130 million in 2018, and 37% of world Internet users have watched Netflix (Statista, 2019d). The total number of monthly active users of YouTube reached 1.9 billion in 2018, and the number of users creating content reached 50 million worldwide. Today, YouTube services are available in 88 countries and in 76 languages (Omnicore, 2019). As people increasingly use mobile streaming media, they no longer subscribe to cable services that are more expensive than streaming media. This phenomenon is called cord cutting. Besides the cheaper prices of streaming media, the time flexibility of mobile media also facilitates cord cutting. As discussed above, mobile media enables users to watch videos during the interstices (short time gaps) between activities. This time flexibility enhances mobile streaming media consumption.

Moreover, most people now use social media apps on mobile platforms. According to comScore, 60% of time spent on social media in the United States is through mobile apps on smartphones, while 6%, 10%, and 2% of time spent on social media is through websites on smartphones, through mobile apps on tablets, and through websites on tablets, respectively. In total, 79% of time spent on social media is through mobile media, and only 21% of time spent on social media is through desktops (comScore, 2017). The time flexibility attribute of mobile media enables people to use social media during many interstices as well as to do other things while simultaneously using social media. Today, media users tend to use their time more efficiently by using interstices and multitasking. Mobile media provides media managers opportunities to meet this demand and keep mobile media evolving in the era of time famine.

With the further diffusion of mobile media and new mobile broadband technologies, such as 5G in many countries, time spent on streaming media and social media via mobile platforms will continue to increase. Another promising area of mobile technology is virtual reality (VR) and augmented reality (AR) via mobile media (IQUII, 2018), something that will be discussed more in chapter 20. The world market value of VR reached $13.9 billion just in 2017, with an important growth of 130.5% compared to 2016. Mobile technology is a strong propellent for the future of VR and AR. The development of VR and AR will bring new opportunities for mobile media companies to develop new products and services to engage audiences. Although the rapid evolution of wireless technologies and diffusion of mobile media provide huge opportunities to the wireless technology industry and media industry, they also bring challenges, discussed more in the following section.

CHALLENGES

Frugal innovations in mobile communication pose a big challenge for mobile technology and device developers in developed countries. For example, the leading brands in the United States and South Korea, such as Apple, Samsung, Verizon, AT&T, and Qualcomm, are starting to lose considerable market share to competitors in China whose technologies are based on or developed from frugal innovations. To cope with these challenges, these mobile technology innovators need to strengthen investments in research and development and maintain their leadership in front-end technologies such as 5G. Moreover, to increase their market share in developing countries, these companies should develop more low-priced technologies that meet the demands of most people in developing countries. Samsung, for example, has begun to provide multiple low-priced smartphones, thus capturing the highest market share in many countries.

Mobile media also bring many challenges for media companies as the changes in media consumption and advertising revenues have a large impact on the media industry. The major challenge comes from fragmentation due to the increasing number of media choices. When traditional media companies provide mobile access to their content, many have questioned whether people will still use the traditional platforms.

Scholars investigated whether mobile media and traditional media platforms substitute or complement each other. Chan-Olmsted, Rim, and Zerba (2013) found that there is a substitution effect between mobile news and print news among young audiences. That is, young people are intensive mobile news users but not likely to read print news. Although evidence also shows a complementary effect between mobile news and print news (e.g., Winter & Alpar, 2018), the time budget framework suggests a substitution relationship as well. The actual time consumption patterns of different media platforms support the substitution relationship. In other words, people probably will spend more time on mobile media and less time on traditional media. As advertising revenues go along with the time consumption trends, loss of audiences and advertising revenues are the huge challenges for traditional media companies.

In order to succeed in the mobile media era, a media content production company should identify the characteristics of its target audiences who consume media content via mobile. However, as the public are more concerned with their privacy and personal information, it is harder to obtain information about personal characteristics of mobile users. Moreover, because mobile users are more likely to consume mobile content during the time gaps between activities, it is challenging to predict their mobile media use patterns. Notwithstanding these challenges, future mobile practitioners and media managers can use the following action plan to effectively reach mobile audiences.

ACTION PLAN

1. Complete a thorough audience analysis in order to identify the characteristics of a target audience most likely to consume media content via mobile.
2. Create content according to your target audience's time budget by considering how they will utilize mobile media in their daily lives and differentiate mobile media content from content created for other platforms.
3. Attract advertisers by providing them the data of audience characteristics as well as their mobile and traditional media consumption patterns.

KEY TAKEAWAYS

1. Mobile media and mobile broadband have diffused faster than computer and fixed broadband in many countries, abridging the digital divide in the world.
2. Time spent on mobile media consumption is second to TV and much higher than other media platforms.
3. Media content providers use mobile media as the new platform to distribute content.
4. Mobile communication technology innovators in developed countries should develop low-cost mobile technologies that meet the huge demands in developing countries.

CONCLUSION

Mobile devices, especially smartphones, have diffused rapidly over the past decade. As the global mobile divide—the gap of mobile media penetration rates between different countries—still exists, media practitioners and managers should be concerned with issues of equality and access. With the rapid diffusion of mobile media in the world, an increasing number of people use mobile media for Internet access. The worldwide average time spent on the mobile Internet is much more than that of the desktop Internet. This is attributed to the rapid diffusion of mobile broadband, which enables advanced Internet applications. The adoption rate of mobile broadband is much higher than that of fixed broadband. The rapid diffusion of mobile broadband stimulates media content consumption via mobile. Mobile media consumption time is only second to TV and much more than time spent on other media platforms. Many media content providers use mobile media as the new platform to distribute their content.

Scholars have applied theories to explain the diffusion of mobile media. They suggest that the diffusions of mobile media and mobile broadband are constrained by consumers' income budget and time budget. Time budget is a perspective that explains why people spend time and who would spend more time on mobile media. This perspective is pertinent because people across the world spend a large proportion of their time on media. The advantage of mobile media is that people can utilize the small interval of time between doing other things to consume mobile media content. This advantage explains why people use most streaming media and social media on mobile devices.

Frugal innovation is a specific type of innovation that is developed in developing countries with a lack of resources, affordability, and infrastructure but can address specific needs of the target populace. It is different from the high-end innovations that have been developed in developed countries, where abundant resources, sufficient affordability, and mature infrastructure are available. Many mobile devices designed and produced in developing countries, especially China, are frugal innovations. These low-priced mobile devices are sold in huge numbers in many developing countries. Furthermore, the price of mobile broadband, which uses low-priced mobile communication infrastructure technologies, is very low in many developing countries. Both the low-priced mobile devices and mobile broadband facilitate the rapid diffusion of mobile media in the world, especially in developing countries.

Frugal innovations in mobile media pose a huge challenge for the developers of high-end mobile media technologies as low-priced mobile devices and infrastructure technologies have increasingly seized the global market share. Consequently, high-end mobile devices and infrastructure technologies have lost their market shares. The high-end mobile communication technology developers need to develop low-priced products that help them capture more shares in the world market.

The next generation of mobile communication, 5G technology, will significantly facilitate the diffusion of VR and AR in various industries, discussed more in chapter 20. With the progress of 5G networks, as well as VR and AR technologies, the mobile technology industry and media industry will have many opportunities to develop new products and services. On the other hand, these new technologies will bring new challenges and further transform these industries. Those who can effectively seize the new opportunities and overcome the new challenges will be successful in the future.

To succeed in the future mobile world, mobile practitioners and managers should achieve a comprehensive understanding of three trends in mobile communication. The first trend is the rapid diffusion of mobile technologies, especially frugal technologies, around the world. Theories such as DIT, TAM, and consumption model help media managers understand this trend. The second trend is that media companies use mobile media as their major content distribution channel, which is closely connected to the third trend—that people spend more time on mobile media for media consumption. These trends further transform media industries as audiences and advertising revenues move from traditional media platforms to mobile media. To capture mobile media audiences, practitioners need to know their mobile usage patterns. Time budget provides an insightful perspective to study these patterns.

In summary, this chapter discusses the phenomena and trends of mobile media across the world and the theories that explain these trends. It is important for mobile content providers to study their audiences from a time budget perspective and understand the relationship between their audiences' time allocations and frequencies for mobile content consumption. This understanding will help content producers create mobile content and help salespeople promote mobile content. For mobile device manufactures, attention must be turned to their consumers' needs for frugal devices. Those companies that focus on research and development and high-end innovations need to develop their marketing strategies to highlight the values of their products and services. As mobile media clearly points out trends in media consumption, the next chapter discusses the future of media management practices—specifically, the trends, opportunities, and challenges in virtual reality, second screening, big data, integrating traditional and new media management and practices, as well as career development and education for future media managers.

REFERENCES

Bankmycell.com. (n.d.). *How many phones are in the world?* https://www.bankmycell.com/blog/how-many-phones-are-in-the-world

Bhatti, Y. A., & Ventresca, M. (2013, January 19). *How can "frugal innovation" be conceptualized?* SSRN. https://papers.ssrn.com/sol3/papers.cfm?abstract_id=2203552

Castells, M., Mdernandez-Ardevol, M., & Liu, J. L. (2007). *Mobile communication and society: A global perspective*. The MIT Press.
CBS. (2019). *Pick a plan*. https://www.cbs.com/all-access/subscription/plan
Cendrowski, S. (2016, January 25). Why Chinese smartphone makers come to America. *Fortune*. http://fortune.com/2016/01/25/why-chinese-smartphone-makers-come-to-america
Chan-Olmsted, S., Rim, H., & Zerba, A. (2013). Mobile news adoption among young adults: Examining the roles of perceptions, news consumption, and media usage. *Journalism and Mass Communication Quarterly, 90*, 126–147.
Chu, W. L., Wu, F. S., Kao, K. S., & Yen, D. C. (2009). Diffusion of mobile telephony: An empirical study in Taiwan. *Telecommunications Policy, 33*, 506–520.
comScore. (2017, March 22). *2017 U.S. cross-platform future in focus*. https://www.comscore.com/Insights/Presentations-and-Whitepapers/2017/2017-US-Cross-Platform-Future-in-Focus?
Converse, P. E. (1968). Time budgets. In D. Sills (Ed.), *International encyclopedia of the social sciences* (pp. 42–47). Macmillan.
Counterpoint. (2018a, November 17). *China smartphone market share: By quarter*. https://www.counterpointresearch.com/china-smartphone-share
Counterpoint. (2018b, November 20). *US smartphone market share: By quarter*. https://www.counterpointresearch.com/us-market-smartphone-share/
Davis, F. D. (1989). Perceived usefulness, perceived ease of use, and user acceptance of information technology. *MIS Quarterly, 13*, 319–340.
DeviceAtlas. (2019, January 8). *Android v iOS market share 2019*. https://deviceatlas.com/blog/android-v-ios-market-share#us
Dimmick, J., Feaster, J. C., & Hoplamazian, G. J. (2010). News in the interstices: The niches of mobile media in space and time. *New Media & Society, 13*, 23–39.
Ejectejecteject. (2019, July 30). *24 tablet market share statistics and analysis*. https://www.ejectejecteject.com/statistics/24-tablet-market-share-statistics-and-analysis
European Commission. (2018, March 13). *Mobile broadband prices in Europe 2017*. https://ec.europa.eu/digital-single-market/en/news/mobile-broadband-prices-europe-2017
Ezell, S., Atkinson, R., Castro, D., & Ou, G. (2009, March 6). *The need for speed: The importance of next-generation broadband networks. The Information Technology & Innovation Foundation*. SSRN. http://dx.doi.org/10.2139/ssrn.1354032
Frank, L. D. (2012). An analysis of the effect of the economic situation on modeling and forecasting the diffusion of wireless communications in Finland. *Technological Forecasting and Social Change, 71*, 391–403.
Gruber, H., & Koutroumpis, P. (2011). Mobile telecommunications and the impact on economic development. *Economic Policy, 26*, 387–426.
Gupta, R., & Jain, K. (2012). Diffusion of mobile telephony in India: An empirical study. *Technological Forecasting & Social Change, 79*, 709–715.
Hossain, M., Simula, H., & Halme, M. (2016). Can frugal go global? Diffusion patterns of frugal innovation. *Technology in Society, 46*, 132–139.
Hwang, J., Cho, Y., & Long, N. V. (2009). Investigation of factors affecting the diffusion of mobile telephone services: An empirical analysis for Vietnam. *Telecommunications Policy, 33*, 534–543.
IEEE. (2017, October). *IEEE 5G and beyond technology roadmap white paper*. https://5g.ieee.org/images/files/pdf/ieee-5g-roadmap-white-paper.pdf
International Data Corporation. (2019). *Smartphone vendor market share*. https://www.idc.com/promo/smartphone-market-share/vendor
International Telecommunication Union. (2019). *Statistics*. https://www.itu.int/en/ITU-D/Statistics/Pages/stat/default.aspx
IQUII. (2018, January 4). *From augmented reality to mobile reality: It's the smartphone that drives augmented reality*. Medium. https://medium.com/iquii/from-augmented-reality-to-mobile-reality-its-the-smartphone-that-drives-augmented-reality-31ae65b44958
Jackel, M., & Wollscheid, S. (2007). Time is money and money needs time: A secondary analysis of time-budget data in Germany. *Journal of Leisure Research, 39*, 86–108.
Kalba, K. (2008). The adoption of mobile phones in developing countries: Global diffusion and the rural challenge. *International Journal of Communication, 2*, 631–661.

Kim, Y. J., & Sim, J. B. (2012). Acceptance-diffusion strategies for tablet-PCs: Focused on acceptance factors of non-users and satisfaction factors of users. *ETRI Journal, 34,* 245–255.

Koetsier, J. (2018, February 23). Mobile advertising will drive 75% of all digital ad spend in 2018: Here's what's changing. *Forbes.* https://www.forbes.com/sites/johnkoetsier/2018/02/23/mobile-advertising-will-drive-75-of-all-digital-ad-spend-in-2018-heres-whats-changing

Kwong, R. (2010, October 17). Bandit phone king has the last laugh. *The Financial Times.* http://www.webcitation.org/5tcXbg9AL

Larson, D. M., & Shaikh, S. L. (2004). Recreation demand choices and revealed values of leisure time. *Economic Inquiry, 42,* 264–278.

Lee, J. H., & Kim, J. (2014). Socio-demographic gaps in mobile use, causes, and consequences: A multi-group analysis of the mobile divide model. *Information, Communication & Society, 17,* 917–936.

Lee, M., & Cho, Y. (2007). The diffusion of mobile telecommunications services in Korea. *Applied Economics Letters, 14,* 477–481.

Lee, S., Lee, S., & Chan-Olmsted, S. (2017). An empirical analysis of tablet PC diffusion. *Telematics and Informatics, 34,* 518–527.

Lin, X. (2017, October 21). *5G communications: What companies are leading in 5G technologies?* Quora. https://www.quora.com/5G-Communications-What-companies-are-leading-in-5G-technologies

Loo, B. P. Y., & Ngan, Y. L. (2012). Developing mobile telecommunications to narrow digital divide in developing countries? Some lessons from China. *Telecommunications Policy, 36,* 888–900.

McCarthy, N. (2018, August 23). China now boasts more than 800 million Internet users and 98% of them are mobile. *Forbes.* https://www.forbes.com/sites/niallmccarthy/2018/08/23/china-now-boasts-more-than-800-million-internet-users-and-98-of-them-are-mobile-infographic

Mir, M., & Dangerfield, B. (2013). Propagating a digital divide: Diffusion of mobile telecommunication services in Pakistan. *Technological Forecasting & Social Change, 80,* 992–1001.

Molleryd, B., Markendahl, J., & Makitalo, O. (2009). *Analysis of operator options to reduce the impact of the revenue gap caused by flat rate mobile broadband subscriptions.* Thorngren. http://thorngren.nu/wp-content/uploads/2010/04/Molleryd_B_et_al_2009_Analysis_of_operator_options.pdf

New York Times. (2019). *Digital subscriptions.* https://help.nytimes.com/hc/en-us/articles/115015852367-Digital-subscriptions

Okazaki, S. (2006). What do we know about mobile Internet adopters? A cluster analysis. *Information & Management, 43,* 127–141.

Omnicore. (2019). *YouTube by the numbers: Stats, demographics & fun facts.* https://www.omnicoreagency.com/youtube-statistics

Organisation for Economic Co-operation and Development. (2009). *Mobile broadband: Pricing and services.* http://www.oecd.org/sti/broadband/43280727.pdf

Papacharissi, Z., & Zaks, A. (2006). Is broadband the future? An analysis of broadband technology potential and diffusion. *Telecommunications Policy, 30,* 64–75.

Pearce, K. E., & Rice, R. E. (2013). Digital divides from access to activities: Comparing mobile and personal computer Internet users. *Journal of Communication, 63,* 721–744.

Prieger, J. (2013). The broadband digital divide and the economic benefits of mobile broadband for rural areas. *Telecommunications Policy, 37,* 483–502.

Rogers, E. M. (2003). *Diffusion of innovations* (5th ed.). Free Press.

Rubin, J., Flowers, N. M., & Gross, D. R. (1986). Adaptive dimensions of leisure. *American Ethnologist, 13,* 524–536.

Srinuan, C., Srinuan, P., & Bohlin, E. (2012). An analysis of mobile Internet access in Thailand: Implications for bridging the digital divide. *Telematics and Informatics, 29,* 254–262.

Statcounter. (2019). *Mobile vendor market share Africa.* https://gs.statcounter.com/vendor-market-share/mobile/africa

Statista. (2019a). *Number of tablet users worldwide from 2013 to 2021.* https://www.statista.com/statistics/377977/tablet-users-worldwide-forecast

Statista. (2019b). *Global market share held by leading smartphone vendors from 4th quarter 2009 to 3rd quarter 2018.* https://www.statista.com/statistics/271496/global-market-share-held-by-smartphone-vendors-since-4th-quarter-2009

Statista. (2019c). *Mobile share of global digital video plays from 3rd quarter 2013 to 1st quarter 2018.* https://www.statista.com/statistics/444318/mobile-device-video-views-share
Statista. (2019d). *Netflix: Statistics & facts.* https://www.statista.com/topics/842/netflix
Thompson, H. G., Jr., & Garbacz, C. (2007). Mobile, fixed line and Internet effects on global productive efficiency. *Information Economics and Policy, 19*, 189–214.
Tripathi, P. (2018, May 7). *Smartphone users in India 2018: 16% YoY growth is the highest.* Daze Info. https://dazeinfo.com/2018/05/07/smartphone-users-in-india-2018-2022-growth
Winter, P., & Alpar, P. (2018). On the relationship between print and mobile channels for newspapers. *Electronic Markets, 28*, 79–92.
The World Bank. (n.d.). The world development indicator. *Data Catalog.* https://datacatalog.worldbank.org/dataset/world-development-indicators
Worldwide Web Foundation. (2018, September 11). *Mobile broadband pricing data.* Web Foundation. https://webfoundation.org/research/mobile-broadband-pricing-data
Yamakawa, P., Rees, G. H., Salas, G. M., & Alva, N. (2013). The diffusion of mobile telephones: An empirical analysis for Peru. *Telecommunications Policy, 37*, 594–606.
Zenith Media. (2019). *26% of media consumption will be mobile in 2019.* https://www.zenithmedia.com/26-of-media-consumption-will-be-mobile-in-2019
Zhang, X. (2017). Exploring the patterns and determinants of the global mobile divide. *Telematics and Informatics, 34*, 438–449.
Zhang, X., & Ha, L. (2016). Mobile news consumption and political news interest: A time budget perspective. *Journal of Applied Journalism and Media Studies, 5*, 277–295.
Zheng, H., & Liu, S. (2019). *ZTE on its best way to 5G.* ZTE. https://www.zte.com.cn/global/about/magazine/zte-technologies/2017/1/en_752/461950

PART V

THE FUTURE OF MEDIA MANAGEMENT

CHAPTER 20

Diffusion of Virtual Reality in Local Television News

Douglas A. Ferguson, College of Charleston
Clark F. Greer, Liberty University

LEARNING OBJECTIVES

1. Understand the impact of virtual reality on local television news.
2. Apply the concept of diffusion theory to better understand virtual reality convergence.
3. Identify key takeaways for news media managers to use when creating a virtual reality strategy.

Emerging technologies are changing how local television stations gather and disseminate news. One recent technology is virtual reality (VR). It is important that future scholars and practitioners understand the extent to which local TV stations adopt VR as part of their media operations so that new business models can be developed to maximize convergent opportunities. VR for local news comes in many forms. It can be as simple as a 360-degree video that does not require special equipment. At the other end of the spectrum is a virtual reality headset paired with haptic response for an enhanced, enveloping experience. An example would be the Oculus Quest device proposed by Facebook founder Mark Zuckerberg in 2018 (Vanian, 2018). Touch controls on Oculus devices add another sense to visual stimulus.

Perhaps the best way to understand how far VR has advanced is to look back at early attempts and observations. An editorial, primarily dealing with print media, in *Journalism and Mass Communication Quarterly* argued that technologies such as VR were contributing to "watershed moments" in news (Marron, 2015, p. 351). For example, in November 2015, the *New York Times* inserted Google Cardboard VR viewers into an edition of the paper that was delivered to more than a million of its subscribers (Wohlsen, 2015). The *Des Moines Register* used VR to produce a series of stories about farming

(Hoey, 2015). Those uses of VR provide the ability for news audiences to experience news situations and settings (Marron, 2015).

Nonny de la Peña had previously created the first virtual reality journalism stories with her 2012 *Hunger in Los Angeles*, which mixed narrative, news values, and technology storytelling (Stubbs, 2018). Kurz (2016) notes that virtual news sets and augmented reality will be game changers for the future of TV news. Virtual content enables audiences to be participants versus simply observers and even offers the ability for viewers to choose the path in a story rather than follow linear storytelling (Koski, 2015). Industry forecast reports have revealed growing public acceptance of VR receivers (International Data Corporation, 2018; Martin, 2017). When Facebook in 2014 spent $2 billion for the Oculus Rift VR headset, many observers began to take notice (Wood, 2018).

Virtual techniques are not solely tools of professional news organizations. The Annenberg School at University of Southern California teaches students practical applications of augmented reality and VR as well as the use of 360 video in journalism (Hur, 2017). Additionally, the Knight Foundation partnered with Google News Lab and the Online News Association to sponsor a competition in the use of virtual reality for news to deliver stories through "immersive storytelling" (Preston & Zenni, 2017, para. 1).

Recent developments in virtual technologies may be setting the stage for different approaches to news, both print and broadcast. Some newspapers remain very active at the close of the decade. For example, McClatchy operates a New Ventures Lab, which demonstrated its digital environment plans at the Capital Region AR VR Accelerator in Sacramento, California (Anderson, 2019). Before we can ever understand such cutting-edge developments, however, we should take a closer look at how one news outlet has experimented with VR storytelling through 360-degree journalism.

CASE STUDY

The easiest VR format to experience without VR goggles or other equipment is basic 360-degree journalism, similar to Facebook photos that allow the viewer to rotate the view of a still frame. *USA Today* introduced VR storytelling with the following definition: "Virtual reality is a computer-generated experience that can simulate physical presence in real or imagined environments. Quite simply, virtual reality can put you there, wherever there may be" (USA Today, n.d., para. 1). By manipulating a computer mouse and cursor, the viewer can rotate the video in a nearly endless array of viewpoints. The website (https://www.usatoday.com/vrstories) gives examples of 360-degree experiences in full motion: inside a race car, inside a fighter jet, through the streets of Havana, and attending a political rally. Words cannot describe the experience; you are encouraged to take a quick look at the website.

Although *USA Today* maintains the website, the documents regarding the "current" state of VR journalism are only as current as 2015. Using the Internet archive Wayback Machine, we can also experience the early predictions back then (Doyle, 2015). Doyle acknowledges that consumer acceptance of VR would be slow but opines that traditional media were eager to "avoid repeating their slow adoptions of the Internet and mobile devices" (Doyle, 2015, p. 5). Although his reported prediction was 10 to 38 million devices by 2018, the number actually sold worldwide by then was much higher. Sony alone sold 50 million headsets worldwide by 2018, not counting the 30 million sold to PlayStation users (Fogden, 2018). Still, technology observers (e.g., Fogden, 2018) were not entirely convinced there was widespread demand.

Television networks and their affiliated stations began taking note of how newspapers were receiving attention for their VR storytelling and thus began to experiment on their own. In particular, ABC News established a website (https://abcnews.go.com/VR) that captured the kind of stories attempted by *USA Today* but focused on documentary-style news stories with more narration. An example is "Inside the Hermit Kingdom: VR Journey in North Korea," which attracted 17 million 360-degree views in the first 48 hours. The ABC link lives on, but McDonald (2017) is dead. The same web address presented 15 additional stories, including a trip to Chernobyl and a California marijuana harvest. Downloading the Jaunt VR app allowed someone to watch the video inside Google Cardboard, a very inexpensive VR device designed to hold a cell phone connected to ordinary earbuds. While only a simulation of "true VR" devices, the experience was arguably better than rotating one's view of a stationary screen, a difference left unanswered by current research. While virtual reality is a new media technology, its emergence and adoption are fairly consistent with other forms of technology. It is important for future practitioners to understand both traditional theories and emerging applications.

Something Old

Herz and Rauschnabel (2018) have explored the diffusion of VR devices and concluded that VR adoption intention is the highest when potential buyers expect to enjoy a strong sense of virtual embodiment (the sensation of being another person) and virtual presence (the sensation of being at another place), while only one of these conditions might have a negative effect. Diffusion has been studied in many ways, even throughout this handbook, but most theoretical foundations originate with the work of Everett Rogers and diffusion theory.

DIFFUSION THEORY

Diffusion is how any innovation is communicated over time among members of a social system (Rogers, 1995). Rogers explained five perceived characteristics of an innovation that influences its adoption: (1) relative advantage, (2) compatibility, (3) complexity, (4) observability, and (5) trialability. All characteristics except complexity are positively related to adoption. The adoption of VR devices by news organizations requires strong participation from media managers.

Relative advantage is often associated with a cost/benefit analysis in which individuals or organizations determine whether it is in their best interest to adopt an innovation (Rogers, 1995). An important aspect of this characteristic is audience size, which is usually a crucial issue for television broadcasters. The number of viewers whom a video platform can attract is typically linked to increased revenue from advertisers or subscribers.

Local TV stations face several concerns when it comes to adopting various types of digital technologies. These include how to create revenue from social media, realizing the potential for mobile technologies, and being more innovative in newscasts (Knight Foundation, 2018). Another tool for TV stations is artificial intelligence (AI). Internally, the use of AI can facilitate faster searches when researching story archives, providing a means of adapting content for different delivery platforms, and analyzing social media (Pallanich, 2019). At the same time, stations still must deal with monetizing content and determining whether the advantages of using AI systems are worth the cost of implementation (Pallanich, 2019).

Compatibility is related to the extent to which the innovation is similar to existing objects or practices (i.e., how well it fits "values, past experiences, and need of potential adopters") (Rogers, 1995). A high degree of compatibility tends to reduce the level of uncertainty toward the innovation. Because stations already have experience with posting to their websites, there is an assumed degree of congruence in delivering content via VR. Supplying downloads to dedicated VR devices could be easily accomplished with a television medium that preproduces its news stories. Despite its technical compatibility, giving viewers a 360-degree experience may create problems related to the central content of a story. Compared to stories produced in 2D, stories that give viewers a 360-degree perspective might take their focus of attention away from what the story producer intends (Bösch, Gensch, & Rath-Wiggins, 2018). Therefore, stations that want to venture into 360-degree storytelling need to determine how to produce content differently to ensure the viewer is directed to the central visual.

Complexity is associated with the level of simplicity or complexity in using the innovation (Rogers, 1995). Television stations interested in implementing VR will need to understand the technological side of news dissemination and gathering. As noted above, complexity is negatively associated with adopting an innovation, so the higher the perceived complexity of the innovation, the lower the tendency to adopt the innovation. A news director who perceives VR as too complex is less likely to implement the technology. News directors might view the entire process as too much trouble. For example, creating graphics for a virtual set or even a partly virtual environment is only part of the task of creating a newscast without a physical set. For WTHR in Indianapolis, it meant time to reach a comfort level at coordinating the station's robotic cameras with the graphics (Irish, 2018). WRAL's use of virtual reality for its 2018 Winter Olympics program required time for rehearsals to ensure coordination of anchors, cameras, and graphics (Capitol Broadcasting Company, 2018).

Trialability is the ability for a potential adopter to try an innovation before deciding whether to adopt (Rogers, 1995). Additionally, this provides an opportunity to see how the innovation works in the potential adopter's particular situation. However, as Rogers (1995) notes, some innovations are more difficult to try than others. Local television stations might perceive that implementing VR is too difficult to try because it requires additional technology. Audience members who have adopted VR headsets might be ready for local news, but the station must bear the risk of costly cameras and training. Another yet-unanswered question is what it might take for consumers with VR devices for game playing to wear them for watching the news. One might assume that gamers and news addicts occupy groups with little overlap. Perhaps those who do both activities consider their time spent in entertainment seeking greatly different than that spent in information seeking.

Observability relates to how well potential adopters can see an innovation in use (Rogers, 1995). News directors can observe other stations' use of new technology but without being able to observe results in relation to television audiences. The issue is the extent to which adoption of VR by other stations in a market may influence other news directors' choice to implement new methods for news gathering and dissemination. VR is still fairly rare, mostly adopted by metropolitan daily newspapers (see Marron, 2015). Judging from the static website for *USA Today*, even major newspapers are not producing much new content. This chicken-or-egg question concerning which comes first is yet unanswered.

In addition to the perceived characteristics of an innovation, organizations also adopt innovations based on three types (Rogers, 1995). Adoption from the optional perspective means the organization does not sense a need to adopt or is not mandated to do so. Under collective adoption, the decision to implement an innovation is based on consensus. The third type of innovation adoption in an organization is authority driven. In that instance, a few people who are in authority positions make the decision to adopt. In the case of VR, broadcast television stations that are part of a station group might fall under either collective or authority drive, depending on the amount of participation the local news director has in the decision process.

Now that we understand how an "old" theory of media adoption, diffusion theory, can be applied to local television newsrooms' VR adoption, let's turn our attention to new trends in virtual reality literature and practice. Key to the use of VR is the notion of giving audiences an immersive experience. The notion of "immersive" has two components: placing the viewer in a specific environment and allowing the person to be a part of what they are viewing (Vettehen, Wiltink, Huiskamp, Schaap, & Ketelaar, 2019). Bebawi and Evans (2019) focus their attention on technologies and their uses by foreign correspondents, but their observations are appropriate when understanding local TV stations' consideration of VR. Bebawi and Evans (2019) also stress the necessity of news workers adapting to changing environments, including the type of content and the notion of enhancing the value of what is delivered to audiences. For example, they noted that VR would allow correspondents to be present in a physical location while virtually being in another place.

Something New

Cost is a crucial issue in station management deciding if adopting VR technology is to their advantage. Equally important is whether implementation of these technologies means anything to viewers, even if stations can handle the financial aspect of acquiring the equipment. One study examined attitudes of viewers about the use of "immersive technologies," in this case 360 video, as compared to a traditional presentation of news stories (Vettehen et al., 2019, p. 91). The researchers found that viewing 3D stories increased the "sense of presence, enjoyment, and credibility" that viewers had in stories they watched in a 2D format (p. 30). According to these findings, the enhancements may be worth the investment of time and money.

Similarly, an experiment by Kang, O'Brien, Villarreal, Lee, and Mahood (2019) examined whether there were differences for study participants who only offered their perspective about news viewing experiences but did not view the stimulus story, compared with a group that viewed the story in a traditional format, a group that viewed the story in VR through a headset, and another group that viewed a 360-degree video on a phone. They found that there were higher levels of telepresence for VR and 360 viewers than the other two groups. The 360 group also perceived the story as more credible than participants in the traditional viewing group. Especially interesting was that viewers had a more immersive experience, even the group that did not use a VR headset to view the story. Findings of this experiment suggest that news organizations do not need to rely on headsets for VR but that they can provide content for phones to enhance viewer experiences. From this we can surmise that stations will not necessarily need to wait until VR headsets surpass the 50 million mark in the early 2020s (O'Malley, 2019) to continue experimenting with forms of VR that are less device intensive.

Virtual technologies are only one side of the equation for television stations. Other research has considered immersive journalism from the perspective of the user. Shin and Biocca (2018) find that engagement in a VR story is dependent on an individual's desire to engage with the story. Context of the story was also a factor in the immersive experience. The researchers conclude that the viewing experience from a virtual story is not simply the use of technology but also depends upon user motivations and level of participation. The story remains the key element. Shin and Biocca (2018) also note that the use of VR can enhance viewers' empathy. Additionally, content should include topics of interest that have meaning for the individual.

One task of journalists is to connect the news consumer to the story (Reis & Coelho, 2018). Immersive journalism is one means of achieving that goal. At the same time, however, there are concerns about the use of virtual technologies for reporting and storytelling. One concern is ethics regarding how segments of an event are chosen for inclusion within a story, which has long been an issue faced by journalists (Reis & Coelho, 2018). Other concerns include using virtual reality to elicit an emotional response on the part of viewers and the potential for manipulation of content that gives a sense of reality (Bailenson, 2018). For investigative reporting, one question is how placing the viewer in a story affects its content as well as the user's experience (Bösch et al., 2018). As more TV stations experiment with immersive storytelling, we predict that standards will evolve (especially when professional societies begin to get involved). One example is a collaborative effort between PBS and the Knight Foundation, in which best practices are examined (PBS, 2018).

Television networks and local stations are using VR in a variety of ways to add value for their viewers. The Weather Channel (TWC) anchors and sports personalities have used mixed reality technology to virtually transport themselves to a football stadium prior to a game to discuss how various weather conditions affect a game (Weather Group, 2018). The intent of TWC was to use the technology as a means of teaching viewers about weather. At previous times, TWC has used mixed reality to show the effects of tornados, floods, and wildfires. For the flood scenario, TWC helped viewers visualize the impact of Hurricane Florence on objects and people as the level of water increased, virtually, from the beginning of the storm to reaching several feet deep (Feldman, 2019). We imagine that other channels will take note of innovations made by TWC and develop their own enhanced reporting.

On a local level, television stations are using a combination of physical and computer-generated elements to enhance digital effects for viewers. KABC and WFAA are two stations that use virtual reality graphics to give viewers a better picture of weather events (Romano, 2018). WTHR uses both augmented and virtual reality for its newscasts (Irish, 2018). For example, the station creates virtual scenes by chroma keying on an "L-shaped" wall that "adds dimension and depth" to visuals (Irish, 2018, para. 15). One main benefit of this technique is the reduced cost of creating realistic video stories that provide audiences with a more engaging representation of a particular environment. Sending a video crew into a danger zone is not worth the risk to human life.

WRAL in Raleigh, North Carolina, offers viewers a variety of content on multiple platforms, including through a Roku app that features live newscasts and other news content; plus, the station streams sports and news on its website (Morrison & Carlson, 2018). In addition, the station has its own AR/VR production facility that has a dual use. On one hand, the studio enables anchors to appear in distant locations and provides for the insertion of graphics. On the other hand, the studio is used as a means of producing content for outside businesses. During the 2018 Winter Olympics, the station used VR to place the anchors in a snow-covered environment (Capitol Broadcasting Company, 2018). It's evident that the reduced cost of building physical sets will encourage news managers to use VR in more innovative ways.

Competition between television stations in a given market has historically driven decisions regarding news production and the adoption of innovations. For large market stations, technology is a factor in that competition (Irish, 2018). Stations are increasingly using drones for news, and they are being more intentional with social platforms, although research shows there is less innovation associated with mobile technologies (Papper, 2018). More research is needed to explore the use of VR technology.

Mark Effron, a broadcast news veteran and journalism teacher, says stations are not sensing an urgency to innovate, which could have negative consequences down the road (Morrison & Carlson, 2018). Former CBS News president Andrew Heyward noted in an interview with Nieman Lab that innovating "is not an opportunity, it's a necessity" if stations want to reach new audiences (Schmidt, 2018, para. 29). Beyond the technology itself, stations are realizing the need to produce content for audiences that consume news through a variety of platforms (Irish, 2018). For example, reaching younger audiences has long been the goal of news organizations. Innovative technology is already in their young hands, and we predict newer forms of news content should appeal to their sense of (and desire for) novelty. Perhaps linear stories lack something nowadays. Clearly, new technologies are not always beneficial to news organizations. VR is no exception, as it comes with many opportunities and challenges for future media managers.

Opportunities and Challenges

Scholarly research about the implementation of technologies in local television news is largely delineated by four time periods that reflect overall trends in innovation development and the emergence of linear and digital communications in the industry: traditional, online, social, and immersive. Diffusion of journalistic technologies that are commensurate with the traditional phase has largely corresponded with content and the tools used to gather news, while dissemination of news to audiences remained linear. With each new high-tech innovation, however, the chance to innovate is almost imperative. Each provides a "new" opportunity for media managers to innovate new technologies.

TRADITIONAL OPPORTUNITIES

One traditional means of obtaining news was through satellite-delivered sources and station satellite news gathering (SNG) equipment. A survey of news directors in the late 1980s found that almost three-quarters of stations used satellite sources, but only around 16% had SNG equipment (Lacy, Atwater, & Powers, 1988). Respondents indicated that the technologies made their newscasts better and improved news content.

Another study examined the extent to which television stations used weather reporting technologies as a promotion tactic (Daniels & Loggins, 2010). Radar, satellite maps, and "short-term forecasts" were three of the most featured forms of content on 95% of the stations' weather reports (p. 30). Results also showed that weather branding was the most important to the top stations in the markets studied. Stations with 360-degree cameras mounted on masts to provide a look at the weather would provide a comparative advantage to stations with ordinary cameras.

Another issue is whether emerging technologies affect news content. One study qualitatively examined four decades of TV news packages produced by a local TV station (Cummings, 2014). The analysis showed there was little difference in the organization of stories across time, although the number of edits increased, and the length of edits decreased with the use of digital tools. However, the question remained whether technology was the reason for the change versus other factors, such as culture. Not all stories are visual, but increased use sometimes helps justify the investment of scarce resources in expensive equipment.

ONLINE

A number of studies examined how television stations were implementing the web and related technologies. For example, Kiernan and Levy (1999) analyzed the content of TV station websites and found that stations were more prone to provide local rather than national and international news on their websites. There was some differentiation between affiliates, but only for international and local news, civic information, and archived content. They found that competition was not a factor in site differences. Other research noted that TV station websites had a relatively high level of interactivity through clickable objects and links, as well as audiovisual content, and opportunities for viewers to post comments (Bucy, 2004).

Another consideration in technology adoption by local television is the role of budgets, such as in the use of the Internet (Chan-Olmsted & Ha, 2003). Results of the study showed that "customer relations management" was the highest perceived use of the web (p. 606). Respondents viewed the Internet as a way to enhance station offerings and to find out about viewers rather than to use the technology in advertising.

An additional factor is the impact of technologies on news workers, particularly given the emergence of mobile platforms. According to research by Reinardy and Bacon (2014), online tools create a sense that news workers were being required to do more but with fewer personnel and organizational resources. There also were more concerns about the quality of stories than with posting the stories online. Respondents who rated their support system as high also had higher "work quality" (p. 141). Other research revealed that television stations were not fully implementing web features, especially with regard to interactively seeking ideas for news stories (Gregson, 2008). Sites contained more features that promoted the station than those that promoted the newscast. Only a small percentage of stations highlighted the newscast for a particular day.

A subsequent study analyzed the websites of stations affiliated with ABC, CBS, NBC, and Fox (Cleary & Bloom, 2011). More than two-thirds of the websites provided a way for viewers to share station content. Nearly one-half featured user-generated content (UGC), but extent of UGC was not related to ownership, market size, or network affiliation. Compared with a study from 2009, stations were still relying on text and photos for web content. Although the web has provided opportunities for audience connections (Bucy, 2004), research discussed above found that this platform remained largely linear with little interactivity tied to newscasts (Gregson, 2008).

SOCIAL

Over the last decade, stations have included a variety of social media in their repertoire of communication strategies. Although online and social are both digital and web based, what differentiates the two technology segments is the inherent characteristics of social platforms as a means of connecting and building relationships with target audiences (Greer & Ferguson, 2011a). One issue for media scholars and practitioners is the effect that social networks have on TV stations and their news operations. An early study of social media and local television examined whether stations were using Twitter as a promotion and branding tool (Greer & Ferguson, 2011b). Findings revealed differences between commercial and public stations. Commercial entities offered more tweets overall, with a predominance of news content, while public stations featured more promotion tweets. However, less than a quarter of stations used the platform for breaking news, and few stations used Twitter to promote their newscasts. Other research similarly showed that few tweets on TV and newspaper Twitter sites contained cross-promotions, interactivity / engagement with followers, or promotional content, although TV stations were more active in "cross-promotion than newspapers" (Meyer & Tang, 2015, p. 249).

Moon and Hadley (2014) examined how much Twitter was used for news sourcing by top TV networks and newspapers. They found that the social network was used as a news-gathering tool, but journalists still relied on traditional sourcing techniques. Television networks were more active in using Twitter for story sources than were newspapers. One might expect networks and their large-market affiliates to invest first in something like virtual reality storytelling.

Given TV's visual composition, it is not unexpected that TV stations would utilize social networks that consist primarily of that characteristic. For example, an analysis of TV station Pinterest sites found that stations tended to post more pins on lifestyle boards than they did on promotion boards (Ferguson & Greer, 2015). Lifestyle (which represented the highest percentage of boards) and community boards also had more followers than boards that promoted the station. In contrast, a study of TV station Instagram sites found that around a third of the posts consisted of news, followed by station promotion. Site visitors interacted more with news posts than they did with content that showed reporters, anchors, and other behind-the-scenes visuals of the station (Greer & Ferguson, 2017).

IMMERSIVE

Of course, the foregoing discussion has established VR as the most highly relevant development among news-related technologies. As already noted in this chapter, some networks and stations are experimenting with the use of virtual reality. This technology is actually divided into three different concepts: virtual reality, augmented reality (AR), and mixed reality (MR). Virtual reality places individuals in a created environment, typically through the use of goggles, such as Oculus Rift (Jones, 2017; McKalin, 2014). For TV news, VR often consists of giving audiences a 360-degree view of a story versus placing the individual in an "immersive experience" (Watson, 2017, para. 4). The concept of virtual is also being used to denote the use of digital sets in combination with physical objects for newscasts (Kurz, 2015). In contrast, AR combines virtual environments with real objects and settings for user interaction (McKalin, 2014). Mixed reality uses a combination of VR and AR but with digital content that is superimposed on a viewer's reality, such as virtual objects in a room with which the person may interact (Rivera, 2017).

Based on research focused on the use of technology in TV news over the four time periods, there are several antecedents that are pertinent to today's media management practice. One is that technology improves the content of news (Lacy et al., 1988), despite concerns about quality when news personnel work across multiple platforms (Reinardy & Bacon, 2014), and whether technologies affect story organization (Cummings, 2014). Future research and news media practices should examine or experiment with the organizational structure of news stories with and without VR technology. Station characteristics also may serve as antecedents to technology adoption. This includes ownership, market size, and network affiliation, which Cleary and Bloom (2011) find were not associated with the presence of user-generated content. Kiernan and Levy (1999) also note that competition was not an issue in TV station websites.

Opportunities present challenges for tradition-bound organizations. We find compelling evidence that change is coming when the oldest forms of print journalism are leading the way for TV news broadcasters. It is worthwhile to look at these challenges in the next section.

CHALLENGES

The diffusion of emerging technologies continues to change how local television stations gather and disseminate news. Over the past two decades, research has examined how stations have evolved from relatively simple online distribution points through websites (e.g., Cleary & Bloom, 2011; Gregson, 2008; Kiernan & Levy, 1999) to enhanced connectivity of social media (e.g., Ferguson & Greer, 2015; Greer & Ferguson, 2011a; Moon & Hadley, 2014). More recently, academic and industry researchers have turned their attention to issues associated with immersive technologies, such as virtual reality (Koski, 2015). Despite the growing but understated adoption of VR in recent years, few studies have considered the current status of VR implementation in TV newsrooms and rationales for their use.

One key challenge to future media managers is lack of knowledge about the technology. The extent to which VR is being adopted by local TV stations' news departments is still not well examined, largely due to such limited case studies. Examples of VR use in journalism seem to primarily exist in print settings (e.g., Hoey, 2015; Wohlsen, 2015). Indeed, research by Pavlik and Bridges (2013) about the diffusion of AR in news contexts indicates that major newspapers were primary adopters of the technology at the time of their study. During the writing of this book chapter, a respondent called one of the researchers and volunteered his view that he believes newspapers are more interested in VR. His opinion was that newspapers have a greater need to establish a video presence than television stations. Future research must examine perceived need for such presence.

Additionally, stations that have committed to using VR in news contexts appear to be all-in when it comes to implementing the technology. Future research must focus on adoption of the specific innovation. In particular, the diffusion of VR headsets in viewers' homes will likely lead to more immersive storytelling. By 2023, forecasts predict 54 million devices in the United States alone (O'Malley, 2019). As younger audiences become accustomed to using them to play games, the opportunity may arise for news stations to create content that appeals to aging gamers interested in current events. We can expect that stations in major markets will be the first to explore this kind of storytelling.

Finally, the overall general concept of VR is problematic, as nuances between VR, AR, and MR technologies have not been fully differentiated. It is possible that some stations are using virtual sets, while others are experimenting with more advanced technologies (Kurz, 2016). Case studies would offer more in-depth understanding about how stations are using these tools, especially over time, as these innovations diffuse through local TV stations (Kang et al., 2019). At this writing, however, none of the nascent technologies related to VR have taken firm root in the news ecosystem when compared to the diffusion of other new technologies (e.g., the use of drones) adopted by TV stations (Ferguson & Greer, 2019).

There is a growing body of scholarly literature dealing with VR and journalism. Future research should track the diffusion of these VR innovations for TV news over time, especially as the techniques become more commonplace. Also, additional research should examine perceptions and attitudes of TV news audiences regarding whether immersive reporting techniques are enhancing viewers' experiences with stories (Shin & Biocca, 2018). The research process suggests an action plan to reach the desired destination.

ACTION PLAN

1. Take more risks with VR.
2. See how other TV stations and newspapers, and even companies other than media organizations, are using VR.
3. Be willing to adapt to a changing audience.

KEY TAKEAWAYS

1. The diffusion process of VR technology in news media outlets is slow but promising.
2. VR allows media managers to adopt innovations to reach specific goals in news, thus playing a part in a station's strategic planning.
3. Traditional, online, social, and immersive media all illustrate unique trends and patterns to maximize VR adoption.
4. Much more research on the use of VR in news outlets is needed, especially using VR as a stand-alone case study and looking at audience perceptions.

CONCLUSION

This chapter explains how media managers can adopt resources, have specific goals to use VR in news, and make VR a part of the station's strategic planning. According to the limited case studies, news stations using VR are intentional in their adoption of the technology, to the extent that they have planned for its use and the types of resources needed to make it happen.

Diffusion theory helps us understand the slow adoption process of VR by news organizations. As noted by Rogers (1995), relative advantage, compatibility, trialability, and observability are positively associated with innovation adoption, while complexity is a negative factor in the process. Given the newness of VR technology for news, slow and careful adoption should be encouraged. News managers likely want to try out the technology before making an adoption decision, which may be difficult given the fact that VR has not yet been widely used in TV news contexts. In particular, an analysis showed a strong positive correlation between the technology being easy to try and designated market area rank. News managers in smaller-market stations were more concerned about the ability to try the technology before making a commitment to adopt.

Challenges to TV stations are not only in the realm of adopting VR from a technological standpoint. There is also the issue of compatibility when transitioning between traditional and VR story production (Bösch et al., 2018). Implementing VR also adds a layer of complexity to story development and newscasts (Irish, 2018). Trialability might involve more than one level of adoption decision by stations, particularly those that are group owned.

The use of VR in local television offers a number of opportunities for stations. For example, stations should examine the use of virtual reality in retail environments. This tactic could also be a good way for local TV stations to become acquainted with virtual uses and then adapt those techniques for news coverage and storytelling. Use of VR in journalism would mean not just reporting about an event but also providing viewers a broader perspective of a story. Revenue streams are also a concern of local television. Stations with studio space and virtual equipment might be able to monetize their investment by making their VR studio and qualified staff available for outside productions (Morrison & Carlson, 2018).

Immersive technologies can place the viewer into an environment where they can have a broader perspective of a story (Vettehen et al., 2019). Station management might be looking at VR as all or nothing; however, stations should use only as much technology as necessary to begin implementing VR for news. Research shows that 360-degree video on mobile phones enhances a viewer's experience of a story (Kang et al., 2019). Stations do not necessarily need to produce news content that requires viewing on VR headsets to achieve a sense of presence for audiences.

Complexity, such as producing content that requires the use of a headset for viewing, is not necessary when first adopting virtual reality. As Vettehen and colleagues (2019) discovered, using a 360-degree approach is an effective way to give audiences an immersive experience of news stories. Also, stations should seek ways to break out of traditional techniques by determining how to add technology to newscasts. Stations have long used green screens for graphics. The same physical structure can be repurposed for virtual elements. Remember that technology is a tool to give audiences a better experience with stories. Stations should use as much technology as makes sense and that matches the station's needs and budget (Irish, 2018).

Studies in recent years have shown that television news viewership, even locally, continues to decline. Stations might be able to stem some of that downward trend by incorporating VR stories that connect with viewers' interests to encourage engagement (Shin & Biocca, 2018). Stations also have an opportunity to add value to newscast elements. These include instructing viewers about weather situations (Weather Group, 2018) and giving users perspectives of a distant location (Irish, 2018). This moves news and information programming from simple facts to education, thus enhancing the viewer's knowledge and understanding of events and situations.

Studies also show that local TV news is still a popular information source, despite ongoing declines in viewership (Matsa, 2018). News managers at stations are recognizing the need to adapt to reach a changing news audience, particularly in a digital environment (Knight Foundation, 2018; Papper, 2019). One way to make needed changes is to track the platforms viewers are using, which will help stations connect with audiences on their level (Irish, 2018). The challenge is that constant changes require regular assessment of evolving technologies and their users as well as delivering content that most interests viewers. Stations need to rethink their approaches to news given an aging viewership and decreasing number of younger people who watch live broadcast television (Schmidt, 2018).

Another consideration for stations is offering more variety and options for viewers beyond the decades-old means of delivering news. Stations that want to compete in their market might consider VR as a way to enhance their programming. This involves the use of a wide variety of technologies that range from 360-degree video to augmented reality that combines real objects and people with digital graphics (Kurz, 2015) to mixed reality that offers viewer interaction (Rivera, 2017). The keys to success for stations adopting VR for local news are understanding the technologies and the station's audience. In the next chapter, this book will talk about second screening, a significant change in audience viewing and engagement behavior that has brought many changes to traditional media management practices.

REFERENCES

Anderson, M. (2019, April 19). VR learning platform wins competition, lands appointment with investors. *Sacramento Business Journal.* https://www.bizjournals.com/sacramento/news/2019/04/19/vr-learning-platform-wins-competition-lands.html

Bailenson, J. (2018, January 15). How virtual reality can change the journalism industry. *PBS News Hour: Making Sense.* https://www.pbs.org/newshour/economy/making-sense/how-virtual-reality-could-change-the-journalism-industry

Bebawi, S., & Evans, M. (2019). *Living the future of news.* Springer Nature Switzerland AG.

Bösch, M., Gensch, S., & Rath-Wiggens, L. (2018). Immersed journalism: How virtual reality impacts investigative storytelling. In O. Hahn & F. Stalph (Eds.), *Digital investigative journalism: Data, visual analytics and innovative methodologies in international reporting* (pp. 103–111). Springer Nature Switzerland AG.

Bucy, E. P. (2004). Second generation net news: Interactivity and information accessibility in the online environment. *Internal Journal on Media Management, 6,* 102–113. doi: 10.1080/14241277.2004.9669386

Capitol Broadcasting Company. (2018, February 21). *WRAL-TV creates virtual reality set for "the Olympic zone."* https://www.capitolbroadcasting.com/2018/02/21/wral-tv-creates-virtual-reality-set-for-the-olympic-zone

Chan-Olmsted, S. M., & Ha, L. S. (2003). Internet business models for broadcasters: How television stations perceive and integrate the Internet. *Journal of Broadcasting & Electronic Media, 47,* 597–617. doi: 10.1207/s15506878jobem4704_7

Cleary, J., & Bloom, T. (2011). Gatekeeping at the portal: An analysis of local television websites' user-generated content. *Electronic News, 5,* 93–111. doi: 10.1177/1931243111408389

Cummings, D. (2014). The DNA of a television news story: Technological influences on TV news production. *Electronic News, 8,* 198–215. doi: 10.1177/1931243114557596

Daniels, G. L., & Loggins, G. M. (2010). Data, Doppler, or depth of knowledge: How do television stations differentiate local weather? *Atlantic Journal of Communication, 18,* 22–35. doi: 10.1080/15456870903340472

Doyle, P. (2015). Bringing you into the news: The state of virtual reality in journalism [Archive]. https://web.archive.org/web/20151122230121/http://storynext.gannett.com:80/state-of-vr.pdf

Feldman, B. (2019, January 21). The best use of augmented reality right now is the Weather Channel's. *New York Magazine.* http://nymag.com/intelligencer/2019/01/the-weather-channels-augmented-reality-segments.html

Ferguson, D. A., & Greer, C. F. (2015). Pinning and promotion: How local television stations are using Pinterest for branding and audience connectivity. *Journal of Promotion Management, 21,* 64–81. doi: 10.1080/10496491.2014.971210

Ferguson, D. A., & Greer, C. F. (2019). Assessing the diffusion of drones in local television news. *Electronic News, 13,* 23–33. doi: 10.1177/1931243119829430

Fogden, T. (2018, August 30). *Why is VR failing to take off (again)?* Tech.co. https://tech.co/why-is-vr-failing-to-take-off-again-2018-08

Greer, C. F., & Ferguson, D. A. (2011a). Following local television news personalities on Twitter: A uses and gratifications approach to social networking. *Electronic News, 5*, 145–157. doi: 10.1177/1931243111420405

Greer, C. F., & Ferguson, D. A. (2011b). Using Twitter for promotion and branding: A content analysis of local television Twitter sites. *Journal of Broadcasting & Electronic Media, 55*, 198–214. doi: 10.1080/08838151.2011.570824

Greer, C. F., & Ferguson, D. A. (2017). The local TV station as an organizational self: Promoting corporate image via Instagram. *International Journal on Media Management, 19*, 282–297. doi: 10.1080/14241277.2017.1383255

Gregson, K. S. (2008). Missed opportunities: Use of the web to promote the local television newscast. *Journal of Website Promotion, 39*, 102–117. doi: 10.1080/15533610802052837

Herz, M., & Rauschnabel, P. (2018). Understanding the diffusion of virtual reality glasses: The role of media, fashion and technology. *Technological Forecasting and Social Change, 138*, 228–242. doi: 10.1016/j.techfore.2018.09.008

Hoey, A. (2015, May/June). Journalism's emerging platforms. *Columbia Journalism Review*. https://www.cjr.org/the_experiment/journalisms_emerging_platforms.php

Hur, E. (2017, September 1). *Digital journalism class focuses on virtual reality*. Daily Trojan. https://dailytrojan.com/2017/09/01/digital-journalism-class-focuses-virtual-reality

International Data Corporation. (2018, June 19). *Augmented reality and virtual reality are on the VRge of growth, says IDC.* https://web.archive.org/web/20200115130531/https://www.idc.com/getdoc.jsp?containerId=prUS44001618

Irish, E. (2018, June 15). Indy TV news stations take different approaches to set technology. *Indianapolis Business Journal.* https://www.ibj.com/articles/69131-indianapolis-tv-news-stations-take-different-approaches-to-set-technology

Jones, S. (2017). Disrupting the narrative: Immersive journalism in virtual reality. *Journal of Media Practice, 18*, 171–185. doi: 10.1080/14682753.2017.1374677

Kang, S., O'Brien, E., Villarreal, A., Lee, W., & Mahood, C. (2019). Immersive journalism and telepresence: Does virtual reality news use affect news credibility? *Digital Journalism*, 7, 294–313. doi: 10.1080/21670811.2018.1504624

Kiernan, V., & Levy, M. R. (1999). Competition among broadcast-related websites. *Journal of Broadcasting & Electronic Media, 43*, 271–279. doi: 10.1080/08838159909364489

Knight Foundation. (2018, April 5). *Local TV news and the new media landscape*. https://knightfoundation.org/reports/local-tv-news-and-the-new-media-landscape

Koski, O. (2015, Winter). *Virtual reality lets audiences step into the story*. Nieman Storyboard. http://niemanstoryboard.org/stories/virtual-reality-lets-the-audience-step-into-the-story

Kurz, P. (2015, June 18). *Gray TV takes aim at hybrid news sets*. TVNewsCheck. http://www.tvnewscheck.com/article/86270/gray-tv-takes-aim-at-hybrid-news-sets

Kurz, P. (2016, May 19). *Five technologies reshaping TV news*. TVNewsCheck. http://www.tvnewscheck.com/article/94879/five-technologies-reshaping-tv-news

Lacy, S., Atwater, T., & Powers, A. (1988). Use of satellite technology in local television news. *Journalism & Mass Communication Quarterly, 64*, 925–929.

Marron, M. B. (2015). Watershed moments in journalism. *Journalism & Mass Communication Quarterly, 70*, 351–353. doi: 10.1177/1077695815625497

Martin, C. (2017, March 16). *VR, AR headset market growing 58% a year, to reach 99 million devices*. MediaPost. https://www.mediapost.com/publications/article/297258/vr-ar-headset-market-growing-58-a-year-to-reach.html

Matsa, K. E. (2018, January 5). *Fewer Americans rely on TV news; what type they watch varies by who they are.* Pew Research. https://www.pewresearch.org/fact-tank/2018/01/05/fewer-americans-rely-on-tv-news-what-type-they-watch-varies-by-who-they-are

McKalin, V. (2014, April 6). Augmented reality vs. virtual reality: What are the differences and similarities? *Tech Times*. http://www.techtimes.com/articles/5078/20140406/augmented-reality-vs-virtual-reality-what-are-the-differences-and-similarities.htm

Meyer, K. M., & Tang, T. (2015). #social journalism: Local news media on Twitter. *International Journal on Media Management, 17*, 241–257. doi: 10.1080/14241277.2015.1107569

Moon, S. J., & Hadley, P. (2014). Routinizing a new technology in the newsroom: Twitter as a news source in mainstream media. *Journal of Broadcasting & Electronic Media, 58*, 289–305. doi: 10.1080/08838151.2014.906435

Morrison, S., & Carlson, E. (2018, April 18). *From Nieman reports: Reinventing local TV news might require going over the top*. NiemanLab. https://www.niemanlab.org/2018/04/from-nieman-reports-reinventing-local-tv-news-might-require-going-over-the-top

O'Malley, G. (2019, January 31). *VR headsets forecast to reach 54M by 2023*. MediaPost. https://www.mediapost.com/publications/article/331302/vr-headsets-forecast-to-reach-54m-by-2023.html

Pallanich, J. (2019, May 16). *Newsrooms getting smarter about AI*. TVNewsCheck. https://tvnewscheck.com/article/235067/newsrooms-getting-smarter-about-ai

Papper, B. (2018, July 11). *2018 newsroom digital media report*. Radio and Television Digital News Association. https://www.rtdna.org/article/research_2018_newsroom_digital_media_technology

Papper, B. (2019, May 15). *2019 research: Local TV and radio news strengths*. Radio and Television Digital News Association. https://www.rtdna.org/article/2019_research_local_tv_and_radio_news_strengths

Pavlik, J. V. (2019). *Journalism in the age of virtual reality: How experiential media are transforming news*. Columbia University Press.

Pavlik, J. V., & Bridges, F. (2013). The emergence of augmented reality (AR) as a storytelling medium in journalism. *Journalism & Communication Monographs, 15*, 4–59.

PBS. (2018, September 20). *Creating virtual reality journalism: A guide for best practices*. https://www.pbs.org/wgbh/frontline/article/creating-virtual-reality-journalism-a-guide-for-best-practices

Preston, J., & Zenni, N. (2017, July 11). *11 ideas win journalism 360 challenge on immersive storytelling*. Knight Foundation. https://knightfoundation.org/articles/11-ideas-win-journalism-360-challenge-on-immersive-storytelling

Reinardy, S., & Bacon, S. (2014). Feast and famine? Local television news workers expand the offerings, but say they are hungry for quality journalism. *Journal of Media Practice, 15*, 133–145.

Reis, A. B., & Coelho, A. F. V. C. C. (2018). Virtual reality and journalism: A gateway to conceptualizing immersive journalism. *Digital Journalism, 8*, 1090–1100. doi: doi.org/10.1080/21670811.2018.1502046

Rivera, A. (2017, October 9). *Reality check. VR vs. AR vs. MR*. Business.com. https://www.business.com/articles/virtual-vs-augmented-vs-mixed-reality

Rogers, E. M. (1995). *Diffusion of innovations* (4th ed.). Free Press.

Romano, A. (2018, April 24). *Stations take new view of weather*. Broadcasting + Cable. https://www.broadcastingcable.com/news/stations-take-new-view-of-weather

Schmidt, C. (2018, May 16). *What is innovation in local TV news? Andrew Heyward's new mission is to find out*. NiemanLab. https://www.niemanlab.org/2018/05/what-is-innovation-in-local-tv-news-andrew-heywards-new-mission-is-to-find-out

Shin, D., & Biocca, F. (2018). Exploring immersive experience in journalism: What makes people empathize with and embody immersive journalism? *New Media & Society, 19*(11), 1–24. doi: 10.1177/1461444817733133

Stubbs, B. (2018). Virtual reality journalism: Ethics, grammar and the state of play. *Australian Journalism Review, 40*, 81–90.

USA Today. (n.d.). *VR stories: Put yourself inside the story*. https://www.usatoday.com/vrstories

Vanian, J. (2018, September 26). Facebook CEO Mark Zuckerberg debuts the Oculus Quest. *Fortune*. http://fortune.com/2018/09/26/facebook-oculus-quest

Vettehen, P. H., Wiltink, D., Huiskamp, M., Schaap, G., & Ketelaar, P. (2019). Taking a full view: How viewers respond to 360-degree video news. *Computers in Human Behavior, 91*, 24–32. doi: 10.1016/j.chb.2018.09.018

Watson, Z. (2017, April 24). *VR for news: The new reality*. Reuters Institute for the Study of Journalism. https://reutersinstitute.politics.ox.ac.uk/our-research/vr-news-new-reality

Weather Group. (2018, November 16). The Weather Channel and SEC network team up on immersive mixed reality experience [Press release]. http://weathergroup.com/newsroom/2018/11/17/weather-channel-and-sec-network-team-immersive-mixed-reality-experience
Wohlsen, J. (2015, November 9). Google Cardboard's *New York Times* experiment just hooked a generation on VR. *Wired.* https://www.wired.com/2015/11/google-cardboards-new-york-times-experiment-just-hooked-a-generation-on-vr
Wood, L. (2018, November 28). *Global virtual reality (VR) market analysis & forecast to 2027.* Business Wire. https://www.businesswire.com/news/home/20181128005629/en/Global-Virtual-Reality-VR-Market-Analysis-Forecast

CHAPTER 21

Second Screening

Miao Guo, Ball State University

LEARNING OBJECTIVES

1. Understand second screening as a convergence between mass and personal communication.
2. Understand the relationships between second screening and social television, and between second screens and primary television.
3. Identify second-screen user behavior within a media multitasking context.
4. Recognize the business values of second screening to media practitioners and managers.

As mobile devices proliferate through the adoption of smartphones, tablets, and laptop computers, today's audiences increasingly interact with television content through a "second screen" platform. In particular, mobile enhancement apps allow audiences to remotely comment and share information about their favorite shows online. Social media create a new and powerful "back channel," fueling the renaissance of live broadcasting. Mobile and tablet devices empower viewers to experience television whenever and wherever they want (Proulx & Shepatin, 2012). These developments have significantly invigorated the social nature of television viewing, now dubbed social television viewing. The emerging pattern of second screening is meaningful for program producers, broadcasters, and advertisers in their justification of investment in content, retaining and acquiring viewers, enhancing brand affinity and program loyalty, and identifying and marketing to the most valuable audiences.

In today's convergent media environment, second screening has become a larger phenomenon. Second screening involves any time a person simultaneously watches television and uses a digital device (e.g., smartphone, tablet, or laptop computer) to access the Internet, social media platforms, and enhancement apps in order to obtain more information about or discuss the program they are watching (Zúñiga, Garcia-Perdomo, & McGregor, 2015). According to an industry report, around 177.7 million U.S. adults—70.3% of the total population—regularly used another digital device while watching television (Kirkpatrick, 2017). Among those second screeners, 110.5 million used a desktop or laptop to browse the web while watching cable or over-the-top streaming services like Netflix or Hulu, while 162.2 million used a smartphone for second-screen activities (Kirkpatrick, 2017). Moreover, Nielsen discovered how dependent U.S. consumers are on their smartphones when engaging second-screen viewing behavior (Perez, 2018). Shopping, seeking entertainment, and relaxation while watching television are the most popular reasons second screeners access their mobile phones. Smartphone users also increasingly search for information related to actors, plot lines, and athletes or teams while watching television (Clement, 2019).

In reviewing second-screen activities, media practitioners and scholars have suggested various benefits of cross-media engagement for advertisers and broadcasters. From the advertisers' perspective, viewers engaged in a multimedia environment are more likely to remember an advertisement, internalize the message, and be motivated by it than those who are less engaged (Epps, 2009). Advanced web-based technologies and their online applications, especially various social media platforms, are useful in nurturing customer relationships with brands among those who are most tightly engaged with the program. Because more-involved viewers tend to engage in cross-media activities, while less-involved viewers tend to engage through a single screen, advertisers are most interested in targeting cross-media platforms (Harris Interactive, 2008). Hence, the value of advertising grows as viewers connect television programming and marketing message via multimedia platforms.

Viewer engagement with television programs through second screens also offers never-before-possible opportunities for broadcasters to connect with their increasingly fragmented audiences. Major broadcasting and cable networks have adopted real-time platforms such as Twitter to drive tune-in and take advantage of the growing trend of simultaneous television and Internet usage by dispensing online information in tandem with the airing of programs. The ABC network has two of the top-ranked social television shows through second-screen platforms, which allow fans to connect through mobile and online platforms and share their opinions about the shows across their social profiles (Copp, 2019). Here, the use of second-screen devices enhances audience engagement and thus has tremendous marketing potential. Socially engaged viewers are more likely to stick with a show, talk about the show, and spread word of mouth about the show. The "stickiness" achieved through real-time interaction can humanize broadcasters, which enables them to listen to, affirm, and amplify the opinions of their fans.

To fully understand second-screening behavior and its impact, this chapter approaches second-screen activities and technologies from the following perspective. First, one must realize that second screening is an ongoing convergence between mass and personal communication that combines traditional and new media screens. Second, it is vital to understand the relationships between second screening and social television behavior and between primary television screen and second-screen devices. Third, media managers may be better suited to understanding second-screen user behavior and its implications. Lastly, second-screen activities and technologies encompass more than social television. The main concept pivots around bringing broadcasters, advertisers, content producers, and even celebrities together for a deeper, more interactive, engaging, and personalized viewing experience. These relationships are especially important for future media managers. Therefore, there are enormous business values of second screening across different media sectors, which present opportunities and challenges to media practitioners and managers in today's convergent media environment. Let us explore how media companies, such as Televisa and AMC, integrate second screening into their business strategy.

CASE STUDY

Starting in 2015, the Televisa company in Mexico introduced a fully interactive television series called *Logout* by taking advantage of second-screen technology and audience evolution. *Logout* is designed, written, and performed to integrate with an app to enhance audience viewing experience. Automatic content recognition technology allows mobile devices to access interactive and organic content from the television in real time, synchronized with a second-screen platform. The app incorporates various mobile device features, including camera, text, touchscreen, geolocation, and microphone—along with creating opportunities to interact via videos, texts, calls, and video chats.

The second-screen app was designed to appeal to two types of target audience with the most access to smartphones: (1) men and women ages 16–24 years and (2) middle- to upper-middle-class men and women ages 25–44 years. In order to successfully introduce the idea of native content produced with second-screen functionality, offline and online campaigns were implemented to use space on programming and newscasts across all channels, including both Televisa's broadcast and paid television. To encourage people to download the app, Televisa launched a search engine marketing campaign to promote the series. The search website was critical because it gave viewers the chance to access interactive content and learn about the app before attempting to live broadcast. The site had links to stores where the app could be downloaded for different operating systems. To close the circle, each episode began with a brief message or bumper asking viewers to open their apps to interact. An "icon" or "bug" was used to alert viewers when a scene was about to integrate with their device through the app. The mobile campaign contained various actions, including a direct call to download the *Logout* app, a video tutorial, FAQs, and an email contact to report incidents.

This cross-media marketing campaign achieved successful results. The hashtag for the app (#Logout) was popular, and viewers used it to discuss the series on Twitter, Facebook, and Instagram. One viewer called the project a "masterpiece." The first live broadcasting of *Logout* broke records, with 100,000 total downloads across iOS and Android. After nine episodes, the app had reached 540,000 interactions and 640,000 sessions. *Logout* is the first of many projects of its kind, as second-screen experiences are growing, offering new and different ways to interact with Televisa's content and to strengthen viewers' emotional connections with the series. By taking advantage of second-screen technology and audience evolution, *Logout* implied a paradigm shift in presenting television content across different platforms.

Another example of successfully adopting the second-screen experience is American cable network AMC's popular zombie show *The Walking Dead*. The second-screen activities include running a fan video contest on Facebook, an ultimate fan game that is effectively a trivia contest, and implementing a "Watch and Win Sweepstake." In each episode of *The Walking Dead*, there were three commercials devoted to the Watch and Win Sweepstake, urging viewers to visit a link with a large "Enter Contest" button. The prize was the Hyundai Tucson featured on the show at the beginning of the third season, and the car was prominently featured in both app ads and on-air promotions. Here, the second-screen activities, such as social games, story syncs, quizzes, contests, and sweepstakes, brought a variety of opportunities for alternative promotions and online sales.

As digital consumption continues to rise around the world, second screening has become the new norm for global television audiences. It is expected that more media managers will engage with this innovative strategy to incorporate second screens with their programming. It's expected that major players in the media industry will grow digital audiences and position mobile within their content. How to integrate "old" traditional concepts with an effective second-screening strategy will be important for media managers to determine in today's media multitasking era.

Something Old

To decipher the second-screening experience, this section approaches it from three perspectives. First, it should be realized that second screening is an ongoing convergence between mass and personal communication as well as a combination of traditional and new media screens. Second, it is vital to understand the relationship between second screening and social television behavior. Third, there are far more complicated relations between the primary television screens and the second-screen devices in a dual-viewing environment.

CONVERGENCE BETWEEN MASS AND INTERPERSONAL COMMUNICATION

As discussed above, second screening is when individuals utilize digital devices to access the Internet, social media platforms, or enhancement apps to gain additional information or discuss television content while simultaneously watching television (Guo & Holmes, 2016; Zúñiga, Garcia-Perdomo, & McGregor, 2015). Increased second-screening behavior is the outcome of two types of media consumption: television content and digital media, which represents a set of interrelated behaviors and the convergence between mass and interpersonal communication (Perloff, 2015). More specifically, second screening demonstrates the concurrence of mass and interpersonal process, side by side. The social-viewing activities that take place on various second screens indicate that socially shared television viewing can be enjoyed while simultaneously exchanging reactions via social media about television content with coviewers. This is an excellent example of the parallel processes of mass and interpersonal communication and how they can be combined to enhance the entertainment experience (Raney & Ji, 2017).

Moreover, drawing on theories from the communication mediation model (McLeod et al., 1999; Shah et al., 2007) and the cognitive mediation model (Eveland, 2004; Eveland, Shah, & Kwak, 2003), second screening is proposed as a communicative mediating process (Gil de Zúñiga, Molyneux, & Zheng, 2014). Specific to news consumption, second screening has been widely used by audiences during breaking news, live coverage, political debates, and online political participation (Giglietto & Selva, 2014; Zúñiga et al., 2015). In particular, second screening for news consumption is a significant predictor of online political participation and a key link between television news and political engagement as this relationship is fully mediated. The mediation process is indicative of a user's motivation toward information seeking and expression via the website and social media platforms (Zúñiga et al., 2015).

SECOND SCREENING AND SOCIAL TELEVISION

To better understand second screening and its impact, it is necessary to differentiate between second screening and social television. The concept of social television refers to the simultaneous consumption of television alongside social media chatter about the programs (Fossen & Schweidel, 2019). It describes audience engagement, communication, and social interaction while watching television through a variety of social media platforms, including Facebook, Twitter, and Instagram. For example, Twitter and Facebook rank among the top social media platforms that users tend to visit when simultaneously watching television. The degree of social interaction is even higher when it comes to "event television," such as the Super Bowl and Academy Awards (Toy, 2010).

Various motivations drive audiences to engage with social television activities. Researchers identified 10 possible motives behind social television activities (Guo & Chan-Olmsted, 2015), which correspond to previous television viewing motives (Rubin, 1983), Internet use motives (Papacharissi & Rubin, 2000), and YouTube video viewing motives (Haridakis & Hanson, 2009). The first motive, *relaxation*, describes a pleasant rest and relaxation-driven motivation. The second motive, *companionship*, describes a relief from loneliness as one of the reasons behind social television behavior. The third, *passing time*, describes how television audiences use social media to interact with television content out of habit and to occupy time. The fourth motive, *entertainment*, illustrates the experience of social television for amusement and enjoyment. The fifth, *information*, explains how the social engagement experience is derived from being informed. The sixth and seventh motives describe the *arousal* and *escape* motives. The eighth motive, *access*, measures the use of social media to access television content because it is easier and a novel way of searching for information and keeping up with current issues. The ninth motive, *learning*, describes uncovering unknown and useful things as a motivation for social television activities. The last motive, *interpersonal utility*, suggests belonging, inclusion, affection, social interaction, and expressive needs (Guo & Chan-Olmsted, 2015).

This emerging pattern of social television viewing promises to enhance viewer engagement, extend the value of brands and content properties, and open up new advertising opportunities for media managers (Fossen & Schweidel, 2019; Guo & Chan-Olmsted, 2015; Harris Interactive, 2011). Exploring the relationships among television advertising, social television activities, and sales, Fossen and Schweidel (2019) suggest that television programs with high online social television activities are profitable for advertisers. Moreover, social media offers a rare new and attractive potential in improving audience engagement, marketing television content, and enhancing brand affinity. Engaged viewers in a multimedia environment are more likely to remember an advertisement, internalize the message, and be motivated by it than those who are less engaged (Epps, 2009). Hence, social television engagement behavior has a significant positive impact on program loyalty, audience satisfaction, and the likelihood of product purchase (Guo & Chan-Olmsted, 2015).

While the terms *social television* and *second screening* are often used interchangeably, they are, in fact, two different experiences: social television is a subset of second screening. HBO's *Game of Thrones* app is probably the best example of this relationship, as it allows viewers to become better acquainted with each character when they appear on screen as well as their relationships to other characters. It is a great application for a show with such a large cast and helps draw viewers deeper into the programming. Another good example is sport broadcasting, such as football games. If football team supporters use a second device while watching the game, those spectators are found to be particularly interested in "functional" services such as statistics but less into social or even gaming activities (Pfeffel, Kexel, Kexel, & Ratz, 2016). Despite these experiences all happening on second screens, there is nothing particularly "social" about the activities involved; viewers are interacting with the app but not with each other. Instead, they are simply enhancing their television viewing experience. Therefore, second screening encompasses a lot more than just social television. The main concept pivots around bringing broadcasters, advertisers, content producers, audiences, and even celebrities together for a deeper, more interactive, engaging, and personalized viewing experience.

RELATIONSHIP BETWEEN SECOND SCREENS AND PRIMARY TELEVISION

When examining the relationship between traditional television screens and second-screen devices, multitasking behaviors among second screen users vary significantly. Audio information combined with text tends to overwhelm individual channels. However, the combination of audio with a relevant visual image demands less time to process the information (Chandler & Sweller, 1992). A dual-coding theory asserts that memory can be enhanced when corresponding visual and verbal information are received simultaneously and paired in working memory (Paivio, 1986). Yet, researchers found that while the television screen is the primary device and receives a majority of the user's cognitive attention, a concurrently used second device can either interrupt or complement the user experience (Vaccari, Chadwick, & O'Loughlin, 2015). It is important for media managers to note that using enhancement apps while watching television may enhance or diminish cognitive processing, depending on the alignment between the two content sources (e.g., television audio and mobile screen content).

By investigating visual attention distribution between the television screen and second screens through eye-tracking experiments, Guo and Holmes (2016) discovered that the distribution of gaze time across screens differed depending on whether the television content was programming or commercials. During commercials, the share of gaze time on the television fell, while the share of gaze time on the second screen increased. Results suggest that the second screen could garner considerable visual attention during commercials, which may be associated with lower engagement with television during these periods (Guo & Holmes, 2016). Nielsen also reported that most of the activities (71%) that take place on second screens while watching television are related to the show content. Second screening actually augments the overall television viewing experience (Perez, 2018).

Combining an audience attention approach with a cognitive perspective, diverse results of the relations between the second screen and television screen exist. The hierarchy between the "first" television screen and "second" screens becomes less certain, and the media multitasking behavior makes it unclear which device is primary and which is complementary. With the increasingly prevalence of concurrent use between television and an ancillary device, media managers today may be less interested in whether the use of a second screen distracts or complements the primary device's usage and more focused on which type of device attracts the most attention and which is complementary.

Something New

All forms of media consumption, including both live television broadcasting and digital media, share the goal of generating audiences. Therefore, media practitioners and managers benefit greatly by understanding second-screen viewing patterns and their multidimensional behaviors. Latest industry reports confirm that smartphones are the most popular second screens when watching television, followed by laptops, desktops, and tablets (Perez, 2018). Mobile devices, especially smartphones, have become an increasingly common part of people's daily television routine (Kirkpatrick, 2017). Obtaining more information about show content, using social media to write or read posts related to the show, and searching for information about product features advertised in the show are among the top second-screen activities (Ali, 2018).

UNDERSTAND SECOND-SCREEN VIEWING PATTERNS

As a means to assess second-screen viewing patterns, it is valuable to find out when audiences typically use their second screens to interact with different genres of programs, such as news, sports, dramas, reality shows, and sitcoms. For sport events, second-screen activities happen frequently while or after viewers watch the games. Viewers also tend to interact with reality television shows through their second screens while simultaneously watching them on traditional television. However, for news, dramas, and sitcoms, second screeners are more likely to engage in their media devices and online apps after watching these shows. Interestingly, the majority of second screeners prefer to use mobile devices to interact with television content, regardless of genre, synchronously and asynchronously. Moreover, sports programming and reality television shows seem more easily to stimulate real-time interaction than other television genres.

IDENTIFY SECOND SCREENERS' MULTIDIMENSIONAL BEHAVIOR

Five dimensions have been found to explain the different ways television viewers use second screens to engage with television content: utility, control, interaction, influence, and attention. The first dimension, *utility*, is a self-education process describing use of the second screen to satisfy curiosity and interest about a program or to gain a sense of security through knowledge. For example, television viewers tend to use their second screens to search for program-related information and updates and access biographies/backgrounds of characters/players of the shows. The utility dimension characterizes participatory behavior in relation to the core programming and/or ancillary information about program content. It is less interactive or social but nevertheless critical, because second screeners start showing interest in the program and initiate a social engagement process. Furthermore, the "social shows" could be core programming and/or ancillary materials and information, which supplement, extend, or expand viewers' overall knowledge, including critiques, gossip about the stars, back-scene interviews, and television promos.

The second dimension, *control*, demonstrates the extent to which individual viewers feel "in charge" of their television viewing experience. This dimension signifies how the second screen user has versatile choices and control over their viewing platform, time, and place. Empowered by mobile, personal media devices, television viewers can access television content through a range of portals, including (1) broadcast/cable network websites (e.g., nbc.com, usanetwork.com), (2) broadcast/cable network apps (e.g., ABC Watch, HBO Go), and (3) specific show apps (e.g., *The Walking Dead, Grey's Anatomy*). In recent years, a growing number of media companies have launched their own network or show-specific companion apps. These official websites and companion apps enrich linear television viewing, providing a variety of enhancements such as online fan communities, live event interaction, and online merchandise.

The third dimension, *interaction*, indicates the degree of social interaction viewers develop with programs as well as program personnel like creators, writers, and characters through Twitter. Such engagement behaviors include (1) following and reading the show tweets on Twitter and (2) writing or commenting on the show tweets on Twitter. The participation of celebrities/characters and other personnel of television programs in Twitter interaction could prompt involvement with new audiences who might not be interested in other show-centered activities and further stimulate a two-way social interaction. Twitter, therefore, has been recognized as one of the best social media venues to enliven social conversations surrounding television programs across diverse locations. Media managers, therefore, need to embrace Twitter (or other social media) to drive viewer engagement.

The fourth dimension, *influence*, measures the degree of identification and belonging. This helps explain the meaningful influence users feel when discussing television programs on social media platforms such as Facebook. Such typical activities include (1) "liking" the shows on Facebook, (2) interacting with friends about the shows on their own Facebook pages, and (3) posting or commenting on show posts on Facebook. The influence dimension involves peer-to-peer interaction between audiences of the program and a potential meaningful nonaudience. Driven by the relationship-focus and identity-management dynamics on Facebook, signaling one's personal preferences or "liking" a show suggests the viewer draws on the program as part of self- and social identity as well as a way of adding meaning to relationships with others. In addition, influence opportunities also exist when a show solicits viewers' status updating, opinion input, and program sharing in social networks. These activities influence a broader range of people, regardless of whether they are the target audiences of the program. In this sense, the viewer becomes an ambassador on behalf of the television brand to advocate, recommend, and personally promote television content.

The fifth dimension, *attention,* indicates the degree of focused attention on the second-screen television experience. In other words, it lets media managers understand how focused (or not) audiences are on their second-screen television viewing. Concentration of attention is manifested by such engagement behaviors during second-screen viewing as (1) blocking out events around them, (2) "losing themselves" while watching the show (known as "narrative immersion"), (3) avoiding interacting with others, and (4) losing track of time. Corresponding to visual attention distributed between the television screen and the second screen, the focused attention dimension signals the degree of users' mental concentration while performing second-screen activities. In addition, this dimension could be indicative of users' perceptions of their external environment. There is great social functionality delivered by the second screen, but mobile devices can also serve as a "buffer," creating one's own space in managing relationships with others and external surroundings.

Many media professionals and managers are interested in identifying second screeners' viewing patterns and multidimensional behavior. As a behavior-oriented measure of audience experiences, these five dimensions—utility, control, interaction, influence, and focused attention—decipher second-screen viewing simultaneously at the content and platform levels. These five aspects also demonstrate different functionalities delivered by various digital devices. The utility and control dimensions indicate that the second screen can empower television viewers with access to core programming and/or information. The dimensions of interaction and influence show how second screens can transform a shared and sharing viewing pattern into a real social television experience.

Mobile devices have significantly facilitated social dialogues and interaction between audiences and media figures via social media. In other words, the second-screen engagement experience can deepen the relationship between audiences and branded television content and extend that relationship to media figures and other audience members. The focused attention dimension signifies that the second screen can be a focus point used to manage the user's relationship with others and external environments. In summary, this explication process presents media managers an aggregate, vivid profile of cross-media multitasking viewers, who have actively engaged with a second monitor of different screen sizes while watching television. Media managers, therefore, should take advantage of the capability of each media device to create and distribute program content that best serves their audience's needs.

Opportunities and Challenges

As discussed above, it is vital to fully understand the behavior of second screeners, the relationship between second screening and social television, and relationships between the primary television screen and the second screen for media managers to create a deeper, more interactive, engaging, and personalized viewing experience for their audiences. The main purpose of creating second-screen experiences for viewers, apart from expanding the fan base and viewership in general, is monetization. Almost half the U.S. marketing decision makers believe that the second screen is one of the top factors that limit the success of their television advertising campaigns, and a growing number of marketers are embracing a cross-device approach in efforts to drive an increase in conversations (Talbot, 2019). The multidimensional behavior of second-screen platforms highlights the growing importance of cross-platform advertising campaigns in reaching targeted and involved audiences. Media managers today have to face the opportunities and challenges brought by second screening.

OPPORTUNITIES

At present, second screen social television viewing is gradually evolving into a ubiquitous consumption pattern among television viewers. This provides a great opportunity for advertisers, as they can target television audiences in a highly engaged environment by extending their commercial messaging in particular shows to social media channels and mobile devices. Marketers who fully utilize cross-media platforms are able to boost the value of advertising. Therefore, second screening may create several new opportunities, including targeted advertising, online sales and mobile commerce, and audience research due to big data available through second-screen platforms.

TARGETED ADVERTISEMENTS

The combination of television content and ancillary information on second screens yields great opportunities for advertisers and digital marketers. Second screening enables media managers to serve highly targeted, personalized ads synchronized with the first screen. If those ads are able to be coordinated appropriately, they are more likely to result in a successful conversion. Such strategies should incorporate companion app ads, sponsored tweets, Facebook posts, or Instagram hashtags. Common practices are to display at the bottom of the television screen tweets about television programming and contests that require sending short messages or posting on social media. Such ads may offer coupons or discounts to viewers who respond on social media and bring them to a website or require them to download apps that synchronize with television content.

Sports fans, most notably fantasy sports enthusiasts, are also found to be tethered to a second screen during live broadcasting (Pfeffel et al., 2016). Suppose a sports fan is watching a football game and switches to a mobile device to search for a player's stats. Here, the marketer can send the fan a digital coupon, an ad for a newsletter signup, or even a targeted ad for a local store where the player's jersey is being sold. When the target audience is using multiple screens simultaneously, this gives marketers and advertisers an opportunity to be creative on the second screen in ways that reinforce the message coming from the first screen in the media multitasking context (Talbot, 2019). In essence, the key of successful second-screen advertising is to create mobile ads and ad experiences that are relevant to first-screen content that captures more of consumers' attention.

ONLINE SALES AND MOBILE COMMERCE

In terms of online sales and mobile commerce, easy access to second screens empowers television viewers to take immediate actions after seeing an ad. Those activities include searching for product reviews and prices, expressing opinions on social media, or placing an order on the advertiser's website. Clearly, second screening offers a valuable opportunity for television advertisers to combine post-ad spikes in an online or social context to the individual television ad that caused them. Researchers confirmed that there is a detectable spike of brand search and price search online after a regular ad insertion within national and local television broadcasts (Du, Xu, & Wilbur, 2019). Nearly all the immediate response occurs within five minutes of an ad spot. In addition, managers should note that online chatter about the program before an ad's airing could decrease online traffic to the advertiser's website but increase online purchases, leading to an overall net positive effect on online sales (Fossen & Schweidel, 2019). Online chatter about the retailer following an ad's airing increases subsequent online purchases on the retailer's website. As such, media managers and marketers should shift their focus to the second screen and offer viewers a selection of items featured on their television screens for online sales or mobile commerce opportunities.

In practice, Target, a retail giant in the United States, has converted product placement on television into an online shopping experience through various second-screen platforms, which brings advertising and product placement to a whole new level. Target has collaborated with TBS's comedy *Cougar Town* and had certain Target products featured in the show. When an episode aired on TBS, it was simultaneously transmitted on ShopCougarTown.com. Therefore, if viewers saw a Target product they liked while watching the show, they could view the online simulcast on their mobile phones or tablets to locate the product by clicking a flashing red square nearby. This is an excellent example of how managers and marketers can move beyond the historical confines of an ad break, engage consumers with the premium television content experience, and generate new sales opportunities through second-screen activities.

BIG DATA AND AUDIENCE ANALYTICS

Products, services, and memberships are primary sources of second-screen monetization. However, the technology provides value that may be just as, if not more, profitable to companies—big data. Viewer behaviors in social media and second-screen apps are part of the big data puzzle and, if handled properly, provide extremely valuable and actionable insights to advertisers and content providers. At the same time, media organizations today are competing for attention in an ever-more-competitive and constantly changing environment. They must adopt new methods of audience research through media analytics that inform the creation, distribution, and marketing of media content. Changing media consumption behaviors and organizational activities have produced a plethora of digital data that can be measured and analyzed to generate significant strategic insights. In the end, analysis of this data may help create better products for broader audiences and generate additional revenue per viewer.

Specifically, by using big data and audience analytics generated from second screening, content creators, service providers, and broadcasters could better understand complex consumption behaviors and develop the best product and promotional strategies to attract and retain viewers, subscribers, and users. For example, big data and audience analytics have provided insights into the redesign of ABC's WATCH app. "It is really an example of how we looked at analytics to make our decision," said Disney / ABC Television Group executive vice president Albert Cheng in an interview (Graser, 2014). The aggregated data from second-screen platforms in tandem with traditional demographics data can be used for personalized advertising in the right context, at the right time, in the right place. Therefore, it is valuable for optimizing cross-platform ad campaigns and strengthening the message of the commercial. Simply put, big data and audience analytics make it possible to understand who uses a second screen when and where to deliver the right message through the right channel.

CHALLENGES

Efficient monetization of second-screen technologies and applications depends on the ability of media companies to deliver real value to consumers by offering a new level of interactivity and serving tailored ads to meet each second screener's interests. However, the advancement of technologies may bring several uncertainties and challenges to professionals and managers across different media sectors, such as broadcast, advertising, telecommunications, and more. Technologies such as artificial intelligence (AI), virtual reality (VR), augmented reality (AR), application programming interface, 360-degree video, machine learning, and facial recognition have been experimented with and applied to various media businesses in order to enhance audience immersive experience. For example, advanced personalized content recommendation technologies can enable content aggregators to collect news content and information from third-party providers and use AI algorithms to personalize content and offer tailored newsfeed services. Using natural language processing and computer vision, those mobile news apps on second screens could further fine-tune their models with users' continuous interactions with the app, which has gradually reshaped people's news consumption behavior.

These technological advancements and the evolution of audience behavior demand a combined effort from content creators, broadcasters, advertisers, audiences, and other related stakeholders to generate a shared vision for how the second screen should develop further, making the second screen a full-fledged part of the overall experience rather than an optional extra. Television companion apps have been an important growth area for both commercial and public television. They should place increasing emphasis on higher-quality second-screen apps capable of driving engagement and retaining viewership in the long run. To achieve those goals, these apps will have to offer unique value and functionality accessible instantly by all eligible audiences. For instance, second-screen apps may eventually include elements of face-to-face interaction via conferencing for deeper immersion and direct communication between friends, fans, and even actors / hosts.

The creative partnership between television broadcasters and advertisers is critical to fund this growth and to meet those challenges. As the television industries increasingly compete against alternative distribution platforms while facing fragmented audiences with decreasing loyalty, it is vital for television broadcasters and advertisers to develop a long-term relationship with their viewers through cross-platform strategies. For media practitioners and managers, the issue of whether and how television broadcasters and advertisers should devote resources to develop second-screening strategies must be addressed. It is expected that there will be more partnerships between television and technology companies in the near future, impacting all stakeholders in the television industry, including content producers, cable / broadcast networks, local television stations, cable / satellite system operators, and advertisers.

Tech-savvy audiences have proved resistant to traditional, intrusive television commercials. Therefore, second-screen interaction works best when it taps in to the desires and motivations of second screeners, and the most successful multiscreen experiences are driven by organic viewer activities. Second screening depends on the future viewing habits of the millennial and post-millennial generations. These groups of viewers watch fewer hours of linear television than other audience groups. However, it is still not clear that this trend will continue as those generations become aged. Although significant challenges remain to overcome, media managers should be aware that television has entered into a new age, closely intertwined with enhancement apps, social networks, and concepts like second- or multiscreen content consumption. Based on this understanding, the following action plan should help future managers integrate second screening into their media business strategies.

ACTION PLAN

1. Develop personalized, immersive experiences for audiences by offering higher-quality second-screen content, services, and functionalities.
2. Utilize big data and digital analytics to continuously track and measure audiences' media multitasking behavior.
3. Seek continuous collaboration among broadcasters, advertisers, audiences, and other related stakeholders to further integrate second screening in media business strategies.

KEY TAKEAWAYS

1. Second screening should be understood as a convergence between mass and interpersonal communication.
2. Social television activities are a subset of second-screening behavior, while the majority of social television takes place on second-screen platforms.
3. The hierarchy between the "first" television screen and "second" screens becomes less certain, and the media multitasking behavior makes it unclear, which device is primary and which is complementary.
4. Second screening should be recognized as multidimensional behavior simultaneously happening at the content and platform levels, which includes such dimensions as *utility, control, interaction, influence,* and *attention.*
5. Second screening may present several new opportunities regarding targeted advertising, online sales and mobile commerce, and audience research due to big data available through second-screen platforms.

6. The advancement of technologies like AI, VR, and AR may cause several uncertainties and challenges to professionals and managers across different media sectors, such as broadcast, advertising, telecommunications, and more.

CONCLUSION

As a marriage of convenience between two screens, second screening results in a growing audience size, thus increasing business potential. This chapter examines the key concepts in terms of second screening and social television, discusses the multidimensional behavior of second screeners, summarizes several business opportunities, and examines the challenges associated with technology innovation and audience evolution. The example of Televisa clearly indicates that when television viewers are given an opportunity to access second-screen platforms, their viewership, loyalty, and engagement with television content are amplified. Audience fragmentation, brought on by numerous options for entertainment and information as well as a host of advanced technologies, is a serious management issue for media organizations. Media managers today cannot stop the fragmented marketplace or continuously declining viewership; they can only adapt to those rapid changes.

The second screen is best understood not only as an object or a media device but as a convergence experience or process that combines mass and interpersonal communication. For legacy and digital media organizations, the best way to take advantage of second screening is to build on the organizations' strategic plans and objectives in conjunction with technology innovation and audience evolution. Unlike traditional "passive" audiences, today's audiences are defined as active, motivated, and goal oriented. To identify potential audiences, managers need a clear understanding of audience research and to recognize that a plethora of digital data can be measured and analyzed to generate strategic insights. For example, real-time audience measurement metrics are now achievable by applying automatic content recognition technology into smart televisions, set-top boxes, smartphones, and tablets. The measurement data is essential to quantify audience consumption behavior. In the end, big data and audience analytics could help create better products for broader audiences and generate additional revenue streams.

Although stakeholder optimism is high, it is still unclear if second screening is a complementary feature to the television screen or if it will become a dominant platform to replace primary television viewing. When it comes to audience attention in a cross-device scenario, researchers reveal that concurrent streams of information add extra mental effort to engage and generally result in poorer performance in comprehension tasks (Fox, Rosen, & Crawford, 2009). Multiscreen multitasking is sometimes criticized as the inability of the young generation to stay focused. Nevertheless, enhancement apps used by second-screen users while watching television may enhance or diminish cognitive processing, depending on the alignment between the two content sources (e.g., television audio and mobile screen content). Therefore, cross-platform advertising campaigns require more contextual rich data that help enhance engagement using cross-media techniques within the right context at the right time. In modern cross-device scenarios, these effects are likely exacerbated—we sit with the device in our laps; therefore the second screen is in the peripheral of our vision as we watch television (and vice versa).

After years of incubation, second screening is finally prevalent across digital media audiences, and second-screen viewing trends have become increasingly prevalent across the globe. Among the top 10 countries having second screen audiences, Norway and Turkey are at the top of this list with a 76% multiscreeners rate. Australia and New Zealand have around 75% second screeners, followed by Netherlands (73%) and Colombia (72%) (Ali, 2018). Although large reservoirs of potential opportunities remain untapped within this union of screens, media practitioners and managers today should recognize that the success of future television depends on involving mobile and social engagement and being designed to encourage genuine viewer participation around the world. As one can imagine, the increased engagement of media audiences on personal devices produces a vast amount of data for analysts to decipher. Chapter 22, "Big Data and Entrepreneurship," will focus on the role big data plays in media management in a convergent age.

REFERENCES

Ali, A. (2018, November 13). *The second screen viewing trend that's reshaping marketing*. Curatti. https://curatti.com/second-screen-viewing-trend

Chandler, P., & Sweller, J. (1992). The spilt-attention effect as a factor in the design of instruction. *British Journal of Educational Psychology, 62*, 233–246.

Clement, J. (2019, January 29). *Second screen usage—statistics and facts*. Statista. https://www.statista.com/topics/2531/second-screen-usage

Copp, E. (2019, February 12). *6 brands tapping in to the power of second screen social*. Hootsuite. https://blog.hootsuite.com/second-screen-social

Du, R. Y., Xu, L., & Wilbur, K. C. (2019). Immediate responses of online brand search and price search to TV ads. *Journal of Marketing, 83*, 81–100.

Epps, S. R. (2009). *What engagement means for media companies*. Slideshare. http://www.slideshare.net/ad_crystal/forrester-what-engagement-means-for-media-companies

Eveland, W. P. (2004). The effect of political discussion in producing informed citizens: The roles of information, motivation, and elaboration. *Political Communication, 21*, 177–193. doi: 10.1080/10584600490443877

Eveland, W. P., Shah, D. V., & Kwak, N. (2003). Assessing causality in the cognitive mediation model: A panel study of motivations, information processing and learning during campaign 2000. *Communication Research, 30*, 359–386.

Fossen, B. L., & Schweidel, D. A. (2019). Social TV, advertising, and sales: Are social shows good for advertisers? *Marketing Science, 38*, 274–295.

Fox, A. B., Rosen, J., & Crawford, M. (2009). Distractions, distractions: Does instant messaging affect college students' performance on a concurrent reading comprehension task? *Cyberpsychology Behavior, 12*, 51–53.

Giglietto, F., & Selva, D. (2014). Second screen and participation: A content analysis on a full season dataset of tweets. *Journal of Communication, 64*, 260–277. doi: 10.1111/jcom.12085

Gil de Zúñiga, H., Molyneux, L., & Zheng, P. (2014). Social media, political expression, and political participation: Panel analysis of lagged and concurrent relationships. *Journal of Communication, 64*, 612–634. doi: 10.1111/jcom.12103

Graser, M. (2014, September 24). How big data helped ABC redesign the second screen experience. *Variety*. https://variety.com/2014/digital/news/how-big-data-helped-abc-redesign-the-second-screen-experience-1201312940/

Guo, M., & Chan-Olmsted, S, M. (2015). Predictors of social television viewing: How perceived program, media, and audience characteristics affect social engagement with television programming. *Journal of Broadcasting & Electronic Media, 59*, 240–258. doi: 10.1080/08838151.2015.1029122

Guo, M., & Holmes, M. (2016). Double vision: An eye-tracking analysis of visual attention between television and second screens. In J. V. Pavlik (Ed.), *Digital technology and the future of broadcasting: Global perspectives* (pp. 31–44). Routledge.

Haridakis, P., & Hanson, G. (2009). Social interaction and co-viewing with YouTube: Blending mass communication reception and social connection. *Journal of Broadcasting & Electronic Media, 53*, 317–335.

Harris Interactive. (2008, June 25). *The next wave in media measurement and engagement: Multi-screen engagement study finds greatest advertising value among audiences that cross platforms and are the most engaged.* http://www.businesswire.com/news/home/20080625006000/en/Wave-Media-Measurement-Engagement-Multi-Screen-Engagement-Study

Harris Interactive. (2011, June 25). *Are the online marketing efforts of TV shows and programs worthwhile?* https://theharrispoll.com/marketers-are-increasingly-spending-time-money-and-creativity-to-reach-their-audiences-in-non-traditional-ways-a-recent24-7-wall-st-harris-poll-on-social-media-and-television-set-out-to-see-if-thes/

Kirkpatrick, D. (2017, November 8). *US adults' "second-screen" while watching TV*. Marketing Dive. https://www.marketingdive.com/news/emarketer-70-of-us-adults-second-screen-while-watching-tv/510341

Leavy, D. (2010, October 14). *Television and social media: A marriage made in heaven?* http://www.navigatenewmedia.com/Home/Article.aspx?100029

McLeod, J. M., Scheufele, D. A., & Moy, P. (1999). Understanding deliberation: The effects of discussion networks on participation in a public forum. *Communication Research, 26*, 743–774. doi: 10.1177/009365099026006005

Paivio, A. (1986). *Mental representation: A dual coding approach*. Oxford University Press.

Papacharissi, Z., & Rubin, A. M. (2000). Predictors of Internet use. *Journal of Broadcasting & Electronic Media, 44*, 175–196.

Perez, S. (2018, December 12). *Nielsen: The second screen is booming as 45% often or always use devices while watching TV*. TechCrunch. https://techcrunch.com/2018/12/12/nielsen-the-second-screen-is-booming-as-45-often-or-always-use-devices-while-watching-tv

Perloff, R. M. (2015). Mass communication research at the crossroads: Definitional issues and theoretical directions for mass and political communication scholarship in an age of online media. *Mass Communication & Society, 18*, 531–556. doi: 10.1080/15205436.2014.946997

Pfeffel, F., Kexel, P., Kexel, C. A., & Ratz, A. (2016). Second screen: User behavior of spectators while watching football. *Athens Journal of Sports, 3*, 119–128.

Proulx, M., & Shepatin, S. (2012). *Social TV: How marketers can reach and engage audiences by connecting television to the web, social media, and mobile*. Wiley.

Raney, A. A., & Ji, Q. (2017). Entertaining each other? Modeling the socially shared television viewing experience. *Human Communication Research, 43*, 424–435. doi: 10.1111/hcre.12121

Rubin, A. M. (1983). Television uses and gratifications: The interactions of viewing patterns and motivations. *Journal of Broadcasting, 27*, 37–51.

Shah, D. V., Cho, J., Nah, S., Gotlieb, M. R., Hwang, H., Lee, N. J., . . . & McLeod, D. M. (2007). Campaign ads, online messaging, and participation: Extending the communication mediation model. *Journal of Communication, 57*, 676–703.

Talbot, P. (2019, February 26). Why TV advertisers need a second screen strategy. *Forbes*. https://www.forbes.com/sites/paultalbot/2019/02/26/why-tv-advertisers-need-a-second-screen-strategy

Toy, T. (2010, July 26). *How social media is affecting our television viewing habits and dictating what we watch.* ImaginativePRO Blog. http://tommytoy.typepad.com/tommy-toy-pbt-consultin/2010/07

Vaccari, C., Chadwick, A., & O'Loughlin, B. (2015). Dual screening the political: Events, social media, and citizen engagement. *Journal of Communication, 65*, 1041–1061.

Zúñiga, H. G. D., Garcia-Perdomo, V., & McGregor, S. C. (2015). What is second screening? Exploring motivations of second screen use and its effect on online political participation. *Journal of Communication, 65*, 793–815.

CHAPTER 22

Big Data and Entrepreneurship

M. Laeeq Khan, Ohio University

LEARNING OBJECTIVES

1. Understand big data analytics and the role of data scientists in media management.
2. Understand the importance of big data analytics for entrepreneurship.
3. Identify the opportunities and challenges brought by big data and social analytics in media management and business.

Having identified media management and business in a dynamic, globalized landscape of emerging technologies, we turn our attention to the future of media management practice and research. *Big data* is one of the most popular terms of our times and has gained considerable importance. The huge wave of digital transformation impacting individuals, organizations, governments, and societies has transformed how we live, work, interact, and entertain. The pervasive use of the Internet increases the importance of big data and makes a huge mark on the global economy. According to a *Forbes* article, the worldwide big data analytics market is expected to grow to more than $203 billion in 2020 (Press, 2017).

Big data not only impacts industry practice but also changes the way media scholars engage research. In 2018, there were more than one million academic peer-reviewed publications that utilized big data as a method. It is perhaps one of the most important technological changes in the past decade, as we now know more about audience behavior than ever before.

The growth in the volume of data, with the advancement of computing storage and processing power, has heralded a new era where better connectivity between two points further leads to an information explosion. The age of social media has propelled the rise of big data as individuals participate in the generation and dissemination of data at an unprecedented scale. There is no doubt that virtually every field, from business to sports to journalism to politics, has been transformed by data.

It is argued that big data as a field of study is interdisciplinary in nature, comprising elements of mathematics, statistics, informatics, communication, and business. In fact, big data's reach and impact is so widespread that various other disciplines are also compelled to study big data's role, especially in the area of predictive analytics. Furthermore, artificial intelligence and machine learning are transforming various domains as they cater to the requirements of different forms of businesses, such as health care, telecommunications, and financial services. All businesses, whether big or small, need to make strategic decisions; and big data and social analytics can help them make those decisions.

Not only are media industries increasingly dependent on social media for distribution of their content, but the Internet has also become a vital part of their overall strategy. The Internet and big data have led to the rise of newer realities whereby successful media companies rely on the data advantage to compete. While access to data and its efficient utilization is a desire of many in the industry, only a select few have managed to deploy and utilize it effectively and thus thrive on the data advantage. Netflix is a classic example of how a company used data to its advantage.

CASE STUDY

Netflix emerged as a disrupter in the film industry, debuting the opportunity for subscription-based mail-order DVDs. It was one of the first media platforms that recognized new media audiences aren't as interested in owning a personal media content library as they are in gaining access to various titles at a reasonable rate. Additionally, Netflix users do not have to take time out of their day to drive to a rental store, like they did with Blockbuster movie stores. Instead, Netflix was built on a model that would automatically deliver the next movie title in a personalized user queue to the doorstep of every subscriber. While today Netflix offers digital streaming, along with various other media conglomerates, including Amazon, Hulu, and Apple, its ability to utilize big data to reach fans is unmatched.

In addition to offering a more convenient and sought-after service to customers, Netflix proved itself a savvy tech company when it began developing its own algorithms. These personalized, relevant recommendation systems pushed audiences away from larger Blockbuster hits (titles with a large competition) and toward lesser-known library titles that were only available on Netflix (Richards & King, 2013). Thus, Netflix began introducing a new business model to the previously bottlenecked film industry.

Netflix employs some of the smartest software engineers to develop algorithms to personalize its streaming service. Its recommendation development is based on a combination of machine learning, algorithms, and creativity (Blattmann, 2018). According to Todd Yellin, Netflix's vice president for product innovation, Netflix uses complex data to develop the algorithms it uses, including "what people watch, what they watch after, what they watch before, what they watched a year ago, what they've watched recently and what time of day" (Blattmann, 2018, p. 2). While Netflix doesn't have access to more big data than other streaming giants, for example, YouTube, some suggest that the reason it has been so successful is due to its ability to analyze the numbers in every new media production decision (Wu, 2015). This is perhaps one of the greatest takeaways of big data: it is only as useful as the sense that you are able to make from the numbers.

Today, Netflix serves more than 137 million subscribers with over $15 billion in sales (Markman, 2019). Each of these users comes with a wealth of data that producers can use to improve the user experience. This information guides almost every aspect of the streaming service, including future production, recommendation systems, and even cover art to the content users see. Big data is reported to have saved Netflix $1 billion a year in value from customer retention (Markman, 2019). The success of Netflix is largely due to the company's ability to combine traditional mass media research methods with emerging new big data trends.

Something Old

Any industry that deals with customers, employs machines, uses content, moves things, and involves money is set to be transformed by big data (Davenport, 2014). In other words, marketing, supply chain, human resources, manufacturing, finance, and information technology are all the types of business functions that already are, or will be, impacted by big data. It is therefore evident that tapping in to the potential of big data and leveraging the potential of analytics can significantly increase the productivity and overall competitiveness of a business. When data is used as a strategic asset, real-time analysis can aid informed decision making. This may also lead to greater efficiencies that result from identifying and eliminating operating and production inefficiencies and improving customer experience. One of the biggest drivers of success in media companies using big data is a unique old-fashioned entrepreneurial mindset.

ENTREPRENEURS AND DATA ANALYTICS

Entrepreneurs historically rely on rudimentary observations, intuitions, and their gut feeling to make important judgments. Today, they are compelled to look into data and analytics to make informed decisions in a competitive world. Data analytics is concerned with sifting through vast amounts of structured and unstructured data to tell an effective story for better decision making. Determining patterns and trends and finding hidden meanings in data is both an art and a science. This move toward data and analytics can also be attributed to the increased reliance on the Internet and e-commerce. Each and every activity online results in the generation of vast amounts of data.

Generation of online data is only one part of the larger puzzle. To make better decisions, organizations need to process raw data into something more meaningful and understandable. Finding meaningful information is often challenging, like finding a needle in a haystack. Therefore, any data not analyzed appropriately proves useless. However, when properly analyzed, data can not only provide immense intelligence but also empower effective decisions that help media companies prosper and compete. From a practical standpoint, it isn't the size or volume of data that in itself serves as the advantage; rather it is what can be done with this data, the insights derived from this data, and the business value attained that matters. Companies such as Amazon, Netflix, Apple, Google, Baidu, and Alibaba thrive on data and analytics. In fact, data and analytics are at the core of their business strategy and operations.

While big data proves an inherently new hot topic, it is consistent with the entrepreneurial mindset of many media industries that have risen before. Its position within media measurement is similar to other quantitative measurements we used in the past. Now let's explore the historic definition of big data and place it within the long historical trajectory of media research.

DEFINING BIG DATA

In the media business field, the use of the term *big data* often generates awe and sometimes confusion about what it entails. This is mainly due to big data's primary emergence in the computer science and informatics fields. Ancient civilizations also collected and analyzed information (later referred to as data). Today, data is essential to how new knowledge is created. "Data provide the key inputs to systems that individuals, institutions, businesses, and the sciences employ in order to understand, explain, manage, regulate, and predict the world we live in and are used to create new innovations, products, and policies" (Thatcher, Eckert, & Shears, 2018, p. 3).

It's important for media managers to understand that while big data is mostly unstructured, once it is tamed and processed, big data can enable media companies to better understand audience behaviors, likes and dislikes, and viewing and purchasing patterns, and possibly predict their future viewing and purchasing behaviors (Puschmann & Burgess, 2014). Davenport (2014) defines *big data* as "a catchall term for data that doesn't fit the usual containers" (p. 1). Furthermore, big data tends to exist in a nonstatic manner, meaning that we can witness the constant, ongoing, and fast-flowing pouring of data from various sources, in particular social media, that makes it difficult to contain or store big data in one place. Therefore, to exploit and analyze big data, media practitioners need to develop or cultivate methods and techniques that allow analysts to keep abreast of this continuously flowing nature of big data. Media managers need to allocate resources to employing big data in their strategy development and decision making.

When it comes to the definition, big data can be understood as big and complex. However, just calling it big would not do it justice. Data volume or size of data can be relative. What is big for some may be relatively small for others. Big data is therefore described in terms of the three Vs: volume, velocity, and variety (see figure 22.1) (Laney, 2001). Kaplan and Haenlein (2019) describe big data as "characterized by huge amounts (volume) of frequently updated data (velocity) in various formats, such as numeric, textual, or images/videos (variety)" (p. 17). Although the three Vs—volume, velocity, and variety—do a decent job explaining the complexities of big data, others have described big data through six Vs: volume, velocity, variety, veracity, value, and venality (Davenport, 2014). What matters most is that media organizations are not only getting a large volume of data; they are also getting it fast, in complex formats, and from a variety of sources. Later in this chapter, we will talk about the emerging challenges brought by the veracity, value, and venality of big data to media managers in today's convergent environment.

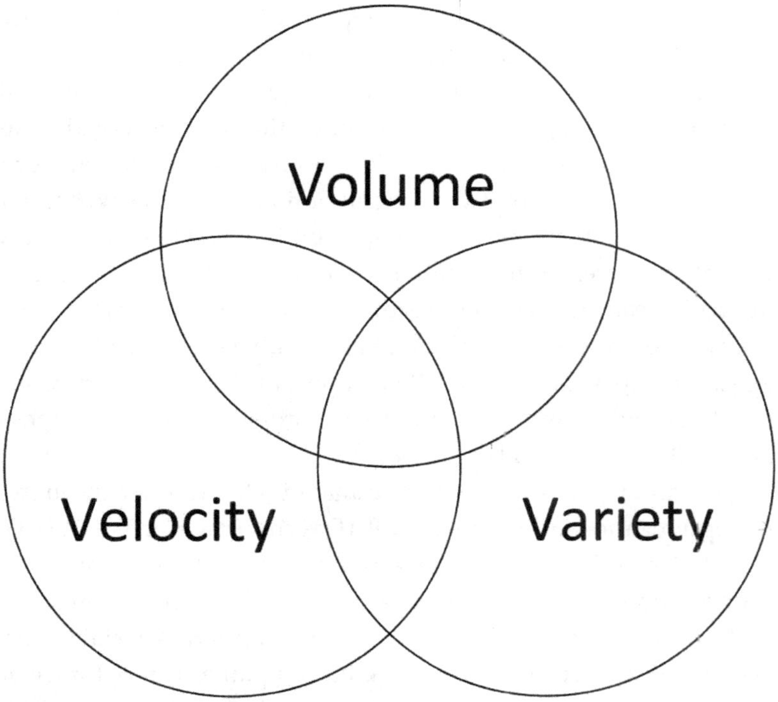

FIGURE 22.1. The Three Vs of Big Data

BIG DATA ANALYTICS

Big data and analytics are deeply linked to each other (Watson, 2014). Big data analytics can help media organizations develop new strategies and more effective tactics to conduct and enhance business and to exactly cater to what their audiences want and need. To derive value from data, analytics techniques must be employed. Such analytics can include regression analysis, simulation, machine learning, visualization, and more.

Analytics can be further broken down into three different areas: descriptive analytics, predictive analytics, and prescriptive analytics. Descriptive analytics involves collecting and processing historical data to describe the past and current situation. Examples of descriptive data analytics include facts and figures about sales, customer interactions, financial performance, and other reports about what happened, how and where it happened, and so on (Davenport & Harris, 2017). Traditional ratings reports from Nielsen are an example of descriptive analytics.

Predictive analytics is about predicting what can happen in the future; the emphasis is not on surface-level observations but on predicting the next course of action. Examples of predictive analytics include statistical analyses, forecasting and predictive modeling, and informing about what will happen next (Davenport & Harris, 2017). The Netflix recommendation system mentioned earlier in this chapter is a good example of predictive analytics. Netflix uses predictive analytics to provide movie recommendations for users based on their past viewing behaviors.

Prescriptive analytics suggests the best way to deal with a situation or the best way to approach a specific circumstance. More like a doctor prescribing some course of action or the exact medicine to take (Davenport & Kim, 2013), prescriptive analytics often results in building advanced systems that automate the analytics processes. This is achieved through machine learning algorithms, experimental techniques, simulations, and various mathematical optimization measures that are leveraged to aid decision making. In other words, prescriptive analytics comprises computational programs that select the best or optimal solution from several options while also keeping in view the limitations of particular situations. For example, building on the advantage of big data, retailers are employing prescriptive analytics to receive specific instructions about what they need to do instead of managers reading complicated forecast reports (Woodie, 2016). Retailers can learn about the price that would give them the highest level of profitability. Logistics companies such as UPS can provide specific instructions (based on analytics) about how, what, and where to drive in order to deliver packages in the most efficient manner (Davenport, 2014).

Media organizations can use prescriptive analytics to prescribe through experimental design and optimization techniques as well (Davenport & Harris, 2017). For example, prescriptive analytics can be employed by a media company to determine the best social engagement opportunity. Social media managers are able to utilize optimization tools to know exactly how much money to spend on advertising across social media platforms. Depending on the overall business goals, media companies can optimize allocation of time and human resources to deal with customer queries and create targeted content on social platforms (Hausman, 2013).

Hopefully, now you have understood that data can be of various types. Media organizations can gather web data such as page views, time spent on a site, customer searches, and more. They can also capture data from social platforms such as Facebook, Twitter, blogs, and so on. These data could be in the form of text, images, or videos. Data can also be about the location of individuals, known through addresses, GPS, and IP addresses. Media managers can use all forms of data in strategic combinations to make decisions in today's convergent environment.

TRAINING

Big data helps point to overall trends in audience behavior. Data scientists are able to watch patterns of media consumption and use this information to help predict what will be popular in the future. However, big data can't help producers answer every question they have about audiences. Most important, content managers will need to be trained in additional hybrid methodologies to help them understand *why* audiences may be behaving in certain ways. Like most research methodologies, big data works best when triangulated with other methodologies, particularly qualitative research methods. However, it does invite a new type of researcher to media businesses: the data scientist.

Something New

Industries across the globe are facing increasing competition and uncertainty as technological advances open new avenues of growth. Media and entertainment industries in particular are in a state of flux as converging technologies present new challenges. As media consumers have greater choices and power to get content from various sources, media companies are faced with the challenge of making the most of razor-thin profits. This process often involves harnessing the potential of big data with a better understanding of what data can do for them. The creation of more advanced and newer job roles in the form of data scientists, analysts, and machine learning experts demands an investment in such resources, both human and technological.

Capitalizing on the promise of predictive and prescriptive analytics, media companies are better able to target their advertising dollars, optimize creation and scheduling of media content, find new markets and revenue sources, and get better content recommendations that prevent churn. However, in order to achieve the benefits of big data, media companies must employ skilled experts who are able to properly implement such predictive and prescriptive techniques.

THE ROLE OF DATA SCIENTISTS

People who conduct big data analytics are referred to as "data scientists." In an article published by *Harvard Business Review* in October 2012, titled "Data Scientist: The Sexiest Job of the 21st Century," Thomas Davenport and D. J. Patil (2012) discussed the importance of data scientists in finding treasure in "messy, unstructured data" and that there is a shortage of such people. This holds true even today, as we notice a high demand for skilled data scientists who can make sense of big data through sophisticated analytics techniques. It is also important to note that our field needs media managers who can work with data scientists and use their analytics to help make strategic business decisions. How to balance data and creativity is a major challenge faced by all media managers in today's convergent environment.

Data scientists are viewed as the dominant contributors to the emergent field of big data. In particular, data scientists are believed to possess the skills necessary to utilize and sort out data. According to Davenport (2014), "[Data scientists] extract the data from obscure locations, write programs to turn unstructured into structured data, analyze the data, interpret the results, and advise executives on what to do about it—all in short order and with a sense of urgency" (p. 110).

Capturing big data, as Davenport (2014) argues, can be done much more easily with software and applications. However, it is the task of processing and structuring data that tends to require expertise from data scientists. While it is impossible to deny the significant role of data scientists, to exploit big data means an effort to collaborate among stakeholders (e.g., media managers, marketers) in order to make sound decisions (Davenport, 2014). A successful business requires teamwork, and a business that capitalizes on big data is not exempt from this axiom.

Davenport (2014) explicitly argues for a need to "combine data science activities with traditional data management virtues" (p. 137). Within this context, big data clearly operates in ways that solicit innovation and collaboration and encourage both start-ups and large media corporations to stay on top of their games if they hope to survive, thrive, and prosper within today's convergent environments. Furthermore, to be successful and to act on new opportunities provided by big data, adaptation and more effective ways of management are to be considered.

IMPORTANCE OF BIG DATA ANALYTICS FOR ENTREPRENEURSHIP

It is vital to understand the link between big data analytics and entrepreneurship. Churchill (1992) defines entrepreneurship as "the process of uncovering and developing an opportunity to create value through innovation and seizing that opportunity without regard to either resources (human and capital) or the location of the entrepreneur—in a new or existing company" (p. 586). From another viewpoint, Peter Drucker (1970) views entrepreneurship as something related to taking risks, creating something new—new values, new products/services, new organization or business, new wealth. In the information age, the traditional concept of entrepreneurship takes the meaning of new innovation, a commitment to change and adaptation when facing new realities of big data. Entrepreneurs and media managers need to be ready and prepared to collect data, process and analyze it, and visualize it to tell a compelling story that helps them make better decisions.

For many entrepreneurs who are still not utilizing big data, there is a need to recognize the potential advantages of utilizing big data in the media industry. Big data has gradually changed the way media companies operate and has provided them with invaluable and overarching opportunities to improve their products and services. The modern entrepreneurial mindset ought to embrace and utilize big data resources. A large part of the success of Amazon, Google, Facebook, and Netflix can be attributed to their approach toward data and analytics and how they steer themselves based on data advantage. In this way, effective and strategic use of big data can provide a media company with a competitive edge.

Today, entrepreneurship stands at a crossroads. Analytical approaches need to be at the heart of media management, requiring constant change, learning, and acquisition of essential skills that are relevant in the data analytics landscape (Sedkaoui, 2018). In other words, there needs to be a realization among media organizations that the latest technological challenges can be best met by situating and creating timely and insightful responses. Such responses can be in the form of effective analytics-focused business strategies and plans that can allow such companies to compete in an intensely competitive media environment. Capitalizing on the potentials of big data can further foster predictions regarding business trends. In particular, media organizations that do not understand the impact of big data on the contemporary business world are likely to lag behind (Davenport, 2014). Each media market holds unique opportunities for utilizing big data.

MUSIC

Similar to most big media revolutions, music was at the forefront of the big data trend. Streaming platforms such as Pandora and Spotify created algorithms to use an audience's preferences and settings to suggest new music. Even the downloading pioneer Napster included personal recommendation filters. Today, SoundCloud, Apple Music, and YouTube have become leaders in utilizing big data. Music production has also heavily relied on big data to make decisions, though with much less confidence. For example, music producers are choosing new artists based on their following and engagement on these streaming platforms. Big data helps offset risks by offering deals to artists with a steady following. Using big data to track new artists is a double-edged sword. On the one hand, users are able to use recommendation systems to discover music that they may otherwise never hear of. On the other hand, recommendation systems are inherently tied to a popularity bias. It can be increasingly difficult for new and niche artists to break through. Artists who are the most savvy with their social media promotion will gain the most traction in this system.

While people rely on big data to keep their music familiar, as well as fresh and interesting today, they may not necessarily own these digital formats. Digital media must be presented at a low cost through subscription services or a tiered system of payments. It is important to note that consumers are becoming more critical about how music services utilize their personal data. As most music platforms rely on steady revenue support, many have used big data to profile and track individuals and then sell their personal information to external parties (Heitner, 2018). Privacy and data security are an emerging issue in the music industry, a topic that will be addressed in greater detail later in this chapter.

FILM

Unlike music, film has been slow to adapt to changes and opportunities brought by big data. Hollywood has historically shied away from risk taking by offering products for microsegments of the population. For the most part, big data hasn't done much to change this on the big screen. As discussed in the case study above, big data has allowed alternative paths for content distribution to video-on-demand streaming services, such as Netflix, Hulu, and Amazon. Netflix is able to use big data to predict what people want to watch next in the queue and what they will want to see in the future. The ability to use big data to inform Netflix-produced programming is one of the most effective uses of big data in media management.

That's not to say that studios in Hollywood are not using big data in their metrics. Interestingly, Smith (2018) reports studios are now adding a postproduction process where audiences are asked to complete real-time opinion assessments after a movie has been shown. Results from these data help inform final decisions, such as targeting specific demographics in marketing campaigns, developing appealing trailers, and pushing distribution to specific geographic areas. Playing to the crowd is not a new concept in film, but big data can provide a higher level of confidence in their judgments (Smith, 2018). Nonetheless, it can create the same self-fulfilling prophecy where the same types of productions are being reproduced over and over, as audiences don't always know what they like until they have been exposed to something new.

SOCIAL MEDIA

Social media analytics have gradually brought changes to the media industries. Journalists are now encouraged to engage audiences through social media platforms, and preferential treatment is given to those who are able to garnish the most "likes" for their posts. Perhaps no industry is as influenced by big data as marketing and advertising. While focus group and survey research have proven difficult and expensive for media practitioners to conduct in the past, social media provides more in-depth information to media managers today with virtually no effort on the part of media practitioners. For example, Facebook has a free, powerful analytics tool, Facebook Insights. Facebook

Insights is easily accessed through any business page and can track page likes, views, reach, audience demographics, and more. It has even begun providing information on its sister platform, Instagram.

On the other hand, Twitter has taken a different approach to data management. Twitter is interested in the data licensing business, acquiring more than $70 million in licensing payments in 2013 (Edwards, 2014). While some data is free and accessible to users, depending on the size and relevance of key word searchers, Twitter will charge to track hashtags or archives of the site.

There are many new ways in which various media utilize and adapt to big data. While big data provides many new opportunities for media managers, it is not without challenges. Let's explore the opportunities and challenges media managers encounter when developing big data strategies to meet their business needs.

Opportunities and Challenges

Advances in data capture, storage, and processing create notable hype around the potential of analytics. Media businesses and organizations that have properly employed big data analytics have already reaped immense benefits. Benefits in the form of cost reductions and improved efficiencies provide a competitive edge in the global business environment. However, we also witness challenges in data privacy, security, and rampant online misinformation.

OPPORTUNITIES

Data analytics is a "value generator for entrepreneurial opportunities" (Sedkaoui, 2018, p. 1). However, for such value to be generated, media organizations must have clear objectives. Big data has the potential to bring immense cost reductions, significant improvements in computing task efficiencies, better online user behavior predictions, enhanced engagement, and more. Among these, media managers should pay attention to three major opportunities brought by big data and analytics: (1) understanding and connecting with audiences, (2) predicting audience behavior, and (3) exploring trends and improving efficiency.

UNDERSTANDING AND CONNECTING WITH AUDIENCES

Big data helps media organizations better understand their audiences. Through market research and analytics, organizations can understand how their audiences behave online (and offline). By understanding audience interactions, they can better plan their marketing strategies and engage with their audiences more effectively. Large data sets can be mined for critical and timely information for decision making. Historical data about audience interactions and customer transactions can also inform media companies when developing their business strategies. Studying audiences or customers for factors that drive their consumption behaviors helps media managers make better decisions. Once it is understood who and where the audiences are, the next logical step is to connect with them. Connecting with audiences and better engaging with them allows for more targeted advertising. We have discussed how to connect with audiences and consumers in detail in chapter 7, "Marketing and Branding," in this book.

PREDICTING BEHAVIOR

Data analytics can help media managers predict audience behavior and plan accordingly. Planning ahead for customer needs can be crucial in a competitive world. Recommendation systems also help companies "think ahead" and thereby target customers based on their needs. By studying customer transaction data, for example, companies can predict what they would be most interested in next. This will lead to the difference between a successful company that relies on data and analytics to compete and a media organization that does not fully utilize its data potential.

EXPLORING TRENDS AND IMPROVING EFFICIENCY

Effective data analytics can help media managers better manage costs and operations. By having immediate answers to critical questions, decisions can be made in a timely manner. Instead of sifting through a myriad of records of raw data, insights gained through analytics can aid efficient and effective decision making. Accordingly, media managers can identify important trends. There are a number of prominent examples where big data analytics has helped organizations perform better. At a general level, supermarkets and pharmacies have loyalty cards for their customers, through which stores can track purchasing habits and sift through their data to create customized store offerings (Thatcher, Shears, & Eckert, 2018).

Since time is of the essence, the time required to carry out day-to-day operations within a company is being shortened with the help of data analytics. A case in point is U.S.-based department store Macy's merchandise pricing optimization system. The system has reduced the process of price calculation from 27 hours to just one hour (Davenport, 2014). Such time savings and increased efficiencies brought by data analytics has enabled Macy's to compete effectively through improved and timely marketing and overall cost reductions.

When Starbucks introduced a new coffee, it was naturally concerned about customer response; data and analytics based on social media reactions to the new coffee informed the Starbucks management team that, although customers liked the taste of the new coffee, they were not happy with the high price (Watson, 2014). Similarly, based on data and analytics, Target predicted whether some of its female shoppers were pregnant and sent them store coupons for pregnancy-related items (Duhigg, 2012).

As discussed in the case study, Netflix serves as one of the most compelling examples of big data analytics success. Netflix rose to prominence as a global company for online content creation and distribution with presence in more than 190 countries and revenues in excess of $8 billion in 2016 (Davenport & Harris, 2017). Netflix is known for successfully harnessing the power of data through effective analytics whereby it understands customer behaviors and buying patterns and turns this knowledge into a competitive advantage by offering movie recommendations and personalization for each customer (Davenport & Harris, 2017).

CHALLENGES

While big data and analytics have brought many opportunities to media management, media managers also need to address the various challenges related to data. Below, we will discuss three major data analytics challenges faced by the media industry: (1) privacy and security, (2) misinformation and fake news, and (3) extracting data value.

PRIVACY AND SECURITY

With the rapid rise of data volume and variety, issues of privacy and security are also bound to increase. As mentioned above, privacy is one of the most important issues faced by our information-dependent societies today. How much data should governments and media organizations have access to? How will private user data be used by media companies and advertisers? Are there effective safeguards in place to protect user data from misuse and unauthorized use? The above-mentioned example of Target using personal data to predict pregnancy and push related targeted advertising is a case in point where personal privacy seemed to have been compromised, bringing up questions about ethics. We have discussed ethical issues and concerns in the big data era in detail in chapter 9 in this book.

It is observed that citizens do not sufficiently understand or give enough attention to how their data is being used by organizations. This points toward a general lack of understanding and awareness about the costs associated with the rise in data analytics, especially in the realm of social media.

MISINFORMATION AND FAKE NEWS

Fake news has existed in the information ecosystem of various societies in the forms of rumors, gossip, and propaganda (Burkhardt, 2017). The advent of big data has complicated the situation because the rapid flow of information and its sheer volume make it hard to differentiate credible information from false data. Technological advancements, pervasive use of social media, and clickbait advertisements are some of the factors that exacerbate the flow of misinformation and fake news. Media managers need to ensure that data does not include fake information; otherwise good value cannot be derived from it.

Dealing with widespread misinformation on social media requires a thorough evaluation of the information gained as well as new approaches and strategies. Such strategies include more individualized analytics and system-based algorithms. Information verification strategies by individuals require Internet skills such as knowing how to search for information, share information, and verify it.

EXTRACTING DATA VALUE

Another challenge of big data in media management is the lack of structure. Most big data, especially that emanating from social media, lacks structure. In other words, data first has to be organized in rows and columns to make sense of it. Extracting value from data can be hard, and much of the challenge is because of a lack of understanding at the managerial level about the potential value that can be derived through big data analytics (Morabito, 2015). From a technological perspective, a lack of internal and external consistency of analytical and database systems adds to the level of complexity and inhibits the extraction of value from available data streams (Sedkaoui, 2018).

Extracting data value is also part of media managers' responsibility to implement a big data analytics strategy (Davenport & Harris, 2017). History is filled with examples of how complacency or a lack of understanding of timely vision led to failure. Photographic film companies were not able to fully comprehend the threat from digital photography, just as movie rental companies like Blockbuster were not able to foresee the rise of digital streaming companies like Netflix (Davenport & Harris, 2017).

While privacy concerns, misinformation, and an inability to extract data value are huge challenges to future media practitioners, each of these should improve as scholars, managers, and citizens become increasingly savvy. Big data is still relatively new. It is refreshing to see media literacy courses and basic online courses being implemented into K–12 education. While it is always challenging to ensure the quality and value of data, big data have made personalization, customization, and user-generated content the norm. The more media practitioners are able to cater to these features, the more connected to and engaged with their audiences they will be. Media managers should use the following action plan as a guide as they develop a big data strategy.

ACTION PLAN

1. Hire and train skilled data scientists who understand the company's goals.
2. Never break audience trust for the sake of obtaining data. Be transparent about how you are going to use data and user information to increase revenue. Protect the privacy and security of your audience.
3. Use big data during almost every media preproduction, production, and postproduction process.
4. Remember to also rely on qualitative and hybrid methodologies to better understand why your audience may be behaving in certain ways.

KEY TAKEAWAYS

1. Big data is best characterized as a huge volume of frequently updated data in various formats, including numeric, textual, and images/videos.
2. The application of big data has proven a major disruptor in today's media marketplace, especially in the music, film, and advertising industries.
3. Media managers are able to use big data to better understand audience behavior and better connect them to their products.
4. Many key challenges still exist in big data, including extracting value data, the rapid spread of misinformation, and privacy/security concerns of audiences.

CONCLUSION

Data and analytics lie at the heart of the digital revolution. Capitalizing on data and leveraging the power of analytics for entrepreneurship and various other uses hinges on a carefully planned and sustained effort. Big data is already an integral element of the overall business strategy of many media organizations, and it is expected to become even more important for managers at various types and sizes of business in an increasingly competitive and convergent environment. It is believed that by the end of 2020, the big data volume is expected to surpass 44 trillion gigabytes or 44 zettabytes (EMC, 2014). This indicates a major challenge in terms of data volume and complexity but also an opportunity to be seized.

Here we can unequivocally see time and speed as the two integral components of big data. In order to turn big data into something useful for media businesses, analytics must be carried out swiftly so that these data can be efficaciously categorized and structured. Media organizations that do not try to stay on top of their analysis of these data might occupy a disadvantaged position. Davenport (2014) highlights the possibility of big data to provide media organizations with more information and materials about how customers react and behave toward certain products, therefore leading to the proliferation of advertisements, products, and services that are customized and created for particular segments of these customers.

While technology allows media organizations to gather more data, more attention should be paid to how entrepreneurs adapt to a big-data environment and how they make sense of and structure big data. Such a change that embraces big data analytics requires "considerable imagination, courage, and commitment" (Davenport, 2014). Within this context, one can understand the interplay of various and disparate factors that can work together to make the best out of big data. Big data's appeal to businesses, corporations, and organizations stems from the notion that big data can reduce cost as well as contribute to the development of new ways to improve data gathering and collection.

While many media companies have embraced big data and analytics as part of their strategic mix, a large number still lag behind in the full utilization of the data advantage. It is clear that big data analytics enables informed decision making. Now businesses must cultivate a culture that values data. The advent of cloud-based computing has lowered the barriers to adopting big data analytics. This has certainly opened up more opportunities, especially for small and medium-sized entrepreneurial ventures, as they too can embrace analytics technologies to their advantage.

It is worth remembering that in the globally competitive world, only the smartest survive. Being smart implies that companies and organizations are agile, embrace change, and inculcate new solutions that help them make informed decisions in a timely manner. Since data is being constantly generated, opportunities also continually expand.

Media scholars are beginning to incorporate big data into their research. Results are being met with a combination of enthusiasm and skepticism. On one end of the spectrum, it is finally possible for the average researcher to deal with data sets that are affordable and include a representative sample. One the other end, new waves of research illustrate that data size really doesn't matter at all (Davenport, 2014). Instead, what you do with your analysis matters much more. Academics must be careful not to rely solely on big data, especially those generated on social media. It must be carefully considered which populations are included in and excluded from these measurements. However, as more PhD programs train future data scientists in big data measurements, the results should only improve.

Big data has proven to be one of the biggest drivers of success in today's media management practices. However, we must be cautious; just because something is new doesn't mean that it is better. The next chapter will explore the best way to merge "new" concepts and trends in media management with more traditional "old" foundations.

REFERENCES

Blattmann, J. (2018, August 2). *Netflix: Binging on the algorithm*. UX Planet. https://uxplanet.org/netflix-binging-on-the-algorithm-a3a74a6c1f59

Burkhardt, J. M. (2017). How fake news spreads. *Library Technology Reports, 53*(8), 10–13.

Churchill, N. C. (1992). Research issues in entrepreneurship. In D. L. Sexton & J. D. Kasarda (Eds.), *The state of the art of entrepreneurship* (pp. 579–596). PWS-KENT.

Davenport, T., & Harris, J. (2017). *Competing on analytics: Updated, with a new introduction: The new science of winning*. Harvard Business Press.

Davenport, T. H. (2014). *Big data @ work: Dispelling the myths, uncovering the opportunities*. Harvard Business Review Press.

Davenport, T. H., & Kim, J. (2013). *Keeping up with the quants: Your guide to understanding and using analytics*. Harvard Business Review Press.

Davenport, T. H., & Patil, D. J. (2012, October). Data scientist: The sexiest job of the 21st century. *Harvard Business Review*. https://hbr.org/2012/10/data-scientist-the-sexiest-job-of-the-21st-century

Drucker, P. (1970). Entrepreneurship in business enterprise. *Journal of Business Policy, 1*, 3–12.

Duhigg, C. (2012, February 16). How companies learn your secrets. *New York Times*. http://www.nytimes.com/2012/02/19/magazine/shopping-habits.html

Edwards, J. (2014, April 15). Twitter is quietly building a $100 million business in big data. *Business Insider*. https://www.businessinsider.com/twitter-100-million-big-data-business-2014-4

EMC. (2014, April 9). *Digital universe invaded by sensors* [Press release]. https://www.emc.com/about/news/press/2014/20140409-01.htm

Hausman, A. (2013, May 21). *Prescriptive analytics in social media: Optimize your processes*. Social Media Today. https://www.socialmediatoday.com/content/prescriptive-analytics-social-media-optimize-your-processes

Heitner, D. (2018, June 7). Big data is revolutionizing the music industry. *Inc*. https://www.inc.com/darren-heitner/big-data-is-revolutionizing-music-industry-here-are-lessons-for-your-business.html

Kaplan, A., & Haenlein, M. (2019). Siri, Siri, in my hand: Who's the fairest in the land? On the interpretations, illustrations, and implications of artificial intelligence. *Business Horizons, 62*, 15–25. doi: 10.1016/j.bushor.2018.08.004

Laney, D. (2001). *3D data management: Controlling data volume, velocity and variety*. META Group.

Markman, J. (2019, February 25). Netflix harnesses big data to profit from your tastes. *Forbes*. https://www.forbes.com/sites/jonmarkman/2019/02/25/netflix-harnesses-big-data-to-profit-from-your-tastes

Morabito, V. (2015). *Big data and analytics: Strategic and organizational impacts* (pp. 177–180). Springer International Publishing. https://link.springer.com/book/10.1007%2F978-3-319-10665-6

Press, G. (2017, January 20). 6 predictions for the $203 billion big data analytics market. *Forbes*. https://www.forbes.com/sites/gilpress/2017/01/20/6-predictions-for-the-203-billion-big-data-analytics-market

Puschmann, C., & Burgess, J. (2014). Metaphors of big data. *International Journal of Communication, 8*(20), 1690–1709.
Richards, N. M., & King, J. H. (2013). Three paradoxes of big data. *Stanford Literature Review Online, 66*, 41.
Sedkaoui, S. (2018). How data analytics is changing entrepreneurial opportunities. *International Journal of Innovation Science, 10*, 274–294.
Smith, R. (2018, March 31). *How should film function in the age of big data?* Medium. https://medium.com/@ryanmsmith/how-should-film-function-in-the-age-of-big-data-fb97e01818b0
Thatcher, J., Eckert, J., & Shears, A. (Eds.). (2018). *Thinking big data in geography: New regimes, new research*. University of Nebraska Press.
Watson, H. J. (2014). Tutorial: Big data analytics: Concepts, technologies, and applications. *CAIS, 34*, 65.
Woodie, A. (2016, February 11). *How retailers are benefiting from prescriptive analytics*. Datanami. https://www.datanami.com/2016/02/11/how-retailers-are-benefiting-from-prescriptive-analytics
Wu, T. (2015, January 27). Netflix's secret special algorithm is a human. *The New Yorker*. https://www.newyorker.com/business/currency/hollywoods-big-data-big-deal

CHAPTER 23

Old vs. New

Sabine Baumann, Jade University of Applied Sciences

LEARNING OBJECTIVES

1. Understand traditional practices of media management and how media management has evolved in academia and business.
2. Identify relevant and obsolescent media management roots in convergent times.
3. Highlight the factors that lead to pitfalls and success of media management in today's convergent media environment.

Media industries were among the first businesses affected by digital transformation and the ensuing sectoral convergence. This includes not only different types of media platforms but also telecommunication and new information technology. While media firms struggle to develop their business models for digital production and distribution of original creative content, companies in various other industries also realize that a digital content strategy is central to their business (Ots, Nyilasy, Rohn, & Wikström, 2015). Therefore, it is a fascinating and important moment to study and practice media management.

Media management is a hybrid discipline with foundations in management science, media and communication theories, and, more recently, computer science and engineering. Each discipline comes with its intellectual and ideological heritage, specific assumptions, and distinctive priorities and values. In addition, media management is an international area of interest in academia and, particularly, in business, both strongly influenced by cultures, media structures, and policies (Brown, 2016; Picard, 2005). For example, TV shows with a global appeal such as *Idols* have been adapted to local cultures. National ownership regulations in a country may also prevent foreigners from owning a TV station.

Media organizations produce and distribute highly complex products and services resulting from creative work that is based on information, ideas, literacy, and artistic endeavors. Their goods "are at the same time symbolic goods, public goods, club goods, experience goods, talent goods, multipurpose goods and goods for dual markets"

(Lowe, 2016, p. 5). Media products and services have always been a very noticeable part of daily life. For example, TV networks schedule programs around audience availability and family activities. With the increasing use of the Internet and mobile technologies, media have become almost ubiquitous while giving more freedom to consumers.

The media business of the past, although volatile in terms of business growth, was very stable and consistent in terms of value creation and business models. Yet, the current ecology is a high-velocity business environment characterized by strong volatility, uncertainty, complexity, and ambiguity. Emerging technologies brought new entrants and led to increasing competition between established players (print, TV, radio, etc.) as well as between new and old media sectors. In this context, legacy media struggle to cope with the rapid changes in a convergent environment, with an infamous history of misinterpreting effects of technologies on their existing business models or underestimating competitors emerging from the start-ups. For example, the music industry misjudged the disruption by peer-to-peer platforms, resulting in Apple's domination in music downloads. Furthermore, competitors often come from related telecommunication, information technology, consumer electronics, media, and entertainment industries (Baumann & Hasenpusch, 2014; Hasenpusch & Baumann, 2017).

As a consequence, media markets have become increasingly fragmented. Industry boundaries are blurred more than ever before. The question "What is a media company?" no longer has a fixed answer. Historically, media companies controlled the creation and consumption of media products via limited distribution channels (Deuze, 2016) and ultimately defined themselves through the channel(s) for which they supplied media products and services. Today, media industries are characterized by media abundance rather than scarcity and increasingly diversified, personalized, and idiosyncratic patterns in media consumption via a plethora of platforms and channels (Picard & Lowe, 2016). To succeed in today's converged environment, media firms need to continuously adapt. They must develop their dynamic capabilities and rethink traditional business models to include new and more integrated revenue streams (Lowe, 2016). Now, let's discuss the case of Wolters Kluwer (WK), an excellent example of how a science publisher adapted itself to add data analytics and information technology to its portfolio.

CASE STUDY

Wolters Kluwer, a traditional publisher of textbooks, academic journals, and professional publications, has transformed its business in the past decades in response to media convergence. According to its mission statement, WK is "a global provider of professional information, software solutions and services. [Their] work at Wolters Kluwer helps to protect people's health, prosperity, safety, and legal rights while building better professionals in business" (Wolters Kluwer, 2019a).

WK's products and services distinctly aim at helping customers solve business problems. WK's website states that it positions itself as an enabler for professionals in health care, tax, finance, and law. It provides customers with not only comprehensive information but also software and analytics tools as well as consulting services (Wolters Kluwer, 2019b).

What this implies in practice is that WK offers software solutions to directly support its clients' businesses with information services. For example, instead of merely supplying accounting firms with the information that a new tax law has come out (WK's legacy business model), WK now provides each accounting firm with the new tax law combined with a data-driven product-service to approach these clients. "Expert solutions—in compliance, collaboration, internal and external audit management, corporate performance management and firm management—integrate deep domain knowledge with workflows to ensure compliance, improved productivity, effective management, and strengthened client relationships" (Wolters Kluwer, 2019c). In essence, WK now helps its customers lead their businesses more easily and efficiently by relieving them from cumbersome tasks.

WK's digital transformation is based on a clear business strategy developed over the past two decades focusing on products in four sectors: health, tax and accounting, governance risk and compliance, and legal and regulatory affairs. In addition, it has implemented its 2016–2018 strategy, which is equally focused on three overarching goals: expanding market coverage, delivering expert solutions, and driving efficiencies and engagement. In order to achieve digital transformation, WK has been heavily investing in digitization while selling its businesses outside the strategic core area. As Nancy McKinstry, CEO and chairman of Wolters Kluwer, explains in an interview in January 2019, "Once we had identified the portfolio we wanted, we targeted our acquisitions to digital businesses and talent. In all, we have sold €1 billion ($1.14 billion) worth of businesses and we have acquired €1.3 billion ($1.48 billion). The result is that in 2018, around 90 percent of our total revenues came from digital products and services" (Unger, 2019).

Another focus of WK is technology innovations in combination with in-depth understandings of its customers' business processes to create values—"but we are also innovating with technology. It's very important to us. We are already embedding AI, robotic process automation, and natural language processing in our products. When you build products with those kinds of advanced technologies, to spot opportunities for improvement you have to really understand what your professional customer does, in terms of their workflow. That's our strength" (Unger, 2019). The shift in WK's business also comes with extensive changes in the workforce. While the number of employees in domain-specific (i.e., content) areas has fallen dramatically, WK has proactively recruited computer and data scientists and business specialists in their identified topic areas. "We have been increasing our ranks of data scientists quite dramatically; in fact, we've more than doubled the teams" (Unger, 2019).

The Wolters Kluwer case demonstrates a number of best practices. It is important to understand your clients' businesses and unique challenges. Only when you are able to derive a full-service solution that improves your client's business can your product compete in today's and tomorrow's marketplace. WK has changed from a pure content-based company to a content, technology, and platform player. It made difficult decisions around reducing the domain-specific content business while extending the technology-driven service package offering. At the same time, WK created a culture of employee-led innovations and constantly invested in new product and service research and development. In sum, it is important to note that WK has developed and implemented a clear digital business strategy to transform from a legacy media player to a media technology company. It deploys a portfolio of media solutions based on the latest technologies around AI, robotic process automation, and natural language processing in combination with in-depth domain knowledge to provide highly valuable services to customers. With this example of an already transformed publishing company in mind, we will now explore some of the old practices of media management that are still viable in today's changing media environment.

Something Old

As a discipline, media management and economics are fairly young. While early scholars started investigating media markets in the 1940s (Albarran, 2018), media management research did not take off until the last two decades of the 20th century. Today, scholars no longer treat media economics and media management separately but instead perceive them as two sides of the same coin. While this presents a new perspective on media management theories, it is important to understand what is managed at different levels: media companies provide media products to be distributed and sold in the marketplace. This comprehensive view captures the significant differences between media products and general products and services. Some "old" media management traditions still remain relevant today.

MEDIA MANAGEMENT TRADITIONS

What are media companies? This question has been debated in the field for quite a long time. Answers typically mention creativity in the forms of idea generation, literary narratives, or artistic expression as central to the activities of media companies (e.g., Küng, 2007; Picard, 2005). Product and service innovation is a must for any type of company, but in media, these innovations must flow constantly because audiences always expect novel content—in media such as newspapers or TV, on a daily basis. As Küng (2007) states, "Media organizations live ultimately by the content they create, with 'create' being the operative word. The act of content generation is the sector's fundamental activity and raison d'être, and their requirement for creativity is constant" (p. 26).

Legacy media companies revolved around the medium they used in producing, aggregating, bundling, and distributing content. Print media organizations (i.e., newspapers, magazines, and books) used paper to publish and were aptly named publishers. Broadcasters in TV and radio applied broadcasting devices for their content producing and distributing activities, while film studios, music, and game publishers used records, CDs, DVDs, film, cassettes, or cartridges. This list clearly indicates that media has always been a very diverse sector, where each media subsector had evolved differently with specific market settings, regulations, technologies, and organization types (Küng, 2007).

Furthermore, operating the equipment for content creation and distribution was typically performed by media professionals, as these operations required special knowledge and training (Hess, 2014). The arrival of the Internet and mobile devices has brought easy-to-use functionalities that allow users to become producers and distributors for any medium. As such, a new type of media company emerged: the online and mobile platform operator that collects, combines, and distributes content generated by platform users (Albarran, 2018; Evens, 2010; Hess, 2014).

TRADITIONAL MEDIA BUSINESS MODELS

Media companies and conventional product-producing and service-delivering organizations differ in their objectives. Media products not only have financial outcomes but also serve as cultural goods that represent societal values (Baumann, 2013). Media companies generate most of their revenues through three sources: selling media products and services to audiences, selling media content to advertisers, and selling media content or services to other companies. Typically, they provide packages that include information and entertainment (content) services and advertising (Wirtz, 2011). Before the introduction of the Internet, competition in many media subsectors was limited or even nonexistent, often reinforced by access restrictions to the market or subsidies. In such an environment, media companies benefited from high margins, regardless of their management competencies (Lowe, 2016). Nevertheless, diversification has been a must for companies offering media products with a high uncertainty of demand and/or extensive sunk costs (Hang & van Weezel, 2007).

Traditional media business's revenue generation derived largely from customer spending (product purchases and subscriptions) and advertising. Media such as books, films, and recorded music focused mostly on product sales. Newspapers and magazines relied on a mixture of sales and advertising, whereas broadcasters depended primarily on advertising revenues or—in the case of public service media—public funding (Daidj & Jung, 2011; Mierzejewska & Shaver, 2014).

In the traditional media environment, media companies commonly rely on the so-called blockbuster model in which a small number of successful products finance the losses of many unsuccessful ones (Küng, 2007; Picard, 2005). Media managers must be able to manage these failures while still creating sustainable business conditions and keeping up morale. Yet, in the digital era, sales in the long tail (Anderson, 2006) have now become viable propositions for media products as sunk costs are lower and distribution and storage do not involve costly physical media. It should be noted that media companies today are operating in a global environment. While media organizations need to adapt to the global marketplace, they typically develop locally adapted versions of their products. Digitization has spurred moves toward overseas and consequently brought challenges in media management (Hollifield, 2001).

DUALITIES IN MEDIA ORGANIZATIONS

Media products and services are created as single products and/or on an ongoing basis (Picard, 2005). The former are singular and unique creations, such as books and movies, while the latter products and services are concept driven, such as newspapers and TV programs, which are continuously filled with new content. While single creation products are typically produced in project settings, continuous media products represent structured, coordinated, and mostly time-constrained efforts (DeFillippi, 2009; Picard, 2005). Consequently, the management challenges differ in that continuous creation requires excellent process and fixed-cost management of the production facilities, while single creations focus more on project management and managing unit cost for the media product, including the typically extensive marketing activities (Picard, 2005). The constant product innovation requires flexible structures, and work in media companies is often organized around temporary projects for specific tasks (Lundin & Norbäck, 2016) that overlap the hierarchical organizational structures of the media entity.

Besides their dual product characteristics, media organizations bear other dualities. Media organizations must support creative processes as well as bottom-line-oriented management functions. As such, they contain structural-functional and product-induced differences (Aris & Bughin, 2012). Clashes of creative ideals and economic reality are often inevitable. The dual structure—for example, an editor in chief and a managing director in a publishing house sharing responsibility—can often create conflict. In addition, the multitier market structure for media products and services poses additional challenges, as typically at least two, if not more, of these markets need to be served simultaneously (Baumann, 2013).

MEDIA CUSTOMERS

Consumer behavior and the success of media products and services are incredibly difficult to predict (Hang, 2018; Picard, 2005). The music industry was flabbergasted when consumers downloaded poor-quality ringtones for $2.99 while rejecting full-fledged high-quality songs for 99 cents. TV formats such as *Idols* or *I'm a Celebrity . . . Get Me Out of Here!* were questioned by media managers who did not believe in their success and would rather have invested in other ventures. *Idols*, in particular, has been a huge success in that not only was the TV format successful through the call-in revenues, but it also came with spin-off products such as the music, magazines, books, and other merchandise. Reuses of content (e.g., songs on the show are made available on CD, on video, and as stream; see Küng, 2007) and product spin-offs where the content idea is used in another media subsector (e.g., making a film version of a book) are unique properties of media products (Picard, 2005).

It is noteworthy that consumers can choose from a tremendous oversupply of content, which provides them with significant market power, in combination with the blockbuster business model or where media products are financed through advertising. The time audiences invest in consuming media products and services far exceeds that of other products. With media fulfilling functions of information, leisure, and mood making, consumers have a special relationship with media products and services (Wirtz, 2011).

MEDIA MARKET STRUCTURES AND COMPETITION

Many smaller companies formed the typical market structure until the 1970s before merging into larger conglomerates (Albarran, 2018). We saw an unprecedented consolidation in the media industry in the 1980s and 1990s. Despite restrictions in ownership, by the middle of the 2000s, huge organizations with complex substructures were the norm for media asset ownership (Ozanich, 2006), raising questions of excessive market dominance (Chambers & Howard, 2006). In Europe, public service broadcasting was established during the first half of the 20th century as publicly owned nonprofit institutions with specific sociocultural and pro-democracy obligations. Controversies ensued regarding the best balance of public ownership, regulation, the ideal of editorial autonomy, and the best revenue model. Public service broadcasters are significant actors in their domestic markets who produce a relatively large proportion of original content (Nissen, 2013).

The Internet and mobile technologies brought new competitors from the telecommunication and information technology (IT) sectors as well as newly founded start-ups that have entered into the media markets within just the last decade (Hasenpusch & Baumann, 2017). As the telecommunication and IT sectors converge with the media and entertainment industries (Wirtz, 2011), new technologies, such as improved broadband, digitalization, upgraded wireless and mobile connections, smartphones and other hybrid digital devices, enhanced digital content quality, and availability of user-friendly, web-enabling software applications lead to new media distribution channels as well as a huge range of new, digital-native media products (Albarran, 2018; Bartosova, 2011). As a result, convergence makes it more difficult to define media markets (Ozanich, 2006) and has reraised the question of what a media company is and how it should be managed (Evens, 2010). The next section of this chapter will therefore investigate new management concepts for a convergent era.

Something New

Although the media business models have always been driven by enabling technologies for their production and distribution processes (Küng, 2007), the media marketplace has greatly changed with the extreme growth of technology-driven competitors (Baumann, 2020; Oliver, 2018). Likewise, consumers have adopted interactive digital media applications and online platforms with unprecedented speed and now publish user-generated content (UGC), hence becoming *prosumers* (other labels are *pro-ams, amafessionals, produsers*). Today's audiences are involved in content cocreation with peers (participatory media or peer content) (Deuze, 2016; Küng, 2007). This new ecosystem of convergent media players has evolved into a broad content service industry (Cestino & Berndt, 2018) that assembles legacy media, technology players, Internet service providers, communication operators, and UGC applications that all compete for profits while providing values to consumers (Bartosova, 2011; Evens, 2010; Küng, 2017).

MANAGING CONVERGENT MEDIA

From a management perspective, technology diffusion breaks down the "insulated silos determined by their content format and delivery system" (Mierzejewska & Shaver, 2014, p. 47), to cross-media settings where, for example, print media now also offer audiovisual content via their websites and apps. This means the former dominance of distribution channels for particular types of content has been replaced by convergent media settings of "any media, any time, any device." Needless to say, this profoundly changes the understanding of what a media company is as well as the related media management practices.

MEDIA PRODUCT OFFERINGS: FROM PUBLISHING AND BROADCASTING TO PLATFORMS

Legacy media leave their silos to provide content across all distribution channels. Platform operators join them as both partners and competitors in the media ecosystem as they start offering original content, especially in giving noninstitutional media actors such as bloggers and other user-generated content providers market access. These new industrial platform players include the hyper-sized digital disrupters—Facebook, Amazon, Apple, Netflix, and Google (FAANG) as well as smaller digital media businesses, such as BuzzFeed, Snap, and Spotify (Albarran, 2018; Evens, 2010; Küng, 2016). In addition, other companies from the IT and telecommunication sectors, such as Comcast and AT&T, no longer solely provide Internet and mobile transmission services but have extended their companies to include original content creation and acquisition. The former sector of media and entertainment (ME) is now aptly called TIME (Telecommunication, Information Technology, Media, and Entertainment) (Hasenpusch & Baumann, 2017; Wirtz, 2011). Consequently, legacy media companies experience an extensive loss of control, and media managers have to deal with growing complexity, uncertainty, and volatility (Baumann & Hasenpusch, 2016; Evens, 2010; Lowe, 2016; Picard & Lowe, 2016).

Today's media consumers have abundant choices as they choose from a growing array of multimedia devices, multiplatform and streaming media providers, and constant social media interactions. They expect media to follow their multitasking and increasingly mobile-centric lifestyles and to provide immediate relevancy for their ongoing activities (e.g., information for problem solving, entertainment for leisure, social media for communication), allowing them to access and conveniently consume content on any device, on any platform, at any time. As a result, media companies face continuous audience fragmentation, ensuing content segmentation, and increasing competition (including from both media and nonmedia activities) for attention. On the positive side, more audience interaction channels also mean more media touch points between brands and consumers and opportunities for content enhancement (Chan-Olmsted & Wolter, 2017).

Due to increasing audience fragmentation, mass media production and distribution are now complemented by niche products, which, however, are distributed—if possible, on demand—via a multitude of devices and platforms (Chan-Olmsted & Wolter, 2017; Deuze, 2016; Küng, 2007). The platform approach differs considerably from the traditional publishing-broadcasting approach in which media companies controlled the entire content creation and distribution process (Bartosova, 2011). In the platform approach, media companies operate an IT-based platform to attract and distribute content, and they charge fees for platform access and activities. Content is provided by the platform users (e.g., members of other organizations) and distributed to other recipients via online and mobile media. The platform owner does not have to create content but is responsible for attracting enough content from other sources and ensuring the content quality (Hess, 2014). In addition, digital platforms allow content rights owners to offer their content directly to end users, essentially cutting out former intermediaries in content distribution (e.g., CD sales, bookshops) (Bartosova, 2011; Evens, 2010).

BUSINESS MODELS: CHANGING REVENUE AND FINANCE STRUCTURES

Traditional media businesses relied largely on customer spending and advertising revenues. With advertising budgets moving to online media, the traditional players receive much smaller slices of the pie (Lowe, 2016) because technology companies (e.g., Google and Facebook) currently take up most of this revenue stream. On the plus side, more companies that incorporate interactivity generate new revenues through transaction charges or by offering advertisers a click-through merchandise ordering service. Furthermore, as mentioned in the previous chapter, data collection and analytics provide unprecedented opportunities for targeted advertising.

In terms of media content, the "idea of free" instilled by early online content access has created unwanted customer practices of avoiding payment. Introducing paywalls helps recoup ground by reinstating consumer payments or, in the case of free local newspapers, moving from the advertising-only to a mixed user payment/advertising revenue model (Olsen & Solvoll, 2018). Generic news content payments are hard to come by as long as the content can be accessed for free through other channels, but willingness to pay for exclusive high-quality content has been increasing. Other media, such as gaming companies, benefit as they can now offer subscriptions for their online games, sell virtual products, or charge for in-game advertising (Mierzejewska & Shaver, 2014). In terms of financing, especially for artistic media products, crowdfunding has emerged as another trend (Freeman, 2017). Crowdfunding accumulates contributions from audiences in return for ownership in media product creation or, in some cases, as a donation to fund a media project (Baumann & Brüning, 2017).

Digital technology now allows even amateurs to film, record, and produce almost any type of content and then publish UGC via online and mobile platforms. As a consequence, media not only lose their content gatekeeping function but still have to cover the cost of their infrastructure while losing audiences to prosumers. Feasible news organizations have started to incorporate UGC into their news products (Mierzejewska & Shaver, 2014).

Technological changes have also altered the geographic scope of media markets. In the predigital era, content delivery was restricted to specific geographic areas due to limited technological reach or market regulations for most content other than books, films, and recorded music. Digital content can now be consumed worldwide and hence bypass geographic distribution limitations (Küng, 2007; Mierzejewska & Shaver, 2014).

It should be noted that media companies have been affected by the changes in information and communication technologies to a higher degree than organizations in other industries, because as Cardoso and Moreno (2016) write, "information and digital content are the business" (p. 223). Consequently, the media product itself is becoming digital, or previously necessary physical components of a media product are removed from the value creation chain (Achtenhagen, 2017). Nevertheless, media consumption still requires a viewing, reading, or listening device, but these devices tend to be multifunctional in that they support all consumption methods. In terms of business model adaptations, media companies have to decide how far they want to diversify their business into the digital world and how they plan to generate revenues from their digital businesses (Evens, 2010; Hess, Matt, Benlian, & Wiesböck, 2016).

Looking at a broader picture, the business ecosystems surrounding media companies (i.e., the set of actors that contribute to their value proposition) have changed considerably. The term *ecosystem* conveys the notion that firms are embedded into evolving systems in which actors from different industries mutually influence each other through innovation, competition, and collaboration (Kapoor, 2018).

Complementarities and interdependencies between actors are simultaneously present in a business ecosystem. Functions performed by two or more actors that create or enhance the media company's value proposition are called complementarities. They represent an economic relationship between offers in terms of the potential value creation for users. Interdependencies between actors exist because their offers are connected within the system-level architecture. Hence, they represent a structural relationship between the actors' offers through their role in the value creation of the final product (Jacobides, Cennamo, & Gawer, 2018; Kapoor, 2018).

In the case of media business ecosystems, actors contribute to the media product or service, for example, by supplying photographs for an article or website that are incorporated into the product (interdependency). Downstream complement offers are not integrated into the final "product" by the media company but instead by users who, for example, select the game to be installed on a game console. Technology changes have disrupted traditional media business ecosystems as the traditional media's value creation chains are replaced by more fluid value creation networks (Doyle, 2016). Consequently, media companies need to embrace horizontal interfirm relationships and strategic alliances as well as increasing specialized modularization on a vertical level. These specialized companies can concentrate on their own offers and connect to other actors via market transactions rather than through full vertical integration. For legacy media, this strategy indicates a shift away from instituting and controlling a series of activities in the value creation chain to establishing cooperation and bilateral agreements with other actors in the business ecosystem (Evens, 2010).

Digital transformation is a complex process that affects many or all functions within a media company. Media managers have to simultaneously balance the exploration into media product and service innovation and the efficient exploitation of their firms' resources. While the latter ensures current operations, the former helps achieve the necessary organizational agility for successful digital business transformation (Baumann, 2013; Hess et al., 2016). From a strategic media management perspective, this requires the development of dynamic capabilities (Lowe, 2016; Oliver, 2016) as managing and adapting company resources and capabilities is essential to remain competitive and to sustain in the long run. However, this process of adaption necessitates considerable resource investment for transformational initiatives and necessary organizational learning (Hess et al., 2016; Oliver, 2016). The next section presents opportunities and challenges of managing the digital transformation toward a convergent media environment.

Opportunities and Challenges

Almost three decades after the introduction of the Internet, the structures of a new media ecosystem are becoming more distinctive. Legacy incumbents need to transform their content and business models as well as their organization structure (Bartosova, 2011). This digital transformation comes with considerable opportunities and challenges in media management practices.

OPPORTUNITIES

In terms of business models, media companies have to continually develop new content and service offerings across multiple local markets while also addressing a triple market interface under conditions of increasing volatility. Although content remains a core element of media business, the offering now has to fit consumer lifestyles (any content, any platform, any time) and focus on the complete customer experience for convergent media across multiple platforms. Interactivity is a must as audiences want to become involved (if they so choose) in any aspect of the value creation from design to content creation to distribution.

Each of these touch points provides opportunities for customer interaction. Media companies will also need to collaborate with e-commerce companies. For example, magazines of Gruner + Jahr are now developing branded products, the sales of which contribute strongly to fund the journal. *Schöner Wohnen*, an interior design magazine, now publishes a catalog with furniture, carpets, paintings, flooring, and other home decor in which the items are arranged as stylishly as in the magazine. It is important to note that in the media industry, the new models supplement the existing ones but rarely fully displace them. Nevertheless, they affect the operation and revenue generation of traditional media organizations (Deuze, 2016).

In a business-to-consumer market, the speed of technology adoption is generation driven. This means that older consumers often stick to or only gradually replace their customary devices, allowing continued viability of the older business models. For example, older viewers mostly watch TV on traditional big screens or read books. Although these business models will not crash overnight, media practitioners need to watch out for the tipping point when an increasing share of younger generations pressures the old business model into the niche space, while interactive and convergent media business models take center stage.

Business-to-business media markets experience even swifter changes. Business customers expect full-service solutions that far exceed the current focus on content products. The Wolters Kluwer example in this chapter demonstrates that the media company not only needs in-depth knowledge of its clients' business processes but must also apply the latest technologies, such as automation, robotics, and AI, into their business practices. Assessing, integrating, and exploiting these and other digital technologies present some of the most prevalent opportunities (as well as challenges) that media companies currently face (Hess et al., 2016), especially given the plethora and speed of technological innovations that supplement or undermine existing technologies. Media companies, therefore, have to constantly adapt to new technologies and realign or abandon existing ones (Deuze, 2016).

Media managers must determine how proactive and innovative they want to and can be in their approach to new technology given the usual resource constraints and the high risk associated with these decisions. However, waiting and seeing is not an option in today's fast-paced media environment, as the next offer is just a click, app, or platform away. Managers of legacy media companies have to transform the corporate culture from a content-based product company to that of a player in the technology and platform sector. Managing this transition sometimes involves tough decisions of closing or selling unprofitable content business while growing organically, and/or through acquisitions, in the digital arena.

Traditionally, advertising revenues in linear media relied on the number of eyeballs or ears that could be reached through a particular medium. Although the legacy measurement systems had some inherent flaws, measuring audience engagement for convergent media is even more difficult, as discussed in chapter 4; there are currently no metrics that are conceptually and methodologically adequate (Chan-Olmsted & Wolter, 2017). Nevertheless, the increasing viability of metrics, personalization of media products, development of innovative data-driven offerings, and targeted advertising will advance even further in creating better value for paying customers. In addition, better predictability of audience behavior reduces risks associated with investing in the wrong kind of content.

Advertising products increasingly become commodities. Therefore, innovative forms of advertising (e.g., storytelling) and integrated advertising concepts (e.g., around customer journeys) are needed (Küng, 2017). These require revamping the advertising ecosystem in that advertisers become strategic partners, and pricing is based on performance (Achtenhagen, 2011). While the multiplatform approach unquestionably extends opportunities for content consumption, it is also boosting brand extension strategies through recycling and repurposing of media content (Doyle, 2015). Nevertheless, although digital technologies and data analytics offer many opportunities for enhanced business models and revenue streams, personalized content and advertising as well as customers' integration into the value creation ecosystem all come with unique challenges.

CHALLENGES

As explained above, media business ecosystems are affected by continuous disruption induced by technology changes and the traditional media's value creation chains replaced by more fluid value creation networks. These typically transcend the traditional boundaries of media content providers by including technology players, telecommunication firms, software developers, consumer electronics manufacturers, and others. These ecosystems are driven by both competition and collaboration. On the one hand, streaming companies such as Netflix and Amazon heavily invest in producing original content after media companies such as Disney pulled back content from their platforms and consequently directly compete with traditional content providers for audience share. Telecoms are also investing in offering content of their own by acquiring media companies (e.g., AT&T bought Time Warner for $85 billion) and at the same time want to monetize the content they are transporting to their fixed and mobile networks. On the other hand, all old and new media players increasingly collaborate as consumers progressively reevaluate their content needs and question multiple subscriptions.

Customer experience management far exceeds content partnerships because the audience expects an attractive and, in particular, a consistent experience across all channels and media devices. This includes optimal usability through responsive platform designs and availability of preferred content choices regardless of the channels and devices they use.

The latest trend in media ecosystems involves collaborating with your customers, such as codeveloping content. In the Wolters Kluwer case, the company closely collaborates with tax accountancies to develop full-service software solutions for clients, and WK's offer far exceeds those of the traditional content provider.

In order to ensure long-term profitability, media companies must be able to monetize their products and services. The challenge is that the more consumers move to mobile platforms, the larger the chunk of revenues (e.g., from advertising) claimed by technology companies such as Google and Facebook. Content sales are hampered by reverting the for-free mentality of consumers in news media and cannibalization effects in traditional media, for example, lower-margin e-books substituting print book sales (Prostka, Shehu, & Clement, 2018).

Content licensing constitutes a large part of media business both as a means of monetizing one's own original content and acquiring content from other sources/platforms. Although intellectual property management was already difficult in traditional media business models due to the multitude of national and international regulations, it has become excessively complex and complicated in a digital environment. Content is being consumed by switching devices and access modes, while the content offering needs to be simultaneously adapted to the usage setting. Adaptations range from different content combinations depending on devices or subscription models to compliance with licensing contracts of the content provider or local regulations subject to the location of the user/device. Digital ledgers based on blockchain technologies are being discussed as possible solutions to quickly identify content owners and grant rights to licensees, but the technology is not yet mature. Most of the enhanced digital business propositions rely on some form of data analysis and exploitation for target products, services, and/or advertising. However, regardless of their improved customer experience, consumers become increasingly worried about data privacy and security issues.

One of the central management challenges of the digital transition is establishing a corporate culture that accepts permanent change as the new norm. Media managers and practitioners have to get accustomed to working in multidisciplinary teams and integrating agile organizational responses to changes (Küng, 2017). A complete change of mindset is needed as media companies have to embrace technology and accept that market success now relies as much (if not more) on data analysis and technology applications as it does on excellent content. Exceptional skills are required to understand the technological developments (e.g., automation, robotics, AI) and their business potentials as well as the implications for managing changes when entering the new digital territory. Difficult decisions will involve reducing domain-specific (i.e., content-creating) staff while recruiting a strong engineering workforce to implement a digital strategy. As the cultures of content and engineering are very different, building a successful integrated culture brings additional challenges but could also be a starting point for a growth trajectory if employees treat this as an opportunity for permanent learning and hence personal development. The permanent-learning mindset determines the scope of full immersion of all employees into idea sharing, constant innovation, and the necessary momentum and agility for the digital transition (Küng, 2017).

The digital transformation provides media organizations with manifold business opportunities but also comes with considerable management challenges. The following action plan can be used for media managers to navigate this route toward digital transition.

ACTION PLAN

1. Invest in digitization.
2. Monitor the digital marketplace, audience behavior, and technology developments.
3. Leverage new technology in media businesses, such as automation, robotics, and AI.
4. Develop use cases, design customer experiences, and create superior customer value.
5. Form alliances that help develop business ecosystems.
6. Build a strong leadership and corporate culture.

KEY TAKEAWAYS

1. Disruption is the new norm faced by media managers in today's convergent environment.
2. Data and technology are key to success in media management practices.
3. Change comes faster than media managers and practitioners think and prepare for.
4. Be aware of content silos, and also think about how to integrate convergent media solutions in creating customer values.
5. Involve the customer in your value creation decisions.
6. Think in terms of business ecosystems, and find partners outside of the media industry.
7. Think coopetition (i.e., collaboration and competition).
8. Excellent media managers are needed for the digital transition.

CONCLUSION

Media industries have been among the earliest and most affected sectors influenced by digitization. Digitization affects not only media organizations' operational processes but also their products and value creation, as any media product can and will eventually be digitized. Unfortunately, news media fell into the trap of offering their product for free on the Internet, while advertising funding remained minimal. This resulted in customer expectations that are difficult to change. Willingness to pay has increased for exclusive and high-quality content, but the bulk of advertising goes to the digital behemoths, such as Google and Facebook. Likewise, the music industry underestimated peer-to-peer platforms, which allowed Apple to initially dominate music downloads. Looking at these two media industries among many other examples, media companies have had their fair share of digital strategy disasters and are now actively exploring new business strategies.

TABLE 23.1. Actions and Related Objectives for Digital Transformation

Action	*Objectives*
Invest in digitization	Survival; competitive advantage
Monitor markets, audience behavior, and technology developments constantly	In-depth knowledge; access to data; ability to prepare, explore, and exploit business potential
Leverage technology: automation, robotics, AI	Creating innovative business models with benefits for your customers
Develop use cases, design customer experiences, and create superior customer value	Helping your customers solve problems, run their business better, and create an engaging customer experience
Form alliances/develop media business ecosystems	Creating integrated, hassle-free customer solutions
Develop leadership and corporate culture	Increased agility; digital mindset

Table 23.1 summarizes the must-dos for media managers and associates the above action plan with organizational objectives toward digital transformation. Without major investment into digitization, media companies will lose their competitive advantages and eventually cease to exist in today's fast-changing environment. New and adaptations of existing business models require in-depth knowledge of the markets, audience behavior, and the latest technical developments. By leveraging automation, robotics, and AI, media companies can create innovative business models with true benefits for their customers that are based on use cases that incorporate excellently designed customer experiences. Providing integrated, hassle-free customer solutions requires alliances with all relevant partners and developing the respective media business ecosystems. Finally, media practitioners who are knowledgeable in technology and data analytics need to develop leadership and a corporate culture with a digital mindset in order to increase the agility of their organization (Baumann, 2020).

The Wolters Kluwer example showed the importance of understanding the customer and all aspects of their media usage and service needs in order to provide a full-service solution. WK transformed from a pure content-based company to a content, technology, and platform player by not being afraid to make difficult decisions around reducing the domain-specific content business while extending the technology-driven service package offering. This is complemented by a culture of employee-led innovation and constant investments in research and development and innovative products and services.

Another important lesson to be learned from WK is that the niche strategy can be very successful if you cannot and do not want to compete in the media mass market that is dominated by the FAANG conglomerates. Nevertheless, some legacy media organizations have—though often painfully—successfully followed the digitization trajectory and are effectively holding their ground against the behemoths in their own niches. Also, it is a myth that traditional media businesses are all dead. Some media, such as music and newspapers, have been affected faster than others but are still very much alive, although they had and still have to adapt their business models. Traditional TV will still survive for quite some time but due to generational transitions will eventually be constrained to a niche.

Although digitization puts pressure on legacy business models, it has also helped save costs for manufacturing, distributing, storing, and disposing of physical media products, such as books, CDs, and DVDs. In addition, digital copies are easy to reproduce and distribute, thus making small-volume business viable (e.g., leveraging the back catalog). Data analytics of online and mobile content usage provide unique personalized marketing opportunities—direct marketing on steroids. However, the multiplatform approach and mobile distribution extend opportunities for content consumption but not necessarily greater diversity of content nor pluralism, because often content, particularly those from high-profile content providers, are merely recycled or repurposed to further increase their market share (Doyle, 2015).

Finally, it can be said that the digital transformation requires strong leadership and a change in corporate culture that embraces changes and disruption as a norm and where employees regard constant learning as an opportunity rather than a threat. Otherwise, lacking agility and missing innovation will prevent the necessary adaptions to new technology and data-driven business models. Media business ecosystems will favor actors who are open to diversity and thinking outside the box.

As this chapter demonstrates, managing convergent media in practice is dynamic, full of exciting developments, and paved with many failures and increasing successes. The next chapter presents a comprehensive examination of traditional and convergent skills needed for media practitioners and managers in a convergent environment. It will also point out how academics can better prepare future practitioners to keep up with the speed of the digital transformation in media environments.

REFERENCES

Achtenhagen, L. (2011). Managing media companies: Harnessing creative value by Annet Aris and Jacques Bughin. *International Journal on Media Management, 13*, 149–151. doi: 10.1080/14241277.2011.578027

Achtenhagen, L. (2017). Media entrepreneurship: Taking stock and moving forward. *International Journal on Media Management, 19*, 1–10. doi: 10.1080/14241277.2017.1298941

Albarran, A. B. (2018). Media management and economics research: A historical review. In A. Albarran (Ed.), *Handbook of media management and economics* (2nd ed.) (pp. 3–16). Routledge.

Anderson, C. (2006). *The long tail: How endless choice is creating unlimited demand*. Penguin Random House.

Aris, A., & Bughin, J. (2012). *Managing media companies: Harnessing creative values* (2nd ed.). Wiley.

Bartosova, D. (2011). The future of the media professions: Current issues in media management practice. *International Journal on Media Management, 13*, 195–203. doi: 10.1080/14241277.2011.576963

Baumann, S. (2020). Guest editor's introduction: Strategic media management at a junction. *Journal of Media Business Studies, 17*, 1–12. doi: 10.1080/16522354.2020.1740564

Baumann, S. (2013). Adapting to the brave new world: Innovative organisational strategies for media companies. In T. Storsul & A. H. Krumsvik (Eds.), *Media innovations. A multidisciplinary study of change* (pp. 77–92). Nordicom.

Baumann, S., & Brüning, H. (2017). Attention, crowd: We need your money! Start-ups' communicative appearances on crowdfunding platforms. In M. Friedrichsen & Y. Kamalipour (Eds.), *Digital transformation in journalism and news media, media management, media convergence and globalization* (pp. 107–114). Springer International Publishing.

Baumann, S., & Hasenpusch, T. C. (2014). Konvergierende Technologien—konvergierende Geschäftsmodelle: Hybrid TV und Multiscreen (Converging technologies—converging business models: Hybrid TV and multiscreen). *Think CROSS-Change MEDIA. Crossmedia im Jahr*, 11–27.

Baumann, S., & Hasenpusch, T. C. (2016). Multi-platform television and business models: A Babylonian clutter of definitions and concepts. *Westminster Papers in Communication and Culture, 11,* 85–102. doi: 10.16997/wpcc.219

Brown, C. (2016). Media management: A critical discipline? In G. F. Lowe & C. Brown (Eds.), *Managing media firms and industries: What's so special about media management?* (pp. 83–100). Springer.

Cardoso, G., & Moreno, J. (2016). Technology management and business models. In G. F. Lowe & C. Brown (Eds.), *Managing media firms and industries: What's so special about media management?* (pp. 223–239). Springer.

Cestino, J., & Berndt, A. (2018). Institutional limits to service dominant logic and servitisation in innovation efforts in newspapers. *Journal of Media Business Studies, 14,* 188–216. doi: 10.1080/16522354.2018.1445163

Chambers, T., & Howard, H. H. (2006). The economics of media consolidation. In A. B. Albarran, S. M. Chan-Olmsted, & M. O. Wirth (Eds.), *Handbook of media management and economics* (pp. 363–385). Lawrence Erlbaum Associates.

Chan-Olmsted, S. M., & Wolter, L.-C. (2017). Perceptions and practices of media engagement: A global perspective. *International Journal on Media Management, 20,* 1–24. doi: 10.1080/14241277.2017.1402183

Daidj, N., & Jung, J. (2011). Strategies in the media industry: Towards the development of co-opetition practices? *Journal of Media Business Studies, 8,* 37–57. doi: 10.1080/16522354.2011.11073530

DeFillippi, R. (2009). Dilemmas of project-based media work: Contexts and choices. *Journal of Media Business Studies, 6,* 5–30. doi: 10.1080/16522354.2009.11073493

Deuze, M. (2016). Managing media workers. In G. F. Lowe & C. Brown (Eds.), *Managing media firms and industries: What's so special about media management?* (pp. 329–341). Springer.

Doyle, G. (2015). Multi-platform media and the miracle of the loaves and fishes. *Journal of Media Business Studies, 12,* 49–65. doi: 10.1080/16522354.2015.1027113

Doyle, G. (2016). Managing in the distinctive economic context of media. In G. F. Lowe & C. Brown (Eds.), *Managing media firms and industries: What's so special about media management?* (pp. 175–188). Springer.

Evens, T. (2010). Value networks and changing business models for the digital television industry. *Journal of Media Business Studies, 7,* 41–58. doi: 10.1080/16522354.2010.11073514

Freeman, M. (2017). Funding and management in the media convergence era: Introduction. *International Journal on Media Management, 19,* 103–107. doi: 10.1080/14241277.2017.1300478

Hang, M. (2018). Media entrepreneurship. In A. Albarran (Ed.), *Handbook of media management and economics* (2nd ed.) (pp. 259–272). Routledge.

Hang, M., & van Weezel, A. (2007). Media and entrepreneurship: What do we know and where should we go? *Journal of Media Business Studies, 4,* 51–70. doi: 10.1080/16522354.2007.11073446

Hasenpusch, T. C., & Baumann, S. (2017). Strategic media venturing: Corporate venture capital approaches of TIME incumbents. *International Journal on Media Management, 19,* 77–100. doi: 10.1080/14241277.2017.1280040

Hess, T. (2014). What is a media company?: A reconceptualization for the online world. *International Journal on Media Management, 16,* 3–8. doi: 10.1080/14241277.2014.906993

Hess, T., Matt, C., Benlian, A., & Wiesböck, F. (2016). Options for formulating a digital transformation strategy. *MIS Quarterly Executive, 15,* 123–139.

Hollifield, C. A. (2001). Crossing borders: Media management research in a transnational market environment. *Journal of Media Economics, 14,* 133–146. doi: 10.1207/S15327736ME1403_1

Jacobides, M. G., Cennamo, C., & Gawer, A. (2018). Towards a theory of ecosystems. *Strategic Management Journal, 39,* 2255–2276. doi: 10.1002/smj.2904

Kapoor, R. (2018). Ecosystems: Broadening the locus of value creation. *Journal of Organization Design, 7*(12), 1–16. doi: 10.1186/s41469-018-0035-4

Küng, L. (2007). Does media management matter? Establishing the scope, rationale, and future research agenda for the discipline. *Journal of Media Business Studies, 4,* 21–39. doi: 10.1080/16522354.2007.11073444

Küng, L. (2016). Why is media management research so difficult—and what can scholars do to overcome the field's intrinsic challenges? *Journal of Media Business Studies, 13,* 276–282. doi: 10.1080/16522354.2016.1236572

Küng, L. (2017). *Going digital: A roadmap for organisational transformation.* Reuters Institute. https://reutersinstitute.politics.ox.ac.uk/our-research/going-digital-roadmap-organisational-transformation
Lowe, G. F. (2016). Introduction: What's so special about media management? In G. F. Lowe & C. Brown (Eds.), *Managing media firms and industries: What's so special about media management?* (pp. 1–20). Springer.
Lundin, R. A., & Norbäck, M. (2016). Projectification in the media industries. In G. F. Lowe & C. Brown (Eds.), *Managing media firms and industries: What's so special about media management?* (pp. 367–382). Springer.
Mierzejewska, B., & Shaver, D. (2014). Key changes impacting media management research. *International Journal on Media Management, 16,* 47–54. doi: 10.1080/14241277.2014.954439
Nissen, C. S. (2013). What's so special about public service media management? *International Journal on Media Management, 15,* 69–75. doi: 10.1080/14241277.2013.785737
Oliver, J. J. (2016). Dynamic media management capabilities: A case study. In G. F. Lowe & C. Brown (Eds.), *Managing media firms and industries: What's so special about media management?* (pp. 293–308). Springer.
Oliver, J. J. (2018). Strategic transformations in the media. *Journal of Media Business Studies, 25*(8), 1–22. doi: 10.1080/16522354.2018.1546088
Olsen, R. K., & Solvoll, M. K. (2018). Reinventing the business model for local newspapers by building walls. *Journal of Media Business Studies, 15,* 24–41. doi: 10.1080/16522354.2018.1445160
Ots, M., Nyilasy, G., Rohn, U., & Wikström, P. (2015). Media business studies as we see it: Why does it matter, for whom, and how do you get published? *Journal of Media Business Studies, 12,* 103–106. doi: 10.1080/16522354.2015.1054699
Ozanich, G. W. (2006). Media finance and valuation. In A. B. Albarran, S. M. Chan-Olmsted, & M. O. Wirth (Eds.), *Handbook of media management and economics* (pp. 601–621). Lawrence Erlbaum Associates.
Picard, R. G. (2005). Unique characteristics and business dynamics of media products. *Journal of Media Business Studies, 2,* 61–69. doi: 10.1080/16522354.2005.11073433
Picard, R. G., & Lowe, G. F. (2016). Questioning media management scholarship: Four parables about how to better develop the field. *Journal of Media Business Studies, 13,* 61–72. doi: 10.1080/16522354.2016.1176781
Prostka, T., Shehu, E., & Clement, M. (2018). Cannibalisation effects in the early market stage of e-books—an analysis of the German book market. *Journal of Media Business Studies,* 4(2), 1–19. doi: 10.1080/16522354.2018.1481490
Unger, D. (2019). *Making critical decisions with confidence.* Strategy+Business. https://www.strategy-business.com/article/Making-Critical-Decisions-with-Confidence/
Wirtz, B. W. (2011). *Media and Internet management.* Gabler.
Wolters Kluwer. (2018). *Our strategy.* https://wolterskluwer.com/company/about-us/strategy.html
Wolters Kluwer. (2019a). *Company website.* https://wolterskluwer.com
Wolters Kluwer. (2019b). *Products & services.* https://wolterskluwer.com/products-services
Wolters Kluwer. (2019c). *Tax & accounting.* https://wolterskluwer.com/products-services/our-portfolio/tax-accounting.html

CHAPTER 24

Looking Forward

Roger Cooper, Ohio University
L. Meghan Mahoney, West Chester University
Tang Tang, Kent State University

LEARNING OBJECTIVES

1. Summarize traditional skills to prepare for a career in media business.
2. Identify convergent soft skills necessary for media practitioners and aspiring media managers to succeed in a convergent media environment.
3. Suggest university adaptations necessary in order to meet these new market demands.
4. Explore how to best prepare for career advancement in the field through the 12 attributes of extraordinary media professionals model.

This book was designed to prepare media practitioners and aspiring media managers for a successful career in dynamic and ever-changing media landscapes. Hopefully, it has taught foundational principles that should be the core of every strategic decision, as well as key disruptions that future practitioners must adapt toward in today's convergent media environment. While it is difficult to predict how tomorrow's technologies will impact the field, this chapter will look forward to a post-convergence era and make critical suggestions to thrive in these dynamic professions.

Media industries are characterized by high competition and unemployment, less occupational stability and security, lower median pay, and ill-defined pathways to employment and success relative to most professions (Cooper & Tang, 2010). They require a complex combination of technical, creative, collaborative, and problem-solving skills. These challenges should not deter media professionals from a future in media management but rather inspire aspiring media practitioners to develop and incorporate the vast array of skills needed to *thrive* over time. While the so-called hard skills are certainly important to effectively carry out specific tasks, soft skills emerge as equally, if not more, important qualities needed in the uncertain career environments described above.

For example, interviews for jobs at media companies are untraditional. Rather than strict assessments of hard skills, interviewers look for qualities that are difficult to detect on a résumé, as the company seeks new hires who can grow and adapt to challenges and be adept at multiple tasks. While many young professionals expect there to be an "interrogation" during an interview, it is instead a *conversation* used to help determine how the applicant might assimilate into the company's culture and serve as a potential solution for the short- and long-term goals of the company. Let's explore how a media giant, Google, "interviews differently" (Popomaronis, 2019) in order to vet candidates that will help maintain Google's competitive status in the industry.

CASE STUDY

Google has consistently been cited on the Best Place to Work list (Glass Door, 2020). It is no surprise that many of the brightest, most innovative, and creative professionals vie for each position listed within the company. Google had an acceptance rate of 0.2% for every position available in 2019, with candidates often completing up to 25 interviews over six to nine months to land a single job (Popomaronis, 2019).

What skills were hiring committees searching for in this arduous process? Clearly, Google employees must be at the top of their class and possess savvy media and technological skills. However, assessing the latest media software and SEO development in candidates was not the focus of these interviews. Instead, the process was reserved for assessing something that Google has termed "Googleyness" in candidates, defined as enjoying fun, intellectual humility, and comfort with ambiguity (Meisenzahl, 2019).

> Attributes like enjoying fun (who doesn't), a certain dose of intellectual humility (it's hard to learn if you can't admit that you might be wrong), a strong measure of conscientiousness (we want owners, not employees), comfort with ambiguity (we don't know how our business will evolve, and navigating Google internally requires dealing with a lot of ambiguity), and evidence that you've taken some courageous or interesting paths in your life. (Bock, 2015)

While Google is constantly revamping its interview process, it is clear that the company is also taking untraditional measures to bring in candidates who already have the needed technological skills and using the interview as an opportunity to assess how well candidates work in group settings and incorporate feedback into their own work process. Brainstorming and problem solving are key to tackling interview questions. One candidate was reportedly asked, "How many uses are there for a traffic cone?" and was expected to develop an innovative and comprehensive list of options (Moran, 2017). This unusual approach to interview questions helps recruiters better understand how candidates react in unpredictable situations and use their personal past experiences to help solve problems.

More media companies are taking a similar approach, where they bring in candidates who already showcase the technological hard skills, as well as maintain a creative portfolio to succeed at a job, and they use the interview process as an opportunity to better understand the candidates' motivation, personality, and process. What other unexpected soft qualities do media companies value in candidates? Meisenzahl (2019) lists (1) doing the right thing; (2) being proactive; (3) valuing coworkers; (4) having a sense of humor; and (5) being simply kind, friendly, and approachable as a few examples of qualities that are important to succeed in media fields.

It may seem as though future media managers need to have it all: strong technological, creative, and problem-solving tendencies. While this is true to a certain extent, many of these qualities can be trained and mastered with a proactive approach. Below we will explore some "old" approaches to media education as well as new strategies for improving soft skills to help you land your dream career in media business.

Something Old

Having a clearly defined and tangible goal, researching the requirements for landing an entry-level position, and acquiring the necessary training and experience remains a strong strategy for achieving employment in media business. While there are many hard skills (technical) and soft skills (e.g., interpersonal) that employers are searching for in candidates, with enough motivation and proper guidance, aspiring candidates are able to position themselves positively in tomorrow's media marketplace.

Currently, media companies predict a 50% skills gap in the workforce, primarily citing new digital technologies as a primary issue (Bartosova, 2011; Skillset, 2009). A career in media management today requires convergent multiplatform skills that combine effective leadership with innovation, creativity, and understanding of technology, and the analytical skills to understand audience interests and to translate that into appropriate business intelligence (Bartosova, 2011). Below we will explore best options for mastering foundational skills that will advance any media career, including writing, content creation, and strategic thinking. While these may be the same skills that have always been the core of media companies, there are many new converged formats to which practitioners need to adapt.

WRITING

Strong writing is still a foundation for all aspects of media relations, digital marketing, and client communication (Portersfield, 2017). With an increasingly mediated and global media marketplace, much critical communication to businesses happens through writing. Media practitioners and managers must be able to communicate clearly and adapt writing strategies for a variety of audiences (or stakeholders). In addition to being one of the most sought-after skills for media practitioners, it is also one of the most difficult to teach. Future practitioners should highlight writing skills on their résumé and provide numerous examples of writing across media platforms in their digital portfolio. Of perhaps greater value is to *demonstrate* good writing skills through a cover letter and electronic communication, which are often the first impression provided to prospective employers or key contacts.

Strong writing skills still fuel the industry. While English and journalism programs used to focus on developing student writing, many of these skills are mastered through general education curriculum and upper-level communication assignments today. Writing assignments in a post-convergence era should focus on compact formats and engaging storytelling as well as how to communicate within a business setting. Everything from advertising to entertainment to daily informational newsletters are competing for audience attention. Good stories will help keep a brand in focus and hold the attention of audiences.

CONTENT CREATION

Engaging storytelling in a digital environment requires strong multimedia skills. Increasing visual literacy in students should be the foundation of any media curriculum. Tomorrow's practitioners are expected to carry a "backpack" skill set of content creation using graphic, photography, and video production skills. Traditionally, aspiring content creators have entered specialty programs where they select, focus on, and master a single genre of multimedia. While it is still important for employees to understand their skills and areas that bring greatest passion, they should prepare themselves across a wide variety of modalities and software. This is especially true, as it is uncertain what technological changes the future will bring, and this range of skills and training will help cultivate lifelong, highly adaptable technological learners. One example of such versatility is a career in social media marketing. Companies now look to younger professionals to write compelling content, create graphics, shoot photos, and produce short-format videos for social media posts. Rather than hiring a separate employee for each of these skills, tomorrow's social media marketers are expected to have a backpack skill set where they are able to do many of these things at a high level.

In order for students to best adapt in a post-convergent environment, it is important for classrooms to change as well. Aspiring professionals should seek out programs that encourage content creation in a traditional computer laboratory setting but also allow the opportunity to leave the classroom with digital and video cameras to capture real-world material (Wilhelm, 2005). Primarily sitting at desktop computers for training seems counterintuitive, as most convergent digital media content is created and consumed through mobile media.

Students should seek training that facilitates mastery of basic theoretical knowledge of concepts and provides the opportunity to perform the skills. Media training must shift from traditional face-to-face lecture-style classes to more active workshops and blended, flipped, and online modalities of learning. Much of media content creation relies on practice and trial and error. Students must be given the opportunity to practice, try out new ideas, and make mistakes. They must be out "in the real world" gathering information, encouraged to create and collaborate outside of strict classroom structures (e.g., student production organizations) and especially at media internships. Rather than simply turning in final polished projects, students should receive guidance throughout the entire process.

Tomorrow's media professionals must have practiced working under pressure and tight deadlines (Wenger & Owens, 2012). Most positions in the media industry require proactive and independent work. Practitioners will create organizational messages with no editor or filter. They must learn to curate content quickly, under pressure, with minimal errors, on their own. Otherwise, aspiring media practitioners will encounter additional roadblocks and / or missed opportunities for jobs and advancement.

STRATEGIC THINKING

Strategic thinking requires an understanding of the basic long-term goals and objectives of an enterprise and the adoption of courses of action and the allocation of resources for carrying them out. Various techniques will help facilitate such processes, including periodically confirming an organization's mission, setting short- and long-term goals and objectives, developing plans of action, allocating resources, deploying strategies, monitoring results, and reassessing the corporate mission (Nickols, 2016). Media managers must be strategic in nature and always consider where an organization is currently positioned, where it would like to advance, and the necessary steps that will help achieve this process.

Quality content means nothing if not disseminated effectively or if it is out of sync with the company's brand. A core of any media program should be establishing strategic thinking and research into the process of future practitioners. Media strategy, marketing, SEO, analytics and data management, and user experience design are all essential elements for aspiring media practitioners to succeed in today's convergent environment (Digital Marketing Institute, 2019). While these skills used to be taught in isolation from each other, today's professionals should hold basic interdisciplinary knowledge of each and understand how they connect in a business strategy.

While digital technology skills are important, it is necessary for media managers to also have strong business management skills (Royle & Laing, 2014). They must be able to take strategic measures to understand their brand, mission, and goals; delegate tangible steps for daily operations; and have the proactive personality to manage various employees. Additionally, media managers must have the necessary research skills to measure the success of such efforts. While a convergent media environment has brought new possibilities for metrics, such as big data, the ability and importance of analytic thinking for media managers has not changed.

ADDITIONAL FOUNDATIONS

It is equally important for young or aspiring media professionals to use their formative education years to obtain as much applied work experience through internships and media entry jobs as possible to bolster their portfolio and network of relationships. Tomorrow's media companies are searching for a combination of tech-savviness and a motivation to learn. Work experience directly impacts the ability of college students to get industry jobs after graduation (Wenger & Owens, 2012). This allows employers to see tangible examples of your skills and will better allow candidates to answer questions about how they approach various work environments. The more applied work experience that candidates obtain, the more "seasoned" they become. This also helps candidates make more accurate, informed distinctions about their own career path.

Moreover, each of these professional experiences is an opportunity to learn from established practitioners in the field, to find career mentors, and to obtain written and verbal recommendations within these highly connected small-world professions.

Building strong relationships (or networking) is just as important today as it was 30 years ago, and no computer-mediated communication is able to replace the power of knowing someone who can connect you to the right person or position. A recent study by Mowbray, Hall, Raeside, and Robertson (2018) found that individuals with no work experience related to their target job roles faced heavier barriers to the market than those with direct contacts. This research suggests that mobility is self-generating during the job search process, and work experience helps provide access to a widening pool of contacts in your relationship network.

The importance of gaining experience and having a strong relationship network illustrates the importance of both hard and soft skills for career success in media business. Hard skills may help you land an internship or potential entry-level opportunity, but soft skills will play a critical role in gaining access and advancement. As illustrated by the Google case study above, many media firms rely on an arduous interview process to better assess soft skills. As such, media programs should implement "new" soft skill assessment and criteria into their curriculum. Let's explore some of these approaches below.

Something New

Soft skills are more difficult to define, measure, and improve on. They often refer to personality traits, social graces, facility with language, personal habits, friendliness, and optimism (Schulz, 2008). Soft skills tend to complement hard skills, which are the technical requirements of a job. However, soft skills are often more important in regard to whether a person succeeds with a company. Future academic programs need to do a better job of teaching soft skills if students are to succeed in the evolving media industry (Zehr, 1998).

However, this does bring up the question of whether a person's individual traits and habits can even be improved or if they are ingrained into an individual's natural personality. Research tends to treat personality traits as "dispositional" (i.e., one either has the trait or doesn't). While there might be certain dispositional tendencies that influence our behavior, important soft skills can at least be enhanced through self-recognition and active motivation to improve or develop them (Schulz, 2008). However, one needs to clearly understand why the improvement will be beneficial in order to undertake the development. Often, there are important gaps between what media companies really seek in new employees and what aspiring professionals believe they need. It's critical for curricula in media programs to communicate what these important differences are and why they are critical to succeed in tomorrow's media industries.

IMPORTANCE OF SOFT SKILLS

While cognitively based measures of success such as IQ, GPA, SAT, and college test scores are important, media industries rely very strongly on criteria beyond simple knowledge and intelligence. In a study by Cooper and Tang (2010), media professionals were asked what they believe the most important attributes are for career success in the industry. Adaptability, reliability, being articulate, persistence, and resourcefulness emerged as the top attributes for career success (Cooper & Tang, 2010). These items can be characterized as soft skills and are rarely assessed directly in a traditional classroom setting.

In today's convergent media environment, employers increasingly place the highest importance on items that can be categorized as soft skills and the lowest importance on cognitively based measures of academic reputation (Finch, Hamilton, Baldwin, & Zehner, 2013). Many hard skills can be taught through additional training by employers. However, soft skills are more difficult to improve, and many companies may not feel like they have the time or resources to train or change a candidate's personality. Let's explore some of the most critical soft skills for media professionals to master in a post-convergent era and some classroom strategies for assessing and improving them below.

GROUP ENVIRONMENT

Business executives are especially interested in soft skills that help facilitate an environment of collaboration and group cohesion. Courtesy, flexibility, and teamwork were cited as top business skills employers seek (Robles, 2012). Though media convergence brought much automation and streamlining to businesses, most departments still run with multiple individuals who rely on each other in order to produce a product. If these personalities don't get along or prove ineffective at working together, it will be very difficult to achieve strategic goals.

Basic interpersonal skills such as self-awareness, relationship building, conflict management, and commitment to diversity will make the work environment more productive and enjoyable. Research illustrates that teams of people who work well together produce better and more effective technical solutions, thus resulting in more satisfied customers (Bancino & Zevalkink, 2007). It is difficult for media practitioners to reach their creative potential when they are working in a conflict-ridden environment. Consider the difference in satisfaction between group projects that you may have been assigned in your own career training. The most fruitful group dynamics are those that include various individuals with different talents, attitudes, and worldviews who all work together to achieve a common goal.

ENTERPRISING

Tomorrow's media industries highly rely on freelancers and managers within a larger organization. This new positioning requires an increase in entrepreneurial and enterprising skills (Bartosova, 2011). Individuals with an enterprising attitude are most likely to achieve in the new media environment (Wenger & Owens, 2012). There are many reasons for this, but it is clear that business executives do not want to micromanage employees. Instead, they hope to hire individuals who understand the company's mission and are able to work proactively to help achieve goals.

How do media programs teach and assess enterprising attitudes in students? Students should seek out professors who provide various industry case studies that help illustrate the types of conflicts and challenges that businesses will potentially face as well as the many different strategies for how managers could respond. Each part of the enterprising process (brainstorming, development, presentation, report writing) should be taught and assessed with a plethora of instructor feedback to help guide the process. Yet, it is important to note that overly strict grading rubrics and strident examples to follow are red flags for hampering creativity. While assessment and project expectations should be clear, students should be given the opportunity to complete an assignment based on their ideas, resulting in a unique end result. For this to work well and be fair to students, instructors should not have a "one-size" answer that they are expecting when grading.

Keogh and Galloway (2004) suggest that the only way students will apply media theory to media management practices is if they understand the connection. Therefore, it is important to connect theoretical concepts with how companies and entrepreneurs use them in the real world. Critical components of an effective group process should also be taught. It is important for members of a group project to delegate responsibilities across multiple group members, each contributing based on their own experiences and strengths. Sufficient communication should be encouraged among group members so that everyone involved is aware of what the other members are doing and there is an opportunity for each member to fulfill multiple roles.

Multitasking is key to an enterprising attitude (Wenger & Owens, 2012) and is a key competency required for today's work environment, especially given the technological advancements in media industries (Lindbeck & Snower, 2000; Sanderson, Bruk-Lee, Viswesvaran, Gutierrez, & Kantrowitz, 2013). Students must have practice taking on more than one responsibility and role within a group project and be active participants in planning and executing multiple moving portions that aid in the final product. Clearly not all multitasking efforts result in quality production. The ability to assess the quality of work, as well as when you are overwhelmed and need to delegate or ask for support, is better learned in the classroom than in a real-life professional scenario.

INTEGRITY

Perhaps the most difficult soft skill to teach and assess is integrity. Media industries are wrought with scandal and stories of employees doing anything to remain competitive and increase profits. Concerns about the media industries prioritizing profits over public service have historically given rise to proposals for a more professional model of journalism education (Macdonald, 2006). This is especially true in an era of media convergence, with growing concerns regarding misrepresentation, manipulation, access, privacy, and accuracy across media industries (Tanner, Phillips, Smyth, & Tapsall, 2005). It is important that future media managers are held to greater integrity standards than previous generations.

Chapter 9 discussed the most critical ethical issues facing the media business today and offered directions for future practitioners. Specifically, the field needs to continue to prioritize accuracy, privacy, and transparency in decisions. Audiences must be seen as partners rather than solely profit ventures. Media programs must integrate ethical business case studies, uphold journalism oaths in curriculum, and offer various service opportunities for students. As traditional media and journalism programs turn toward content writing and digital production training, it is important that these ethical standards are not lost in the curriculum. It should be noted that simply teaching students strong ethical standards is not enough. They must also be taught strategies for combatting unethical situations that they may encounter as future media practitioners and leaders. Integrity requires confidence, gumption, and the ability to stand up for what is right, even if it means a loss of profits.

In addition to formal training, you should also be cognizant of life experiences, such as internships or volunteer opportunities, that can improve soft skills. Candidates must go into an interview prepared to tell a compelling story about how unique experiences have contributed to their development and make them an interesting person. Cite specific examples that demonstrate your ability to work well with others, problem solve through an enterprising attitude, and maintain integrity and ethical standards.

Opportunities and Challenges

It is clear that media professions represent a dynamic, unpredictable journey. Young professionals and future leaders need a broad array of hard and soft skills to build a successful long-term career. The pathway's lack of clear definition can seem especially overwhelming to young or aspiring professionals. Some give up not because they lack skills or talent but because they need to activate the full assortment of tools to be equipped for the journey ahead. In pathways that are so often ill defined, ever evolving, and highly competitive, more than cognitive ability, talent, and hard skills are necessary. A deeper set of personal qualities provide many opportunities, added distinctiveness, as well as challenges to young media professionals and future industry leaders.

THE ATTRIBUTES OF EXTRAORDINARY MEDIA PROFESSIONALS

The term *attribute* is used to describe a set of interrelated qualities or characteristics that consistently emerge as important determinants of long-term success and growth in media-related professions. The significance of attributes is that they serve to *drive and sustain* the acquisition of talents and skills / knowledge (specific information for a specific job / profession) needed to enter, advance, and, ultimately, achieve extraordinary things. For example, an individual with a "passion" for something (i.e., an intense love or desire) is going to be driven to learn and retain the specific skills and gain requisite knowledge necessary to gain entry into the area of interest. Contrast this with a person who may be intelligent but is not passionate. Will this person be motivated to fight through the thicket of competition and obstacles likely to be in the way? Stated another way, visualize the *dis*passionate media professional. In any media or creative industry, will this person be motivated to develop the hard skills necessary to navigate effectively through these industries? Will *dis*interest attract people and employment opportunities?

OPPORTUNITIES

The triangulation of attributes with skills and knowledge is a vital link in the chain for the optimally prepared, extraordinary media professional. This critical link, if applied and developed, can provide valuable distinctions for young professionals who will eventually become managers and leaders. The true "genius" of *extraordinary* media professionals is usually not that they are "born" with innate artistic or business talent or excessively high intelligence but that they have accessed a compelling set of attributes that distinguish them from the average media professional (or, perhaps, the *former* media professional). The *real* "talent" is the ability to discover and develop the attributes that enable individuals to succeed in an uncertain, ever-evolving, highly competitive set of industries (Cooper, forthcoming).

Figure 24.1 represents a visualization of how critical soft skills, when combined with tangible hard skills, can help media professionals become *extraordinary* over time. Individually, each attribute is important to media-related professions. Collectively, the 12 attributes, functioning as an integrated *system* of attributes, generates synergistic levels of understanding and momentum toward long-term success in media professions. More important, these attributes are *dynamic* in that they offer no true end point. Personal and professional development is approached as a never-ending pursuit because your ongoing development will lead to new opportunities and challenges, including those as managers and leaders.

Distilled to its essence, the media professions seek smart-working, motivated, passionate, well-rounded, solution-oriented people who are adaptable, reliable, eager to learn and grow, and enjoyable to be around. These individuals do what it takes, within correct principles, to successfully get the job—big or small—done. The *extraordinary* professional gains access to the people and resources to achieve and contribute at levels greater than the sum of the individual attributes. This builds inner confidence and greater capacity to gain more access to people, resources, and opportunities. The model is organized into "arenas of attributes" labeled "big picture," "active," "enduring," and "reinforcing." Below is further illustration of how these important attributes function to enable high levels of achievement and long-term success.

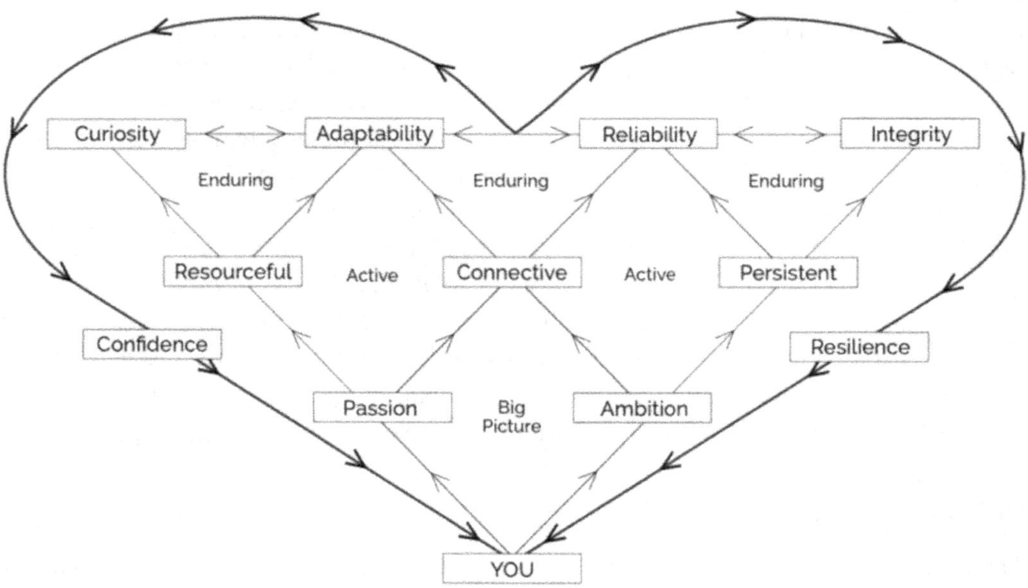

FIGURE 24.1. 12 Attributes of Extraordinary Media Professionals
Source: Cooper, forthcoming.

THE BIG PICTURE ATTRIBUTES

The big picture starts with *you* and is built on connecting who you are to your *passion(s)*; an ongoing thirst to succeed (*ambition*); and an ability to *connect* with people, ideas, and audiences/users/buyers. These four elements form a diamond that serves as an "activation agent" for other elements of the model. Big picture attributes are foundational characteristics that guide your overall approach and direction toward career choice and development.

Of all the important qualities and attributes to be described, *you* remain the most critical, instigating element in the professional (and personal) development equation. Just as attaining a strike in bowling is next to impossible without hitting the head pin, success in the highly competitive, uncertain media industries starts with the unique attributes that you bring to any and every situation. Understanding who you are, what you are good at and interested in, and why you are pursuing a career in media professions is of utmost relevance. What makes you an interesting person? What is unique about you? What stories do you have to tell? What events or defining moments led you to choose a career (and life) in media or creative professions? What skills or aptitudes seem to come "naturally" to you? Your own uniqueness, plus the talents and skills you bring, are critical elements of your own personal development and success. You require a clear understanding of your own personal "story," *why* (not "how") you seek to embark on or continue a career in these professions, and how this impacts the values and ambitions that lead to your career choices. Your own unique personal attributes, in addition to others described in this book, might range from humility to competitiveness to a sense of humor to an innate (or highly developed) talent to exceptional intelligence, or any number of other key attributes. It's critical to *accurately* understand what those unique "talents" are and how they connect to your own values and aspirations.

Passion represents a key "prerequisite" in the big picture to attain extraordinary success in media professions. Across the various industries—film, television, recording, gaming, digital, publishing, and all associated fields—"having a passion" is an often-cited quality or attribute of highly successful media professionals. Why? Success and achievement in the competitive, uncertain media industries is next to impossible without having an emotionally driven desire (or *love*) to do this work. Thus, passion is not merely about "wanting to" work in some area of the media professions but represents the *having to* within the individual. It is an internalized value that is central, fundamental, and essential to develop the other key attributes necessary to be "extraordinary" in media-related professions. Think of passion as a kind of emotion muscle memory. Someone with a passion for something carries an emotional attachment to whatever and whoever they are passionate about and thus is willing to do more than someone who is not emotionally invested. Thus, connecting your specific passions to your career is incredibly important.

Extraordinary media professionals also exhibit *ambition*, an essential "want to" in the big picture for media professionals. People who are ambitious have a drive to achieve and succeed. Although passion is critical, it's often not enough to achieve success. For example, you can have a passion (or "love") for television, but this isn't sufficient to develop a successful *career* in television. Ambition, therefore, is critical in the big picture to develop a successful career because a drive to succeed will help overcome inherent challenges and obstacles.

Being *connective* not only completes the diamond of big picture attributes but also represents the *central nervous system* for the entire attributes model. *Connective* refers to the ability to build relationships and develop a network of contacts, which is crucial within highly collaborative media professions. *Connective* also implies a desire to connect with audiences/users/buyers with content that makes an emotional and/or intellectual impact. The importance of being connective cannot be overstated, and the extraordinary media professional recognizes how important this is when working in people- and audience-driven industries. An individual who connects effectively creates opportunities that are often far more powerful than a strong résumé or simple display of talent. While these prerequisites are important to the big picture of media management success, there are many active attributes that may provide challenges to professionals looking to enter the field.

CHALLENGES

Big picture attributes are critical, but not sufficient, for long-term success. These must eventually manifest themselves into attributes of *quality action*. The next three attributes—*resourcefulness, connectiveness,* and *persistence*—represent core active attributes as a result of the individual's effective orientation to the big picture. As the model shows, passion and ambition serve as the basis/foundation for a set of *active* attributes that are critical to success.

THE ACTIVE ATTRIBUTES

The active attributes bring your skills and talents to life, allowing you to "activate" knowledge, skills, and talents to a high level, which creates professional opportunity in addition to personal development. Your passion for a career in the media industries is enhanced by the desire to resourcefully "figure it out." Resourceful people, fueled by their passions, are creative problem solvers (i.e., solution oriented) with the ability to act imaginatively. Being *persistent* or having the ability and willingness to "stick it out," fueled by one's ambition to succeed, is consistently cited as a key attribute for the media professions due to their competitive, uncertain nature. Together, the ability to "figure it out" (resourcefulness) and "stick it out" (persistence) are critical to build leverage and advance in the media professions.

The ability to persist toward difficult goals and to resourcefully problem solve carry limited value if you're unable to "connect" these efforts with people and organizations. Thus, being *connective* remains a central fiber for the active attributes—and the entire model—and carries power for young professionals and future managers. Being connective is particularly relevant in industries centered on communication and collaboration. Whether pitching a script idea, working collaboratively on a production, or convincing people to invest money in your idea (or *you*), the ability to connect effectively with others opens up vital avenues and opportunities. Thus, persistent individuals, fueled by their ambitions, find ways to develop connections, even when times are tough. Resourceful professionals, fueled and activated by passion, build connections through being viewed as a *solution*.

THE ENDURING ATTRIBUTES

The ability to connect with people, to resourcefully problem solve, and to persist toward goals leads to an additional set of attributes that are important as you embark on a career and also function to help you grow and endure within these dynamic professions. The enduring attributes of *curiosity, adaptability, reliability,* and *integrity* are critical in and of themselves and do not merely depend on the successful functioning of other attributes in the model. The desire to continually learn and grow (curiosity), the ability and willingness to adapt to gradual or sudden changes or demands in work or industry environments (adaptability), being a reliable "go-to" person, and demonstrating a strong value system and reputation (integrity) provide the platform for long-term success.

As the model shows, adaptability completes an "active diamond" that includes passion, resourcefulness, and connectiveness, while reliability completes an "active diamond" of ambition, persistence, and connectiveness. *Adaptability* and *reliability* hold this more central presence because media professionals rate these two attributes as the *most important* for career success (Cooper & Tang, 2010). Moreover, passion in the big picture is aided by the ability to adapt to new technologies, business practices, and specific situations that will inevitably occur through the course of one's career. Put another way, the inability to adapt can have a profound negative impact on sustained advancement. Being someone who can be consistently "counted on" (reliability) in a variety of situations (whether working as a young professional or as an executive) builds positive reputation and, as a result, leverages success and distinction.

Ongoing *curiosity* about people, stories, industry trends, processes, and/or technology breeds "well-roundedness" through *habitual interest* in a range of areas that can provide knowledge, understanding, and connection among people and concepts. People who display curiosity ask questions and continually seek to know more about things connected to the media industries yet also have outside interests that help feed or embellish these core interests. Simply put, those with a broad knowledge base have multiple lenses or perspectives to draw from, have greater abilities and orientation to develop innovative solutions, have better *analytical* tools that are critical in a dynamic set of industries, and are better able to adapt to changing situations. The result of having curiosity is the ability, orientation, and inclination to *grow* in knowledge over the short and long term.

Integrity is a product of your reputation through connections, demonstrated reliability, problem-solving skills, and perceptions of who you are and what you bring to a situation. Professionals quickly learn just how shockingly small the media world is. A strong, positive reputation and *earned integrity* is the product of a value system that allows the media professional to "sleep well at night" but also enables opportunities to arise because you and your performance and values have proven to be strong.

THE REINFORCING ATTRIBUTES

Development of the various big picture, active, and enduring attributes—individually and in tandem—are reinforcing and lead to greater levels of personal confidence and professional reputation. These encourage continual pursuit of career goals, access to opportunities, and development of the key attributes. These arrows point back to *you* as they clarify self-distinctions about who you are (as you continue to develop personally and professionally), what you might want to pursue (and lead), and your willingness and opportunities to connect (with people and audiences). All additionally reinforce the big picture, active, and enduring skills needed to build and enhance your personal and professional success over the long term.

Confidence is a product of earned self-assuredness as a result of developing important big picture, active, and sustaining attributes. Confident media professionals come to trust their own abilities and instincts and believe they can accomplish whatever it is they set out to do. This makes an individual (i.e., *you*) more likely to take risks and less likely to be deterred by temporary setbacks. Confidence develops as a result of successful interactions and perpetuates itself toward greater distinction within media professions.

For the extraordinary media professional, *resilience* deepens your capacities to handle challenges and bounce back from setbacks. Resilience is optimally manifest through a strong system of values that remain steadfast in challenging conditions. The phrase "What doesn't kill you makes you stronger" is an overstatement of fact in the technical sense yet carries a profound truth that helps many media professionals thrive in the industry. Or, as American author Carol Orsborn (1997) states, "Mastering the art of resilience does much more than restore you to who you once thought you were. Rather, you emerge from the experience transformed into a truer expression of who you were really meant to be."

IMPACT OF DEVELOPING THE 12 ATTRIBUTES

The model's combination of big picture, active, enduring, and reinforcing attributes reflects a continuous, never-ending progression toward personal development and greater distinction in the media professions. This model visualizes how attributes might work as a *system* to produce extraordinary results over time. In other words, your successful career is made possible by what is uniquely you, enabled by your passion, ambition, and ability to connect; activated with resourcefulness, persistence, and connections you make; endure with curiosity, adaptability, reliability, and integrity; and then is reinforced by earned confidence and resiliency. The extraordinary media professional is optimally in control of destiny, confident navigating the uncertain paths ahead, and continually seeking to use the attributes to ever greater effect. The journey will, at times, be challenging and uncertain, but you'll be better equipped to handle the challenges and difficulties ahead. Regardless of your specific interests within the media professions, you will be able to—over time—complete virtually any goal, idea, or aspiration. You will be enterprising and industrious, motivated and energetic, and optimally equipped to navigate, even *thrive*, in the media industries. Effective application of these attributes makes the young or aspiring professional "feel" successful (even if the financial rewards trail initially) and will encourage more experienced professionals to become successful leaders in the industry.

Work to apply and/or improve these personal attributes. Find avenues through which you can enhance your own problem-solving skills and challenge yourself to grow. Actively connect with current professionals (or other aspiring professionals) who might provide insight and opportunity to enhance your own growth. Be that person who has an unquenchable curiosity about people, trends, and processes so that you can adapt to most any change and be viewed as *the* highly reliable "go-to" person. And do this while remaining true to your core values. These attributes will help enable your extraordinary career in the media professions.

ACTION PLAN

1. Develop a 30-second personal pitch that clearly conveys "who you are" if a media professional or interviewer asks you to "tell me about yourself."
2. Schedule an informational meeting with a current media professional to gain insight into the professional's career and their advice about building a career.
3. Read industry trade publications or aggregated media industry resources at least once a week to learn about the latest media industry news and trends.
4. Describe how your interest or passion for a career in media started.

KEY TAKEAWAYS

1. Foundational skills, such as project management, writing, networking, and technical skills, will continue to be important for future media practitioners.
2. "Soft skills" are emerging as important indicators for career success in media industries.
3. Many media companies, including Google, are adapting interview processes to assess soft skills and problem-solving abilities.
4. The ability to actively, genuinely build a network of relationships is of critical importance to your long-term career.
5. In the "small world" of media industries, a positive reputation and ability to adapt to inevitable changes is of utmost importance.

CONCLUSION

The business of media has undergone a series of industry transformations. Currently, media professionals are addressing the age of convergent disruption through a stage of experimenting, but the field is attempting to enter the final stage of stable structure by closing a gap between the demands of the current industry and the training of new hires. Competitive media firms, such as Google, are beginning to hire differently in order to assess the problem-solving and soft skills of potential candidates. It is important that future practitioners develop new digital technological competencies across multiple platforms and software. Specifically, candidates should develop digital portfolios that highlight their mastery of foundational skills such as writing, content creation, and strategic thinking.

Strong writing remains a foundation for all aspects of media businesses. This, combined with a "backpack" skill set of content creation, including graphic, photography, and video production skills, will be an asset to any media firm. Finally, media managers must be strategic in nature and always consider where an organization is currently positioned, where it would like to advance, and the necessary steps that will help achieve this process.

In order to meet these demands, aspiring professionals should seek out training that shifts from traditional face-to-face lecture-style classes to more active workshops and blended, flipped, and online modalities of learning. Students should also actively create and collaborate outside traditional classrooms. There should be great opportunities for students to work with vocational clients through project-based learning that will lead to a strong digital portfolio, work experience, and networking. It is important for future professionals to be proactive in these efforts.

While these foundational skills remain imperative for a successful career in the media industry, media professionals still cite a deficit in soft skills. Aspiring practitioners should work on improving group work dynamics, develop an enterprising attitude, and uphold integrity standards. Courtesy, adaptability, and teamwork are cited as top business skills necessary to succeed in tomorrow's marketplace (Robles, 2012). Problem-solving, multitasking, and critical thinking skills are also essential. There are many steps that students can take to develop a portfolio that demonstrates examples of soft skill development.

The 12 attributes of extraordinary media professionals (and the accompanying visual model) serve as a useful tool to understand and apply key personality attributes in the service of professional growth and development in the media professions. The 12 attributes function as an integrated system of attributes that will foster and aid long-term success in media professions. It is important for aspiring practitioners to understand how "big picture," "active," "enduring," and "reinforcing" attributes work together to ensure a media professional who is both well prepared and extraordinary in nature.

Young professionals and future media leaders should embrace the challenges ahead. There's a reason why so many people want to work in media. The opportunities to affect and influence people through story (however defined) is indeed a special pursuit—and responsibility. Your ability to grow personally and professionally through these challenges will be worth the effort. It is impossible to predict what the future of media technologies, convergence, and industry disruptions has in store for media managers. However, with the right foundational tools, and a passion for adaptation and learning, the field of media management is an appealing career choice for creative and business minds alike. Hopefully, this book offered insights into media management today and future trends. Still, the media landscape is constantly evolving. We hope this book will prove to be only a start in the continual merging of media management and business as well as provide a useful guide for the advanced tools and practical experience needed to tackle the convergent disruptions of today's rapidly evolving media industries.

REFERENCES

Bancino, R., & Zevalkink, C. (2007). Soft skills: The new curriculum for hard-core technical professionals. *Techniques: Connecting Education and Careers, 82*(5), 20–22.

Bartosova, D. (2011). The future of the media professions: Current issues in media management practice. *The International Journal on Media Management, 13*, 193–201.

Bock, L. (2015). *Work rules! Insights from inside Google that will transform how you live and lead.* Twelve Publishing.

Cooper, R. (Forthcoming). *12 attributes of extraordinary media professionals*. Rowman & Littlefield.

Cooper, R., & Tang, T. (2010). The attributes for career success in the mass communication industries: A comparison of current and aspiring professionals. *Journalism & Mass Communication Educator, 65*, 40–55.

Digital Marketing Institute. (2019). *The most in-demand transferable skills in digital marketing.* https://digitalmarketinginstitute.com/en-us/blog/the-most-in-demand-transferable-skills-in-digital-marketing

Finch, D. J., Hamilton, L. K., Baldwin, R., & Zehner, M. (2013). An exploratory study of factors affecting undergraduate employability. *Education+Training, 55*, 681–704.

Glass Door. (2020). *Best places to work 2020.* https://www.glassdoor.com/Award/Best-Places-to-Work-LST_KQ0,19.htm

Keogh, W., & Galloway, L. (2004). Teaching enterprise in vocational disciplines: Reflecting on positive experience. *Management Decision, 42*, 531–541.

Lindbeck, A., & Snower, D. J. (2000). Multi-task learning and the reorganization of work. *Journal of Labor Economics, 18*, 353–376.

Macdonald, I. (2006). Teaching journalists to save the profession: A critical assessment of recent debates on the future of US and Canadian journalism education. *Journalism Studies, 7*, 745–764.

Meisenzahl, M. (2019, October 31). Google made a small but important change in 2017 to how it thinks about "Googleyness," a key value it looks for in new hires. *Business Insider*. https://www.businessinsider.com/google-googleyness-hiring-training-guide-change-2019-10

Moran, G. (2017, September 10). 6 ex-Googlers share how they landed the job. *Fast Company*. https://www.fastcompany.com/40458298/6-ex-googlers-share-how-they-landed-the-job

Mowbray, J., Hall, H., Raeside, R., & Robertson, P. (2018). Job search information behaviours: An ego-net study of networking amongst young job-seekers. *Journal of Librarianship and Information Science, 50*, 239–253.

Nickols, F. (2016). Strategy, strategic management, strategic planning and strategic thinking. *Management Journal, 1*(1), 4–7.

Orsborn, C. (1997). *The art of resilience: 100 paths to wisdom and strength in an uncertain world.* Three Rivers Press.

Popomaronis, T. (2019, April 17). *Here's how many Google interviews it takes to hire a Googler*. CNBC. https://www.cnbc.com/2019/04/17/heres-how-many-google-job-interviews-it-takes-to-hire-a-googler.html

Portersfield, H. (2017, February 1). *Why writing should be the most sought-after skill in PR*. PRSA. https://apps.prsa.org/Intelligence/Tactics/Articles/view/11790/1138/Why_Writing_Should_Be_the_Most_Sought_After_Skill#.XhybTC2ZN1M

Robles, M. M. (2012). Executive perceptions of the top 10 soft skills needed in today's workplace. *Business Communication Quarterly, 75*, 453–465.

Royle, J., & Laing, A. (2014). The digital marketing skills gap: Developing a digital marketer model for the communication industries. *International Journal of Information Management, 34*(2), 65–73.

Sanderson, K. R., Bruk-Lee, V., Viswesvaran, C., Gutierrez, S., & Kantrowitz, T. (2013). Multitasking: Do preference and ability interact to predict performance at work? *Journal of Occupational and Organizational Psychology, 86*, 556–563.

Schulz, B. (2008). The importance of soft skills: Education beyond academic knowledge. *Journal of Language and Communication, 2*(1), 146–154.

Skillset. (2009). *Creative media workforce survey 2008*. Sector Skills Council for Creative Media. https://www.screenskills.com/media/1412/creative_media_workforce_survey_report_2008.pdf

Tanner, S., Phillips, G., Smyth, C., & Tapsall, S. (2005). *Journalism ethics at work*. Pearson.
Wenger, D. H., & Owens, L. C. (2012). Help wanted 2010: An examination of new media skills required by top US news companies. *Journalism & Mass Communication Educator*, *67*(1), 9–25.
Wilhelm, L. (2005). Increasing visual literacy skills with digital imagery: Successful models for using a set of digital cameras in a College of Education. *T.H.E. Journal*, *32*, 24–26.
Zehr, M. A. (1998, February 18). New office economy putting greater demands on schools. *Education Week*, *17*(23), 7.

Index

About the Contributors

Rasha Allam, assistant professor and associate chair at the Department of Journalism and Mass Communicationat the American University in Cairo (AUC), is a graduate of the Department of Journalism and Mass Communication (BA, 2002; MA, 2005), School of Global Affairs and Public Policy at the AUC. She is an honorary alumnus of the Annenberg School for Communication at University of Pennsylvania and a graduate of the Oxford University program of media laws and regulations. Her doctorate in business administration is from Maastricht School of Management (2011) with specialization in media management. Allam has a range of experience in teaching; her areas of specialization include media management, media economics, and mass media laws and regulations. Allam's research interests include Egyptian and Arab media management systems, Arab broadcast media laws, policies and regulations, media monitoring, and media and elections in the Middle East. Allam also worked as media consultant with international organizations such as UNESCO, USAID, and the Carnegie Foundation. Dr. Allam serves on the editorial board of *Journalism Practice* academic journal.

Sabine Baumann is professor for business administration in the College of Management, Information, Technology at Jade University, Germany. Before rejoining academia, Dr. Baumann worked in senior management positions for Bertelsmann, Germany's largest media conglomerate. In 2016, she received the Barry Sherman Teaching Award of the Media Management, Economics and Entrepreneurship (MMEE) division of the Association for Education in Journalism and Mass Communication. She has served on the board of the MMEE division and the European Media Management Association. Dr. Baumann's interdisciplinary research addresses digital transformations of business models and strategic exploitations of network structures. Her work has been published in journals such as the *Journal of Media Business Studies, International Business and Economics Review*, the *Journal of Business Economics*, and the *International Journal on Media Management*. Recently, Dr. Baumann served as guest editor for a special issue on strategic media management for the *Journal of Media Business Studies* (https://www.tandfonline.com/doi/full/10.1080/16522354.2020.1740564) and edited *Teaching Strategic Management: A Hands-on Guide to Teaching Success* (2020).

Roger Cooper (PhD, Indiana University) is director of Ohio University's Semester in Los Angeles program and author of the forthcoming book *12 Attributes of Extraordinary Media*

Professionals: How to Navigate Your Road to Success (Rowman & Littlefield). His research and teaching focus on professional development for the media and creative industries.

Michael Devlin (PhD, University of Alabama, 2010) is an associate professor in the School of Journalism and Mass Communication at Texas State University. His research interests lie in the intersection of advertising, sports, and media effects, focusing on the cognitive, affective, and behavioral effects of fan identification and its impact on sponsorships, endorsements, branding, and advertising campaigns. His research has been published in journals such as *Journal of Broadcasting and Electronic Media, Communication and Sport, International Journal of Sport Management and Marketing, Journal of Sports Media,* and *International Journal of Sport Communication*. He serves on the editorial board for *Communication and Sport* and has held leadership positions in the International Communication Association's Sport Communication Interest Group.

Douglas A. Ferguson received his PhD from Bowling Green State University before coming to the College of Charleston as the first department chair for the Department of Communication. Dr. Ferguson later served three years as director of graduate studies of the Master of Arts in Communication program, which he helped start. He has taught three different online courses and is the author of textbooks and scholarly works focusing on communication technology.

Kim Fox (MA, Ohio University) is a professor of practice in the Department of Journalism and Mass Communication at the American University in Cairo in Cairo, Egypt. She primarily teaches audio production and other journalism courses. Her research interests are podcasting/radio/audio, social media, pedagogy, and media representations. Fox and coauthors David O. Dowling and Kyle J. Miller received the Broadcast Education Association's (BEA) 2019 Diversity and Inclusion Research Award for their paper "A Curriculum for Blackness: Podcasts as Discursive Cultural Guides." Fox is the executive producer of the award-winning *Ehky Ya Masr (Tell Your Story Egypt)* podcast, a narrative nonfiction podcast about life in Cairo, Egypt. The podcast won BEA's Diversity and Inclusion Creative Award in 2019 for the episode "Ramadan across Social Classes in Cairo." Her work in audio also includes facilitating workshops in Beirut, Lebanon; Budapest, Hungary; Bishkek, Kyrgyzstan, and other countries. Fox was the recipient of the 2018 Scripps Howard Foundation's Visiting Professor in Social Media and was embedded at WCPO-TV in Ohio. Other fellowships include the National Association of Television Program Executives, National Public Radio, Reynolds Business Journalism, and the Kopenhaver Center. Her service commitments include positions on the board for the BEA, the Association of Independents in Radio, and the Arab U.S. Association for Communication Educators and in a leadership position for the Association for Education in Journalism and Mass Communication's Commission on the Status of Women.

Richard A. Gershon (Ohio University) is professor of media management and telecommunications in the School of Communication at Western Michigan University. Dr. Gershon is an internationally recognized scholar, having authored eight books and more than 50 journal articles and book chapters. His most recent works include *Media, Telecommunications and Business Strategy*, 3rd ed. (2020) and *Digital Media and Innovation: Management and Design Strategies in Communication* (2017). Dr. Gershon is a Fulbright scholar, having held visiting appointments at the University of Navarra, Spain, and Nihon University, Japan. Dr. Gershon has twice been selected for national teaching honors, including the Steven H. Coltrin Professor of the Year Award by the International Radio and Television Society and the Barry Sherman Award for Teaching Excellence by the Management and Economics division of the Association for Education in Journalism and Mass Communication. Dr. Gershon is a founding member of the Information and Telecommunications Education and Research Association, where he served as the organization's first president. Dr. Gershon is one of a select number of professors who has been recognized by Western Michigan University's College of Arts and Sciences in each of its three major award categories: the Faculty Achievement Award in Teaching (2005), Research and Creative Activities (2015), and Professional and Community Service (2017).

Clark F. Greer (PhD, Bowling Green State University, 2000) is an online adjunct professor of communication. Prior to that role, he taught for more than two decades as a full-time communication faculty member at three institutions. His research interests include content and effects of emerging media and social platforms on the public and on traditional media. He has published articles in several journals, including *Electronic News, Journal of Radio and Audio Media, Journal of Broadcasting and Electronic Media, The International Journal on Media Management, Journal of Promotion Management, Newspaper Research Journal, Convergence: The Journal of Research into New Media Technologies,* and *Public Relations Review*. He also has served as a reviewer for journal articles. In addition, he served on the Broadcast Education Association Festival of Media Arts.

Miao Guo (PhD, University of Florida, 2012) is associate professor of telecommunications at Ball State University. Her research interests include audience behavior analysis, data analytics, and emerging media technologies. She has published articles in *Journal of Broadcasting and Electronic Media, International Journal on Media Management,* and *Journal of Media Business Studies, Media and Communication,* among others. Her teaching interests include audience analytics, communication research, digital media marketing and promotion, media management and economics, and telecommunication programming at both the graduate and undergraduate level. Dr. Guo's research work has been funded by the industry (e.g., Time Warner Company) and academic professional associations. She is the recipient of the 2016 Broadcast Education Association (BEA) New Faculty Research Award and 2013 Association for Education in Journalism and Mass Communication (AEJMC) Emerging Scholar Award. Dr. Guo is a faculty fellow of the National Association of Television Program Executives, International Radio and Television Society, and AEJMC's Institute for Diverse Leadership. She is a social media visiting professor of Scripps Howard Foundation and ANA Educational Foundation. She has held leadership positions in the College of Communication, Information and Media as well as professional associations like the BEA and AEJMC.

María Elena Gutiérrez-Rentería earned a doctorate in public communication from the Universidad de Navarra and is a professor in the School of Communication at the Universidad Panamericana in Guadalajara, México. Her bachelor's degree is in business and finance, and she has a degree in anthropology and ethics. Dr. Gutiérrez-Rentería participated as a visiting professor of the College of Media and Communication at Texas Tech University in the United States. She was a member of the National System of Researchers in Mexico. Her work has been published in the *International Journal on Media Management, Palabra Clave, Revista de Comunicación,* and *Journal of Spanish Language Media* and in the books *A Research Agenda for Media Economics, Handbook of Media Management and Economics, Value-Oriented Media Management, Media Management and Economics Research in a Transmedia Environment, The Handbook of Spanish Language Media,* and *The Palgrave Handbook of Global Radio.* Gutiérrez-Rentería currently serves on the editorial board of *The International Journal on Media Management* and is the author of the Mexican country profile published each year by Reuters Institute for the Study of Journalism at Oxford University.

Louisa Ha (PhD, Michigan State University, 1994) is editor in chief of *Journalism and Mass Communication Quarterly,* professor at the School of Media and Communication, and founder and leader of the Emerging Media Research Cluster at Bowling Green State University. She has published 70 refereed journal articles and many invited book chapters. She received the Emerald Research Grant to study knowledge creation and dissemination in rural Nigeria and won the Special Commendation for Research of value to the developing world, and the 2009 Literati Network Awards for Excellence for her article published in *Management Decision.* Her 2007 edited book, *Webcasting Worldwide: Business Models of an Emerging Global Medium,* was the recipient of the 2007 Association for Education in Journalism and Mass Communication's Robert Picard Book Award. Her latest edited books are *The Audience and Business of YouTube and Online Videos* and *Asian Women Leadership: A Cross-National and Cross-Sector Comparison.* Her research interests are audience research, media management, media technologies, online videos and advertising, and comparative communication.

Todd Holmes (PhD, University of Florida, 2015) is an assistant professor of entertainment media management (EMM) at California State University Northridge. He is the option head for the EMM program and teaches courses in media management, media research, and audience analysis. He has published research in the *Journal of Media Business Studies* and has presented award-winning papers at both national and international media conferences. His research interests include the effectiveness of online and mobile video advertising, innovation adoption by media firms, advertising sales management, branding, and marketing strategy. Holmes has held leadership positions in the Broadcast Education Association and the Association for Education in Journalism and Mass Communication. He is also an industry consultant and has worked as a project manager on a four-year longitudinal study that Nielsen conducted on the media consumption habits of college students. Prior to entering academia, Holmes worked for more than a decade as a senior account executive in television and radio advertising as well as telecommunications.

Kelly Kaufhold (PhD, University of Texas at Austin, 2011) is an associate professor of digital media innovation. He teaches and researches in the Media Innovation Lab in the School of Journalism and Mass Communication at Texas State University. Kaufhold worked as a multiplatform journalist for two decades and now teaches multimedia and data journalism with an extensive emphasis on storytelling using smartphones. His research has appeared in *Broadcasting and Electronic Media, Journalism and Mass Communication Quarterly, International Journal on Media Management, Newspaper Research Journal, Journalism Practice, The International Journal of Interactive Communication Systems and Technologies,* and *International Journal of Internet Science*. He has also won numerous conference research awards and served as a research officer in multiple divisions of the Association for Education in Journalism and Mass Communication.

M. Laeeq Khan (PhD, Michigan State University, 2014) is a faculty and the founding director of the Social Media Analytics Research Team Lab in the Scripps College of Communication at Ohio University. He has more than a decade of experience in teaching and researching media effects, digital engagement, and data analytics. Khan's research employs quantitative, qualitative, as well as latest analytics techniques in areas as diverse as health, business, government, sports, media literacies, and digital inequalities for effective data storytelling. He has published articles in *Telematics and Informatics, Computers in Human Behavior, Behavior and Information Technology, Computers in Education, International Journal of Communication, Information Communication and Society,* and *Government Information Quarterly*. Khan's administrative and research experience is global; he has worked on managerial and consulting positions in hospitality, health, and media organizations.

Maria A. Kopacz (PhD, 2007, University of Arizona) is an associate professor in the Department of Communication and Media at West Chester University. Her research interests center on the intersection of emerging media technologies, empowerment of marginalized groups, community building, and social change. She has published articles in *New Media and Society, Journal of Broadcasting and Electronic Media, Communication Quarterly,* and *Human Communication Research.*

Carlos López-Hernández is a research professor at the School of Business and Economics, Universidad Panamericana, Guadalajara Campus. His research interests include negotiation and strategy implementation. He obtained his PhD in management of organizations from the Universidad Popular Autónoma del Estado de Puebla. López-Hernández has a master's degree in business from Ipade Business School, México. He has been a member of Mexico's National Research System since 2018. Currently, he is the vice president of Academics at Universidad Panamericana, in Guadalajara, México.

Buddy Love is working toward his master's degree in media industry studies at the University of North Texas, where he also serves as a teaching and research assistant. While he has yet to narrow his research focus, contributions such as those found in this book are allowing him to hone his skills and experiment with his interests in the different media fields.

Jenn Burleson Mackay (PhD, University of Alabama, 2008) is an associate professor in the Department of Communication at Virginia Tech. Her research looks at the ethics of journalists and the influence of new technology on journalism. She is coeditor of the journal *Electronic News* and edited a special issue of the *Electronic Journal of Communication*. Her work has been published in several journals including *Electronic Journal of Communication, Journal of Mass Media Ethics, Newspaper Research Journal, Journalism and Mass Media Quarterly, Journalism Studies,* and *Journalism Practice*. She has held leadership positions in the Association for Journalism and Mass Communication.

L. Meghan Mahoney (PhD, Ohio University, 2011) is associate professor in the Department of Communication and Media at West Chester University of Pennsylvania. She regularly publishes research on issues related to new media audiences, social media, and marketing messages for behavior and social change, most recently in the *Journal of Media Education, Journal of Intercultural Communication, Journal of Medical Internet Research, Journal of Development Communication,* and *Journal of Media and Communication Studies*. She also coauthored *Strategic Social Media: From Marketing to Social Change*. Meghan served as chair of the Management, Marketing and Programming Division of the Broadcast Education Association and as social media coordinator for the Eastern Communication Association Convention. She is a faculty fellow of the National Association of Television Program Executives.

Drew McDaniel is professor in the School of Media Arts and Studies at Ohio University. Professor McDaniel has written extensively on media in Asia and on technology in media and communication. His book publications include *Electronic Tigers of Southeast Asia: The Politics of Media, Technology, and National Development, Broadcasting in the Malay World, Fundamentals of Audio Production,* and *Fundamentals of Communication Electronics,* among others. For more than 30 years, he held an additional appointment as staff consultant at the Asia-Pacific Institute for Broadcasting Development, a UN-chartered agency in Kuala Lumpur, Malaysia, that provides research and training assistance across the region. He held an appointment as Distinguished Scholar in Residence at the University of Queensland in Australia in 2008, and in 2011 he held a Wee Kim Wee School of Communication and Information Endowed Visiting Professorship at Nanyang Technological University in Singapore.

Andrea L. Meluch (PhD, Kent State University, 2016) is an assistant professor of business and organizational communication in the School of Communication and Department of Management at the University of Akron. Her research focuses on the intersections of health, organizational, and instructional communication. Specifically, she is interested in issues of organizational culture, mental health, and social support. She has published in *Communication Studies, Communication Education, Southern Communication Journal, Qualitative Research in Medicine and Healthcare, Journal of Communication in Healthcare,* and *Journal of Communication Pedagogy*. She has also authored or coauthored more than a dozen book chapters and encyclopedia entries.

Gregory Newton (PhD, Indiana University, 2001) is associate dean for graduate studies, research, and creative activity in the Scripps College of Communication and associate professor in the School of Media Arts and Studies at Ohio University. His research interests include legal and management issues related to the creation, distribution, and marketing of media content; freedom of expression and restrictions on offensive content; and media ownership policies and regulations. He has published articles in *Journal of Communication, Journal of Broadcasting and Electronic Media, Journal of Media Business Studies, Journal of Radio Studies, Journal of Applied Communication Research, Journal of Promotion Management,* and *International Journal on Media Management.* He has also contributed chapters to *Media Programming Strategies and Practices* and *Media Promotion and Marketing for Broadcasting, Cable, and the Internet* and entries in the *Encyclopedia of Radio* on "Localism" and "College Radio." Greg is a past president of the Broadcast Education Association and has been a faculty fellow of the National Association of Television Program Executives and International Radio and Television Society.

Anthony Palomba (PhD, University of Florida, 2015) is a visiting assistant professor at the Darden School of Business at University of Virginia. His research interests include consumer behavior, branding, and marketing behind television, video games, and film. He has published articles in *Journal of Media Business Studies, Journal of Retailing and Consumer Services, Computers in Human Behavior, Entertainment Computing,* and *Games and Culture* as well as several book chapters, including "Esports Communication" and "Esports Marketing," for an upcoming textbook titled *Esports Business Management.* Anthony has previously been honored as a faculty fellow at the National Association of Television Program Executives, a faculty fellow at the Television Academy Foundation, and an industry attendee at the Electronic Entertainment Expo Conference. He currently serves as a co-research chair of the Media Management, Economics, and Entrepreneurship Division at the Association for Education in Journalism and Mass Communication.

Ronen Shay (PhD, University of Florida, 2015) is an assistant professor of communications and media management at the Gabelli School of Business at Fordham University. Dr. Shay's research is focused on contemporary challenges in the fields of media management, strategic communication, and technology diffusion. His research includes papers written on windowed distribution strategies, modeling return on investment for social media marketing, and the factors affecting mobile media device adoption among U.S. audiences. His published works include articles in the *International Journal on Media Management, Journalism and Mass Communication Quarterly, The Handbook of Media Branding, Journal of Communication and Emergent Technologies, Games and Culture, Palabra Clave, The Handbook of Media Management and Business,* and the forthcoming *Media Business Models: Connecting Media to Their Markets.* Dr. Shay has presented his research at the Association for Education in Journalism and Mass Communication, Broadcast Education Association, and the International Communication Association's national conferences as well as international symposiums including the University of Zurich's summit on media branding, the Sixth Media and the Public Sphere International Conference, and the World Media Economics and Management Conference. His industry experience includes project management roles at Rogers Communications, North by Northeast, and start-up Random Sounds.

Brandon T. Sweitzer (MA, University of Akron) is a professor of communication at Kent State University and the University of Akron. He is also helping Aultman College of Nursing and Health Sciences expand their degree program by developing and teaching communication-based courses such as Business and Professional Communication and Interpersonal Communication. Sweitzer is currently enrolled in the PhD program at Ohio University and will receive his PhD pending the completion of his dissertation. His dissertation involves the development of an empirical model of mediation that provides insight into the relationship between media effects and an individual's perception of their congruency with public opinion in a social media ecosystem. His research interests include cross-cultural communication, computer-mediated communication, strategic social media, media management and the intersection of media effects, and interpersonal interactions found on social media sites. He has several award-winning papers and has presented his work at the Ohio Communication Association, the Broadcast Education Association, and the International Communication Association.

Tang Tang (PhD, Ohio University, 2008) is professor in the School of Media and Journalism and School of Emerging Media and Technology at Kent State University. Her research interests include uses and effects of emerging media technologies and sport communication. She has published articles in *Journal of Broadcasting and Electronic Media, Mass Communication and Society, Computers in Human Behavior, International Journal on Media Management, Communication and Sport, International Journal of Sport Communication, Journalism and Mass Communication Educator*, and others. She also coauthored *Strategic Social Media: From Marketing to Social Change* and coedited *Handbook of Media Management and Business*. Tang is a faculty fellow of the Television Academy, National Association of Television Program Executives, and International Radio and Television Society and has held leadership positions in the Broadcast Education Association and the International Communication Association. She also serves on the editorial boards of *Communication and Sport, International Journal of Sport Communication, Chinese Journal of Communication*, and *Ohio Journal of Communication*.

Rob Upchurch earned his master's degree from the Department of Media Arts at the University of North Texas. His focus areas are media industry studies and practicum. He currently produces podcasts that inform through entertainment and is engaged in the ever-growing prospects of mobile media.

Heather L. Walter (PhD, State University of New York at Buffalo, 1999) is director and associate professor in the School Communication at the University of Akron. Her research interests include conflict management in organizations, health advocacy, and social network analysis. Her publications have appeared in *Communication Quarterly, Communication Research Measures, Journal of Magazine and New Media Research, Media Education Research Journal*, and *The Ohio Communication Journal*. She has authored or coauthored more than a dozen book chapters and coedited *Converging Conversations across Contexts*. She also serves on the editorial board for *The Ohio Journal of Communication* and *CF Research News* and on the board of trustees for the Cystic Fibrosis Foundation.

Quan Xie (Ph.D., Ohio University, 2015) is assistant professor of advertising at the Temerlin Advertising Institute, Southern Methodist University. Her primary research interests center on the effects and implications of digital technology in advertising and digital marketing communications. She has published articles in the *Journal of Advertising, International Journal of Advertising, Journal of Interactive Advertising, Journal of Research in Interactive Marketing, Journal of Product and Brand Management,* and *International Journal of Strategic Communication,* among others. Quan has held leadership positions in the Broadcast Education Association. She is the recipient of the Association of National Advertisers–Educational Foundation Visiting Professor Fellowship and the American Academy of Advertising Research Fellowship Grant. She serves on the editorial review board for *International Journal of Advertising*. She also served as a video director for the sports presentation team at the 2008 Beijing Olympics and Paralympics.

Xiaoquan Zhang (PhD, Bowling Green State University; Tsinghua University) is an associate professor in the Department of Media Arts at University of North Texas. His research interests are media management and economics, media technology and policy, media reputation of corporations, and audience research. His work has been published in *Communication Research, Journalism and Mass Communication Quarterly, Telematics and Informatics, Telecommunications Policy, Time and Society, Journalism Studies, Journal of Applied Journalism and Media Studies,* and *Corporate Reputation Review*. His monograph *The Measurement of Media Reputation* was published in 2019. His work also gained four research paper awards from the Association for Education in Journalism and Mass Communication and six research paper awards from the Broadcast Education Association.

CPSIA information can be obtained
at www.ICGtesting.com
Printed in the USA
BVHW011129101120
592733BV00012B/3

9 781538 115305